Strategic Customer Relationship Management in the Age of Social Media

Amir Khanlari
University of Tehran, Iran

A volume in the Advances in Marketing, Customer Relationship Management, and E-Services (AMCRMES) Book Series

BUSINESS SCIENCE Reference
An Imprint of IGI Global

Managing Director: Lindsay Johnston
Managing Editor: Austin DeMarco
Director of Intellectual Property & Contracts: Jan Travers
Acquisitions Editor: Kayla Wolfe
Production Editor: Christina Henning
Development Editor: Caitlyn Martin
Cover Design: Jason Mull

Published in the United States of America by
Business Science Reference (an imprint of IGI Global)
701 E. Chocolate Avenue
Hershey PA, USA 17033
Tel: 717-533-8845
Fax: 717-533-8661
E-mail: cust@igi-global.com
Web site: http://www.igi-global.com

Library of Congress Cataloging-in-Publication Data

Strategic customer relationship management in the age of social media / Amir Khanlari, editor.
pages cm
Includes bibliographical references and index.
Summary: "This book provides a variety of strategies, applications, tools, and techniques for corporate success in social media in a coherent and conceptual framework offering the resources necessary to adopt and implement social CRM strategies within their organizations"-- Provided by publisher.
ISBN 978-1-4666-8586-4 (hardcover : alk. paper) -- ISBN 978-1-4666-8587-1 (ebook : alk. paper) 1. Customer relations--Management. 2. Customer relations--Technological innovations. 3. Social media--Economic aspects. I. Khanlari, Amir, 1981-

HF5415.5.S77 2015
658.8'1202854678--dc23

2015012060

This book is published in the IGI Global book series Advances in Marketing, Customer Relationship Management, and E-Services (AMCRMES) (ISSN: 2327-5502; eISSN: 2327-5529)

British Cataloguing in Publication Data
A Cataloguing in Publication record for this book is available from the British Library.

Advances in Marketing, Customer Relationship Management, and E-Services (AMCRMES) Book Series

Eldon Y. Li
National Chengchi University, Taiwan &
California Polytechnic State University, USA

ISSN: 2327-5502
EISSN: 2327-5529

Mission

Business processes, services, and communications are important factors in the management of good customer relationship, which is the foundation of any well organized business. Technology continues to play a vital role in the organization and automation of business processes for marketing, sales, and customer service. These features aid in the attraction of new clients and maintaining existing relationships.

The Advances in Marketing, Customer Relationship Management, and E-Services (AMCRMES) Book Series addresses success factors for customer relationship management, marketing, and electronic services and its performance outcomes. This collection of reference source covers aspects of consumer behavior and marketing business strategies aiming towards researchers, scholars, and practitioners in the fields of marketing management.

Coverage

- E-Service Innovation
- Cases on CRM Implementation
- Mobile services
- Legal Considerations in E-Marketing
- CRM strategies
- Social Networking and Marketing
- Ethical Considerations in E-Marketing
- Text Mining and Marketing
- Customer retention
- Relationship marketing

IGI Global is currently accepting manuscripts for publication within this series. To submit a proposal for a volume in this series, please contact our Acquisition Editors at Acquisitions@igi-global.com or visit: http://www.igi-global.com/publish/.

The Advances in Marketing, Customer Relationship Management, and E-Services (AMCRMES) Book Series (ISSN 2327-5502) is published by IGI Global, 701 E. Chocolate Avenue, Hershey, PA 17033-1240, USA, www.igi-global.com. This series is composed of titles available for purchase individually; each title is edited to be contextually exclusive from any other title within the series. For pricing and ordering information please visit http://www.igi-global.com/book-series/advances-marketing-customer-relationship-management/37150. Postmaster: Send all address changes to above address.

Titles in this Series

For a list of additional titles in this series, please visit: www.igi-global.com

Maximizing Commerce and Marketing Strategies through Micro-Blogging
Janée N. Burkhalter (Saint Joseph's University, USA) and Natalie T. Wood (Saint Joseph's University, USA & Edith Cowan University, Australia)
Business Science Reference • copyright 2015 • 354pp • H/C (ISBN: 9781466684089) • US $225.00 (our price)

Trends and Innovations in Marketing Information Systems
Theodosios Tsiakis (Alexander Technological Educational Institute of Thessaloniki, Greece)
Business Science Reference • copyright 2015 • 357pp • H/C (ISBN: 9781466684591) • US $225.00 (our price)

Analyzing the Cultural Diversity of Consumers in the Global Marketplace
Juan Miguel Alcántara-Pilar (University of Granada, Spain) Salvador del Barrio-García (University of Granada, Spain) Esmeralda Crespo-Almendros (University of Granada, Spain) and Lucia Porcu (University of Granada, Spain)
Business Science Reference • copyright 2015 • 404pp • H/C (ISBN: 9781466682627) • US $200.00 (our price)

Engaging Consumers through Branded Entertainment and Convergent Media
Jose Marti Parreno (Universidad Europea de Valencia, Spain) Carla Ruiz Mafe (Universidad de Valencia, Spain) and Lisa Scribner (University of North Carolina Wilmington, USA)
Business Science Reference • copyright 2015 • 354pp • H/C (ISBN: 9781466683426) • US $205.00 (our price)

Handbook of Research on Integrating Social Media into Strategic Marketing
Nick Hajli (Newcastle University Business School, UK)
Business Science Reference • copyright 2015 • 440pp • H/C (ISBN: 9781466683532) • US $310.00 (our price)

Customer Relationship Management Strategies in the Digital Era
Süphan Nasır (Istanbul University, Turkey)
Business Science Reference • copyright 2015 • 322pp • H/C (ISBN: 9781466682313) • US $200.00 (our price)

Handbook of Research on Effective Advertising Strategies in the Social Media Age
Nurdan Öncel Taşkıran (Ondokuz Mayıs University, Turkey) and Recep Yılmaz (Ondokuz Mayıs University, Turkey)
Business Science Reference • copyright 2015 • 509pp • H/C (ISBN: 9781466681255) • US $335.00 (our price)

Understanding Consumer Behavior and Consumption Experience
Rajagopal (EGADE Business School, Tecnologico de Monterrey, Mexico) and Raquel Castaño (EGADE Business School, Tecnologico de Monterrey, Mexico)
Business Science Reference • copyright 2015 • 303pp • H/C (ISBN: 9781466675186) • US $185.00 (our price)

This book is gratefully dedicated:
To the loving memory of my father, Alireza Khanlari.
To my mother, Azam Ajrian, who has supported me in all my endeavors.
To my wife, Mahsa Vaziri, who provides meaning to my life.

Table of Contents

Detailed Table of Contents

conversations driven by peer groups, industry professionals, prospects, customers and competitors. The objective of this chapter is to explore the opportunities analytics provides to organizations in terms of converting social CRM data into useful insights for designing CRM strategies.

The purpose of this chapter is studying that technology, such as customer relationship management systems and social media, improves the understanding of how to manage interactions with customers in today's digital era. Iran's auto industry has passed the first states of a new born auto industry (assembling the imported parts) and before the revolution, some of the car factories were upgraded to factories with the ability of design and production of spare parts. In order to examine the research model, data was gathered from survey of car representatives of IRAN. Participants included different levels in sales. Data was collected using an emailed link to an online survey supported by two reminder emails. 843 respondents completed the 130+ item. No significant difference between the data was evidenced. Results show that CRM and social media positively influence customer orientation activities, which in turn positively impact sales performance. Managerial implications are provided regarding the potential power CRM and social media has on sales performance.

This study has explored organizations' motivations to adopt Facebook for customer relationship management purposes. Interviews with twenty small to medium sized Australian organizations in this study showed that market pressures, direct customer service, brand promotion, and testing and experiencing are among key motivations for organizations to begin having presence on the Facebook. Ease of use, ease of receiving customers' feedback, availability of rich tools, and the opportunity to reach a large number of potential and existing customers are found to be amongst the key benefits of such presence. Furthermore, the findings show that dealing with negative comments, finding qualified human resources, ensuring the reliability of Facebook policies, and scalability of Facebook pages are some of the key issues that organizations have experienced with using this website for managing relationship with their customers.

This book chapter is aimed at finding out how SMEs in Ghana employ electronic customer relationship management (E-CRM) to improve their business performance.Case studies were used and five companies were selected and their managers interviewed. The study found that there is a growing awareness among SME owners about social media platforms. It also found that SME owners use such platforms for marketing and e-CRM purposes. The most reported social platforms used for e-CRM were found to be Facebook, WhatsApp and Instagram. Regarding the effectiveness of these platforms for marketing and e-CRM, the SME owners interviewed intimated that they are fast, convenient, and cost effective marketing platforms. This study concludes that SMEs in Ghana are aware of and use mostly free internet platforms such as Facebook, WhatsApp and Instagram for e-CRM. Specifically, SMEs use such platforms to share information with clients and build and maintain relationships.

Social media has been widely adopted world-wide, especially by young generations, and has become an integral part of today's society. As a popular Web 2.0 application, social media has significantly affected our daily life; from communication to education, from entertainment to business life. With a large percentage of young adults using social media in daily life, social media has become present in nearly all aspects of the higher education, ranging from admission to education in the classroom. Despite the many benefits and advantages, while many universities actively use social media, some lag behind in adopting this technology, especially in developing countries. The main aim of this chapter is to investigate the presence of social media in Web sites of the higher education institutions in Istanbul and analyze how they use it.

The chapter analyzes gamification conception presenting different perspective towards gamification. Game elements, game mechanics and game dynamics are discussed within the chapter as a main component gamification. Customer relations development stages are presented analyzing acquisition, retention and enchantment stages. The proposed conceptual model describes game elements impact on customer relations development and perceived value. The proposed model empirical validation results in Lithuania market are discussed.

This chapter explores the affective role of Web 2.0 on customer knowledge management (CKM) in two ways. At first, a new conceptualization of customer knowledge regarding knowledge "for", "from" and "about" customer is introduced through categorizing them in a detailed typological manner. The second part, attempts to find the relationship between Web 2.0 and three types of customer knowledge in a way that demonstrates each type of customer knowledge could be supported by using any kind of Web 2.0 tools. These parts are integrated as a comprehensive model which is named "Grape Model". This model encompasses different types of customer knowledge in detail as "grapes" which is related to Web 2.0 tools as "leafs" which support encompassed grapes. The"Grape Model" was applied in four different Iranian industries so as to evaluate each industry in making benefits from CKM and using Web 2.0 tools in order to facilitate the CKM process.

Facebook as the greatest social network has offered a new marketing tools for companies, agencies, organizations and even people like celebrities. We are witnessing a growing trend in emergence of online brand communities both in and out of social media. However, one of the important aspects that needs to be magnified is how brand's fans participate in their favorite brand pages? This study tries to answer questions like this. We introduce new variables which should be counted in the 3M model of personality in order to stimulate brand fans to participate on the brand page more than before. Entertainment, monetary and normative incentives are introduced as potential variables which affect situational traits of participants. Finally, we advise brand managers to not forget about entertainment mixed with promotions or representation of products over their online brand community; entertainment along with monetary and normative incentives can motivate fans to participate.

Effectiveness of websites is largely dependent on the quality of the website. The biggest share of the quality`s new concept is that the technical aspects of products and services combines with customers usage and understanding. Therefore websites evaluation based on the maximum usage and perception of the customers is considered an important issue to announce to the related organizations the success of website from customers' views. This customer relationship need a kind of management that first step of that for future decision needs knowledge about the websites features, customer insight and the position of websites among the competitors. One of the available media is the online news websites which their success is highly dependent on the relationship of their users. In this article achieving the information of websites is automatic and without the intervention of human so that the instant evaluation could be possible and used method is TOPSIS combined with information entropy to rank 791 news website which have most visitors of the Iranian users based on Alexa ranking report.

Extant research has been focusing on the effectiveness of social media in driving consumer engagement and interaction. However, little research has examined how social media influences firms' Customer Relationship Management. This chapter fills this gap by proposing a conceptual framework to capture the impact of social media on traditional Customer Relationship Management in the context of consumers' organic food purchasing. Specifically, this study investigates how social media influences the purchase behavior of loyalty program members and non-loyalty program members. This study also examines the effectiveness of different types of social media content on consumer purchase behavior of organic food.

Nowadays, the concept of brand community is tied with media. So, the new concept of social media based brand community without constraint of geography is built. In this chapter, we investigate the effects of social media based brand community on elements of the customer centric model, brand loyalty and brand equity through its antecedents (i.e., brand loyalty, brand trust, perceived quality, brand awareness/ association). An online survey with 170 users of brand community of Cinere Company on Facebook was conducted and path analysis technique was applied for data analysis. The results show that brand community of Cinere on social media has positive effects on all elements of the customer centric model. customer/ other customer and customer/ brand relationships have positive effects on brand loyalty with mediating role of brand trust; and loyalty, perceived quality, brand awareness/association have positive effects on brand equity. Interestingly, brand trust contributes only indirectly to brand equity. Finally, implications for practice and future research opportunities are discussed.

This chapter explores the influence of social media in Customer Relationship Management that leads to Customer loyalty. The social media in restaurant is recognized as an essential component of the customer satisfaction and therefore it is a cornerstone of the success of CRM and customer loyalty through social media nowadays. The purpose of this chapter is to investigate how Restaurant industry can harness the power of social media by utilizing CRM that leads to Customer loyalty. The problem is approached applying both the restaurants perspective and the customer perspective. The recent explosion in social media usage, combined with the transformation of the consumer into a "consume' activist", has permanently changed the relationship between a restaurant and its customers. There were two interviews conducted for 384 restaurants collected and analyzed for the research. The results proved that Social media can be an excellent channel for building long-lasting customer relationships in restaurants.

Preface

The mixture of social media and Customer Relationship Management that known as social CRM enables brands to truly listen to their customers more than ever before. It enhances the traditional CRM by listening for and engaging with social media conversations, tracking new leads from social media posts and moving them into the sales funnel.

As an emerging discipline, interpretations of Social CRM vary, but the most frequently quoted definition is from Paul Greenberg. He defined it as "a philosophy and a business strategy, supported by a technology platform, business rules, workflow, processes and social characteristics, designed to engage the customer in a collaborative conversation in order to provide mutually beneficial value in a trusted and transparent business environment. It's the company's response to the customer's ownership of the conversation."

Social CRM is a new approach for organizations that want to optimize the potential of social interactions to get closer to customers. Considering high usage of social networks, businesses are feeling extreme pressure to be where their customers are. Social CRM uses high potential of social media to develop relationships among different stakeholders includes employees, customers and businesses. But getting started with social CRM is comparable to other IT projects. Being multifaceted process, implementing this concept has a high risk and uncertainty. The most common factors associated with social CRM project failures may be included no clear strategy, no measurable objectives, or adopting technology without strategy, defined processes and organizational alignment. So, there is a need for resources and texts to addresses all aspects of this discipline. This book looks to discuss and address the comprehensive view to this emerging discipline includes Tools, Techniques and Strategies.

This book provides a variety of strategies, applications, tools and techniques of CRM proposed to different businesses for success in the social media in a coherent, conceptual framework. This conceptual framework provides an advanced and categorized variety of strategies, applications and tools by investigating their infrastructures, CSFs, required specializations, development processes, implementation methods, advantages, disadvantages, challenges, and futures.

The book approach is both practical and scientific to be useful for academicians and practitioners as well. It has been organized into two sections: Strategies & Applications such as Social Business Model and Strategy, Social CRM Analytics, Impact of social CRM on Sales Performance, Adoption of Facebook for CRM, e-CRM Practices of Micro, Small and Medium Enterprises, Social Media in Higher Education Institutions, Gamification impact on customer relationship; and Customer Learning & Engagement such as CKM 2.0, Fan Personality and Participation in Social CRM, News websites quality from customer insight, using Social media to influence CRM and loyalty,Social brand communities and brand loyalty, Electronic Word Of Mouth in Social Networks.

The book is useful for upper-level students, Interdisciplinary researchers, academicians, professional and practitioners, scientists, executive managers and consultantsof marketing and CRM in profit and non-profit organizations.The book contains 14 chapters written by professional researchers coming from academic and industrial fields. The chapters in section 1 make an overview of social CRM strategies and applications in different industries and businesses.

According to changing in economic environment and emergence of social business, the need to investigation of the differences and similarities between traditional business and social businesses is shown. Since the business model is one of the essential tools to understand how to do business, to study social business models is one of the areas of research that in this research is covered. The purpose of chapter 1, "Social Business Model and Strategy" is to define social business and its difference with conventional business type. It reviews the recent literature about social business evolution and definition, then it goes through social business model literature review and for run a social business the definition and models of conventional business models should be redefined. Finally it compares the different Social business models and introduces the social business components. At the end there are two cases from Grameen group one of the leading social groups in the world.

Social CRM entails the premise of customer relationship management channelizing the latent power and potential of social media platforms to enhance customer engagement. Social CRM encompasses a community-based environment in which the control and rules of engagement in the relationship with organizations has shifted from the unidirectional ways of traditional CRM directly to the customer who has the power to influence others in his social network. Marketers are expending efforts and devising new strategies to understand the field of social media and networks to demystify and understand consumer behaviors, patterns of engagement and attitudes and then harness the gained insights for business value. Analytics can help marketers in analyzing social CRM data to identify the most valuable insights from conversations driven by peer groups, industry professionals, prospects, customers and competitors. Chapter 2, "Social CRM Analytics: Gaining Customer Insights for Designing Social CRM Strategies" is to explore the opportunities analytics provides to organizations in terms of converting social CRM data into useful insights for designing CRM strategies.

Iran has recently been placed in the top 20 country car producers in the world. Iran's auto industry which started from the 1959 has passed the first states of a new born auto industry (assembling the imported parts) and before the revolution, some of the car factories were upgraded to factories with the ability of design and production of spare parts. The chapter 3, "The Impact of CRM & Social Media Technologies on Customer Orientation Process and Sales Performance" studies that technology, such as CRM systems and social media, improves the understanding of how to manage interactions with customers in today's digital era. The authors examine how customer focused technology (CRM/social media) and customer orientation process impacts sales performance. Results show that CRM and social media positively influence customer orientation activities, which in turn positively impact sales performance. Managerial implications are provided regarding the potential power CRM and social media has on sales performance.

Chapter 4, "Adoption of Facebook for Customer Relationship Management for SMEs: Exploring the Underlying Motivations"explores organizations' motivations to adopt Facebook for customer relationship management purposes. Interviews with twenty small to medium sized Australian organizations in this study showed that market pressures, direct customer service, brand promotion, and testing and experiencing are among key motivations for organizations to begin having presence on the Facebook. Ease of use, ease of receiving customers' feedback, availability of rich tools, and the opportunity to reach a large number of potential and existing customers are found to be amongst the key benefits of such presence. Furthermore, the findings show that dealing with negative comments, finding qualified human resources, ensuring the reliability of Facebook policies, and scalability of Facebook pages are some of the key issues that organizations have experienced with using this website for managing relationship with their customers.

The main aim of the chapter 5, "Electronic Customer Relationship Management (e-CRM) Practices of Micro, Small and Medium Enterprises" is to find out how SMEs in Ghana employ electronic customer relationship management (e-CRM) to improve their business performance. Case studies were used and five companies were selected and their managers interviewed. The study found that there is a growing awareness among SME owners about social media platforms. It also found that SME owners use such platforms for marketing and e-CRM purposes. The most reported social platforms used for e-CRM were found to be Facebook, WhatsApp and Instagram. Regarding the effectiveness of these platforms for marketing and e-CRM, the SME owners interviewed intimated that they are fast, convenient, and cost effective marketing platforms because they give them the opportunity to upload pictures, videos and textual information which clients are able to access. In addition, respondents stated that the internet (Facebook in particular) allows them to do real time marketing, monitor and record statistics on the number of people who might have seen their products and services online.

Social media has been widely adopted by people, especially young generations, and has become an integral part of today's society. As a Web 2.0 application, social media has significantly affected our daily life; from communication to education, from entertainment to business life. With a large percentage of young adults using social media in daily life, social media has become present in nearly all aspects of higher education, ranging from admission to education in the classroom. Despite the many benefits and advantages, while many universities actively use social media, some lag behind in adopting this technology. Chapter 6, "The Use of Social Media in Higher Education Institutions in Turkey: A Case of Istanbul" investigates the presence of social media in Web sites of higher education institutions in Istanbul and analyze how they use it.

Chapter 7, "Gamification impact on customer relationship development in virtual environment" analyzes gamification conception presenting different perspective towards gamification. Game elements, game mechanics and game dynamics are discussed within the chapter as a main component gamification. Customer relations development stages are presented analyzing acquisition, retention and enchantment stages. The proposed conceptual model describes game elements impact on customer relations development and perceived value. The proposed model and empirical validation results in Lithuania market are discussed.

Section 2 contains 7 chapters about Customer Learning and Engagement in the social media era.

Chapter 8 titled "CKM 2.0, Integrating Web 2.0 into Customer Knowledge Management" explores the affective role of Web 2.0 on customer knowledge management (CKM) in two ways. At first, a new conceptualization of customer knowledge regarding knowledge "for", "from" and "about" customer is introduced through categorizing them in a detailed typological manner. The second part, attempts to find the relationship between Web 2.0 and three types of customer knowledge in a way that demonstrates each type of customer knowledge could be supported by using any special kind of Web 2.0 tools. These two parts are integrated as a comprehensive model which is named "Grape Model". This model encompasses different types of customer knowledge in detail as "grapes" which is related to different Web 2.0 tools as "leafs" which support encompassed grapes. In this chapter, Web 2.0 tools are introduced as powerful tools for enhancing the capabilities of CKM in organizations. In addition, the "Grape Model" was applied in four different Iranian industries so as to evaluate each industry in making benefits from CKM and using Web 2.0 tools in order to facilitate the CKM process.

Facebook as the greatest social network has offered a new marketing tools for companies, agencies, organizations and even people like celebrities. Chapter 9, "The Effects of Fan Personality on Participation in Social Media Based Brand Community: Role of Personality on Participation in the Social Media" witnesses a growing trend in emergence of online brand communities both in and out of social media. However, one of the important aspects that need to be magnified is how brand's fans participate in their favorite brand pages? This chapter tries to answer questions like this andintroduces new variables which should be counted in the 3M model of personality in order to stimulate brand fans to participate on the brand page more than before. Entertainment, monetary and normative incentives are introduced as potential variables which affect situational traits of participants. Finally, the chaptersuggests brand managers to not forget about entertainment mixed with promotions or representation of products over their online brand community; entertainment along with monetary and normative incentives can motivate fans to participate.

Success and effectiveness of websites is largely dependent on the quality of the website. The biggest share of the quality`s new concept is that the technical aspects of products and services combines with customers usage and understanding. Therefore websites evaluation based on the maximum usage and perception of the customers is considered an important issue to announce to the related organizations the success of website from customers' views. This customer relationship need a kind of management that first step of that for future decision needs knowledge about the websites features, customer insight and the position of websites among the competitors. This ranking and evaluation should be performed in a special activity domain so that the first place of website rank determines among its other competitors. One of the available media is the online news websites which their success is highly dependent on the relationship of their users. In chapter 10, "Study of the automatic evaluation of websites quality from customer insight: a Case study of the most visited NEWS websites as influential social media tool" achieving the information of websites is automatic and without the intervention of human so that the instant evaluation could be possible.

Extant research has been focusing on the effectiveness of social media in driving consumer engagement and interaction. However, little research has examined how social media influences firms' Customer Relationship Management.Chapter 11, "Social Media, Customer Relationship Management and Consumers' Organic Food Purchase Behavior“ fills this gap by proposing a conceptual framework to capture the impact of social media on traditional Customer Relationship Management in the context of consumers' organic food purchasing. Specifically, this chapter investigates how social media influences the purchase behavior of loyalty program members and non-loyalty program members. It also examines the effectiveness of different types of social media content on consumer purchase behavior of organic food.

Nowadays, the concept of brand community is tied with media. So, the new concept of social media based brand community without constraint of geography is built. Chapter 12, "The effects of social media based brand communities on brand loyalty and brand equity: (case study: Cinere Company)" investigates the effects of social media based brand community on elements of the customer centric model, brand loyalty and brand equity through its antecedents (i.e., brand loyalty, brand trust, perceived quality, brand awareness/ association). An online survey with 170 users of brand community of Cinere Company on facebook has been conducted and path analysis technique used for data analysis. The results show that brand community of Cinere on social media has positive effects on all elements of the customer centric model. customer/ other customer and customer/ brand relationships have positive effects on brand loyalty with mediating role of brand trust; and loyalty, perceived quality, brand awareness/association have positive effects on brand equity. Interestingly, brand trust contributes only indirectly to brand equity. Finally, implications for practice and future research opportunities are discussed.

Chapter 13 titled "Using Social media to influence CRM and loyalty: Case Study of Restaurant Industry" investigates how integrating social media channels into existing Client Relationship Management platforms can influence customer service and customer loyalty. It used a mixture of both qualitative and quantitative research methods. The research method chosen was a single unique case study with interviews, observations and surveys as the data collection methods. The chapter used and built upon theoretical knowledge in the field of CRM, Social Media, customer service and loyalty, Restaurant industry in order to help the process of gathering empirical data. There were two interviews conducted for 384 restaurants collected and analyzed for the research. This chapter will bring value to everyone who wants first to understand what is CRM, its underlying principles and criticisms. And secondly having a wide overview and knowledge of linking social media to CRM practices aligned with customer services and customer loyalty.

Social networks as new form of popular and widely used communities especially among Iranians are considered as a place to talk about brands and share users comments, experiences and interests and they can play more prominent role in their own and others informed choices. Chapter 14, "Electronic Word of Mouth Marketing: Relationship between Brand Loyalty and Electronic Word Of Mouth in Social Marketing Networks" finds a logical relationship between loyalty to a brand (good/ service) on one hand, and participating in electronic word of mouth marketing and individuals' identification through specific brands (Adidas brand in present study) on the other. Regarding objective methodology and nature and data collection method, this chapter is an applied descriptive and surveying study. Research results showed a significant and positive correlation between brand loyalty and participating in eWoM and also consumer brand identification. Model presented in this chapter explains the same process. Research results showed a significant and positive correlation between brand loyalty and participating in eWoM and also consumer-brand identification.

As mentioned, there are not enough references to addresses all aspects of this discipline include strategies, business models, process, applications and tools. This book looks to discuss the comprehensive view to this emerging discipline. This comprehensive publication aims to be an essential reference source, building on the available literature in the field of social CRM while providing further research opportunities in this dynamic field for researchers and academicians. And also, it is hoped that this text will provide the resources necessary for professionals to adopt and implement social CRM strategies, process and techniques.

The book enables a variety of business managers to choose the best tools and applications of CRM according to their own strategies in the social media. Companies should align their social CRM strategies with existing CRM implementations.

As mentioned earlier, chapters divided into two sections. First section discusses strategic level problems, challenges and applications that could be useful for top-level managers to develop best strategies for managing customer relationships in social media environment. At this section, Strategies, business models and some applications in businesses are discussed which could be helpful to directors to select most suitable business models and strategies for their business based on customer knowledge, needs and expectations, and also use knowledge and experiences from cases and applications to how social media can enhance relationships with their customers.

At the second section, the chapters focus and emphasize on solutions for managing customer knowledge and also engage them more in business processes and increase their loyalty. Social CRM has high potential and power to drive customer engaging in business processes and also get knowledge from transactions, feedbacks and relationships. The proposed models and frameworks can useful to make loyalty programs, customer clubs and customer knowledge management more effective.

The book also helps professors, students, and researchers in fields of marketing, IT and CRM to further their knowledge on the Social CRM. Along these chapters, the reader is faced with the discussions and confirmation of the relevance and impact of this hot topic, providing researchers, and scholars with some of the most advanced research developments, solutions, state-of-the-art enabling technologies, discussions, applications, and case studies. As an academic tool, it can be a support to disciplines of post-graduate studies on IT, CRM, Marketing.

Hope to find it useful and enjoy your study!

Amir Khanlari
University of Tehran, Iran

Acknowledgment

The editor would like to acknowledge the help of all the people involved in this project and, more specifically, to the authors and reviewers that took part in the review process. Without their support, this book would not have become a reality.

First, the editor would like to thank each one of the authors for their contributions. Our sincere gratitude goes to the chapter's authors who contributed their time and expertise to this book.

Second, the editor wish to acknowledge the valuable contributions of the reviewers regarding the improvement of quality, coherence, and content presentation of chapters. Most of the authors also served as referees; we highly appreciate their double task.

Amir Khanlari
University of Tehran, Iran

Section 1

Social CRM:
Strategies and Applications

Chapter 1
The Impact of Social Business Strategies in Creating Empirical Social Business Models

Siavash Moheb
University of Tehran, Iran

Ali Golrokh
University of Tehran, Iran

ABSTRACT

The purpose of this chapter is to define social business and its difference with conventional business type. Governments could not address all the social problems. Because they don't have the knowledge ore the money to do so.however big enterprises have much more resources. Social business is form at the intersection pf social needs and business expertise. Also corporates want to have a good publicity through social responsibility.social business can help them to run social responsibility process through a sustainable approach. The articles reviews the recent literature about social business evolution and definition. And then it goes through social business model literature review to run a social business the definition and models of conventional business models should be redefined. Finally it compare the different Social business models and introduces the social business components in the end there are two cases from Grameen group one of the leading social groups in the word.

INTRODUCTION

Mohammad Yunus:" we created a joint venture company with DANONE-a food company that produce diary-.I met the Chairman of DANONE.A chance meeting, I suggested him why don't we create a DANONE - Grameen Company in Bangladesh. He said "to do what" and I said to produce yogurt. For a special purpose.to address the problem of malnutrition among the children of Bangladesh. We put all the malnutrition needed for the children and put them in the yogurt and make it very cheap so that poor can afford it.If they eats the yogurt twice a week for a year they will regain their full health. The DANONE chairman agreed. I said it will be a social business.he said "what is a social business? "I explained in this

DOI: 10.4018/978-1-4666-8586-4.ch001

kind of business you can invest but cannot take any dividends. You can take back all of your investment back but after that it stop the profit will go back to expand the company to reach out for more children because it's driven by a social objective and he said "I agree"

The example above was the story of one the most successful social business experiences in bangladesh. in this case they tried to solve malnutrition problem among the children of Bangladesh. The Grameen group used the expertise of DANONE and tackle to solve the malnutrition problem. The story of this cooperation is in the final case of this chapter.

In today's business world many corporates aim to invest in solving social problems. However the investment usually has no impact and it's just spend as a part of the budget. A comprehensive social business model can guide the enterprises to manage their donations and investment in way that has most possible impact on social problems. According to European commission social businesses have SME's problems alongside with their own specific problems. "Social enterprises should be able to benefit from the advantages of the internal market just as much as other businesses. This applies, of course, to large enterprises which may be able to expand at continental level or even only across the borders of their country, but small social enterprises, which mainly have their roots solely in local activities, are also directly affected by the rules of the internal market on bank regulation, access to structural funds or public procurement. Above all, social enterprises have difficulty finding funding, for which their needs vary according to their level of development (conceptual support, development of pilot projects or prototypes, large-scale development)."

The paper tries to review the best Social Business (SB) models and provides a conceptual business model to reduce such obstacles in running social business

LITERATURE REVIEW

Part I: Business Model

Business model definition: surprisingly the business model is often studied without explicitly defining the concept.(Zott 2010) this lack of exact definition has led to confusion. The origins of the business model concept can be traced back to Chandler's seminal book '*Strategy and Structure*' from 1962. Strategy, Chandler states, "can be defined as the determination of the basic long-term goals and objectives of an enterprise, and the adoption of courses of action and the allocation of resources necessary for carrying out these goals" (Chandler 1962, 13).After Chandler's discussions the Ansof matrix was developed and for a long time it remained the main framework for developing a business model. Andrew's work (1980) on corporate strategy also develop the business model concept. The emergence of developing a prevalent business model concept has since the advent of internet in mid-1990's.the number of articles addressed business models has increased exponentially. The emergence of dot com companies in late 90's led to search for definitions of a business model. For so –called highly competitive Chaharbaghi*et al.* (2003) identify three interrelated strands which form the basis of a meta-model for business models: characteristics of the company's way of thinking, its operational system, and capacity for value generation. This definition was on the basis of Porter's work.

In 2004 a comprehensive model proposed by Osterwalder which named canvas business model. This model built blocks for the activities taken applying a business strategy.

Osterwalder's work and thesis (2010, 2004) propose a single reference model based on the similarities of a wide range of business model conceptualizations. With his business model design template, an enterprise can easily describe their business model. This business model consist of four main areas: Infrastructure, Offering, Customers and Finances.

- Infrastructure
    - Key Activities: The most important activities in executing a company's value proposition. Key Resources: The resources that are necessary to create value for the customer. They are considered an asset to a company, which are needed in order to sustain and support the business. These resources could be human, financial, physical and intellectual.
    - Partner Network: to make synergy and increase the level of productivity companies usually make strategic alliance and a network of partners
- Offering
    - Value Propositions: The collection of product and services provide by company to fulfill the need of customers. According to Osterwalder, (2004), a company's value proposition is what distinguishes itself from its competitors
        - The value propositions may be:
        - Quantitative- price and efficiency
        - Qualitative- overall customer experience and outcome
- Customers
    - Customer Segments: a company should not produce a product /service for all the society but instead it should chooses what part of society to sell to. segmentation can be applied by various basis like (product or service offered, by industry, by demographics, Geographically, by profession, By lifestyle, By interest) the important note is that each segment must be very similar within the group and be distinctly different from other segments
    - Channels: A company can deliver its value proposition to its targeted customers through different channels. Effective channels will distribute a company's value proposition in ways that are fast, efficient and cost effective. An organization can reach its clients either through its own channels (store front), partner channels (major distributors), or a combination of both.
    - Customer Relationships: To ensure the survival and success of any businesses, companies must identify the type of relationship they want to create with their customer segments. Various forms of customer relationships include:
        - Personal Assistance: Assistance in a form of employee-customer interaction. Such assistance is performed either during sales, after sales, and/or both.
        - Dedicated Personal Assistance: The most intimate and hands on personal assistance where a sales representative is assigned to handle all the needs and questions of a special set of clients.
        - Self Service: The type of relationship that translates from the indirect interaction between the company and the clients. Here, an organization provides the tools needed for the customers to serve themselves easily and effectively.
        - Automated Services: A system similar to self-service but more personalized as it has the ability to identify individual customers and his/her preferences. An example of this would be Amazon.com making book suggestion based on the characteristics of the previous book purchased.

        - Communities: Creating a community allows for a direct interaction among different clients and the company. The community platform produces a scenario where knowledge can be shared and problems are solved between different clients.
        - Co-creation: A personal relationship is created through the customer's direct input in the final outcome of the company's products/services.
- Finances: this part of business model is consist of two main steps.Cost Structure and Revenue Stream.
    - Cost Structure: This describes the most important monetary consequences while operating under different business models. A company can be cost –driven which means it puts all its endeavor to minimize the cost. On the other hand the company can be value driven which tries to maximize the value for customers.
    - Revenue Streams: The way a company makes income from each customer segment. Several ways to generate a revenue stream
        - Asset Sale - (the most common type) Selling ownership rights to a physical good. e.g. Wal-Mart
        - Usage Fee - Money generated from the use of a particular service e.g. UPS
        - Subscription Fees - Revenue generated by selling a continuous service. e.g. Netflix
        - Lending/Leasing/Renting - Giving exclusive right to an asset for a particular period of time. e.g. Leasing a Car
        - Licensing - Revenue generated from charging for the use of a protected intellectual property.
        - Brokerage Fees - Revenue generated from an intermediate service between 2 parties. e.g. Broker selling a house for commission
        - Advertising - Revenue generated from charging fees for product advertising.[16]

In early 2000's the concept of bottom line pyramid was proposed which turned the attention to other segment of society and led to concepts like Social responsibility through the evolution of Corporate Social responsibility the Social Business concept has emerged.

Part II: Social Business: The Evolution of Corporate Social Responsibility

Porter and Kramer (2006, 2011) highlighted the mutual relation between social responsibility and profit making business. They stated that "successful corporations need a healthy society (and) at the same time a healthy society needs successful companies" (Porter and Kramer 2006, p. 83)." The companies have learned that giving effort to solve the society problems can help them to develop their own business. Through this relation a new paradigm is emerging. A connection between private enterprises and the public interest that produces profitable and sustainable change for both sides. This paradigm is the creating shared value (CSV) approach.

This approach has shown it's important since the entrance of multinational companies in developing countries.These countries present a good opportunity for investing and business. However they face a lot of social problems which can be addressed by such powerful companies.it should be mentioned that this new role of companies changes their main strategy-being profit oriented-.Porter and Kramer note that "the concept of shared value blurs the line between for-profit and nonprofit organizations. New kinds of hybrid enterprises are rapidly appearing"(2006,2011)

These hybrid enterprises needs new business models. Hence the corporate social responsibility turns into social entrepreneurship(SE) and social business (SB).the main goal of SE is to find a way to reach the low-income market (Mahlouji and Anaraki 2009).

A further analysis by Sánchez and Ricart (2010) identifies two types of business model configurations that can be implemented to reach the low-income market:

- *Isolated* business models are characterized by an exploitation strategy, which leverages the firm's own resources and capabilities for seeking efficiency;
- *Interactive* business models are characterized by an exploration strategy, which leverages on external resources and fosters learning and innovation processes.

Following the Bottom Of Pyramid theory proposed by Prahalad (2004), which is based on the concept of "serving the poor profitably", it is now evident that profitability in Low Income Customer could only be achieved if companies change their traditional opinions toward developing countries by no longer regarding them as territories to exploit but as uncharted territories (or as entirely different markets) characterized by good producers and good consumers with specific needs, which in turn could be satisfied through specific and innovative businesses (Austin et al. 2007). Importantly, it is necessary to "turn Low income customers (LIC) into partners" (Marwaha et al. 2005), as doing so could result in profits for both the company and the LIC. BOP scholars often argue that, to be successful, solutions must be co-created by the exogenous actors and the poor. These researches shows that a new kind of business is needed. Mohammad Yunus called this new type of business a Social business (2006).the main goal of this business is to serve the poor while being sustainable. "The free market and spread of wealth through this market is not flawed but it is too limited" (yunus 2006) we see lots of examples in today's world which free market has failed. Let think that any business man has two incentives to work.first to maximize profit and second to solve a social problem. The first one is called profit maximizing enterprise (PME's) and the second one is called Social business enterprise (SME's).with this new definition conventional business models can help to adjust the imbalance of wealth in the world and to reduce poverty.

The second category business man is called social entrepreneur who put his energy time and efforts to address a social problem whilst conducting his own business. This definition enlarges the span that an entrepreneur can work.it says that you can run a business and serve the society as well.

Every year the companies donate a huge amount to charities as a part of their social responsibility.as Yunus says this a dollar donated to a charity is spend and that's it. But if we put that dollar in a process that can produce more dollars for that social purpose it is much better. Each corporate can bridge a social problem to its expertise and provide a solution to that problem. Through this approach the company can make a sustainable social business with no actual cost. Because that sub SME of company can cover its own cost and return the initial investment too.in case below we see that how corporates can use their expertise to create a successful social business

SOCIAL BUSINESS DEFINITION

The definition of Social business and social entrepreneurship differs in the recent literature. However the core definition is to run a sustainable business that serve the poor.

For UNDP and EMES, social enterprises may be defined as "private, autonomous, entrepreneurial organizations providing goods or services with an explicit aim to benefit the community. They are owned or managed by a group of citizens, and the material interest of capital investors is subject to limits. Social enterprises place a high value on their autonomy and on economic risk-taking related to ongoing socioeconomic activity. Social enterprises are either legally prohibited from distributing profits or are structured to exclude profit as the main goal" (UNDP/ EMES 2008, p. 18)

Mohammad Yunus (2010) stated "Social business is a non-dividend company to solve a social problem".as said by Yunus in the example above in a social business the objective is to solve a social of problem instead of making more profit. The important part is the difference between a SB and charities or NGO's.In a social business the company is self-sustainable. Which means it can provide the money for its activities through its own business while NGO's activities depend on the money that others donate. Corporates has tried to play a role in society through NGO's and donating charity. The term used for such activities is social responsibility of an enterprise. However such activities were not that much effective. Something ongoing action was needed to address the society problems.

Furthermore, Yunus (2008) proposed a second typology of the social business model: a profit-making company that is owned by poor people. In this case, even if the business is profit oriented, it could be considered a social business because it is permitted to improve the social condition of low-income people.

A broader definition of SE was also given recently by the European Commission (2011), which considers the social enterprise to be "an operator in the social economy whose main objective is to have a social impact rather than make a profit for their owners or shareholders. It operates by providing goods and services for the market in an entrepreneurial and innovative fashion and uses its profits primarily to achieve social objectives. It is managed in an open and responsible manner and, in particular, involves employees, consumers and stakeholders affected by its commercial activities" (p. 2)

Social Business is a business:

- Created and designed to address a social problem.
- A non-loss, non-dividend company, i.e.(Yunus 2007)

1. It is financially self-sustainable, and
2. Profits realized by the business are reinvested in the business itself (or used to start other social businesses), with the aim of increasing social impact, for example expanding the company's reach, improving the products or services or in other ways subsidizing the social mission.

SOCIAL BUSINESS AND CONVENTIONAL BUSINESS

Companies are seeking more ways to address the challenges of society. And the social companies and communities are seeking for the business expertise to solve the social problem.at the intersection of these two the social business is created. This is how a hybrid enterprise is made. On a span form 100% charity companies to profit oriented companies, social businesses placed somewhere in between (see Figure 1). Here is the chart that shows the position of social business.

Figure 1. Social businesses are placed beetween NGO's and Profit oriented Business-Source: BCG Analysis

	NGO	Business inspired NGO	Social business	Balanced (social profit business	Business
Primary objective	Social impact	Social impact	Social impact	Social impact and commercial success	Commercial success
Product/service price for sale	No	YES	YES	YES	YES
Business model	Maximizing social impact	Maximizing social impact	Maximizing social impact	Maximizing social impact	Ensuring social standards
	Funded through donations	Partially Funded through donations	Financially sustainable	Maximizing profit	Maximizing profit
			Social entrepreneurs		

The Grameen team defines social business as non-dividend business that like NGO's its main purpose is to address a social problem.it is a subset of social entrepreneurship defined by Mair and Marti(2005) as 'a process involving the innovative use and combination of resources to pursue opportunities to catalyze social change and/or address social needs'. Unlike NGO, it's a no loss no dividend self-sustaining company which can produce its own operating costs. Hence the social business is a new form of business which lies somewhere between profit maximizing and non-for-profit business (see Figure 2).

Figure 2. Greeman definition of social business

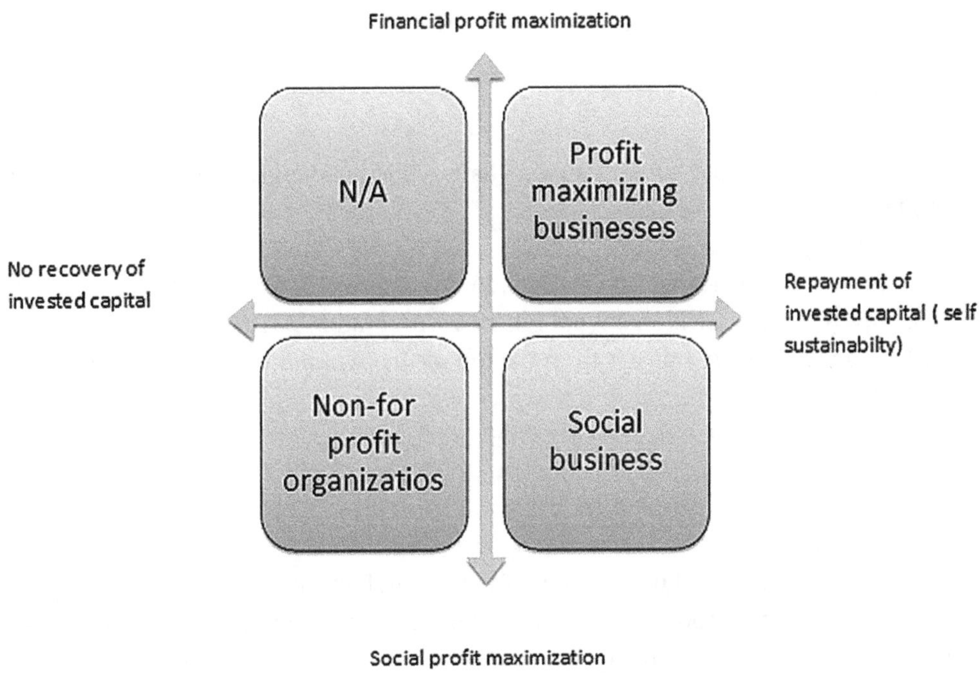

SOCIAL BUSINESS PRINCIPLES

Yunus and Grameen research team propose 7 principles of social business.

These were developed by Prof. Muhammad Yunus and Hans Reitz, the co-founder of Grameen Creative Lab:

- Business objective will be to overcome poverty, or one or more problems (such as education, health, technology access, and environment) which threaten people and society; not profit maximization.
- Financial and economic sustainability.
- Investors get back their investment amount only; no dividend is given beyond investment money.
- When investment amount is paid back, company profit stays with the company for expansion and improvement.
- Environmentally conscious.
- Workforce gets market wage with better working conditions.
- Do it with joy.

Through Bottom of pyramid theory an inclusive business model along with social business model is the most suitable framework that can fulfill the social business goals. The inclusive business model can provide an opportunity to conduct a business while addressing the social problems. Inclusive businesses are based on models with which to "include the poor on the demand side as clients and customers, and on the supply side as employees, producers and business owners at various points in the value chain. They build bridges between business and the poor for mutual benefit. The benefits from inclusive business models go beyond immediate profits and higher incomes. For business, they include driving innovations, building markets and strengthening supply chains. And for the poor, they include higher productivity, sustainable earnings and greater empowerment."(UNDP 2008, p. 2).

The main characteristics through inclusive model are:

- CO-value creation.

The company generates value within its own chain while generating value with its suppliers and-partners.(UNPD 2008)

- Economic growth is considered, in any case, to be the primary driver for the companies that develop inclusive businesses (International Finance Corporation 2010).
- Knowledge and technology transfer from the top of the pyramid to the bottom and from the bottom to the top.

METHODOLOGY

Through reviewing the background information of the research the author tries to provide a conceptual model and identify the main components of a Social Business model. The paper also tries to give a frame work to run such a business through reviewing successful cases in recent years.

Social Business Models

Now that we learn what a social business really is its time to learn how we can start a SME from the beginning. The important part is that we understand the between the key assumptions of conventional business and social business to establish social business model. We review two major concepts in designing a social business model.the first on is for Prof Yunus of Grameen group (see Figure 3) and second one chengue-ludlow.finally we review the European commission model

A conventional business consists of three major parts.

1- Value proposition: which defines customers and what product and service we offer them that they value.
2- Value constellation: that is, the answer to the question: 'How do we deliver this offer to our customers?' This involves not only the company's own value chain but also its value network with its suppliers and partners.
3- These two components join together if they can provide the profit expected.

A review on new literature of business models indicates that the researchers could not adjust hybrid enterprises with the conventional business model so they had to change it some way. Here are three business models for social business:

GRAMEEN MODEL FOR A SOCIAL BUSINESS

The Grameen social business model has five major parts (see Figure 4). Three of these five are similar to conventional business models.

1. Challenging conventional wisdom and basic assumption: Most research on business model innovation underlines the radicalism of this type of innovation, which is defined as the capacity to create new strategies which modify the rules of the competitive game in an industry.it indeed needs a review of the common assumptions in the industry. The creation of Grameen bank could be a great example. Mohammad Yunus says he finds out about a problem by a village woman. The problem

Figure 3. Source: Muhammad Yunus ET all's; building social business models (2010)

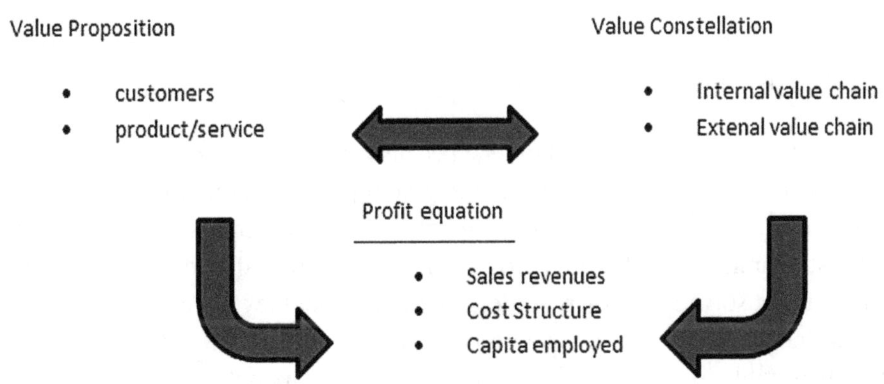

Figure 4. Grameen social business framework

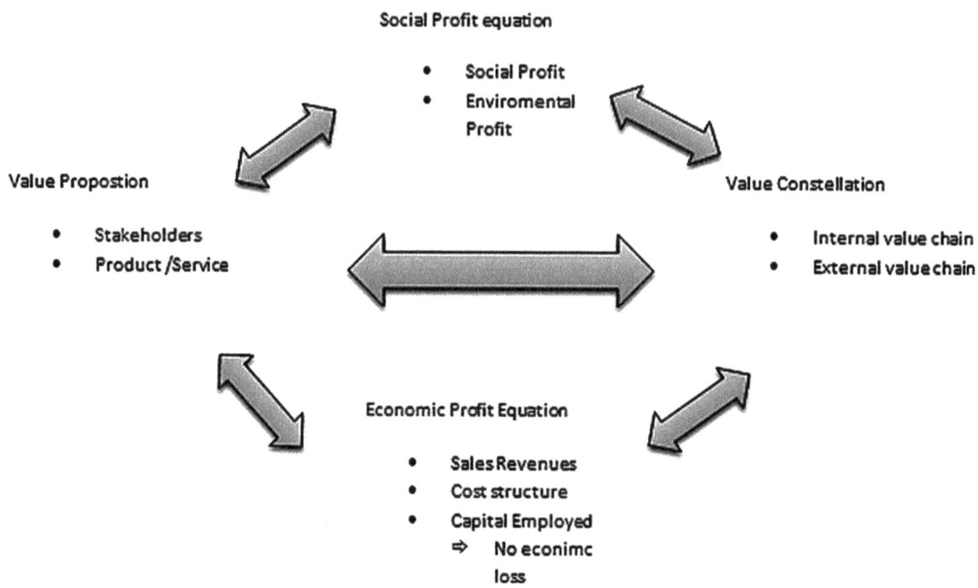

was that village people in Bangladesh have to sell their entire product at a ridiculously low price to moneylenders to make some money. They couldn't use banks because they do not have an acceptable credit and even worse they were illiterate. The conventional banks focus on wealthier parts of the society and simply omitted the poor village people. Hence the Grameen bank was established to give loan to these segments of society and soon it can make profit and make a self-sustaining social business. The Grameen bank breaks the conventional rules of bank which neglect the poor segments of society.

2. Finding complementary partners: like the GM Eye care center a company Grameen cannot run a business by itself. Because it doesn't have the expertise and skill to do it. And the doctors and hospitals didn't have the knowledge of management and the network of Grameen. The cooperation of these two can make such a successful social business.
3. Undertaking continuous experimentation: strategic experiments are vital to the expansion and continuing he business.to be radical corporate you need to always revise the situation and strategies you have already made for the business plan.

These three factors were similar to conventional business factors. The following to is what make a business model specific for social businesses

4. Favoring social profit-oriented shareholders: because the investment require the time and power of top management and the top managers should give report to shareholders.by investing in a social business the profit will reduce so all the shareholders must feel that they are a part of it and it must be shown that their investment is going to return in long term and also does social responsibility. If this problem is not solved then shareholders might feel that they are cheated. DANONE Grameen corporate which mentioned before is a good example." As the CEO of a publicly-held company, Riboud is answerable to his DANONE's shareholders, but he risked being

Unable to provide clear evidence of how the resources used in the Grameen DANONE experiment Maximize value for them. So, in order to avoid alienating skeptical shareholders, DANONE developed another innovation by disconnecting the funding of Grameen DANONE from the stock market. The company created a publicly-trade mutual fund with a special mission to give investors social benefits rather than financial benefits and gave DANONE's shareholders the option of joining if they wished. "(Yunus et al-2010)

5. Specifying social profit objectives clearly: there is always a possibility in a social business for occurring a conflict between social goals and financial goals. For example in DANONE - Grameen case in 2008 the price of milk raised dramatically and the DANONE - Grameen project was stuck in choosing financial goals or social goals.

To avoid such problems goals of the project must be mentioned explicitly in the first place. Because in conventional business the implicit and obvious goal is always maximizing profit. The Grameen DANONE's mission statement is very explicit: 'to bring daily healthy nutrition to low income, nutritionally deprived populations in Bangladesh and alleviate poverty through the implementation of a unique proximity business model.

THE SOCIAL BUSINESS FRAMEWORK

According to Grameen researchers this frame work is suggested for conducting a social business

Chengue-Ludlow Model for a Social Business

In this model a broader span of businesses are in SME's category compared to Grameen models.

This model says that there are three fundamental ways that social impact can be created through trading activities:

1. Model One: Engage in a trading activity that has no direct social impact, make a profit, and then transfer some or all of that profit to another activity that does have direct social impact (the 'profit generator model')
2 Model Two: Engage in a trading activity that does have direct social impact, but manage a trade-off between producing financial return and social impact (the 'trade-off model')
3 Model Three: Engage in a trading activity that not only has direct social impact, but also generates a *financial return in direct correlation to the social impact created (the 'lock-step model')*

Model One: 'Profit Generator'

In this model the main motivation is the financial incentive.it means that the corporate runs the business to maximize profit and then it allocate a percentage of profit to a social cause. It can be seen, therefore, that a social investment in Model One involves two 'bets' – (I) that the business will in fact make a profit; and (ii) that the profit generated is then effectively used to achieve social impact.

In Model One, therefore, the financial risk of the investment is disconnected from the likelihood of achieving social impact. Examples of Model One include (but are not limited to):

- For-profit businesses with CSR programmers
- Charitable foundations investing their endowments in mainstream financial markets
- Trading subsidiaries of charities (e.g. Oxfam shops)
- 'Ethical' bottled water companies – which give a percentage of their profits to developing charitable projects (e.g. Belu Water, Thirsty Planet)
- A hedge fund which gives a slice of its profits to a charitable foundation (e.g. Children's Investment Fund)

Model Two: 'Trade-Off'

In this model the business itself does not have social impact but there is balance between social impact and profit of the business and by increasing one the other one must decrease. Unlike Model One, social impact is integral to the very nature of the trading activity of Model Two. Even if no financial return is achieved, some social impact will occur by virtue of the existence of the trading activity.

Examples of Model Two include:

- Fair trade businesses
- Microfinance institutions
- Firms that employ the disabled, ex-offenders or other disadvantaged people
- Ethical Property Company

Model Three: 'Lock-Step'

In this model, not only does the trading activity itself have direct social impact, but that social impact increases or decreases in lock-step and in parallel with financial returns. These corporates are producing a service or product for a social impact.so it is obvious that they should participate in a competitive environment where there are other substitute products. They have an advantage of being a social business which is positive image in customer's mind. But their rivals have the advantage of profit maximizing which means they can do anything (even sometimes unethical) to defeat our product.

Examples of Model Three include:

- Cooperatives
- Wind farms
- Abel & Cole Organic Food

The three models enable the managers to conduct their business according to the market environment and affordable risks they can take... Other commentators have described how charitable capital might be applied more efficiently for social impact by adopting socially responsible investment ('SRI'), mission-connected investment ('MCI') and programed-related investment ('PRI'). We believe that the Three Models help investors to differentiate between potential investments with an apparent social benefit, and to think through the risks and returns of these opportunities.

European Commission Model: in comparison with Grameen model this model consider a wider range of business as social ones.EC do not restricts the enterprise to reinvest all the profit in the business. But the main goal (social goal) must always be met.

We can summarize the social business models through the business type span in the beginning of the chapter

In Figure 1 we have five type of business models. Yunus model is a pure social business. However the European commission Model covers a wider range of business models and it includes social business and social profit business. The Ludlow model contains even broader span form business NGO inspired to social profit business.

However he all of these models have a core incentive which is to have a social impact and be sustainable as much as possible

Analysis

In the beginning of chapter the main problem was to address the social problems through businesses. By reviewing the literature it was obvious that all the researchers in this field had tried to change the components of conventional business model and change the components relations to fulfill social business needs.

To meet practical goals a framework to run a social business (after choosing the business model) has been brought. This frame work is BCG suggestion based on Grameen group experiences in Bangladesh

At Yunus et al (2010 social business mode the suggested component are: Value proposition (stakeholders and product/service), social profit equation (social profit and environmental profit), value constellation (internal value chain and external value chain) and economic profit equation (sales revenues, cost structure, and capital employed)

Also Osterwalder and Pigneur's (2010) in canvas model suggest these components: customer segment, Key resources, key partners, key activities, value proposition, clients, competitors, channels, cost and revenue.in canvas reinvented model for social business these changes are made:

Beneficiary Segments: Clearly identify who your beneficiary segments are -- even if they aren't paying you and there is no place for them in the regular business model canvas

Social and Customer Value Proposition: Ensure that you have laid out a compelling rationale that will drive your customers to buy without forgetting about your impact on society

Impact Measures: Develop clear thinking around what kind of social impact you're creating and how it could be measured

Surplus: Plan and communicate what happens with profits and where you aim to reinvest them

By reviewing these two business models and suggestion of European Commission the components below are suggested to make a social business model for a business

1. Value proposition
2. Market segment: the part of society who face a social problem
3. Governance: set of laws and processes that manage the stakeholders and company relations
4. Surplus: how company manage the revenue.it can reinvest it like Yunus model or it can distribute some of the profit between stock holders

5. Profit equation: revenue model of company
6. Social value equation: the way company create social benefit
7. Ecosystem: the competence and social context

DEVELOPING A SUCCESSFUL SOCIAL BUSINESS

Boston consulting group (BCG) has made a frame work based on Grameen bank experiences. This five step frame work (see Figure 5)

1. Choosing the right focus area
2. Designing a successful business model
3. Continuously learning and adapting
4. Building efficient and sustainable operations
5. Managing for impact

1. Choosing focus area: like any other business the first thing is to specify the problem you want to address.remember the GM eye care center. After hearing about the problem prof.Yunus went among those people to understand the **root cause** for the problem. And then he established Grameen bank. He also cheeked what other banks do to introduce something new to the market that can solve the problem and have the business advantage at the same time

Figure 5. Developing a social business

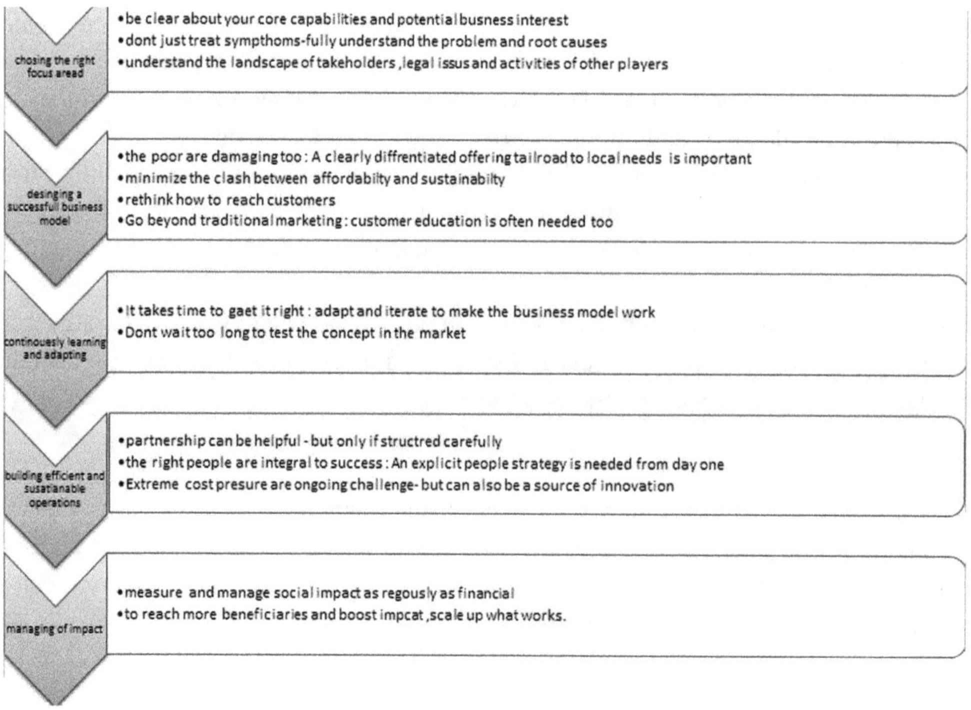

When companies trying to address a social problem their baseline is to take look at their own core capabilities

For example the Grameen voila company was a joint venture between Grameen bank and voila water company. The problem was that a great portion of Bangladesh population drink contaminated water with arsenic. They use it even if they knew it contains arsenic. After some research different reason were found for this problem. The results showed that not only the people needs clean source of water but they need some changes in their behavior in usage of water

2. Designing a Successful Business Model

An effective business model–with a clear value proposition–is as important to a social business as it is to a commercial business. The challenges that the social business model must tackle, however, are exceptionally difficult, particularly in the context of a developing country.

"Social businesses–as any other businesses–need a clearly differentiated product with a unique selling proposition." – Kazi Huque, CEO of Grameen Intel Social Business

BCG's survey of managing directors at social businesses in Bangladesh revealed that chief among these challenges is gaining a deep understanding of the specific needs of the target population in order to design a clearly differentiated solution that meets those needs. Developing a product/service to poor people does not mean to reduce quality. You have to cut down the price while presenting an acceptable quality.

There are three main ways of pricing in a SB. The first one is to set the lowest price in the market. The price should be that low that the poorest people become willing to use that service/product. But we must know that there is a limit to the price we set and sustainability of corporate must be considered. The second method is to put a premium price. But they convince poor people to pay such price they should be informed about the quality they receive. The third way of pricing is to differentiated prices for different segments of poor people. The key part is to recognize the segments and affordability of them

Three other challenges were consistently mentioned: achieving a price point that the targeted population can actually afford, physically reaching those most in need, and generating sufficient demand for the new offering. An effective business model must explicitly address these four challenges

3. Continuously Learning and Adapting

One thing we consistently hear from people who have been involved with social businesses is that getting the business model right is an iterative learning process that involves time and effort, trial and error.

You should always be prepared to take much longer step than you initially expected.the learn and approach cycle has to major ways (I) rapid market entry which means learning what to do by experiencing and doing the business (ii) through advance planning: which obviously means predicting all the possible events and have a plan for them 'while both ways are valuable you should never wait too long for your concept works in market.

"We learned that it doesn't really help you to plan more and more and more–your plan is going to be wrong." – Jochen Ebert, managing director of DANONE India

4. Building Efficient and Sustainable Operations

You expect the social business to cover the initial investment and make profit for further expansion. But this goal can be achieved only if you plan your social business efficiently. Common problems that can occur during a social business are: weak partnership, having a high-performance work force is vital, dealing with an ongoing cost pressure,

"Social business creates a common platform for the public sector, the private sector, and NGOs to work together on the resolution of social problems...This demilitarized zone allows collaboration modes, creativity, and a correlation of solutions which no other modality allows." – Emmanuel Faber, co-COO and vice chairman, DANONE Group

The joint venture of two companies must turn into a strategic alliance.two corporates (like DANONE and Grameen) should be integrated in all of their top decision making parts in their cooperation.this helped them to avoid goal conflicts in long term and build a strong partnership.

A high-performance group of worker who are both familiar with social concepts and have high-level of expertise is vital to every step of business.

There is always an ongoing pressure to control the cost. Because of the low price services of such business the corporate always seeks for new ways of cutting the cost. This could be a source of innovation for itself

5. Managing the impact: this is where you can tell whether your SME was successful or not. The two measures for this conclusion is the real social impact and self-sustainability.for this measurement you need a full annual report of your business

This measurement should be exact in numbers. For example in Grameen voila case the money that people spend for clean water should be measured and also the reduction of arsenic in water usage has to be measured in numbers

Another important factor to increase impact is to scale up your business

Big companies can reach people in many countries, deliver products to remote areas, learn in one place, and take knowledge to all other countries." – John E. Davies, general manager, Intel World Ahead Program

There are three routes to increase scale:

- *Local scale-up* aims to reach a broader customer base in a given country. For instance, Grameen Shakti plans to expand from more than 1 million solar home systems sold in 2012 to a cumulative installation base of more than 2 million units by 2015.
- *Portfolio extension* enhances the portfolio of a social business by adding new products or services. For instance, Grameen Distribution has expanded its portfolio with new social products, such as BASF Grameen mosquito nets.
- *International expansion* involves transferring a social business to another region or country. While none of the businesses highlighted in this report have yet taken this step, it is certainly an option for those that have reached significant national scale.

CONCLUSION

We can summarize the social business models in two main group

1. Pure social business as Yunus state. A non-loss non dividend business which is sustainable and is run to address a social problem. All the profit from such business is reinvested to expand the business
2. Social business by European commission definition which covers a broader range. The corporate can give stack holders part of the profit as long as it meets the social goal. An inclusive strategy help to do so

If an enterprise want to increase its social responsibility level it can choose to have an inclusive strategy or the Grameen social business model. The company could choose the low income customer as their main segment and shift the strategy to an inclusive business model.it also have to link the components of social business strategy in a way that insure the sustainability of corporate.

It should be considered that Social business have benefits for both society and business.

"Imagine a world in which electricity reaches even the most remote rural families in developing countries–those living far from today's existing grid system–and provides them a means of working and studying late into the evenings. Imagine further that this electricity is green energy–solar home systems or biogas plants, for example. And imagine it were sold to the customers–most of whom live on less than $2 a day–for a price that makes the business financially sustainable and keeps it from depending on ongoing aid payments. Impossible, you might say. And then you might travel to Bangladesh and come across Grameen Shakti, a social business that is thriving on just such a business model. "Yunus (2008)

Through social business you can address almost any social problem in the society. Not only has the society received the benefits this business is a great experience for business corporates too (see figure-6). They learn a lot and make tons of innovations to run such cooperation with social corporates.

Figure 6. Social business benefits

Social benefits	Business benefits
Provide innovative solutions to social problems	Create greater lasting social impact than traditional donation-based corporate social responsibility programs
Create results that last well beyond the initial investment	Provides new opportunities for learning and innovation
Empower beneficiaries by transforming them from	Improve employee motivation and retention
Leverage the business mindset to increase efficiency	Offer the potential for a positive impact on the brand

Further Research

The performance of a conventional business model is measured by return of capital (ROI) however the goal of a social business is to address a social problem andit is not easy to measure how a social problem is solved. For example in Grameen DANONE case the purpose is to address the malnutrition problem. The change in mal nutrition problems for children in Bangladesh can take several years.so measuring the business model annually is somehow impossible. Relevant indicators are needed to measure the social change after running the social business project. For example in this case an experiment must be done on children each year and their state of health must be measured.

Another interesting issue is that companies conducting business in social area do not have the kind of rivalry companies in conventional business.in social business enterprises share their experiences to help one another solve social problems. When there is no contest to be the best social business company the incentives may decrease in time and this could reduce the productivity of company

Social Business Case

Case 1: The Grameen DANONE Case

Case Study: Grameen DANONE

Created in 2006, Grameen DANONE is a 50-50 joint venture between the Grameen Group and the French Group DANONE, one of the world's leading healthy food companies. (Number one in the worldwide market for fresh dairy products and number two in bottled water, DANONE had 2008 revenue results ofV15.2 billion.) DANONE has been involved in a dual commitment to business success and social responsibility for the past 30 years, over which its mission has evolved from: 'bringing health through food 'in early 2000 to 'bringing health through food to a maximum number of people 'currently.

Echoing its two partners' mission statements, Grameen DANONE's goal is to 'help the children of Bangladesh to be healthy 'by offering them 'a nutritious and healthy product which they may consume on a daily basis'. The value proposition meant that, to be effective, its product had to be affordable eon a daily basis -for poor families who represented a radically different target market from DANONE's conventional high-end consumers. 'Shoktidoi' (literally, 'yoghourt which makes one strong') was created to achieve this goal. Made from cow's milk and date molasses enriched with micronutrients, Shoktidoi contains calcium and proteins essential for children's growth and bone strength. Thanks to its pricee6 BDT (approximatelyV6 cents) per container even the poorest Bangladeshi families could purchase it regularly.

The business model is still being fine-tuned. In terms of the value constellation, the whole value

Chain again had to be questioned. The three main processes of the value constellation supply, production and distribution needed to be radically revisited. Grameen DANONE favored using locally available ingredients for several reasons: to reduce raw materials costs (no import fees, simplified logistics, etc.), to minimize fossil energy consumption (reduced transportation), and to promote local community development and counter rural exodus. To avoid competing with other milk purchasers, and so as to limit any increases in already high milk prices, Grameen DANONE had to structure the upstream market, and chose to develop micro-farms to form part of its own supply network. Micro-credits were offered by the Grameen Bank to potential owners of dairy cattle, who received a guaranteed annual fixed price and veterinary advice to help improve quality and output. As far as production is concerned, the Grameen

DANONE factory at Bogra in northern Bangladesh is small (500 square meters in surface area) and has a capacity which is approximately one thirtieth of DANONE's typical European factory, so the production process has been simplified to the extreme and slightly automated. Door-to-door distribution and sales are handled by the 'Grameen ladies', who can reach 200 households per day and, although illiterate, have been trained to deliver a nutritional message. Again, they act as small-scale entrepreneurs: they are not employees of Grameen DANONE but use credit from Grameen Bank to buy in their product stock and receive a commission for each yoghourt they sell unsold items are not taken back. As well as this door-to-door distribution system, Grameen DANONE sells Shoktidoi via existing (mostly food) stores. The standard advertising model (press and television-based ad campaigns) was not deployable, due to the lack of conventional media penetration in rural Bangladesh. But Grameen DANONE was fortunate to get the support of Zinedine Zidane, the internationally famous French soccer player, who visited the factory and contributed to a spectacular launch for the brand.GrameenDanone is still fine tuning its business model in Bogra; there is no doubt that through experimentation, changes will occur to improve the current model

Case 2: Grameen Veolia

Veolia Water (a subsidiary of Veolia Environnement), is the world's leading provider of water services with a 2008 turnover of V12.6 billion. In March 2008, Veolia Water created a joint venture with the Grameen Bank e Grameen Veolia e with the aim of providing affordable access to drinking water for rural populations in Bangladesh, many of whom had previously been obliged either to buy bottled water, or to drink polluted surface water or even water tainted with arsenic. For several years previously, Veolia Water had been developing solutions to allow access to drinking water for vulnerable people in urban areas, but had not yet tackled the problems of isolated rural areas. As with other developed country water service operators, Veolia Water's conventional business model consisted of recycling and purifying unclean water and billing consumers for their water consumption.

But the rural people of Bangladesh cannot afford water points in their own homes, so Veolia and Grameen shared their knowledge and resources to experiment with a new business model. By the end of 2008 they had built a factory and a whole water supply network in Goalmari, a fairly densely populated rural area. The value proposition was to provide safe drinking water at an affordable price to the inhabitants. The value constellation challenged Veolia's conventional business model in several ways. First, the cost of water treatment was to be reduced as much as possible in order to offer the cheapest price, so the factory was kept simple, and it was decided to recycle surface water as a less costly option. While the drinking water it produced would not meet current US or European norms, it did nonetheless meet World Health Organization standards. Second, three different water access modes needed to be implemented: inside people's homes, at the village's public drinking fountain, or by distributing water cans, which were dispatched to the most isolated villages by rickshaws driven by Grameen-financed entrepreneurs (a distribution mode that was a first for Veolia). Finally, new payment facilities needed to be implemented and a system of prepaid cards is being established. Grameen Veolia is currently fine tuning this business model, and expects to roll it out over Bangladesh and other countries in the coming years.

REFERENCES

Boston Consulting Group. (2011). *The power of social business: Lessons from Grameen experiences.* retrieved July 16 2014 from https://www.bcgperspectives.com/content/articles/corporate_social_responsibility_poverty_hunger_power_social_business

Brugmann, J., & Prahalad, C. (2007). *Concreting business's new social compact.* Boston: Harvard BusinessReview.

Canvas Business Model. (n.d.). Retrieved September 15 2014 from http://businessmodelgeneration.com/canvas/bmc

European Commission. (2011). *Social business initiative creating a favourable climate for social enterprises, key stakeholders in the social economy and innovation. section(2011) 1278 final.* Retrieved September 8 2014 from http://ec.europa.eu/internal_market/social_business/docs/COM2011_682_en.pdf

European Union. (2012). *Financing social impact-Funding social innovation in Europe –Mapping the way forward.* Author.

Mahlouji, H., & Anaraki, N. (2009). Corporate social responsibility towards social responsible innovation: A dynamic capability approach. *International Review of Business Research Papers, 5*(6), 185–194.

Mair J, Schoen. O. (2005). *Social entrepreneurial business models: an exploratory study.* Workingpaper. IESE Business School Madrid 610.

Michelini, L., & Fiorentino, D. (2012). New business models for creating shared value. *Social Responsibility Journal, 8.*

Muhammad, Y., Moingeon, B., & Lehmann-Ortega, L. (2010). Building Social Business Models: Lessons from the Grameen Experience. *Long Range Planning, 43*, 308-325.

Muhammad, Y. (2008). *A world without poverty: social business and the future of capitalism.* Public Affairs.

Organization for Economic Co-Operation. and. development (OECD). (2010). *SMEs, Entrepreneurship and Innovation.* Retrieved September 1 2014 from "http://www.oecd.org/document/16/0,3746,en_2649_33956792_44938128_1_1_1_1,00.html

Porter, M. E., & Kramer, M. R. (2011). Creating shared value. *Harvard Business Review, 89*(1), 62–77.

Social Innovation Europe. (2012). *Financing social impact.* Retrieved September 1 2014 from http://ec.europa.eu/enterprise/ newsroom/cf/itemdetail.cfm?item_id=5582&lang=en

United Nations Development Programmed (UND) & European Research Network (EMES). (2008). Social enterprise: a new model for poverty reduction and employment generation. Retrieved August 28, 2014, from http://europeandcis.undp.org/ourwork/poverty/show/02F5569C-F203-1EE9-BD529F7FE21C9320

Volkmann, Tokarski, & Ernst. (2012). Social Entrepreneurship and social business. Springer Gabler.

KEY TERMS AND DEFINITIONS

Business Model: A general long term frame work helps a company to peruse and reach its long term goals.

Bottom of Pyramid Theory: Giving attention to the largest but poorest segment of the society as new customers through new technology.

Hybrid Enterprises: New form of enterprises which are society and profit oriented rather than purely profit oriented.

Profit Oriented Business: Conventional type of business that its main goal is to earn gain more profit and does not care about environment causes or society problems.

Social Business: A non dividened type of business that address a social problem and its profit is reinvested in the company.

Social Responsibility: and ethical framework that organziations hsat to act for the benfit of the society and help addressing social issues.

Sustainable Business: type of business that can cover its own cost and and does not need charities like NGO's.

Chapter 2
Social CRM Analytics:
Gaining Customer Insights for Designing Social CRM Strategies

Prerna Lal
International Management Institute, India

ABSTRACT

Social CRM entails the premise of customer relationship management channelizing the latent power and potential of social media platforms to enhance customer engagement. Social CRM encompasses a community-based environment in which the control and rules of engagement in the relationship with organizations has shifted from the unidirectional ways of traditional CRM directly to the customer who has the power to influence others in his social network. Marketers are expending efforts and devising new strategies to understand the field of social media and networks to demystify and understand consumer behaviors, patterns of engagement and attitudes and then harness the gained insights for business value. Analytics can help marketers in analyzing social CRM data to identify the most valuable insights from conversations driven by peer groups, industry professionals, prospects, customers and competitors. The objective of this chapter is to explore the opportunities analytics provides to organizations in terms of converting social CRM data into useful insights for designing CRM strategies.

INTRODUCTION

The advent and prevalence of information and Web-based technologies resulting in the emergence of the digital era has made the business environment very competitive as well as tough to survive for all players–enterprises, small and medium businesses and multi-location corporations. The forces arising from digitization, the emergence of the new digital marketspace, liberalism, intense competition, and demanding customers are forcing businesses to consider customers as a basis of profitability and progressive development (Sen & Sinha, 2011). On the other hand, technological innovations are reducing time-to-market, thereby eroding product differentiation and customer loyalty (Gupta & Jain, 2014). Organizations use customer relationship management (CRM) to address these issues by focusing on

DOI: 10.4018/978-1-4666-8586-4.ch002

identifying new customers and attracting them as well as ensuring that they maintain relationship with their existing customers. The objective of this is to ensure a sustainable relationship which is equally valuable for customers as well as for the organizations. To achieve this, organizations need to ensure that they are able to identify right customers, which can be targeted with appropriate offers conveyed through appropriate channels (Sen & Sinha, 2011; Swift, 2001).

Getting closer to customers is essential for organizations. According to Korn Ferry Marketing Pulse survey (2014), ability to create sustainable and engaging customer relationships while improving the customer experience is one of the top priorities of organizations. This is also endorsed by Consumer Goods Forum and KPMG International in their annual Global Top of Mind Survey (2014), which suggests that designing a digital strategy for engaging consumers through mobile and digital platforms is a top-of-mind concern for organizations. Nowadays organizations are adopting social media to do just that.

There has been a recent explosion of social media tools, services and strategies. As a result, the ways, methods and approaches of engaging and communicating with customers have changed quite dramatically. Social media is the emerging phenomenon which encompasses a whole slew of varied sources of online information. These new outlets and mediums initiated, created, circulated and used by consumers are used as educational and informational aids to know more about brands, products, services and personalities (Blackshaw & Nazzaro, 2004; Mangold & Faulds, 2009). To be sure, the advent of communication between consumers has been emulated in the market with better attuning by the producers and marketers of goods, products and services (Mangold & Faulds, 2009). Organizations have to cotton on to this shift and embrace a new strategy. Social CRM is the new strategy which delineates the approach needed - that of recognizing that instead of managing customers at micro-levels, businesses need to create a platform that will aid customers to share their experience which will be of great value to the organizations. Enterprises and businesses need to devise and design social CRM experiences that will explore the features of social media. The endeavor would be to provide credible value to customers for the time they are spending in giving their views, sharing their experiences, and endorsing the products or services consumed.

Today, social media is becoming a hub of customer activity, and this hub has brought millions of users together. Online social networks create a huge repository of data by capturing every single post created on these sites (e.g., Twitter, Pinterest, or Facebook) in a form of a digital footprint. Further, when somebody browses through these posts, they add to the data trail. It is amazing to look at the speed of adoption of social media by consumers as well as businesses. The growth of two major social sites Facebook and Twitter can vouch for this trend. Facebook has 1.44 billion monthly active users as of March 31, 2015 (Facebook, 2015) while Twitter has 288 million monthly active users, and it observes 500 million Tweets per day as of March 31, 2015 (Twitter, 2015). According to the study conducted by eMarketer in 2012 on worldwide social network users, count of Internet users will grow from 2.3 billion in 2012 to 3.6 billion by 2017, which will be more than 40% of the world's projected population (eMarketer, 2013).

Managing and analyzing this huge set of data is challenging because of its varied format (text, audio, and video) and unstructured nature (blogs, tweets, comments, etc.). This is where analytics can help organizations. Analytics holds enormous capabilities for analyzing customers' interactions on social media. It can help organizations in understanding customers, their preferences, and predicting their reactions to the new products or promotional strategies. Further, this analysis can be used by organizations for designing their Social CRM strategy for getting closer to customers.

The purpose of this chapter is threefold. First, we will try to understand the difference between social CRM and traditional CRM. In addition, we will discuss the role of social CRM in managing customer relationships. The second purpose of the chapter is to understand different tools and techniques of analytics. The final and most significant contribution of this chapter is in presenting ways in which analytics can help managers in designing Social CRM strategies.

SOCIAL CRM

Introduction of social media has brought a paradigm shift in managing customer relations. Conventional CRM framework is focused on the organization where standard processes are used to capture substantial information about customers (Verhoef et al., 2010). Management of customer information requires a lot of attention as it plays a key role in interacting with customers throughout the customer lifecycle. CRM helps in integrating a firm's marketing activities and managing every single aspect of customer interaction with the firm starting from prospecting, acquisition, retention, in addition to value enhancement (Rigby and Ledingham 2004;Saini, Grewal, & Johnson, 2010). The most popular definition of CRM is given by Payne and Frow, (2005, page 168) as:

CRM is a strategic approach that is concerned with creating improved shareholder value through the development of appropriate relationships with key customers and customer segments. CRM unites the potential of relationship marketing strategies and IT to create profitable, long-term relationships with customers and other key stakeholders. CRM provides enhanced opportunities to use data and information to both understand customers and co-create value with them. This requires a cross-functional integration of processes, people, operations, and marketing capabilities that is enabled through information, technology, and applications.

CRM aims to systematically and proactively manage the customer relationship from start to finish happening through numerous channels involving direct contact with customers (Reinartz, Krafft, & Hoyer, 2004). During this process, a large amount of customer data is captured, which is leveraged by organizations to increase customer lifetime value. In traditional CRM, organizations are in the main role and they are ones talking to the customers whereas customers can react to this by accepting or rejecting the product or service. Further, this reaction can only be captured by their purchase behavior (Berger, Sorensen, & Rasmussen, 2010; Malthouse, Haenlein, Skiera, Wege, & Zhang, 2013).

On the other hand, Social CRM provides a very collaborative environment where customers can interact not only with organizations but also with other customers through social media. We can define Social CRM in a number of ways, but the most widely accepted definition of Social CRM is the one given by Paul Greenberg (PGreenblog, 2009 July 6) as:

Social CRM is a philosophy and a business strategy, supported by a technology platform, business rules, workflow, processes and social characteristics, designed to engage the customer in a collaborative conversation in order to provide mutually beneficial value in a trusted and transparent business environment. It is the company's response to the customer's ownership of the conversation.

As illustrated in Table 1, there are some fundamental differences between social CRM and traditional CRM. We will now go through each of these areas in the following sections.

Table 1. Traditional CRM vs. Social CRM

	Traditional CRM	Social CRM
Analysis	Data driven	Content driven
Focus	Process Centric / Operationally focused.	Conversation centric / Community focused.
Interaction	Customer interaction through organization defined channels.	Customer interaction through customer-driven dynamic channels
Time	The business hour	Customer sets the hour.
Touch points	Phone, fax, email, service center, letters, personal contact, company's website, SMS, instant messaging, chat.	Auctions, video sharing, microblogs, podcast, price comparison websites, wikis, social networks, blogs, widgets, photo sharing forums, slide sharing, reviews and ratings in retail sites, social bookmarking, wish lists, RSS

Origin of traditional CRM systems lies in the need for having a central system to store customer records. Soon it became an important source for customer data tracking. Organizations could now use this data for different functional areas and for distinctive purposes. On the other hand, social CRM evolved based on the need to attract the attention of social customers. These are the customers who are social media savvy and browse through social media platforms and outlets for making decisions regarding purchase as well as for sharing their experiences. By doing so they create a lot of content, which is vital for organizations. They can use it to understand customers' reactions regarding their products or new promotional schemes. Thus, content is the foundation of social CRM analysis. Organizations need to ensure that such content is created which conveys the message strongly and is easy for the target customers to consume. This will compel prospects to start a conversation with the organization. Organizations can choose to create content in any format ranging from a Webinar, a video related to product or service features on Youtube, or a podcast (Leary, 2009).

Focus of today's customer relationship is shifting from being process-centric to conversation-centric. The type of information we gather regarding customers from traditional CRM systems is nothing compared to the one which we capture in a social CRM environment. Customers use social media channels, online communities, blogs, review sites to share their experience, concerns, etc. This certainly is a shift from one-to-one relationship with particular organizations to more collaborative experience with other customers/communities (Rohra & Sharma, 2012). Experiences and views shared by customers on social media can be used to understand their buying behaviors but this is not the only reason for analysis. Instead organizations can use this data to identify how their views influenced the buying patterns of other customers following them on the social media platform. Thus, now the challenge for organizations is to identify people who influence the behavior in an online environment and encourage them to become promoters of their products. These people are no one but customers who are also very active on social media platforms such as popular industry bloggers.

Social media savvy customers are now turning away from traditional unidirectional communication channels (television, radio, newspapers, trade magazines) to social media where they have more of a say (Zafra, 2013). Social media give them flexibility of searching for products, going through reviews, interacting with other customers through blogs, social networking sites, etc. and making informed decisions (Rashtchy et al., 2007; Lempert, 2006; Vollmer & Precourt, 2008). Doing all this at their own convenient time is an added benefit provided by the social media to the customers. Since reviews are posted by customers at their own will they are considered more trustworthy than paid campaigns run by organizations (Foux, 2006).

Flexibility to communicate with organizations, other customers or communities at any time is another encouraging factor in case of social CRM. This eliminates the barrier of traditional CRM systems where there is a constraint on reaching the organization during a specific time, i.e. 9 am to 5 pm (Morgan, 2010). Thus, social media is rapidly becoming the first choice for the consumers for sharing their views regarding different products and services (Mangold & Faulds, 2009). Social media provides wide range of interaction points ranging from blogs, social networking sites, microblogs, content sharing (audio, video, images, photographs, or movies). This has changed the manner in which consumers accept as well as respond to the information regarding products or services (Singh, Veron-Jackson, & Cullinane, 2008). Organizations need to ensure their presence in a social environment to communicate and collaborate with customers (Li & Bernoff, 2008). Business needs to focus on accepting social media not only to shape virtual communities, but also to leverage it for customer retention and value enhancement. With so much to gain, companies need to capitalize on social media to reach to current and potential customers (Baird & Parasnis, 2011).

Thus, Social CRM is providing a better platform for organizations to manage customer relations than traditional CRM in terms of analysis of data where the focus is more on the customer's view of products or services rather than the organization's view. Where the interaction is not limited between customers and organizations but customers are encouraged to interact with each other any time and through any media.

ANALYTICS

In an uncertain economic environment, organizations cannot afford to make wrong or slow decisions. The digital economy has brought with it a torrent of data, which are being generated by all organizations across industries. This data, if analyzed prudently, can be used by organizations to strengthen their competitive advantage (Ernst &Young, 2012). Many experts see analytics as providing a tool for insights into this data which enables executives to make informed decisions with confidence (Fuloria, 2011). By streamlining the decision making process, organizations can improve their agility and ability to flourish in an environment of constant change (Ernst & Young, 2014).

Analytics if implemented prudently can give greater visibility into the organizational data. Further, analytics provide capabilities to analyze data be it measuring and monitoring financial or operational performance, analyzing data related to business processes, as well as predicting results, which can be used for planning and improving business outcomes (IBM, 2013).

HOW ANALYTICS WORKS

Large organizations invest millions of dollars for designing proficient data-management strategies to ensure right data acquisition, which will lead to effective management and analysis of the acquired data and lead to better decisions related to organizational management and business operations. (Davenport, 2006). Implementation of an analytics platform requires a lot of planning in terms of collating data from various sources and ensuring that it is complete and ready for applying analytical techniques. Figure 1 represents various steps involved in the data-management life cycle of analytics implementation namely:

Figure 1. Analytics Framework

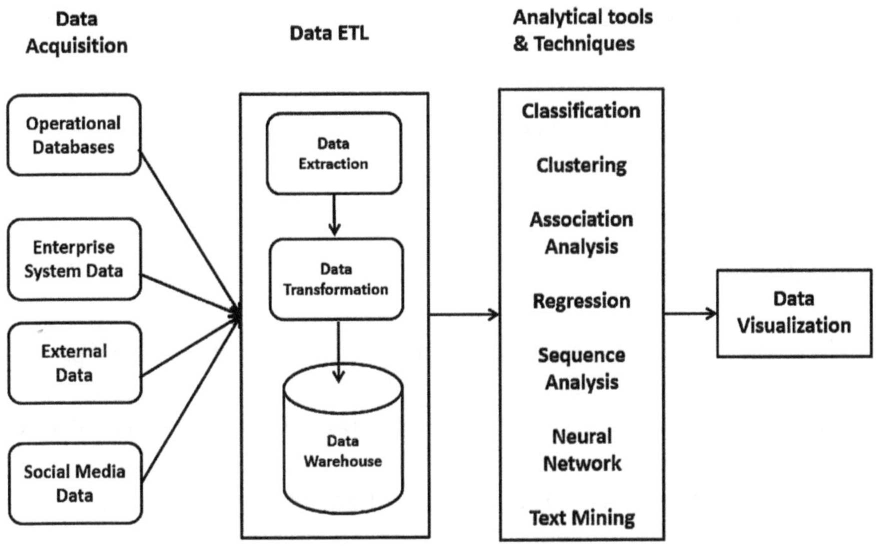

(1) data acquisition, (2) data extraction, transformation & loading (ETL), (3) data analysis using analytical tools and techniques, (4) data visualization.

Data-management process starts with creating or acquiring data. The objective is to determine what data is needed. The source can be data from any operational database, enterprise systems, or from social media. Next, this data has to go through Extraction Transformation and Loading (ETL) process. Extracting data from its source is a fairly straightforward task but cleaning and transforming data requires a well-thought out process to be followed. Data cleaning ensures data is complete as well as correct. This is done by checking missing, duplicate, or incorrect values captured and stored in various applications. Once they are identified, a decision is taken regarding how to handle these values. For example, whether to delete missing values or impute then with the mean. Cleaned data is then transformed based on business rules, for example; representing product codes in specific combination of text and numbers. Further, business logic is developed to map data from various sources to a single data repository called as data warehouse. Once the data is cleaned and transformed it is then put into the data warehouse so that it is ready to use. This is not a onetime process as data needs to be updated in data warehouse on regular intervals defined according to the nature of data (Han & Kamber, 2006; Inmon, 2005). The construction of a data warehouse is a significant but not a necessary step for applying analytical techniques. In case there is no data warehouse, analytics techniques can be applied directly on the data extracted from different sources (Davenport, 2006).

When data is ready for the analysis, a number of analytical techniques can be applied on it for understanding trends, identifying patterns and predictions. These techniques are an amalgam of techniques related to the domain of data mining, artificial intelligence and statistics such as: classification, clustering, association, sequences, neural networks and text mining. Organizations can use powerful tools that allow them to develop their own analysis, or they can select analytics product suites offered by organizations such SAS, IBM, SAP, Oracle, Tableau, Tibco, etc.

The final step in data management is the representation of results. In case of analytics, data visualization is used to do that rather than using tables for displaying results. Data can be visualized through pictures and graphs. Tools like Tableau can help in presenting data in different graphical formats such as bar charts, line graphs, pie charts, ring charts, scatter plots, stacked area charts, network diagrams, bubble charts, tree diagrams, maps, etc. Visual representation of data helps in understanding information more easily and quickly. Managers involved in decision making process appreciate data visualization as it enables them to find relationship between thousands of variables which are not obvious and cannot be spotted easily and quickly (SAS, 2014).

ANALYTIC TECHNIQUES

Analytical techniques are designed to explore large data sets in search of consistent patterns and systematic relationships between variables. This is done by generating models by using available data and then validating the findings by applying these models on a new dataset. There are number of different analytical techniques available which can be applied depending upon the dataset as well as kind of analysis required (Hill & Lewicki, 2007). Analytics encompasses usage of analytical techniques to discover previously unknown, effective patterns and associations in the large data set. Analytical tools and techniques takes account of statistical models, machine learning methods as well as data mining models which helps in analysis and prediction (Phyu, 2009). Table 2 represents different types of analytical techniques that can be used by organizations. We will now discuss each of these techniques in detail in the following sections.

Classification technique is used to assign items of a data set in predefined target categories or classes. This process requires a database with records that are labeled with predefined classes. System then uses this database to develop the model which will be able to assign class to the new record (Baloglu & Ak-

Table 2. Analytical techniques

Technique	Description	Example
Classification	Used to predict an event or likelihood of an occurrence of an event when there are two possible outcomes for the event (Ngai, Xiu, & Chau, 2009).	Churn prediction
Clustering	Used to analyze data patterns and identify groupings of customers. New customers are subsequently scored against created clusters (Jain, Murty, & Flynn, 1999).	Behavioral segmentation
Association / Affinity	Used to detect associations between discrete events, products, or attributes (Chen, Chiu, & Chang, 2005; Liou & Tzeng, 2010; Sánchez, Vila, Cerda, & Serrano, 2009; Xintong, Hongzhi, Song, & Hong, 2014).	Recommender systems implementation, market-basket analysis
Regression analysis	It is a useful technique for investigating relationships between the variables as well as identifying the impact of one variable upon other variables.	Predicting customer re-purchase decision or response to the marketing campaign.
Sequence analysis	Used to detect associations over time, generate summary of sequences occurring frequently such as Web path followed etc. (Mabroukeh & Ezeife, 2010).	Web path analysis
Neural Network	Neural network represents a computing system which is made up of a number of simple, highly interconnected processing elements which process information by their dynamic state response to external inputs (Bloom, 2005; Caudill, 1987; Chen, Khoo, & Yan, 2002; Kim, Street, Russell, & Menczer, 2005; Larasati, DeYong, & Slevitch, 2012; Zhang, Liang, Li, Zheng, & Berry, 2011).	Market segmentation, customer segmentation, customer churn
Text Mining	Text mining is useful in deriving significant insights from text-based content posted on social media such as Twitter, Facebook, Blogs (Botzenhardt, Witt, & Maedche, 2011; Chang, Lin, & Wang, 2009; Gamon, Aue, Corston-Oliver, & Ringger, 2005; Hu & Liu, 2004; Mostafa, 2013; Pang & Lee, 2008).	Sentiment analysis, customer voice analysis

tas, 2010; Qi & Davison, 2009). Marketers may use this technique to classify customers on the basis of demography or to predict possible churn timely and respond quickly (Lu &Ph, 2002).

Clustering is a procedure to create groups of records having similar attributes (Colet, 2000). The process starts by creating clusters and then each cluster is further analyzed to define its attributes. This results in getting interesting and unanticipated group of clusters which can be used for designing business strategies. Marketers can use this technique to identify distinct group of customers and then design marketing and promotion strategies specifically for them (Aggarwal & Zhai, 2012; Prasad, 2011; Vicari & Alfó, 2014).

Association analysis aims to formulate rules based on the patterns generated for a given business process. A very popular example of association rule is one in the area of sales of products wherein we can generate rules to identify the probability of a customer purchasing product A will also purchase product B. In today's online business environment this technique is applied to implement recommendation systems. These recommendation systems use association rules to understand the browsing patterns of users and based on their past behavior will suggest items or services that perfectly suits to their taste (Changchien & Lu, 2001; Wang & Shao, 2004; Zhang, 2007).

Regression analysis is a very useful technique for investigating relationships between variables. Typically, it helps in identifying casual effect of one variable upon other (Sykes, 2000). If applied appropriately, one can identify important variables that should to be used to predict the outcome correctly. In case of customer data, regression can be applied to access the chances of customer purchasing the product again or responding to the email marketing campaign.

Sequence analysis is implemented to recognize as well as analyze a sequence of events taking place in a particular time frame (Schulz, 2014). Organizations pay attention in analyzing sequences as they need to understand which path a customer follows for getting information regarding a product or service before taking a decision to buy a product. Thus, organizations can use this analysis to design strategies to enable personalization, increase conversion of customers from browsers to buyers, etc. (Doherty, 2000).

Neural Network is a powerful data modeling tool that is capable to capture and represent complex input/output relationships. Neural networks have the competence to explore complex set of data and produce highly accurate predictive models (Hui, 2000; Phyu, 2009; Shieh, Yan, & Chen, 2008). Organizations can use neural networks either for market or customer segmentation in addition to predicting customer churn rate.

Text Mining is a method of generating meaningful information from text. It involves deriving patterns and trends, which can be useful in numerous ways. In marketing, application of text mining is in the form of sentiment analysis wherein models are built to analyze posts available on social media to understand customers opinion (Fan, Wallace, Rich, & Zhang, 2006; Stavrianou, Andritsos, & Nicoloyannis, 2007; Yang, Akers, Klose, & Barcelon Yang, 2008). Sentiment analysis can help in analyzing whether customer's view about new products or a new promotion campaign is positive, negative or neutral (Thelwall, Buckley, Paltoglou, & Cai, 2010).

Though numbers of different analytical techniques are available, and each of them has their own merits, often they are used in combination to develop a model. For example, retail stores can apply clustering technique to identify customer groups having similar attributes and further implement association rules analysis to identify associations between purchasing behaviors of each cluster. This will help them in developing a specific promotion strategy for each cluster wherein chance of the conversion rate is higher. Hence, in the following section, we will try to understand how these techniques can be implemented in the social media environment to analyze customer data and design business strategies accordingly.

DESIGNING CRM STRATEGIES THROUGH SOCIAL CRM ANALYTICS

The application of Analytics in CRM is an emerging trend in the global economy. Development of competitive strategy needs a strong foundation of customer data analysis. This foundation can help them in acquiring potential customers and retaining existing ones. CRM analytics can examine customer data consisting demographics and behavioral patterns, which will help them in improving customer satisfaction levels.

Customer analytics, qualified with insights from social media data, can aid organizations in understanding the entire customer life cycle. This becomes more important when customers are exposed to the social platform, which can influence their decisions at every stage. Thus, understanding the customer life cycle becomes the very first step for developing social CRM strategy.

Forrester defines the customer life cycle as: "*customers' relationship with a brand as they continue to discover new options, explore their needs, make purchases, and engage with the product experience and their peers*" (Nobel, 2010). Customer life cycle can be represented in four steps: Prospecting & Lead Generation, Acquisition, Retention, and Value Enhancement (Reinartz et al., 2004; Winer, 2001). Figure 2 represents application of analytical techniques in different phases of the customer life cycle.

Prospecting and Lead Generation

Refining customer relations and optimizing CRM strategy lays on the foundation of understanding the customer base. Segmentation is the best way to do that. Once segmentation is done, next step is lead scoring, which helps marketers to figure out whether their leads comprises right kind of people (explicit

Figure 2. Application of Social CRM Analytics throughout Customer Life Cycle

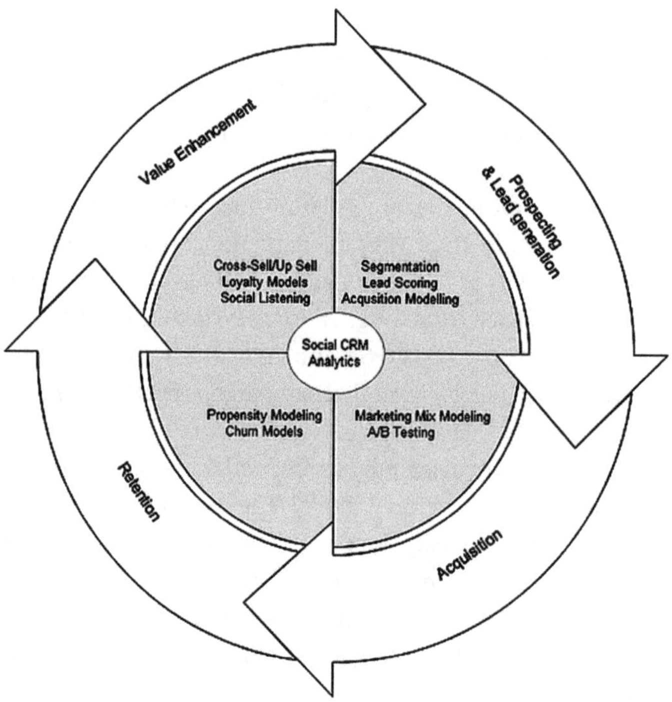

scoring) and even more important to know if they are the one displaying right level of interest (implicit scoring) in the product or service offered by the organization (Eloqua, 2014). Finally, marketers will work on acquisition modeling for identifying how to attract customers.

Analytic techniques such as classification, clustering and neural networks can help in creating segments. We can classify customers by profession, geographic location, qualification, age, sex, etc. While in case of online social environment, customer segmentation can be done based on how they use social media. A study done by Forester Research suggests that customers can be grouped as creators, conversationalists, critics, collectors, joiners, spectators, and inactives (Bernoff & Anderson, 2010). Understanding this will help in identifying potential prospects for existing as well as new products or services. Further, customers can be grouped on the basis of the platform the customer is using. For example, one group of customers may prefer Twitter and others may prefer phone calls. Customers in a social media era use varied platforms. The platform that a customer uses often posits the power of social media segmentation. Proven and benchmarked marketing practices call for rolling out marketing campaigns on all available platforms. It is important to note that all customers may not be on the same platform nor are they on all platforms. It does not make sense to build an elaborate Twitter campaign that delivers no value simply because your customers are not on Twitter. The old adage still holds true: Every market is unique and different and every customer is different. Over time, marketers have come to realize the power, reach and expanse of social media and now understand that social medial allows them to create customized experiences for their customers. The key is to customize for your customers; reach some of them thru Twitter or some of them thru LinkedIn so that each customer feels like one of a kind. Broaden the group of prospects in this manner.

The focal point of lead scoring is to ensure generation of sales-ready leads. In case of an online social environment, this starts with the collection of conversations trending online other than on an organization's website (Pergolino, 2011). These conversations can take any form ranging from a comment on a blog, tweet regarding product, query posted on Linkedin, etc. Once you have collected data now you can use analytic techniques like text mining, association and sequence analysis for developing lead scoring mode.

Lead-scoring models reveal critical aspects related to the discovery of a message by an individual along with the source of message. In addition to that it will also help in analyzing the complete cycle of buying a product starting from identifying when customer entered in the loop and searched for the product and finally made a purchase. Lead-scoring models also have the capabilities wherein they can be used to identify customers who started the process but left in the middle and expressed interest in the competitor's offerings. Demand generation and lead management not only increase conversion rates but also reduce direct marketing costs.

Acquisition

Analytics can help in identifying appropriate customers for different categories of products or services. This will help organizations in identifying strategies to attract these customers using a message designed especially for them and delivered through appropriate media to ensure maximum impact on the prospective customers. Analytics can help in developing right marketing-mix models to plan optimal spend levels across each channel. Given the rise of social media as a platform to extend marketing campaigns and reach consumers through dialogues with brands' marketing mix, modeling becomes ever more critical. Organizations cannot stay on one singular channel; instead they need to be flexible and capable of shifting strategies in real-time for marketing optimization. Analytics can help them in this with strong real-time statistical analytical methods (Cole, 2011).

Organizations test various marketing inputs, such as messaging and content with online and offline testing methods before rolling out initiatives on a larger scale. A/B and multivariate testing, in addition to site optimization, prove popular with digital marketers that plan online testing programs (Sridharan, 2012). Analytics can help in tracking test results and segment the results by other parameters such as the country, the type of visitors, browsers, etc., For example, we can use Google analytics to create customer segmentation using techniques like classification, clustering, neural network and their response for different test cases.

Retention

Nowadays customers are not ready to compromise on anything be it price, value for money or quality of a service. Intense competition in the market force organizations to compete based on these as customers won't hesitate to switch brands or service providers if they feel better options are there in the market. Ultimate word-of-mouth communication through social media is also contributing to the declining level of loyalty as an individual's decision regarding switching to different brands can have extensive and quick impact on others (Accenture, 2011). If you really want to retain your customers in a cost-effective manner you need to ensure that you are keeping track of customers' views posted on social sites. For this, organizations need to understand future behavior through propensity models, further arrest customer iteration through churn models.

Using predictive techniques, coupled with the existing historical knowledge of customers, to build propensity models that help marketers predict the likelihood that a customer will respond to an offer or message and convert. For example, retailers include propensity models to identify best segments based on channels. These channels include store, online retail website, or a digital media which comprises SMS, emails, online advertising, or mobile applications. Propensity models are essentially created on the foundation of RFM model which incorporates analysis on the basis of recency- recent purchases by the customer, frequency- how often customer visits the store, and what is the monetary value of the customer. In case of social media we can relate it to how updated a customer is about the product, how frequently s/he purchases products and expresses views and finally how s/he behaves online and what his/her social media status is (Sridharan, 2012). We can use classification techniques to get customer insights and predict likelihood of future purchase patterns. Text mining can be done to analyze experiences of customer and understand their satisfaction or dissatisfaction for the product or service. This helps identify early signs of defection and allows firms to preempt customer churn with corrective actions, such as win-back or reactivation programs. Based on the insights extracted in the early stages of the customer's life cycle, personalized customer treatments are designed to elicit specific next best actions. For example, an online retail store delivers a contextually tailored experience on its portal using banner ads that deliver next best offers that adjust automatically to customer queries.

Value Enhancement

Expand the breadth of customer interaction with cross-sell, upsell, and affinity models. Cross-sell, upsell, and affinity models determine the additional products and services to offer customers based on their relationship with the firm. Analytical techniques like cluster analysis, sequence analysis can be used to analyze customer history of interactions though service requests, product use, and other online social media interactions. On the other hand, customer loyalty models can be developed to increase depth of relationship. Analytical techniques, such as association analysis, sequence analysis; clustering and sentiment analysis can be used for designing retention strategy.

Finally, in online environment organizations can capture valuable customer feedback through voice of customer (VoC) analysis. Voice of customer analysis allows firms to close the loop on customer experience management using customer insights (Sridharan, 2012). Organizations can capture customers' voice through blogs, review websites, discussion forums, etc. Further, text mining can analyze this unstructured text and provide insights such as, what a customer thinks about a particular brand, features they like or dislike, whether their experience was good or bad, etc.

CHALLENGES

Achieving success in applying analytics on social CRM data is not free of challenges. First and the most important are dealing with the noise present in the large set of social CRM data. This noise is in a form of conversations or posts on the social sites which are not significant at all for the analysis. Organizations need to use specialized listening platforms for the identification of relevant conversations as well as sentiments associated with them. This is an iterative plus a very complex process and if not done correctly then may lead to wrong decisions (Rohra & Sharma, 2012).

The second challenge is related to the quickness shown in giving the response especially regarding posts where customers are either giving wrong information or sharing their bad experiences related to products or service. This is important because any response posted on social platform travels fast and may receive strong reactions from customers. Therefore, organizations need to make sure that these responses are tackled properly much before they damage the reputation of brand in the market (Rohra & Sharma, 2012). On the other hand, organizations should also not miss an opportunity to thank customers who are posting positive reviews so that they may be converted into brand ambassadors (Ashenden, 2014).

Technology is the third challenge every organization faces while dealing with varied and multiple social media platforms. Dealing with the technological changes every third month is a challenge and need to be managed effectively while adopting social CRM strategies. Not only this, organizations need to decide cautiously which technology they should use to connect with the customers. Decisions related to technology acceptance may either help or hinder the success of social CRM adoption (Dorsey, 2012).

CONCLUSION

Every interaction with customers leaves a trail of data. Such data, if analyzed judiciously, becomes assets. It can then generate a richer picture of everything from a customer's product choices and channel preferences to when, how, and why they want to interact with the organization. Evolution of social media has introduced new business models, marketplaces and new channels of customer interaction. Today, opinions floated on social media are significantly driving the buying decisions for large segments of customers. It is imperative for enterprises to communicate, interact, transact, and serve customers across varied channels ranging from stores, call centers, Web, social networks, and mobile phones. The Social Customer expects organizations to listen and respond promptly and provide uniform service treatment irrespective of the channel. The end-to-end customer experience is a key differentiator that has a major influence on the customer's buying decisions, brand impressions and sustainability of customer relationships.

Social CRM analytics plays a key role in understanding customer behavior through the customer life cycle. Analytical tools can help organizations in designing strategies for increasing customer engagement and providing a superior customer experience. While there will be some challenges and pitfalls associated with rolling out the social CRM analytics initiatives, overall the benefits far outweigh the pitfalls. Key pillars for enabling Social CRM analytics include analyzing customers' conversations and sentiments, and identify customer needs thereby enriching their profile.

REFERENCES

Accenture. (2011). *Maximizing Customer Retention: A Strategic Approach to Effective Churn Management* [PDF document]. Retrieved from http://www.accenture.com/SiteCollectionDocuments/PDF/Accenture-Maximizing-Customer-Retention.pdf

Aggarwal, C., & Zhai, C. (2012). Mining text data. *Mining Text Data*, *4*(2(63)), 889–903. doi:10.1007/978-1-4614-3223-4

Ashenden, P. (October 31, 2014). Social customer service: the benefits and challenges. [Web log comment]. Retrieved from https://eptica.wordpress.com/2014/10/31/meeting-rising-customer-expectations-on-social-media/

Baird, C. H., & Parasnis, G. (2011). *From social media to Social CRM: What customers want The first in a two-part series* [PDF document]. Retrieved from http://public.dhe.ibm.com/common/ssi/ecm/en/gbe03391usen/GBE03391USEN.PDF

Baloglu, A., & Aktas, M. S. (2010). BlogMiner: Web blog mining application for classification of movie reviews. In *5th International Conference on Internet and Web Applications and Services*, ICIW 2010 (pp. 77–84). doi:10.1109/ICIW.2010.19

Berger, J., Sorensen, A. T., & Rasmussen, S. J. (2010). Positive Effects of Negative Publicity: When Negative Reviews Increase Sales. *Marketing Science*, *29*(5), 815–827. doi:10.1287/mksc.1090.0557

Blackshaw, P., & Nazzaro, M. (2004). *Consumer-Generated Media (CGM) 101: Word-of-mouth in the age of the Web fortified consumer* [PDF document]. Retrieved from http://www.brandchannel.com/images/papers/222_cgm.pdf

Bloom, J. Z. (2005). Market segmentation. A neural network application. *Annals of Tourism Research*, *32*(1), 93–111. doi:10.1016/j.annals.2004.05.001

Botzenhardt, A., Witt, A., & Maedche, A. (2011). A Text Mining Application for Exploring the Voice of the Customer. In *Proceedings of the Seventeenth Americas Conference on Information Systems* (pp. 1–11). Retrieved from http://aisel.aisnet.org/amcis2011_submissions/274

Caudill, M. (1987). Neural Networks Premier Part I. *AI Expert*, *2*(12), 46–52.

Chang, C. W., Lin, C. T., & Wang, L. Q. (2009). Mining the text information to optimizing the customer relationship management. *Expert Systems with Applications*, *36*(2 PART 1), 1433–1443. doi:10.1016/j.eswa.2007.11.027

Changchien, S. W., & Lu, T. C. (2001). Mining association rules procedure to support on-line recommendation by customers and products fragmentation. *Expert Systems with Applications*, *20*(4), 325–335. doi:10.1016/S0957-4174(01)00017-3

Chen, C. H., Khoo, L. P., & Yan, W. (2002). A strategy for acquiring customer requirement patterns using laddering technique and ART2 neural network. *Advanced Engineering Informatics*, *16*(3), 229–240. doi:10.1016/S1474-0346(03)00003-X

Chen, M. C., Chiu, A. L., & Chang, H. H. (2005). Mining changes in customer behavior in retail marketing. *Expert Systems with Applications*, *28*(4), 773–781. doi:10.1016/j.eswa.2004.12.033

Cole, Z. (2011, December 7). Social Business: Using Marketing Mix Modeling to Maximize ROI. *Socialbusinessnews.com*. Retrieved from http://www.socialbusinessnews.com/marketing-mix-model/

Colet, E. (2000). Clustering and Classification: Data Mining Approaches. *Tabor Communications*. Retrieved from http://www.tgc.com/dsstar/00/0704/101861.html

Davenport, T. H. (2006). Competing on analytics. *Harvard Business Review*, *84*(1), 98–107, 134. http://doi.org/Article PMID:16447373

Doherty, R. (2000). Click stream reporting & analysis for Website optimization [PDF document]. Retrieved from http://www.sascommunity.org/seugi/SEUGI2000/doherty_clickstream.pdf

Dorsey, P. (2012, April 13). *Social Media Is Not Social CRM, but It Can Be With These Five Steps*. Retrieved from http://www.marketingprofs.com/articles/2012/7627/social-media-is-not-social-crm-but-it-can-be-with-these-five-steps#ixzz3Pl049bv9

Emarketer (2013, June 18). *Social Networking Reaches Nearly One in Four Around the World*. Retrieved from http://www.emarketer.com/Article/Social-Networking-Reaches-Nearly-One-Four-Around-World/1009976#sthash.gcLXWxbW.dpuf

Ernst & Young. (2012). *Driving a competitive advantage with advanced analytics* [PDF document]. Retrieved from http://www.ey.com/Publication/vwLUAssets/CAI_advanced__analytics_final/$FILE/CAI_advanced%20_analytics_final.pdf

Facebook (2015). *Statistics*. Retrieved on March 31, 2015 from http://newsroom.fb.com/company-info/

Fan, W., Wallace, L., Rich, S., & Zhang, Z. (2006). Tapping the power of text mining. *Communications of the ACM*, *49*(9), 76–82. doi:10.1145/1151030.1151032

Foux, G. (2006, May 8). *Consumer-generated media: Get your customers involved*. Retrieved from http://www.highbeam.com/doc/1G1-145500854.html

Fuloria, S. (2011). *Building Sustainable Competitive Advantage with Advanced Analytics* [PDF docment]. Retrieved from http://www.cognizant.com/InsightsWhitepapers/Building-Sustainable-Competitive-Advantage-with-Advanced-Analytics.pdf

Gamon, M., Aue, A., Corston-Oliver, S., & Ringger, E. (2005). Lecture Notes in Computer Science: Vol. 3646. *Pulse: Mining customer opinions from free text* (pp. 121–132). Springer; doi:10.1007/11552253_12

Gupta, S., & Jain, A. (2014). *Customer Lifetime Value Analytics in Retail Banking – Staying Competitive and Profitable* [PDFdocument].Retrived from http://www.genpact.com/docs/resource-/customer-lifetime-value-analytics-in-retail-banking---staying-competitive-and-profitable

Han, J., & Kamber, M. (2006). *Data Mining: Concepts and Techniques*. Waltham, MA: Morgan Kaufmann.

Hill, T., & Lewicki, P. (2007). *Statistics: Methods and Applications*. Tulsa, OK: StatSoft.

Hu, M., & Liu, B. (2004). Mining and summarizing customer reviews. In *Proceedings of the 2004 ACM SIGKDD international conference on Knowledge discovery and data mining KDD 04* (Vol. 04, p. 168). http://doi.org/ doi:10.1145/1014052.1014073

Hui, S., & Jha, G. (2000). Data mining for customer service support. *Information & Management*, *38*(1), 1–13. doi:10.1016/S0378-7206(00)00051-3

IBM. (2013). *The Case for Business Analytics for Midsize Firms* [PDF document]. Retrieved from http://www-03.ibm.com/innovation/us/engines/assets/ibm-business-analytics-case-study-1-22-13.pdf

Inmon, W. H. (2005). *Building The Data Warehouse*. Indianapolis: Wiley.

Jain, A. K., Murty, M. N., & Flynn, P. J. (1999). Data clustering: A review. *ACM Computing Surveys*, *31*(3), 264–323. doi:10.1145/331499.331504

Kim, Y., Street, W. N., Russell, G. J., & Menczer, F. (2005). Customer Targeting: A Neural Network Approach Guided by Genetic Algorithms. *Management Science*, *51*(2), 264–276. doi:10.1287/mnsc.1040.0296

Korn Ferry Survey. (2014, August 12). *Korn Ferry Survey: CMOs' Top Priority Remains How to Best Engage with Customers*. Reterived from http://www.kornferry.com/press/15191/

KPMG. (2014). Transforming for growth: *Consumer business in the digital age* [PDF document]. Retrived from http://www.kpmg.com/Global/en/IssuesAndInsights/ArticlesPublications/global-consumer-executive-top-of-mind-survey-2014/Documents/top-of-mind-survey-2014-v2.pdf

Larasati, A., DeYong, C., & Slevitch, L. (2012). The Application of Neural Network and Logistics Regression Models on Predicting Customer Satisfaction in a Student-Operated Restaurant. *Procedia: Social and Behavioral Sciences*, *65*, 94–99. doi:10.1016/j.sbspro.2012.11.097

Lempert, P. (2006). Caught in the Web. *Progressive Grocer*, *85*(12), 15–28.

Li, C., & Bernoff, J. (2008). *Groundswell: Winning in a world transformed by social technologies*. Boston: Harvard Business Press.

Liou, J. J. H., & Tzeng, G. H. (2010). A Dominance-based Rough Set Approach to customer behavior in the airline market. *Information Sciences*, *180*(11), 2230–2238. doi:10.1016/j.ins.2010.01.025

Lu, J. (2002). *Predicting Customer Churn in the Telecommunications Industry — An Application of Survival Analysis Modeling Using SAS* [PDF document]. Retrieved from http://www2.sas.com/proceedings/sugi27/p114-27.pdf

Mabroukeh, N. R., & Ezeife, C. I. (2010). A taxonomy of sequential pattern mining algorithms. *ACM Computing Surveys*, *43*(1), 1–41. doi:10.1145/1824795.1824798

Malthouse, E. C., Haenlein, M., Skiera, B., Wege, E., & Zhang, M. (2013). Managing customer relationships in the social media era: Introducing the social CRM house. *Journal of Interactive Marketing*, *27*(4), 270–280. doi:10.1016/j.intmar.2013.09.008

Mangold, W. G., & Faulds, D. J. (2009). Social media: The new hybrid element of the promotion mix. *Business Horizons*, *52*(4), 357–365. doi:10.1016/j.bushor.2009.03.002

Morgan, J. (2010, November 3). *What Is Social CRM?* Retrieved from http://www.socialmediaexaminer.com/what-is-social-crm/

Mostafa, M. M. (2013). More than words: Social networks' text mining for consumer brand sentiments. *Expert Systems with Applications*, *40*(10), 4241–4251. doi:10.1016/j.eswa.2013.01.019

Ngai, E. W. T., Xiu, L., & Chau, D. C. K. (2009). Application of data mining techniques in customer relationship management: A literature review and classification. *Expert Systems with Applications*, *36*(2), 2592–2602. doi:10.1016/j.eswa.2008.02.021

Nobel, S. (2010, August 12). *It's Time To Bury The Marketing Funnel. Forrester Research.* Retrieved from http://www.forbes.com/2010/12/08/customer-life-cycle-leadership-cmo-network-funnel.html

Pang, B., & Lee, L. (2008). Opinion Mining and Sentiment Analysis. *Foundations and Trends® in Information Retrieval*, 2(1–2), 1–135.

Payne, A., & Frow, P. (2005). A Strategic Framework for Customer. *Journal of Marketing*, *69*(4), 167–176. doi:10.1509/jmkg.2005.69.4.167

PGreenblog. (2009, July 06). *Time to Put a Stake in the Ground on Social CRM.* Retrieved from http://the56group.typepad.com/pgreenblog/2009/07/time-to-put-a-stake-in-the-ground-on-social-crm.html

Phyu, T. N. (2009). Survey of Classification Techniques in Data Mining. In International MUlticonference of Engineers and Computer Scientists (Vol. I, pp. 18–20).

Prasad, P. (2011). Generating Customer Profiles for Retail Stores Using Clustering Techniques. *International Journal on Computer Science and Engineering*, *3*(6), 2506–2510.

Qi, X., & Davison, B. D. (2009). Web page classification: Features and algorithms. *ACM Computing Surveys*, *41*(2), 1–31. doi:10.1145/1459352.1459357

Rashtchy, F., Kessler, A. M., Bieber, P. J., Shindler, N. H., & Tzeng, J. C. (2007). The user revolution: The new advertising ecosystem and the rise of the Internet as a mass medium [PDF document]. Minneapolis, MN: Piper Jaffray Investment Research; Retrieved from http://people.ischool.berkeley.edu/~hal/Courses/StratTech09/Lectures/Google/Articles/summary-user-revolution.pdf

Reinartz, W., Krafft, M., & Hoyer, W. (2004). The customer relationship management process: Its measurement and impact on performance. *JMR, Journal of Marketing Research*, *41*(3), 293–305. doi:10.1509/jmkr.41.3.293.35991

Rigby, D. K., & Ledingham, D. (2004). CRM done right. *Harvard Business Review*, *82*(11), 118–129. PMID:15559450

Rohra, G., & Sharma, M. (2012). *Social CRM - Possibilities and Challenges* [PDF document]. Retrieved from http://www.tcs.com/SiteCollectionDocuments/White%20Papers/ConnectedMarketing_Whitepaper_Social_CRM%E2%80%93Possibilities_Challenges_0912-1.pdf

Saini, A., Grewal, R., & Johnson, J. L. (2010). Putting market-facing technology to work: Organisational drivers of CRM performance. *Marketing Letters*, *21*(4), 365–383. doi:10.1007/s11002-009-9096-z

Sánchez, D., Vila, M. A., Cerda, L., & Serrano, J. M. (2009). Association rules applied to credit card fraud detection. *Expert Systems with Applications*, *36*(2 PART 2), 3630–3640. doi:10.1016/j.eswa.2008.02.001

SAS. (2014). *Data Visualization: Making Big Data Approachable and Valuable* [PDF document]. Retrieved from http://www.sas.com/content/dam/SAS/en_us/doc/whitepaper2/sas-data-visualization-marketpulse-106176.pdf

Schulz, F. (August 19, 2014). *Path analysis with SAS Visual Analytics* [Web log comment]. Retrieved from http://blogs.sas.com/content/sascom/2014/08/19/path-analysis-with-sas-visual-analytics/

Sen, A., & Sinha, A. P. (2011). IT alignment strategies for customer relationship management. *Decision Support Systems*, *51*(3), 609–619. doi:10.1016/j.dss.2010.12.014

Shieh, M. D., Yan, W., & Chen, C. H. (2008). Soliciting customer requirements for product redesign based on picture sorts and ART2 neural network. *Expert Systems with Applications*, *34*(1), 194–204. doi:10.1016/j.eswa.2006.08.036

Sridharan, S. (2012). *How analytics derives customer life cycle management* [PDF document]. Retrieved from http://contentz.mkt3838.com/lp/10371/367751/How_Analytics_Drives_Customer%20Life-cycle%20Management_Nov%202012_2.pdf

Stavrianou, A., Andritsos, P., & Nicoloyannis, N. (2007). Overview and semantic issues of text mining. *SIGMOD Record*, *36*(3), 23. doi:10.1145/1324185.1324190

Swift, R. S. (2001). *Accelerating Customer Relationships: Using CRM and Relationship Technologies*. Upper Saddle River, NJ: Prentice Hall.

Sykes, A. O. (2000). An Introduction to Regression Analysis. In E. Posner (Ed.), *Chicago Lectures in Law and Economics*. Chicago, IL: Foundation Press.

Thelwall, M., Buckley, K., Paltoglou, G., Cai, D., & Kappas, A. (2010). Sentiment Strength Detection in Short Informal Text. *Journal of the American Society for Information Science*, *61*(12), 2544–2558. doi:10.1002/asi.21416

Twitter (2015). Twitter usage. Retrived on March 31, 2015 from https://about.twitter.com/company

Verhoef, P. C., Venkatesan, R., McAlister, L., Malthouse, E. C., Krafft, M., & Ganesan, S. (2010). CRM in data-rich multichannel retailing environments: A review and future research directions. *Journal of Interactive Marketing*, *24*(2), 121–137. doi:10.1016/j.intmar.2010.02.009

Vicari, D., & Alfó, M. (2014). Model based clustering of customer choice data. *Computational Statistics & Data Analysis*, *71*, 3–13. doi:10.1016/j.csda.2013.09.014

Vollmer, C., & Precourt, G. (2008). *Always on: Advertising, marketing, and media in an era of consumer control*. New York: McGraw-Hill.

Wang, F. H., & Shao, H. M. (2004). Effective personalized recommendation based on time-framed navigation clustering and association mining. *Expert Systems with Applications*, *27*(3), 365–377. doi:10.1016/j.eswa.2004.05.005

Winer, R. S. (2001). A Framework for Customer Relationship Management. *California Management Review*, *43*(4), 89–105. doi:10.2307/41166102

Xintong, G., Hongzhi, W., Song, Y., & Hong, G. (2014). Brief survey of crowdsourcing for data mining. *Expert Systems with Applications*, *41*(17), 7987–7994. doi:10.1016/j.eswa.2014.06.044

Yang, Y., Akers, L., Klose, T., & Barcelon Yang, C. (2008). Text mining and visualization tools - Impressions of emerging capabilities. *World Patent Information*, *30*(4), 280–293. doi:10.1016/j.wpi.2008.01.007

Zafra, I. (2013, August 22). *Traditional vs. Social CRM: What's The Difference*? Retrieved from http://www.spi-global.com/blog/think-tank/traditional-vs-social-crm-whats-the-difference/

Zhang, X. Z. (2007). Building personalized recommendation system in E-Commerce using association rule-based mining and classification. In *Proceedings of the Sixth International Conference on Machine Learning and Cybernetics*, ICMLC 2007 (Vol. 7, pp. 4113–4118). doi:10.1109/ICMLC.2007.4370866

Zhang, Y., Liang, R., Li, Y., Zheng, Y., & Berry, M. (2011). Behavior-based telecommunication churn prediction with neural network approach. In *Proceedings - 2011 International Symposium on Computer Science and Society, ISCCS 2011* (pp. 307–310). doi:10.1109/ISCCS.2011.89

ADDITIONAL READING

Acker, O., Gröne, F., Akkad, F., Pötscher, F., & Yazbek, R. (2011). Social CRM: How companies can link into the social web of consumers. *Journal of Direct. Data and Digital Marketing Practice*, *13*(1), 3–10. doi:10.1057/dddmp.2011.17

Adomavicius, G., & Tuzhilin, A. (2001). Using data mining methods to build customer profiles. *Computer*, *34*(2), 74–81. doi:10.1109/2.901170

Anderson, J. L., Jolly, L. D., & Fairhurst, A. E. (2007). Customer relationship management in retailing: A content analysis of retail trade journals. *Journal of Retailing and Consumer Services*, *14*(6), 394–399. doi:10.1016/j.jretconser.2007.02.009

Bijmolt, T. H. A., Leeflang, P. S. H., Block, F., Eisenbeiss, M., Hardie, B. G. S., Lemmens, A., & Saffert, P. (2010). Analytics for Customer Engagement. *Journal of Service Research*, *13*(3), 341–356. doi:10.1177/1094670510375603

Choudhury, M. M., & Harrigan, P. (2014). CRM to social CRM: The integration of new technologies into customer relationship management. *Journal of Strategic Marketing*, *22*(2), 149–176. doi:10.1080/0965254X.2013.876069

Coltman, T. (2007). Why build a customer relationship management capability? *The Journal of Strategic Information Systems*, *16*(3), 301–320. doi:10.1016/j.jsis.2007.05.001

Ferguson, B. R. (interviewer) & Sundaresan, N. (Interviewee). (2013, June 25). *How eBay Uses Data and Analytics to Get Closer to Its (Massive) Customer Base* [interview transcript]. Retrieved from http://sloanreview.mit.edu/article/how-ebay-uses-data-and-analytics-to-get-closer-to-its-massive-customer-base/

Ganapathy, S., Ranganathan, C., & Sankaranarayanan, B. (2004). Visualization strategies and tools for enhancing customer relationship management. *Communications of the ACM*, *47*(11), 92–99. doi:10.1145/1029496.1029500

Greenberg, P. (2010). The impact of CRM 2.0 on customer insight. *Journal of Business and Industrial Marketing*, *25*(6), 410–419. doi:10.1108/08858621011066008

Iyer, L. S., & Raman, R. M. (2011). Intelligent Analytics : Integrating Business Intelligence and Web Analytics. *International Journal of Business Intelligence Research*, *2*(1), 31–45. doi:10.4018/jbir.2011010103

Lichtenstein, S., Bednall, D. H. B., & Adam, S. (2008). Marketing research and customer analytics: Interfunctional knowledge integration. *International Journal of Technology Marketing*, *3*(1), 81. doi:10.1504/IJTMKT.2008.017341

Min, H., Min, H., & Emam, A. (2002). A data mining approach to developing the profiles of hotel customers. *International Journal of Contemporary Hospitality Management*, *14*(6), 274–285. doi:10.1108/09596110210436814

Mosadegh, M., & Behboudi, M. (2011). Using social network paradigm for developing a conceptual framework in CRM. *Australian Journal of Business & Management Research*, *1*(4), 63–71.

Öztaysi, B., Sezgin, S., & Özok, A. F. (2011). A measurement tool for customer relationship management processes. *Industrial Management & Data Systems*, *111*(6), 943–960. doi:10.1108/02635571111144982

Persson, A., & Ryals, L. (2014). Making customer relationship decisions: Analytics v rules of thumb. *Journal of Business Research*, *67*(8), 1725–1732. doi:10.1016/j.jbusres.2014.02.019

Ren, S., Sun, Q., & Shi, Y. (2010). Customer segmentation of bank based on data warehouse and data mining. In *ICIME 2010 - 2010 2nd IEEE International Conference on Information Management and Engineering* (Vol. 5, pp. 349–353). doi:10.1109/ICIME.2010.5477693

Ribarsky, W., Xiaoyu Wang, D., & Dou, W. (2014). Social media analytics for competitive advantage. *Computers and Graphics (Pergamon)*, *38*(1), 328–331. doi:10.1016/j.cag.2013.11.003

Rygielski, C., Wang, J. C., & Yen, D. C. (2002). Data mining techniques for customer relationship management. *Technology in Society*, *24*(4), 483–502. doi:10.1016/S0160-791X(02)00038-6

Saarijärvi, H., Karjaluoto, H., & Kuusela, H. (2013). Customer relationship management: The evolving role of customer data. *Marketing Intelligence & Planning*, *31*(6), 584–600. doi:10.1108/MIP-05-2012-0055

Schmidt, A., & Hoyer, J. (2012). Social CRM. *ERP Management*, *8*(2), 32–35.

Scullin, S. S., Fjermestad, J., & Jr, N. C. R. (2004). E-relationship marketing: Changes in traditional marketing as an outcome of electronic customer relationship management. *Journal of Enterprise Information Management*, *17*(6), 410–415. doi:10.1108/17410390410566698

Shankar, V., & Winer, R. S. (2006). When customer relationship management meets data mining. *Journal of Interactive Marketing*, *20*(3-4), 2–4. doi:10.1002/dir.20062

Stodder, D. (2012). Customer Analytics in the Age of Social Media. *The Data Warehousing Institute Research*, (Third Quarter), 1–41.

Trainor, K. J., Andzulis, J., Rapp, A., & Agnihotri, R. (2014). Social media technology usage and customer relationship performance: A capabilities-based examination of social CRM. *Journal of Business Research*, *67*(6), 1201–1208. doi:10.1016/j.jbusres.2013.05.002

Tsai, C. F., & Lu, Y. H. (2010). Data Mining Techniques in Customer Churn Prediction. *Recent Patents on Computer Science*, *3*(1), 28–32.

Tuzhilin, A. (2012). Customer relationship management and Web mining: The next frontier. *Data Mining and Knowledge Discovery*, *24*(3), 584–612. doi:10.1007/s10618-012-0256-z

Wang, P., & Swanson, E. B. (2008). Customer relationship management as advertised: Exploiting and sustaining technological momentum. *Information Technology & People*, *21*(4), 323–349. doi:10.1108/09593840810919662

KEY TERMS AND DEFINITIONS

Analytics: Analytics involves studying historical data and analyzing it systematically resulting in discoveringmeaningful patterns in data, which can help in identifying trends and predict future.

Association Analysis: Association analysis when applied on a data set of transactions helps in discovering rules that indicate the likely occurrence of an item based on the occurrences of other items in the same transaction data set.

Clustering: Clustering is the task of grouping or creating clusters from a set of objects in such a way that objects in one cluster are meaningful and display similar characteristics in comparison to other clusters.

Lead scoring: Lead scoring is a methodology used to rank prospects by adding or subtracting points on a scale based on their attributes (e.g. demographics, behavior, etc.) for representing the perceived value of each lead to the organization.

Sentiment analysis: It is a method of computationally identifying and categorizing opinions expressed in a piece of text with the help of natural language processing and computational linguistics. This analysis helps in identifying the writer's attitude (positive, negative or neutral) towards a particular topic.

Social CRM: Social Customer Relationship Management is use of social media tools and techniquesby the organizations with an objective to attract, attain, and engage with their customers.

Social Listening: Social listening is the procedure of monitoring digital media channels for the identification and assessment of stakeholders views regarding the organization so as to devise a strategy that will better influence consumers.

Chapter 3
The Impact of CRM and Social Media Technologies on Customer-Orientation Process and Sales Performance

Mahdi Sheykhlar
Islamic Azad University, Iran

Rozita Shahbaz Keshvari
Islamic Azad University, Iran

ABSTRACT

The purpose of this chapter is studying that technology, such as customer relationship management systems and social media, improves the understanding of how to manage interactions with customers in today's digital era. Iran's auto industry has passed the first states of a new born auto industry (assembling the imported parts) and before the revolution, some of the car factories were upgraded to factories with the ability of design and production of spare parts. In order to examine the research model, data was gathered from survey of car representatives of IRAN. Participants included different levels in sales. Data was collected using an emailed link to an online survey supported by two reminder emails. 843 respondents completed the 130+ item. No significant difference between the data was evidenced. Results show that CRM and social media positively influence customer orientation activities, which in turn positively impact sales performance. Managerial implications are provided regarding the potential power CRM and social media has on sales performance.

1. INTRODUCTION

Iran's auto industry which started from the 1959 has passed the first states of a new born auto industry (assembling the imported parts) and before the revolution, some of the car factories were upgraded to factories with the ability of design and production of spare parts. After the revolution, due to the shortage of qualified engineers and closure of car factories, we had a great downfall in auto production. The car

DOI: 10.4018/978-1-4666-8586-4.ch003

industry tried to survive but, because of the war it faced another shock and auto production experienced another slump. In addition, by the first 15 years until 1993 it was mainly producing some outmoded cars (with the out of date technology of 20 years before).

Auto industry which was started up by two production lines at the two strands of the Atlantic Ocean in 1896, today, after 150 years has reached an annual production of 50,500,000 cars and involves nearly 100,000,000 employees.

Before the advent of super markets and automobile, people shopped from their neighborhood general store. This relationship between the buyer and the seller was highly personalized as the proprietor not only recognized his /her customers by name and by face, but also knew about his/her customers preferences and wants. As the population grew and people moved towards urban centers, this idyllic customer relationship disappeared. The reason behind the transition was the introduction of large superstores which benefitted from economies of scale and mass marketing to provide cheaper and standardized goods. Customers now became fickle, moving to the supplier who offered the cheapest price or the greatest number of features.

The auto industry is amidst an era of marketing disruption. Traditional advertising models and budgets are withering. Consumers' time and attention have quickly transitioned to social and digital platforms. Interspersed among those platforms are growing ranks of brand advocates and detractors who share their purchase and ownership experiences through text, photo and video postings on their personal networks. That process alone is having significant influence on purchase decisions.

The percentage of people who pause to share their purchase and ownership experiences using social and digital platforms is growing significantly. The process is always on and relentless. It's a new playing field for automakers, dealers, and suppliers. The sum of connected experiences shared online and how they influence transactions is what we refer to as social selling.

As a result, Customer Relationship Management (CRM) evolved as an important business tool in the last several years. It is a simple concept that focuses on marketing to each customer individually rather than marketing to a mass of people or firms. The main purpose of this one-to-one approach is to analyze previous purchases, wants and preferences of a customer in order to formulate new offers that are likely to be accepted.

In the extremely fluid and unstable world of social media, Social CRM is not the latest marketing "trend" or simply an elevation of traditional CRM, kitted out with a fashionable adjective. It is the adaption of companies' organization and brands' communication to a new Customer Relationship Management landscape. E-reputation and community management – still very new and evolving disciplines – are generally perceived as communication-related functions and activities. Social CRM goes further: it has made its way into the heart of current thinking in Commercial Management, Customer Services, Communications, IT, etc.

Social CRM is changing the scale and perspective of brand involvement in social media. What was once a Communications department issue is now becoming an organizational challenge for any company that claims to be "customer-centric". Social CRM is the connection between social media and a company's internal and external communication systems. The question for companies is no longer whether to engage with social media, but rather how to engage with it. Companies that have already started implementing Social CRM strategies rapidly see the impact on their internal processes.

In an article predicting 2012 CRM market trends, analysts pointed out that CRM will allow companies to become more customer-centric and that integrating social media with CRM will be essential for organizations (Schiff, 2012). Technology is useful for enhancing the customer relationship and in capturing competitive advantages (Bharadwaj, Varadarajan, & Fahy, 1993). Technology can help improve the operating process of an organization and, thus, improve its performance. In order to extract value from technology, organizations need to build a framework and processes to deliver value to the customer.

2. LITERATURE REVIEW

Greenberg (2009) stated in his study that the term "social media" has been used in several contexts related to different technologies and what they can accomplish. Social media may be defined as the production, consumption and exchange of information across platforms for social interaction.Using a similar approach but without explicitly defining social media.

Andzulis, Panagopoulos & Rapp, (2012) explained in his study that all customers are now "customer benefits" and that every interaction is an integral part of a new collaboration between the company and the customer, yielding CRM 2.0.

According to CREDOC (2009), 57% of French Internet users consult the opinions of other users before purchasing various products and services. Specifically, these new media enable conservations between customers about such topics as products and company reputations.

Mangold & Faulds (2009) stated that before the development of social networks, companies retained control over the messages that they diffused and the time in which customers would have access to them. Companies lose "control" once a message is broadcast as it is recovered by customers who will comment on, share or question it. The customer can "talk" directly with the brand and other customers.

Manish Parihar (Jan, 2012) founded that although the traditional touch points with the customer are to stay, but the new generation online tools have radically changed in the way that companies connect and relate to their customers the concept of customer experience management has been an extension of the new-age customer relationship management.

Lehmkuhl Tobias & Jung Reinhard (Jun, 2013) stated in their study that the triggers of SCRM are technological advancements and societal changes leading to an empowered web user. Persons are engaged in a public and direct dialogue with organizations and their peers in order to derive personal utilitarian and affective value. SCRM added to that point by facilitating customer engagement as a means to establish mutually /beneficial relationships.

2-1. Customer Relationship Management

The customer is the only source of the companies present profit and future growth. CRM can be thought of as a marketing approach that is based on customer information. The relationship between a company and its customers involves continuous bi-directional communication and interaction. CRM involves managing this relationship so it is profitable and mutually beneficial. Management: CRM is not an activity only within a marketing department, it involves continues corporate changes in culture and strategies. CRM requires a comprehensive change in the organization and people. CRM used in business for identifying the new selling opportunities. Also it deliver instant, company-wide access to customer histories. CRM has emerged as a popular business strategy in today's competitive environment. It is a discipline that enables the companies to identify and target their most profitable customers. It involves new and advance marketing strategies that not only retain the existing customers but also acquire new customer. There are three key elements to successful CRM initiatives: people, business process, and technology.

CRM activities allows for increased call center efficiency, improved close rates, marketing processes, improved customers profiling and targeting, reduced cost, increased share of customer and profitability. CRM provides enhanced opportunities to use data and information to both understand customers and co-create value with them. This requires a cross-functional integration of processes, people, operations, and marketing capabilities. In this new Era, product centric approach changes into the customer centric approaches, the focus of marketers has shifted towards their customers and more deliberately on their experiences, which will be elaborated in subsequent sections (Megha Y. Patil, 2014)

2-2. Social Media

The world is becoming "global" from global and is squeezing its economic, social and political boundaries thus giving it a common platform for development.The convergence of the media has expanded the usage of internet that gave birth to social media. The term "social media "has been used in several contexts related to different technologies and what they can they accomplish. Social media may be defined as the production, consumption and exchange of information across platforms for social interaction. Social media has taken the web world by storm.It has completely revolutionized the ways communication used to take place even a decade ago. It makes use of web-based technologies to transform and media monologues into social media dialogues. This technology is mostly of grate interest to those that are interested in search engine optimization and Internet marketing. The social media technology also supports the democratization of knowledge and information transforming people from mere content customers to content producers. People now rely more on social to learn about events and influenced more than ever by their peers. As a result, Social Medias now play a significant role in forming public opinion. In the age of the web 2.0 and almost present broadband internet connections, a large majority of the online public are communicating with each other through a new medium. Apart from e-mail and instant messengers, they communicate through the medium of blogs, micro blogging websites and social networking websites like face book, Twitter, LinkedIn and many others. (Ahuja, 2010).

2-3. Social Media CRM (SCRM)

SCRM is a Social Customer Relationship Management. The integration of social media with customer relationship management (CRM) strategies-is the next frontier for organizations that want to optimize the power of social interactions to get closer to customers. With the worldwide explosion of social media usage, business is feeling extreme pressure to be where their customers are. The social CRM from technological standpoint bridges social media with the traditional CRM. Social media holds unprecedented potential for companies to get closer to get closer to customers and, by doing so, facilitate increased revenue, cost reduction and efficiencies. Businesses are rapidly embracing social media not only to build virtual communities, but also to create innovative social commerce programs, improve customer care and streamline customer research. With so much to gain, companies need to invest the effort to understand how to break through the noise and offer current and potential customers a reason out to them via social media. The blend of social media and customer relationship management (social CRM) enables your brand to truly listen to your customers more than ever before. It enhances your traditional CRM by listening for and with social media conversations, tracking new leads from a Tweet or Face book post and moving them into your sales funnel. Social media continuously generate hoards of information so that it becomes difficult for enterprises to monitor them. As a result, an increasing number of CRM developing companies of CRM developing companies are now offering social media integration their CRM. CRM customization allows your social media accounts to be linked and managed through your customer relationship management software.It helps businesses in devising business strategy using the insight gained from societies. The benefits offered by SCRM or social CRM are:

- Improved peer–to-peer interaction in offering customer support.
- Market feedback research.
- Idea management.
- Brand positioning and promotion.
- Product launching.

CRM helps business in streaming operation and improve customer dealing. Integration of social media to it further enforced its usefulness in helping businesses to connect and serve their customers better. Customer channels have to identify before a company can build and manage its customer relationships via social networks. Once done, the full potential of Social CRM can be realized: because nowadays, customers like to use the social networks to share information about themselves and their interests. Social CRM in the current state is just a beginning of the larger shifts that are likely to take place on the foundation stone of today`s emerging directions (Megha Y. Patil, 2014).

A number of companies have successfully adopted the new paradigm, and proved that social CRM can have a very significant beneficial effect on each of the functional areas of a business. Social CRM applications encourage participation among various stakeholders in order to support sales, marketing, as well as customer and business processes. It engages customers in different scenarios, such as, ideas for innovation, development of new products and services, word-of-mouth marketing, price comparisons and product reviews.

Some of the largest brands have increased their digital spend and have started experimenting with social media to engage with the customer and provide an improved customer experience. Examples of companies using social media include Bank of America, which has been successfully running customer services via Twitter and Dell in the Hi Tech industry, which has used social media effectively to drive sales and increase revenue.

2-4. Customer-Oriented Technology

The advancement of technology allows sales-focused organizations to manage customer information effectively in order to better understand their unique needs and provide a solution that meets those needs. Panagopoulos defines sales technology "as any information and communication technology employed by the sales organization to conduct its essential activities". The central focus of CRM is "to leverage customer data creatively, effectively and efficiently to design and implement customer-focused strategies" (Hansotia, 2002). Initially, CRM was considered an information technology customer solution, a type of sales force automation. Now, CRM strategy is considered a "holistic approach to managing customer relationships to create shareholder value" (Payne & Frow, 2005, p. 168). Evolving into a mix of relationship marketing and relevant technology, use of platforms such as CRM can potentially generate profitable, long-term relationships with customers. The CRM aim is three fold, 1) improve data regarding the customer from a host of different inputs, not just from the sales force, 2) improve relationships, and 3) co-create value with clients.

Recent research has focused on specific sales technology, such as customer relationship management (Tanner, Ahearne, Leigh, Mason, & Moncrief, 2005; Rapp, Agnihotri and Forbes, 2008) and sales force automation tools (SFA). Ahearne, Jelinek, and Rapp (2005) reported in previous studies that CRM systems improve the sales professional's ability to collaborate internally with peers and communicate clearly with clients. Sales-based CRM technology tools are designed to help sales professionals manage customer relationships (Hunter & Perreault, 2007) by improving communication, learning more about the clients' needs, and creating customized solutions for the customer. Organizations are also integrating use of social media tools to reach new markets and gain an improved understanding of prospects and existing customers. When managing customer relationships and experiences, sales organizations are leveraging social media to perform sales-related tasks, such as prospecting and sharing of information on product and services (Panagopoulos, 2010). Today, sales-focused firms have integrated social media tools, such as Linked-In, Facebook, and Twitter, into their business process to directly communicate with prospective buyers and create deeper conversations. To stay current and competitive, organizations may find it critical to add a social media strategy to their existing CRM initiative. Social media tools, whether in the form of blogs, Facebook, or Twitter, offer interactions between buyer and seller. This new era of creating conversations may develop more meaningful relationships with customers and, potentially, result in a more profitable relationship. In order for these technologies to benefit stakeholders, sales professionals must accept and employ the technology within their job function (Venkatesh, Morris, Davis & Davis, 2003; Rodriguez & Honeycutt, 2011). In fact, the value of any technology investment to an organization is mainly determined by the way the technology is used and applied (Kohli & Grover, 2008).

Customer-oriented technologies, such as CRM and social media, are expected to positively impact performance and activities within the organization.

2-5. Customer Orientation Processes and Sales Performance

The marketing literature suggests that customer orientation is a cornerstone in the theory and practice of marketing management (Saxe & Weitz, 1982; Jaworski and Kohli, 1993). Ruekert (1992) defines this orientation as the "degree to which the organization obtains and uses information from customers, develops a strategy which will meet customer needs, and implements that strategy by being responsive to customers' needs and wants". Different processes relate to customer orientation: customer satisfaction, after-sales services, personalized services to key customers, and commitment to deliver high value to customers (Narver & Slater, 1990). Researchers argue that customer orientation is not only a set of processes, but a culture that stresses the customer as the center of strategic planning and execution and that is important to create superior value for an organization (Narver & Slater, 1990; Deshpande et al., 1993; Jaworski, Kohli & Sahay, 2000; Steinman, Deshpande, & Farley, 2000). Organizations with higher customer orientation are better able to respond to customers' demand with goods and services (Deshpande et al., 1993). Those companies also indicate a continuous and proactive disposition toward identifying and meeting demands (Han, Kim, & Srivastava, 1998). Researchers found that increased customer orientation within an organization results in improved business performance (Narver & Slater, 1990; Jaworski & Kohli, 1993; Van Egeren & O'Connor, 1998; Yilmaz, Alpkan, & Ergun, 2005).

Thus, customer-oriented processes involve many facets, including understanding clients' needs and sharing and aligning information to create a value proposition that satisfies customers.

Past research on the relationship between technology and performance has been well documented and supported (Stoddard, Clopton, & Avila, 2006; Hunter and Perreault, 2007; Rodriguez and Honeycutt,

2011). Due to the increased use of technology from the sales perspective, current research has focused on the relationship between technology and sales performance. Johnston and Marshall define sales performance as "behavior evaluated in terms of its contribution to the goals of the organization". Ahearne, Jelinek, and Rapp (2005) reported that CRM technology improves the sales professional's ability to communicate clearly with prospects and clients and establish new business.

However, other researchers found that the link to performance is not always direct, and can depend on environmental settings (Hartline & McKee, 2000). There is still a need in the literature to better understand the impact of customer orientation on firm's benefits (Brady & Cronin, 2001). In this paper, we attempt to understand the direct influence of customer-oriented processes on sales performance, while considering the impact of CRM and social media use.

2-6. Key Terms and Definitions

2-6-1. Social Media

Social media tools are computer and web-based tools and softwares that people use them to share, exchange and create information and files, photos and videos in visual networks. People use computer, laptop, tablet and mobile for creating or sharing a subject, idea or picture, and sometimes other people, see that and comment their opinion or viewpoint about it. Social media is an inexpensive tool for communicate with people and promotion. You can use this tool for broadcasting news in a very short time to a large number of audiences.

2-6-2. CRM

CRM or Customer Relationship Management is a field of management that uses strategies, methods and softwares to keep, manage and process customer data and records to improving and growing the quality of relation between the organization and their customers in order to keeping present customers and increasing customer loyalty. It works with recognizing the customer needs, and making products and services matching their needs, and also providing good customer services.

2-6-3. Customer Orientation

Customer orientation means a business put goals of marketing plans based on providing product or services to meet what new consumer wants. It includes a set of activities applied by sales and services staffs in order to provide consumer needs and enhance their satisfaction.

2-6-4. Organizational

A group of people working together to achieving goals using software and hardware. An organization has a structured system managed by management team, defining and handling relations between staffs and activities. Every member of this system has particular tasks and responsibilities and altogether processing system inputs to make its output and reach the goals.

2-6-5. Performance

Performance is the production of valid results. It is the accomplishment of a given task measured against preset known standards of accuracy, completeness, cost, and speed.

2-6-6. Organizational Performance

An analysis of a company's performance as compared to goals and objectives. Organizational performance comprises the actual output or results of an organization as measured against its intended outputs (or goals and objectives).

2-6-7. Sales

Providing products or services in exchange for receiving money from whom that want it. Without sales no business can be alive.

2-6-8. Industry

The manufacturing or technically productive enterprises in a particular field, country, region, or economy viewed collectively, or one of these individually. A single industry is often named after its principal product. Every business that can be isolated from others, is an industry.

2-6-9. Auto Industry

Every companies or organizations that prepare products or services related to auto and car, such car manufacturing companies, companies produce auto parts, companies that provide car services or organizations that sell cars.

3. RESEARCH MODEL AND HYPOTHESES

Customer-oriented technologies, such as CRM and social media, help organizations support and create strong relationships with customers and support the firm's customer orientation. The authors posit that the real value of customer-oriented technologies lies in the way customer orientation processes use the information provided by the platforms to enhance the customer's experience. Customer orientation subsequently drives improved sales performance because firms can tailor their offerings to suit customer needs. Previous research shows that customer orientation is positively associated with a firm's performance (Narver & Slater, 1990; Van Egeren & O'Connor, 1998; Jaworski et al., 2000; Yilmaz et al., 2005). As the preceding discussion suggests, better customer-oriented processes facilitated by CRM and social media should enable a firm to improve its sales performance. The research model is shown in Figure 1.

Customer-oriented technologies, such as CRM and social media, are used to collect customer data from all customer contact points and create proper customer-oriented marketing responses (Payne & Frow, 2005). Accumulating this customer insight can be used to boost the quality of the customer experience (Plakoyiannaki & Saren, 2006). CRM and social media applications enable firms to customize their of-

Figure 1. Customer orientation mediation model

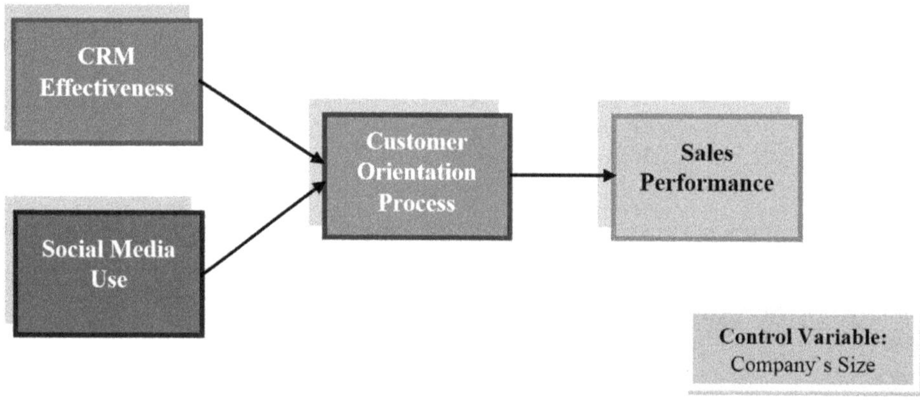

ferings for each customer. By accumulating information across customer interactions and processing this information to discover hidden patterns, CRM and social media applications help firms customize their offerings to suit the individual tastes of their customers and improve customer engagement (Woodcock, Green, & Starkey, 2011).

In order to achieve higher benefits, well designed customer-orientation processes are needed to enable sales performance level benefits. Therefore, we expect customer-oriented processes (such as measuring customer satisfaction, obtaining feedback from customers, and adapting to changes in customers' needs) to positively impact sales performance. Customer orientation implies having an understanding of the customers to be able to offer them greater added value (Narver & Slater, 1990). Organizations with higher customer orientation will be able to design business processes that are strongly oriented to improve employee understanding of the customers (Bang, 2005). This is why we expect customer orientation processes are likely to positively impact sales performance. Organizations should be equipped with strong customer-oriented technologies (CRM & social media) to effectively employ customer-oriented processes for optimal level marketing and sales activities, which eventually may result in higher performance. Hence, we hypothesize that:

H1: CRM has a positive relationship on customer-orientation.
H2: Social media has a positive relationship on customer-oriented processes orientation.
H3: Customer oriented processes has a positive relationship on sales performance

4. RESEARCH METHODS

4-1. Data Collection

In order to examine the research model, data was gathered from survey of car representatives of IRAN that answer to this survey by email. Participants included different levels in sales. Data was collected using an emailed link to an online survey supported by two reminder emails. Data were collected within a 3 month period. 843 respondents completed the 130+ item. No significant difference between the data was evidenced.

4-2. Measures

Customer orientation was measured on a 7-item Likert scale. We specified customer orientation as a formative first-order construct. The measurement items were selected and refined to ensure that the selected formative measures for customer orientation did not overlap and covered all characteristics of the constructs. The indicator specification process resulted in a set of subjective measures for customer orientation. CRM effectiveness and social media use was measured using a 3-item scale. All performance measures used a 7-point scale.

The car company size is included as a control variable to account for any contextual differences that may influence the sales performance across the sample.

4-3. Results

Partial Least Squares (PLS) was used to analyze the data. PLS is well suited to handle highly complex predictive models (Jöreskog & Wold, 1982) with formative constructs as is the case with this model. The results of the PLS analysis are presented in the following discussion.

4-4. Measurement Model

Appropriate validation procedures were followed to evaluate both reflective and formative measures in the model. We examined internal consistency, convergent validity, and discriminate validity to check the measurement validity of reflective constructs (Straub, 1989; Gefen and Straub, 2005). Both discriminate validity and multicollinearlity were examined for formative measures.

The internal consistencies of the reflective measures were evaluated using Cronbach's alphas. All constructs had Cronbach's alpha values greater than 0.6, the recommended threshold for exploratory research (Nunnally & Bernstein, 1994). Table 1 displays the Cronbach's alpha values for all the reflective constructs.

Principle component factor analysis with varimax rotation was used to evaluate discriminate validity of the reflective measures. This approach examines whether the theorized items group together on appropriate constructs and discriminate across multiple constructs with minimal cross loading among factors. The criterion used in the analysis was a factor loading greater than 0.45, and eigen values greater than 1.0. The results in Table 2 show that the items for the independent variables converge on three constructs as originally designed.

Confirmatory factor analysis in SmartPLS (Ringle, Wende & Will, 2005) was used to validate the measurement model. One control variable, sales organization size, was included in the model for the confirmatory factor analysis test. We also examined the convergent and discriminant validity of the re-

Table 1. Test and measurement reliability

Construct	Cronbach's alpha
Social Media	0.733
CRM Effectiveness	0.891
Sales Performance	0.907

Table 2. Factor analysis results

Loading	Component		
Items	Social Media	CRM Effectiveness	Sales Performance
SM1_dm	0.786		
SM2_bp	0.653		
SM3_bo	0.715		
CRM1_p		0.827	
CRM2_qi		0.811	
CRM3-da		0.901	
OP1_cp			0.927
OP2_na			0.936
OP3_nq			0.894
OP4_cr			0.906
OP5_qa			0.882

Notes: Principal components method was used for extracting the components and Varimax was the rotation method. All factor loadings below 0.45 were suppressed.

flective constructs. Convergent validity is supported as indicated by Average Variance Extracted (AVE) for each construct being greater than the recommended 0.5 in all cases (Gefen & Straub, 2005). In addition, strong convergent validity is evident as the items load highly on their own constructs (Table 3). Discriminant validity was evaluated by assessing the square root of the AVEs to ensure that it is greater than the correlation among the constructs. The higher AVE for a construct indicated that more variance is shared between the construct and its items than with other constructs (Fornell & Larcker, 1981; Chin, 1998). The inter-construct correlation matrix in Table 4, with square root of AVE on the diagonal, indicated satisfactory discriminate validity of all the constructs. Furthermore, Cronbach's alpha for all reflective constructs exceeded 0.6, and the composite reliability of all reflective constructs exceeded 0.7, indicating adequate internal consistencies of the constructs.

For the formative construct, the outer model weights were examined. The results shown in Table 5 indicate acceptable outer model weights. Multicollinearity among indicators was also checked since it can cause an insignificant model. The variance inflation factor (VIF) was used to assess any multicollinearity problems. VIF values below 3.3 are indicative of an absence of multicollinearity (Diamantopoulos & Siguaw, 2006). The VIF value for the customer orientation processes was below the threshold value of 3.3. Therefore, multicollinearity is not a problem in the formative construct.

4-5. Structural Model

A bootstrapping resampling method was used to assess the structural model. The R^2 values in the model range from 0.122 to 0.347. Additionally, all paths are statistically significant at the 0.05 level and are in the expected direction. Therefore, the proposed model is considered to have good predictive power. The path coefficient of each hypothesized relationship and its statistical significance was examined to determine the support for the hypothesis. The path coefficient between CRM technology and customer

Table 3. Reflective constructs reliability and loadings

Social Media	**Composte Reliability = 0.752** **Cronbach's alpha = 0.733**	**AVE = 0.622**
	Loading	**T-Value**
SM1_dm	0.703	13.558***
SM2_bp	0.692	10.288***
SM3_bo	0.724	8.018***
CRM Effectiveness	**Composte Reliability = 0.905** **Cronbach's alpha = 0.891**	**AVE = 0.847**
	Loading	**T-Value**
CRM1_p	0.882	26.173***
CRM2_qi	0.926	48.667***
CRM3-da	0.917	42.501***
Sales Performance	**Composte Reliability = 0.931** **Cronbach's alpha = 0.907**	**AVE = 0.898**
	Loading	**T-Value**
OP1_cp	0.922	46.551***
OP2_na	0.97	54.806***
OP3_nq	0.923	52.323***
OP4_cr	0.884	40.604***
OP5_qa	0.936	47.887***

*p<0.1, **p<0.05, ***p<0.01

Table 4. Inter-construct correlation matrix

#		1	2	3
	Social Media	0.78		
	CRM Effectiveness	0.34	0.88	
	Sales Performance	0.31	0.37	0.72

Table 5. Formative measures weights assessment

Customer Orientation	Weights	T-Value
CO1_wb	0.166	2.402*
CO2_fp	0.152	1.965**
CO3_a	0.124	2.229**
CO4_fv	0.176	2.663***
CO5_ci	0.338	2.374***
CO6_af	0.247	2.154**
CO7_ac	0.491	3.22***

*p<0.1, **p<0.05, ***p<0.01

orientation was 0.412 (t= 4.85, pb.001), while that between social media and customer orientation was 0.237 (t=3.51, pb.001). We also found customer orientation to be positively associated with sales performance 0.355 (t=4.63, pb.001). The PLS structural model results are shown in Figure 2.

5. CONCLUSION

The coming years will see more integration of social media to customer management platform. The integration procedure depends upon the social media maturity level of your organization with companies at the initial stage needing more comprehensive social media plans. These brands are using social media as a meaningful way to develop relationships with their customers and publicity of their products. Customers are connecting and having conservations about enterprises through social media, whether enterprises are actively engaged or not, and brands risk being raised if they fail to participate. Social CRM is an opportunity for organization to become customer centric. It contents the new communication and collaboration medium of social media to improve the existing business processes of marketing, sales & services. Technology will play a vital role in taking social CRM to take next level of maturity. It is concluded that social networks holds unprecedented potential for companies to get closer to customers facilitate increased in revenue, cost reduction and so on.

This study delivers several contributions. First, it provides evidence that customer technology, such as CRM and social media, positively impacts customer-orientated processes. These processes include understanding customers, adapting to customers changing needs, measuring customer satisfaction, and aligning customer needs with sales and marketing activities. Organizations adopting CRM strategies, both traditional and social, need to practice customer-oriented behaviors in order to have these technologies platforms affect bottom-line sales performance. Before implementing customer-oriented technologies, car companies need to create business practices that build and maintain profitable relationships. It is too easy for organizations to get caught up in technology investment without first defining and practicing customer orientation and establishing proper customer-oriented business processes.

Figure 2. Customer orientation mediation model results

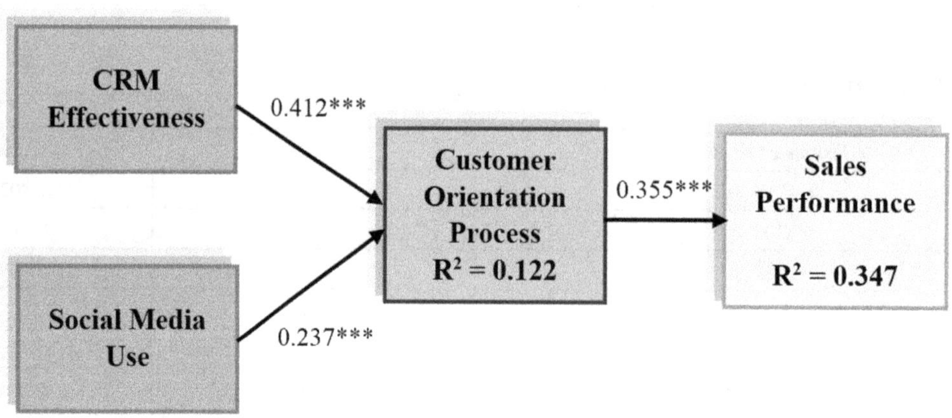

*p<0.1, **p<0.05, ***p<0.01

Second, the findings provide justification for investing in both CRM and social media technology as it leads to improved customer orientation processes in the firm. Business-to-business organizations need to implement both CRM technology and social media and ensure the technologies integrate well with one another. Integration of both CRM and social media leads to improved customer oriented processes, which in turn may lead to a number of benefits: improved sales and marketing alignment, access to decision makers, shorter sales cycles, and better collaboration with customers. This type of integration will more effectively capture conversations and truly provide a 360-degree view of the client. "Social media adds a new dimension by recording the interaction and conversation with the client. Organizations should capture the most relevant and valuable information from social media and integrate this communication with the firm's current CRM workflow" (Rodriguez, Peterson, & Krishnan, 2012, pg. 378).

Third, effective utilization of sales-focused technology, in the form of CRM and social media, starts with understanding customer processes. Firms with higher customer orientation are more competitive due to the level of understanding of their clients' needs and buying habits. This understanding combined with integration of CRM and social media results in more successful firm performance. The study also makes a pioneering contribution to the existing research that has mostly been focused on sales force automation technology. To date, it appears no other studies have empirically examined both CRM and social media practices and tied them to performance with such a large cross-sectional sample.

In today's competitive environment, organizations need to focus on delivering high value to their customers through focused, customer-oriented business processes. New CRM and social media technologies have changed the way organizations interact with customers and have allowed enhanced understanding of customers' needs and concerns (Marshall, Moncrief, Rudd, & Lee 2012; Rodriguez, Peterson, & Krishnan, 2012). These new technologies have enabled customers to communicate effectively with organizations and to improve the relationships between the buyer and seller. In this research, we assessed the positive impact of CRM and social media on customer orientation processes (i.e., processes focused on customer satisfaction and commitment) which, in turn, positively impacts sales performance. Traditional and Social CRM should be tightly integrated into both marketing and sales strategy, in order gain a deeper understanding of customers, develop further commitment and loyalty, which in time will increase overall sales performance.

REFERENCES

Ahearne, M., Jelinek, R., & Rapp, A. (2005). Moving Beyond the Direct Effect of SFA Adoption on Salesperson Performance: Training and Support as Key Moderating Factors. *Journal of Marketing Development and Competitiveness*, *8*(1), 2014.

Ahuja, V., & Medury, Y. (2010, March 23). Corporate blogs as e-CRM tools-building customer engagement through content Management. *Journal of Databases Marketing & Customer Strategy Management*, *17*(2), 91–105. doi:10.1057/dbm.2010.8

Bang, J. (2005). *Understanding customer relationship management from managers' and customers' perspective: Exploring the implications of CRM fit, market orientation, and market knowledge competence.* (Ph.D. dissertation). University of Rhode Island, Kingston, RI. Retrieved May 06, 2012, from ABI/INFORM Global.

Bharadwaj, S. G., Varadarajan, P. R., & Fahy, J. (1993). Sustainable Competitive Advantage in Service Industries: A Conceptual Model and Research Propositions. *Journal of Marketing*, *57*(Oct), 83–99. doi:10.2307/1252221

Brady, M. K., & Cronin, J. (2001). Customer Orientation: Effects on Customer Service Perceptions and Outcome Behaviors. *Journal of Service Research*, *3*(3), 241–251. doi:10.1177/109467050133005

Chin, W. W. (1998). *The Partial Least Squares Approach for Structural Equation Modeling in Modern Methods for Business Research*. Mahwah, NJ: Lawrence Erlbaum Associates.

Deshpande, R., Farley, J. U., & Webster, F. E. (1993). Corporate Culture, Customer Orientation, and Innovativeness in Japanese Firms: A Quadrad Analysis. *Journal of Marketing*, *57*(1), 23–37. doi:10.2307/1252055

Diamantopoulos, A., & Siguaw, J. A. (2006). Formative versus Reflective Indicators in Organizational Measure Development: A Comparison and Empirical Illustration. *British Journal of Management*, *17*(4), 263–282. doi:10.1111/j.1467-8551.2006.00500.x

Diamantopoulos, A., & Winklhofer, H. M. (2001). Index Construction with Formative Indicators: An Alternative to Scale Development. *JMR, Journal of Marketing Research*, *38*(2), 269–277. doi:10.1509/jmkr.38.2.269.18845

Fornell, C., & Larcker, D. (1981). Evaluating Structural Equation Models with Unobservable Variables and Measurement Error. *JMR, Journal of Marketing Research*, *18*(1), 39–50. doi:10.2307/3151312

Gefen, D., & Straub, D. W. (2005). A Practical Guide to Factorial Validity Using PLS-Graph: Tutorial and Annotated Example. *Communications of the AIS*, *16*(5), 91–109.

Han, J. K., Kim, N., & Srivastava, R. K. (1998). Market Orientation and Organizational Performance: Is Innovation a Missing Link? *Journal of Marketing*, *62*(4), 30–45. doi:10.2307/1252285

Hansotia, B. (2002). Gearing up for CRM: Antecedents to Successful Implementation. *Journal of Database Marketing*, *10*(2), 121–132. doi:10.1057/palgrave.jdm.3240103

Hartline, M. D. III, Maxham, J. G. III, & McKee, D. O. (2000). Corridors of Influence in the Dissemination of Customer-Oriented Strategy to Customer Contact Service Employees. *Journal of Marketing*, *64*(2), 35–50. doi:10.1509/jmkg.64.2.35.18001

Hunter, G., & Perreault, J. W. D. Jr. (2006). Sales Technology Orientation, Information Effectiveness, and Sales Performance. *Journal of Personal Selling & Sales Management*, *26*(2), 95–113. doi:10.2753/PSS0885-3134260201

Hunter, G. K., & Perreault, W. D. Jr. (2007). Making Sales Technology Effective. *Journal of Marketing*, *71*(1), 16–34. doi:10.1509/jmkg.71.1.16

Jaworski, B., Kohli, A. K., & Sahay, A. (2000). Market-driven versus driving markets. *Academy of Marketing Science Journal*, *28*(1), 45–55. doi:10.1177/0092070300281005

Jaworski, B. J., & Kohli, A. K. (1993). Market Orientation: Antecedents and Consequences. *Journal of Marketing*, *57*(July), 53–70. doi:10.2307/1251854

Jelinek, R., Ahearne, M., Mathieu, J., & Schillewaert, N. (2006). A Longitudinal Examination of Individual, Organizational and Contextual Factors on Sales Technology and Adoption and Job Performance. *Journal of Marketing Theory and Practice*, *14*(Winter), 7–23. doi:10.2753/MTP1069-6679140101

Johnston, M. W., & Marshall, G. W. (2006). *Churchill/Ford/Walker's Sales Force Management*. Boston: McGraw-Hill/Irwin.

Jöreskog, K. G., & Wold, H. (1982). The ML and PLS Techniques for Modeling with Latent Variables: Historical and Comparative Aspects. In H. Wold & K. Jöreskog (Eds.), *Systems Under Indirect Observation: Causality, Structure, Prediction* (Vol. I). Amsterdam: North-Holland.

Jun, M. & Cai, S. (2010). Examining the Relationships between Internal Service Quality and its Dimensions, and Internal Customer Satisfaction. *Journal of Marketing Development and Competitiveness*, *8*(1), 95.

Kohli, R., & Grover, V. (2008). Business Value of IT: An Essay on Expanding Research Directions to Keep up with the Times. *Journal of the Association for Information Systems*, *9*(1), 23–39.

Krafft, M. (1999). An Empirical Investigation of the Antecedents of Sales Force Control Systems. *Journal of Marketing*, *63*(July), 120–134. doi:10.2307/1251779

Li, D., Chau, P. Y. K., & Lai, F. (2010). Market Orientation, Ownership Type, and E-Business Assimilation. *Evidence from Chinese Firms Decision Sciences*, *41*(1), 115–145. doi:10.1111/j.1540-5915.2009.00261.x

Luo, K., Hsu, M., & Liu, S. (2008). The Moderating Role of Institutional Networking in the Customer Orientation-Trust/Commitment Performance Causal Chain in China. *Journal of the Academy of Marketing Science*, *36*(2), 202–216. doi:10.1007/s11747-007-0047-z

Marshall, G. W., Moncrief, W. C., Rudd, J. M., & Lee, N. (2012). Revolution in Sales: The Impact of Social Media and Related Technology on the Selling Environment. *Journal of Personal Selling & Sales Management*, *32*(3), 349–363. doi:10.2753/PSS0885-3134320305

Mathieson, K., Peacock, E., & Chin, W. W. (2001). Extending the Technology Acceptance Model: The Influence of Perceived User Resources. *The Data Base for Advances in Information Systems*, *32*(3), 86. doi:10.1145/506724.506730

Megha Y. Patil, (2014), Social Media and Customer Relationship Management. *Journal of Business and Management,* (IOSR-JBM) PP 27-32

Narver, J. C., & Slater, S. F. (1990). The Effect of Market Orientation on Business Profitability. *Journal of Marketing*, *54*(4), 20–35. doi:10.2307/1251757

Nunnally, J. C., & Bernstein, I. H. (1994). *Psychometric Theory*. New York: McGraw-Hill.

Oliver, R. L., & Anderson, E. (1994). An Empirical Test of the Consequences of Behavior- and Outcome-Based Sales Control Systems. *Journal of Marketing*, *58*(October), 53–67. doi:10.2307/1251916

Panagopoulos, N. (2010). *Sales Technology: Making the Most of Your Investment*. New York: Business Expert. doi:10.4128/9781606491171

Payne, A., & Frow, P. (2005). A Strategic Framework for Customer Relationship Management. *Journal of Marketing*, *69*(October), 167–176. doi:10.1509/jmkg.2005.69.4.167

Piercy, N. F., Cravens, D. W., & Morgan, N. A. (1997). Sources of Effectiveness in the Business-To-Business Sales Organization. *Journal of Marketing Practice: Applied Marketing Science*, *3*(1), 43–69. doi:10.1108/EUM0000000004320

Plakoyiannaki, E., & Saren, M. (2006). Time and the Customer Relationship Management Process: Conceptual and Methodological Insights. *Journal of Business and Industrial Marketing*, *21*(4), 218–230. doi:10.1108/08858620610672588

Rapp, A., Agnihotri, R., & Forbes, L. P. (2008). The Sales Force Technology Performance Chain: The Role of Adaptive Selling and Effort. *Journal of Personal Selling & Sales Management*, *28*(4), 335–350. doi:10.2753/PSS0885-3134280401

Ringle, C. M., Wende, S., & Will, A. (2005). Smart PLS 2.0 (beta). Hamburg, Germany, Retrieved from http://www.smartpls.de

Rodriguez, M., & Honeycutt, E. (2011). CRM's Impact on B2B Sales Professionals' Collaboration and Sales Performance. *Journal of Business-To-Business Marketing*, *18*(4), 335–356. doi:10.1080/1051712X.2011.574252

Rodriguez, M., Peterson, R. M., & Krishnan, V. (2012). Social Media's Influence on Business-to-Business Sales Performance. *Journal of Personal Selling & Sales Management*, *32*(3), 365–378. doi:10.2753/PSS0885-3134320306

Ruekert, R. W. (1992). Developing a Market Orientation: An Organizational Strategy Perspective. *International Journal of Research in Marketing*, *9*(3), 225–245. doi:10.1016/0167-8116(92)90019-H

Saxe, R., & Weitz, B. (1982). The SOCO scale: A measure of the customer orientation of salespeople. *JMR, Journal of Marketing Research*, *19*(August), 343–351. doi:10.2307/3151568

Schiff, J. L. (2012). *CIO Magazine, 8 CRM Trends You Need to Watch*. Retrieved January 28, 2013, from: http://www.cio.com/article/print/699311

Steinman, C., Deshpande, R., & Farley, J. U. (2000). Beyond Market Orientation: When Customers and Suppliers Disagree. *Journal of the Academy of Marketing Science*, *28*(Winter), 109–119. doi:10.1177/0092070300281010

Stoddard, J. E., Clopton, S. W. & Avila, R. A. (2006). An Analysis of the Effects of Sales Force Automation on Salesperson Perceptions of Performance. *Journal of Selling and Major Account Management*, 38-56.

Straub, D. W. (1989). Validating Instruments in MIS Research. MIS Quarterly. *Journal of Marketing Development and Competitiveness*, *8*(1), 2014.

Strong, C. (2006). Is Managerial Behaviour a Key to Effective Customer Orientation? *Total Quality Management and Business Excellence*, *17*(1), 97–115. doi:10.1080/14783360500249687

Tanner, J. E., Ahearne, M., Leigh, T. W., Mason, C. H., & Moncrief, W. C. (2005). CRM in Sales-Intensive Organizations: A Review and Future Directions. *Journal of Personal Selling & Sales Management*, *25*(2), 169–180.

Van Egeren, M., & O'Connor, S. (1998). Drivers of Market Orientation and Performance in Service Firms. *Journal of Services Marketing*, *12*(1), 39–58. doi:10.1108/08876049810202357

Venkatesh, V., Morris, M. G., Davis, G. B., & Davis, F. D. (2003). User Acceptance of Information Technology: Toward a Unified View. *Management Information Systems Quarterly*, *27*(3), 425–478.

Woodcock, N., Green, A., & Starkey, M. (2011). Social CRM as a business strategy. *Journal of Database Marketing & Customer Strategy Management*, *18*(March), 50–64. doi:10.1057/dbm.2011.7

Yilmaz, C., Alpkan, L., & Ergun, E. (2005). Cultural determinants of customer- and learning-oriented value systems and their joint effects on firm performance. *Journal of Business Research*, *58*(10), 1340–1352. doi:10.1016/j.jbusres.2004.06.002

Chapter 4
Adoption of Facebook for Customer Relationship Management for SMEs:
Exploring the Underlying Motivations

Babak Abedin
University of Technology, Sydney, Australia

ABSTRACT

This study has explored organizations' motivations to adopt Facebook for customer relationship management purposes. Interviews with twenty small to medium sized Australian organizations in this study showed that market pressures, direct customer service, brand promotion, and testing and experiencing are among key motivations for organizations to begin having presence on the Facebook. Ease of use, ease of receiving customers' feedback, availability of rich tools, and the opportunity to reach a large number of potential and existing customers are found to be amongst the key benefits of such presence. Furthermore, the findings show that dealing with negative comments, finding qualified human resources, ensuring the reliability of Facebook policies, and scalability of Facebook pages are some of the key issues that organizations have experienced with using this website for managing relationship with their customers.

INTRODUCTION

With currently more than 60% of Internet users involved in social networking sites (SNSs) and three SNSs appearing in the world's top 10 visited websites in 2013, more organizations use SNSs' tools for advertisement and communication with users. Social networking sites such as Facebook enhance the level of collaboration between users by allowing them to connect with friends or colleagues, recommend links, and use software applications

Social relationship management has been defined as technology enabled and supported business strategy, which is supported by business processes and social characteristics to engage customers in a collaborative discussion for providing mutually beneficial values (Greenberg, 2010). Social CRM is

DOI: 10.4018/978-1-4666-8586-4.ch004

supported by organizational strategies and culture as well as technology platforms and processes, and facilitates engagement and establishes mutually beneficial relationships (Lehmkuhl & Jung, 2013). Increasing customers loyalty and building a long term relationship with them is an essential objective of CRM systems and social networking sites present a new communication channel and structure for organizations to create value through expanding and supporting long term relationships (Friedrichsen, 2013). Gu et al. (2011) suggest that Facebook enable organizations to increase customers' loyalty through impacting on customers' perceived value, satisfacion, and their knowledge about products and services.

Kaplan and Haenlein (2010) have argued that organizations have not been able to successfully adopt social media and social networking sites. A succeflul adoptation is not just creating a Faceboook presence, it is rather effectively use SNSs such as Facebook as CRM tools. One reason behind unsuccessful adoption of social media is a lack of understanding of the potential various configurations of SNSs. Organizations have mainly focused more on establishing, maintaining and updating their SNS presence than trying to drive people to it (AIMIA & SENSIS, 2012). While traditional relation systems were under the control of organizations to manage relationships with customers, with Facebook organizations are no longer in control of this relationship (Baird & Parasnis, 2011; Erfani et al., 2013). Instead, customers have now the power to drive the conversation, and therefore organizations need to use new strategies to recognize the importance of Facebook by addressing social aspect of relationship management on these websites (Trainor et al., 2014).

The current research attempts to investigate how organizations use Facebook, as the largest SNSs, for managing relationship with customers, and also to explore organizations' motivations for adoption of Facebook. In particular, this study is trying to answer what are the factors and motivations for organizations to adopt Facebook for managing relationship with customers?

RESEARCH PROBLEM AND BACKGROUND

Social networking sites are web-based services that allow individuals to (1) construct a public or semi-public profile within a bounded system, (2) articulate a list of other users with whom they share a connection, and (3) view and traverse their list of connections and those made by others within the system (Erfani et al., 2013). SNSs are slightly different in mechanism, but most of them support their members with various tools and features to enable them to build a sense of community in an informal and friendly way (Boyd & Ellison, 2011). Through an SNS, people interact with each other in a common information space and participate in a variety of interactive and social activities such as posting information, photo sharing, tagging, organizing events, and so on (Greenberg, 2010).

While the use of SNSs for customer relationship management has widely been increased, it is yet unclear how organizations use SNSs such as Facebook for establishing and managing relationship with customers. The current research is a preliminary study that attempts to investigate how organizations use Facebook for managing relationship with customers, and also to explore organizations' motivations for adoption of Facebook. In particular, this study is trying to answer the following main question: *What are the underlying motivations for organizations to adopt Facebook as a CRM tool?*

The paper proceeds as follows. In the next section, the capabilities of the social networking sites and Facebook in developing relationship with members are reviewed. The paper then presents results of in-depth interviews with Australian organizations regarding their experiences in using Facebook to communicate with their customers. Lastly, the findings of the study are discussed, and underlying motivations for adopting Facebook as a CRM tool and the spectrum of social CRM adoption.

SOCIAL NETWORKING SITES AND CUSTOMER RELATIONSHIP MANAGEMENT

SNSs have been defined as computer-mediated communication environments, serving as new channels for communication and collaboration by individuals who are eager to share and explore resources (Sun & Wu, 2012; Abedin, 2011; Kwon & Wen, 2010; Koh & Kim, 2004). Compared to traditional CRM systems, SNSs are slightly different in mechanism but most of them support their members with various tools and features that enable them to build a sense of community in an informal and friendly way (Pallis et al., 2014). People use SNSs such as Facebook to interact with each other in a common information space and participate in diverse interactive and social activities such as posting, photo sharing, tagging, and organizing events (Pallis et al., 2014). While younger individuals initially used Facebook, recently older people have also been actively involved in using these websites (Boyd & Ellison, 2011).

The value for organizations comes from how a platform is used than anything else. Culnan et al. (2010) have argued that organizations need to use platforms for additional values beyond just distribution of information for users. For example, Table 1 provides some understanding about how organizations can use virtual environment platforms such as Facebook to enhance relationship with customers and create a virtual environment through forming communities on these environments.

As currently the largest SNSs, the large number of users has made Facebook a great place for businesses to communicate and stay in touch with their existing and potential customers (Abedin & Jafarzadeh, 2013). Facebook facilitate group formation around shared purposes and interests and allow people to create massive interactions which have not been possible before. People's interest in a product or a company on Facebook is visible to their friends, which may consequently encourage their friends to follow the company's social network page or advertisement. Facebook allows businesses to filter and target members based on demographic information and therefore better reach potential customers for a specific product or service (Karjaluoto & Leinonen, 2009). Social network sites such as Facebook provide many ways for organizations to cultivate and develop relationships with members. According to Kent and Taylor (1998) and Taylor et al. (2001), organizations should develop relationships with members on online communities through three strategies:

- Firstly, organizations should use Facebook to describe their history and activities, to link their profile to their website, and to provide pictures and videos to allow members to establish a connection with the organization.

Table 1. Sources of value created by virtual environments (adopted from Culnan et al., 2010)

Activity Supported	Source of Value
Branding	Drive traffic, royalty and retention, viral marketing
Sales	Revenue
Service and support	Cost savings, revenue, satisfaction
Product development	Revenue

- Organizations should then establish the usefulness of their Facebook profiles by posting news items and visual content about the organization and its products, services and causes, and using the message board or discussion forum to communicate with members and answer their questions.
- Finally, it is important that organizations make their Facebook profile an interactive environment where they develop relationships with members and create a space where members feel they are part of a community. For example organizations should provide a calendar of offline and online events and allow members to get involved in different ways.

Through initiatives such as group buying, co-purchasing, and spreading word of mouth, Facebook has enabled organizations to establish and strengthen relationship with customers (Wu et al., 2013; Chu & Kim, 2011). In a recent study, Rishika et al. (2013) have found that customer participation in organizations' social networking sites increases the frequency of customer visits. Organizations should integrate knowledge from their customers' transactional relationship with their social networking site participation to improve customer relationship and to better understand customer needs and preferences. Thus, it appears that the power is now with individuals who share information, pictures, and videos related to products with or without organizations' permission (Rishika et al., 2013; Kietzmann et al., 2011). Organizations now need more than before to be aware of, and be prepared for, the challenges and opportunities that social networking sites like Facebook provide for communication and interaction with customers, and establishing strong bonds with them through information and resource exchange (Wellman, 1997).

Yet, while the power of Facebook is clear, more research is needed to explore organizations experience with it, and also to understand strategies that are needed to effectively engage with customers and to respond to opportunities and threats presented by this website (Kim et al. 2009).

RESEARCH DESIGN AND METHODOLOGY

Organizations have different levels of willingness to adopt innovations and normally there are fewer adopters at the early stages of diffusion of the innovation than the later stages. The literature suggest that characteristics of adopters and extent of the adoptions as well as characteristics of the technology and of the environment under which an organization is operating should be considered for assessing diffusion of a new technology or innovation (Gruber H, Pantelis, 2013; Gulati & Williams, 2011). Gulati & Williams (2011) have reviewed the factors that may impact decisions about technology adoptions and suggest that such decisions will depend on both the characteristics of the adopters as well as the characteristics of the innovation and the environment. Based on the results of Gulati & Williams (2011) three groups of characteristics have been considered for this paper for understanding the decision making about Facebook adoption: (i) organizational characteristics (intention and resources), (ii) innovation characteristics (benefits versus risks), and (iii) adoption characteristics (how the innovation being used). These three groups of characteristics were used to structure the interview questions.

The research method of the study is interview method that allows exploring new phenomena including opinions, perceptions, and reality in order to explore organizations' motivations for adoption of Facebook for the purpose of customer relationship management. The interview guide of the study contains a list of questions and prompts designed to guide the interview in a focused yet flexible and conversational manner. To enhance the quality of the research attempts were made to illuminate interviewees' subjective meanings, actions and social contexts, as understood by them, Therefore the two of the three distinct inquiry elements recommended by Patton (1999) have been introduced including 'techniques and methods for gathering and analysing qualitative data (see below) as well as credibility, competence, and perceived trustworthiness of the researcher. Confirmation from the interviewees was sought about disambiguation and clarification of the issues raised by them during the interviews. Two open-ended questions were developed for each of the above three groups of characteristics for understanding the decision making process in relation to the Facebook adoption. Twenty small to medium sized Australian organizations were interviewed for this study as the unit of analysis. Snowball sampling was used to recruit participants for the interviews. Table 2 shows their background information.

The participants in the interviews were social media or marketing managers, who were directly involved in, or responsible for, their organizations' Facebook campaign. Approval from each company was gained prior to conducting the interviews. Interviews were conducted at interviewees' workplaces and on average each interview took 1.5 hours with frequent elaboration and clarification on the responses. Interview notes were typed after each interview and where the notes were not clear, the audio recordings were used. NVivo software was used for open coding of the interview data. The objective of the coding was to capture themes expressed by the interviewees. Each audio transcript was documented into distinct statements and then each coded into multiple emerging themes. Coding started with no predefined code list, as this is primarily an exploratory study with the intention to discover new themes and codes (Niazi et al., 2006). Interviews were continued until the themes for each question were stabilized and the same themes recurred in subsequent interviews. This ensured that interviews would continue until repetitive results are achieved or no new factors/themes were discovered.

ADOPTION DECISION FACTORS

As discussed earlier, three groups of characteristics have been considered in this study for understanding organizations' decision making about Facebook adoption: (i) organizational characteristics, (ii) innovation characteristics, and (iii) adoption characteristics. Two interview questions have used for the each of these groups. These characteristics have been used to structure motivations and factors that may influence organizations' decision about adopting and using Facebook for CRM purposes.

The rest of this section outlines the findings of interviews, and then section 5 describes the distribution of adoption of Facebook by the participating organizations:

1.1. Organizational Characteristics

Organizational characteristics represent organizations' purpose and intention for using Facebook for customer relationship management, which can help to identify resources that are needed for achieving

Table 2. Interviewees' background information

Organization size			Organizational role		
20=<	>20; <=100	>100	SNS manager	Marketing manager	SNS analyst
10	8	2	8	8	4

these purposes. The first interview question was therefore looking for when and why organizations' presence started on Facebook.

The interviewees expressed a variety of reasons for their presence. Below is the aggregation of organizations' motivation for embarking on a presence on Facebook in the order of priority. No pre-arranged categories was provided to the interviewees, however at times, the interviewers had to intervene by requesting further clarification and rewording of the emerging themes for both better understanding of the interviewees' intentions as well as for the purpose of standard reporting of the results:

1. Market pressure: Since many people are already on Facebook and also several competitors have already had their presence on this website, organizations found it necessary to begin a presence on the Facebook. Eighteen participants explicitly pointed out that it is becoming a trend for organizations to have an active presence on Facebook and that customers increasingly tend to interact with the organizations through these sites. "So we found some of our competitors were on Facebook and they were doing a good job to connect with customers. We felt we had no choice but to do something!" said a social media manager of an educational institute. He continued by saying: "in fact my position did not exist at the time we were thinking about creating a page on Facebook, but as our campaign became bigger, this position was created to take care of social media related activities". Since majority of the participating organizations started late on their Facebook presence, longitudinal studies will provide more accurate rating for this factor.
2. Direct customer service: Organizations also realized that as the number of Facebook members and the time they spent on the website was rapidly increasing, it has become an attractive marketing channel (and in some cases a preferred channel) for providing a variety of services to customers, as well as maintaining effective communications with them through updated news and events. About 75% of the research participants explained that since their audiences are mainly people who actively use Facebook, their organization needed to integrate their current customer service systems with their Facebook business page to provide consistent and swift responses to the customers. For example, a marketing manager of an IT company in Sydney believed that "we have an active phone customer support and everyday we respond to many calls from customers. Yet, [a few years ago] we realized that customers increasingly use Facebook, so we decided to have an active presence on Facebook and integrate our phone customer support with our Facebook business page"
3. Brand promotion: Another reason for having a presence on the Facebook was the opportunity to promote brand, both nationally and internationally. Fifteen research participants agreed that Facebook helps with branding through viral marketing and friends' recommendations. For small organizations in particular this would be a cost effective opportunity to promote their brand, as a marketing manager of a small leisure center said "Facebook made it possible for small businesses like ours to promote our brand in a way that we previously were not able to afford". Yet, promotion of brands was not a primary benefit perceived by one skin-body care business in this study, as they use a private and secure Facebook page and only accept new members by invitation.
4. Testing and experiencing: Five out of twenty participants in the study were unsure how Facebook could help their business. Yet, they have decided to begin a presence on this website and to experience how it could benefit their business and facilitate communication with their customers. A good example of this was an IT manager of a sport facility, who encouraged the business to try Facebook, even though he was initially unsure about the value of the website: "Three years ago we just decided to give it a go! Our customers liked it, so we thought why not us!"

1.2. Innovation Characteristics

Innovation characteristics represent what an innovation is and what benefits and risks are associated with it. Thus, the participating organizations in this study were asked about pros and cons of using Facebook for customer relationship management. This resulted in exploring seven key challenging issues and eight benefits as summarized in Table 3 and outlined below:

As for the benefits, ease of use of Facebook was found as the key advantage and motivation for organizations to embark on having a presence on the Facebook. After that, participants believed that social networking sites in general and Facebook in particular are the future of communication with customers since many individuals prefer to communicate with organizations through these websites. As one of research participants stated:

"In early 2000s almost all businesses were expected to have a website. Today, if you sell to individuals, customers ask about your Facebook-page address. At least today it is much easier to run and use Facebook than setting up a new website ten years ago!"

Furthermore, since Facebook allows customers to directly interact with organizations, it would enable organizations to receive customers' feedback and questions without any intermediaries or barriers. Facebook also provides a variety of free rich tools, such as many applications, multimedia and text sharing tools, which enable organizations to use interactive and appealing content for customers. Another advantage is that Facebook enables organizations to reach a large number of new members through a variety of ways such as advertising and viral marketing. By getting them to join their business page, organizations can build a closer relationship with current and new customers by regularly updating them with products and events information. For example, for a small leisure business:

"Facebook is very useful to stay in touch with your customers by getting them to 'like' your page. As customers talk about us and our services, we can not only customize our services, but to attract new customers via our Facebook page and our promotion for new Facebook members".

Using the above benefits, organizations can further promote their brand amongst current and new customers. And lastly, Facebook enables organizations to use their business page to create a community in which people constructively share ideas. A sense of community amongst customers encourages them

Table 3. Pros and cons of using Facebook for customer relationship management

Frequency	Pros	Cons
High (as experienced by 75% or more of the participating organizations)	Ease of Use Ease of receiving feedback Rich tool Reach new customers Building relationship Promotion of brand	Negative comments Reliability of Facebook policies Facebook scalability Qualified human resources
Medium (as experienced by 25% to 75% of the participating organizations)	Sense of community Future of communication	Time and resource consuming Measuring ROI Maintain anonymity

to participate in online discussions and contribute in an organization's product and service development, which consequently may foster brand awareness and relationship building with customers.

Seven issues were also raised by the participating organizations in using Facebook for CRM purposes. Customers' negative comments were one of the main issues which almost all participating organizations had to deal with. Facebook allows members to post negative, and in some cases offensive, comments on business pages and it potentially may get viral before the organization has even an opportunity to respond to them. However, according to the experience of Twenty per cent of the interviewees, negative comments are opportunities for organizations to not only quickly become aware of an issue within their business, but to establish a closer relationship with customers by acknowledging the problem and demonstrating a real commitment to address the problem.

Next was the participants' concern about recruiting experts and finding qualified human resources. Twelve interviewees explicitly mentioned that networked campaigns need dedicated people with a strong passion about working in dynamic environments 24/7; and this has been one major concern expressed by all of the respondents. Furthermore, scalability of services on Facebook was another concern, since some of the interviewees found it difficult to scale up the level and the diversity of their activities and services on their Facebook page. For fifty percent of organizations in this study one reason for a lack of scalability of services was a low level of reliability on Facebook policies. As noted by one of the research participants, Facebook's ultimate goal is to make money and increase profitability, the website may make sudden changes to their services which consequently may significantly impact the way organizations use Facebook.

Maintaining anonymity of customers was another concern for those organizations with longer history of presence on the Facebook. They reported instances where customers would prefer not to publicize their posts on an organization's page. For example, customers may prefer to keep their identities confidential when they share personal or medical related questions or concerns. This will make it difficult for organizations with a public Facebook page to allow customers to choose whether or not they wish to make it available for their friends.

Next, almost half of the research participants believed that use of Facebook for communication with customers has been more time and resource consuming than they originally expected. In order for an organization to regularly update its business page, constantly responding to customers' posts, and integrating their business page with existing customer service systems, it needs a dedicated team with a significant level of financial and time investment. While many organizations are willing to invest in their Facebook campaign, the question for them is to what extent such investment may pay off. This in turn will lead to the last issue addressed by the respondents, which is, finding a way to measure return on investment (ROI) on Facebook presence and the associated activities. Participants believed that they would be more encouraged to invest additional time and resources on their Facebook advertisement campaigns if they knew how much this investment would pay off.

Despite a comprehensive list of benefits provided by the respondents it seems that the low level of spending on Facebook advertising can be explained by the challenges that it provides to the organizations, particularly the SMEs.

1.3. Adoption Characteristics

Adoption characteristics examine how organizations adopt an innovation. Two questions were considered for adoption characteristics. The first question looked into how organizations use Facebook to communicate with their customers, and the degree to which Facebook has been integrated into their current CRM practices. The second question examined whether organizations undertake formal or informal performance measurement for using Facebook for CRM purposes.

The results have shown that the most common way for organizations to communicate with their customers through Facebook is to create a Facebook page and to provide information about products and services, events, invitations, videos, and pictures. Some participating organizations emphasized that they regularly posted promotions and special offers as well as free give-away information in order to attract regular visitors and maintain an ongoing relationship with the latter. In addition, three participating organizations linked their Facebook business page to their company website and other related community weblogs. This has helped them to update their customers with weblog updates and also to expose their organization's Facebook page to other communities and attract new members. Furthermore, two organizations regularly run competitions and invite celebrities to their Facebook business page. Members then were able to interact with the celebrities through asking questions, posting comments, receiving updates, and getting involved in discussions. This initiative on average tripled their Facebook and website traffic and helped these organizations to strengthen their relationship with current customers and also to attract new customers.

Facebook Insights provides a set of tools and metrics that allows organizations to assess their performances. Metrics such as number of likes, number of times a post is shared by members, number of comments, and number and the trend of the page visits can be viewed with a click of a mouse. Only ten per cent of organizations were unaware of these tools and never used them. Ninety per cent used these tools to measure the performance of their Facebook activities. Number of likes, number of page visits, and number of comments was amongst the most popular measurements used by the participants.

CONCLUSION AND FUTURE STUDIES

The growing popularity of social networking sites has encouraged many organizations to embark on establishing a presence on social networking sites and, in particular, on Facebook. Despite the ease of creating a business page on Facebook and using its content generation tools, many organizations are still unaware or unsure about challenges and opportunities that they may face when using Facebook to communicate with their potential and current customers. Effective use of Facebook allows organizations to create an online community in which customers can develop a strong sense of community and belonging. This sense of community may encourage customers to get more involved in conversations and content development. One interviewee revealed that in their Facebook page members normally respond to each other's inquiries much faster than the organization. Some customers also actively contributed to the development of new products by commenting on the design and functional features of particular products. This kind of behaviours was mainly motivated by the organization's close relationship with customers through being honest with customers about their product characteristics, price and complaints.

The findings of this paper show that organizations have embarked on having a presence on the Facebook mostly to promote their brand, establish a closer relationship with their customers and to make sure they are not left behind their competitors. Results also point to seven main issues that organizations need to tackle. These are: negative comments, reliability of the Facebook policies, maintaining anonymity, time and resource consumption, Facebook scalability, measuring ROI, and qualified human resources. Future studies are needed to investigate ways and strategies that help organizations to deal with the above issues in order to improve efficiency and effectiveness of their social CRM. Furthermore, this study explores a number of key benefits that motivate organizations to use Facebook for managing relationship with s. These include ease of use, easy to receive feedback, benefits from having powerful online tools, future of communication, good way to reach new users, building relationships, promotion of brand, and sense of community. Exploring the above factors in turn will allow future studies to investigate the role and impact of these factors on organizations' performance of their social CRM systems. Research could also be undertaken to use a combination of the above factors to develop guidelines for strategic social CRM planning.

REFERENCES

Abedin, B. (2011). Web 2.0 and Online Learning and Teaching: A Preliminary Benchmarking Study, *Asian. Social Science*, *7*(11), 5–12.

Abedin, B., & Jafarzadeh, H. (2013). Attracting and retaining customers on Facebook business pages: A Content Analysis of an Online Discussion Forum. *International Journal of Technology Marketing*, *8*(3), 304–315. doi:10.1504/IJTMKT.2013.055340

AIMIA & SENSIS. (2012). *What Australian people and businesses are doing with social media*. Retrieved from https://www.sensis.com.au/about/our-reports/yellow-social-media-report-2014

Baird, C. H., & Parasnis, G. (2011). From social media to social relationship management. *Strategy and Leadership*, *39*(5), 30–37. doi:10.1108/10878571111161507

Boyd, D. M., & Ellison, N. B. (2011). Social Network Sites: Definition, History, and Scholarship. *IEEE Engineering Management Review*, *38*(3), 16–31. doi:10.1109/EMR.2010.5559139

Chu, S. C., & Kim, Y. (2011). Determinants of consumer engagement in electronic word of mouth (eWOM) in social networking sites. *International Journal of Advertising*, *30*(1), 47–75. doi:10.2501/IJA-30-1-047-075

Culnan, M. J., Mchugh, P. J., & Zubillaga, J. I. (2010). How Large U.S. Companies Can Use Twitter and Other Social Media to Gain Business Value. *MIS Quarterly Executive*, *9*(4), 243–260.

Erfani, S. S., Abedin, B., & Daneshgar, F. (2013), Investigating the impact of Facebook use on cancer survivors' psychological well-being. *Proceedings of the Nineteenth Americas Conference on Information Systems*, Chicago, Illinois, August 15-17, 1-7.

Friedrichsen, M. (2013). Social Media in Companies. Integrated Approach for a Social Media Strategy. In M. Friedrichsen & W. Muhl-Benninghaus (Eds.), *Handbook of Social Media Management Media Business and Innovation* (pp. 25–47). doi:10.1007/978-3-642-28897-5_3

Greenberg, P. (2010). The impact of CRM 2.0 on insight. *Journal of Business and Industrial Marketing*, *25*(6), 410–419. doi:10.1108/08858621011066008

Gruber, H., & Pantelis, K. (2013). Competition enhancing regulation and diffusion of innovation: The case of broadband networks. *Journal of Regulatory Economics*, *43*(2), 168–195. doi:10.1007/s11149-012-9205-4

Gu, R., Oh, L. B., & Wang, K. (2011). Determinants of Loyalty for Social Networking Sites. Exploring the Grand Challenges for Next Generation E-Business. *Lecture Notes in Business Information Processing*, *52*, 206–212.

Gulati, G. J., & Williams, C. B. (2011). Diffusion of innovations and online campaigns: Social media adoption in the 2010 U.S. congressional elections. Proceedings of *6th General Conference of the European Consortium for Political Research*, Reykjavik, Iceland. doi:10.2139/ssrn.1925585

Gulati, G. J., & Williams, C. B. (2013). Social Media and Campaign 2012: Developments and Trends for Facebook Adoption. *Social Science Computer Review*, *31*(5), 577–588. doi:10.1177/0894439313489258

Kaplan, A. M., & Haenlein, M. (2010). Users of the world, unite! The challenges and opportunities of Social Media. *Business Horizons*, *53*(1), 59–68. doi:10.1016/j.bushor.2009.09.003

Karjaluoto, H., & Leinonen, H. (2009). Advertisers' perceptions of search engine marketing. *International Journal of Internet Marketing and Advertising*, *5*(1), 95–112. doi:10.1504/IJIMA.2009.021952

Kent, M. L., & Taylor, M. (1998). Building dialogic relationships through theWorldWideWeb. *Public Relations Review*, *24*(3), 321–334. doi:10.1016/S0363-8111(99)80143-X

Kietzmann, J. H., Hermkens, K., Mccarthy, I. P., & Silvestre, B. S. (2011). Social media? Get serious! Understanding the functional building blocks of social media. *Business Horizons*, *54*(3), 241–251. doi:10.1016/j.bushor.2011.01.005

Kim, S. H., Yang, K. H., & Kim, J. K. (2009). Finding critical success factors for virtual community marketing. *Service Business*, *3*(2), 149–171. doi:10.1007/s11628-008-0059-x

Koh, J., & Kim, Y. G. (2004). Knowledge sharing in virtual communities: An e-business perspective. *Expert Systems with Applications*, *26*(2), 155–166. doi:10.1016/S0957-4174(03)00116-7

Kwon, O., & Wen, Y. (2010). An empirical study of the factors affecting social network service use. *Computers in Human Behavior*, *26*(2), 254–263. doi:10.1016/j.chb.2009.04.011

Lehmkuhl, T., & Jung, R., (2013). Towards Social CRM–Scoping the Concept and Guiding Research. *proceedings of BLED 2013*, 190-205.

Niazi, M., Wilson, D., & Zowghi, D. (2006). Critical Success Factors for Software Process Improvement Implementation: An Empirical Study. *Software Process Improvement and Practice*, *11*(2), 193–211. doi:10.1002/spip.261

Pallis, G., Zeinalpour-Yazti, D., & Dikaiakos, M. D. (2011). Online social networks: Status and trends. *Studies in Computational Intelligence*, *331*, 213–234.

Patton, M. Q. (1999). Enhancing the Quality and Credibility of Qualitative Research. *Health Services Research*, *34*(5), 1189–1208. PMID:10591279

Rishika, R., Ashish, K., Ramkumar, J., & Ram, B. (2013). The Effect of Customers' Social Media Participation on Visit Frequency and Profitability: An Empirical Investigation. *Information Systems Research*, *24*(1), 108–127. doi:10.1287/isre.1120.0460

Sun, T., & Wu, G. (2012). Traits, predictors, and consequences of Facebook self- presentation. *Social Science Computer Review*, *30*(4), 419–433. doi:10.1177/0894439311425978

Taylor, M., Kent, M. L., & White, W. J. (2001). How activist organizations are using the Internet to build relationships. *Public Relations Review*, *27*(3), 263–284. doi:10.1016/S0363-8111(01)00086-8

Trainor, K. J., Andzulis, J., Rapp, A., & Agnihotri, R. (2014). Social media technology usage and relationship performance: A capabilities-based examination of social CRM. *Journal of Business Research*, *67*(6), 1201–1208. doi:10.1016/j.jbusres.2013.05.002

Wellman, B. (1997). For A Social Network Analysis Of Computer Networks: A Sociological Perspective on Collaborative Work and Virtual Community. In *SIGCPR '96 Proceedings of the 1996 ACM SIGCPR/SIGMIS Conference on Computer Personnel Research*. ACM.

KEY TERMS AND DEFINITIONS

Customer Relationship Management (CRM): An information system for maintaining and managing relationship with customers.

Facebook: A popular SNS which is available for public for making connection with friends and sharing information and multimedia content.

Social CRM: Technology enabled business strategy to engage customers in a collaborative discussion for providing mutually beneficial values.

Social CRM Adoption: The use and utilization of CRM systems by organizations.

Social Networking Sites (SNSs): Web-based services that allow individuals to construct a public or semi-public profile, articulate a list of other users with whom they share a connection, and view and traverse their list of connections and those made by others within the system.

Chapter 5
Electronic Customer Relationship Management (E-CRM) Practices of Micro, Small, and Medium Scale Enterprises in Ghana

Rebecca Baah-Ofori
University of Professional Studies Accra, Ghana

George Amoako
Central University College Accra, Ghana

ABSTRACT

This book chapter is aimed at finding out how SMEs in Ghana employ electronic customer relationship management (E-CRM) to improve their business performance.Case studies were used and five companies were selected and their managers interviewed. The study found that there is a growing awareness among SME owners about social media platforms. It also found that SME owners use such platforms for marketing and e-CRM purposes. The most reported social platforms used for e-CRM were found to be Facebook, WhatsApp and Instagram. Regarding the effectiveness of these platforms for marketing and e-CRM, the SME owners interviewed intimated that they are fast, convenient, and cost effective marketing platforms. This study concludes that SMEs in Ghana are aware of and use mostly free internet platforms such as Facebook, WhatsApp and Instagram for e-CRM. Specifically, SMEs use such platforms to share information with clients and build and maintain relationships.

INTRODUCTION/BACKGROUND

An important aspect of running a business is the ability to attract and retain clients who will patronize the goods or services being offered.In other words, businesses cannot survive without clients or customers. When customers are pleased with the products or services being offered, there is the possibility for

DOI: 10.4018/978-1-4666-8586-4.ch005

them to return to an organisation for more of such goods or services. However, no matter how good a company's products are, that company will not be guaranteed continued patronage if it has dissatisfied clients due to poor service experience. In a world of fierce business competition, a company's inability to implement measures to satisfy and retain clients will be to that company's own detriment. Thus, good client relations is essential to the survival of a business. In other words, building relationships with clients through regular, accurate communications is key to successful CRM (Luck & Lancaster, 2003).

The need to maintain relationships with customers led to the development of the concept of Customer Relationship Management (CRM) which refers to the ability of a company to implement certain strategies that are meant to build and strengthen relationships with customers with the hope of raising long term profits for the company. In the words of Farooqi and Dhusia (2011), customer relationship management is a "comprehensive sales and marketing approach to building long term customer relationship management and improving business performance." So that, the aim of managing relationships with customers is not entirely for immediate gains but rather, for long term increasing of a firm's profit margin. Bradshaw and Brash (2001) describe customer relationship management as "a management approach which enables organisations to identify, attract and increase retention of profitable customers by managing and retaining relations with them."Again, the concept of customer relationship management suggests that companies place extreme value on satisfying the needs of current clients in order to retain them and placing mechanisms in place in order to attract potential clients. Some of these mechanisms have been the provision of telephone and fax numbers with which clients can contact a company, the creation of client service desks and the designation of particular person(s) to attend to the needs of clients (Bradshaw & Brash, 2001).

The advent of the internet has meant the creation of an additional tool with which businesses can engage their clients and a general improvement in the customer relationship management practices of organisations. The use of the internet in Customer Relationship Management has resulted in the term: Electronic Customer Relationship Management (E-CRM) which according to Blery and Michalakopoulos (2006) refers to the use of the internet to implement CRM strategies. E-CRM is the use of ICT tools by organisations as a means of building potentially long lasting relationships with customers (Kotorov, 2002). Businesses have taken advantage of the internet to showcase their products in a creative, attractive and at a relatively cheaper cost (Hamid, Cheng & Akhir, 2011). This is largely due to the fact that most clients find the internet as a convenient way of shopping and scouting for good deals comfortably, without having to be physically present in shops. Indeed, some businesses are entirely internet based without a physical business address. What this means is that aside managing relationships with clients who may be physically present to patronise a firm's products, there is the need for businesses to adapt and manage relationships with those who do business with them online (Hamid, 2008).

This process of establishing and maintaining relationships with clients using internet platforms is what has been termed as electronic customer relationship management. Its key characteristics include the use of the internet to communicate brand information, gather customer information and answer customers' enquiries (Luck & Lancaster, 2003; Rich, 2000). Generally, e-CRM is geared toward the provision of "a consistently superior customer experience" (Reichheld & Schefter, 2000).E-CRM can be done using channels such as websites, emails, voice portals and SMS (Skououdis, 2003).The rationale for the adoption of e-CRM varies from company to company. However, some reasons for the adoption of e-CRM include a desire to offer better services, improve communication and build stronger relationships (Blery & Michaakopoulos, 2006). Even though some scholars argue that the benefits of e-CRMcan best be described as weak and complex (Fienberg, Kandam, Hokama & Kim,2002), there is a strong evidence to the contrary. For instance, e-CRM has been found to improve efficiency (through the provision of better customer service), increase profitability, improve sales, create customer satisfaction and customer loyalty and reduce cost(Blery & Michaakopoulos, 2006;Lyoyd,Scullin, Allora, & Fjermestad, 2001; Feinberg et al., 2002).

Despite the identified benefits of e-CRM, it has been argued that research into the phenomenon has focused on the experiences of large firms or organisations with just a handful of studies focusing on Small and Medium Scale Enterprises (SMEs) (Wahlberg, Strandberg, Sundberg & Sandberg, 2009). Yet, SMEs contribute enormously to the development of the current global economy. Defined differently by different scholars, SMEs have been categorised according to size, assets and method of production (Abor & Quartey, 2010). The consensus however seems to be that SMEs typically have a small market share, are independent an often managed by one person who takes all the major decisions. Nevertheless, the European Commission for instance, defines SMEs based on the number of employees with the breakdown as follows:

- 0-9 employees: micro enterprise
- 10-99 employees: small enterprise
- 100 – 499 employees: medium enterprise

SMEs have also been defined as firms with 1-50 workers (Mead & Liedholm, 1998). Such firms are a major source of employment and income in both advanced and developing countries; contributing to GDP, creating jobs and employing people. In Ghana, SMEs are said to provide 85% of manufacturing employment, account for 92% of local businesses and contribute about 70% of Ghana's GDP (Steel& Webster, 1991; Aryeetey, 2000). Just as is the case in most other developing countries, SMEs in Ghana help in human resource development and ultimately contribute to the alleviation of poverty (Cook & Nixson, 2000; Agyapong, 2010).

This immense contribution of SMEs to national development is acknowledged by the Government of Ghana and this is evidenced in the institution of a National Board for Small Scale Industries (NBSSI) in 1985. The board was set up under the Ministry of Trade, Industry and Presidential Special Initiatives with the mandate to promote the growth and development of Micro and Small Enterprises (MSEs) in the country. Currently, the NBSSI has set up Business Advisory Centres (BACs) in the District capitals across Ghana to provide business development services for micro and small enterprises in the country. The NBSSI has a breakdown of SMEs into minor categories as follows:

- Micro enterprises: employing less than 5 people
- Small enterprises: employing 5-29 people
- Medium enterprises: employing 30-99 people
- Large enterprises: employing 100 and over people.

No matter the classification, Mensah (2004) argues that Ghanaian MSMEs "are dominated by one person, with the owner or manager taking all major decisions, the entrepreneur having possible limited formal education, limited access to and use of new technology, limited access to and use of market information and credit from the formal baking sector, weak managerial skills, lack of technical knowhow, etc." Though this description exudes gloom, it is unfortunately a true reflection of the state of most Ghanaian small scale businesses. For instance, Abor and Quartey (2010), list a number of factors that confront SMEs as including: low access to technology, limited access to international markets, legal barriers limiting their development/growth, weak institutional capacity, little or no managerial skills and training and limited or no access to finance. In spite of these challenges, SMEs continue to be established for a number of reasons including but not limited to the need to increase revenue, the need to work on one's own or be independent, a desire to improve one's standard of living and for personal growth and satisfaction (Benzing & Chu, 2009).

In a developing country like Ghana, characterised by low economic growth, low education quality, an inability of even the educated youth to obtain jobs (partly due to the absence of a link between the education received and the requirements of the job market), youth unemployment and graduate unemployment, most young people resort to self-employment/entrepreneurship to earn a decent living (Yarquah & Baafi-Frimong, 2011). Thus, there is a current trend of unemployed and in some cases, employed youth creating micro and small businesses either as part time or full time ventures. Yet, such ventures continuously have to grapple with challenges such as funding and a lack of managerial skills which eventually affects how they run their small scale set ups (Educational Research Network for West and Central Africa, 2008).Typically, they engage in activities such as dress making, hairdressing and barbering, catering, electrical repairs, carpentry and other crafts, plumbing and masonry as well as merchandising and retail (Agyapong, 2010).In recent times, there is also a rise in the number of small set ups offering a range of services in event management, photography, footwear, among others.

O'Toole (2003) writing on e-relationships in small businesses argues that small firms are traditionally characterised by independent ownership and management. This, in addition to other challenges related to resource acquisition and inadequate technical expertise, ultimately limits their ability to effectively market their goods and services. Yet, the marketing and customer relationship efforts of SMEs has been found to be grounded in building personal relationships with clients (Harrigan, Ramsey & Ibbotson, 2011). The availability of the internet means that SMEs have to be innovative and move from personal contacts to the adoption of internet tools as a way of boosting business. Harrigan, Ramsey and Ibbotson (2008) suggests that SMEs adopt e-CRM because it gives them a broader platform to compete with larger firms, helps to improve their business, improve communication with clients who are increasing purchasing online and obtain customer data faster. Over time, the documented benefits or advantages SMEs have gleaned from adopting e-CRM include its potential to facilitate new market penetration, capturing of client data, building stronger online relationships, improved efficiency, reduced marketing costs, increased profitability and improved customer loyalty (Harrigan et al., 2008; Harrigan et al., 2011).

In spite of these benefits, studies demonstrate that in terms of e-CRM a general adoption of the internet for doing business, most SMEs ether under-utilize the internet's potential to boost their business or are confronted with countless challenges associated with internet use. O'Toole (2003) for instance argues that small businesses use the internet for basic marketing. This view is shared by Verhees and Meulenberg (2004) who suggest that SMEs use e-CRM for general communication efforts, ignoring other equally important features such as gathering customer intelligence. Some challenges to IT and e-CRM adoption by small businesses include a reduction in face to face communication, a general absence of clients' trust in terms of sharing information online, resource constraints (financial and skills) and differences in consumers preferred mode of being contacted for business(Hamid, Cheng & Akhir, 2011; Harrigan et al., 2008).

Ghana has a huge youth unemployment challenge and there are demands on young people to develop entrepreneurial skills. To this end, there are several young people who have set up businesses which serve either as the sole income source or as complements to some other source of income. Given all the challenges some of these firms are facing (as enumerated above), this study seeks to examine how those SMEs are using methods such as e-CRM to market, attract and maintain customers for increased profit and business sustainability. E-CRM has several aspects but the study sought to specifically seek answers to the following research questions:

RQ1. What e-CRM practices are Ghanaian SMEs engaged in?
RQ2. What benefits are Ghanaian SMEs obtaining from practicing e-CRM?
RQ3. What are the challenges Ghanaian SMEs face in implementing e-CRM?

LITERATURE REVIEW

Research on e-CRM covers several aspects of the phenomenon and has particularly examined the issue from the point of view of large firms. Typically, issues examined include what e-CRM is, the rationale for implementing e-CRM, the technology needed to implement it, the benefits/ advantages companies have gleaned from having implemented the technology and the challenges that accompany implementing e-CRM practices. This section reviews such literature in addition to those that discuss e-CRM in SMEs.

E-CRM: What Is It?

Electronic Customer Relationship Management emanates from the original phenomenon Customer Relationship Management which has been described as the ability to develop close relationships with clients through paying attention to individual clients' needs, solving those needs with the hope to keep them satisfied and loyal to a company (Peppard, 2000; Thompson & Moscardini, 2002). At the most basic level, perhaps the definition that makes most meaning is that e-CRMisCRM with the use of technology. In other words, the main difference between the more established Customer Relationship Management (CRM) and the relatively new Electronic Customer Relationship Management (E-CRM) is that in CRM, relationships are built through traditional channels such as telephones, fax machines and retail outlets while for e-CRM, relationships are built through internet technologies in addition to traditional channels like the aforementioned ones (Farooqi & Dhusia, 2011). Electronic customer relationship management(e-CRM) has also been defined as the use of internet technologies to facilitate the development and management of customer relationships (Chaston & Mangles, 2003). Thus, relationship building using internet technologies is essential to e-CRM.

Yet, it has been argued that simply having access to the internet and engaging customers at some level will not guarantee successful e-CRM. Bradshaw and Brash (2001) have intimated that for e-CRM to be successful, it should be incorporated into a larger strategy to build and maintain relationships with clients and not be an ad hoc activity. To this end, businesses are expected to anticipate the ability of e-CRM to create added value and actively pursue the practice for value creation in order to be successful (Day & Hubbard, 2003). Tools for e-CRM include e-mails, websites, online promotional campaigns, browser based applications which allow the exchange of information between businesses and their clients. With such web based platforms, customers and businesses are able to exchange information such as product information, purchase conditions, product preview, FAQs, complaints, orders, customer service, company history or profile using web features such as chat, electronic bulletin board and links (Feinberg et al.,

2002; Farooqi & Dhusia, 2011). Aside the information exchange, the use of advanced internet tools can also help businesses to capture and integrate customer data in order to serve them better (Ross, 2005).

Benefits of E-CRM in General

Research into the benefits of e-CRM has suggested that it helps businesses to be more efficient, improves sales, creates value and saves costs (Adebanjo, 2003). The argument here is that e-CRM has the potential to save time in terms of the duration used to contact clients and respond to their needs. The time saved also often results in reducing administrative and operational costs. For instance, clients' inquiries can be responded to almost immediately such that businesses would be able to spend time on other productive things. In terms of adding to profitability, e-CRM has been found to increase a business' profits because it leads to more satisfied and content clients who in turn do more business with a company thus, leading to increased profits (Sims, 2000; Scullin, Alora, Lloyd & Fejermestad, 2002).

Barriers to E-CRM

Most barriers to e-CRM border on challenges with e-CRM implementation and the negative effects e-CRM has on attempts to actually build relationships. E-CRM has been found to reduce face-to-face relationships and in some cases led to a total destruction of already established customer relationships (Gillen, Durkin & McGowan, 2000). Another barrier to e-CRM stems from customers' reluctance to share certain personal details online due to a lack of trust for online security systems (Tagliavini, Ravarini & Antonelli, 2001; Day & Hubbard, 2003). Another barrier to e-CRM is lack of resources. That is, e-CRM implementation has financial and technical skills requirements which may not always be available to companies especially for SMEs.

What Is an SME?

Small and Medium Scale Enterprises (SME) have received attention in the literature for several reasons. Undoubtedly, this attention to SMEs is as a result of several factors including the fact that SMEs are a major source of employment in many economies worldwide and yet are often faced with countless challenges that threaten their survival. These challenges include limited access to finance (Cook & Nixson, 2000), poor management skills, little or no expertise in handling equipment and technology, regulatory issues and limited access to international markets (Aryeetey, 2001; Abor & Quartey, 2010). In developing countries, SMEs are widely appreciated for their contribution to the growth of the local economies through job creation and income generation (Schmitz, 1995). In Ghana, they're present about 92% of Ghanaian businesses and contribute about 70% to Ghana's GDP and over 80%to employment (Ntsika, 1999; Abor & Quartey, 2010).

Nevertheless, opinions on what constitutes an SME vary significantly. While some have based definitions on the size of firms, others have based it on the number of people employed. Jordan, Lowe and Taylor (1998) define an SME as having less than 100 employees while Michaelas, Chittenden and Poutziouris (1999) define SMEs as employing less than 200 employees. The United Nations Industrial Development Organisation (UNIDO) has set different criteria for determining SMEs in developed and developing countries. For developing countries, SMEs have been sub-categorised into various groups as follows:

- Large - firms with 100 or more employees
- Medium - firms with 20-99 employees
- Small - firms with 5-19 employees
- Micro - firms with less than 5 employees (See Elaian, 1996).

Similar classification systems exist in Ghana with the Ghana Statistical Service classifying SMEs based on the number of employees. For instance, it classifies firms with less than ten employees as small-scale enterprises while firms with more than ten employees are classified as either medium or large (Kayanula & Quartey, 2000). The National Board for Small Scale Industries (NBSSSI), a body mandated to promote and develop SMEs in Ghana also has its classification as follows:

- **Micro enterprises:** employing less than 5 people
- **Small enterprises:** employing 5-29 people
- **Medium enterprises:** employing 30-99 people
- **Large enterprises:** employing 100 and over people.

Thus, the definition varies and perhaps it can concluded that in terms of number of people employed, SMEs in Ghana consist of firms which employ less than 100 people (www.nbssi.org).

Key features of SMEs include the fact that emphasis is placed on building and maintaining personal relationships with stakeholders including customers, suppliers and employees. Thus, whether it is through traditional channels of communication or word of mouth communication, SMEs survive on building relationships and creating awareness of the key business through those relationships (Harrigan et al., 2008). However, SMEs are also noted as having negative challenges such as limited financial resources, limited technical expertise, limited access to large markets, poor management and inadequate marketing skills (Carson & Gilmore, 2000; Doole, Grimes & Demack, 2006; Walsh & Lipinski, 2009). While the noted challenges may be described as internal, there also some external threats to the survival of SMEs. These include broader legal and economic controls which SMEs have little or no control over; often leaving them unable to effectively compete and influence suppliers and distributors in particular (Kocak & Abimbola, 2009).

In developing countries such as Ghana, the characteristics of SMEs have been enumerated as typically consisting of single/ one person businesses (usually owned by women) which are engaged in activities such as retailing, trading or manufacturing (Fisher & Reuber, 2000). In addition, SMEs in the country according to Abor and Quartey (2010) can be categorised into urban and rural enterprises. The urban ones are either organised or unorganised with the organised businesses comprising SMEs with registered offices and paid employees while the unorganised ones have no rented places and formal employees but rather operate from open spaces, temporary structures or from the confines of their homes with few or no salaried employees. Rural enterprises comprise largely of family enterprises, women engaged in food processing and other activities such as soap making, textile and leather works, timber and mining, furniture, etc. (Kayanula & Quartey, 2000; Osei, Baah-Nuakoh, Tutu & Sowa, 1993).

THE INTERNET, E-CRM AND SMEs

Traditionally, marketing in SMEs have focused largely on face-to-face communications and networking primarily through word of mouth communications which sometimes proved ineffective (Ritchie & Brindley, 2005) due to time and resource constraints (Stokes, 2000). The internet has been found to particularly reduce most of the challenges faced by SMES as it grants them, among others, the ability to compete on a wider scale with other SMEs and even with larger organisations (McCole& Ramsey, 2005). Yet, not all SMEs are tapping into this immense resource to promote their businesses (Ramsey, Ibbotson, Bell & Gray, 2004) which can be used to complement traditional relationship building and marketing activities (Ab Hamid & Kassim, 2004).

Barriers to E-CRM in SMEs

All the barriers to e-CRM implementation on a larger scale also apply to the SME situation. Examples of such barriers include those related to resources, a reduction in face-to-face relationships and personal businesses which is a key feature of SMEs as well as a lack of trust for online security and sharing information online (O'Toole, 2003). It has been argued that e-CRM destroys the social part of relationship management in SMEs (Gillen, Durkin & McGowan, 2000). An additional problem for the SME situation is the often reluctance of SME owners to adopt internet technologies for general purposes and for e-CRM in particular. Because most SMEs are run by a single person, those persons often have to single-handedly take tough decisions on behalf of a firm. Often, such people tend to lack the technical expertise or knowledge pertaining to understanding the rationale for the adoption of internet technologies and the benefits that stand to be derived from adopting internet technologies. In most cases, this prevents an adoption of internet technologies completely (McGowan & Durkin, 2002). Also, the nature of the SME or the nature of products and services on offer also determine whether e-CRM will be adopted. It has been argued that SMEs offering services are more likely to use internet technologies; hence, are more likely to engage in e-CRM than SMEs who are not offering services (Riquelme, 2002). Nevertheless, it is important for SMEs to seriously inculcate the use of internet technologies into their business not only as a communication tool but also as a means of improving marketing and building closer ties with customer. That way, the growth of e-CRM is assured (Lawson-Body & O'Keefe, 2006).

Benefits of E-CRM in SMEs

Despite the challenges enumerated above, SMEs obtain several benefits from e-CRM adoption. While several studies have documented the benefits to be derived from e-CRM in large organisations, there is still much room for more work on how SMEs can take advantage of e-CRM. McGowan, Durkin, Allen, Dougan and Nixson (2001) states that perhaps the most noteworthy benefit e-CRM offers most SMEs is the ability to transcend geographical borders. In the light of the fact that most SMEs operate within an often limited sphere, the internet and e-CRM grants them the opportunity to show the world what their core business entails and also relate and serve clients on an international scale. This view of the internet and e-CRM helping to build open international markets and build relationships with clients beyond the physical/ geographic location of SMEs has been widely supported (Hamill & Gregory, 1997; Berthon, Page & Pitt, 1996; Danie & McInerney, 2005; Matthews & Healy, 2008). Harrigan et al., (2008) also state that by using e-CRM, SMEs can be able to capture valuable client data which can be used to better serve the needs of clients with the ultimate aim of ensuring their survival. According to Harrigan et al. (2008), this is possible since the data captured can also facilitate the development of personal relationships with clients online. Capturing the information or details of clients has also been found as an efficient way of being able to better tailor products and services to clients. Once a business knows the demographics and psychographics of clients, it becomes easier to develop products and services which will best suit their needs (Day & Hubbard, 2003; Chaston & Mangles, 2003). E-CRM's enables businesses to personalise goods and services for clients. This can also lead to improved communications and improved customer service. Harrigan et al., (2008); Bradshaw & Brash, 2001; McGowan and Durkin, 2002). Better served customers have been found to be more satisfied and loyal to the companies they do business with (Reichheld & Sasser, 1990; Ragins & Greco, 2003).

Note must be made however that some studies argue that e-CRM does not ultimately lead to customer loyalty. The basis for such argument is that it is difficult for companies to achieve loyalty; hence, e-CRM can best be described as leading to minimal customer loyalty (Ab Hamid & Kassim, 2004). Regardless of this, the recognition of e-CRM as leading to customer loyalty, whether maximum or minimum is what, perhaps, should be most important. Some studies have also concluded that in SMEs, e-CRM should be seen as an innovative marketing strategy which helps SMEs to manage customer information in order to improve communication with them (Harrigan et al.,2011;O'Cass&Weerawardena, 2009; O'Dwyer, Gilmore & Carson, 2009; Street & Cameron, 2007).

The review of literature clearly shows that a lot of studies have sought to examine the nature, benefits and challenges for practicing e-CRM in large organisations and SME contexts. However, there appears to be a dearth of literature concerning how e-CRM is practiced particularly in developing country contexts. This paper sought to fill this gap by undertaking a study into e-CRM activities of SMEs in Ghana (a West African developing country). The next section discusses the methodology adopted for the study.

METHODOLOGY

The study was based on qualitative research approach. Symon and Cassel (1998) suggest that qualitative research dwells more on interpretation, subjectivity and examining phenomena in their context. Yin (2003) is of the view that qualitative research, among other things, allows researchers to represent the views and perspectives of research participants in real world contexts. Though there are several variations in qualitative research, the case study approach was used for this qualitative study. Yin (2003) maintains that case studies give researchers the opportunity to wholly investigate the characteristics of real life events or situations. A further distinction is made between intrinsic, instrumental and collective case studies. Intrinsic case studies are used by researchers to examine a single case due to its unique features which are believed to be worth studying. Instrumental case studies enable researchers to use a case to examine an issue other than the case itself. In other words, the case is used to build knowledge/ understanding of other issues of interest. Collective case studies on the other hand are described as studying several cases in order to be able to compare individual cases and also develop a better understanding of any given phenomenon (Yin, 2011). Given the limited literature available on e-CRM in Ghanaian SMEs, this study wanted to examine how SMEs practices e-CRM; and examine particularly the benefits gained and the challenges faced in implementing e-CRM. To do this, the study adopted the case study approach which helps researchers to focus on particular phenomena or events in their natural setting (Stake, 1995; Mankelow & Merrilees, 2001). The study can be said to have used collective case study because multiple cases were used in an attempt to understand how e-CRM is practiced in SMEs in Ghana. Even though the decision on the number of cases to include for case study research is often left to the discretion of the researcher, (Romano, 1989), Gillham (2000) recommends the use of multiple sources of evidence as part of case study research. Scholars including Wong and Merrilees (2005) have suggested an inclusion of more cases till the data reaches a point of saturation.

In this study, five cases were studied. The authors wish to state that the five cases selected were not because the cases were the best examples available. Rather, the selection of these cases was based on convenience and a readiness of SME owners to partake in the study. An initial email was sent out to ten of the most visible SMEs on Facebook, Ghana's most popular social media platform. The e-mails introduced the researchers and the purpose of the study. However, only two out of the ten SMEs which were initially contacted expressed a desire to partake in the study. The researchers then used the snowballing method, to reach other SME owners through these initial two. This led to an additional four SME owners agreeing to take part in the study. However, only five SMEs owners were finally able to respond with an indication to participate in the study. All five cases were included in the study because of differences in the core nature of the businesses they were engaged in: fashion (bags, shoes, and jewellery), event management and photography services. Thus, researchers acknowledge that the five cases used, though most convenient, may not be the best examples of cases of e-CRM in SMEs. Nevertheless, the authors believe the findings from the five cases can provide adequate insights into e-CRM in SMEs in Ghana. Going by the NBSSI's classification of SMEs n Ghana, it can be concluded that all the cases examined were micro enterprises, employing an average of three people at the time of the study. As far as the researchers are concerned, the study of the micro enterprises represent the best cases of small industries trying to tap into the internet as a resource to improve business practices.

The business owners who agreed to partake in the study were asked to provide a convenient time at researchers could meet and conduct interviews. At the stipulated times, interviews were held separately for each of the SME owners who had consented to be part of the study. After assuring each participant of confidentiality, interviews were held with them to solicit their views on a range of e-CRM issues. The interviews, which lasted an average of twenty minutes, were recorded, using a tape recorder, with the consent of participants. Tape recordings of the interviews were later transcribed for further analysis. For the analysis, all the transcripts were first compiled by the researchers who jointly looked for any emergent themes or patterns based on the research questions. Thus, the transcribed data was organised according to issues such as how e-CRM is practiced by SMEs, the benefits they have accrued from implementing e-CRM as well as the challenges encountered in e-CRM implementation. The observations made after the presentation of findings are presented after an outline of the profiles of the five cases used for the study.

Brief Profiles of SMEs Studied

- **Bayabs:** This is an accessories enterprise which makes bags, shoes, slippers and ribbons, etc. out of African print/textile. The company's owner says she set up the enterprise initially as a part time enterprise but has now become a full time venture. It has been in existence for a year and currently employs five people. The company currently serves both local and international clientele.
- **Éclat Events:** It is an event planning and management company which focuses on planning and coordinating functions such as weddings, parties, and other social events for clients. Éclat also has tables, chairs, canopies, etc. for rental. At the time of the interview, it had been in existence for a year.

- **Miquifire Events:** the company has been in existence for three years and has branding, event organisation and coordination, wedding management and stage production as the core business. It currently has 2 employees and 12 assistants.
- **ANKBO Designs:** the company has been in existence for the past 15 years. It is a fashion and accessories business owned by two sisters. The enterprise deals primarily in fabric and bead purses, bags and jewellery (earrings, necklaces, bangles, bracelets and brooches). The business employs one permanent employee and occasionally recruits 3-5 part time employees when extra hands are needed in order to meet deadlines.
- **Genesiz Multimedia:** is an events management and professional photography business that has been in existence for 5 years. The core functions of the business include events coordination, media planning, and photography. It currently employs 6 people.

FINDINGS AND DISCUSSIONS

This section presents the findings of the study and discusses them in relation to the literature reviewed. Each sub-heading represents a theme which addresses any one of the research questions posed.

Traditional Marketing and CRM Tools Employed by SMEs

Traditionally, the most important traditional marketing tool for the SMEs studied was creating awareness through word of mouth either personally or through their friends and acquaintances. That made it easier for individuals to share information quicker. The event planners also mentioned participating in trade shows or fairs as means of exhibiting their services and rental facilities. Traditionally, the SMEs studied highlighted that they stayed in contact generally with clients through telephone calls or text messages aimed at finding out about their welfare and satisfaction with goods and services delivered. Table 1 below summarises respondents' responses on the traditional marketing and CRM tools used in their businesses.

The Internet as a Marketing and E-CRM Tool

The study found that the SME owners studied were aware of and used social media platforms for marketing and e-CRM purposes. The most reported platforms were Facebook, WhatsApp and Instagram as indicated in Table 2. Only one SME had a website. The suggestion seems to be that most SMEs in Ghana perhaps do not have the capital to invest in more personalised internet platforms such as websites which require huge initial costs and monthly payments for maintenance. Thus, they resort to more public, cheaper, easily accessible platforms such as Facebook, Instagram and WhatsApp which only require internet connection to work. In terms of using these platforms for e-CRM purposes, even though one SME reported that it has been a bit slow using the internet to build relationships, majority of them indicated that the chat features available on the platforms enabled them to interact with clients; leading to the establishment of relationships both for the short and long term. This finding was at variance or inconsistent with that of Frempong (2007) who suggests that SMEs in Ghana have a low regard for incorporating the internet in their business activities. Undoubtedly, this study shows that SMEs in Ghana are fully aware of the business gains that they can make with the help of the internet.

Table 1. Traditional marketing and customer relationship management tools of SMEs and the type of communication exchanged between SMEs and their clients

Marketing Tools	CRM Tools	Type of Communication
Awareness creation through word of mouth communication	Telephone calls	Client welfare
Personal selling by business owners, friends, acquaintances and family members	Text Messages	Extent of satisfaction with goods and services provided
Exhibitions		

Source: case study interviews

Table 2. E-CRM Platforms and the type of communication between SMEs and their clients

e-CRM Platform	Type of Communication on all the e-CRM platforms
Facebook	Pictures/samples of products Information about upcoming events/deals/products Responding to client enquiries/orders How to make payment for purchases Contact details Terms of agreement of service and delivery
WhatsApp	
Instagram	
Website	

Source: case study interviews

For most of these SMEs, these platforms served as the first point of contact between them and their clients. They reported using the platforms to upload pictures of their wares while customers used them to make further enquiries. The more they interacted with particular clients through the chat features and emails, the easier it was to build more solid friendships and relationships. Harrigan et al. (2008) make a distinction between SMEs using the internet to communicate and using it to build relationships. However, this study suggests that such a distinction is unnecessary because building relationships with customers thrives on communication. Thus, the more businesses communicate with clients, the easier it is for them to form and manage relationships with them.

Determinants of Successful E-CRM in SMEs

The SME owners interviewed were however quick to add that relevant communications and transparency helps to sustain relationships over time with clients. In their opinion, transparency was most likely achieved by sticking to agreed time schedules for delivering goods ordered or apologising to customers for any delay in delivery. According to them, transparency was also achieved by providing quality goods and excellent services based on earlier agreed on specifications and updating clients on progress made with their orders. Thus, to a large extent, even though they used various tools to contact their clients, it was evident that the content of the interaction had to be relevant to clients in order to build customer trust and sustain relationships. This finding was not different from that of Bradshaw and Brash (2001) who suggest that even though it is good to manage customer relationships generally, what is most important is to ensure that the information shared on platforms is consistent and meets the needs of customers. In their view, customers prefer a reliable, efficient service and it is up to businesses to do so efficiently and in a memorable manner. Figure 1 sums up the authors' construct of the determinants of successful e-CRM in SMEs in Ghana.

Figure 1. Determinants of successful e-CRM in SMEs
Authors' construct

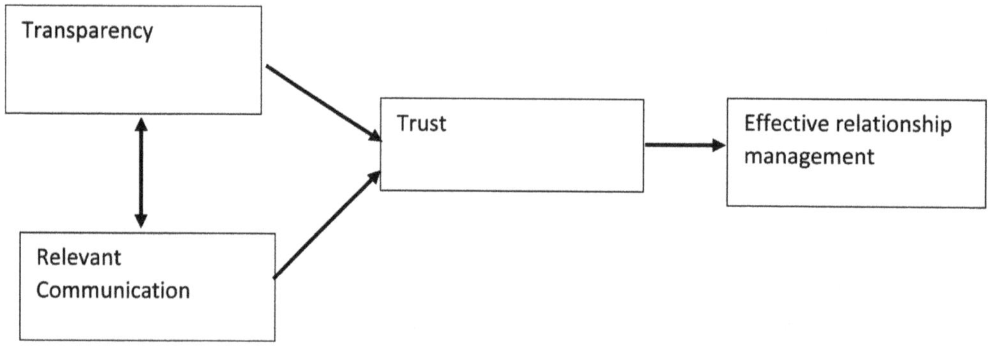

Benefits of E-CRM

Regarding the effectiveness of these platforms for marketing and e-CRM, the SME owners interviewed intimated that they are fast, convenient, and cost effective marketing tools because they give them the opportunity to upload pictures, videos and textual information which clients are able to access. In addition, respondents stated that the internet (Facebook in particular) allows them to do real time marketing, monitor and record statistics on the number of people who might have seen their products and services online. Facebook in particular was reported to be a very time efficient means of marketing. These words of one respondent perhaps captures how SME owners feel about the internet and marketing:

"It saves us space and the laborious task of walking from door to door to market products. Without facebook, we would have had to pay huge sums of money to television stations in order to market our products. However, facebook gives us the opportunity to advertise our product at a very low price (all you sometimes need is money to buy internet credit and you are in business) and we are able to reach a larger audience both within and outside Ghana. Also, the pages are open so everyone gets to see the pictures we post and we get contacted by interested people. With social media, people are visually stirred and so usual updates on what you've been up to and tips that may be of interest to them. This helps with marketing." (Source: Bayabs)

With relationship marketing, respondents reported that the internet helped to reach larger audiences in an easier and less expensive way. They also suggested that the internet enables them to interact and share messages with clients and receive instantaneous feedback from them in the comfort of their shops and homes. In the words of another:

"People from other countries like the United States, England and Nigeria are able to see our products and buy from us. I have had calls and messages from people in these countries asking to buy my products. A man saw a flyer of a programme designed by our company on facebook and followed up all the way from Tema to Legon campus to get our contact and eventually offered a business deal." (Source: Miquifire Events).

It appears the most important benefit the studied SMEs perceive to be obtaining from e-CRM was that it helped them build relationships with customers on the international scene. Thus, confirming assertions by Harrigan et al. (2008) that e-CRM in SMEs facilitate entry into new markets and internationalisation. To a large extent, the finding also seems to suggest that perhaps, SMEs are under-exploiting other potential benefits of e-CRM such as capturing client data and improved efficiency (O'Toole, 2003).

Type of Information Exchanged

Luck and Lancaster (2003) intimate that the idea of managing client relationships thrives on regular information exchange. The study asked SME owners to indicate the kinds of information exchanged on their internet platforms which would typically be found by visitors to their internet platforms. It was found that they provided information about pictures and videos of items, how to make purchases (especially from outside Ghana), contact details, location and directions and in some instances, tips on how to use purchased items. On the other hand, customers usually sought information about prices quotes, details of products or services, location, delivery/response time, payment mode or procedure, and terms of agreement. Concerning how long it takes to respond to enquiries, respondents indicated that depending on the nature of information being sought, the time of day the enquiry is received, they responded to enquiries almost instant responses or within 48 hours. Most of them shared the view that quick responses showed that clients could rely on businesses; thus fostering stronger relationships.

Challenges of E-CRM in SMEs

Though the respondents demonstrated that the internet had helped SMEs to initiate some form of e-CRM and were able to enumerate the benefits they are deriving from marketing and e-CRM, they admitted that there were some challenges which inhibited their e-CRM efforts. As shown in Table 3 below, the challenges SMEs encountered in terms of practicing e-CRM included a fear of being unable to provide online customers with accurate and relevant information as they claimed to have difficulties determining whether the information posted would be beneficial to clients. One major challenge they reported encountering was the tendency of other people to steal pictures of designs posted online and either pass it off as their own or steal the designs and replicate them for profit. One person put it this way:

"We have had an issue where someone stole a picture of a necklace from our page, photo shopped our brand's name out of it and sent the picture to friends telling them that they could order those necklaces from them." (Source: Ankbo Designs)

Table 3. Challenges to practising e-CRM in SMEs

Challenges
Poor internet services
Lack of online security/trust
Determining what information would be relevant to clients
Stealing of original ideas/designs/samples by competitors
Difficulties in responding to client inquiries promptly

Source: Case Study interviews

The issue of lack of trust in internet relationships was a challenge as respondents indicated that customers exhibited traits of being sceptical about their ability to deliver and fearing that they would be duped of their money. Thus a lack of trust in the online platforms appeared to be a major issue for the SMEs studied. On the one hand, businesses feared their competitors would access their ideas and designs online while on the other hand, customers exhibited some amount of mistrust for the businesses they were dealing with. This is not surprising since security concerns online has been cited as one challenge to ICT usage among SMEs in Ghana (Frempong, 2007). They also indicted information overload as another challenge e-CRM presented. This was explained as a situation where they were unable to respond to the large quantities of information transmitted online every second. For them, the large amount of information received often leaves them confused as to which one to answer first. Perhaps this situation arises because SMEs are noted for lacking the requisite expertise and/or skills to effectively handle such situations (Chiware & Dick, 2008). Lastly, poor internet service was a common identified challenge in e-CRM implementation among SMEs. This finding wasn't surprising since it was consistent with those of Frempong (2007) and Frempong and Essegbey (2006). To solve these challenges, respondents called for a stricter enforcement of copyright laws and the provision of better internet service.

CONCLUSION AND RECOMMENDATION

This study set out to examine e-CRM practices in SMEs in Ghana. Specifically, it sought to determine the kind of e-CRM practices Ghanaian SMEs are engaged in, the benefits Ghanaian SMEs are obtaining from practicing e-CRM and investigated whether the SMEs faced any challenge (s) in implementing e-CRM. Using the case study approach, the owners of 5 SMEs were interrogated on the e-CRM activities of their businesses. Though findings may not be generalizable to the entire SME population in Ghana, they provide insights into what the situation could be among SMEs in the country. Based on the findings of the study, this study concludes that SMEs in the country are aware of and use mostly free internet platforms such as Facebook, WhatsApp and Instagram to share information with clients using the chat and messaging features; a situation that eventually leads to the formation and sustenance of relationships. Also, the e-CRM information shared usually centred round exchanges on product types, modes of payment, how to obtain products, etc. The study also concludes based on the findings that e-CRM in SMEs thrives on two main things: transparency in dealing with clients and the sharing of relevant communication with clients. This is because SME owners interviewed intimated that transparency and relevant communication creates trust between SMEs and their clients and trust also leads to the building and maintenance of relationships.

The study also concludes that the most outstanding benefit of e-CRM by SMEs in Ghana was that it helped them establish relationships with clients on a global scale. Nevertheless, other identified benefits were that e-CRM led to efficient service delivery, better customer service, improved marketing, access to a larger market and a greater brand awareness. In terms of challenges encountered in the implementation of e-CRM, the study notes that the absence of security of doing business online and the existence of poor internet services were the main factors inhibiting the smooth execution of e-CRM among SMEs in Ghana.

Recommendations

This study has demonstrated that SMEs in Ghana stand to gain immensely from e-CRM. Thus, there is a need for greater awareness creation among SME owners to the effect that they need not invest huge capital into the establishment of e-CRM platforms but can use public ones which are available at no real cost for both marketing and relationship building. In terms of improving trust in online security, it is recommended that the relevant bodies put in more effort to instil public confidence in doing business online. Also, the NBSSI and other public agencies could educate SMEs about copyright laws and how they could patent their ideas and designs to protect them from being stolen. Then again, given the immense contribution of the internet to businesses in this era, it is important for service providers to be held accountable for the provision of stable internet connection to encourage internet use particularly among small businesses. Lastly, it is recommended that further research be carried out with a larger sample size to further interrogate the issues explored in this study.

Main Focus of Chapter

This book chapter focuses on how SMEs are taking advantage of media platforms such as Facebook, WhatsApp and Instagram to develop effective customer relationship with their clients in Ghana. The chapter also highlights on some benefits and challenges of implementing E-CRM in Ghana.

REFERENCES

Ab Hamid, N. R., & Kassim, N. (2004). Internet technology as a tool in customer relationship management. *Journal of American Academy of Business*, *4*(1/2), 103–108.

Abor, J., & Quartey, P. (2010). Issues in SME development in Ghana and South Africa. *International Research Journal of Finance and Economics*, *39*, 218–228.

Adebanjo, D. (2003). Classifying and selecting e-CRM applications: An analysis-based proposal. *Management Decision*, *41*(6), 570–577. doi:10.1108/00251740310491517

Agyapong, D. (2010). Micro, Small and Medium Enterprises' activities, income level and poverty reduction in Ghana – A synthesis of related literature. *International Journal of Business and Management*, *5*(12), 196–205. doi:10.5539/ijbm.v5n12p196

Aryeetey, E. (2001). Priority Research Issues Relating to Regulation and Competition in Ghana. Centre on Regulation and Competition Working Paper Series. *Management Decision*, *41*(6), 570–577.

Benzing, C., & Chu, H. M. (2009). A comparison of the motivations of small business owners in Africa. *Journal of Small Business and Enterprise Development*, *16*(1), 60–77. doi:10.1108/14626000910932881

Berthon, P., Page, M., & Pitt, L. (1996). Analysing and reducing customer defections. *Long Range Planning*, *29*(6), 821–834. doi:10.1016/S0024-6301(97)82819-1

Blery, E. K., & Michalakopoulos, M. G. (2006). An e-CRM application in the telecommunications sector: A case study from Greece. *EUROMED Journal of Business*, *1*(2), 5–14. doi:10.1108/14502190610750135

Bradshaw, D., & Brash, C. (2001). Managing customer relationships in the e-business world: How to personalize computer relationships for increased profitability. *International Journal of Retail & Distribution Management*, *29*(12), 520–530. doi:10.1108/09590550110696969

Carson, D., & Gilmore, A. (2000). SME Marketing Management Competencies. *International Business Review*, *9*(3), 363–382. doi:10.1016/S0969-5931(00)00006-8

Chaston, I., & Mangles, T. (2003). Relationship marketing in online business-to-business markets: A pilot investigation of small UK manufacturing firms. *European Journal of Marketing*, *37*(5/6), 753–773. doi:10.1108/03090560310465134

Chiware, E. R. T., & Dick, A. L. (2008). The use of ICTs in Namibia's SME sector to access business information services. *The Electronic Library*, *26*(2), 145–157. doi:10.1108/02640470810864055

Cook, P., & Nixson, F. (2000). *Finance and small and medium-sized enterprise development*. Institute for Development Policy and Management, University of Manchester.

Coviello, N. E., Brodie, R. J., & Munro, H. J. (2000). An investigation of marketing practice by firm size. *Journal of Business Venturing*, *15*(5-6), 523–545. doi:10.1016/S0883-9026(98)00035-4

Dangayach, G. S., & Deshmukh, S. G. (2005). Advanced manufacturing technology implementation: Evidence from Indian small and medium enterprises (SMEs). *Journal of Manufacturing Technology Management*, *16*(5), 483–496. doi:10.1108/17410380510600473

Daniel, T. A., & McInerney, M. L. (2005). E-commerce and the 'reluctant' small business owner: How technology is changing the business model for small and medium-sized enterprises (SMEs). *The International Journal of Applied Management and Technology*, *3*, 183–206.

Day, S. G., & Hubbard, J. K. (2003). Customer relationships go digital. *Business Strategy Review*, *14*(1), 17–26. doi:10.1111/1467-8616.00240

Doole, I., Grimes, T., & Demack, S. (2006). An exploration of the management practices and processes most closely associated with high levels of export capability in SMEs. *Marketing Intelligence & Planning*, *24*(6), 632–647. doi:10.1108/02634500610701690

Educational Research Network for West and Central Africa. (2008). Graduate unemployment in Ghana: possible case of poor response of university programmes to the demands of the job market. Project report. Ghana.

Elaian, K. (1996). Employment implications of small scale industries in developing countries: Evidence from Jordan. *Science. Technology and Development*, *14*(1), 80–101.

Farooqi, R., & Dhusia, D. K. (2011). A comparative study of CRM and e-CRM technologies. *Indian Journal of Computer Science and Engineering*, *2*(4), 624–627.

Feinberg, R. A., & Kadam, R. (2002). E-CRM web service attributes as determinants of customer satisfaction with retail websites. *International Journal of Service Industry Management*, *13*(5), 432–451. doi:10.1108/09564230210447922

Feinberg, R. A., Kadam, R., Hokama, L., & Kim, I. (2002). The state of electronic customer relationship management in retailing. *International Journal of Retail & Distribution Management*, *30*(10), 470–481. doi:10.1108/09590550210445344

Fischer, E., & Reuber, R. (2000). *Industrial clusters and SME promotion in developing countries. (3)*. Commonwealth Secretariat. doi:10.14217/9781848597266-en

Frempong, G. (2007). Trends in ICT usage by small and medium scale enterprises in Ghana. *ATDF Journal*, *4*(1), 3–10.

Frempong, G. K., & Essegbey, G. O. (2006). Ghana Case Study. InC. Stork and S. Esselaar (Eds.). Towards an African e-Index: SME e-Access and Usage in 14 African Countries. Witwatersrand, South Africa: Link Centre.

Gillen, J., Durkin, M., & McGowan, P. (2000). *Exploring the role of branding in the developmentof trust online*. Paper presented at the Irish Academy of Management Conference, Dublin.

Gillham, B. (2000). *Case study research methods*. London: Continuum.

Hamid, N. R. A. (2008). Consumers' behaviour towards internet technology and internet marketing tools. *International Journal of Communication*, *2*(3), 195–204.

Hamid, R. A., Cheng, A. Y., Akhir, R. M. (2011). Dimensions of E-CRM: an empirical study on hotels' web sites. *Journal of Southeast Asian Research. 2-15.*

Hamill, J., & Gregory, K. (1997). Internet marketing in the internationalisation of UK SMEs. *Journal of Marketing Management*, *13*(1-3), 9–28. doi:10.1080/0267257X.1997.9964456

Harrigan, P., Ramsey, E., & Ibbotson, P. (2008). E-CRM in SMEs: An exploratory study in Northern Ireland. *Marketing Intelligence & Planning*, *26*(4), 385–404. doi:10.1108/02634500810879296

Harrigan, P., Ramsey, E., & Ibbotson, P. (2011). Critical factorsunderpinning the e-CRM activities of SMEs. *Journal of Marketing Management*, *27*(5/6), 503–529. doi:10.1080/0267257X.2010.495284

Jordan, J., Lowe, J., & Taylor, P. (1998). Strategy and financial policy in U.K. small firms. *Journal of Business Finance & Accounting*, *25*(1/2), 1–27. doi:10.1111/1468-5957.00176

Kayanula, D., & Quartey, P. (2000). The Policy Environment for Promoting Small and Medium-Sized Enterprises in Ghana and Malawi. Finance and Development Research Programme. Working Paper Series, Paper No 15. IDPM, University of Manchester.

Kelley, L. L., Gilbert, D., & Mannicom, R. (2003). How e-CRM can enhance customer Loyalty. *Marketing Intelligence & Planning*, *21*(4), 239–248. doi:10.1108/02634500310480121

Kımıloğlu, H., & Zaralı, H.HandeKimilog˘lu. (2009). What signifies success in e-CRM? *Marketing Intelligence & Planning*, *27*(2), 246–267. doi:10.1108/02634500910945011

Kocak, A., & Abimbola, T. (2009). The effects of entrepreneurial marketing on born global performance. *International Marketing Review*, *26*(4/5), 439–452. doi:10.1108/02651330910971977

Kohlbacher, F. (2006). The use of qualitative content analysis in case study research. *Forum Qualitative Sozialforschung/Forum: Qualitative. Social Research*, *7*(1), 21. http://nbn-resolving.de/urn:nbn:de:0114-fqs0601211

Kotorov, R. (2002). Ubiquitous organization: Organizational design for e-CRM. *Business Process Management Journal*, *8*(3), 218–232. doi:10.1108/14637150210428934

Lawson-Body, A., & O'Keefe, T. (2006). Interorganisational relationships in the context of SMEs B2B E-commerce. *Journal of Electronic Commerce in Organizations*, *4*(4), 1–28. doi:10.4018/jeco.2006100101

Lawson-Body, A., & O'Keefe, T. P. (2006). Interorganizational Relationships in the Context of SMEs' B2B E-Commerce. [JECO]. *Journal of Electronic Commerce in Organizations*, *4*(4), 1–28. doi:10.4018/jeco.2006100101

Lee-Kelley, L., Gilbert, D., & Mannicom, R. (2003). How e-CRM can enhance customer loyalty. *Marketing Intelligence & Planning*, *21*(4/5), 239–249. doi:10.1108/02634500310480121

Luck, D., & Lancanster, G. (2003). E-CRM: Customer relationship management in the hotel industry. *Managerial Auditing Journal*, *18*(3), 213–231. doi:10.1108/02686900310469961

Mankelow, G., & Merrilees, B. (2001). Towards a model of entrepreneurial marketing for rural women: A case study approach. *Journal of Developmental Entrepreneurship*, *6*(3), 221–235.

Matthews, S., & Healy, M. (2008). From garage to global: The Internet and international market growth – An SME perspective. *International Journal of Internet Marketing and Advertising*, *4*(2/3), 179–196. doi:10.1504/IJIMA.2008.017021

McCole, P., & Ramsey, E. (2005). E-business in professional SMEs: The case of New Zealand. *Journal of Small Business and Enterprise Development*, *12*(4), 528–544. doi:10.1108/14626000510628207

McGowan, P., & Durkin, M. G. (2002). Toward an understanding of internet adoption at the marketing/entrepreneurship interface. *Journal of Marketing Management*, *18*(3/4), 361–377. doi:10.1362/0267257022872451

McGowan, P., Durkin, M. G., Allen, L., Dougan, C., & Nixon, S. (2001). Developingcompetencies in the entrepreneurial small firm for use of the internet in the management of customer relationships. *Journal of European Industrial Training*, *25*(2/4), 126–136. doi:10.1108/EUM0000000005443

Mead, D. C., & Liedholm, C. (1998). The dynamics of micro and small enterprises in Medium-Sized Enterprises in Developing Countries. *World Development*, *26*(1), 61–74. doi:10.1016/S0305-750X(97)10010-9

Mensah, S. (2004). A review of SME financing schemes in Ghana. UNIDO Regional Workshop of Financing SMEs, 15-16 March, Accra, Ghana.

Michaelas, N., Chittenden, F., & Poutziouris, P. (1999). Financial policy and capital structurechoice in U.K. SMEs: Empirical evidence from company panel data. *Small Business Economics*, *12*(2), 113–130. doi:10.1023/A:1008010724051

Ntsika.(1999). State of Small Business in South Africa. *SARB Quarterly Bulletins; and StatsSA Releases*, South Africa.

O'Cass, A., & Weerawardena, J. (2009). Examining the role of international entrepreneurship,innovation and international market performance in SME internationalisation. *European Journal of Marketing, 43*(11/12), 1325–1348. doi:10.1108/03090560910989911

O'Dwyer, M., Gilmore, A., & Carson, D. (2009). Innovative marketing in SMEs. *European Journal of Marketing, 43*(1/2), 46–61. doi:10.1108/03090560910923238

O'Toole, T. (2003). E-relationships-emergence and the small firm. *Marketing Intelligence & Planning, 12*(2), 115–122. doi:10.1108/02634500310465434

Osei, B., Baah-Nuakoh, A., Tutu, K. A., & Sowa, N. K. (1993). Impact of structural adjustment on small-scale enterprises in Ghana. In A. H. J. Helmsing & T. H. Kolstee (Eds.), *Structural Adjustment, Financial Policy and Assistance Programmes in Africa*. London: IT Publications. doi:10.3362/9781780445908.004

Peppard, J. (2000). Customer relationship management (CRM) in financial services. *European Management Journal, 18*(3), 312–327. doi:10.1016/S0263-2373(00)00013-X

Ragins, J. E., & Greco, J. A. (2003). Customer relationship management and e-business: More than a software solution. *Review of Business, 24*(1), 25–30.

Ramsey, E., Ibbotson, P., Bell, J., & Gray, B. (2004). A projectives perspective of international 'e' services. *Qualitative Market Research: An International Journal., 7*(1), 34–47. doi:10.1108/13522750410512868

Reichheld, F. F., & Sasser, J. W. E. (1990). Zero defections: Quality comes to services. *Harvard Business Review, 68*(5), 105–111. PMID:10107082

Reichheld, F. F., & Schefter, P. (2000). E-loyalty: Your secret weapon on the web. *Harvard Business Review, 68*(5), 105–113. PMID:10107082

Rich, M. K. (2000). The direction of marketing relationships. *Journal of Business and Industrial Marketing, 15*(2/3), 170–191. doi:10.1108/08858620010316877

Riquelme, H. (2002). Commercial internet adoption in China: Comparing the experience of small,medium and large business internet research. *Electronic Networking Applications and Policy, 12*(3), 276–286. doi:10.1108/10662240210430946

Ritchie, B., & Brindley, C. (2005). ICT adoption by SMEs: Implications for relationship and management. *New Technology, Work and Employment, 20*(3), 205–217. doi:10.1111/j.1468-005X.2005.00154.x

Romano, C. (1989). Research strategies for small business: A case study. *International Small Business, 7*(4), 5–43.

Romano, N. C., & Fjermestad, J. (2002). Electronic customer relationship management: An assessment of research. *International Journal of Electronic Commerce, 6*(2), 61–113.

Ross, D. (2005). E-CRM from a supply chain management perspective. *Information Systems Management, 22*(1), 37–44. doi:10.1201/1078/44912.22.1.20051201/85737.5

Schmitz, H. (1995). Collective efficiency: Growth path for small-scale industry. *The Journal of Development Studies, 34*(4), 529–566. doi:10.1080/00220389508422377

Scullin, S., Allora, J., Lloyd, G. O., & Fjermestad, J. (2002, April). Electronic customer relationship management: benefits, considerations, pitfalls and trends. In *Proceedings of the IS One World Conference, Las Vegas, Nevada*. 3-5.

Simpson, M., Padmore, J., Taylor, N., & Frecknall-Hughes, J. (2006). Marketing in small and medium-sized enterprises. *International Journal of Entrepreneurial Behaviour and Research*, *12*(6), 361–387. doi:10.1108/13552550610710153

Sims, D. (2000). A new ROI for new economy CRM and just why doesn't high-tech get it? http://www.crmguru.com

Skouloudis, M. (2003, October). E-CRM vs CRM.*Magazine Ne.O*, 32-33.

Stake, R. (1995). *The Art of Case Study Research*. Newbury Park, CA: Sage.

Stake, R. E. (2000). Case studiesCase studies. In N. K. Denzin&Y. S. Lincoln (Eds.).Handbook of qualitative research, 435-453. Thousand Oaks: Sage.

Steel, W. F., & Webster, L. M. (1991). *Small Enterprises in Ghana: Responses to Adjustment Industry. Series Paper, No. 33*. Washington, DC: The World Bank Industry and Energy Department.

Stokes, D. (2000). Entrepreneurial marketing: A conceptualisation from qualitative research. *Qualitative Market Research: An International Journal*, *3*(1), 47–54. doi:10.1108/13522750010310497

Street, C. T., & Cameron, A. F. (2007). External relationships and the small business: A review ofsmall business alliance and network research. *Journal of Small Business Management*, *45*(2), 239–266.

Symon, G. E., & Cassell, C. E. (1998). *Qualitative methods and analysis in organizational research: A practical guide*. London: Sage Publications Ltd.

Tagliavini, M., Ravarini, A., & Antonelli, A. (2001). An evaluation model for electronic commerce activities within SMEs. *Information Technology Management*, *2*(2), 211–230. doi:10.1023/A:1011417703063

Thompson, E., & Moscardini, N. (2002). Gartner's CRM Vision: A Roadmap for customer- centric transformation.Garthner Symposium ITXPO, San Diego, California.

Verhees, F. J. H. M., & Meulenberg, M. T. G. (2004). Market Orientation, Innovativeness, Product Innovation, and Performance in Small Firms. *Journal of Small Business Management*, *42*(2), 134–154. doi:10.1111/j.1540-627X.2004.00102.x

Wahlberg, O., Strandberg, C., Sundberg, H., & Sandberg, K. (2009). Trends, topics and under researched areas in CRM research- a literature review. *International Journal of Public Information Systems*, *3*, 191–208.

Walsh, M. F., & Lipinski, J. (2009). The role of the marketing function in small and medium sized enterprises. *Journal ofSmall Business and Enterprise Development*, *16*(4), 569–585. doi:10.1108/14626000911000929

Wong, H. Y., & Merrilees, B. (2005). A brand orientation typology for SMEs: A case research approach. *Journal of Product and Brand Management*, *14*(3), 155–162. doi:10.1108/10610420510601021

Yarquah, J. A., & Baafi-Frimpong, S. (2011). Social cost of educated youth unemployment in Ghana and its implications for education. *Centrepoint Humanities Edition.*, *14*(1), 122–143.

Yin, R. K. (2003). Case study research: designs and methods (3rd ed.). Thousand Oaks, CA: Sage.

Yin, R. K. (2011). *Applications of case study research.* California: Sage.

Zontanous, G., & Anderson, A. R. (2004). Relationships, marketing and small business: An exploration oflinks in theory and practice. *Qualitative Market Research: An International Journal*, *7*(3), 228–236. doi:10.1108/13522750410540236

ADDITIONAL READING

Harrigan, P., Ramsey, E., & Ibbotson, P. (2008). E-CRM in SMEs: An exploratory study in Northern Ireland. *Marketing Intelligence & Planning*, *26*(4), 385–404. doi:10.1108/02634500810879296

Harrigan, P., Ramsey, E., & Ibbotson, P. (2011). Critical factorsunderpinning the e-CRM activities of SMEs. *Journal of Marketing Management*, *27*(5/6), 503–529. doi:10.1080/0267257X.2010.495284

Kımıloğlu, H., & Zaralı, H.HandeKimilog˘lu. (2009). What signifies success in e-CRM? *Marketing Intelligence & Planning*, *27*(2), 246–267. doi:10.1108/02634500910945011

Steel, W. F., & Webster, L. M. (1991). *Small Enterprises in Ghana: Responses to Adjustment Industry. Series Paper, No. 33.* Washington, DC: The World Bank Industry and Energy Department.

Swift, R. S. (2001). *Accelerating Customer Relationships using CRM and Relationship Technologies.* Englewood Cliffs, N.J: Prentice Hall.

Wilson, H., Daniel, E., & McDonald, M. (2002). Factors for Success in Customer Relationship Management CRM) Systems. *Journal of Marketing Management*, *18*(1-2), 193–219. doi:10.1362/0267257022775918

Winer, R. S. (2001). A framework for customer relationship management. *California Management Review*, *43*(4), 89–105. doi:10.2307/41166102

Xu, M., & Walton, J. (2005). Gaining customer knowledge through analytical CRM. *Industrial Management & Data Systems*, *105*(7), 955–971. doi:10.1108/02635570510616139

Yin, R. K. (2011). *Qualitative Research from Start to Finish.* New York: The Guilford Press.

KEY TERMS AND DEFINITIONS

CRM: Customer relationship management is a comprehensive sales and marketing approach to building long term customer relationship management and improving business performance.

E-CRM: Electronic Customer Relationship Management emanates from the original phenomenon Customer Relationship Management which has been described as the ability to develop close relationships with clients through paying attention to individual clients' needs, solving those needs with the hope to keep them satisfied and loyal to a company's business.

Facebook: Facebook is a popular free social networking website that allows registered users to create profiles, upload photos and video, send messages and keep in touch with friends, family and colleague.

Ghana: Officially called the Republic of Ghana, is a sovereign multinational state and unitary presidential constitutional democracy, located along the Gulf of Guinea and Atlantic Ocean, in the subregion of West Africa. Ghana is the 82nd largest country in the world and 33rd largest country on continental Africa by land mass, and Ghana has a land mass of 238,535 km, with 2,093 kilometres of international land borders. The country is bordered by the Ivory Coast in the west, Burkina Faso in the north, Togo in the east and the Gulf of Guinea and Atlantic Ocean in the south. The word *Ghana* means "Warrior King".

Instagram: Is an online mobile photo-sharing, video-sharing and social networking service that enables its users to take pictures and videos, apply digital filters to them, and share them on a variety of social networking services, such as Facebook, Twitter, Tumblr and Flickr.

Internet: The Internet is a global system of interconnected computer networks that use the standard Internet protocol suite (TCP/IP) to link several billion devices worldwide. It is a *network of networks* that consists of millions of private, public, academic, business, and government networks, of local to global scope, that are linked by a broad array of electronic, wireless, and optical networking technologies. The Internet carries an extensive range of information resources and services, such as the inter-linked hypertext documents and applications of the World Wide Web (WWW), the infrastructure to support email, and peer-to-peer networks for file sharing and telephony.

SMEs- Small and Medium Enterprises: SMEs in Ghana consist of firms which employ less than 100 people.

WhatsApp: WhatsApp is a proprietary, cross-platform instant messaging subscription service for smartphones and selected feature phones that uses the internet for communication. In addition to text messaging, users can send each other images, video and audio media messages as well as their location using integrated mapping features.

Chapter 6
The Use of Social Media in the Higher Education Institutions in Turkey:
A Case of the Higher Education Institutions in Istanbul

Ali Acılar
Bilecik Şeyh Edebali University, Turkey

ABSTRACT

Social media has been widely adopted world-wide, especially by young generations, and has become an integral part of today's society. As a popular Web 2.0 application, social media has significantly affected our daily life; from communication to education, from entertainment to business life. With a large percentage of young adults using social media in daily life, social media has become present in nearly all aspects of the higher education, ranging from admission to education in the classroom. Despite the many benefits and advantages, while many universities actively use social media, some lag behind in adopting this technology, especially in developing countries. The main aim of this chapter is to investigate the presence of social media in Web sites of the higher education institutions in Istanbul and analyze how they use it.

INTRODUCTION

Together the Internet and the Web have profoundly affected our life for the past decades. Today, we can use the Web for searching information, communication, education, business and entertainment. The World Wide Web has evolved greatly through the years since it was invented. Before Web 2.0, the World Wide Web was mainly consisted of static content. In the time of Web 1.0, Web sites are very limited and there was no interaction between users and Web sites in the early years of the Internet. The earliest Web sites provided little opportunity for two-way communication, perhaps at best providing a mailing address, e-mail, or phone number for any further contact (Andzulis, Panagopoulos, & Rapp, 2012). In

DOI: 10.4018/978-1-4666-8586-4.ch006

addition to static content, today's Web sites enable people to collaborate, share information, and create new services and content online (Laudon & Laudon, 2012, p. 272). Web 2.0 is generally considered as the current stage of the Internet's development (Constantinides & Stagno, 2011). The term Web 2.0 refers to a collection of second generation Web-based technologies and services, many of which are designed to facilitate collaboration and sharing between users (Kennedy et al., 2007). There is a common acceptance in the literature that the concept of "Web 2.0" was born with a conference brainstorming session between O'Reilly and MediaLive International (O'Reilly, 2005). According to Laudon and Laudon, (2012, p. 272) Web 2.0 has four characteristic features, such as: interactivity, real-time user control, social participation (sharing), and user-generated content. The main technologies and services behind Web 2.0 features include cloud computing, software mashups and widgets, blogs, RSS, wikis, podcasting, social networking services, social bookmarking services and file sharing (Laudon & Laudon, 2012, p. 273; Kennedy et al., 2007).

Web 2.0 can be considered as the platform for the evolution of social media (Kaplan & Haenlein, 2010). According to Kaplan and Haenlein (2010) "Social media is a group of Internet-based applications that build on the ideological and technological foundations of Web 2.0, and that allow the creation and exchange of User Generated Content." According to Holotescu and Grosseck (2012) social media is about transforming monologue into dialogue, free access to all types of information, transforming Internet users from mere readers to creators of online content, and interacting in the online world so as to form new personal or business relationships. Social media comprises a wide range of a new generation of Internet applications and encompasses tools that allow individual and collective publishing; sharing of multimedia such as images, audio and video; and the creation and maintenance of online social networks (Constantinides & Stagno, 2011; Bennett et al., 2012). The broad term, social media, has been used to apply to a variety of technologies, including wikis, blogs, microblogs, social networking sites, virtual worlds, and video-sharing sites (Kane, Alavi, Labianca, & Borgatti, 2014). These online social technologies can also be accessed on mobile phones, tablets and other mobile devices. Mobile devices and the use of social media presented new opportunities for interaction, provided opportunities for collaboration, allowed students to engage in content creation and communication using social media and Web 2.0 tools with the assistance of constant connectivity (Gikas & Grant, 2013). Today, online social media applications have been integrated into the daily practices of many users around the world, supported by different websites, tools, and networks (Oberer & Erkollar, 2012). As accessibility to the Internet and social media from mobile devices has become more available, the popularity of social media has increased and people started to share more content on social network sites.

Social networking has become very popular during the past few years, and it has an important role in most people's life nowadays (Zaidieh, 2012). The term "Social Network" corresponds to "a network of relationships between different information processing entities such as people, groups, and organizations" (Hosny & Fatima, 2012). Boyd and Ellison (2008) defines social network sites as "web-based services that allow individuals to (1) construct a public or semi-public profile within a bounded system, (2) articulate a list of other users with whom they share a connection, and (3) view and traverse their list of connections and those made by others within the system." With providing tools for posting messages, sharing photos, creating personal pages and groups, social networking sites, such as Facebook, Twitter, Instagram, LinkedIn, etc., bring people together and allow them to communicate by making new friends, exchanging ideas and engaging in similar interests (Hosny & Fatima, 2012).

In recent years, the use of social media has become so widespread worldwide, especially among young generations. Today, as a new way of communication and interaction, social media is an important part of daily life of many young adults and students (McCarthy & McCarthy, 2014; Magro, Sharp, Ryan, & Ryan, 2013). According to the Pew Research survey results, more than 70 percent of online adult participants and 89 percent of the young adult participants (between 18 and 29 years old) use a social networking site (As of January 2014) in the United States.

According to the Internet World Stats (2014), Internet penetration rate is 46.3 percent of the population in Turkey and the use of social media is widespread in the Turkish population. GlobalWebIndex Wave 11 reported that 97 percent of the Internet users in Turkey have a social network account, Facebook and Twitter have the highest penetration rates; 93 percent of the Internet users own a Facebook account and 72 percent of the Internet users own a Twitter account (Global Digital Statistics, 2014). Akyıldız and Argan (2011) found that only 6.2 percent of undergraduate students have no Facebook account among 1300 students in Turkey. These statistics indicate that the use of social media in the higher education institutions in Istanbul to interact with their audiences is a necessity in today's highly competitive world, not a luxury.

The strong capabilities of social media are affecting many areas of life, including business operations, communication, social networking, and even education (Tuten & Marks, 2012; Tess, 2013). Social media has radically changed the nature of communication in organizations and outside organizations (Mayfield, 2011; Zailskaite-Jakste & Kuvykaite, 2012). Despite the widespread use of social media among people, firms have been slower to adopt social media at the organizational level, but are quickly seeing the potential value in their use (Andzulis, Panagopoulos, & Rapp, 2012). Today, as the concept of social media is an important issue for many business executives, companies struggle with how to adopt social media into their business models and strategy, and decision makers try to identify ways in which firms can make profitable use of social media applications (Kaplan & Haenlein, 2010; Andzulis, Panagopoulos, & Rapp, 2012).

THE USE OF SOCIAL MEDIA IN THE HIGHER EDUCATION INSTITUTIONS

The higher education institutions are significantly affected from the emergence of Web 2.0 tools in all around the world. In parallel with the developments of Web 2.0 technology, they have become more popular in the everyday lives of students over the years (Bennett et al., 2012). The important changes in the global environment had a direct impact over the higher education institutions and forced them to rethink their general strategy and to tailor their marketing efforts in order to better suit the student-customer information and communication needs (Alexa, Alexa, & Stoica, 2012). It is necessary to rethink the higher education environments based on the use of online social network applications like Facebook, YouTube or Twitter, in accordance with the skills and learning needs of students (Holotescu & Grosseck, 2012). In recent years, social media has an increasing influence on higher education (Oberer & Erkollar, 2012) and have managed to attract the attention of the higher education institutions as a mean to connect with students (Bélanger, Bali, & Longden, 2013). To succeed in today's fast-changing world, the higher education institutions are in the position of having to adapt to external conditions created by widespread adoption of popular technologies such as social media, social networking services and mobile devices (Kukulska-Hulme, 2012). Today, the increased presence of social media in the higher education is essential in order to get in touch with prospective and current students (Selwyn, 2012; Beqiri, 2014). Several studies investigated the use of Facebook in education as the primary social networking site in the world, and according to Magro, Sharp, Ryan and Ryan (2013) these studies can be classified into four categories such as: 1) student and faculty interactions, 2) the effect of student individual differences on adoption and usage, 3) student-to-student collaboration, and 4) social network sites impact on individual learning.

Social media has affected the higher education in number of ways from education to office operation, from student life to public relations of universities (Hrastinski & Dennen, 2012). The higher education institutions are using social media for different activities and purposes, such as gathering and sharing information, showcasing student and faculty work, broadcasting special events, emergency notifications and creating a dialogue in addition to communicating with their students or prospective students (Alexa, Alexa, & Stoica, 2012; Chai-Lee, 2013).

Social software applications, such as wikis, social networking and bookmarking sites, are increasingly being used in higher and further education to support teaching and learning processes (Schroeder, Minocha, & Schneider, 2010). There are many potential benefits of these applications in the higher education environment for both students and educators. In addition to allowing students to learn interactively and collaboratively, these social software applications provide students with social and cognitive stimulation and also add to the interaction between students and educators (Schroeder, Minocha, & Schneider, 2010). Online social networks can be appropriated and repurposed to support teaching and learning delivery in educational institutions (Hamid, Chang, & Kurnia 2009). According to Hamid, Chang and Kurnia (2009) specifically, four online social network activities, content generating, sharing, interacting and collaboratively socializing are relevant in the education context. General-interest social networks can be used as a valuable tool for the dissemination and communication of science, as transmitters from many to many (Freire, Rogel, & Rodríguez, 2014). Veletsianos (2012) investigated scholars' naturalistic practices in social networks in general, and on Twitter in particular. And Veletsianos (2012) found that scholars participating on Twitter (1) shared information, resources, and media relating to their professional practice; (2) shared information about their classroom and their students; (3) requested assistance from and offered suggestions to others; (4) engaged in social commentary; (5) engaged in digital identity and impression management; (6) sought to network and make connections with others; and (7) highlighted their participation in online networks other than Twitter.

Today, distance education, especially online, is becoming more widespread (Naqvi & Ajiz, 2006; Neuhauser, 2003). Online web-based learning has made learning content much more freely and instantaneously available to students who can download course materials such as notes and readings with a single mouse click (Bosch, 2009). Distance education as a primary means of instruction in the higher education is expanding significantly at the college and university level (Brady, Holcomb, & Smith, 2010). And, an increasing number of higher education instructors are beginning to combine distance education delivery with social network sites (Brady, Holcomb & Smith, 2010).

As social media use increases among the members of the society, educators are challenged to think differently about how to communicate with their audiences (Hanson et al., 2011). Social media is changing the nature of relationships with information and knowledge in education (Selwyn, 2012). Social media is increasingly visible in the higher education institutions as instructors look to technology to mediate and enhance their instruction with a media-rich environment as well as promote active learning for students (Nyangau & Bado, 2012; Rodriguez, 2011; Tess, 2013). The instructional potential for Web 2.0 technologies has led to many recent applications in the higher education including social networking, microblogging, wikis and blogging (Bennett et al., 2012). Social media offers many opportunities to universities connect with students where they are most comfortable and promote their universities in exciting ways such as in video sharing sites (Cappex.com, 2010; Wilson, 2013). Veletsianos (2012) stated that "Scholars participate in online social networks for professional purposes. In such networks, learning takes the form of participation and identity formation through engagement in and contribution to networked practices."

Social media applications have also important potentials for the teamwork studies among students in universities. Rasiah (2014) stated that the use of Facebook in a team-based pedagogy setting significantly enhanced the teaching and learning process from the perspective of the educator, and found that Facebook provided a rich team-based learning environment that was used to channel the students' creativity.

Among the functional areas of a business, marketing is one of the most dramatically affected by the social media. Due to the widespread acceptance of social media, social media has become an important factor of influence in buying behavior (Constantinides & Stagno, 2012). Addition to actively use social media in education, marketing, recruiting, admissions, alumni relations, and fund-raising staff have been among the first to use social media on many higher education institutions (Wilson, 2013).

Higher education institutions are involved in marketing themselves in order to build up a good image, to improve the level of satisfaction of students and the stake holders, to gain competitive advantage and to increase their market share (Ross, 2014). Today, in addition to the traditional branding efforts, the higher education institutions are embracing other innovative marketing mediums, such as social media (Bélanger, Bali, & Longden, 2013). The Internet and social media offer a new way to universities to present its brand to current students, prospective students, parents, faculty members, and community members (Peruta, Ryan, & Engelsman, 2013). The Internet and social media have introduced new alternative ways to the universities for recruiting students. Higher education institutions show increased interest in the potential of social media as a marketing tool for reaching and attracting prospective students (Constantinides & Stagno, 2012; Reuben, 2008). Social media offers alternative ways to reach out to potential students for the higher education admissioners (Nyangau & Bado, 2012). Therefore, social media is capable of being a very potent recruitment aid (Lubbe et al., 2013). Using social media as a higher education marketing tool is an attractive proposition, because of positive past experience in the business sector on the results of social media marketing and the high adoption rates of social media by the younger generation (Constantinides & Stagno, 2012).

Typically youths between 14 and 19 years old enter a higher education institution and this age group started to use the Internet and social media at an early age (Greenwood, 2012; Liang, Commins, & Duffy, 2010). This generation, which has variously been referred to as the 'Net Generation', 'Digital Natives' and 'Generation Y' are claimed to be very different comparing to their parents in their familiarity with technologies and the regularity with which they use them (Kennedy et al., 2007). According to Kennedy et al., (2007) some commentators have claimed that their use of technology during their developmental years has changed the way that they learn and perhaps even the physiology of their brains. For increasingly diverse student populations, social networking and the use of mobile devices are an unquestionable part of how they learn (Kukulska-Hulme, 2012). Therefore, with such a large percentage of prospective students using social media in some capacity, the higher education institutions clearly must adapt their recruiting techniques to this generation (Greenwood, 2012; Hayes, Ruschman, & Walker, 2009).

Social media applications can also be used as an orientation tool for new students by the higher education institutions. University Web sites and social media profiles are very important information sources for prospective and incoming students. The higher education institutions can use social media tools that feature student contributions to help welcome prospective students to the campus community (Wilson, 2013). After new students arriving to the university, social media tools can be used for distributing information about events, activities, and deadlines, as well as interactive communication devices that students can use to ask questions of staff or of other students who are equipped with information, experience, and additional resources (Wilson, 2013). DeAndrea et al. (2012) reported that a student-centered social media site designed to enhance students' perceptions of social support prior to their arrival on campus increased students' perceptions that they would have a diverse social support network during their first semester at college.

Even though, higher education institutions remain slow to adapt social media (Peruta, Ryan, & Engelsman, 2013), there are some good examples of using social media in the higher education institutions, such as Harvard University's social media site (http://www.harvard.edu/social-media). It is ranked on the top of the studentadvisor.com's Top 100 Social Media Colleges list in 2015 (http://www.studentadvisor.com/top-100-social-media-colleges).

Although there are various studies about the use of social media among young people and students, studies on the institutional use of social media by the higher education institutions are limited. The major objective of this study is to investigate the presence of social media in Web sites of the higher education institutions in Istanbul and analyze how they use it.

METHODOLOGY

There are 52 higher education institutions in Istanbul listed in the Board of Higher Education's Web site. Of these, eleven are state institutions including three military academies, and remaining 41 are private higher education institutions including four vocational schools. The author visited each of the 52 institutions' Web sites in 15th and 16th of June 2014. After entering a higher education institution's Web site, a full screen shot of the main page of Web site was captured by Webpage Screenshot v13.11, a Google Chrome plug-in, and saved as pdf. Each higher education institution Web site was reviewed for social network sites utilized and the phrases "social media" and "social network" are searched using Web site search box and the institutional social network site profile pages linked from the higher education institutions Web site was captured and saved. Presentation web sites for prospective students were also reviewed for social network sites, if linked to main page of the higher education institution's Web site. Each higher education institution was given credit for incorporating a particular social network site if there was text, banner, logo or a picture anywhere on the Web site linking the user to the institution's respective official social network site page, as done by Greenwood (2012). Only official institutional social network site profile pages were considered. Department and division social network site profile pages were not counted.

Findings

All of the higher education institutions in this study have an active Web site. It is found that total of fourteen social network sites are linked on the Web sites of the higher education institutions in Istanbul. These are Facebook, Twitter, Google+, YouTube, Vimeo, Pinterest, Instagram, Linkedin, Flickr, Foursquare, Yammer, Vine, Tumblr and Dailymotion. Among them, the most used four sites are Facebook, Twitter, YouTube, and Google+. It is found that generally the higher education institutions in Istanbul list their social network site links on the main page of their Web sites.

It is apparent from Table 1 that Facebook and Twitter are the most linked social network sites on Web sites by the higher education institutions in Istanbul. As Facebook and Twitter have the highest penetration rates in Turkey, their adoption by the higher education institutions in Istanbul is in line with

Table 1. Spread of social network sites linked

Social Network Sites	Number of Higher Education Institutions	%
Facebook, Twitter	46	88.46
YouTube	32	61.54
Google+	13	25.00
Instagram	11	21.15
Flickr, LinkedIn	7	13.46
Vimeo, Pinterest, Foursquare	4	7.69
Tumblr	2	3.85
Dailymotion, Vine, Yammer	1	1.92

expectations. 88 percent of them (46 higher education institutions) linked their Facebook and Twitter profile page on their Web sites. Among them, 45 higher education institutions linked Facebook and Twitter together. It is found that generally the higher education institutions in Istanbul made Facebook and Twitter together available to their Web site users. After Facebook and Twitter, YouTube is the third most popular social network site among the higher education institutions. 62 percent of the higher education institutions link their YouTube profile on their Web sites. These findings suggest that Facebook, Twitter and YouTube are the most popular social network sites among the higher education institutions in Istanbul. Apart from these social network sites, other social network sites are linked by less than 5o percent of the higher education institutions. Google+ was linked by thirteen higher education institutions, Instagram was linked by eleven higher education institutions, Flickr and LinkedIn were linked by seven higher education institutions, Vimeo, Pinterest and Foursquare were linked by four higher education institutions, Tumblr was linked by two higher education institutions, Dailymotion, Vine and Yammer were linked by one higher education institution.

Number of social network sites linked by the higher education institutions in Istanbul are vary between zero to eleven. As Table 2 shows, ten higher education institutions linked four social network sites together, eleven higher education institutions linked three social network sites together and twelve higher education institutions linked only two social network sites together on their Web sites. The higher education institutions using social media in tandem with their web sites are generally using two, three or four social network sites together. One higher education institution linked the total of its eleven social network site profile pages. 47 higher education institutions (90%) linked at least one social network site on their Web sites and nearly 65 percent of higher education institutions linking social network sites linked at least three social network sites on their Web sites. There were no link(s) to any social network sites on five higher education institutions including all three military academies and one newly established university. Remaining higher education institution showed three social network site logos on its Web site but there was no link. Military academies preferred not to link any social network sites on their Web sites for some reasons.

Some higher education institutions joined more than one social network site but they have not used at all or have not used effectively. For example one institution joined Vimeo, two years ago but there was not even a video shared on its profile. Another higher education institution joined Tumblr and also there was not a picture or video loaded. No pictures and videos were found on five higher education

Table 2. Number of social network sites linked by the higher education institutions

Number of Social Network Sites Linked	Number of Higher Education Institutions	%
11	1	1.92
7	4	7.69
6	2	3.85
5	6	11.54
4	10	19.23
3	11	21.15
2	12	23.08
1	1	1.92
0	5	9.62

institutions' Google+ account. Because most of the higher education institutions in Istanbul are newly established after the year 2000, it is difficult for them to focus on social media medium while dealing with other problems.

In this study it is found that the higher education institutions in Istanbul prefer linking social network sites on their Web sites rather than preparing a separate Web page to social media. It is found that only one higher education institution using a Web page dedicated to social media and it was very limited.

According to Zailskaite-Jakste and Kuvykaite (2012), the most negative aspect of social media is the lack of information control. Opinions and discussions initiated by consumers through social media have an important impact on brand image and cannot be overlooked (Bélanger, Bali, & Longden, 2013). Results of the unprepared entry to social media by the education institutions could be devastating. In this study, it is found that some disturbing negative comments were written by members on three higher education institutions' social network site profiles about the institution, such as "Zincirlikuyu cemetery is more lively", "Welcome to serenity house", "It is written as .... university, it is read as regret", "It is just so boring, I can go blind because of it", "like a high school", "... my biggest mistake in my life." "... one of my fault too". There was no response at all from the institutions for these comments, seems that they have not aware of the negative comments. It is sure that such comments can damage institutions' reputation and adversely affect the decisions of prospective students. Also, not responding a negative comment could result in hurting an institution's brand (Bélanger, Bali, & Longden, 2013). But, it can be possible for the higher education institutions to cruise through user generated content in the social networking sites by promoting positive feedback and mending negative feedback (Bélanger, Bali, & Longden, 2013). Therefore, before selecting social media channels, every institution should plan social media implementation process (Zailskaite-Jakste & Kuvykaite, 2012). It is important to have an appropriate social media marketing strategy in place for the higher education institutions for clear reasons such as that having a social media marketing strategy would allow the universities to keep social media accounts easily transferable between different employees and would also help a university to keep its social media efforts aligned with other running marketing campaign (Bélanger, Bali, & Longden, 2013).

CONCLUSION AND DISCUSSION

Social media has gained great popularity among people and become an integral part of significant portion of young adults all over the world. It is widely accepted that young generation is more familiar with the Internet, mobile technologies and social media than their parents. With the widespread acceptance of social media in the society, social media has also become present in nearly all aspects of the higher education, ranging from admission to education in the classroom. The Internet and social media have introduced new ways to the universities for recruiting students.

In this study, the Web sites of the higher education institutions in Istanbul were reviewed for social media use. While all 52 higher education institutions have a Web site, 47 of them (90%) link at least one social network site profile page of its own on their Web sites. Facebook and Twitter are the most linked social network sites on Web sites by the higher education institutions in Istanbul. Following Facebook and Twitter, YouTube is the third most popular social network site. The higher education institutions using social media in tandem with their Web sites are generally using two, three or four social network sites together. In general, Facebook and Twitter are used together by the higher education institutions. The higher education institutions in Istanbul prefer linking social network sites on their Web sites rather than preparing a separate Web page for social media.

Before entering a social media channel, the higher education institutions should have a strategic plan for this medium. Disturbing comments on institution's social network site profile by members and not responding them can damage universities' reputation and adversely affect the decisions of prospective students.

REFERENCES

Akyıldız, M., & Argan, M. (2011). Using online social networking: Students' purposes of Facebook usage at the university of Turkey. *Journal of Technology Research*, *3*, 95–104. Retrieved from http://www.aabri.com/manuscripts/111085.pdf

Alexa, E. L., Alexa, M., & Stoica, C. M. (2012). The use of online marketing and social media in higher education institutions in Romania. *Journal of Marketing Research & Case Studies*, 1-9. Retrieved 13 August, 2014, from http://www.ibimapublishing.com/journals/JMRCS/2012/721221/721221.pdf

Andzulis, J., Panagopoulos, N. G., & Rapp, A. (2012). A review of social media and implications for the sales process. *Journal of Personal Selling & Sales Management*, *32*(3), 305–316. doi:10.2753/PSS0885-3134320302

Bélanger, C. H., Bali, S., & Longden, B. (2014). How Canadian universities use social media to brand themselves. *Tertiary Education and Management*, *20*(1), 14–29. doi:10.1080/13583883.2013.852237

Bennett, S., Bishop, A., Dalgarno, B., Waycott, J., & Kennedy, G. (2012). Implementing Web 2.0 technologies in higher education: A collective case study. *Computers & Education*, *59*(2), 524–534. doi:10.1016/j.compedu.2011.12.022

Beqiri, G. (2014). The impact of social media on higher education in Kosovo: The student's perspective. *Academic Journal of Interdisciplinary Studies*, *3*(2), 155–163.

Bosch, T. E. (2009). Using online social networking for teaching and learning: Facebook use at the University of Cape Town. *Communicatio*, *35*(2), 185–200. doi:10.1080/02500160903250648

Boyd, D. M., & Ellison, N. B. (2008). Social network sites: Definition, history, and scholarship. *Journal of Computer-Mediated Communication*, *13*(1), 210–230. doi:10.1111/j.1083-6101.2007.00393.x

Brady, K. P., Holcomb, L. B., & Smith, B. V. (2010). The use of alternative social networking sites in higher educational settings: A case study of the e-learning benefits of ning in education. *Journal of Interactive Online Learning*, *9*(2), 151–170.

Cappex.com. (2010). *Establishing a benchmark for social media use in college admissions*. 2010 Social Media and College Admissions Study, Retrieved 01 July, 2014, from http://www.cappex.com/media/EstablishingABenchmarkForSocialMediaUse.pdf

Chai-Lee, G. (2013). *The use of social media in education: A perspective*. Paper presented at 2nd International Higher Education Teaching and Learning Conference. Retrieved 23 June, 2014, from http://www.curtin.edu.my/tl2013/PDF/The%20Use%20of%20Social%20Media%20in%20Education_%20A%20Perspective.pdf

Constantinides, E., & Stagno, M. C. Z. (2011). Potential of the social media as instruments of higher education marketing: A segmentation study. *Journal of Marketing for Higher Education*, *21*(1), 7–24. doi:10.1080/08841241.2011.573593

DeAndrea, D. C., Ellison, N. B., LaRose, R., Steinfield, C., & Fiore, A. (2012). Serious social media: On the use of social media for improving students' adjustment to college. *The Internet and Higher Education*, *15*(1), 15–23. doi:10.1016/j.iheduc.2011.05.009

Freire, F. C., Rogel, D. R., & Rodríguez, C. (2014). Presence and impact of Andean universities in online social networks. *Revista Latina de Comunicación Social*, *69*, 571–592.

Gikas, J., & Grant, M. M. (2013). Mobile computing devices in higher education: Student perspectives on learning with cellphones, smartphones & social media. *The Internet and Higher Education*, *19*, 18–26. doi:10.1016/j.iheduc.2013.06.002

Global Digital Statistics. (2014). *We are social's snapshot of key digital indicators*. Retrieved 29 November, 2014, from http://etonpreneurs.com/uploads/Global%20Social,%20Digital%20&%20Mobile%20Statistics,%20Jan%202014.pdf

Greenwood, G. (2012). Examining the presence of social media on university web sites. *Journal of College Admission*, *216*, 24–28.

Hamid, S., Chang, S., & Kurnia, S. (2009). Identifying the use of online social networking in higher education. In *Proceedings ASCILITE*. Auckland: ASCILITE. Poster presentation (pp. 419-422). Retrieved 19 January, 2015, from http://www.ascilite.org.au/conferences/auckland09/procs/hamid-poster.pdf

Hanson, C., West, J., Neiger, B., Thackeray, R., Barnes, M., & McIntyre, E. (2011). Use and acceptance of social media among health educators. *American Journal of Health Education*, *42*(4), 197–204. doi:10.1080/19325037.2011.10599188

Hayes, T. J., Ruschman, D., & Walker, M. M. (2009). Social networking as an admission tool: A Case study in success. *Journal of Marketing for Higher Education*, *19*(2), 109–124. doi:10.1080/08841240903423042

Holotescu, C., & Grosseck, G. (2012). An empirical analysis of the educational effects of social media in universities and colleges. In *Proceedings of the 8th International Scientific Conference eLearning and Software for Education (eLSE)*, Bucharest: Editura Universitara. Retrieved 20 January, 2014, from http://www.ceeol.com/aspx/getdocument.aspx?logid=5&id=1b3dcdac-c6c7-4ea5-b1aa-de9f0fd45a23

Hosny, M. I., & Fatima, S. (2012). Facebok in education: Students, teachers, and library perspectives. *Journal of Computing*, *4*(6), 78–86.

Hrastinski, S., & Dennen, V. (2012). Social media in higher education: Introduction to the special issue. *The Internet and Higher Education*, *15*(1), 1–2. doi:10.1016/j.iheduc.2011.11.004

Internet World Stats. *Internet Stats and Facebook Usage in Europe*. Retrieved 29 November, 2014, from http://www.internetworldstats.com/stats4.htm

Kane, G. C., Alavi, M., Labianca, G., & Borgatti, S. P. (2014). What's different about social media networks? A framework and research agenda. *MIS Querterly*, *38*(1), 274–304.

Kaplan, A. M., & Haenlein, M. (2010). Users of the world, unite! The challenges and opportunities of social media. *Business Horizons*, *53*(1), 59–68. doi:10.1016/j.bushor.2009.09.003

Kennedy, G., Dalgarno, B., Gray, K., Judd, T., Waycott, J., Bennett, S.,... Churchward, A. (2007). The net generation are not big users of Web 2.0 technologies: Preliminary findings. In *Proceedings ASCILITE*. Singapore: ASCILITE. Retrieved 23 June, 2014, from http://www.ascilite.org.au/conferences/singapore07/procs/kennedy.pdf

Kukulska-Hulme, A. (2012). How should the higher education workforce adapt to advancements in technology for teaching and learning? *The Internet and Higher Education*, *15*(4), 247–254. doi:10.1016/j.iheduc.2011.12.002

Laudon, K., & Loudon, J. (2012). *Management information systems: Managing the digital firm* (12th ed.). Prentice Hall.

Liang, B., Commins, M., & Duffy, N. (2010). Using social media to engage youth: Education, social justice, & humanitarianism. *Prevention Researcher*, *17*(5), 13–16.

Lubbe, J., Roets, L., van Tonder, S., & Wilkinson, A. (2013). Social media: A method to recruit students into undergraduate nursing programmes. *Gender & Behaviour*, *11*(2), 5402–5411.

Magro, M., Sharp, J. H., Ryan, K., & Ryan, S. D. (2013). Investigating ways to use Facebook at the university level: A Delphi study. *Issues in Informing Science and Information Technology*, *10*, 295–311.

Mayfield, T. (2011). A commander's strategy for social media. *Joint Force Quarterly*, *60*(1), 79–83.

McCarthy, R. V., & McCarthy, M. M. (2014). Student perception of social media as a course tool. [IS-EDJ]. *Information Systems Education Journal*, *12*(2), 38–46.

Naqvi, S. J., & Ajiz, M. A. (2006). Attitudes toward WebCT and learning: An Omani perspective. *Issues in Informing Science and Information Technology*, *3*, 435–444.

Neuhauser, C. (2005). A five-step maturity model for on-line course design. In *Proceedings of 19th Annual Conference on Distance Teaching and Learning*. Retrieved 19 January, 2015, from http://www.uwex.edu/disted/conference/Resource_library/proceedings/03_80.pdf

Nyangau, J. Z., & Bado, N. (2012). Social media and marketing of higher education: A review of the literature. *Journal of the Research Center for Educational Technology*, *8*(1), 38–51.

O'Reilly, T. (2005). *What is Web 2.0: Design patterns and business models for the next generation of software*. Retrieved 27 March, 2014, from http://www.oreillynet.com/pub/a/oreilly/tim/news/2005/09/30/what-is-web-20.html

Oberer, B., & Erkollar, A. (2012). Social media integration in higher education. cross-course google plus integration sown in the example of a master's degree course in management. *Procedia: Social and Behavioral Sciences*, *47*, 1888–1893. doi:10.1016/j.sbspro.2012.06.918

Peruta, A., Ryan, W., & Engelsman, R. (2013). Social media branding strategies for higher education: Comparing Facebook pages and Web sites, *The International Journal of Technology. Knowledge in Society*, *9*, 11–23.

Pew Research Internet Project. (n.d.). *Social networking fact sheet*. Retrieved 13 August, 2014, from http://www.pewinternet.org/fact-sheets/social-networking-fact-sheet/

Rasiah, R. (2014). Transformative higher education teaching and learning: Using social media in a team-based learning environment. *Procedia: Social and Behavioral Sciences*, *123*, 369–379. doi:10.1016/j.sbspro.2014.01.1435

Reuben, R. (2008). *The use of social media in higher education for marketing and communications: A guide for professionals in higher education*. Retrieved 23 June, 2014, from http://doteduguru.com/wp-content/uploads/2008/08/social-media-in-higher-education.pdf

Rodriguez, J. E. (2011). Social media use in higher education: Key areas to consider for educators. *MERLOT Journal of Online Learning and Teaching*, *7*(4), 539–550.

Ross, D. S. (2014). Junior college students' expectations on choosing institutions for higher education and institutions marketing strategies for admissions. *Abhinav National Monthly Refereed Journal of Research in Commerce & Management*, *3*(5), 23–27.

Schroeder, A., Minocha, S., & Schneider, C. (2010). The strengths, weaknesses, opportunities and threats of using social software in higher and further education teaching and learning. *Journal of Computer Assisted Learning*, *26*(3), 159–174. doi:10.1111/j.1365-2729.2010.00347.x

Selwyn, N. (2012). *Social media in higher education*. Retrieved 11 July, 2014, from http://www.educationarena.com/pdf/sample/sample-essay-selwyn.pdf

Tess, P. A. (2013). The role of social media in higher education classes (real and virtual) - A literature review. *Computers in Human Behavior*, *29*(5), A60–A68. doi:10.1016/j.chb.2012.12.032

Tuten, T., & Marks, M. (2012). The adoption of social media as educational technology among marketing educators. *Marketing Education Review*, *22*(3), 201–214. doi:10.2753/MER1052-8008220301

Veletsianos, G. (2012). Higher education scholars' participation and practices on Twitter. *Journal of Computer Assisted Learning*, *28*(4), 336–349. doi:10.1111/j.1365-2729.2011.00449.x

Wilson, C. D. (2013). Making connections: Higher education meets social media. *Change: The Magazine of Higher Learning*, *45*(4), 51–57. doi:10.1080/00091383.2013.806201

Zaidieh, A. J. Y. (2012). The use of social networking in education: Challenges and opportunities. *World of Computer Science and Information Technology Journal*, *2*(1), 18–21.

Zailskaite-Jakste, L., & Kuvykaite, R. (2012). Implementation of communication in social media by promoting studies at higher education institutions. *Inzinerine Ekonomika-Engineering Economics*, *23*(2), 174–188.

KEY TERMS AND DEFINITIONS

Blog: A truncation of the Weblog. A web site that serves individuals for publishing their posts chronologically.

Cloud Computing: Accessing computer processing power, data, software and other services over a network, principally the Internet, instead of local computer's resources.

Internet: Global network of networks that use universal standards to connect several billion devices all over the world.

Mashup: A web page or web application that combines data from more than one online source under a unified graphical interface.

RSS: Abbreviation for Rich Site Summary. RSS allows subscribers' computers to receive up-to-date web contents, news and updates from Website.

Social Media: Social media refers to Web-based platforms that allow people to create, share, and/or exchange digital contents in the Internet.

Social Networking Site (SNS): SNS is an online platform to build online community or social networks among people on the Internet.

Web 1.0: Web 1.0 is accepted as the first stage in the World Wide Web, which consists of static web sites.

Web 2.0: Web 2.0 refers to the second stage in the World Wide Web. Web 2.0 allows people to collaborate and interact each other with web-based services such as social networking sites, video sharing sites, blogs, and wikis.

Wiki: A collaborative Web site that allows visitors to make changes and contributions on content.

Chapter 7
Gamification Impact on Customer Relationship Development in Virtual Environment

Rimantas Gatautis
Kaunas University of Technology, Lithuania

Audrone Medziausiene
Kaunas University of Technology, Lithuania

ABSTRACT

The chapter analyzes gamification conception presenting different perspective towards gamification. Game elements, game mechanics and game dynamics are discussed within the chapter as a main component gamification. Customer relations development stages are presented analyzing acquisition, retention and enchantment stages. The proposed conceptual model describes game elements impact on customer relations development and perceived value. The proposed model empirical validation results in Lithuania market are discussed.

INTRODUCTION

Intensifying competition demands from companies to find new ways to create value and develop relations with customers. Since 2010 the new gamification conception started gaining popularity between companies. The main idea of the conception was to use same principles which are embedded in games development for companies' services and activities oriented towards customers design. This conception is gaining popularity and according Gartner (2011) "by 2014, more than 70 percent of Global 2000 organizations will have at least one "gamified" application". However gamification is still new phenomena and has more practical evidences. Meanwhile, Boer, Geerts and Adriani (2013) estimate that the current market of gamification is worth $10 billion worldwide and forecast that within 5 years it could exceed

DOI: 10.4018/978-1-4666-8586-4.ch007

the entertainment game market which is estimated at $70 billion. TechNavio (2014) report forecast the global gamificiation market to grow 68.4% over the next four years (from 2013 to 2018).

Following the growing popularity of gamification approach various companies developed different platforms and software providing new opportunities to deploy gamification in enterprises activities. The most popular platform is Badgeville claiming to be "the #1 gamification platforms for enterprise". Other important gamification platforms providers are Comarch, 500Friends, Dopamine and Gigya. The growing number of platforms offering gamification services demonstrate the importance of this phenomena.

Although this is a relatively new concept, many authors trying to define gamification concept emphasize similar features of this process. Taking into account various researchers perspectives we define gamification as the process when the game mechanics, elements and dynamics is applied in everyday situations (Zichermann and Linder, 2010), which are not directly related to the games (Bunchball, 2010) and occurs in a non-game context (Deterding, Dixon, Khaled and Nacke, 2011). Gamification is used to create an engagement process, which allows users to obtain higher perceived value from the company. Companies apply gamification in order facilitate consumers engagement, participation and motivation (Bunchball, 2010).

Typically gamification is associated with companies marketing activities with the ultimate goal to deliver greater value to customers. Companies deploy gamification in various marketing activities such as advertising, new products development, marketing research. Customers relationship management is also an area there gamification can be successfully deployed. Looking from consumer relationship management perspective gamification in particular drives consumers' engagement. Gamification brings brands and companies close to consumer. Many companies such as Coca-Cola, Nike, Starbuck deploy gamification in their activities.

Burke (2014) outline the importance of cloud solutions, mobile technologies, socialization, and information as future forces which will have huge impact on gamification in the future. The gamification will be intensively used by companies, by educational institutions, by public organizations in the future. With the growing penetration of smart devices gamification based activities will be accessible any tine for consumers.

Taking this into consideration within this chapter we aim to analyze gamification conception, to describe main conceptual construct of gamification, to underline gamification and customer relations development connection and propose gamification impact on customer relations development model.

GAMIFICATION AND CUSTOMER RELATIONS DEVELOPMENT

Gamification Conception

Gamification is a new conception and the term gamification was started to be used from 2010, though Meloni Gruener (2012) claims that gamification and elements have been asserted in corporate marketing activities. In fact, authors argue that since 2010 had been started exploration of gamification and the first attempts to explain gamification in enterprise's activities. The researchers and practitioners had been started to explain how gamification can be used in not related game activities and what impact this concept could have to formation of relationship with consumers.

Gamification is complicated phenomena and various researchers used different theories explaining gamification. Typically self-determination theory, intrinsic and extrinsic motivation theory, situational relevance theory, situated motivational affordance theory, universal design for learning, user-centric design theory, transtheoretical model of behavior changes are used for analyzing and explaining gamification. There are several different perspectives when researchers aim to define gamification as conception. According to Zichermann (2011) gamification is the usage of gaming techniques and elements in order to motivate consumers and to encourage them to perform a desirable action (Zichermann, 2011).

Chorey (2012) explains gamification as a concept that is based on usage of gaming techniques and elements in not related activities, in order to make them more attractive and entertaining. Author states that one of the most important tasks of usage of gaming techniques is to create activity, where consumers could perform activities or tasks to be fun and company could achieve their goals.

Hamari and Lehdonvirta (2010) also note, that applying of gaming techniques become a part of each innovative and expanding company's marketing. According to the authors 'gamification' is elements of game (such as achievement badges, ladders, points and so on.) and the use of game mechanics in order to achieve goals of the company. Gamification is used in processes and activities not linked with games in order to encourage users to perform certain actions and to "bind" to the company or the company's products and services. In 2010 when marketing practitioners used the term "gamification" they had in mind a tool that would "tie" the consumers and encourage the desired behavior of consumers. According to the authors, the use of game technology helps businesses not only to create value for consumers, but it also helps to increase number of both new and loyal users.

According to Bunchball (2010), the essence of "gamification" is to use game mechanism which is not directly linked to events or actions of the games, thus changing people's behavior. "Gamification" is a concept by which using the technical elements of the game, as well as game mechanics and dynamics are integrated into an online community and marketing activities in order to increase the interest and involvement of the participants. The authors argue that "gamification" is to interest customers and encourage their participation, as well as sharing the achievements of certain activities or community. The authors note that particularly well-used game technology can help the companies to achieve the set goals.

Deterding, Dixon, Khaled, Nacka (2011) also agree that "gamification" concept can be defined as the usage of the game elements and mechanisms in non-gaming context. The authors argue that the use of gaming technology occurs when the various activities that are not directly related to the games, such as points, meeting status, i.e. these activities interact with game elements and game mechanisms. In this context, it is very important to the companies to determine what game elements and mechanisms can be used and what impact it could have on consumer behavior.

Zichermann ir Linder (2010) in the book "Game Based Marketing: Inspire Customer Loyalty Through Rewards, Challenges and contests", says that "gamification" is the usage of game mechanics and elements in everyday situations. The authors present a model of social networks „Foursquare", where users play (compete) with each other by providing information about the visited places (posts, comments, ratings or even format by uploading relevant images). This involvement (the game) promote consumer willingness to take a leadership position in the relevant topic (on site), resulting in getting the satisfaction and recognition of other users. For the active steps users get different points and virtual "badges" that show the status of other users. In this context, the social network „Foursquare" uses game technology by encouraging the involvement of users, based on the desire to dominate and be recognized.

Deterding, et al. (2011) state that the use of game techniques is associated with the „passing through a certain way"(implementing action of a particular scenario in terms of the company). In today's business environment, the consumers get a lot of information about a variety of goods and services, which results in the short-term interest in them. In this context game techniques are used in order to encourage the interest itself, and then the process of consumers' involvement to make it playful and attractive. If the game is related to a product or service, it can increase consumer both the perception and the received bit. In particular, the use of gaming technology enables companies to create a more attractive and playful suggestions, resulting in the company gaining advantage over competitors. In turn, users simply link it with the added benefit - the opportunity to make some fun activities.

Deterding et al. (2011) notes that application of the game techniques are very closely related to psychology. Companies, applying gaming mechanisms, are seeking to understand the relationship between the individual characteristics of a player and corresponding elements of the game, the game scenarios and game dynamics. Users have different characteristics and different needs, which results to motivate them and incorporate gaming techniques it is necessary to apply them in the context of different outcomes, different scenarios or different elements of the game. The authors note yet that the most of consumers are mostly motivated and involved by a certain social status. However, in many cases the individual needs are asserted by desire to win, to compete, to be recognized, to get some reward for their achievements, and other needs that are associated with the game elements.

Werbach, Hunter (2012) argues that the use of gaming techniques can lead users' involvement and participation in activities such as the evaluation of certain content, sharing content with others, content rating, rating sites, shopping, certain operations and others. All of these activities can be directed to the creation of value for the company. All of these activities can be directed to the creation of value for the company. Hamari (2011) notes that thanks to modern technological advances, "gamification" concept is to more and more apply by companies. Game technique allows you to increase the use of the sold goods or services, since the use of the technique increase the client's involvement in the buying process, they are more interesting to perform certain actions.

According to Deterding (2011) game technique is associated with:

- Use (not extension);
- Design and design elements (not game development technology);
- Elements (in than full-fledged games);
- Characteristics of the game (not the same game);
- Game is not directly related to contexts (for usage of specific possibilities).

Based on this concept, the company has to evaluate all technical solutions of the games – design, elements, and game's performance. As an alternative theory Werbach and Hunter (2012) identify the pyramid of gamification. According to the authors, the use of game technology includes elements such as mechanics, components and dynamics. The interaction of all these components forms a "gamification" concept. Connecting and using these tools, enterprise can use this game technique in almost any activity.

Gamification is constantly drawing attention of researchers and practitioners and according Gartner technology hype cycle gamification reached peak of expectations in 2013. This raised several approaches to gamification, discussing them as gamification 1.0, gamification 2.0 and recently gamification 3.0. However these approaches were more related to practical applications of tools deployed in gamification. The most radical perspective to gamification was proposed by Deterning (2014) defying gamification as "critical, transformative, socio-technical systems design practice for motivational affordances in the service of human flourishing".

Werbach, Hunter (2012) state the components of games are user involvement methods which are used in the context of games. Components of the game make the game exciting, fun to play and motivate players to engage in activities, which are used in game technique. According to the authors, these components enable the use of gaming technology with activities not relayed to games and to motivate consumers and encourage them to take the desired actions. The authors point out the following game elements that are closely related to the game mechanics, dynamics, complementary to them and reach the desired results - Achievements; Avatars; Badges; Fighting against the strongest (boss); Collections; Fight battles; Unlock the content; Gifts; Leaders; Levels; Points; Search for answers; Social status; Team; Virtual goods and gifts.

Wu (2011) states that the game elements could be called the interface of the game and the players themselves, in order to make the game itself or the games not directly related to activities at works, more interesting, more engaging, and joyful. The aim of elements of the game is to direct desired consumer behavior favorable to them and to meet the needs of consumers.

Game mechanics is a tool created by game designers that complements and enhances the activities in which the technique used to play, the content. Game mechanics are often manifested as a certain reward system, which includes points, award badges, levels, virtual goods, and so on. It is important to note that the game mechanics does not make the product or service in a particular game, it's just an activity that uses the concept of gaming mechanics (Zichermann Linder, 2010).

According to Werbach, Hunter (2012), the mechanics of the game is the use of game technology component that models and encourages users to explore and learn on their own opportunities through feedback. Game mechanics can be very simple and predictable, it is important that the affected user in the desirable direction and making the user to perform actions that the company expects. There are various game mechanics, and game designers are still discovering and creating new ones. In practice there are an infinite number of ways to motivate people to perform certain actions. Creative use of game mechanics can be achieved with different results, and the author states that it is possible for almost all, (with games not related activities) to apply games mechanics.

Werbach, Hunter (2012) identifies the following examples of game mechanics, which are closely related to the component of the game:

- Points. This is one of the successful elements using of gaming technology. Accumulating points is one of the basic needs of people, and this is a great way to meet their needs. The collected points can be used to purchase certain items, unlocking some hidden content, or simply collected points without any additional motive. Points might be awarded to users when they perform certain activities or tasks. These actions may have different attributes, so the different steps have to be given a different number of points.
- Levels. Levels are often a match of a certain number of points, so the user collecting the required number of points is assigned the next level, or it is moved to the next level. Reaching a certain level, the user must be able to use the collected points for the purchase of virtual goods (such as clothing, weapons, and a virtual player, etc.), obtaining a discount on other purchases or simply points can be exchanged to any product or service. Often, new options or features are provided to a player when he/she reaches a higher level. Similarly, along with the points and achievements, the most important are the elements of used game mechanics.

- Leaders. Leaders encourage the pursuit of glory, when one's name is visible and memorable to others, as well as the promotion of competition and collection points and achievements. Leaders can occur in different ways, for example, blog with the title page to post the most popular blogs or within a certain period of time people wrote a title. The aim of these signs is the same as in case of the usual games - to exalt the most successful users.
- Achievements. Achievements reflect the performance of certain tasks. They can be both virtual and real. Achievements fill wills to make the game more complex, allows measuring the progress status and encourages players to collect points. Achievements and points can be published on leader's signboards to encourage competition among the participants. Achievements and goals give people the feeling that he/she is going in a purposeful way. They can be given as achievement badges and trophies. In general terms, it is appropriate to provide some of the achievements for the performed first tasks, in such a way the player will be more and more integrated, and he will find a growing interest in how things work (for example, blog site should give some badge of achievement or trophy for a man who for the first time put a blog in the system). Steps between certain achievements have still to rise, increasing the user's motivation to collect points or reach a new level.
- Contests. Contests allow users to challenge not only for themselves but also for others. When each user makes certain tasks, a user that has collected the most points is awarded, while others receive consolation prizes. This can help to connect the experience of one user with the other users' experiences and encourage sociability. For example, a certain internet community in one month post photos and vote for your favorite. After a month of collecting, the photo which collected most votes is placed in a permanent place in the community home page and the photos of all other participants are displayed in random order. In these actions the company pleases all your customers and stakeholders and it can be said, it does not cost anything.
- Virtual goods. Although the points are collected for fun, but often points are used to buy certain virtual goods. Virtual goods can vary widely, depending on the system, involving the users. However, most of this is for a product that allows the user to express personality. For example.: blogging site which can be user avatar clothes, new color themes or user profile, the ability to upload larger and higher-quality images, and so on. Werbach, Hunter (2012) argues that the personality and unique sense of expression is one of the strongest needs of the user.

Chorney (2012) argue that the used tool by game mechanics complements and enhances the game content. The mechanics are a virtual award system. It can be such things as points, achievement badges, levels, virtual goods, and so on.

According to Kim (2009), the game mechanics is a set of tools and systems that game designer can use to enhance the player experience and make it more interesting, joyful and engaging content. It argues that social exchanges and collecting of certain achievements and pursuit is an example game mechanics.

Bunchball (2011) argue that the game mechanics are a number of actions, behavior and control of the compound, which is used to make playing certain activities. These elements are used together to create a compelling, binding and an engaging user experience. The author identifies the following these games mechanics:

- Points;
- Levels;

- Challenges;
- Virtual gifts and achievements;
- Leaderboards.

The most extensive list of game mechanics is presented by Badgeville, company providing gamification solutions. Badgeville outline 24 game mechanics - achievements, appointments, behavioral momentum, blissful productivity, bonuses, cascading information theory, combos, community collaboration, countdown, discovery, epic meaning, free lunch, infinite gameplay, levels, loss aversion, lottery, ownership, points, progression, quests, reward schedules, status, urgent optimism, virality. Each of game mechanics is characterized by type, benefits and player's personality type. Player's personality type usually refers to Richard Bartle's proposed player types framework - achievers, explorers, killers and socialites.

Despite of very high variety of game mechanics exist it is still not enough to attract customer. People are different and they are motivated by different things. Some of the game mechanics presentation techniques work well for a group of users, but the other group, they can't work, and almost completely exclude them. Also, people get bored with the routine and doing the same action. In this case, the dynamics of gaming experience that reflects the needs of the players and encourage them to pursue further goals and enhance consumer emotions.

Game dynamics - this is a great painting, which further determines a certain activity, which uses game technology scenarios (Werbach, Hunter, 2012). According to the authors, at the highest point of satisfaction when a certain level, or upshot, game dynamics are used to enhance the user-experience feelings and emotions. According to the authors, the most important dynamics of the game are as follows:

- Constraints (certain restrictions or forced withdrawal);
- Emotions (curiosity, competitiveness, frustration, happiness);
- Stories (consistent, constant, continuous storyline);
- Progression (user, as a player growth and development);
- Relationships (social interaction creates feelings of friendship, status, altruism).

Werbach, Hunter (2012) asserts that the dynamics of the game is one of the main aspect of the games technologies usage, which should draw maximum attention, in order to reach the goal, however, should never be directly integrated into a dynamic business that is easy to understand the dynamics, as in this case, the objectives will not be achieved.

Factors Driving Consumers' Involvement into Gamified Activities

Factors that drive consumers' participation in the games can be divided into two broad categories: internal and external motivating factors. Reiss (2004) argues that the internal motivating factors contribute to make a certain action on the inherent properties, for example, out of curiosity. External motivating factors contribute to make a number of steps to achieve the result, and to be for decoration or to receive a reward. External factors can have any kind of direct expression of the prize as money or other material values. Reiss (2004) identify 16 key internal motivating factors that encourage to perform certain actions:

- Recognition. The desire to be recognized.
- Curiosity. Willingness to learn.

- Eating. Demand for food.
- Family. The desire to grow up children.
- Honor. The desire to be loyal to the ideas of a group of traditional ethical and moral norms.
- Idealism. The need to create a public good.
- Independence. Need to be an individual.
- Order. The need to create an organized and stable environment.
- Physical activity. The need to train and be physically active.
- Strength. Desire to influence (including leadership and leadership).
- Romance. The need to be loved.
- Preservation. The desire to collect and store data.
- Social contact. The need to have friends and friendly relations.
- Social status. The desire to be important to a certain group.
- Peace. The need to be safe.
- Revenge. Willingness to answer and win.

In order to apply the gaming technology successfully, enterprises need to consider and to make sure, that at least some of these internal motivators will be met.

Ariely (2008) states that the movement from the external motivators, such as money, points, or other material containing expressions gifts toward internal motivating factors is an important step in moving the market closer relationship to the social relationships with consumers.

Deterding (2011) ir McGonigal (2011) agree that the internal motivating factors are more important and have a greater impact on consumer behavior than external factors. The authors argue that the use of gaming techniques and the use of such an external factor motivating the status of the grant or award, keep in mind that the game would allow consumers to pleasant feelings and meet their internal needs and motivating.

Gaming technology concept is to use both internal and external motivating factors, thus increasing user engagement and motivation to perform the desired actions. Internal motivating factors come from internal users, and allow the user to decide whether these factors have an impact on him or not.

External motivating factors occurs when someone encourages the user to perform an action on it directly not related the properties from the outside, such as: rise to the next level, points, achievement badges, awards, carried out the mission, rating (Dabbish, 2010).

The authors argue that external motivating factors may have a negative impact on the real cause of the conflict, when they are the main motivating factors for using "gamification" concept, so you should always keep in mind to connect the internal motivating factors that allow consumers the joy of recognition and social status and meet their internal needs.

Factors that facilitate consumer participation in the games can be divided into two categories: internal motivating factors and external motivating factors Reiss (2004). Deterding (2011), and McGonigal (2011) agree that the internal motivating factors are more important and have a greater impact on consumer behavior than external factors. Gaming technology concept is to use both internal and external motivating factors, thus increasing user engagement and motivation to perform the desired actions Dabbish (2010).

Harrel (1999) argues that increasing competition results more and more different consumer expectations. Every time a company rejoices client it starts creating new expectations. Typically, for each item, price, promotion and distribution of the change in the customer's expectations may change. The main challenge for companies is to create a marketing strategy that provides customers with high but realistic expectations. The company is required to do more than what competitors are doing and expect customers.

According Bunchball (2011) factors motivating players might be connected with various game technics to drive players' engagement:

- Desire to achieve status might be driven by points, challenges virtual gifts, leaderboards, etc.
- Achievements might be driven by challenges and virtual goods.
- Self-expression might be driven by challenges.
- Competition might be driven by points, levels, challenges, leaderboards, and gifts.
- Altruism might be driven by points, challenges and leaderboards.

As mentioned above factors driving involvement into games allowed identifying different types of players. R.Bartel proposed different players types represents different motivation and needs in games context:

- Achievers are goal oriented players and are driven by game goals. The goals are achieved through collecting points, badges, progressing through levels, challenges, etc. Explorers are driven by interest to know more about the issue and as much as they can. In gamification context this relates to virtual construct–including mapping its geography and understanding the game mechanic and dynamics.
- Killers are the type of players which main interest is to cause distress on other players. Distress causing leads to satisfaction gain from inflicting anxiety and pain on others players in virtual game world.
- Socializers are driven by socialization motives, so their main interest is to use the virtual game world to socialize with their fellow gamers.

Successful gamification is built on these factors and keeps users engaged. G. Zichermann as the key drivers for successful gamification identifies feedback, friends and fun.

Customer Relationship Management

Companies always look for possibilities to attract more and loyal consumers. This activities are mainly assigned to marketing departments and depending on marketing orientation companies deploy various activities. Since 1990 new marketing paradigm called relationship marketing gained wide recognition and adoption. The conception outlines importance of building relations with consumer and information and communication technologies in particular can support companies' effort in this area. Relationship marketing aims to develop close and beneficial relations with consumers.

Rao and Perry identifies 5 stages of relations with consumer development – relations inflation, relations establishment, relations development, relations nurturing and relations dissolvent.

An alternative approach for relationships with consumers in cyberspace development process suggest elements such as acquisition, retention and enhancement. Successful previous customer relationship development process allows you to get higher returns from customers, as they obtain a higher value.

Alrubaiee, Nazer (2010) argues that the acquisition phase requires enterprises to evaluate critically their possibilities, identify the targeted customer segments. According to the authors, for the company it is very important to listen to a consumer and potential views of the stakeholders, to identify customers' needs and expectations. Companies must developed right image that is attractive to potential users, and users would interest organization or its products and services.

Egan (2008) argues that at the acquisition stage, organizations have to convince the user that their needs and expectations will be implemented purchasing of the goods or services offered by the company. Also at this stage the company has to provide prospects and evaluate how future changes in consumer needs and expectations. According to the author, attracting stage company to improve the interaction with the user interface and the organization itself and the user to obtain more information about each other's values, norms and aspirations.

In Day and Hubbard (2002) opinion retention phase is associated with growing mutual benefit and interdependence. Company focuses on consumer retention through collaboration, trust, commitment and exchange of information. Egan (2008) argues that the maintenance phase of the users feel they get a higher value for the company and feel valued.

Alrubaiee, Nazer (2010) argues that trust is the basis for future cooperation, consisting of two main elements: 1) confidence in the integrity of a partner; 2) confidence in the goodwill of the partner. Integrity - is the belief that the partner, will his word, and kindness - is the belief that the partner is interested in the welfare of the organization and not unexpected actions that will have a negative impact on the organization. Trust also gets a lower perception of anxiety and knowing what to expect from the organization. Trust promotes the benefits of user commitment, and hence loyalty.

According to the authors, the pursuit of commitment is an important of relations between to the pursuit customers relationship, based on relying on the communication between the exchange partners continuity. Obligations between the exchange partners are important ensuring their long-term relationship.

Day and Hubbard, in 2002 stated that the satisfaction of customer describes his emotional condition and the quality of relationships with. The authors argue that there is a close relationship between satisfaction and service quality: a good quality of service raises customer satisfaction.

According to the authors, communication helps to achieve higher goals. Correctly communicating with users is the increased satisfaction and confidence as well as increasing their obligations to the Company. Communication is essential to the successful transaction, to create and maintain long-term relationships.

Negi, Ketema (2010) argues that in the enhancement stage, the company strives to create all the conditions that users would like to become active visitors, the company would be useful and bring material benefits to the company. At this stage, the company will also investigate alternative relationships with existing customers options, i.e. evaluate the relationship with their replacement costs, and consumer prospects.

Robinson, Neeley, Williamson (2011) argues that a good relationship with consumers drives user satisfaction. Happy customers become loyal and recommend the organization, its products or services for other consumers. Nevertheless, among the loyal customers there are huge differences. Users can be less satisfied, satisfied and highly satisfied with the organization. Even small frustration can affect loyal customers. Therefore, customer loyalty and retention is becoming increasingly important. It can be argued that the organization, through customer relationship management, aim at the creation of consumer confidence, based on a long-term relationship. So, relationship is one of the most important determinant of loyalty.

Companies dedicating great efforts to the development of relations with customers are investing in the development of higher-value to customers (Sen Sinha, 2011). Relations with customers help resolving specific individual customers or customer segments needs and to collect information, which can be used to build stronger relations and offer greater value to consumers. According to the authors, the development of relationships with customers and their needs clarification is directly proportional to the added value delivered to consumers.

Uncles, Dowling, Hammond (2003) asserts that established relationships with customers allows the gathering and management of complex data information structures. Having this information companies get better understanding about customers, provide better targeted and more concentrated solutions, and make smarter decisions that will provide additional value for consumers.

Das (2012) claims that the company's most important tools to develop satisfied customers is a personal service and sales. Of course, that products are followed by various services which supports offerings package. The service package consists of a primary and secondary service services set.

Ueno (2006) asserts that the value for the consumer may be interpreted as the basis of all marketing decisions, because the provision of greater value to the consumer to be considered one of the most important competitive advantage and increase user loyalty. In many cases additional services helps delivering value and strengthening relationship with consumers.

GAMIFICATION IN CONSUMERS RELATIONSHIP MANAGEMENT

Conceptual Model of Gamification Impact on Consumer Relations Development and Perceived Value

The conceptual model of gamification for customer relationship development would allow finding out the most important games elements that influence customer relationship development at different stages. The empirical validation of the model allow to define in which relationship stage, which games elements provide the highest motivation for the customer to perceive value of goods and services

Conceptual model of gamification deployment for relationship development was developed basing on Werbach, Hunter (2012) pyramid conception and Negis, Ketema (2010) model of customer relationship development.

The proposed model (see Figure 1) explains gamification impact on consumer relations development and perceived value and loyalty. Basing on this model the empirical validation will allow identify which game elements proposed by Werbach, Hunter (2012) are the most important in different costumer relationship development stages. Also, proposed model will help to find out what elements of a consumer's point of view create the most value. It is assumed that the creation of greater value for customers by utilizing game elements to increase customer's loyalty.

Basing on literature review we provide the following game elements:

- Points - the game progress, reflected in the figures;
- Achievements - goals;
- Avatar - The visual presentation of the player in a virtual environment;
- Badges - visual reflection of achievement;
- Content Unlocking - elements that appear only when it is to achieve certain goals;
- Gifts - gratuity for the execution of a task or achievement;
- Leaderboards - visual player progress and achievements of reflection;
- Level - the player progress in certain steps;

Figure 1. Conceptual gamification deployment in consumers' relation development in virtual environment model

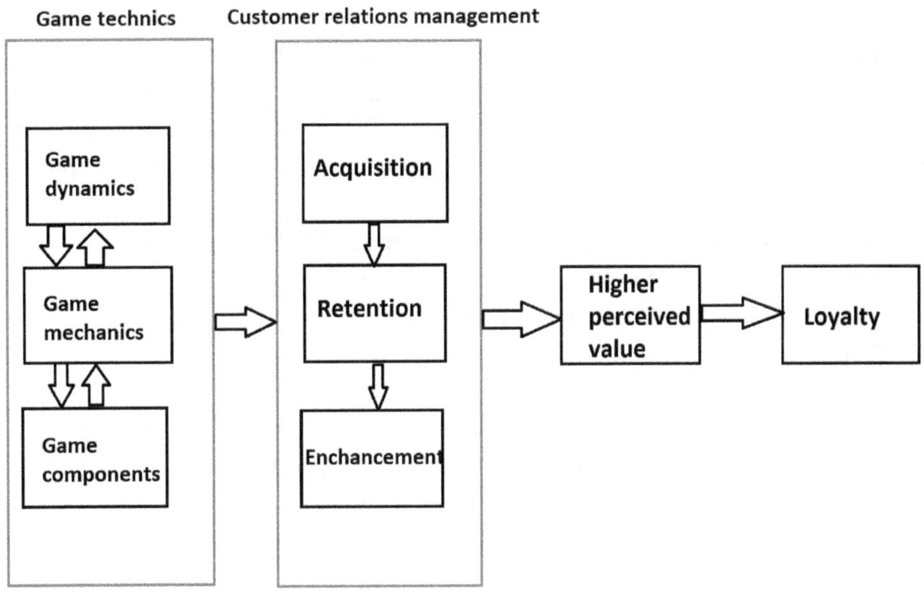

- Social status - the status or the player gained an advantage during the game;
- Team - a group of players who are together to achieve certain goals;
- Virtual goods - assets acquired during the game with the real or virtual value.

Werbach, Hunter (2012) notes, that points, gifts and badges are the most suitable for the consumer's cell constructs convincing and tie, because these elements are used together to create a compelling, binding and an engaging experience for consumers. Also, these customers' elements satisfy Reiss (2004) isolates the internal and Ariely (2008) external motivating factors.

Deterding et al. (2011) argue that teams' levels, social status, giving the company should use the retention phase, since at this phase the company is important to demonstrate the interdependence of consumers. According Deterding et al. (2011) trust and commitment are the most important characteristics of the stage so levels, teams, and social status may facilitate achieving the desired objectives and customers affection. The retention phase should be satisfactory internal motivating factors for consumers, such as the recognition of the social status of the peace (Reiss, 2004).

Werbach, Hunter (2012) argues that virtual gifts and avatars are the most suitable game elements for the enhancement stage, when the users want to get feedback and to perform certain actions that are related to the company's proposed acquisition of goods or services.

Achievements, leadership publication, unlocking the content –these are game elements should be used to increase the perceived value to the consumer (Bunchball, 2011). According to the author, these game technical users satisfy both internal and external motivating factors for companies that run into appropriate use of specific elements of games can increase customer satisfaction and commitment.

Empirical Validation of Model

Empirical evaluation will consider all game elements and their impact on different customer relations development stages and on perceived value. Empirical validation will allow identify if Werbach, Hunter (2012), Deterding, et al. (2011) defined game elements have the different importance in different relationship development stages, and which elements provide the higher perceived value to consumers. However empirical validation will be performed in Lithuania where gamification approach is taking just initial steps.

The research constructs were development basing on literature review and overview of research related to different constructs are presented in Table 1.

Basing on literature review and proposed conceptual model we proposed several hypothesis for empirical validation (see Figure 2).

H1. Points, gifts and badges, as game elements, have the highest impact in acquisition phase.
H2. Teams, levels, leaderboards, as game elements, have the highest impact in retention phase.
H3. Virtual goods and avatars, as game elements, have the highest impact in enhancement phase.
H4. Achievements, social status and content unlock, as game elements, have the highest impact on perceived value of service/product.

The proposed research instrument (questionnaire) was tested by Cronbach-alpha test in order to find out internal consistency between proposed research constructs. The Cronbach-alpha coefficient was determined for every construct. The proposed construct is considered appropriate if Cronbach-alpha coefficient is higher comparing to 0.7. (see Table 2).

Table 1. Research constructs

Research Construct	Researchers Analyzed Construct
Point construct	Bunchball (2011), Werbach, Hunter (2012), Cook (2006)
Achievement construct	Cook (2006), Werbach, Hunter (2012)
Avatar construct	Werbach, Hunter (2012)
Badges construct	Werbach, Hunter (2012)
Content unlock construct	Werbach, Hunter (2012)
Gifts construct	Werbach, Hunter (2012)
Leaderboard construct	Bunchball (2011), Cook (2006), Werbach, Hunter (2012)
Level construct	Bunchball (2011), Cook (2006), Werbach, Hunter (2012), Chorney (2012)
Social status construct	Deterding, Dixon, Khaled, Nacke (2011)
Team construct	Werbach, Hunter (2012)
Virtual good construct	Bunchball (2011), Cook (2006), Chorney (2012)
Acquisition construct	Das (2012)
Retention construct	Das (2012), Griffin (2002)
Enhancement construct	Robinson, Neeley, Williamson (2011)
Higher perceived value construct	Sen, Sinha (2011), Ueno (2006), Dovalienė (2005)

Figure 2. Hypothesis of empirical validation

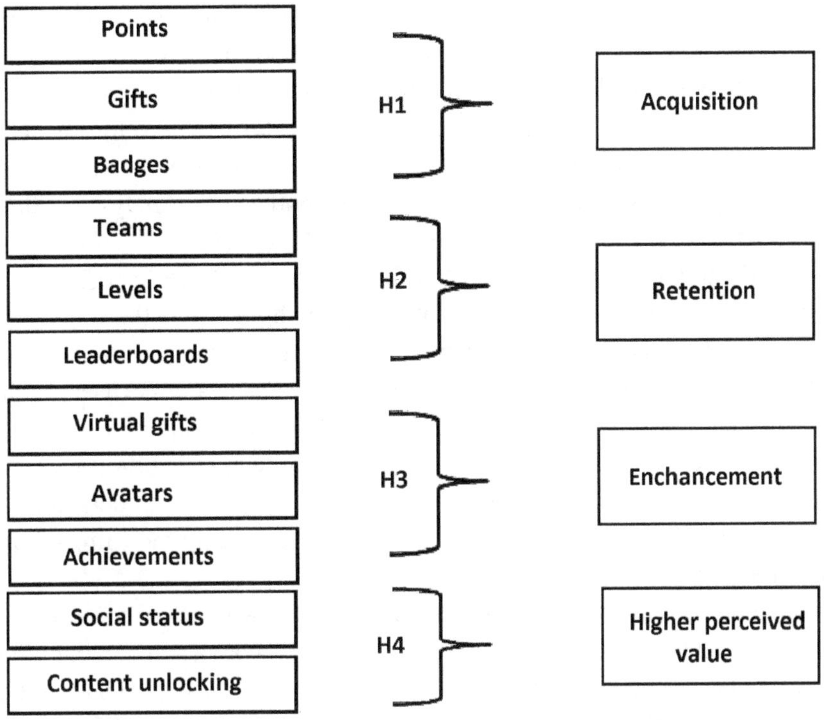

Table 2. Cronbach's Alpha coefficients for constructs

Constructs	Cronbach's Alpha	N. of Items
Acquisition construct	0,829	33
Retention construct	0,903	33
Enhancement construct	0,819	22
Higher perceived value construct	0,744	11

The received Cronbach's Alpha coefficients values are higher than 0,7. Considering this result we may state constructs questions are appropriate and reflect constructs. The obtained data might be used for further analysis.

231 respondent participated in the survey. The demographic characteristics of participants were following - 66.6% man and 33.4% women. Most of respondents were 18-25 years old.

In order to determine the relations between game elements and different stages of consumer relations development and perceived value as well the correlation analysis was used. During the research the proposed construct was assigned as dependable variables (Y) and different game elements were assigned as independable variables (X). Spearman correlation coefficient was used to assess the relation between variables.

The correlation analysis was performed in order to assess Hypothesis 1. Analysis of the data show the statistically strong relation between virtual goods, teams, levels, content unlock and leaderboards and acquisition stages. Accordingly Spearman coefficients were following - $\varrho=0.751$, $\varrho=0.708$, $\varrho=0.74$, $\varrho=0.808$ and $\varrho=0.784$.These relations are statistically significant because probability (p) is higher than 0.05.

Summarizing we can state that the most intensive correlation relation is between content unlock and customer relation development at acquisition stage. During the analysis statistically strong relation between points, gifts and badges as game elements and customer relation development acquisition stage were not identified, so hypothesis H1 was rejected. In the following linear regression analysis only virtual goods, teams, levels, content unlock and leaderboards elements will be used for impact assessment will be considering assessing their impact on customer relations development acquisition stage.

The correlation analysis was used in order to assess Hypothesis 2. Analysis of the data shows the statistically strong relation between virtual goods, teams, levels, achievements and leaderboards. Accordingly Spearman coefficients were following $\varrho=0.843$, $\varrho=0.852$, $\varrho=0.723$, $\varrho=0.72$ and $\varrho=0.787$. These relations are statistically significant because probability (p) is higher than 0.05.

Summarizing we can state that the most intensive correlation relation is between virtual goods elements and customer relations development retention stage. Virtual goods encourage users to share information with other users. The analysis allowed identifying statistically strong relation between teams, levels and leaderboards as game elements and customer relations development retention stage, so Hypothesis 2 is confirmed. In the following linear regression analysis only teams, achievements, levels, virtual goods, leaderboards elements will be considered will be considering assessing their impact on customer relations development retention stage.

The correlation analysis was used in order to assess Hypothesis 3. Analysis of the data shows the statistically strong relation between badges, achievements, gifts, teams and content unlocking. Accordingly Spearman coefficients were following $=0.712$ $\varrho=0.747$, $\varrho=0.78$, $\varrho=0.838$ and $\varrho=0.732$. These relations are statistically significant because probability (p) is higher than 0.05. The strongest relation is between team element and customer relation development enhancement stage.

Summarizing we can state that the statistically strong relation is between virtual goods, avatars as game elements and customer relation development enhancement stage were not identifies, so Hypothesis 3 is rejected. In the following linear regression analysis only badges, achievements, gifts, teams, content unlock as game elements will be considering assessing their impact on customer relations development enhancement stage.

The correlation analysis was used for Hypothesis 4 assessment as well. Analysis of the data shows the strong relation between social status, virtual goods, avatars as game elements and perceived value. Accordingly Spearman coefficients were following $\varrho=0.721$ $\varrho=0.808$, $\varrho=0.776$. These relations are statistically significant because probability (p) is higher than 0.05. The strongest relation is between virtual goods and perceived value.

During the analysis statistically strong relation between achievements and content unlocking were not identified, however statistically strong relation were identified between social status and perceived value. Basing on these results Hypothesis 4 is partially accepted. In the following linear regression analysis only social status, virtual goods and avatars as game elements will be considering assessing their impact on perceived value.

The results of linear regression analysis demonstrate leaderboards have the highest impact on customer relations development in acquisition stage in virtual environment. (Beta = 0,809).

Considering the different games elements importance in retention stage of customers relations development, the highest impact is cause by teams game element (Beta = 0,832).

The correlation analysis results demonstrated that there is a significant relation between teams, levels, leaderboards and retention stage of consumer relations developments. Linear regression analysis shows all three game elements statistically significant.

Considering the enhancement stage, the highest impact on this stage is caused by achievement game element (Beta = 0,814).

From the point of view of perceived value perspective the highest impact on it has virtual goods game element (Beta = 0,875).

Hypothesis 4 was accepted only partly. As demonstrated linear analysis social status element also have significant impact on perceived value.

FUTURE RESEARCH DIRECTIONS

The proposed model identified the key game elements impact different customer relations developments stages as well as perceived value. The analysis of game elements was chosen as game elements are easily identified by user, which leads to empirical data collection. Further research should investigate game mechanics and game dynamics impact on customer relationship development, but this requires customers' to dedicate some time for gamified companies activities and only after customers get engaged they might be interviewed for data collection.

The performed research has several limitation which might be explored in further research. Current research was done in Lithuania between young age respondent. Further research might address different age groups as well other countries and report different results from different age respondents as well as different culture respondents.

The presented research addressed customer relations development perspective, however gamification application is broad from company perspective. Companies might deploy gamification in various marketing activities (product development, market research, advertising, consumer engagement, etc), human resources management activities, project management, etc. Marketing area is probably the most attractive area for practitioners and academia, but it is also important to explore new gamification application areas.

CONCLUSION

Gamification is new concept explaining how game techniques can be deployed in enterprise activities. Basing on various researchers and practitioners perspectives gamification concept can be defined as the usage of the game elements and mechanisms in non-gaming context. Werbach and Hunter proposed (2012) systematic approach to gamification suggesting gamification pyramid containing game components, game mechanics and game dynamics.

Game elements can be called user involvement methods, which are used in the context of games. The mechanics of the game is the use of game technology component that models and encourages users to explore and learn on their own opportunities through feedback.Game dynamics are most high level conventional elements in a game or gamified system.

Gamification most often is deployed to increase engagement of users which leads to additional value creation and delivery. This often is considered as part of enterprise customer relation management activities, although gamification successfully can be deployed in other enterprises marketing activities such as market research, advertising, etc.

The proposed model explains gamification impact on consumer relations development and perceived value and loyalty. Basing on this model the empirical validation will allow identify which game elements proposed are the most important in different costumer relationship development stages. The conceptual model was validated in Lithuania market.

As demonstrate empirical results points, gifts and badges does not have an impact in the acquisition stage of customer relations development so enterprises should not concentrate on these elements deployment as enterprises goal probably will not be achieved. However using these games elements in synergy leads to average impact which might lead to enterprise goals achievement. In the consumers acquisition stage other game elements such as virtual goods, teams, levels and content unlock should be used as these elements have the highest impact on consumer relations development.

Teams and leaderboards as game elements have significant impact on consumer relations development at retention stage. Linear regression analysis demonstrated that combination of these two elements with levels game element also will have significant impact on consumer. Enterprises should also consider using achievements and virtual good elements which have strong impact on consumer relations development at retention stage.

Used in combination virtual good and avatars as game elements have strong impact on consumer relations development at enhancement stage. Enterprises at that stage should also consider using badges, achievements, gifts, teams and content unlock as moderate or strong impact having game elements.

Social status is the game component which has the highest impact on consumer perceived value, so this element should be deployed in all stages of consumer relations development.

REFERENCES

Alrubaiee, L., & Al-Nazer, N. (2010). Investigate the impact of relationship marketing orientation on customer loyalty: The customer's perspective. *International Journal of Marketing Studies*, *2*(1), 155–174. doi:10.5539/ijms.v2n1p155

Ariely, D. (2008). *Predictably Irrational: The Hidden Forces That Shape Our Decisions*. New York, NY: Harper Collins.

Blohm, I., & Leimeister, J. M. (2013). Gamification - Design of IT-Based Enhancing Services for Motivational Support and Behavioral Change. *Business & Information Systems Engineering*, *5*(4), 275–278. doi:10.1007/s12599-013-0273-5

Brodie, R. J., Hollebeek, L. D., Juric, B., & Ilic, A. (2011). Customer engagement: Conceptual domain, fundamental propositions, and implications for research. *Journal of Service Research, 14*(3), 252–271. doi:10.1177/1094670511411703

Bunchball, I. (2010). *Gamification 101: An Introduction to the Use of Game Dynamics to Influence Behavior.* White paper.

Burke, B. (2014). *Gamify: How gamification motivates people to do extraordinary things*. Bibliomotion, Inc.

Chorney, A. I. (2012). *Taking The Game Out Of Gamification*. Dalhousie Journal of Interdisciplinary Management.

Das, D. (2012). PREMASA Model: An Integrated Approach To Customer Relationship Management. *IEM International Journal of Management & Technology*, *2*(1), 111–118.

Deterding, S. (2014). Eudaimonic Design, or: Six Invitations to Rethink Gamification. In M. Fuchs, S. Fizek, P. Ruffino, & N. Schrape (Eds.), *Rethinking Gamification*. Meson press.

Deterding, S., Dixon, D., Khaled, R., & Nacke, L. (2011). From game design elements to gamefulness: defining gamification. In *Proceedings of the 15th International Academic MindTrek Conference: Envisioning Future Media Environments*. Tampere, Finland. doi:10.1145/2181037.2181040

Deterding, S., Sicart, M., Nacke, L., O'Hara, K., & Dixon, D. (2011, May). Gamification. using game-design elements in non-gaming contexts. In CHI' 11 Extended Abstracts on Human Factors in Computing Systems. Vancouver, BC, Canada.

Groh, F. (2012). Gamification: State of the Art Definition and Utilization. In N. Asaj, B. Konings, M. Poguntke, F. Schaub, B. Wiedersheim, & M. Weber (Eds.), *Research Trends in Media Informatics*. Institute of Media Informatics Ulm University.

Grönroos, C. (1994). From marketing mix to relationship marketing: Towards a paradigm shift in marketing. *Management Decision*, *32*(2), 4–20. doi:10.1108/00251749410054774

Gummesson, E., Lehtinen, U., & Grönroos, C. (1997). Comment on" Nordic perspectives on relationship marketing. *European Journal of Marketing*, *31*, 10–16.

Hallowell, R. (1996). The relationships of customer satisfaction, customer loyalty, and profitability: An empirical study. *International Journal of Service Industry Management*, *7*(4), 27–42. doi:10.1108/09564239610129931

Hamari, J. (2011). Perspectives from behavioral economics to analyzing game design patterns: loss aversion in social games. In *Proceedings of the CHI 2011 Social Games Workshop*, Vancouver, BC, Canada.

Hamari, J., & Järvinen, A. (2011). *Building customer relationship through game mechanics in social games. Business, Technological and Social Dimensions of Computer Games: Multidisciplinary Developments*. Hershey, PA: IGI Global.

Hamari, J., & Lehdonvirta, V. (2010). Game design as marketing: How game mechanics create demand for virtual goods. *International Journal of Business Science & Applied Management*, *5*(1), 14–29.

Hunicke, R., LeBlanc, M., & Zubek, R. (2004, July). MDA: A formal approach to game design and game research. In *Proceedings of the AAAI Workshop on Challenges in Game*.

Huotari, K., & Hamari, J. (2011). Gamification" from the perspective of service marketing. *CHI 2011 Workshop Gamification*.

Järvinen, A. S. (2009). *Games without frontiers: methods for game studies and design*. VDM Verlag Dr. Müller.

Kappen, D. L., & Nacke, L. E. (2013, October). The kaleidoscope of effective gamification: Deconstructing gamification in business applications. In *Proceedings of the First International Conference on Gameful Design, Research, and Applications*. ACM Press. doi:10.1145/2583008.2583029

McGonigal, J. (2011). We Don't Need No Stinkin' Badges: How To Reinvent Reality Without Gamification. GDC Vault. Retrievedfrom http://www.gdcvault.com/play/1014576/We-Don-t-Need-No

Negi, R., & Ketema, E. (2010). Relationship marketing and customer loyalty: The Ethiopian mobile communications perspective. *International Journal of Mobile Marketing.*, *5*(1), 113.

Neill, W. (2013). *Gamifying Marketing: Fusing games with consumer transactions to sustain engagement and accurate choices*. Sydney: University of New South Wales.

Nguyen, B., & Mutum, D. S. (2012). A review of customer relationship management: Successes, advances, pitfalls and futures. *Business Process Management Journal*, *18*(3), 400–419. doi:10.1108/14637151211232614

Payne, A., & Frow, P. (2005). A strategic framework for customer relationship management. *Journal of Marketing*, *69*(4), 167–176. doi:10.1509/jmkg.2005.69.4.167

Reiss, S. (2004). Multifaceted nature of intrinsic motivation: The theory of 16 basic desires. *Review of General Psychology*, *8*(3), 179–193. doi:10.1037/1089-2680.8.3.179

Richards, K. A., & Jones, E. (2008). Customer relationship management: Finding value drivers. *Industrial Marketing Management*, *37*(2), 120–130. doi:10.1016/j.indmarman.2006.08.005

Sen, A., & Sinha, A. P. (2011). IT alignment strategies for customer relationship management. *Decision Support Systems*, *51*(3), 609–619. doi:10.1016/j.dss.2010.12.014

Von Ahn, L., & Dabbish, L. (2008). Designing games with a purpose. *Communications of the ACM*, *51*(8), 58–67. doi:10.1145/1378704.1378719

Werbach, K., & Hunter, D. (2012). *For the Win: How Game Thinking Can Revolutionize Your Business*. Wharton Digital Press.

Werbach, K., & Hunter, D. (2012). *How game thinking can revolutionize your business*. Wharton Digital Press.

Winer, R. S. (2001). A framework for customer relationship management. *California Management Review*, *43*(4), 89–105. doi:10.2307/41166102

Wu, M. (2011). Gamification from a Company of Pro Gamers.Retrieved from http://community.lithium.com/t5/Science-of-Social-blog/Gamification-from-a-Company-of-Pro-Gamers/ba-p/19258

Zichermann, G., & Cunningham, C. (2011). *Gamification by design: Implementing game mechanics in web and mobile apps*. O'Reilly Media, Inc.

Zichermann, G., & Linder, J. (2010). *Game-based marketing: inspire customer loyalty through rewards, challenges, and contests*. John Wiley & Sons.

KEY TERMS AND DEFINITIONS

Achievements: Are game element reflecting performance of certain tasks. Achievements are used to increasing the player's motivation to collect additional points or reach new level.

Acquisition: Is the set of methodologies and systems to manage customer prospects and inquiries generated by a variety of marketing techniques.

Avatar: Game element related to the visual presentation of the player in a virtual environment.

Badges: Is game element representing visual reflection of achievement. Badges as well as points are used to elevate status by demonstrating talents, expertise and achievements of players.

Content Unlocking: Game element demonstrating additional game mechanics and appearing only when certain tasks are implemented or goals achieved.

Customer Relations Management: Are company dedicated for interactions with current and future customers.

Enhancement: Is the activities organization take for creating additional and enchanted value for customer.

Game Dynamics: Decisions which further determines a certain activity, which uses game technology scenarios.

Game Elements: Are user involvement methods, which are used in the context of games.

Game Mechanics: Is the use of game technology component that models and encourages users to explore and learn on their own opportunities through feedback.

Gamification: Is usage of gaming techniques and elements in order to motivate consumers and to encourage them to perform a desirable action.

Gift: Game element associated with opportunities to demonstrate gratuity for the execution of a task or achievement.

Leaderboards: Is game element representing the most active players in terms of collecting points or achieving higher level. Leaderboards announcement encourage other players to get more engaged into game.

Level: Game element typical is assigned for a certain number of points and demonstrating player achieved certain stage of difficulty.

Points: Are gamification element typically assigned for player when he performs certain task or activities. Points can be collected or purchased or used to unlock new challenges. Points are reflected in figures.

Retention: Is the activity that a selling organization undertakes in order to reduce customer defections.

Social Status: Is game element related to the status or the player gained an advantage during the game. Status is the rank or level of a player. Players are often motivated by trying to reach a higher level or status.

Team: Is game element representing a group of players who are together to achieve certain goals.

Virtual Good: Is game elementallowing player to express their personality.

APPENDIX

Table 3. Linear regression between game elements and acquisition stage of customer relation development in virtual environment

	B	Standard e.	Beta	t	Sig.
Teams	7.12	0.474	0.704	15.006	0.000
Levels	7.969	0.463	0.751	17.226	0.000
Virtual goods	10.553	0.614	0.751	17.191	0.000
Leaderboards	**8.358**	**0.402**	**0.809**	**20.813**	**0.000**
Content unlock	10.15	0.503	0.8	20.168	0.000

Table 4. Linear regression between game elements and retention stage of customer relation development in virtual environment

	B	Standard e.	Beta	t	Sig.
Teams	**11.005**	**0.484**	**0.832**	**22.733**	**0.000**
Levels	8.515	0.747	0.602	11.395	0.000
Virtual goods	13.045	0.883	0.707	14.779	0.000
Achievements	12.686	0.731	0.754	17.344	0.000
Leaderboards	10.551	0.558	0.781	18.917	0.000

Table 5. Linear regression between game elements and enhancement stage of customer relation development in virtual environment

	B	Standard e.	Beta	t	Sig.
Gifts	6.641	0.485	0.671	13.685	0.000
Badges	6.964	0.488	0.686	14.258	0.000
Teams	7.341	0.439	0.741	16.721	0.000
Achievements	**9.304**	**0.438**	**0.814**	**21.221**	**0.000**
Content unlock	8.356	0.499	0.742	16.748	0.000

Table 6. Linear regression between game elements and perceived value in virtual environment

	B	Standard e.	Beta	t	Sig.
Social status	3.649	0.192	0.782	18.991	0.000
Virtual goods	**4.186**	**0.153**	**0.875**	**27.357**	**0.000**
Avatars	3.392	0.206	0.737	16.498	0.000

Section 2

Social CRM:

Customer Learning and Engagement

Chapter 8
CKM 2.0: Integrating Web 2.0 into Customer Knowledge Management

Fatemeh Najafloo
University of Tehran, Iran

Hatef Rasouli
University of Tehran, Iran

Mehdi Shamizanjani
University of Tehran, Iran

ABSTRACT

This chapter explores the affective role of Web 2.0 on customer knowledge management (CKM) in two ways. At first, a new conceptualization of customer knowledge regarding knowledge "for", "from" and "about" customer is introduced through categorizing them in a detailed typological manner. The second part, attempts to find the relationship between Web 2.0 and three types of customer knowledge in a way that demonstrates each type of customer knowledge could be supported by using any kind of Web 2.0 tools. These parts are integrated as a comprehensive model which is named "Grape Model". This model encompasses different types of customer knowledge in detail as "grapes" which is related to Web 2.0 tools as "leafs" which support encompassed grapes. The"Grape Model" was applied in four different Iranian industries so as to evaluate each industry in making benefits from CKM and using Web 2.0 tools in order to facilitate the CKM process.

INTRODUCTION

CRM is a process designed to collect data related to customers, to grasp features of customers, and to apply those qualities in specific marketing activities. Researchers suggest that CRM is an information industry term for methodologies, software, and usually Internet capabilities that help an enterprise manage customer relationships in an organized way. It focuses on leveraging and exploiting interactions with the customer to maximize customer satisfaction, ensure return business, and ultimately enhance

DOI: 10.4018/978-1-4666-8586-4.ch008

customer profitability (Kumer and Stavropoulos, 2007). Knowledge management is fundamentally about a systematic approach to manage intellectual assets and other information in a way that provides the company with a competitive advantage. Awad and Ghaziri (2004) gave a useful definition of knowledge management (KM) as:

- Using accessible knowledge from outside sources;
- Embedding and storing knowledge in business processes, products, and services;
- Representing knowledge in databases and documents;
- Promoting knowledge growth through the organization's culture and incentives;
- Transferring and sharing knowledge throughout the organization; and
- Assessing the value of knowledge assets and impact on a regular basis.

Rollins and Halinen (2005) regard CKM as an integrated management approach with an ongoing process of generating, disseminating, and using customer knowledge and propose a theoretical framework of CKM that integrates CRM processes. In contrast to customer relationship management (CRM) and general KM, CKM has the following five basic styles: "prosumerism, team-based co-learning, mutual innovation, communities of creation, and joint intellectual property" (Gibbert et al., 2002).

Nowadays, researchers propose that knowledge-enabled customer relationship management (CRM) or customer knowledge management (CKM) is the way to succeed. CKM is an area of management where knowledge management (KM) instruments and procedures are applied to support the exchange of customer knowledge within an organization and between an organization and its customers, in order to improve CRM processes such as customer service, customer retention and relationship profitability (Rollins et al., 2005). CKM **is** a dynamic recycling process of acquiring and refining valuable customer data by means of various paths and methods, and sharing the generated customer knowledge across the organization. Through this process the organization promotes and optimizes the customer relationships in the customer oriented organizational model, frame and environment (Feng & Tian, 2005). Salomann et al. (2005) defines CKM as the utilization of knowledge "for", "from" and "about" customers in order to enhance the customer relating capability of organizations. Most of previous studies have focused on these three mentioned types of customer knowledge. Hence they have not considered sub-types of each customer knowledge in order to investigate different types of them in details so as to provide a comprehensive typological model of customer knowledge which is centralized through three main types of customer knowledge "for", "from" and "about". By taking into account this fact, it`s a critical process through which the identification different types of customer knowledge for each of knowledge "for", "from" and "about" customer through a typological model as mentioned above. This valuable work actually could dramatically strengthen organizations in CKM.

One of the recent emerged technologies in which is applied to provide organizations with utilizing and facilitating the process of KM is Web 2.0 or social software tools. Against the backdrop of recent trends in web technologies such as web 2.0 applications, KM has entered a new age of development with tremendous opportunities (Johnston, 2008). Among various emerging topics of KM, business practitioners and academic researchers have begun to shift their attentions to customer knowledge management (CKM) and social software. The emerging web 2.0 and social software applications open up a new horizon for companies to engage in a more exciting and meaningful relationship with customers (Zhang, 2011). Regarding social software tools like social network, capabilities and specification of each Web

2.0 tool is a critical issue that can help organizations to realize the benefit of each social software tool so as to gain the most advantage.

Firms have recently started to implement social software in exploiting and managing customer knowledge assets. Integrating social software on their electronic storefronts, firms can create virtual communities of interests for current and potential customers to interact with each other and share information and knowledge about their products and services (Zhang, 2011). As a matter of fact, Social software tools could be applied for each type of customer knowledge (knowledge for, from and about customer) according to capability of each social software tool. Indeed the relationship between CKM and social software within organizations has not been explored yet in previous research. The purpose of this research is to find the relationship between each type of customer knowledge through a robust typological model with each Web 2.0 tools. In reality none of the previous studies have focused on finding the relationship between CKM and social software tools as is introduced in this chapter since all types of customer knowledge and the most important Web 2.0 tools are regarded as a comprehensive model.

THEORETICAL BACKGROUND

Customer Knowledge

Customer knowledge is at the origin of most improvements in customer value (Rowley, 2002). Rowley (2002) assumed that customer knowledge is an essential intangible asset for any enterprise, because it enables them to regroup and create value. Dobney (2008) provides an alternative definitive of customer knowledge, that it is the "collection of information and insight that need to have to build stronger customer relationships". Customer knowledge can be classified as knowledge 'for', 'about' or 'from' the customer (Maswera, Dawson, & Edwards, 2006; Salomann et al., 2005; Su et al., 2006).

Knowledge "For" Customer

Knowledge for customer refers to the customer's knowledge about products, services and the market place in general (García-Murillo & Annabi, 2002; Gibbert et al., 2002; Rowley, 2002). This knowledge is highly valuable as it enables tapping the knowledge pool of the customer and therefore sheds light on the reasons behind customers' buying decisions (García-Murillo & Annabi, 2002). Data, information or knowledge for customers can be gained from our other customers, information consulting institutes, our competitors and the company itself to provide information needs of customer (Shamizanjani et al, 2008).

Knowledge "From" Customer

The ideas, thoughts, and information the organization receives from its customers regarding the preferences, creativity, or consumption experience of specific products or services (Desouza and Awazu, 2005). It is customer's knowledge of products, suppliers and markets. This knowledge is highly valuable as it enables tapping the knowledge pool of the customer and therefore sheds light on the reasons behind customers' buying decisions (García-Murillo & Annabi, 2002).

Knowledge "About" Customer

Knowledge "about" customer is a type of knowledge (also data or information which can be analyzed, interpreted and eventually converted to knowledge) that the company attains in order to know its targeted customer better. Companies not only capture knowledge about customers but also purchase data, information and knowledge about customers (Shamizanjani et al., 2008).

Regarding three types of customer knowledge, It`s important and critical to find out other types of customer knowledge in detail in a way that each of them would belong to one of three types of customer knowledge. In fact a more comprehensive typology of customer knowledge is needed while considering knowledge "for", "from" and "about" customer as the base provided for customer knowledge. Indeed the typological model of customer knowledge expands three types of customer knowledge and describes them in more detail in order to make sense each of them. Scholars and practitioners have decomposed customer knowledge in many different types as shown in Table1.

In addition to customer knowledge types mentioned in Table 1, the authors are introduced some other types of customer knowledge for the first time as is shown in Table 2.

As a consequence, regarding different viewpoints of scholars about customer knowledge in additions to authors` point of view, enable us to develop a comprehensive typological model of customer knowledge which is explained in details in next sections.

Table 1. Types of customer knowledge in researchers` point of view

No	Types of Knowledge Management			Reference
1	Knowledge about customer	Potential customers knowledge	Expectation	Day (2000), Davenport et al. (2001)
			Motivation	Day (2000), Davenport et al. (2001)
			Requirements knowledge	Day (2000), Davenport et al. (2001)
		Current customers knowledge	Preferences for products or services	Murillo and Annabi (2002)
			Customers' background	ShamiZanjani et al (2008)
			Demographic	Lee et al. (2006)
			Expectation	Day (2000), Davenport et al. (2001)
			Motivation	Day (2000), Davenport et al. (2001)
2	Knowledge from customer	Environment-related knowledge	Markets knowledge	Murillo and Annabi, (2002)
			Suppliers knowledge	Murillo and Annabi, (2002)
			Competitors' products and services knowledge	ShamiZanjani et al (2008).
		Company-related knowledge	Consumption experience of specific products or services	Desouza, and Awazu (2005)
			Creative ideas about new products and services company	Desouza, and Awazu (2005)
3	Knowledge for customer	Company general knowledge	Company introducing knowledge	ShamiZanjani et al. (2008)
			Company knowledge products	ShamiZanjani et al. (2008)
		Company's environment knowledge	Markets knowledge	ShamiZanjani et al. (2008)
			Government regulation knowledge	ShamiZanjani et al. (2008)
			Suppliers knowledge	Gebert et al. (2003)
			Competitors' products and services knowledge	ShamiZanjani et al. (2008)

Table 2. Types of customer knowledge in authors` point of view

No	Types of Knowledge Management		
1	**Knowledge from customer**	Environment-related knowledge	Government regulation knowledge
2	**Knowledge for customer**	Products and services knowledge	Knowledge about products and services in past
			Knowledge about current products and services
			Knowledge about products and services that will be presented in future

Customer Knowledge Management

Customer Knowledge Management is the application of knowledge management instruments and techniques to support the exchange of knowledge between an enterprise and its customers (Kolbe & Geib, 2005; Rollins & Halinen, 2005; Rowley, 2002), enabling the company to make appropriate strategic business decisions (Rowley, 2002; Su, Chen, & Sha, 2006). CKM can be generally regarded as the processes to capture, share, transfer, and apply the data, information, and knowledge related with customers for organizational benefits. The processes can occur not only among customers and within organizations, but also between organizations and customers (Zhang, 2011). Five styles of CKM as summarised by Gibbert et al. (2002) are identified as:

1. Prosumerism;
2. Team-based co-learning;
3. Mutual innovation;
4. Communities of creation; and
5. Joint IP/ownership.

Each of the above five styles of CKM has its characteristics in the management focus, objectives, processes, systems and performance measurement approaches.

The marketing process view provides a different perspective to look at the CKM process since CKM is about what and how to manage customer knowledge.

Using Wikipedia as an example, Boselli et al. (2008) explore the role of collaborative technologies in supporting and improving service processes and enhancing customer loyalty by identifying and describing certain specific patterns in service development processes. Defining each type of customer knowledge (customer knowledge typology) in one side and gaining benefit from affective technologies like Web 2.0 tools so as to manage customer knowledge on the other side is of high priority for success of CKM process which both are considered in this chapter as a comprehensive model.

Social Software or Web 2.0

Social software has been used when referring to any Internet software which enables groups of people to communicate and to collaborate, from something very familiar such as email, IM and group forms, to new applications such as blogs, SNS, and web based collaborative editing tools (Boyd et al., 2007). The key feature with any social software is that it is easy to use and is usually free at the point of use.

Social software falls under the heading of Web 2.0 applications (Boyd and Ellison, 2007). The Web 2.0 concept was coined officially by Tim O'Reilly and Dale Dougherty (Aharony, 2009). It can be defined as ''the network as platform, spanning all connected devices; Web 2.0 applications are those that make the most of the intrinsic advantages of that platform: delivering software as a continually-updated service that gets better the more people use it, consuming and remixing data from multiple sources, including individual users, while providing their own data and services in a form that allows remixing by others, creating network effects through an 'architecture of participation,' and going beyond the page metaphor of Web 1.0 to deliver rich user experiences'' (O'Reilly, 2005).

This definition has been popular since the first O'Reilly Media Web 2.0 Conference in 2004 (Virkus, 2008), and since then has frequently been cited as the formal definition for the Web 2.0 concept (Serantes, 2009).

As a consequence, during this chapter social software and Web 2.0 are considered as the same notion.

The term "Web 2.0" is not well defined, with numerous definitions in existence (Radcliff, 2007). A number of scholars have attempted to define the Web 2.0, although there is "still a huge amount of disagreement about what Web 2.0 actually means" (O'Reilly, 2005). Some common definitions about web 2.0 according to scholars and researchers` point of view are shown in table 3.

The term Web 2.0 covers a range of software tools which allow users to interact and share data with other users. Actually scholars have mentioned variety of tools using as web 2.0 tools in different cases which are shown in Table 4. As an overall view of this table, it`s obvious that some tools are repeatedly mentioned which shows the importance or effectiveness of them in terms of web 2.0.

Table 3. Definitions of Web 2.0

No	Definitions of Web 2.0	Reference
1	Web2.0 refers to the principles and practice of facilitating information sharing and social interaction by users generating, altering and uploading web-based content whereas its predecessor, Web1.0limitsuserstothe passive viewing and download of largely copyrighted information.	(Liburd, 2012)
2	Aterm associated with "[...] the social use of the Web which allow[s] people to collaborate, to get actively involved in creating content, to generate knowledge and to share information online"	Grosseck (2009)
3	A set of social, economic, and technology trends that collectively form the basis for the next generation of the internet – a more mature, distinct medium characterized by user participation, openness, and network effect.	O'Reilly (2009)
4	The current generation of web-based social networking applications and services designed around architecture of participation and communal collaboration. Web 2.0's authoring tools easily enable users to collaboratively create, share and recreate knowledge from multiple sources, leverage collective intelligence and organize action.	Eijkman (2008)
5	An attitude, not a technology; the network effect; openness; the long tail; trust your users; network as a platform; always beta and small pieces, loosely coupled	Kelly (2008)
6	A global social network that "shifts our focus dramatically away from acquiring information-centred, abstracted second order knowledge into learning as a changing relationship of participation in the world	Eijkman (2008)
7	Web 2.0 is "a space that allows anyone to create and share information online – a space for collaboration, conversation, and interaction; a space that is highly dynamic, flexible, and adaptable.	(Coombs, 2007)
8	Web 2.0 is used to describe web services, formerly provided by software, which rely on the interaction of multiple customers, both as contributors and users of the service itself, to provide the optimal level of service.	(O'Reilly, 2007)
9	Web 2.0 refers to key concepts such as user empowerment, collaboration, active participation, social networking, crowd sourcing, radical transparency, long tail, and rich user experience	(Dearstyne, 2007; O'Reilly, 2005; Tapscott, 2008)

Table 4. Introducing Major Web 2.0 tools

No	Web 2.0 Tools	References
1	Wikis, blogs, forums and Real Simple Syndication (RSS), which strongly support collaboration.	Laughton (2011)
2	Blogs, forums, podcasts, and wikis are the successful implementations of the new generation Web 2.0 technologies. These provide Web 2.0-based applications, programs, and services including web hosting, text-audio-video sharing, communication, social interaction, and many more.	Hossain and Aydin (2011)
3	Wikis, social bookmarking, podcasting, blogs, really simple syndication (RSS), and software as a service (SAAS).	Shu and Chuang (2011)
4	Really Simple Syndication (RSS), blogs, wikis, podcasts, forums and social tagging	Shri Ram et al. (2011)
5	Blogs, calendars, wikis, RSS, image collections, podcasts or vodcasts, social bookmarks, text messages, instant messages, and social networks.	Jeff Howe's (2010)
6	Collaborative publishing sites (Facebook, Bebo, MySpace and Friendster etc), wikis, blogs, social bookmarking sites (del.icio.us, furl, digg etc), and photo sharing sites (flickr, photobucket, etc.).	Harinarayana and Raju (2010)
7	You Tube, Twitter, Facebook, blogs, podcasts, forums, and wikis. It has changed the way entrepreneurs' source and distributes information, enriches the small business service experience and contributes to the value creation process.	Jones (2010)
8	Email, IM, and group forums, to new applications such as blogs, SNS, and webbased collaborative editing tools (Boyd, 2007; Davis, 2003).	Gao et al., (2010)
9	Publication: Weblogs (blogs), wikis, user generated media Syndication: Really simple syndication (RSS) or newsfeeds,social tagging or bookmarking, folksonomies Collaboration: Social networking, peer-to-peer networking,web application program interfaces (APIs) Recombination: mash-ups	Rudman (2010)
10	Blogs, wikis, RSS feeds, socially-based applications such as Facebook, Myspace, YouTube, Flickr and many others.	Ribie`re et al. (2010)
11	Blog, wiki, photo-sharing, social book-marking, IP telephony, videoconference, etc.	Law et al., (2010)
12	Blogs, wikis, podcasts, tags, and social networks	Michael et al.,(2010)
13	Social networking, blogging, wikis, RSS feeds and heightened interactive functionality on the web	Joint (2009)
14	Blogs, wikis, social networks, RSS, tagging	Levy (2009)
15	Blogs, wikis, social networking web sites, such as Facebook and Flickr, and social bookmarking sites, such as Delicious, and 3D environments such as Second Life are examples of some of the tools that are being used to share and collaborate in educational, social, and business contexts.	Minocha (2009)
16	Blogs, wikis, tags, RSS feeds, social bookmarking tools and AJAX	Sudzina (2009)
17	Blogs, wikis, social networking web sites, such as Facebook and Flickr, and social bookmarking sites, such as Delicious, and 3D environments such as Second Life	Minocha (2009)
18	RSS feeds/Syndication/Atom, Blogs, Wikis, Social bookmarking and resource sharing, Social networking sites, Media sharing,Mashups	Jane Secker (2008)
19	Blogs, wikis, RSS, podcasts and videocasts, mashups, social sharing services, communication tools, social networks, folksomonies and tagging, and virtual worlds.	Kelly (2008)
20	Twitter, Facebook, MySpace, wikis, Google Docs, and blogs which allow the exchange of thoughts via the web without restrictions of time or place.	Samuel Kai-Wai Chu and David M. Kennedy (2008)
21	Blogs, wikis, social networking, social bookmarking, podcasting	Gray et al., (2008)
22	Blogs, discussion groups, Wikis, music streams with rating features, social networking platforms or picture sharing	Alexander R.M. Schellong (2008)
23	Blogs, wikis, RSS (Really Simple Syndication) and social tagging	Sirje Virkus (2008)
24	Blogs, Social networking services. File-sharing communities. Forums/bulletin board systems. Some sites combine two or more of the above categories. For example, the Twitter web site offers a social networking and (micro)blogging service	Constantinides and Fountain, (2008); Kennedy et al., (2007); Lai and Turban (2008)
25	Communicative: Social networking, Blogs, Audio blogs, Video blogs, IM tools, Podcasts and Web-conferencing) Collaborative publishing: wikis, Documentative (content management):Blogs, Videoblogs, E-portfolios, Open Journalism, Generative:Mashups, VCOPs, Virtual Learning Worlds (VLWs), Interactive:Social bookmarking, RSS, VCOPs, VLWs	McGee and Diaz (2007); Richardson (2007)

Regarding tools which could be ranked according to frequency mentioned in table 3, eight Web 2.0 tools are selected as the most frequently used or mentions tools of web 2.0 which are: Blog, Wiki, Social Network, Social bookmarking, Tag, Podcast, RSS, and Mashup. In fact these tools are considered as Web 2.0 tools which are potentially capable using for managing customer knowledge. In order to find out definitions and descriptions of eight Web 2.0 tools mentioned above, different viewpoints of scholars is provided in the next sections.

Web 2.0 and CKM

The emerging Web 2.0 and social software applications open up a new horizon for companies to engage in a more exciting and meaningful relationship with customers. Firms have recently started to implement social software in exploiting and managing customer knowledge assets. Recent studies have shown increasing interest in the relationships between social software and KM, expounding the special role of social software in disseminating and creating knowledge (Zhang, 2011). For instance, Avram (2006) analyzes how to use social software to regulate the five core KM activities. Efimova (2005) studies how to use weblogs for PKM, particularly "personal knowledge repositories and learning journals or networking instruments". Greenfield (2007) assesses four enterprise social bookmarking solutions and argues that social bookmarking applications can provide a very effective KM platform. Surveying different social software web sites, Chai et al. (2006) analyze and categorize the revenue models of social software including advertising, premium memberships, affiliate programs, donations, and merchandize sale (CNN Money, 2006).

Researchers start to investigate the role of IT for CKM. Bueren et al. (2004) describe how to utilize ITs to support CRM with an integrated CKM process in order to achieve knowledge transparency, knowledge dissemination, knowledge development, and knowledge efficiency. Despite the increasing interests of social software and CKM in recent studies of KM, the economic value of social software for firms is not well understood. Prior research provides solid foundations for understanding the role of social software in KM and the special features of CKM, but there lacks the research investigating social software and CKM jointly. Social software provides various supports for CKM by facilitating CKM processes, promoting the conversions between customers' explicit and tacit knowledge, and providing effective and efficient ways of bonding customers with organizations. (Zhang, 2011). The Web 2.0 environment has provided organizations with a broad range of new tools and strategies for communicating with their customers, and marketers can capitalize on these developments in different ways by actively or passively engaging in the use of these applications as part of their overall marketing strategy (Davidson, 2011).

As mentioned, Web 2.0 tools are capable to manage different types of customer knowledge. Since each of Web 2.0 tools could be applied for special purpose in organization in a way that facilitate and strength the relationship between customer and organization. In next sections the relationship between Web 2.0 tools and CKM will be more explained and discussed by introducing "Grape Model".

THE CONCEPTUAL FRAMEWORK

Integration of Web 2.0 and CKM (CKM 2.0)

In order to find the relationship between Web 2.0 tools introduced in previous sections and the three major types of customer knowledge as is provided by customer knowledge typology (Table 1), it`s critical and influential to comprehend the characteristics of Web 2.0 tools and also specifications of each type of customer knowledge simultaneously so as to develop a robust and comprehensive framework encompassing Web 2.0 tools and CKM. As a matter of fact, combination of these two concepts allows us to introduce a new generation of CKM which is called "CKM 2.0". This concept is mentioned for the first time in the field of CRM, CKM and related literature. Indeed when "CKM 2.0" is mentioned using Web 2.0 tools in CKM processes comes to mind. In fact this model explores the ways of utilizing Web 2.0 tools in managing customer knowledge (from, for and about customer) in organizations which is shown in Figure 1 as the "Grape Model".

Figure 1. CKM 2.0Model (Grape Model)

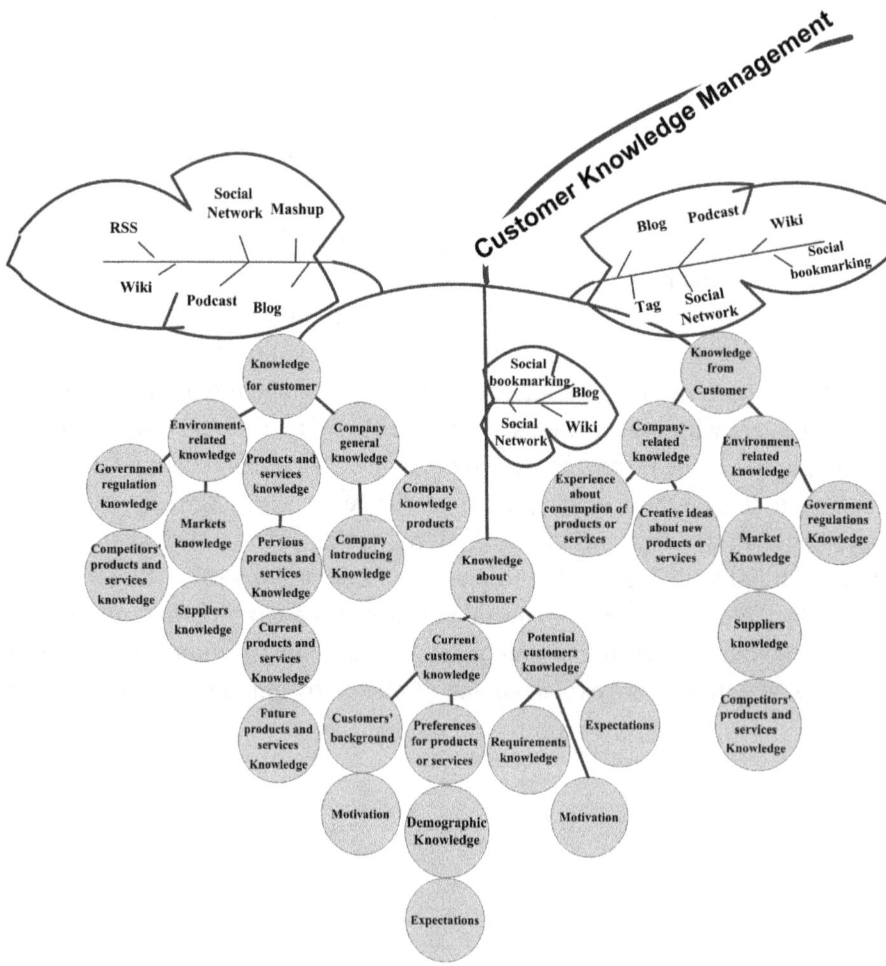

As seen in Figure 1 customer knowledge is decomposed into different types of knowledge for each of knowledge "for" customer, knowledge "from" customer and knowledge "about" customer. In this way these types of customer knowledge can be measured and actually could easily be comprehended because they are more tangible as a result of decomposition. Indeed, through this framework, the relationship between each kind of customer knowledge (For/From/About) and various type of organizational knowledge in different field and viewpoints are clarified. Altogether, considering each type of customer knowledge together, cause to facilitate managing them and also lead the organizations to higher levels of performance in CKM. According to the "Grape Model" in terms of the following items, utilizing Web 2.0 tool for customer knowledge is explained in details.

Blog: Blogs are probably the most popular type of social software. Blogs typically allow creation of new pages, publishing of materials in forms such as text, graphics, audio and video, different presentations of content, facilities for archiving, and mechanisms to allow other authors to add entries or provide feedback on entries (Duffy & Bruns, 2006). As a result blogs are considered as a tool for creating relationship between organization (the author of the blog) in one side and customer as the user of blog on the other side. Actually this mutual relationship facilitates ways of communication for customers so as to express their ideas, point of views and any kind of suggestion of critique about the organization or products and services. Therefore blogs could be used so as to extract knowledge "from" customer and also knowledge "for" customer. Blogs can elicit knowledge "for" customer through publishing information like organizational environment information or current and future products and services. In fact blogs want customers to give their valuable ideas. Blogs can be used to extract knowledge "for" customer through advertising in order to attract positional customers as real customers and can attempt to increase their loyalty by giving suitable and useful information.

Wiki: Wikis are web pages that can be written and edited by anyone, or the wiki can have a restricted group of users with writing and editing privileges (Paul and Chung, 2010). Wiki users can create wiki pages and fill them with a variety of content (e.g. Text, images, graphs, and maps). The characteristics of a wiki as a shared tool fit well with the processes associated with collaborative learning and knowledge management (Nevgi et al., 2006). As mentioned using wikis, users are able to publish or edit any kind of information without any limitations. This capability of wikis enables organizations to extract implicit knowledge of customers in cases of customer`s experience in using products and service. In addition organizations can attempt to gain customer`s ideas about new products and any other similar Knowledge using wikis. Therefore wikis can be considered as a tool for extract knowledge "from" customer and knowledge "for" customer.

RSS: RSS feeds are a technology primarily associated with blogs. They allow users to "syndicate and republish content on the web" (Maness, 2006). RSS in that way would greatly serve the purpose not only for managing information but also reducing the information overload (Harinarayana et al., 2010). Using RSS users are able to access latest topic of news without need to brows different websites. Similarly customers of an organization can be aware of new product and services and any other news of the organization through RSS. In fact RSS is useful for extract knowledge "for" customer.

Social Networking: A social network is an online community of people interacting over such topics as business, culture, and friendship. Before the establishment of social-networking services using the internet in the past decade (Palvia and Pancaro, 2010). Social networks are driven by an individual's need for communication, need for belongingness and affected by gender, personality, education, and attractiveness. (Kiehne, 2004). The main reason for creation of social networks is to provide opportunity for people who have something in common and similar interests to communicate with each other and talk about their ideas and also share them. Organizations can benefit from social networking through creating virtual communities so as to link their potential and current customers to each other and sharing information about experience about usage of goods or services and other similar information. Moreover, organizations can chat and communicate with customers. These capabilities help organizations to gain new and brilliant ideas from customers. In fact Social networking is useful for extract knowledge "for", "from" and "about" customer.

Tag: Tags are labels or keywords to describe features of web content. Tagging is a kind of indexing, but the term "indexing" usually describes work done by professionals, whereas tagging is done by anyone interested in sharing tags (identified terms) to describe a document in a public network space (Lu and Hsiao, 2009). Users can use Tag as a tool to present their imagination and insights about a data object in the form of words. Organizations can use this tool to ask about ideas of customers in different fields of interest and actually use this tool for extract knowledge "from" customer.

Mashup: A mashup, in web development, is a web page, or web application, that uses and combines data, presentation or functionality from two or more sources to create new services (Wikipedia). Mashups are a way to reuse the increasing amount of information being available on the Web; as well as a trend for supporting tools and technologies to make application development in this environment easy (Wilde, 2006). Mashup could be used similar to Google Map to give telephone and address information of organization or information about other branches and plants customers would need it. As a result Mashup can be considered as a tool for extract knowledge "for" customers

Podcast: A podcast is a series of digital media files in audio or video format. It allows users to publish their audio and video recordings on the web episodically and to download them through multiple devices including cell phones, iPods, net books, laptops, desktops, and similar handheld devices (Richardson, 2006). Organizations can create video in order to advertise or show ways of using their products or services and guide customers about the application of products in the best way. Similarly customers are able to use Podcast as a tool to show their own created video of their idea or suggestions. As a consequence, Podcat can be used as a tool to extract knowledge "from" and also knowledge "for" customers.

Social Bookmarking: Social bookmarking is a tool used to mark web pages which a user found relevant, tag them with a keyword which will make them retrievable in the future, and also to send these sites to other users who might find them useful as well (Gordon-Murnane, 2006). In fact, one of the powerful characteristics of this tool is that users can save a collection of resources on web through a database in order to publish or share on web sites automatically. Furthermore users are able to create keywords on the resources in a way that others can use them to find others` comments or ideas. So organization can utilize this tool for extracting knowledge "from" and also knowledge "about" customers.

In accordance with what mentioned above, the "Grape Model" encompasses different types of customer knowledge in detail as "grapes" which is related to different Web 2.0 tools as "leaves" which support encompassing grapes.

RESEARCH METHODOLOGY

This research is implemented in three phases. At the first step, the "Grape Model" is designed by reviewing the background and literature of study which is mentioned earlier in previous sections. By the second step, validation of this model is evaluated via questionnaires answered by experts. At last, application of the CKM through Web2.0 tools (CKM 2.0) in four Iranian companies in different fields of activity is measured using "Grape Model".

The tool utilized for data collection in phases two and three is a questionnaire. Two questionnaires have been designed and distributed in this contribution:

- The first questionnaire is devised for surveying experts in order to validate the proposed model. This questionnaire is distributed and collected among 31 experts. Snowball sampling technique is used for identification of them due to the limitation in number of related experts.
- The second questionnaire is devised to evaluate application of CKM using Web 2.0 tools in four selected Iranian companies. The Method of research in the second part is simple random method.

DATA ANALYSIS AND RESULTS

Validation of "Grape Model"

In order to validate the "Grape Model" 31 experts were asked to fill the questionnaire. This questionnaire consists of three sections. The first section of the questionnaire was designed to elicit the demographic information of the respondents. The second section includes 30 factors and indicators for evaluation of different types of knowledge "for" customer, knowledge "about" customer and knowledge "from" customer. Finally the third part of the questionnaire consists of 16 questions for examining the application of Web 2.0 tools in customer knowledge management. Each question were measured using 5-point likert scales ranging from 1 (least important) to 5 (most important). In fact experts were asked to indicate the perceived importance of the factors and indicators when evaluating different parts of customer knowledge and also using Web 2.0 tools for managing of different types of customer knowledge. The respondents were presented with adequate explanation on what the questionnaire was trying to measure and how they should answer it. There has been an attempt to pervasively search and find the best possible and accessible experts. As a matter of fact, In order to gather expert data, community of practitioners and scholars in the fields of knowledge management, customer relationship management, customer services and also faculty members with considerable experience in research and empirical experience in the field of knowledge management, CKM and CRM are selected through snowball sampling technique.

Reliability Analysis

Reliability analysis (Chronbach's Alpha) was conducted to test the reliability of gathered data with the customer knowledge and using Web 2.0 tools in CKM questionnaire. The results illustrated that the Alpha coefficient is 0.932 that is considered acceptable as an indication of reliability for basic research (Nunnally, 1967).

Data Distribution Test

For the identification of the distribution status of gathered data, the Kolmogorov–Smirnov test was conducted. The results of the Kolmogorov–Smirnov (K–S) test indicated that the distribution of the indicators correspond to the normal distribution (The significance for all of the indicators is more than 0.05). According to the results, the parametric T-Student test was chosen to determine the importance and evaluation of each question.

Determining the Different Types of Each Customer Knowledge (For/From/About)

In order to elicit different parts of each type of customer knowledge the following hypotheses are tested:

- H_0: Experts are not agreeing about each part of customer knowledge in the questionnaire.
- H_1: Experts are agreeing about each part of customer knowledge in the questionnaire.

As the result of the test, since the significance that is less than 0.05, shows the hypothesis H_1 is accepted. This means that average of responses is more than 3 (4 or 5) for each question.

Examining the Importance of Each Type of Customer Knowledge

In order to recognize the importance of each type of customer knowledge according to responses of experts in details, Friedman test in conducted. The results of Friedman test consists of two sections. Since the significance in the first section is less than 0.05 for all tests, then the hypothesis H_1 is accepted. Actually it means that all kinds of customer knowledge, have different importance in expert`s point of view. Results for each customer knowledge (For, from and about) in the second section are demonstrated in Table 5 in details.

Table 5. Average of Importance Ranks for "Knowledge for/from/about customer"

Types of "Knowledge for Customer"	Average of Rank	Rank
Current products and services Knowledge	6.52	1
Future products and services Knowledge	6.27	2
Pervious products and services Knowledge	5.15	3
Competitors' products and services knowledge	5.05	4
Company knowledge products	4.85	5
Market Knowledge	4.75	6
Company introducing Knowledge	4.65	7
Suppliers knowledge	4.05	8
Government regulation knowledge	3.72	9
Types of "Knowledge from Customer"	**Average of Rank**	**Rank**
Competitors' products and services knowledge	4.12	1
Experience about consumption of products or services	3.93	2
Markets knowledge	3.82	3
Creative ideas about new products or services	3.68	4
Suppliers knowledge	3.43	5
Government regulations Knowledge	2.02	6

continued on following page

Table 5. Continued

Types of "Knowledge about Customer"	Average of Rank	Rank
Customers' background	5.35	1
Preferences for products or services	4.98	2
Demographic Knowledge	4.97	3
Motivation	4.60	4
Expectations	4.38	5
Requirements knowledge of potential customers	4.12	6
Motivations of potential customers	3.90	7
Expectations of potential customers	3.70	8

Considering Table 5 it`s obvious that "Current products and services Knowledge" and "Future products and services Knowledge" are more important other types for "Knowledge for customer" in experts` viewpoint. In addition, "Competitors' products and services knowledge" and "Experience about consumption of products or services" are most ranked knowledge types for "Knowledge from customer". Finally the first two ranked knowledge for "Knowledge about customer" are "customers' background" and "preferences for products or services". Also, "Expectations of potential customers" in less important in experts` point of view.

Exploring the Use of Web 2.0 Tools in CKM

In order to clarifying the application of each kind of Web 2.0 tools for each three types of customer knowledge (For/From/About) the following hypotheses are tested:

H_0: Experts are not agreeing about application of determined Web 2.0 tools for managing each types of customer knowledge.

H_1: Experts are agreeing about Web 2.0 mentioned for each part of customer knowledge in the questionnaire.

Since the significance is less than 0.05, the hypothesis H_1 is accepted for each question in this section.

Examining the Importance of Web 2.0 Tools for Managing Different Types of Customer Knowledge

Regarding comprehend the importance of each Web 2.0 tool for managing any type of customer knowledge, Friedman test is conducted similar previous sections. The result of Friedman test indicates that the significance is less than 0.05 for all related tests. It means that application of each Web 2.0 tools for managing any kind of customer knowledge, have different importance in experts` view point. In Table 6, Usage of mentioned Web 2.0 tools is ranked in order to manage customer knowledge.

As mentioned in Table 5, application of social networks for managing knowledge "from" customer and knowledge "about "customer and also using Blogs to managing knowledge "from" customer and knowledge "for "customer are high-ranked Web 2.0 tools by experts. To conclude, social network and

Table 6. Ranks of Web 2.0 tools for managing Customer knowledge

Web 2.0 Tools	Customer Knowledge			Average of Rank	Rank
	For	From	About		
Social Network		√		10.18	1
Social Network			√	9.98	2
Blog		√		9.27	3
Blog	√			9.10	4
Social network	√			9.10	4
Podcast	√			8.87	6
Blog			√	8.73	7
RSS	√			8.73	7
Tag		√		8.13	9
Social Bookmarking			√	8.02	10
Mashup	√			7.93	11
Wiki		√		7.85	12
Wiki	√			7.78	13
Social Bookmarking		√		7.75	14
Wiki			√	7.63	15
Podcast		√		6.93	16

Blogs are more interesting for experts in order to managing customer knowledge. In the contrary, application of Podcast for managing knowledge "from" customer and also Wiki for managing knowledge "about" customer is low-ranked by experts.

SURVEYING THE "GRAPE MODEL" IN FOUR IRANIAN INDUSTRIES

In order to applying the "Grape Model" in Iranian organizations, four industries (Software Industry, Banking Industry, Auto Industry and Cement Industry) are selected. For each of industries, one company is selected since these companies seem to be more knowledge-based and naturally need a well-established relationship with customers. What is more, these companies came from both service-based industries (Software services, Banking) and product-based industries (Auto and Cement). Parskhodro Company for Auto industry, Siman Sepahan for Cement Industry, System Group for Software Industry and Sepah Bank for Banking Industry are chosen. A brief background of each company is summarized in Table 7.

In fact exploring these four industries in Iran, give us a valuable insight so as to evaluate different Iranian companies in gaining competitive advantage over other competitors through usage of CKM advantages and also Web 2.0 tools. In order to evaluate each of companies four questionnaires were designed which were structured in three sections. The first section devoted to extract demographic information of respondents. The second section was used to survey the use of different customer knowledge types which consist of 30 questions and finally the third section to some extend company benefits from using Web 2.0 tools in managing customer knowledge asking 16 questions. Each question was measured using 5-point likert scales ranging from 1 (very low) to 5 (very High). In order to ask respondents to

Table 7. Introduction of Iranian companies

Company	Industry	Date of Establishment	Product/Service Orientation	Size of Company (Number of Employees)	Private/Public	Ranking in Iran
System Group	Software	1987	Service-oriented	1100	Private	Not between Top 100
Sepah Bank	Banking	1925	Service-oriented	35000	Public	21
Siman Sepahan	Cement	1969	Product-oriented	1000	Private	Not between Top 100
Parskhodro	Auto	1960	Product-oriented	7000	Private	46

fill the questionnaires, experts and managers in the fields of knowledge management, marketing and sales, after sales services and CRM of each company were considered as statistical population. Since the statistical population for each of companies ranged from 50 to 110, 45 respondents had chosen using simple random method. A total of 30 out of 45 questionnaires completed by the respondents for each of companies which indicate the rate of 67%. Reliability analysis (Chronbach's Alpha) was conducted to test the reliability of gathered data. Since the value of Chronbach's Alpha is more than 0.90 for all four companies (0.936 for Parskhodro, 0.983 for Siman Sepahan, 0.904 for System Group and 0.934 for Sepah Bank), that is considered acceptable as an indication of reliability for basic research.

Managing Different Types of Customer Knowledge in Iranian Industries

For identification of the distribution status of gathered data, the Kolmogorov–Smirnov test was conducted. Results indicate that the distribution of all the questions for each company correspond to the normal distribution (The significance for all of the questions is more than 0.05). As consequence, the parametric T-Student test was chosen to further analysis and explanations. As a result, the hypotheses are tested similar the previous sections. In Table 8, the usages of each type of customer knowledge are analyzed in details. "√" stands for accepted H_1 hypothesis and also "–"outlines that hypothesis H_1 is not accepted for related type of knowledge.

Table 8. Result of T-Student Test for using different types of customer knowledge in four Iranian companies

	System Group	Sepah Bank	Siman Sepahan	Parskhodro
Types of "Knowledge about customer"				
Customers' background	√	–	–	–
Preferences for products or services	√	–	–	–
Demographic Knowledge	–	–	–	–
Motivation	–	–	–	–
Expectations	√	–	–	–
Requirements knowledge of potential customers	–	–	–	–
Motivations of potential customers	–	–	–	–
Expectations of potential customers	–	–	–	–

continued on following page

Table 8. Continued

	System Group	Sepah Bank	Siman Sepahan	Parskhodro
Types of "Knowledge from Customer"				
Competitors' products and services knowledge	√	–	–	–
Experience about consumption of products or services	√	–	√	√
Markets knowledge	–	–	–	–
Creative ideas about new products or services	–	√	–	√
Suppliers knowledge	√	–	–	–
Government regulations Knowledge	√	–	–	–
Types of "Knowledge for Customer"				
Current products and services Knowledge	√	√	√	√
Future products and services Knowledge	√	–	–	–
Pervious products and services Knowledge	√	√	√	√
Competitors' products and services knowledge	–	–	–	–
Company knowledge products	√	√	–	–
Market Knowledge	√	–	–	–
Company introducing Knowledge	√	√	√	√
Suppliers knowledge	–	–	–	–
Government regulation knowledge	√	–	–	–

By over viewing the Table 8, it seems that System group is more successful in managing customer knowledge in compare of other companies because it`s obvious that this company uses all three types of customer knowledge. Actually only System Group company benefits from knowledge "about" customer. The reason behind this finding refers to this fact that software development processes are knowledge-based and also involving customers in these processes is so essential and influential so as to extract their preferences and interests before and also during the development of software products.

What is more, most of companies benefit from managing customer knowledge in the fields of "Experience about consumption of products or services", "Current products and services Knowledge","Pervious products and services Knowledge" and "Company introducing Knowledge". It also means that managing knowledge "for" customer is more important two other types of customer knowledge. Also there is not enough attention to knowledge "about customer" in Iranian companies.

Application of Web 2.0 Tools for Managing Customer Knowledge in Iranian Industries

As results of T-Student test for evaluating four companies in CKM using Web 2.0 tools, some interesting inferences can be drawn. At first only two companies (System Group and Sepah Bank) use Web 2.0 tools in order to manage customer knowledge. Table 9, shows types of knowledge "for" customer in which is managed through Web 2.0 tools in these two companies.

According to Table 9, Iranian companies exploit Web 2.0 tool in order to manage knowledge "for" customer in compare of other types of customer knowledge. What is more, despite the fact that Sepah Bank is not exploiting "Future products and services Knowledge" type of customer knowledge but this

Table 9. Types of knowledge "for" customer is managed trough Web 2.0 tools in two Iranian companies

Types of "Knowledge for Customer"	Rank	System Group	Sepah Bank
Current products and services Knowledge	1	*	*
Future products and services Knowledge	2	*	–
Pervious products and services Knowledge	3	*	*

bank and also System Group Company both benefit from the first three high-ranked types of knowledge "for" customer. Moreover "Podcast" and "RSS" are Web 2.0 tools utilized for CKM in Iranian companies as is shown in Table 10. In fact, System Group Company benefits from "RSS" for managing knowledge "for" customer and "Podcast" for managing knowledge "for" customer. Furthermore "RSS" for managing "knowledge for customer" is used by Sepah Bank.

As a consequence, "RSS" and "Podcast" are popular Web 2.0 tools in Iranian Industries. In addition, since Sepah Bank utilizes "RSS" and also System Group exploits both "Podcat" and "RSS", it is concluded that Iranian companies use medium-ranked Web 2.0 tools for managing customer knowledge.

According to results of this section, it seems that service-oriented companies (especially System Group Company) more than product-oriented companies benefits from using Web 2.0 tools in managing customer knowledge. This fact demonstrates that service-based companies pay more attention to customer knowledge for delivering services using Web 2.0 tools in order to accelerate and facilitate of CKM process. Another fact to consideration is that service-oriented companies often interact with customers directly and more frequently than product-based companies.

DISCUSSION AND IMPLICATIONS

The main goal of this chapter was to introduce the "Grape Model" as a robust combination of CKM (through introducing a comprehensive typology of customer knowledge) and Web 2.0 which introduces CKM 2.0 as the new generation of CKM which deals with Web 2.0 or Web 2.0 tools to manage different types of customer knowledge. Previous research in the field of customer knowledge had focused on customer knowledge specifically in a way that some types of customer knowledge are considered for especial purposes. In fact they had not attempt to develop a comprehensive model as typology of customer knowledge. This fact has made the subject of the current study very important and influential. For example Paquette (2006) considers customer knowledge as a combination of supply chain knowledge, partner knowledge and customer knowledge. Consequently Murillo & Annabi (2002), introduced a model considered customer knowledge as a part of organizational knowledge that focused on knowledge of products and services and knowledge for helping customers in select and buy products. Similarly, other

Table 10. Result of T-Student Test for using different types

Web 2.0 Tools	Knowledge "for" Customer		Average of Rank	Rank
	System Group	Sepah Bank		
Podcast	*	–	8.87	6
RSS	*	*	8.73	7

researchers have focused on patterns, management processes, and approaches of CKM (e.g. Rowley, 2002; Gebert et al, 2002) In compare of these studies, Shamizanjani (2008) goes even further and emphasizes on a model of CKM which deals with customer knowledge in three layers (knowledge from/for/about customer). For each layer different types of knowledge is recognized. Although this model encompasses various types of knowledge for each three layer, but it seems that they are not in detail enough and as a result this model is not comprehensive. Since little attention has been paid to typology of knowledge of customer in organizations, this study attempted develop a framework so as to enable organizations to evaluate and use of each type of customer knowledge and also give us an insight to identify and manage customer knowledge in a way that the "Grape Model" is introduced as the most comprehensive conceptual model in customer knowledge typology. In fact the "Grape Model" encompasses all types of customer knowledge mentioned in previous researches in addition to some types of customer knowledge which is introduced by authors of this chapter.

In the field of Web 2.0, Researchers have focused on Web 2.0 or Web 2.0 tools in different points of view. For example Fou, Lou and Vang (2008), explored the role of Web 2.0 in creation of social networks and also have surveyed the effects of Web 2.0 on social software structures. Similarly others have introduced Web 2.0 tools in different viewpoints (e.g. Laughton, 2011; Shu and Chuang, 2011; Harinarayana and Raju, 2010; Rudman, 2010; Joint, 2009). In this research eight Web 2.0 tools are introduced according to application and frequency of use of each Web 2.0 tools as mentioned by other researchers. In fact these Web 2.0 tools are mostly used and explored in different fields of interest and propose by a wide range of researchers.

Despite the fact that CKM and Web 2.0 tools has become the field of interest of researchers, but identifying relationship between CKM and Web 2.0 tools in organizations is not paid attention enough and seems to the early steps. In fact According to literature, researchers rarely have considered Web 2.0 and customer knowledge together. Most of researches in this field are devoted to exploring the relationship between Web 2.0 tools and organizational knowledge. For example Avram, G. (2006), has explored the use of social software tools in order to harmonizing the five main steps in knowledge management process. Efimova, L. (2005), surveyed how blogs are used as managing personal knowledge. As a result, all the previous studies deal with social software tools in one side and knowledge management in the other side. On the contrary, Zhang, Z. (2011) has studied the relationship between social software tools and CKM and shows that the optimal level of social software can be obtained under certain conditions and how the level changes with the initial index of customer knowledge base, transactional benefits, and the positive and negative effects of the social software (Zhang, 2011). But this research is not as comprehensive as the "Grape Model". This fact dramatically strengthens and clarifies the importance of this research. In fact this research didn`t focused on use of different Web 2.0 tools according to specifications of them. What is more, Web 2.0 tools are not explored for managing each of three types of customer knowledge for organizations.

As a result, the "Grape Model" seems to be comprehensive in compare of previous models mentioned by researchers in a way that encompasses different type of customer knowledge as a robust and comprehensive typology model for customer knowledge in one side and also the most important and applicable Web 2.0 tools on the other side and provide a meaningful and conceptual relationship between this two sides. As a matter of fact the model of this research focused on utilizing customer knowledge in organizations in a way that gain competitive advantage using Web 2.0 tools.

SUGGESTIONS FOR FUTURE RESEARCH

It is suggested that future research could be conducted to investigate the social and cultural obstacles in using Web 2.0 tools in organizations. What is more surveying the "Grape Model" in a wider population in which encompasses more companies in different field of industries is suggested. In addition, use of the "Grape Model" so as to compare the capability of companies in managing customer knowledge in private and public organizations would be interesting. Moreover exploring risks and challenges in using of Web 2.0 tools and also use it so as to manage customer knowledge is helpful for organizations to overcome probable related obstacles.

REFERENCES

Aharony, N. (2009). Web 2.0 use by librarians. *Library & Information Science Research*, *31*(1), 29–37. doi:10.1016/j.lisr.2008.06.004

Avram, G. (2006). At the crossroads of knowledge management and social software. *Electronic Journal of Knowledge Management*, *4*(1), 1–10.

Awad, E. M., & Ghaziri, H. M. (2004). *Knowledge Management*. Upper Saddle River, NJ: Pearson/Prentice-Hall.

Boselli, R., Cesarini, M., & Mezzanzanica, M. (2008). Customer knowledge and service development, the web 2.0 role in co-production. *Proceedings of World Academy of Science,Engineering, and Technology*, *30*(1), 1–20.

Boyd, D., & Ellison, N. (2007). Social network sites: Definition, history, and scholarship. *Journal of Computer-Mediated Communication*, *13*(1), 7–15. doi:10.1111/j.1083-6101.2007.00393.x

Chai, K., Potdar, V., & Chang, E. (2006). A survey of revenue models for current generation social software's systems. Lecture Notes in Computer Science, 4704, 724-38.

Constantinides, E., & Fountain, S. J. (2008). Web 2.0: Conceptual foundations and marketing issues, *Journal of Direct. Data and Digital Marketing Practice*, *9*(3), 231–244. doi:10.1057/palgrave.dddmp.4350098

Currie, J. P. (2010). Web 2.0 for reference services staff training and communication. *RSR. Reference Services Review*, *38*(1), 152–157. doi:10.1108/00907321011020789

Davenport, T. H., Harris, J. G., & Kohli, A. K. (2001). How do they know their customers so well? *MIT Sloan Management Review*, *42*(2), 63–73.

Davidson, R. (2011). Web 2.0 as a marketing tool for conference centres. *International Journal of Event and Festival Management*, *2*(2), 117–138. doi:10.1108/17582951111136559

Day, G. (2000). Managing market relationships. *Journal of the Academy of Marketing Science*, *28*(1), 24–30. doi:10.1177/0092070300281003

Dearstyne, B. (2007). Blogs, mashups & wikis: Oh, my! *Information Management Journal*, *41*(4), 25–31.

Desouza, K. C., & Awazu, Y. (2005). Maintaining knowledge management systems: A strategic imperative. *Journal of the American Society for Information Science and Technology*, *56*(7), 765–768. doi:10.1002/asi.20149

Dobney.com. (2008). *What is customer knowledge*. Retrieved from www.dobney.com/Knowledge/ck_definition.htm

Duffy, P., & Bruns, A. (2006). *The use of blogs, wikis and RSS in Education: A conversation of possibilities*. Paper presented at the Online Learning and Teaching Conference, Brisbane, Queensland, Australia.

Eijkman, H. (2008). Web 2.0 as a non-foundational network-centric space. *Campus-Wide Information Systems*, *25*(2), 95–104.

Feng, T., & Tian, J. (2005). Customer knowledge management and condition analysis of successful CKM implementation. In *Proceedings of the fourth international Conference on machine learning and cybernetics*, Guanghou.

Gao, Q., Dai, Y., Fan, Z., & Kang, R. (2010). Understanding factors affecting perceived sociability of social software. *Computers in Human Behavior*, *26*(6), 1846–1861. doi:10.1016/j.chb.2010.07.022

García-Murillo, M., & Annabi, H. (2002). Customer knowledge management. *The Journal of the Operational Research Society*, *53*(8), 875–884. doi:10.1057/palgrave.jors.2601365

Gebert, H., Geib, M., Kolbe, L., & Brenner, W. (2003). Knowledge-enabled customer relationship management: Integrating customer relationship management and knowledge concepts. *Journal of Knowledge Management*, *7*(5), 107–123. doi:10.1108/13673270310505421

Gibbert, M., Leibold, M., & Probst, G. (2002). Five styles of customer knowledge management and how smart companies use them to create value. *European Management Journal*, *20*(5), 459–469. doi:10.1016/S0263-2373(02)00101-9

Gordon-Murnane, L. (2006). Social bookmarking, folksonomies and web 2.0 tools. *Searcher*, *14*(6), 26–58.

Gray, K., Thompson, C., Clerehan, R., Sheard, J., & Hamilton, M. (2008). Web 2.0 authorship: Issues of referencing and citation for academic integrity. *The Internet and Higher Education*, *11*(1), 112–118. doi:10.1016/j.iheduc.2008.03.001

Greenfield, D. (2007). Social bookmarking apps provide a new knowledge management platform, eWeek.com, August 12.

Grosseck, G. (2009). To use or not to use web 2.0 in higher education? *Procedia: Social and Behavioral Sciences*, *1*(1), 478–482. doi:10.1016/j.sbspro.2009.01.087

Harinarayana, N. S., & Raju, N. V. (2010). Web 2.0 features in university library web sites. *The Electronic Library*, *28*(1), 69–88. doi:10.1108/02640471011023388

Hossain, M. D. M., & Aydin, H. (2011). A Web 2.0-based collaborative model for multicultural education. *Multicultural Education & Technology Journal*, *5*(2), 116–128. doi:10.1108/17504971111142655

Johnston, R. (2008). Knowledge management in the Web 2.0 age, Associations Now, January, from: www.asaecenter.org/PublicationsResources/ANowDetail. Cfm? ItemNumber1/430024.

Joint, N. (2009). ANTAEUS the Web 2.0 challenge to libraries. *Library Review*, *58*(3), 167–175. doi:10.1108/00242530910942027

Jones, B. (2010). Entrepreneurial marketing and the Web 2.0 interface. *Journal of Research in Marketing and Entrepreneurship*, *12*(2), 143–152. doi:10.1108/14715201011090602

Kasavana, M. L., Nusair, K. H., & Teodosic, K. (2010). Online social networking: Redefining the human web. *Journal of Hospitality and Tourism Technology*, *1*(1), 68–82. doi:10.1108/17579881011023025

Kelly, B. (2008). Library 2.0 and information literacy: the tools. In P. Godwin & J. Parker (Eds.), *Literacy Meets Library 2.0*. London: Facet Publishing.

Kennedy, G., Dalgarno, B., Gray, K., Judd, T., Waycott, J., Bennett, S.,... Churchward, A. (2007). The next generation are not big users of Web 2.0 technologies: Mpreliminary findings, ICT: Providing Choices for Learners and Learning. Proceedings ASCILITE Singapore 2007, from: www.ascilite.org.au/conferences/singapore07/procs/kennedy.pdf

Kiehne, T. P. (2004). Social networking systems: history, critique, and knowledge management potentials, unpublished manuscript, University of Texas, Austin, TX, from: www. ischool.utexas.edu/, i385q/archive/kiehne_t/kiehne (2004)-sns.pdf

Kolbe, L. M., & Geib, M. (2005). Customer knowledge management. *In Proceedings of the 38th Hawaii international conference on system sciences* (HICSS).

Lai, L. S. L., & Turban, E. (2008). Groups formation and operations in the Web 2.0 environment and social networks. *Group Decision and Negotiation*, *17*(5), 387–402. doi:10.1007/s10726-008-9113-2

Lai-Chong Law, E., & Nguyen-Ngoc, A. V. (2010). Analysis of cross-cultural online collaborative learning with social software. *Interactive Technology and Smart Education*, *7*(4), 247–263. doi:10.1108/17415651011096058

Laughton, P. (2011). The use of wikis as alternatives to learning content management systems. *The Electronic Library*, *29*(2), 225–235. doi:10.1108/02640471111125186

Lee, M. K. O., Cheung, C. M. K., Lim, K. H., & Sia, C. L. (2006). Understanding customer knowledge sharing in web – based discussion boards, an exploratory study. *Internet Research*, *16*(3), 289–303. doi:10.1108/10662240610673709

Levy, M. (2009). Web 2.0 implications on knowledge management. *Journal of Knowledge Management*, *13*(1), 120–134. doi:10.1108/13673270910931215

Liburd, J. J. (2012). Tourism research2.0. *Annals of Tourism Research*, *39*(2), 883–907. doi:10.1016/j.annals.2011.10.006

Lindberg, J. O., & Olofsson, A. D. (Eds.). (2010). *Online Learning Communities and Teacher Professional Development: Methods for Improved Education Delivery*. Hershey, PA: IGI Global. doi:10.4018/978-1-60566-780-5

Lu, H., & Hsiao, K. L. (2009). Gender differences in reasons for frequent blog posting. *Online Information Review*, *33*(1), 135–156. doi:10.1108/14684520910944436

Maness, J. M. (2006). Library 2.0 theory: Web 2.0 and its implications for libraries. *Webology*, *3*(2), 1–6.

Maswera, T., Dawson, R., & Edwards, J. (2006). Assessing the levels of knowledge transfer within e-commerce websites of tourist organizations in Africa. *Electronic Journal of Knowledge Management*, *4*(1), 59–66.

McGee, P., & Diaz, V. (2007). Wikis and Podcasts and Blogs! Oh, my! What is a faculty member supposed to do? *EDUCAUSE Review*, *42*(5), 28–41.

Minocha, S. (2009). Role of social software tools in education: a literature review. *Education*˥ + *Training*, *51* (5/6), 353-369.

CNN Money. (2006). *Circuit city enters second life*. Retrieved from http://money.cnn.com/2006/12/15/news/companies/bestbuy sl/index.htm

Nevgi, A., Virtanen, P., & Niemi, H. (2006). Supporting students to develop collaborative learning skills in technology-based environments. *British Journal of Educational Technology*, *37*(3), 937–947. doi:10.1111/j.1467-8535.2006.00671.x

Nunnally, J. C. (1967). *Psychometric Theory*. New York: McGraw-Hill Incorporation.

O'Reilly, T. (2005). What is Web 2.0: design patterns and business models for the next generation of software, *O'Reilly Media Inc*., 30 September, from: www.oreillynet. com/pub/a/oreilly/tim/news/2005/09/30/what-is-web-20.htm

O'Reilly, T. (2009). The war for the web. IT conversations, from: www.itc. conversationsnetwork.org/shows/detail4317.html#

Palvia, S. C. J., & Pancaro, R. (2010). Promises and perils of internet based networking. *Journal of Global Information Technology Management*, *13*(3), 1–10. doi:10.1080/1097198X.2010.10856517

Paquette, S. (2006). Customer Knowledge Management, from http://www.fis.utoronto.ca/phd/paquette/Documents/Paquette%20%20Customer%20Knowledge%20Management.pdf

Paul, R., & Chung, L. H. (2010). Brave new cyberworld: The employer's legal guide to the interactive internet. *The Computer and Internet Lawyer*, *27*(3), 1–20.

Radcliff, D. (2007). Are you watching? *SC Magazine*, *11*, 40–43.

Ram, Anbu K, & Sanjay. (2011). Responding to user's expectation in the library: innovative Web 2.0 applications at JUIT Library. *Electronic Library and Information Systems*, *45* (4), 452-469.

Ram, S Paul Anbu K, J. & Kataria, S. (2011). Responding to user's expectation in the library: innovative Web 2.0 applications at JUIT Library, *Program: electronic library and information systems,* 45(4), 452-469.

Ribie`re, V. Haddad, M. & Vande Wiele, PH. (2010). The impact of national culture traits on the usage of web 2.0 technologies, *the journal of information and knowledge management systems* 40 (3/4), 334-361.

Richardson, W. (2006). *Blogs, Wikis, Podcasts, and other Powerful Web Tools for Classrooms*. Thousand Oaks, CA: Corwin Press.

Rollins, M., & Halinen, A. (2005). Customer knowledge management competence: towards theoretical framework, *Proceedings of the 38th Hawaii International Conference on System Sciences*, Big Island, HI. doi:10.1109/HICSS.2005.180

Rowley, J. (2002). Eight enhancing questions for customer knowledge management in e-business. *Journal of Knowledge Management*, *6*(5), 500–511. doi:10.1108/13673270210450441

Rowley, J. (2002). Reflections on customer knowledge management in e-business, *Qualitative Market Research. International Journal (Toronto, Ont.)*, *5*(4), 80–268.

Roy & Stavropoulos. (2007). *Customer Knowledge Management (CKM) in the e-Business Environment.* (Master`s thesis). Lulea University of Technology.

Rudman, R. J. (2010). Incremental risks in Web 2.0 applications. *The Electronic Library*, *28*(2), 210–230. doi:10.1108/02640471011033585

Salomann, H., Dous, M., Kolbe, L., & Brenner, W. (2005). Rejuvenating customer management: How to make knowledge for, from and about customers work. *European Management Journal*, *23*(4), 392–403. doi:10.1016/j.emj.2005.06.009

Schellong, A. R. M. (2008). Government 2.0 an exploratory study of social networking services in Japanese local government. *Transforming Government: People. Process and Policy*, *2*(4), 225–242.

Secker, J. (2008). Social software and libraries: a literature review from the LASSIE project. *Program: Electronic Library and Information Systems*, *42* (3), 215-231.

Serantes, L. (2009). Understanding the relationship between libraries, young adults and Web 2.0: The necessity of a critical perspective. *Library Review*, *58*(3), 51–237.

ShamiZanjani, M., Rouzbehani, R. & Dabbagh, H. (2008). Proposing a Conceptual Model of Customer Knowledge Management: A Study of CKM Tools in British Dotcoms. *Proceedings of World Academy of Science, Engineering, and Technology*, 28, April, Rome.

Shu, W., & Chuang, Y. H. (2011). The perceived benefits of six-degree-separation social networks. *Internet Research*, *21*(1), 26–45. doi:10.1108/10662241111104866

Su, C. T., Chen, Y. H., & Sha, D. Y. (2006). Linking innovative product development with customer knowledge: A data-mining approach. *Technovation*, *26*(7), 784–795. doi:10.1016/j.technovation.2005.05.005

Tapscott, D. (2008). Viewpoint: Ten talking points for Davos. *Business Week, 16*, 1-16.

Virkus, S. (2008). Use of Web 2.0 technologies in LIS education: experiences at Tallinn University, Estonia. *Program: Electronic Library and Information Systems*, *42* (3), 262-274.

Wilde, E. (2006). *Knowledge Organization Mashups*. Retrieved from http://dret.net/netdret/publications#wil06f

Zhang, Z. (2011). Customer knowledge management and the strategies of social software. *Business Process Management Journal*, *17*(1), 82–106. doi:10.1108/14637151111105599

KEY TERMS AND DEFINITIONS

Blogs: Are probably the most popular type of social software. Blogs typically allow creation of new pages, publishing of materials in forms such as text, graphics, audio and video, different presentations of content, facilities for archiving, and mechanisms to allow other authors to add entries or provide feedback on entries.

CKM: Is a dynamic recycling process of acquiring and refining valuable customer data by means of various paths and methods, and sharing the generated customer knowledge across the organization.

Mashup: Mashup in web development, is a web page, or web application, that uses and combines data, presentation or functionality from two or more sources to create new services.

Podcast: Is a series of digital media files in audio or video format. It allows users to publish their audio and video recordings on the web episodically and to download them through multiple devices including cell phones, iPods, net books, laptops, desktops, and similar handheld devices.

RSS Feeds: Are technologies primarily associated with blogs. They allow users to "syndicate and republish content on the web".

Social Bookmarking: Is a tool used to mark web pages which a user found relevant, tag them with a keyword which will make them retrievable in the future, and also to send these sites to other users who might find them useful as well.

Social Networking: A social network is an online community of people interacting over such topics as business, culture, and friendship. Before the establishment of social-networking services using the internet in the past decade.

Tags: Are labels or keywords to describe features of web content. Tagging is a kind of indexing, but the term "indexing" usually describes work done by professionals, whereas tagging is done by anyone interested in sharing tags (identified terms) to describe a document in a public network space.

Web 2.0: Is "a space that allows anyone to create and share information online – a space for collaboration, conversation, and interaction; a space that is highly dynamic, flexible, and adaptable.

Wikis: Are web pages that can be written and edited by anyone or the wiki can have a restricted group of users with writing and editing privileges.

Chapter 9
The Effects of Fan Personality on Participation in Social Media Based Brand Community:
Role of Personality on Participation in the Social Media

Ali Balapour
University of Tehran

Amir Khanlari
University of Tehran

ABSTRACT

Facebook as the greatest social network has offered a new marketing tools for companies, agencies, organizations and even people like celebrities. We are witnessing a growing trend in emergence of online brand communities both in and out of social media. However, one of the important aspects that needs to be magnified is how brand's fans participate in their favorite brand pages? This study tries to answer questions like this. We introduce new variables which should be counted in the 3M model of personality in order to stimulate brand fans to participate on the brand page more than before. Entertainment, monetary and normative incentives are introduced as potential variables which affect situational traits of participants. Finally, we advise brand managers to not forget about entertainment mixed with promotions or representation of products over their online brand community; entertainment along with monetary and normative incentives can motivate fans to participate.

INTRODUCTION

With advent of social networks and growing number of participants in them (Facebook for instance), it is becoming imperative for brands to move to this platform as well. Many companies such as Burberry recognized the importance of these online brand communities. "In April 2011, Burberry staged a catwalk

DOI: 10.4018/978-1-4666-8586-4.ch009

show in Beijing where live models are mixed with holograms, creating a new and unique experience for its audience. All the videos were immediately posted on YouTube for fans that had missed the shows. This social media strategy helped Burberry to rejuvenate the brand and reposition it as a more fashionable and aspirational one than ever" (Phan et al., 2011).The number of social network users in 2012 was 1.43 billion and it was expected to reach 2.55 billion by 2017 (Emarketer, n.d.), Facebook announced 1.23 billion monthly active users in Dec/2013 (Facebook, n.d.; Wikipedia, n.d.).What people seek in social media are: psychological needs (belongingness, need for interaction), shopping, researching, entertainment & making money (Laroche et al., 2013).People are sharing various types of information like picture, video, text and discussing about politics, economics and consumption-related issues in social networks virtual chatting, bulletin and Customers are at their most open, honest and candid when they are talking to each other about their product opinions and consumption experience; also social networks enable them to have both synchronous (real-time) communication and asynchronous (non-real time) communication (Noble et al., 2012; Sung et al., 2010).

Consumers have compelling stories to share about their brand experiences, seek recommendations and exchange product information with other users of social media (Kapoor et al., 2013).According to Nielsen "Social media plays an important role in how consumers discover, research, and share information about brands and products. In fact 60 percent of consumers researching products through multiple online sources learned about a specific brand or retailer through social networking sites (Nielsen, n.d.). According to Nielsen (n.d.), Internet users are spending more time on Facebook (a massive 7 hours per month on average) than they spend on Google, Yahoo, YouTube, Microsoft, Wikipedia and Amazon combined (Nielsen, n.d.). From a marketer's perspective, this means that their company or product brand needs to be located within Facebook. Consumers are increasingly likely to watch a movie trailer or download a discount coupon if that activity happens inside Facebook, in preference to being pushed to an external website (Harris & Dennis, 2011). We can consider the importance of social media to the extant which companies like old spice shifted it's budgeting from old traditional way to the social campaigns in Facebook, Twitter and Reddit. It helped them rejuvenating the old images of public looks to the brand and now it's one of their most effective customer relationship tools (Datamonitor, n.d.).

"Social Media also plays a key role in protecting brands: 58 percent of social media users say they write product reviews to protect others from bad experiences, and nearly 1 in 4 say they share their negative experiences to "punish companies" (Nielsen, n.d.). Consumers are also bringing their online experiences into their own social networks rather than engaging directly on company websites (offsite social commerce). While social network platforms such as Facebook and LinkedIn started out as meeting spaces for online identity construction, the addition of functionality echoing the reputation and feedback mechanisms of major transaction sites such as Amazon has enabled social networks to develop into full-scale recommendation centers (Costa & McCrae, 1995). In such virtual environments (social networks) users often gather together in sub-groups with a specific brand in its center (Woisetschläger et al., 2008), a brand-related community; consumers sharing their interest for a brand, exchange information and knowledge, or they simply express their affection for this specific brand (Zaglia, 2013).

Brand communities are marked by 3 factors: 1) a shared consciousness, that is, an intrinsic connection members feel with one another. This can also be described as a "we-ness", 2) Rituals and traditions that perpetuate the community's shared history, 3) A sense of moral responsibility which is a felt sense of duty or responsibility to the community as a whole, and to its individual members. A brand is successful when consumer are able to express their personal characteristics through the brand in brand community (Jang et al., 2008; Muniz & O'Guinn, 2001; Wirtz, 2013). Brand communities have proven to be a powerful force, which leaves brand Marketers with an imperative to cultivate relationships with members and to channel the consumers' passions in directions that are helpful to the brand.Two major factor that implicate power of brand communities: 1) As visible consumers of a brand, brand community members can become its best promoters; 2) Because a brand community represents a cohesive group, marketers can treat customers like subscribers or members and develop membership-oriented programs that deepen customer relationships (Kalman, 2014).

Brand communities are relational networks between a parent brand and its members. They potentially exist when brands engage in activities to create and sustain a community around their brand (Samu et al., 2012). Customer-to-customer contact through informal social networking and more formal company-sponsored platforms, such as discussion forums, is an increasingly integral element in building brand communities. There are many benefits to this interaction, such as nurturing brand champions and "super users", and reduced service costs through customer-to-customer solutions for product problems (Noble et al., 2012).They key platform of consumer engagement with brand is now brand pages on social network sites (Tsai & Men, 2013).Consumers join these communities to exchange experiences with other like-minded people fascinated by a specific brand (Woisetschläger et al., 2008). People benefit from participating in online communities, which enable them to get in touch with like-minded others, be entertained, or receive information and advice (Garnefeld et al., 2012). Active member participation is a crucial factor indicating online brand community success because greater participation implies that more members believe that the community fulfills their needs, thus sustaining community growth (Chang et al., 2013).

Brand community members have a strong interest in the product and in the brand. They usually have extensive product knowledge and engage in product-related discussions; they support each other in solving problems and generating new product ideas (Füller et al., 2008). It is argued that consumer creativity, identification with the brand community, and brand-specific emotions and attitudes (passion and trust) as well as brand knowledge are important determinants of consumers' willingness to share their knowledge with producers (Füller et al., 2008). Companies are getting advantage of online communities in their ability to connect likeminded people or businesses but not only the main communities but the sub-communities are expanding at a rapid rate, these sub-communities can be a either disadvantage or advantage (Laroche et al., 2013; Hagel & Armstrong, 1997).Companies such as Delta Airlines, Malaysian Airlines and Avon now permit an entire purchase to be completed without the consumer needing to leave Facebook (Harris & Dennis, 2011). For marketing managers there are 3 to focus on brand community. First, they are important source of market information. Community members usually possess a lot of product knowledge, discuss new product introductions, functionalities of the product, marketing campaigns, or can even have ideas for new product development. Second, brand communities are often considered as distinct market segments. Third, brand communities can play an important role in fostering brand relationships, as their members are strongly committed to the brand and can become brand advocates (Matzler, 2011).

BACKGROUND

Social Network

Socials is a Latin word meaning being united, living with others (Kapoor et al., 2013). The concept of social networks was first introduced by J.A. Barnes (1954), who describes them as connected graphs where nodes represent entities and edges their interdependencies. Entities could be individuals, groups, organizations, or government agencies. The edges could be interactions, invitations, trades, values, etc. (Sherchan et al., 2013). In a technical point of view, social media was earlier termed as 'social software', 'computer mediated communication', 'digital media', 'web 2.0' and 'computer supported cooperative work' (Khong et al., 2013; Solis & Breakenridge, 2009). And defined as "a group of internet based applications that builds on the ideological and technological foundations of Web 2.0, and it allows the creation and exchange of user-generated content" (Kaplan & Haenlein, 2010). Another definition is "an online place where a user can create a profile and build a personal network that connects him or her to other users" (Sung et al., 2010).

Another definition: "the media that is published, created and shared by individuals on the Internet, such as blogs, images, video and more as well as online tools and platforms that allow Internet users to collaborate on content, share insights and experiences and connect for business or pleasure" (Chung & Austria, 2010; Kapoor et al., 2013). Grabner-Kräuter mentioned Brass definition of social network; (Brass et al., 1998) defined a social network as a set of actors and the set of ties representing some relationship or lack of relationship amongst the actors (Grabner-Kräuter, 2009). Web-based social networks, online social media sites, and large-scale information sharing communities are prominent examples of Social Web applications which rely heavily on the opinions, contributions or actions of communities of online users (Zolfaghar & Aghaie, 2011). Social media has become a web of brand related conversations capable of influencing various aspects of consumer behavior including awareness, information acquisition, opinions, attitudes, purchase intention and post-purchase communication (Kapoor et al., 2013; Mangold & Faulds, 2009). Social media is any tool or service that uses the Internet to facilitate conversation and interaction (Khong et al., 2013; Solis, 2010). The development of "Web 2.0" technologies, popularized as social network media, has posed new challenges and opportunities for marketing managers seeking to develop long-term trust in their brands (Palmer & Huo, 2013; Christodoulides et al., 2006).

Virtual Community and Online Brand Community

The combination of both brand community and social media leads to a concept that we call social media based brand community which is a subset of the broader concept of "virtual communities" or online brand communities; but the main differentiator is their platforms. The core platform of social media is Web 2.00 plus User generated or Firm generated content (Laroche et al., 2012). In addition, Virtual brand communities are places where long-term consumer– brand relationships are initiated, maintained and fostered, which in turn strengthen brand loyalty and commitment (Sung et al., 2010). Rheingold introduced virtual community as follow: Virtual communities are social aggregations that emerge from the Net when enough people carry on those public discussions long enough, with sufficient human feeling, to form webs of personal relationships in Cyberspace; Cyberspace, originally a term from William Gibson's science-fiction novel Neuromancer, is the name some people use for the conceptual space where words, human relationships, data, wealth, and power are manifested by people using Computer-mediated communications (CMC) technology (Rheingold, 2014).

The social, communal, and participatory environment of brand SNS pages constitutes virtual brand communities where advertisers can engage consumers at a more intimate and interactive manner, rather than a mere advertising platform (Tsai & Men, 2013). The most cohesive and through definition in our context is what (Muniz & O'Guinn, 2001) introduced: "specialized, non-geographically bound community, based on a structured set of social relations among admirers of a brand." (Laroche et al., 2013;

Muniz & O'Guinn, 2001). For some consumers, brands symbolize values such as quality, status, or reputation and are considered the means for creating a sense of belonging and uniqueness (Sung et al., 2010). With the emergence of new technologies, internet and social media, it is imperative for businesses and customers to find ways to exploit the benefits of both technology and brand community. This results in establishing online brand communities (Laroche et al., 2012). Marketers have come to recognize the importance of the virtual brand community as a consumer-brand relationship-building tool and have become interested in creating and managing virtual communities on their Internet venues (Sung et al., 2010). Brand community represents a form of association embedded in the consumption context positioned around one product. These communities are composed of its member entities and their relationships and are identified by their commonalities which help people share essential resources, i.e. cognitive, emotional or material in nature (Laroche et al., 2012). An Online Brand Community conducts vital brand functions such as sharing information, perpetuating the history and culture of a brand, and providing assistance (Chang et al., 2013). Brand communities were introduced as a solution for serving customers. Brand communities execute important tasks on behalf of the brand. For instance, brand communities support sharing information, perpetuating the history and culture of the brand, and providing assistance to consumers (Laroche et al., 2012).

3M Model of Motivation and Personality

The 3M integrates control theory, evolutionary psychology principles, elements of trait theories, and a hierarchical approach to personality to provide an integrated account of how personality interacts with situations to influence feelings, thoughts, and behavior (Mowen, 2000). The 3M Model integrates four theoretical approaches. First, it describes how traits motivate behavior by employing a control theory framework. Second, it borrows from trait theory the idea that valid and reliable scales can be developed to measure intrapsychic dispositions to behave. Third, ideas from hierarchical models of personality are employed to propose that traits reside in a structure in which more abstract, cross-situational traits influence narrower situation-specific behavioral tendencies, which in turn influence behavior. Finally, the 3M Model borrows concepts from evolutionary psychology to propose that the needs for arousal, for material resources, and for body resources represent highly basic elemental traits (Mowen et al., 2007). The 3m model consists of 4 levels; 1) elemental traits (the big five personality traits), 2) compound traits, 3) situational traits, 4) surface traits.

Elemental Traits: The Big Five Personality Traits

Relying on personality research, we assume that a community member's relationship with the community in total depends on his/her individual personality. The 'Big Five' personality traits consisting of neuroticism, extraversion, agreeableness, openness, and conscientiousness constitute a pattern of traits across individuals (Matzler et al., 2011). Neuroticism is defined as an individual's tendency to experience unpleasant emotions and expect bad things to happen to them. Extraversion is defined as an individual's tendency to express himself/herself socially in an outgoing manner. Openness to experience is defined as the appreciation of alternative perspectives, intellectual curiosity, and the desire of artistic pleasures. Agreeableness is defined as a tendency to be reliable, sympathetic, and cooperative. Conscientiousness is defined as a tendency to plan ahead and be diligent and fair (Özgüven & Mucan, 2013).

McCrae and John (1992) classify various description words used by psychological analysts to nominate 5 factor of traits, yet their meaning or the measurement used for them are pretty much same.Definition of five factors Extraversion: sociable, talkative, gregariousness, assertiveness, activity, outgoing. Agreeableness: sympathetic, altruism, modesty, trusting, forgiving, generous, kind, cooperating, helpful, courteous, being good-natured. Conscientiousness: responsible, dependable, self-discipline, productive, competence, deliberation. Neuroticism: anxiety, fluctuating moods (unstable), self-pitying, worrying, impulsiveness. Openness: imagination & fantasy, wide range of interests, aesthetic, value intellectual matters, curious, attentiveness to inner feelings (McCrae & John, 1992; Matzler et al., 2011). One necessary point to know is, extraverted people more tended to communicate face-to-face, but introverted ones like to communicate through internet or social networks which is fit to them (Özgüven & Mucan, 2013).

Compound Traits

Compound traits result in part from the effects of multiple elemental traits as well as from the effects of culture and subcultures. Compound traits have different properties than the elemental traits; yet, they are composed in part from the effects of multiple elemental traits (Mowen et al., 2007). Compound traits include: need for activity, competitiveness, the need for play, general self-efficacy, task orientation, altruism, need for learning (need for information) and need for interpersonal relationships (Chang et al., 2013; Mowen et al., 2007; Schneider & Vogt, 2012). Social integration involves the sense of belonging, the supportive peer groups, and the enhanced interpersonal connections associated with media usage (Daugherty et al., 2008; Kaye, 2007; Tsai & Men, 2013). An interpersonal relationship is a strong, deep, or close association/acquaintance between two or more people that may range in duration from brief to enduring. This association may be based on inference, love, solidarity, regular business interactions, or some other type of social commitment (Wikipedia, n.d.). Maintaining interpersonal connectivity is related with keeping contact with other people gaining such things as social support and friendship (Lampe et al., 2010).

One important focus of online communities is on guidance and informational support that enhances decision making (Grabner-Kräuter, 2009). (Sung et al., 2010) cite the perceived value of participating in the Apple computer brand community, they found that community members' lurking behaviors in the community contribute to brand loyalty, and that the primary purpose of lurking is to seek out information regarding product function or performance (Sung et al., 2010).

General self-efficacy is: Individuals' belief in their ability to perform well in a variety of situations (Scherbaum et al., 2006). We can suppose self-efficacy means believe in self to be productive, helpful and useful Altruism defined as selflessly seeks to help others (Schneider & Vogt, 2012).

Situational Traits

Situational traits reside at the third level in the hierarchy and represent enduring dispositions to behave within a general situational context. They are influenced by the pressures of the situational environment and by the effects of elemental and compound traits (Mowen, 2000; Mowen et al., 2007). Situational traits used in previous research include: health motivation, health product innovativeness and health locus of control in research on healthy diets, and value consciousness in bargaining proneness research, as well as fashion innovativeness, shopping enjoyment, susceptibility to influence in online word-of-mouth research, and identification with community (Chang et al., 2013). Existence of genuine community based on strong feeling of we-ness (Vock et al., 2013). (Woisetschläger et al., 2008) indicate that identification with community, satisfaction with community, and degree of influence explain most of the variance in consumer participation (Woisetschläger et al., 2008). There are various definitions for social identity (sense of community) or identification with brand and community as follow: individual's sense of sameness with a particular brand (Tuškej et al., 2013). The perception of oneness with or belongingness to some human aggregate (Vock et al., 2013). (Chang et al 2013) Cite the importance of a "sense of community" (SOC), which describes a "spirit of belonging together." Research has found an SOC to be an effective enabler of community success (Chang et al., 2013).

Three important factors involved in participation: identification with community as group level, extraversion as the individual level, and relational trust as relationship level (Chang et al., 2013). Community identification as the key precursors of consumer engagement on SNSs is one of the effective relationship-oriented factors in social media dependency (Tsai & Men, 2013). People also join brand communities to fulfill their need to be identified with groups or symbols they wish to associate with, or that are desirable to them (Laroche et al., 2013). Consumer identification process has a significant impact on individual consumer behavior including: consumer buying-related decisions, brand preference, consumer loyalty, psychological sense of brand community and brand commitment, consumer satisfaction and a higher possibility of repurchase, positive word of mouth and consumers' willingness to pay a price premium (Tuškej et al., 2013). Online Brand Community (simply OBC) identification indicates the strength of perceived closeness and emotional involvement with the OBC. Identification with OBC can be established through community engagement practices such as consumers retelling and sharing milestone memories of the brand and grooming practices dictating the appropriate way to care for the brand (Chang et al., 2013). Two personality traits (i.e., extraversion and openness) that have significant influence on brand passion, creativity, and identification with the community (Füller et al., 2008). Community identification should stimulate group-oriented attitudes and behaviors, including community engagement (Tsai & Men, 2013; Zeng et al., 2009).

Identification with brand community is related to extraversion and agreeableness (Matzler et al., 2011). Brands that make the customer "happy", "joyful" or "affectionate" cause a stronger attitudinal commitment and purchase loyalty (Matzler et al., 2006). Royo-Vela and Casamassima (2011) cite from Gangadharbatla (2008, p. 11), "people join virtual communities to remain in the loop and maintaining relationships with friends and others, irrespective of time and physical space". Thus, it can be presumed that some consumers engage in virtual community activities only for the pleasure of participating in the specific online community they belong to (Royo-Vela & Casamassima, 2011). When social interactions in online communities help participants to accomplish specific tasks, such as solving a problem, validating a decision already reached, or buying a product, online social networks provide instrumental value. Hedonic value relates to the experiential aspects of human consumption in which emotions and feelings of enjoyment or pleasure play a pivotal role (Grabner-Kräuter, 2010).

Entertainment which derives from the fun and relaxation of playing or otherwise interacting with other users. Entertainment refers to the relaxation, enjoyment, and emotional relief generated by temporarily escaping from daily routines. As one of the Facebook members said "for me, entertainment (on Facebook) is an important factor – when I sit in front of the computer all afternoon and work on a project paper, I have about 10 to 20 logins during the afternoon" (Grabner-Kräuter, 2010).

Because people strive to maximize their individual utility, they are motivated to act only when the expected benefits associated with the action exceed their anticipated costs (Datamonitor, n.d.; Palmer & Huo, 2013; Samu et al., 2012). In general, explicit incentives should shift the perceived cost–benefit ratio of an action and affect a person's motivation to perform (Garnefeld et al., 2012). In an online community setting, members anticipate costs of contributing, such as in terms of time and effort. To be motivated to post, a member must receive compensation for these costs, usually in the form of the expected benefits of posting (Garnefeld et al., 2012). Monetary incentives refer to material rewards that community members can consume individually (Garnefeld et al., 2012). Remuneration and empowerment are original motivators identified in the social media literature and were not discussed in prior media research (Muntinga et al., 2011; Tsai and Men 2013). In terms of the social media–specific motivations, remuneration involves participation in online communities where users seek rewards and benefits (e.g., economic incentives such as coupons and promotions) that are constantly shared and distributed through online social networks (Tsai & Men, 2013; Wang & Fesenmaier, 2003).

Monetary incentives weaken social approval incentives because a financial reward eliminates the perception of contributing to the public good as a voluntary moral act that provokes approval. This effect is likely to persist even after the reward expires. Monetary incentives may decrease active members' obligation to adhere to social norms; once they weaken, community norms of reciprocity and solidarity are difficult to reestablish (Garnefeld et al., 2012). Yet monetary incentives may reduce social approval and norm-based incentives. If community members gain social approval when they contribute voluntarily, because they appear to be driven by something other than explicit incentives, then receiving compensation for their contributions would reduce social approval for participation that no longer appears voluntary; explicit normative incentives call on members to adhere to norms or contribute to a common goal. Explicit normative incentives are openly stated inducements to act, according to community principles or norms or in pursuit of a common goal (Garnefeld et al., 2012). Passive members might not respond to explicit normative incentives because they exhibit low levels of commitment to and personal involvement with the community. Reaching a common community goal does not enhance their self-approval because these passive members do not value this goal (Garnefeld et al., 2012). Value consciousness results in bargaining proneness and buying frugality (Mowen, 2000).

Surface Trait

The final level is surface trait which is the most tangible level and it results from combination of elemental, compound and situation traits. Simply the surface trait is dispositions to send and receive information (Chang et al., 2013; Mowen et al., 2007).

THEORETICAL FRAMEWORK AND HYPOTHESES DEVELOPMENT

We are using the 3M model of motivation and personality as our base model, the 4 level of traits and whatever motivate people to send or receive information. In expansion to this model we introduced new factors like monetary and normative incentives and entertainment. These factors has been studied previously and reviewed in literature, in summary Figure1 shows the structure and relationship of the proposed model. The elementary or elemental traits level we used is what had introduced as big five factor of personality earlier, (Mowen, 2000) introduced another 3 factors but we found them not much pertinent to out topic so we decided to leave them for further studies (Mowen, 2000).

Figure1. Model and hypotheses
Note: *to avoid complexity of the model, hypotheses are not shown in the model*

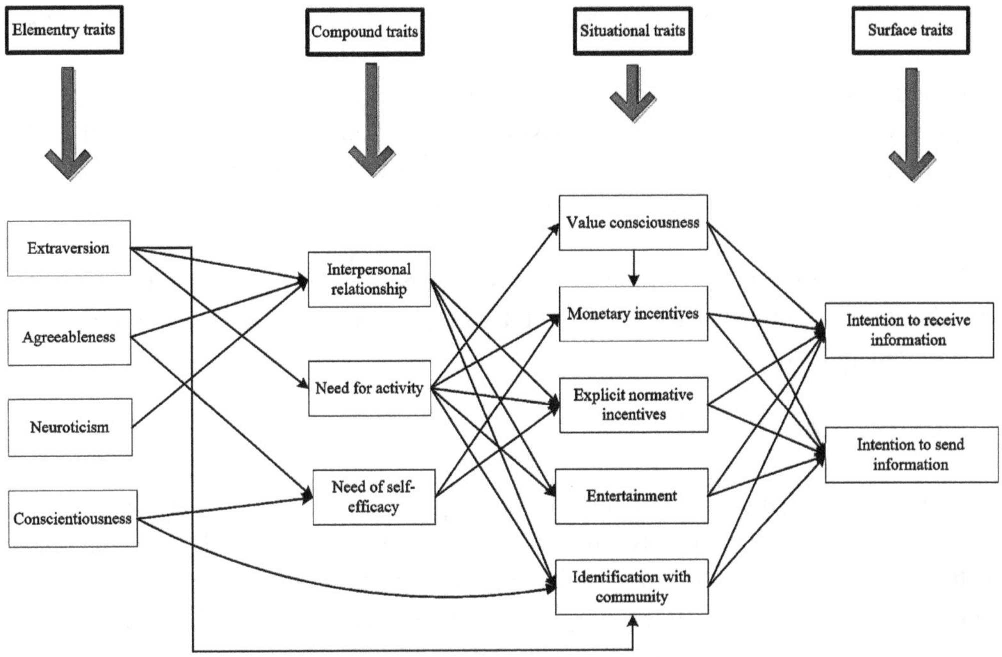

First Level Hypotheses

Extravert people are active, sociable and talkative (McCrae & John, 1992). Thus we hypothesize extravert people have high need for interpersonal relationships & activity (H1a & H1b). Online brand community is a platform for connection and a sense of belonging (Chang et al., 2013). Thus, we hypothesize agreeableness and interpersonal relationships are positively related (H1c). We also hypothesize if agreeable people have need of self-efficacy or not (H1d). To soothe anxiety people seek interpersonal relationship even in online platforms (Chang et al., 2013). Thus we hypothesize Neuroticism and interpersonal relationship should have positive relation (H1e). A person who exhibit high conscientiousness is a productive one, this trait is making a sense with definition of self-efficacy: Individuals' belief in their ability to perform well in a variety of situations (McCrae & John, 1992; Matzler et al., 2011; Scherbaum et al., 2006). So we hypothesize they have positive relation (H1f).

Hypothesis 1a: Extraverted people have higher need for interpersonal relationships.
Hypothesis 1b: Extraverted people have higher need for activity.
Hypothesis 1c: People with agreeable trait have higher need for interpersonal relationships.
Hypothesis 1d: People with agreeable trait have higher need of self-efficacy.
Hypothesis 1e: Neurotic people have higher need for interpersonal relationships.
Hypothesis 1f: People who are more conscientious have higher need of general self-efficacy.

Second Level Hypotheses

Extraversion has significant effect on identification with brand community (Füller et al., 2008). Thus, we hypothesize their relation (H2a).

Conscientiousness can also be described as "We-ness", identification with community described as "the perception of oneness with or belongingness to some human aggregate" (Jang et al., 2008; Muniz & O'Guinn, 2001; Vock et al., 2013; Wirtz et al., 2013). So we hypothesize that Conscientiousness and identification with brand community are positively related (H2b).

Hypothesis 2a: Extraverted people have higher sense of identification with online brand community.

Hypothesis 2b: People who have high conscientiousness, also have higher sense of identification with online brand community.

Third Level Hypotheses

A strong, deep or close association with a group of people in a brand community should be related to sense of belonging to that community (Chang et al., 2013; Wikipedia, n.d.). Thus, we hypothesize that people with a close association with a community have high sense of belonging to it (H3a). Entertainment drives from relaxation of playing or interacting with other users (Lampe et al., 2010). So, we hypothesize that People who have high need for interpersonal relationships looking for entertainment (H3b). We expect a person with strong association with community should have more reaction to inducements to act according to community norms (Garnefeld et al., 2012; Wikipedia n.d.), (H3c).

Consumers retelling and sharing milestone memories of the brand and others can refer to them before buying products (Chang et al., 2013). Community identification plays important role in consumer engagement on brand community (Tsai & Men, 2013). Thus we hypothesize need for activity and identification with community are related (H3d). Relaxation of playing makes sense of entertaining activity (Lampe et al., 2010). So we hypothesize the relations of these two factors (H3e). People with higher activity need expected to have positive reaction to explicit normative and monetary incentives, thus we hypothesize their relation (H3f & H3g). We want to examine relation of need for activity and value consciousness, thus we hypothesis their relation (H3h).

Explicit normative and monetary incentives call on members to contribute in a common goal, on the other hand self-efficacy is "believe in self to achieve that goal" (Garnefeld et al., 2012). Thus, we developed a hypothesis to examine their relations (H3i & H3j).

Hypothesis 3a: People who have high needs for interpersonal relationships have higher sense of identification with online brand community.

Hypothesis 3b: People who have high needs for interpersonal relationships, are more looking for entertainment.

Hypothesis 3c: People who have high needs for interpersonal relationships have positive reaction to explicit normative incentives.

Hypothesis 3d: People who have high needs for activity have higher sense of identification with online brand community.

Hypothesis 3e: People who have high needs for activity, are more looking for entertainment.

Hypothesis 3f: People who have high needs for activity can be motivated with explicit normative incentives.

Hypothesis 3g: People who have high needs for activity can be motivated with explicit monetary incentives.

Hypothesis 3h: People who have high needs for activity are more value conscious.

Hypothesis 3i: People who have high needs of self-efficacy can be motivated with explicit normative incentives.

Hypothesis 3j: People who have high needs of self-efficacy can be motivated with explicit monetary incentives.

Forth Level Hypotheses

Woisetschläger et al. (2008) indicate that identification with community as one of the third factors, which explain most of the variance in consumer participation (Woisetschläger et al., 2008). Thus, we hypothesize identification with online brand community is related to sending and receiving information (H4a & H4b).

Entertainment is considered to be a main factor which lead members to participate in online brand community. So we hypothesize its relationship with intention to send or receive information over online brand community (H4c & H4d).

To be motivated to post, a member must receive compensation for these costs, usually in the form of the expected benefits of posting (Garnefeld et al., 2012). It can be a social approval as normative incentive or a monetary incentive (Tsai & Men, 2013). So, we hypothesize both are related to send and receive information in online brand community (H4e, H4f, H4g & H4h).

Value conscious people seek information to buy high-quality products at a low price (Chang et al., 2013). The hypothesis stated below (H4i). In addition we examine the relation of value conscious people with intention to send information (H4j).

Hypothesis 4a: People who have high identification with the online brand community are more inclined to receive information from the online brand community.

Hypothesis 4b: People who have high identification with the online brand community are more inclined to send information in the online brand community.

Hypothesis 4c: People who find participating in online brand community entertaining are more inclined to receive information from the online brand community.

Hypothesis 4d: People who find participating in online brand community entertaining are more inclined to send information in the online brand community.

Hypothesis 4e: People who get motivated with explicit normative incentives, are more inclined to receive information from the online brand community.

Hypothesis 4f: People who get motivated with explicit normative incentives, are more inclined to send information in the online brand community.

Hypothesis 4g: People who get motivated with explicit monetary incentives, are more inclined to receive information from the online brand community.

Hypothesis 4h: People who get motivated with explicit monetary incentives, are more inclined to send information in the online brand community.

Hypothesis 4i: People who are more value conscious are more inclined to receive information from the online brand community.

Hypothesis 4j: People who are more value conscious are more inclined to send information in the online brand community.

RESEARCH METHOD

Development of Measures

We derived our measures from previous works of Schwarzer and Jerusalem (2004); Goldenberg (1992); Mowen (2000); Costa and McCrae (1995); Garnefeld et al. (2012); Algesheimer et al. (2005) and Chang et al. (2013). For entertainment we have built measures regarding to Lampe et al. (2010); Tsai and Men (2013); Park et al. (2009) and Shao (2009).

To confirm goodness of our measures a pilot study consist of 20 participant conducted. All participants were university students with at least master education. We have been assured that these students do have an active Facebook account and they were following their favorite brand on Facebook. The pilot study showed a great level of reliability and validity for measurement items in addition to some unexpected results which were quiet the same as the main study. Furthermore, 1 Item had been replace and 1 new item had been added to the final survey. The survey had been designed in English and then translated to Persian.

Survey Distribution

We distributed our survey in 3 different Facebook pages, we also added a prize with lottery for winners of every 100 participants. First was a user generated Facebook page, a community of people to ask questions and receive advises for their questions; the page manager donated the money which he took from us for advertising our survey to a cancer charity, then he invited all members to participate in support of children with cancer (explicit normative incentive). The second page was a very popular entertaining page on the Facebook; their manager invited members to participate with promise of a small prize (all paid and supported by our study. The last page were a user generated Gaming brand page called DOTA 2; their manager invited members to participate in our survey with a small gaming prize. The basic requirement for participating in the lottery for prize in all pages were first, sharing and then filling the survey. With this going on, during one month we received over 330 responses via Google forms. However only 286 of them were useful. Out of 49 measurement items, 13 were omitted since they were poorly fit with the model. We didn't want to delay our data gathering more than one month, only because we wanted to avoid any suspicion of un-controlled effects on the study like growing numbers of people who filled the survey twice in order to have a more chance for winning the prize.

Among participants, 35% were female and 63% were male (2% left sexual preferences empty). 12% of sample were under 20 years old, 62% were 20-25 years old, 16% were 26-30 years old and 4% were above 30 years old (6% did not answer to age question). 127 of 286 participants were undergraduate, 69 had Master or PhD degree and the rest has chosen "others" in our education preference's question.

RESULTS

Validity and Reliability

LISREL 8.80 of Jöreskog & Sörbom and IBM SPSS 16 has been used for analyzing data. The results for convergent validity are represented in Table 1. We used the Fornell-Larcker criterion (Fornell & Larcker,

1981) for both convergent and discriminant validity; Cronbach's α used for reliability test of constructs T-values represented in the Table 1 achieved their significance at $\alpha < 0.05$. The confirmatory factor analysis shows a good model ($\chi2$/df (degree of freedom) =1.67; CFI (comparative fit index) =0.97; IFI (incremental fit index) =0.97; NFI (normal fit index) =0.92; NNFI (non-normal fit index) =0.96; GFI (goodness of fit index) =0.86; AGFI (adjusted goodness of fit index) = 0.81; SRMR (standardized root mean square residual) = 0.054; RMSEA (root mean square error of approximation) = 0.049).Table 2 shows the discriminant validity with square root of AVE (average variance extracted) for each construct compared to their shared variances. Neuroticism, Agreeableness and Extraversion are showing weak convergent validity; we assume this is because of local societal culture of IRAN, In that Facebook is widely used but people are reserved when they face with survey or people obtaining information from them, because they are afraid of social network criminals abusing their information. Consequently we expected a slight drop in factor loadings of personality traits and that happened as the results had shown. As their SFL is above 0.5 and their T-values are above 1.96 we decided to keep them in model since they have acceptable loadings and T-value. Another motivation for us to keep these variables is that these variables and their measures have been widely used by previous studies.

Table 1. Measurement items

Measurement items	SFL	T-Value	CR	AVE	α
Extraversion			0.58	0.41	0.57
1. I am a sociable person and I try to communicate.	0.64	10.06			
2. I have a shy personality.	0.63	9.87			
Agreeableness			0.71	0.45	0.69
3. I try to be a trusty person for my friends in their time of need.	0.53	8.18			
4. I almost try to be courteous and kind to others.	0.80	12.50			
5. I sympathize with others' feelings.	0.65	10.19			
Neuroticism			0.67	0.51	0.66
6. I am a very moody person in compare to my friends.	0.63	7.07			
7. I am a temperamental person.	0.78	7.68			
Conscientiousness			0.76	0.52	0.73
8. I try to be precise about everything.	0.82	13.85			
9. I pay attention to details.	0.74	12.36			
10. I am an organized & self-discipline person.	0.57	9.29			
Need for interpersonal relationships			0.68	0.52	0.65
11. I want to be accepted by others around me.	0.83	10.07			
12. I want to be part of the group and be in touch with my friends.	0.58	8.08			
Need for activity			0.85	0.65	0.85
13. I am extremely active in my daily life.	0.79	14.90			
14. I keep busy doing things.	0.81	15.63			
15. My daily schedule is full, and I try to do everything with plan.	0.81	15.55			
Need for self-efficacy			0.79	0.56	0.80
16. I can always manage to solve difficult problems if I try hard enough.	0.70	12.64			
17. I am confident that I could deal efficiently with unexpected events.	0.85	16.20			
18. If I am in trouble, I can usually think of a solution.	0.68	12.01			
Identification with brand community			0.78	0.54	0.77
19. I am very attached to the brand community (simply to their page on Facebook).	0.77	14.68			
20. I see myself as part of the family of brand fan page.	0.81	15.69			
21. If I talk about my favorite brand fan page's event with my friends, I will say "we" plan to do something rather than "they" plan to do something.	0.60	10.62			

continued on following page

Table 1. Continued

Measurement items	SFL	T-Value	CR	AVE	α
Entertainment			0.84	0.63	0.84
22. When I am on my favorite brand page on Facebook, I'm having fun reading posts, watching videos or pictures.	0.80	15.60			
23. Interacting with other brand fan page members makes me have fun and feel relax.	0.81	15.84			
24. When I'm obsessed with watching video, pictures or reading posts on my favorite brand page, I will forget about my personal life problems.	0.77	14.75			
Explicit normative incentives			0.80	0.67	0.80
25. I don't care about reward, I just participate in my favorite brand page, because it gives me the sense of uniqueness & we-ness.	0.84	16.56			
26. I can sense cohesion and solidarity between people of my favorite brand page.	0.79	15.27			
Monetary incentives			0.96	0.94	0.78
27. If my favorite brand page offers a reward for participating I will definitely participate more than usual.	1.27	10.52			
28. If I hear about a community which gives reward for participating, I will definitely participate in their brand page.	0.51	6.97			
Value consciousness			0.78	0.54	0.77
29. I will always track promotions (exp. Discounts) on my favorite brand page.	0.58	10.06			
30. I will read the other members opinion about product or services on my favorite brand page.	0.82	15.72			
31. I will try to evaluate the products & services with the available information on my favorite brand page.	0.78	14.69			
Intention to receive information			0.85	0.66	0.80
32. I will check favorite brand page for the latest news and events.	0.78	14.98			
33. I want to receive new product information from my favorite brand page.	0.88	18.05			
34. I want to receive latest information about promotions (exp. Discounts) from my favorite brand page.	0.76	14.67			
Intention to send information			0.77	0.63	0.76
35. I will comment on most of the posts or videos on my favorite brand page.	0.71	12.53			
36. I will share my experience about products or services with other members on my favorite brand page.	0.87	15.79			
Where: SFL= standard factor loading; CR = construct reliability; AVE = average variance extracted					

Structural Equation Model

Considering the complexity of the model and the time limitation in gathering data, fit indices of the full model are showing acceptable levels. ($\chi 2/df$ (degree of freedom) =2.91; CFI (comparative fit index) =0.91; IFI (incremental fit index) =0.91; NFI (normal fit index) =0.86; NNFI (non-normal fit index) =0.89; GFI (goodness of fit index) =0.76; AGFI (adjusted goodness of fit index) = 0.71; SRMR (standardized root mean square residual) = 0.16; RMSEA (root mean square error of approximation) = 0.082). Figures 2 and 3 show that people with extraversion trait tend to have higher need for interpersonal relationships and activity, thus supporting H1a ($\gamma = 0.18$, $t = 1.99$) and H1b ($\gamma = 0.78$, $t = 9.62$). However, findings show that extraversion is not related to sense of identification with brand community, rejecting H2a ($\gamma = -0.01$, $t = -0.06$). Results showing that people with agreeableness trait tending to have higher need for interpersonal relationships and need for self-efficacy, thus supporting H1c ($\gamma = 0.47$, $t = 5.30$) and H1d ($\gamma = 0.24$, $t = 3.16$). The results showing a poor positive relation between neuroticism trait and the need for interpersonal relationship, thus rejecting H1e ($\gamma = 0.16$, $t = 1.77$). Also, conscientiousness is positively related to need for self-efficacy, results are supporting their relation: H1f ($\gamma = 0.29$, $t = 3.82$);

Table 2. Discriminant validity

EX	AG	NE	CO	IR	NA	NS	IW	EN	NO	MO	VA	RE	SE
AG	0.635												
NE	0.044	0.669											
CO	0.090	0.058	0.709										
IR	0.048	0.058	0.012	0.718									
NA	0.109	0.230	0.000	0.036	0.716								
NS	0.476	0.040	0.063	0.176	0.012	0.803							
IW	0.624	0.063	0.063	0.090	0.014	0.410	0.747						
EN	0.004	0.002	0.006	0.003	0.005	0.000	0.002	0.735					
NO	0.040	0.004	0.000	0.002	0.001	0.008	0.014	0.624	0.794				
MO	0.044	0.000	0.005	0.003	0.001	0.014	0.017	0.723	0.723	0.815			
VA	0.001	0.003	0.008	0.006	0.002	0.006	0.002	0.144	0.102	0.096	0.968		
RE	0.006	0.006	0.004	0.023	0.004	0.004	0.012	0.303	0.397	0.372	0.109	0.734	
SE	0.020	0.000	0.000	0.005	0.004	0.003	0.010	0.397	0.533	0.348	0.130	0.689	0.808

Note: EX = extraversion; AG = agreeableness; NE = neuroticism; CO = conscientiousness; IR = interpersonal relationship; NA = need for activity; NS = need for self-efficacy; IW = identification with brand community; EN = entertainment; NO = normative incentives; MO = monetary incentives; VA = value consciousness; RE = receive information intention ; SE = send information intention

yet, results rejected conscientiousness relation with sense of identification with brand community: H2b ($\gamma = 0$, $t = 0.01$). None of our prediction support the direct relation of traits in elemental level with traits in situational level (relation of extraversion and conscientiousness with sense of identification with brand community.

Our assumption about positive relation of need for interpersonal relationship with identification with brand community, entertainment and explicit normative incentives were wrong. Need for interpersonal relationship were negatively related to sense of identification with brand community H3a ($\beta = -0.08$, $t = -.90$); the other two, entertainment and explicit normative incentives showed no meaningful relation at all: H3b ($\beta = 0.02$, $t = 0.26$), H3c ($\beta = 0.01$, $t = 0.07$). It is in contrast to findings of (Chang et al., 2013), in that they proved a positive relation between need for interpersonal relationship and identification with brand community. We believe that the reason lies within aspects of these two variables, in that identification with brand community is in context of social network where communication is in form of chats and comments, yet interpersonal needs for relationship is in context of real life relations (not virtual worlds, like Facebook). Results show that people with higher needs for activity are more looking for entertainment and they can be motivated by both explicit normative and monetary incentives, thus supporting H3e ($\beta = 0.16$, $t = 2.21$), H3f ($\beta = 0.21$, $t = 2.81$) and H3g ($\beta = 0.16$, $t = 3.18$). However, positive relation between need for activity and sense of identification with brand community had rejected our prediction H3d ($\beta = 0.10$, $t = 0.58$). It is contrary to the findings of (Chang et al., 2013).Perhaps, consumer engagement in brand community does not satisfy their needs for activity. Plus, need for activity were poorly related to value consciousness, thus rejecting H3h ($\beta = 0.12$, $t = 1.66$). People with higher need for self-efficacy are less sensitive to monetary incentives; they are negatively related, thus rejecting our prediction H3j ($\beta = -0.20$, $t = -3.87$). The data could not provide a positive link between higher need for self-efficacy and its relation to motivation explicit normative incentives, H3i ($\beta = -0.01$, $t =$

Figure2. Estimated model

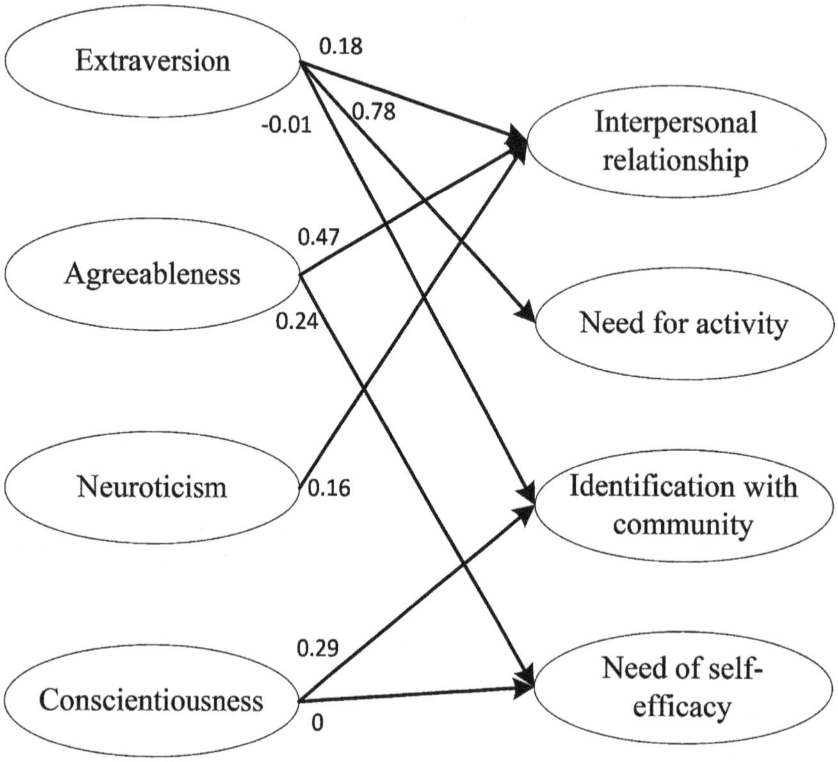

Figure3. Estimated model

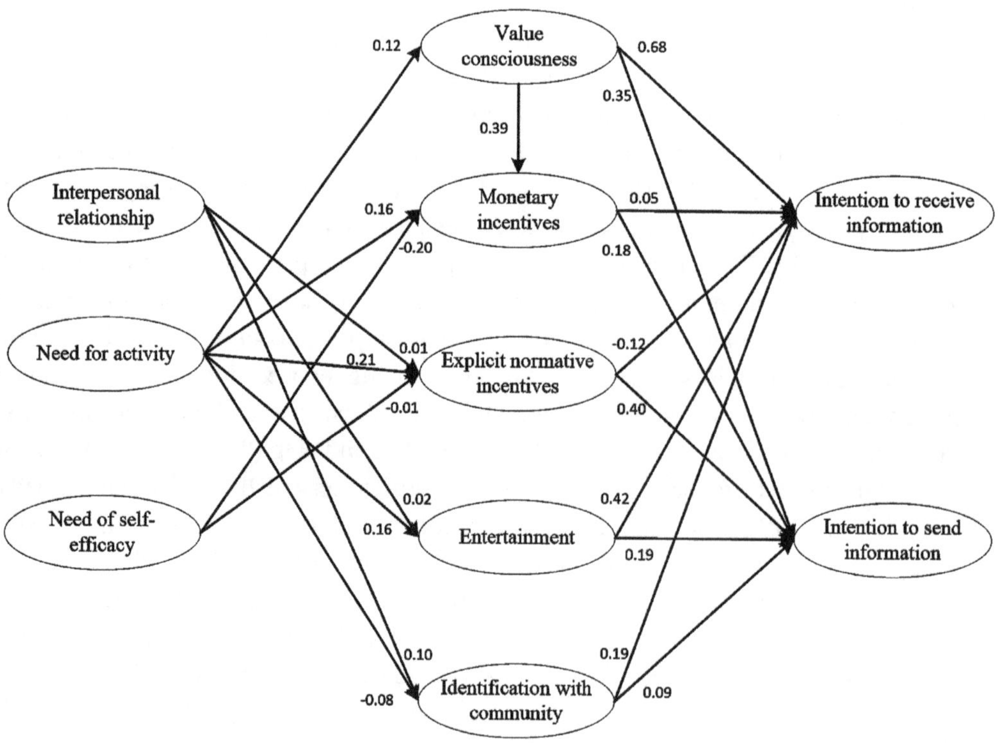

-0.13). It is interesting that any kind of incentives (monetary and normative) could not satisfy people's need for self-efficacy; one explanation could be that self-efficacy exist beyond any incentives to satisfy it; it can only be satisfied internally, and without incentives.

According to our prediction people with sense of identification with brand community are more intended to receive information in online brand communities, thus supporting H4a ($\beta = 0.19$, $t = 3.56$). However, identification with brand community was poorly related to intention to send information on online brand community, H4b ($\beta = 0.09$, $t = 1.42$). This relation had been approved to exist by (Chang et al., 2013), however our data shows a poor relation between identification with brand community and intention to send information; we suggest more investigation on this variable in future studies. People who find participating in online brand community entertaining are more inclined to receive or send information from the online brand community, thus supporting H4c ($\beta = 0.42$, $t = 7.31$), H4d ($\beta = 0.19$, $t = 2.83$). People who get motivated with explicit normative incentives, are more inclined to send information in the online brand community, thus supporting H4f ($\beta = 0.40$, $t = 5.23$). However the relation between explicit normative incentives and intention to receive information were negative, H4e ($\beta = -0.12$, $t = -2.30$). Giving it a second thought, it is logical that normative incentives mostly being used in online brand pages to motivate fans to like, write a comment or share posts, but not for motivating them to receive information. Monetary incentives were successful in motivating people to send information in online brand communities, supporting H4h ($\beta = 0.18$, $t = 2.63$). But, H4g ($\beta = 0.05$, $t = 1.03$) shows that monetary incentives are not related to receiving information. Being more value conscious can incline an individual to send or receive information in the online brand communities, thus supporting H4i ($\beta = 0.68$, $t = 7.66$) and H4j ($\beta = 0.35$, $t = 4.14$).

In short, not only personality traits but other situational factors can play an important role to motivate the participants to engage in online brand community. It is important to mention that we omitted some variables from our base model in process of editing our model. These variables were openness to experience (which exacerbated the model and it's loading factors were under acceptable level, thus showing significantly low reliability and validity), need for information (same as openness to experience this variable also had poor loadings), altruism (omitting this variable improved the full model) and enjoyment (this variable were perfectly related to situational traits and showed very good loading factors along with fitness to the model, however we had to drop one variable from situational level to improve the model and we decided to drop enjoyment out of model).

CONCLUSION

This study used personality traits as predictors of online brand community members and how they affect their attitude in sending and receiving information within the online brand community. The theoretical framework of 3M model has been used with a small modification (adding new variables to the model) (Mowen, 2000). Unlike previous studies, we believe that the context of online brand community does matter. To be more defined, Facebook which is was the main subject of this papers has shown that entertainment, normative and monetary incentives will stimulate participants to send or receive information; this results can vary in YouTube or any other social network. Identification with brand community which has been postulated as main stimulator of members to participate has been rejected by our results. It is deeply rooted in change of views to Facebook; an active brand page in Facebook couldn't maintain a meaningful sense of identification with brand community like the Harley Davidson club does. Perhaps it is deeply rooted in the essence of Facebook which requires entertainment involved but not high sense of identification with brand. So far our study confirmed that specified online brand community websites (like Harley Davidson) are more successful that Facebook brand communities in arousing sense of identification with brand community. On the other hand this study shows that Facebook brand pages can be successful with informing members or getting feedbacks.

People showing extraversion trait have higher needs for activity, this need for activity is associated with positive reaction to entertainment, monetary and normative incentives. Finally, being motivated by monetary and normative incentives can push members to send information, particularly feedbacks; being entertained, they will send or receive information on Facebook brand pages. Thus, Extraversion is significant predictor of information reception and sending in Facebook brand pages.

Extraversion and agreeableness did maintain a positive relation with needs for interpersonal relationships. However interpersonal relationship were stopped and couldn't maintain any relation with "Situational traits". Same scenario happened for Needs for self-efficacy. Despite agreeableness and conscientiousness both showing good relation with needs for self-efficacy, needs for self-efficacy couldn't propose any acceptable relation with situational traits. Neuroticism denied our assumption about its relation with need for interpersonal relationships.

In subject matter of Facebook brand pages, we found that openness to experience is not a good indicator as we omitted it from model, same for neuroticism which is not a significant predictor of participation in Facebook brand pages.

We tried to represent a model that can delineate different variables than previous studies involved in 3M model. The focus of this study was to show that situational traits like normative and monetary incentives or entertainment can motivate participants to share their opinions more than before. For brand page managers it is important to know that they should not omit entertaining posts mixed with their brand products or services on online brand community; It is undeniable that some organizations or agencies were successful to sell their products through Facebook, but they should not forget that people are logging to Facebook to spend their leisure times, meet friends and sometimes watch and read entertaining posts. So, it is incumbent for brands to maintain their relation with their fans via some funny and entertaining posts which can motivate their participants more than before to buy, give feedback or share that post on their wall with their close friends to see (can be a form of word of mouth in Facebook). Because, this study confirms that when people enjoy a post, or when they find it entertaining they will share it.

LIMITATION AND FUTURE RESEARCH

First, we used user-generated pages in our study, in addition we couldn't hire any sponsor from brand pages to support this research; future studies should focus both on user generated contents and brand generated contents. Second, at the time of gathering data, the Facebook decided to put a limitation for free brand pages; only 10% of people who had liked any non-paying page will receive new posts from their favorite page, unless they will visit the page by themselves. Without the second limitation we expected to receive over 400 useful responses which could results in a better model.

Future researches should try to target other social networks, and we strongly suggest YouTube. In addition we couldn't find the relation of the need for interpersonal relationships and need for self-efficacy with situational traits. We recommend a more investigation on this subject with more measurement items involved.

REFERENCES

Algesheimer, R., Dholakia, U. M., & Herrmann, A. (2005). The social influence of brand community: Evidence from European car clubs. *Journal of Marketing*, *69*(3), 19–34. doi:10.1509/jmkg.69.3.19.66363

Chang, A., Hsieh, S. H., & Lin, F. (2013). Personality Traits That Lead Members of Online Brand Communities to Participate in Information Sending and Receiving. *International Journal of Electronic Commerce*, *17*(3), 37–62. doi:10.2753/JEC1086-4415170302

Chang, A., Hsieh, S. H., & Tseng, T. H. (2013). Online brand community response to negative brand events: The role of group eWOM. *Internet Research*, *23*(4), 486–506. doi:10.1108/IntR-06-2012-0107

Christodoulides, G., De Chernatony, L., Furrer, O., Shiu, E., & Abimbola, T. (2006). Conceptualising and Measuring the Equity of Online Brands. *Journal of Marketing Management*, *22*(7-8), 799–825. doi:10.1362/026725706778612149

Chung, C., & Austria, K. "Social media gratification and attitude toward social media marketing messages: A study of the effect of social media marketing messages on online shopping value," *Proceedings of the Northeast Business & Economics Association*, p581, 2010.

Costa, P. T. Jr, & McCrae, R. R. (1995). Domains and facets: Hierarchical personality assessment using the revised NEO personality inventory. *Journal of Personality Assessment*, *64*(1), 21–50. doi:10.1207/s15327752jpa6401_2 PMID:16367732

Datamonitor. (n.d.). Old Spice Case Study: Using Social Media to Revitalise a Brand. Available at: http://www.datamonitor.com/store/Product/old_spice_case_study_using_social_media_to_revitalise_a_brand?productid=CM00056-004

Daugherty, T., Eastin, M. S., & Bright, L. (2008). Exploring Consumer Motivations for Creating User-Generated Content. *Journal of Interactive Advertising*, *8*(2), 16–25. doi:10.1080/15252019.2008.10722139

Emarketer. (n.d.). Social Networking Reaches Nearly One in Four Around the World. Available at: http://www.emarketer.com/Article/Social-Networking-Reaches-Nearly-One-Four-Around-World/1009976#uQhzWqVdJwcM1Eoc.99

Facebook. (n.d.). Facebook Statistics. Available at: http://www.facebook.com/press/info.php?statistics

Fornell, C., & Larcker, D. F. (1981). Evaluating Structural Equation Models with Unobservable Variables and Measurement Error. *JMR, Journal of Marketing Research*, *18*(1), 39–50. doi:10.2307/3151312

Füller, J., Matzler, K., & Hoppe, M. (2008). Brand Community Members as a Source of Innovation. *Journal of Product Innovation Management*, *25*(6), 608–619. doi:10.1111/j.1540-5885.2008.00325.x

Garnefeld, I., Iseke, A., & Krebs, A. (2012). Explicit Incentives in Online Communities: Boon or Bane? *International Journal of Electronic Commerce*, *17*(1), 11–38. doi:10.2753/JEC1086-4415170101

Goldberg, L. R. (1992). The development of markers for the Big-Five factor structure. *Psychological Assessment*, *4*(1), 26–42. doi:10.1037/1040-3590.4.1.26

Grabner-Kräuter, S. (2009). Web 2.0 Social Networks: The Role of Trust. *Journal of Business Ethics, 90*(4), 505–522. doi:10.1007/s10551-010-0603-1

Grabner-Kräuter, S. (2010). Toward a better understanding of trust in web 2.0 social networks. *AMA Winter Educators' Conference*, p313-321,

Hagel, J., & Armstrong, A. G. (1997). *Net gain: Expanding markets through virtual communities*. Boston, MA: Harvard Business School Press.

Harris, L., & Dennis, C. (2011). Engaging customers on Facebook: Challenges for e-retailers. *Journal of Consumer Behaviour, 10*(6), 338–372. doi:10.1002/cb.375

Jang, H., Olfman, L., Ko, I., Koh, J., & Kim, K. (2008). The Influence of On-Line Brand Community Characteristics on Community Commitment and Brand Loyalty. *International Journal of Electronic Commerce, 12*(3), 57–80. doi:10.2753/JEC1086-4415120304

Kalman, D. M. (n.d.). Brand Communities, Marketing, and Media. Available at: http://www.terrella.com/bcmarketingwp2.pdf

Kaplan, A. M., & Haenlein, M. (2010). Users of the world, unite! The challenges and opportunities of Social Media. *Business Horizons, 53*(1), 59–68. doi:10.1016/j.bushor.2009.09.003

Kapoor, P. S., Jayasimha, K. R., & Sadh, A. (2013). Brand-related, Consumer to Consumer, Communication via Social Media. *IIM Kozhikode Society & Management Review, 2*(1), 43–59. doi:10.1177/2277975213496514

Kaye, B. K. (2007). Web Site Story: An Exploratory Study of Blog Use Motivations. In *Blogging, citizenship, and the future of media* (pp. 127–148). New York: Rutledge.

Khong, K. W., Onyemeh, N. C., & Chong, A. Y. (2013). BSEM estimation of network effect and customer orientation empowerment on trust in social media and network environment. *Expert Systems with Applications, 40*(12), 4858–4870. doi:10.1016/j.eswa.2013.02.020

Lampe, C., Wash, W., Velasquez, A., & Ozkaya, E. (2010). Motivations to Participate in Online Communities. *Proceedings of the SIGCHI Conference on Human Factors in Computing Systems*, p1927-1936.

Laroche, M., Habibi, M. R., Richard, M., & Sankaranarayanan, R. (2012). The effects of social media based brand communities on brand community markers, value creation practices, brand trust and brand loyalty. *Computers in Human Behavior, 28*(5), 1755–1767. doi:10.1016/j.chb.2012.04.016

Laroche, M., Habibi, M. R., & Richard, M. O. (2013). To be or not to be in social media: How brand loyalty is affected by social media? *International Journal of Information Management, 33*(1), 76–82. doi:10.1016/j.ijinfomgt.2012.07.003

Mangold, W. G., & Faulds, D. J. (2009). Social media: The new hybrid element of the promotion mix. *Business Horizons, 52*(4), 357–365. doi:10.1016/j.bushor.2009.03.002

Matzler, K., Bidmon, S., & Grabner-Kraüter, S. (2006). Individual determinants of brand affect: The role of the personality traits of extraversion and openness to experience. *Journal of Product and Brand Management, 15*(7), 427–434. doi:10.1108/10610420610712801

Matzler, K., Pichler, E., Füller, J., & Mooradian, T. A. (2011). Personality, person–brand fit, and brand community: An investigation of individuals, brands, and brand communities. *Journal of marketing management*, *27*(9/10), 874-890.

McCrae, R. R., & John, O. P. (1992). An introduction to the five-factor model and its applications. *Journal of Personality*, *60*(2), 175–215. doi:10.1111/j.1467-6494.1992.tb00970.x PMID:1635039

Mowen, J. C. (2000). *The 3m model of motivation and personality: theory and empirical applications to consumer behavior*. Kluwer Academic Publishers. doi:10.1007/978-1-4757-6708-7

Mowen, J. C., Park, S., & Zablah, A. (2007). Toward a theory of motivation and personality with application to word-of-mouth communications. *Journal of Business Research*, *60*(6), 590–596. doi:10.1016/j.jbusres.2006.06.007

Muniz, A. M. Jr, & O'Guinn, T. C. (2001). Brand Community. *The Journal of Consumer Research*, *27*(4), 412–432. doi:10.1086/319618

Muntinga, D. G., Moorman, M., & Smit, E. G. (2011). Introducing COBRAs Exploring motivations for brand-related Social media use. *International Journal of Advertising*, *30*(1), 13–46. doi:10.2501/IJA-30-1-013-046

Nielsen (n.d.). Facebook Users Average 7 hrs a Month in January as Digital Universe Expands. Available at: http://www.nielsen.com/us/en/insights/news/2010/facebook-users-average-7-hrs-a-month-in-january-as-digital-universe-expands.html

Nielsen (n.d.). How Social Media Impacts Brand Marketing. Available at: http://www.nielsen.com/us/en/insights/news/2011/how-social-media-impacts-brand-marketing.html

Noble, C. H., Noble, S. M., & Adjei, M. T. (2012). Let them talk! Managing primary and extended online brand communities for success. *Business Horizons*, *55*(5), 475–483. doi:10.1016/j.bushor.2012.05.001

Özgüven, N., & Mucan, B. (2013). The relationship between personality traits and social media use. *Social Behavior and Personality*, *41*(3), 517–528. doi:10.2224/sbp.2013.41.3.517

Palmer, A., & Huo, Q. A. (2013). Study of trust over time within a social network mediated environment. *Journal of Marketing Management*, *29*(15-16), 1816–1833. doi:10.1080/0267257X.2013.803143

Park, N., Kee, K. F., & Valenzuela, S. (2009). Being Immersed in Social Networking Environment: Facebook Groups, Uses and Gratifications, and Social Outcomes. *Cyberpsychology & Behavior*, *12*(6), 729–733. doi:10.1089/cpb.2009.0003 PMID:19619037

Phan, M., Thomas, R., & Heine, K. (2011). Social Media and Luxury Brand Management: The Case of Burberry. *Journal of Global Fashion Marketing*, *2*(4), 213–222. doi:10.1080/20932685.2011.10593099

Rheingold, H. (n.d.). The Virtual Community: Homesteading on the Electronic Frontier. Available at: http://www.rheingold.com/vc/book/intro.html

Royo-Vela, M., & Casamassima, P. (2011). The influence of belonging to virtual brand communities on consumers' affective commitment, satisfaction and word-of-mouth advertising: The ZARA case. *Online Information Review*, *35*(4), 517–542. doi:10.1108/14684521111161918

Samu, S., Krishnan Lyndem, P., & Litz, R. A. (2012). Impact of brand-building activities and retailer-based brand equity on retailer brand communities. *European Journal of Marketing*, *46*(11/12), 1581–1601. doi:10.1108/03090561211259998

Scherbaum, C. A., Cohen-Charash, Y., & Kern, M. J. (2006). Measuring General Self-Efficacy a Comparison of Three Measures using Item Response Theory. *Educational and Psychological Measurement*, *66*(6), 1047–1063. doi:10.1177/0013164406288171

Schneider, P. P., & Vogt, C. A. (2012). Applying the 3M Model of Personality and Motivation to Adventure Travelers. *Journal of Travel Research*, *51*(6), 704–716. doi:10.1177/0047287512451134

Schwarzer, R., & Jerusalem, M. (1995). Generalized self-efficacy scale. In J. Weinman, S. Wright, & M. Johnston (Eds.), *Measures in Health Psychology: A User's Portfolio. Causal and Control Beliefs* (pp. 35–37). Windsor: NFER-NELSON.

Schwarzer, R., & Jerusalem, M. (2004). General self-efficacy scale. In S. Salek (Ed.), Compendium of Quality of Life Instruments. Cardiff: Centre for Socioeconomic Research, Cardiff University, (Vol.6, Section 2A:1). Haslemere: Euromed Communications (CD-ROM publication).

Shao, G. (2009). Understanding the Appeal of User-Generated Media: A Uses and Gratifications Perspective. *Internet Research*, *19*(1), 7–25. doi:10.1108/10662240910927795

Sherchan, W., Nepal, S., & Paris, C. (2013). A Survey of Trust in Social Networks [CSUR]. *ACM Computing Surveys*, *45*(4), 1–33. doi:10.1145/2501654.2501661

Solis, B. (2010). *Engage! The complete guide for brands and businesses to build, cultivate and measure success in the new web.* New Jersey: John Wiley and sons Inc.

Solis, B., & Breakenridge, D. K. (2009). *Putting the Public Back in Public Relations: How Social Media Is Reinventing the Aging Business of PR.* Upper Saddle River, NJ: FT Press/Pearson Education.

Sung, Y., Kim, Y., Kwon, O., & Moon, J. (2010). An Explorative Study of Korean Consumer Participation in Virtual Brand Communities in Social Network Sites. *Journal of Global Marketing*, *23*(5), 430–445. doi:10.1080/08911762.2010.521115

Tsai, W. S., & Men, L. R. (2013). Motivations and Antecedents of Consumer Engagement with Brand Pages on Social Networking Sites. *Journal of Interactive Advertising*, *13*(2), 76–87. doi:10.1080/15252019.2013.826549

Tuškej, U., Golob, U., & Podnar, K. (2013). The role of consumer–brand identification in building brand relationships. *Journal of Business Research*, *66*(1), 53–59. doi:10.1016/j.jbusres.2011.07.022

Vock, M., Dolen, W., & Ruyter, K. (2013). Understanding Willingness to Pay for Social Network Sites. *Journal of Service Research*, *16*(3), 311–325. doi:10.1177/1094670512472729

Wikipedia. (n.d.). Facebook. Available at: https://en.wikipedia.org/wiki/Facebook

Wikipedia. (n.d.). Interpersonal Relationship. Available at: https://en.wikipedia.org/wiki/Interpersonal_relationships

Wirtz, J., den Ambtman, A., Bloemer, J., Horváth, C., Ramaseshan, B., van de Klundert, J., & Kandampully, J. et al. (2013). Managing brands and customer engagement in online brand communities. *Journal of Service Management*, *24*(3), 223–244. doi:10.1108/09564231311326978

Woisetschläger, D. M., Hartleb, V., & Blut, M. (2008). How to make brand communities work: Antecedents and consequences of consumer participation. *Journal of Relationship Marketing*, *7*(3), 237–256. doi:10.1080/15332660802409605

Youcheng, W., & Fesenmaier, D. R. (2003). Assessing Motivation of Contribution in Online Communities: An Empirical Investigation of an Online Travel Community. *Electronic Markets*, *13*(1), 33–45. doi:10.1080/1019678032000052934

Zaglia, M. E. (2013). Brand communities embedded in social networks. *Journal of Business Research*, *66*(2-2), 216–223. doi:10.1016/j.jbusres.2012.07.015 PMID:23564989

Zeng, F., Huang, L., & Dou, W. (2009). Social Factors in User Perceptions and Responses to Advertising in Online Social Networking Communities. *Journal of Interactive Advertising*, *10*(1), 1–13. doi:10.1080/15252019.2009.10722159

Zolfaghar, K., & Aghaie, A. (2011). Evolution of trust networks in social web applications using supervised learning. *Procedia Computer Science*, *3*, 833–839. doi:10.1016/j.procs.2010.12.137

Chapter 10
Study of the Automatic Evaluation of Website Quality from Customer Insight:
A Case Study of the Most Visited News Websites as Influential Social Media Tool

Molood Arman
University of Tehran, Iran

Hassan Hajipoor
University of Tehran, Iran

Babak Sohrabi
University of Tehran, Iran

ABSTRACT

Effectiveness of websites is largely dependent on the quality of the website. The biggest share of the quality`s new concept is that the technical aspects of products and services combines with customers usage and understanding. Therefore websites evaluation based on the maximum usage and perception of the customers is considered an important issue to announce to the related organizations the success of website from customers' views. This customer relationship need a kind of management that first step of that for future decision needs knowledge about the websites features, customer insight and the position of websites among the competitors. One of the available media is the online news websites which their success is highly dependent on the relationship of their users. In this article achieving the information of websites is automatic and without the intervention of human so that the instant evaluation could be possible and used method is TOPSIS combined with information entropy to rank 791 news website which have most visitors of the Iranian users based on Alexa ranking report.

DOI: 10.4018/978-1-4666-8586-4.ch010

INTRODUCTION

With the rise of internet and its common use in Iran in the early seventies, some of the existing businesses have dramatically changed in nature. One of these businesses was news agencies which formerly had broadcasted their news as a telex to the offices of the newspapers and audio- visual media to be provided to general audience. But gradually with setting up websites they could be able to get users independently and their relationship become without intermediaries and directly. Even with the widespread use of the Internet in world, some of the newspapers and magazines has shut down the printing of their paper copies and distribute their news only via internet. Even newspapers that have retained their printed users have created websites to provide news for their users. The changing nature of the news agencies business can be described as today`s news agencies have become audience themselves alongside their authority role and producing the mother content of other public media, and their influence factors have increased. Based on this information the news organizations and agencies focus their efforts directly on serving better to their target customers in order to provide accurate services based on important information (Ulcina & Lafonte 2000, Peppers 2001).

Customer Relationship Management (CRM) is a general approach to management which is focused on increasing the relationship with customers enabled by IT (Brown 2000, Coningham 2002, Buttle 2004, and Silva & Batista 2007). Customer relationship management can collect and analyze information to produce a vision and insight toward customer behavior and predict their future needs (Silva & Batista 2007). Strategic customer relationship management is focused on developing customer-focused culture. This Culture committed to entice and keep customers by creating and assigning its values better than others. This culture reflects in leadership behaviors, organization's official planning systems and stories associated with the organization.(Richards & Jones, 2008). Then, one of the simplest steps to create this kind of strategic CRM in organization is increasing the quality of customer services more than other competitors and they should know their position on this issue than any other competitor.

The largest share of the new quality concept is that the technical aspects of products and services combine with customers and their perception. Therefore website evaluation is considered important based on the most usage and perception of customers to announce the success of a website from the client's perspective to the relevant agencies (Leonidio & et al., 2011).

To evaluate the quality of websites from customer perspective the aspects that customers are facing gets important, such as the website design, presentation and the times when international evaluation of the website can be influenced by observing the Website. That is why it is recommended that organizations pay attention to the design; website loading time, convenient accessibility, business plan and tasks that they must address them in their website, so that the customer does not get discouraged from the website and eventually the total website view and global prevalence of website does not decrease.

Thus many technical aspects related to website is directly related to user satisfaction and perception of website, this evaluation based on the properties can affect customer decision making as his first visit to website and also may lead to website survival (Leonidio & et al., 2011). According to this matter in the article we were after ranking the news agencies and news websites which have the most Iranian users in internet (based on Alexa statistics) and with regard to the criteria mentioned below.

From last few years social media sites became very important part of the internet. Every online user is using at least one or two social sites. Social news is a kind of social media that refers to websites that are very much in the trend of online community today, wherein users visit these sites to submit and vote on the news, stories, media such as images or other links posted on the site. Basically, these social news websites try to attract customers. These sites are very much useful as great sources of traffic, as well as with users who are into viral marketing. There are some special social news websites like digg, reddit or mixx that everyone has their specific features but as another view, all of news websites today are a kind of social news, because they let people who read their news, vote them and write their opinions and comments about the news and other comments.in the websites with this kind of interaction, organization and owner of these websites have an online relation with their customers. They must do everything to keep this customer relationship active.

The growing deployment of applying Internet in the world has contributed to the increasing rise in the number of websites but that does not necessarily mean the qualitative growth of websites. The demand towards having access to high quality websites for reaching the required information faster, safer and better is the first step to design, create and develop the tools and also the procedures to evaluate the quality of the websites.

In addition every individual and organization needs to have a successful website. Most of the people do a lot along with this need; however, a huge number of them make mistakes in the way of promoting their website, increasing the number of viewers and succeeding. Also the website owners are fond of activities insuring the permanence of these websites in the competitive market. Hence, one of the most important issues being of the major challenges of the managers and the exploiters of the websites is the issue of evaluating the websites. Accordingly, realizing the most effective factors on a specific kind of websites is of the most primary and also the most crucial proceedings to be done for evaluating websites. Furthermore, quantitative modeling of these features mentioning the importance and the weight each of them have in the quality of a website, will help the concerning institutions and the web owners to consider the different aspects of their website on the basis of priority and the mentioned importance and to have a better ranking among their competitors to resolve the problems and shortages.

Also, despite of growing increase of the websites and internet users there is limited number of academic studies reviewing the different criterion of the websites (Hernandez & et al., 2009). There have been a number of ways to evaluate the websites suggested by researchers. But they are still being reviewed (woolrych & et al., 2011). In fact the concept of website evaluating is mostly mistaken with the meaning of assessment in the literature of research. It is important to clarify the range and the objective of the research: is the study on the evaluation of the web or it is evaluating some specific websites? Therefore, is the evaluation goal redesigning the website or it is to rank the websites or reaching the statistics from its features? As a result a different focus is needed for evaluation method based on the goal and the platform (zahran & et al., 2014).

Furthermore, a number of news organizations in Iran are seeking the popularity of the online news between the addressees and is highly fond of evaluating its ranking compared to their other competitors. And this subject of evaluating the position of special career websites has turned to a business for companies which are active in such markets.

About the factors impacting the quality of websites, the evaluation methods, and finally evaluating the websites concerning e-commerce, library and university websites have been studied (Serhat & Cenginz, 2012, Younghwa & Kenneth, 2006 and Hsiu-Fen, 2010). Though, so far for evaluating the news websites noticing assessment principles special for these websites there are rare researches (Kanellopoulos & Kotsiantis, 2012), in the research done by Kanellopoulos & Kotsiantis, also the main focus is not on the Greek news websites, rather it is towards recommendatory systematic designing to accord the news with user's profiles, but primarily they evaluate the Greek news websites on the basis of the factors extracted from Alexa website.

In addition in defining the automatic evaluation the writer's view is basically towards using the online tools of automatic evaluation of websites such as using Webxact 10 (Hasanzade & Navidi 2010) validity check system W3C HTML (Bauer & Scharl, 2000) or the website of measuring tools of the global popularity12(Cho & Adams,2005, Fang 2007, Scowen 2017).and there are few studies concerning the automatic evaluation of websites which has considered the effect of all these principles and influential features on wesites in this automatic evaluation (Lee & Yamada 2009).

In this study an approach is presented for quality evaluation of websites which with its help characterization needed to assess the quality of websites can be extracted autonomously and without the need to use professionals. This approach makes it possible to evaluate websites online and get real-time evaluation. Efforts have been done in the past to evaluate websites are primarily done manually and didn`t have access to the resources necessary to cover all Web sites. Only a limited number of studies aimed at autonomously collecting data to evaluate Web sites have been done and they are not often comprehensive or Regardless of the Website Type have considered similar classification criteria for all sites and are looking for appropriate criteria and have not been limited to a particular group of websites. For instance Schubert & Selz in 1999 extended a tool for online research with a vast list of evaluation criteria. While their results included piles of valuable information, their data set was limited to the evaluation of only 70 different websites. The ultimate goal is to develop a comprehensive analysis and evaluation of hypertext structures framework which is publicly available. However, we need to be aware of the relevant variables to evaluate and classify websites. Thus both the framework and the software prototype imply on practical & measurable criteria definition. These criteria are evaluated and proposed individually for each website by the tool (Bauer & Scharl, 2000). The use of dedicated software agents for Web site evaluation is more efficient and is immune against human interpersonal and intrapersonal errors of human evaluation. Also using thousands of system data is possible and are not limited to samples of tens or hundreds. Normally, these benefits are along with the loss of unquantifiable amounts and data related to customers and human factors. Previous attempts to evaluate Web sites are done manually and didn`t have access to the resources necessary to cover all subjects (Bauer & Scharl, 2000).

LITERATURE REVIEW

Web evaluation studies have viewed the web as a whole concerning exact statistical calculation about the website and presenting the data about web traffic, visibility, connectivity, ranking and the total effect of a website on the web (Zahran et al., 2014). Web analysis performed by Web Analytics Association is to measure, gather, analyze and report from internet data aims the perception and optimizing how to use the web (Fang 2007).

Basically web analysis is a trade tool which websites managers have commenced that by adding a numerator on home pages for observing the web traffic. While, most studies concerning web analysis focus on e-commerce, the applied method can be used for all kinds of websites (Prom, 2007). Two famous tools for web analysis are Google Analytics and Alexa Analytics.

The studies of Link Analysis focuses on the topology of the websites with the assumption that the quality of a website is affiliated with its links. To analyze the links two critical methods are being used: Page Rank and Webometrics.

A huge number of researches have reviewed the structure of web links to optimize the results and have presented the ranking principles. At the time Page & Brin designed Google web browser, they realized the links as positive references and devised a system called Page. Google Page Rank is a link analysis algorithm which has been named after Larry Page giving a numerical version to each hyperlink and each page has a Page rank based on the number and the quality of internal links. Google considers 100 factors when specifying the rate of each page, but the Page Rank is the most important element in ordering the external outcomes.

Scowen (2007) has tested the e-learning websites versus checklist functions and then he has kept them against five ranking systems: searching Google links, Yahoo links, delicious links, the rank of Google and Alexa. Google and Alexa Page Rank are known to realize their correlation with utility of the websites, although none could be known as the main indicator of popularity.

Björneborn (2004) has reviewed the web assessment as studying qualitative concepts of constructing and using data resources, structures and web technologies, extracting book assessment and data evaluation attitudes. In this term web evaluation can be conducted aiming validating the links and presenting its acceptance as a profitable scale for measuring the web. Web assessment has evaluated the international observability and also the impact of an organization or area (country) on the web, but still is a novelty of the research Holmberg and Thelwall (2009).

Most of the web assessment studies have been done in universities, for instance Cybermetrics Lab (2010) which publishes the university web pages since 2004. The other study by Thelwall and Zuccala in 2008 have measured the internal links between European universities. Few of the web assessment studies which were on e-government, also have presented a new way of WIF. The first attempt to measure e-government through web assessment method has been Petricek's who has compared the inventory site in five countries and has illustrated that America and Canada as the major connected sites are more connected to New Zealand and Czech Federation.

Based on the studies in the area of evaluating websites, most of these evaluations have been in the area of e-commerce websites, libraries, universities, e-government, hospitals, hotels, and tourism websites, of course papers such as Kanellopoulos and Kotsiantis (2012) who have evaluated the Greek news websites, Asnafi and Osareh (2007) have evaluated the web-like evaluation of news websites by using the web importance factor and Jowkar and Didgah have evaluated the news website via Correspondence analysis.

In addition to this there are many ways to rank the websites. Common ranking ways are divided into categories: (Lo & Sedhain, 2006)

1. Activity based
2. Reference based
3. Opinion based.

In addition to these the new issue of ranking based on learning has been of the important subjects in the recent years which plays a crucial role in recovering the data especially via search engines.

In the activity based ranking the websites are ranked based on the actions which happen on the websites. The website with the highest traffic or the highest use will be more highly ranked. You can see the samples of such ranking in Alexa, ComScore, Nilson, Ranking.com and websearch. Measuring the web traffic is never easily achieved. Such measuring is tightly dependent on the thing which is measured and the way it is measured. According to the website traffic alone we can distinguish three concepts: the number of the people who have visited the website, the time they spend on the website, and the frequency of which they return to the mentioned website. All these measures are the valid measures of website traffic, in other researches these three concepts have been defined as the following names: (Lee & Leckenby, 1998)

- **Reach:** The number of individual viewers who have visited the website at least once. This shows the expansion of addressees.
- **Frequency:** The average number of the times a viewer visits the site in the period of remeasuring the site.
- **Duration:** The average time that the website viewers spend on the website. This shows the stickiness of the website.

In reference ranking a website is ranked on the basis of the frequency it has been referred through other websites. Probably the more a website is referred the more important that website would be, especially if this reference is via the websites with more authority in the similar subject. Link references are divided into following categories:

1. **Self-Links:** They are linked by themselves.
2. **Foreign Links:** They are referred by other websites
3. **Weighted Foreign Links:** They weigh the links based on the importance of the referred websites.

Google was the first company using the popularity of link in the algorithm of its page rank. Also this method is of the most important factors to recover the data in engine searches.

Opinion ranking uses the user's judgment for ranking the website. The result of such ranking is the feedback resulted from subjective judgment of the panel of the members. Indeed all ranking methods including traffic based and reference based methods are on the basis of the user's opinions but the opinion based ranking clearly and directly is connected with the subjective idea of the viewers. 50 first websites of Times, the first 100 websites of Computer Magazine, the best first 100 websites, etc. are examples of such ranking.

The ideas are taken from the following three items:

1. Ideas from experts' panel
2. The ideas of potential customers
3. The purchase experience or usage of real customers.

In addition, there are some automatic tools to collect web data, these are the software gathering useful information and specifying the potential problems of the website. The first study on the automatic tools was done by Ivory and Chevalier in the year 2002. Brajnik in the year 2004 has implemented diverse kinds of web test tools: access tools such as Bobby, utility tools such as LIFT, operational tools such as TOPAZ, security tools such as WebCPO and also web classifying tools such as WebTango. He mentions the adaption of these tools limited to inexistence of the ways made to compare them and also has suggested that the effectiveness of automatic tools are evaluated automatically. Brajnik (2004) In fact there are many automatic tools both as web based services and desktop applications. An accessible tool based on free public web is http://www.cynthiasays.com/, a product of hisoftware which lets the mentioned URL to be given to that for more analysis or gives a report based on the 508 standards or Web Content Accessibility Guidelines (WCAG) (Zahran & et al., 2014).

Of the success factors of news industry is to satisfy the readers. The news industry is of the most important keys to such prosperity which needs modern technologies such as Customer Relationship Management (CRM). (CRM) is considered as modern technologies which have a vital role in trying to keep the customers and changing them into real, faithful customers. To assert every technology without having the backgrounds the organization will move towards failure. Thus in this research the important factors to evaluate the news websites has been identified from customers point of view according to important indicators for evaluating the quality of news websites and in total according to the results achieved in this research it can be said that the news industry as for the Iranian customers can perform the CRM by doing some activities.

METHOD

The method of this article is based on two main axes, the first axis is collecting data as the indices for evaluation all of which must be automated and with Crawlers and without human factors & the second axis uses the data collected in first axis to rank websites to use autonomous evaluation. These two steps are described as follow:

Step One. Data collection and determining the features needed for quality evaluation:

For collecting websites information and their history the crawler method is used in this study. Also according to the autonomous method of data collection, the following criteria are considered to evaluate the quality of the website:

- Popularity of website is measured by google Page Rank indicator, the number of unique visitors (reach value) to view Web sites and number of pages viewed (Page views value) by the unique user, and delta rate of change (Reach value delta) in the last the number of users in three months.
- Website accessibility which is measured with rating index of the search engine (Seo score), the amount of being indexed on search engines, and website place in the query output of new websites in Google's search engine
- The speed which is measured with Average load time index.
- Navigation which is calculated by total amount of backward link indexes of website
- Presentation which is measured with the error rate in the HTML code of W3C's web site
- Multimedia content which is measured with the average amount of video files, flash, audio and video in the main page of website
- Website history which is measured with the domain age index
- Coefficient of evaluation globally accepted which here is called Alexa traffic rank which are ranking websites based on the users views

These indexes and data have been extracted for 791 news websites that these website were either partially engaged in news such as www.tabnak.ir or www.farsnews.com or sites which are dealing with news related to a special field like www.varzesh3.ir (specialized sports news site) or www.cnet.com (specialized goods and products news site).

Step Two. Ranking websites with combining Topsis and Entropy method

After data collection, the index weight based on the importance of criteria is calculated by information entropy weight method, and according to this weights, the TOPSIS method is used to achieve the final ranking and quality websites evaluation.

The Technique for order preference by similarity to Ideal solution (TOPSIS) was first proposed by Yoon (1980) and Hwang and Yoon (1981) (wang & et.al. 2011). TOPSIS is a proper technique for ranking a number of alternatives via measuring Euclidean distances. This algorithm is based on the fact that best alternative simultaneously have the farthest distance from the negative ideal solution and the shortest distance from the positive ideal distance. Also, these ideal distances to be easily defined based on the benefit and the cost indices. It is assumed that each criterion values is numeric, monotonically increasing or decreasing (Behzadian 2012).

There are a few existing researches that used Entropy method to determine the weight of criterion in the TOPSIS method. (Akyene 2012, Zhang et al., 2012). The detailed applied computational steps are as follows:

1.1.1. Creating the Normalized Decision Matrix

This step allows the indicator's values in different units to be transformed to a common measurable unit. The normalization matrix is useful for comparisons of different criterion and could be calculate by many methods. In this article we calculate it by using the following formula.

$$x'_{ij} = \frac{x_{ij} - \min\limits_{1\le j\le n} x_{ij}}{\max\limits_{1\le j\le n} x_{ij} - \min\limits_{1\le j\le n} x_{ij}}$$

The matrix X' is the normalized matrix of the decision Matrix X, the final value of the x'_{ij} between 0 and 1.

1.1.2. Calculating Criterion Weight

It is obvious that each evaluation criterion is not of equal importance and for MCDM technique, the relative importance of each criterion is necessary to measure. There are many techniques to determine weights: the weighted evaluation technique, the eigenvector method, the weighted least square method, the entropy method, the AHP method and etc. (Huang 2008). The similarity between these methods is that all of them determined by statistical properties. On the other hand, there are other methods for determining weights that are based on the knowledge of experts. The weights are named objective weights and subjective weights respectively. Here, the entropy method is applied to derive the weights of the criteria in the TOPSIS method.

Entropy, in information theory, also known as the average amount of information (Akyene 2012) that is the amount of uncertainty associated with a random variable (Huang 2008). Entropy in information theory usually refers to the Shannon entropy after Claude E. Shannon (1948), although its origin goes back to Pauli and von Neumann (Ueltschi 2006). According to the amount of criterion scattering, the weight of all indices is calculated by information entropy weight. Entropy method for calculating weight is highly reliable and can be easily applied for information measurement (Akyene 2012). In this article, according to normalized decision matrix $X' = \left(x'_{ij}\right)_{m\times n}$, the weight of indices is calculated using following steps:

$$P_{ij} = \frac{1 + x'_{ij}}{\sum_{i=1}^{m}\left(1 + x'_{ij}\right)},\ 1 \le i \le m, 1 \le j \le n$$

The output entropy E_j of the jth criterion was calculated by:

$$E_j = -k \times \left(\sum_{i=1}^{m} p_{ij} \ln p_{ij}\right)$$

where

$$K = \frac{1}{\ln m},\ 1 \le i \le m, 1 \le j \le n$$

Variation coefficient of the jth criterion can be defined by the following equation:

$$G_j = 1 - E_j,\ 1 \le j \le n$$

Note that the smaller E_j is the greater the deviation degree of criterion j. Then, the more information entropy of criterion j provides, the higher the criterion j weight is. Finally, the weight W_j is defined by:

$$W_j = \frac{G_j}{\sum_{j=1}^{n} G_j}$$

Note that $\sum_{1}^{n} W_j = 1$.

1.1.3. Calculating the Weighted Normalized Decision Matrix A

The weighted normalized interval-valued decision matrix $A = \left(a_{ij}\right)_{n\times m}$ is obtained using the following expressions:

$$a_{ij} = W_j \times x'_{ij}$$

1.1.4. Specifying the Positive Ideal Solution V^+ and the Negative Ideal Solution V^-

The positive ideal solution V^+ refers to the best alternative and the negative ideal solution V^- refers to the worst alternative.According to the following formulas the positive and negative ideal solutions of jth criterion can be calculated:

$$V^+ = \left\{ \left(\max_{1 \le i \le m} a_{ij} \mid j \in J \right), \left(\min_{1 \le i \le m} a_{ij} \mid j \in J' \right), \ldots, \left(\max_{1 \le i \le m} a_{ij} \mid j \in J \right) \right\} = \left\{ V_1^+, V_2^+, V_3^+, \ldots, V_n^+ \right\}$$

$$V^- = \left\{ \left(\min_{1 \le i \le m} a_{ij} \mid j \in J \right), \left(\max_{1 \le i \le m} a_{ij} \mid j \in J' \right), \ldots, \left(\min_{1 \le i \le m} a_{ij} \mid j \in J \right) \right\} = \left\{ V_1^-, V_2^-, V_3^-, \ldots, V_n^- \right\}$$

$$J = \{ j = 1, 2, \ldots, n \mid j \in benefit \}$$
$$J' = \{ j = 1, 2, \ldots, n \mid j \in cost \}$$

1.1.5. Determining the Separation of Each Alternative from the Positive and Negative Ideal Solutions

The n-dimensional Euclidean distance as the separation measure of each alternative for both ideal solutions is calculated as follows:

$$d^+_i = \sqrt{\sum_{j=1}^{n} \left(a_{ij} - V^+_j \right)^2} ; 1 \le i \le m$$

$$d^-_i = \sqrt{\sum_{j=1}^{n} \left(a_{ij} - V^-_j \right)^2} ; 1 \le i \le m$$

1.1.6. Calculating the Relative Closeness to the Positive Ideal Solution

This measure is defined as Ci:

$$C_i = \frac{d_i^+}{d_i^- + d_i^+}, 1 \le i \le m; 0 \le C_i \le 1$$

1.1.7. Ranking the Alternatives

According to the relative closeness measure to the positive ideal solution, alternatives could be ranked. The larger relative closeness value, the better the alternative. The best alternative is the one with the higher relative closeness to the positive ideal solution.

All of the above defined formulas have been conducted on 791 news websites by crawlers and the results can be seen on the top 100 sites given by the method used in Table 1 and 2.

RESULTS

First the weight of indicators of evaluation by information entropy method can be observed in Table 1 which as it is seen the Alexa traffic rank with the 0.25 amount and after that google page rank with 0.145 are indicators with the most influence; and changes in users amounts with 0.005 weight is indicator with the least importance. Finally the information of 100 news websites can be seen in Table 2 which by using TOPSIS method among 791 websites shows they have most viewers from Iran and they had best quality with regard to websites evaluation criteria. As can be seen among the 791 reviewed websites, Cnn.com, Reuters.com and Cnet.com websites are the highest ranking respectively.

The order of importance of factors based on Information entropy in ranking news websites according of customer's need is defined below:

1. Alexa Traffic rank
2. Domain age
3. Page rank
4. The position of website in google with Query "وبسايتهاي خبري"[2]
5. Multimedia content
6. Seo score
7. Page views
8. Average Load Time
9. HTML's error
10. Average of indexes in search engines
11. Links backward
12. Number of Unique visitors
13. The rate of unique visitors 'change

As we can see the technical requirements according to the needs of customers for success of websites are the activity duration of websites in this field and the website's credibility that presents in Domain age factor. Another important requirement is the content of websites that has an outstanding effect on search speed and the value of page rank, the position of website in google based on related Query and Alexa traffic rank.

Furthermore, the other technical features as load time of websites, Html's error of websites structure, the number of links are the other important features.

The least important factor between the mentioned criteria is the rate of unique visitor's change.

Table 1. The weight of criteria

Index Name	Multimedia Content	The Position of Website in Google with Query “خبری وبسایت‌های”	Average Load Time	Page Views	Number of Unique Visitors	The Rate of Unique Visitors ‘Change	Links Backward	HTML’s Error	Average of Indexes in Search Engines	Domain Age	Alexa Traffic Rank	Seo Score	Page Rank
Weight of index (Entropy method)	0.08229	0.127485	0.031314	0.043294	0.011912	0.005844	0.013674	0.028891	0.017059	0.170593	0.258915	0.064262	0.144528

Table 2. The raw data of 100 top news websites

Rank	Websites Name	Page rank	Seo Score	Alexa Traffic Rank	Multimedia Content	The Position of Website in Google with Query “خبری وبسایت‌های”	Average Load Time (Second)	Page Views	Number of Unique Visitors	The Rate of Unique Visitors’ Change	Backward Links	HTML’s Error	Average of Indexes in Search Engines	Domain Age (Month)	Separation Measure of Positive Ideal Solution	Separation Measure of Negative Ideal Solution	Closeness to Ideal Solution
1	cnn.com	9	50	1801	29.25	41.81669	2637	3.19	18770	5.6	265479	375	2637	243.4521	758.0203	74566.11	0.010063
2	reuters.com	9	60	3757	8.5	41.81669	3007	2.34	4110	-4.65	149748	252	3007	247.1342	6445.664	68350.23	0.086177
3	cnet.com	8	63	427	12.5	41.81669	3351	2.95	12280	1.9	170452	9	3351	238.0603	25798.62	48857.07	0.345568
4	ghatreh.com	5	57	80	2.75	79	2000	3.86	358	3.5	2966	0	2000	86.63014	37988.17	36818.46	0.507818
5	ruvr.ru	7	76	2777	17.5	41.81669	2587	2.62	560	0.5	14489	251	2587	95.37534	54347.18	20473.95	0.726361
6	vista.ir	3	42	68	4.5	164	1357	3.73	392	19.5	1638	709	1357	0	55924.25	19071.6	0.745698
7	skysports.com	8	57	8925	11.25	41.81669	2058	3.38	1291	-17.69	10156	299	2058	186.937	59457.57	15221.84	0.796171
8	khabarfarsi.com	4	31	34	26.25	1	1789	6.38	576	-8.62	4218	269	1789	72.16438	61898.12	13313.17	0.82299
9	khorasannews.com	5	58	304	14.25	118	1888	4.21	102.1	-6.84	2873	0	1888	145.7753	66287.55	9237.959	0.877684
10	jamnews.ir	4	47	56	19.25	227	2194	4.71	403	-18.72	5159	97	2194	0	67544.66	8173.592	0.892053
11	jahannews.com	5	42	79	23.75	21	2050	5.47	318	-10.95	4773	218	2050	81.0411	67716.47	8025.987	0.894036

continued on following page

Table 2. Continued

Rank	Websites Name	Page rank	Seo Score	Alexa Traffic Rank	Multimedia Content	The Position of Website in Google with Query “خبری وبسایتهای”	Average Load Time (Second)	Page Views	Number of Unique Visitors	The Rate of Unique Visitors' Change	Backward Links	HTML's Error	Average of Indexes in Search Engines	Domain Age (Month)	Separation Measure of Positive Ideal Solution	Separation Measure of Negative Ideal Solution	Closeness to Ideal Solution
12	eqeep.ir	2	44	1860	4.25	41.81669	1611	1.74	19.9	-7.72	152	11	1611	0	67597.04	7902.182	0.895334
13	cbc.ca	8	63	11272	8.5	41.81669	2985	2.21	1457	7.9	62715	31	2985	158.5973	67334.06	7391.865	0.90108
14	mehrnews.com	6	72	42	23.75	58	1265	3.68	690	-6.02	13840	103	1265	133.9397	68919.91	7048.042	0.907223
15	youm7.com	6	52	11646	-0.5	41.81669	3162	4.18	2281	-21.16	14631	676	3162	72.9863	67777.05	6926.988	0.907274
16	tabnak.ir	5	50	12	54.75	6	1594	6.16	1441	-0.43	11806	12	1594	0	69080.7	6925.829	0.908878
17	irna.ir	7	55	110	25.5	13	3811	3.33	321	19.1	12783	55	3811	0	69068.58	6910.68	0.909045
18	forexfactory.com	4	65	4578	0.75	41.81669	2704	3.76	1245	5	3262	0	2704	118.4219	68568.39	6723.273	0.910704
19	afkarnews.ir	5	52	40	21	394	2464	3.13	570	-3.43	5719	300	2464	0	69345.8	6714.676	0.911719
20	aljazeera.net	8	57	6471	20.5	41.81669	4125	2.41	1000	-36.41	32369	0	4125	208.1753	68809.11	6296.919	0.91616
21	asriran.com	6	42	25	0.25	19	3943	5	924	-6.03	9670	12	3943	94.29041	69831.39	6347.007	0.916682
22	sciencemag.org	8	64	14350	3.5	41.81669	3021	1.85	179	-2.14	31946	0	3021	212.2849	68469.25	6187.559	0.91712
23	isna.ir	6	57	37	16.25	56	1566	4.11	727	-0.31	16023	59	1566	0	70006.08	6228.694	0.918296
24	khabaronline.ir	5	57	29	14	139	2175	3.46	857	-2.32	9315	499	2175	0	70093.05	6165.049	0.919155
25	javanemrooz.com	3	55	1115	34.75	41.81669	2648	3.15	33.1	7	987	32	2648	53.88493	70269.6	5847.874	0.923173
26	khabaryaab.com	3	68	3762	9.5	41.81669	1843	2.15	10.7	-5.25	170	29	1843	47.76986	69905.33	5709.297	0.924495
27	tnews.ir	4	63	99	12.75	132	1967	5.21	234	11.1	2563	15	1967	0	70790.34	5680.531	0.925716
28	yjc.ir	6	44	23	24.5	15	1621	4.51	947	-5	65808	29	1621	0	71164.3	5513.572	0.928094
29	jarchi.ir	3	63	119	1.25	41.81669	1713	2.34	289	33	153	0	1713	0	71087.49	5490.87	0.928297
30	irib.ir	7	50	120	14.25	60	1990	3.89	409	-7.29	14172	88	1990	0	71486.64	5250.537	0.931578
31	adinehbook.com	3	70	893	15.5	41.81669	1479	4.21	28.5	175	328	0	1479	106.0603	71315.1	5198.216	0.932061
32	aftabnews.ir	5	55	121	67.75	128	1087	4.84	270	-13.91	4192	7	1087	0	71604.93	5189.471	0.932424
33	farsnews.com	6	55	11	17	2	2030	5.43	1743	-1.49	25681	157	2030	131.4082	72007.43	5002.536	0.93504
34	iribnews.ir	6	52	482	35.75	52	4180	2.63	88.4	1	4080	168	4180	0	71959.61	4906.266	0.936171

continued on following page

Table 2. Continued

Rank	Websites Name	Page rank	Seo Score	Alexa Traffic Rank	Multimedia Content	The Position of Website in Google with Query “خبري وبسايتهاي”	Average Load Time (Second)	Page Views	Number of Unique Visitors	The Rate of Unique Visitors' Change	Backward Links	HTML's Error	Average of Indexes in Search Engines	Domain Age (Month)	Separation Measure of Positive Ideal Solution	Separation Measure of Negative Ideal Solution	Closeness to Ideal Solution
35	iribtv.ir	4	72	941	10.25	41.81669	1285	3.38	29.4	-39.08	1615	105	1285	0	72356.71	4629.666	0.939864
36	seratnews.ir	4	72	153	0	448	2087	4.66	232	-13.43	2834	18	2087	0	72766.36	4636.378	0.940101
37	donya-e-eqtesad.com	6	63	172	6.75	412	999	3.74	187	5	4292	200	999	132.0329	72811.04	4622.217	0.940307
38	nasimonline.ir	4	68	736	94.5	41.81669	3230	2.47	54.3	14	1433	222	3230	0	72569.14	4571.566	0.940737
39	fararu.com	5	52	58	41.5	373	2027	5.49	412	-3.56	3671	290	2027	79.39726	73009.98	4575.508	0.941026
40	pichak.net	5	47	100	11	41.81669	1054	3.69	263	2.9	110456	0	1054	55.36438	73825.61	4626.444	0.941028
41	fardanews.com	5	50	107	15.25	9	1792	5.45	254	-4.93	7465	2	1792	108.8548	73155.15	4521.757	0.941788
42	alalam.ir	6	60	799	16	358	3108	3.39	183	7	5986	193	3108	0	72781.3	4472.592	0.942105
43	al-akhbar.com	6	60	16080	-0.5	41.81669	2170	3.08	172	9	3361	182	2170	127.4301	70372.02	4319.004	0.942175
44	tasnimnews.com	5	54	45	45.25	41.81669	1812	2.99	577	42.9	7351	0	1812	17.85205	73337.07	4487.655	0.942336
45	noorportal.net	4	43	1184	39	41.81669	2906	1.51	31.7	9	1042	0	2906	80.90959	72653.76	4435.749	0.94246
46	entekhab.ir	5	42	57	0	10	3920	4.71	431	-2.2	3043	18	3920	0	73368.26	4463.934	0.942647
47	aftabir.com	4	63	174	40.25	101	4158	2.79	225	-8.3	2440	15	4158	43.52877	73300.53	4450.517	0.942759
48	varzesh3.com	5	55	4	8.25	99	989	7.99	2879	4	8888	642	989	35.37534	73748.45	4417.252	0.943489
49	alef.ir	5	47	73	9.75	11	1724	3.71	382	-2.55	4337	106	1724	0	73662.51	4411.74	0.943493
50	snn.ir	6	64	117	93.25	485	2935	5.47	210	62	3657	143	2935	0	73677.74	4388.34	0.943787
51	rajanews.com	6	52	82	84.75	89	3617	3.61	373	-0.29	7656	471	3617	94.22466	73796.81	4377.289	0.944006
52	qudsonline.ir	6	76	236	15.5	500	1934	2.23	159	-9.07	1729	151	1934	0	73727.3	4356.116	0.944212
53	shafaf.ir	4	68	158	102.75	14	1195	5.24	170	-24.54	11138	7	1195	0	73934.82	4352.716	0.944401
54	afsaran.ir	3	63	177	14	218	2965	5.78	138.7	29	3003	1	2965	0	73904.52	4338.003	0.944557
55	shahrekhabar.com	5	55	28	2.25	35	904	9.07	597	-2.34	1874	15	904	64.2411	74268.15	4357.754	0.944576
56	perspolisnews.com	3	65	339	-0.5	41.81669	3658	5.13	107.8	-9.74	667	52	3658	86.4	73733.73	4318.985	0.944666

continued on following page

Table 2. Continued

Rank	Websites Name	Page rank	Seo Score	Alexa Traffic Rank	Multimedia Content	The Position of Website in Google with Query “خبري وبسايتهاي”	Average Load Time (Second)	Page Views	Number of Unique Visitors	The Rate of Unique Visitors’ Change	Backward Links	HTML’s Error	Average of Indexes in Search Engines	Domain Age (Month)	Separation Measure of Positive Ideal Solution	Separation Measure of Negative Ideal Solution	Closeness to Ideal Solution
57	themeforest.net	7	50	999	13	41.81669	1302	9.82	7760	16.1	53832	11	1302	73.21644	73438.75	4289.045	0.94482
58	khabarpu.com	4	57	55	36	16	1720	6.21	370	-12.24	1132	0	1720	24.85479	74465.61	4340.755	0.944919
59	bultannews.com	5	39	229	0	249	1268	3.26	166	-15.71	3573	129	1268	81.89589	74152.81	4310.893	0.945059
60	parsnews.com	1	75	160	16.5	41.81669	1510	1.97	236	-22.78	637	0	1510	165.5342	74466.33	4315.602	0.945221
61	namehnews.ir	4	45	176	13.25	449	1076	3.33	200	-2.93	1194	0	1076	0	74465.77	4313.935	0.945241
62	khabarkhoon.com	5	55	653	4	134	5935	2.8	56.5	46	725	21	5935	47.04658	73563.58	4259.524	0.945267
63	parseek.com	4	55	192	0.75	32	4031	2.37	185	-11.48	2967	10	4031	140.2521	74234.08	4297.667	0.945275
64	baharnews.ir	5	44	221	36.5	36	1672	4.53	130	36	892	637	1672	0	74314.17	4301.418	0.945285
65	fc-perspolis.com	5	44	218	10.25	69	2731	5.64	122.2	-9.55	3033	6	2731	59.07945	74323.33	4295.278	0.945366
66	farhangnews.ir	4	72	261	21.5	484	2013	3.64	116.5	33	2447	30	2013	0	74258.4	4291.213	0.945369
67	jonoubnews.ir	3	66	186	29	236	2617	2.24	148.6	77	846	0	2617	0	74466.23	4301.333	0.945392
68	akharinnews.com	0	0	226	7.25	184	1595	3.32	203	-25.26	0	0	1595	0	74466.8	4297.993	0.945433
69	musicema.com	5	68	333	44	208	523	2.73	117	-21.94	2001	395	523	64.56986	74270.24	4282.648	0.945481
70	abna.ir	5	72	992	1.75	41.81669	3231	2.54	74	0.9	2987	260	3231	0	73408.75	4228.144	0.94554
71	kayhan.ir	6	48	276	0	41.81669	1124	2.76	148	10	1038	0	1124	0	74465.97	4288.812	0.945542
72	boursenews.ir	5	44	266	0	174	1496	4.79	99.4	7	855	52	1496	0	74466.02	4288.55	0.945545
73	etedaal.ir	4	71	284	0.75	23	1139	3.01	141	-10.36	962	41	1139	0	74466.13	4286.704	0.945568
74	arshnews.ir	3	66	235	26.25	41.81669	3299	4.81	108.5	62	330	0	3299	0	74466.63	4284.85	0.94559
75	irinn.ir	5	57	328	19	44	1720	4.3	99	3	2471	3	1720	0	74312.13	4275.065	0.945601
76	598.ir	4	64	377	65.25	107	1874	4.72	76.3	-29.41	1747	7	1874	0	74263.51	4262.94	0.945713
77	anaj.ir	3	50	393	28.5	41.81669	959	2.8	113	-19.81	727	274	959	0	74303.04	4263.389	0.945735
78	bibaknews.com	4	68	366	19.25	41.81669	2896	2.83	94.1	-17.14	1483	13	2896	41.85205	74266.42	4258.976	0.945763

continued on following page

Table 2. Continued

Rank	Websites Name	Page rank	Seo Score	Alexa Traffic Rank	Multimedia Content	The Position of Website in Google with Query "وب‌سایت‌های خبری"	Average Load Time (Second)	Page Views	Number of Unique Visitors	The Rate of Unique Visitors' Change	Backward Links	HTML's Error	Average of Indexes in Search Engines	Domain Age (Month)	Separation Measure of Positive Ideal Solution	Separation Measure of Negative Ideal Solution	Closeness to Ideal Solution
79	ettelaat.com	6	80	1431	3.75	41.81669	2447	2.73	29	21	2757	7	2447	207.6164	73165.75	4195.465	0.945768
80	javanonline.ir	5	50	927	0	78	1201	3.36	35.9	-22.82	2135	107	1201	0	73608.02	4212.403	0.94587
81	shariyan.com	3	79	383	73.5	41.81669	1876	1.72	107.9	67	254	0	1876	17.62192	74466.45	4256.667	0.945929
82	momtaznews.com	3	48	295	11.25	41.81669	5763	2.84	125	9	618	0	5763	21.66575	74466.14	4254.646	0.945953
83	wikipg.com	2	43	391	33.5	41.81669	2724	2.8	90.7	70	498	0	2724	29.81918	74466.08	4249.033	0.94602
84	footballonline.ir	4	76	406	16.5	41.81669	3003	6.12	69.8	66	492	0	3003	0	74418.53	4243.694	0.946052
85	bazarkhabar.ir	5	76	424	27.75	163	3008	4.07	60.8	-6.52	675	52	3008	0	74411.02	4238.954	0.946104
86	shafaqna.com	4	52	370	16.5	41.81669	5677	2.76	134	-2.37	2519	35	5677	34.45479	74380.16	4237.05	0.946105
87	pnuna.com	3	50	437	6.25	330	3088	3.55	49.2	1	517	70	3088	34.84932	74435.18	4239.945	0.946108
88	almanar.com.lb	4	68	1326	0.25	41.81669	2412	3.34	190	-15.03	5356	3	2412	0	73322.04	4175.093	0.946126
89	weather.ir	6	80	449	35.5	41.81669	2570	1.57	66.5	338	2342	16	2570	0	74465.27	4235.468	0.946183
90	navad.net	5	55	493	54	219	3861	4.03	93.3	-19.08	1620	877	3861	128.3507	74229.92	4222.014	0.946183
91	m2newmedia.com	2	54	499	0	41.81669	952	1.41	5220	60.4	162	0	952	87.74795	74466.47	4234.152	0.946199
92	estekhdamnews.com	2	68	412	23.75	41.81669	4184	3.31	65.5	-26.3	316	1277	4184	24.13151	74466.38	4233.901	0.946202
93	khabardehi.com	2	60	438	8.75	41.81669	3245	1.88	94	-46.31	2239	231	3245	10.78904	74465.37	4233.743	0.946203
94	1doost.com	2	58	477	27.25	41.81669	1793	6.9	56.7	6	750	4	1793	72.9863	74466.11	4233.485	0.946207
95	gamefa.com	2	60	455	20	27	2967	4.65	71.8	-8.31	1311	146	2967	101.8521	74465.82	4231.268	0.946233
96	asrekhodro.com	0	0	503	28.25	53	3260	3.54	77.6	-0.14	0	0	3260	0	74466.95	4217.164	0.946404
97	92.242.195.123	0	0	594	-0.5	41.81669	116	3.8	3.4	25	0	0	116	0	74466.92	4215.624	0.946422
98	enekas.info	3	63	540	-0.5	41.81669	6092	5.66	57.7	-40.15	1083	22	6092	26.16986	74233.28	4196.925	0.946488
99	fcesteghlal.ir	4	61	549	9.75	84	2813	3.54	66.8	-25.57	2554	63	2813	0	74445.28	4208.524	0.946493
100	ilna.ir	6	72	595	0.25	271	1407	2.27	88.4	-13.9	4441	182	1407	0	74463.72	4206.271	0.946533

CONCLUSION

The digital world has come a long way since the early days the World Wide Web. The digital world we are in now is more complicated environment than the physical world. The method of attracting and keeping customers is different from what organization & markets do in real world. One of the channels to communicate with customers in this environments are media and one of them is news websites. In last few years, Customer relationship management is even more important than ever.

Since in this research, the important factors to evaluate the news websites has been identified from customers point of view based on important indicators for evaluating the quality of news websites, we can easily evaluate the list of websites and find the best website with the same target through customer insight. This method helps the organizations and individuals, particularly owners of websites, to understand better their relationships with the customers, because of the numeric rank and numeric measure that was provided.

Furthermore, with the creating this system to assess the quality of this kind of websites that are sort of social media because of their interaction with this readers and for open comments for customers under each news article, we could combine the technical aspects of websites that are one of the important factors to absorbs customers with other factors that are related to peoples, like increasing the view of website and its pages. As this point of view, organization with the perception and understanding the features of sites that are important to attract and keep customers, can take the necessary steps to improve their positions among other competitors.

Also, this method can be improved with extracting and using other features like the number of followers, the number of following, the average number of fav or the average number of like that every websites have in some other kind of popular social media like twitter, facebook or etc.

This kind of real-time evaluation for websites can be extended to other kind of them. Then, as an organization, we can have an overall view of all special kind of websites with my own scope and activity to find important criteria and then focus on them to improve our position for absorption customers, and as a customer we can find the websites that have either good technical quality or other customer views.

The results from this paper show that the technical requirements according to the needs of customers are the errors of websites' structure, multimedia content and the table of contents of websites (position of websites based on related Query). Contents of website impact on search speed and the value of page rank. The errors of websites' structure also is another important element in the design of the user guidance.

Finally, results show that the application of quality function deployment can cause special data and information in web site design for user comfort that has a significant effect on increasing the number of visitors and the success of websites.

REFERENCES

Akyene, T. (2012). Cell Phone Evaluation Base on Entropy and TOPSIS. *Interdisciplinary Journal of Research in Business*, *1*(12), 9–15.

Asnafi, A. R., & Osareh, F. (2007). A study of collaboration among Iranian News Agencies websites using Webometrics methods. *Collnet Journal of Scientometrics and Information Management*, *1*(1), 23–26. doi:10.1080/09720502.2007.10700950

Bauer, Ch., & Scharl, A. (2000). Quantitive evaluation of Web site content and structure. *Internet Research, 10*(1), 31–44. doi:10.1108/10662240010312138

Behzadian, M., Khanmohammadi, O. S., Yazdani, M., & Ignatius, J. (2012). A state-of the-art survey of TOPSIS applications. *Expert Systems with Applications, 39*(17), 13051–13069. doi:10.1016/j.eswa.2012.05.056

Björneborn, L. (2004). *Small-World Link Structures across an Academic Web Space: A Library and Information Science Approach*. Royal School of Library and Information Science, Denmark. Retrieved from http://vip.db.dk/lb/phd/phd-thesis.pdf

Brajnik, G. (2004). Using automatic tools in accessibility and usability assurance. In *User-Centered Interaction Paradigms for Universal Access in the Information Society (pp. 219-234)*. New York, NY: Springer. doi:10.1007/978-3-540-30111-0_18

Brown, S. A., & Coopers, P. W. (2000). *Customer relationship management: A strategic imperative in the world of e-business*. New York, NY: John Wiley & Sons, Inc.

Buttle, F. (2004). *Customer relationship management: Concepts and tools. Butterworth-Heinemann*. Amsterdam: Elsevier.

Cho, J., & Adams, R. (2005). Page Quality: In Search of an Unbiased Web Ranking. In *Proceedings of the 2005 ACM SIGMOD conference* (pp.551-562), Baltimore, MD: ACM.

Cunningham, M. J. (2002). *Customer relationship management: Marketing 04.04(Express Exec.)*. Oxford, United Kingdom: Capstone.

Dominic, P., Jati, H., Sellappan, P., & Nee, G. K. (2011). A comparison of Asian e-government websites quality: Using a non-parametric test. *International Journal of Business Information Systems, 7*(2), 220–246. doi:10.1504/IJBIS.2011.038513

Fang, W. (2007). Using Google Analytics for Improving Library Website Content and Design: A Case Study. *Library Philosophy and Practice, 9*(2), 1–17.

Hernandez, B., Jimenex, J., & Martin, M. J. (2009). Key website factors in e-business strategy. *International Journal of Information Management, 29*(5), 362–371. doi:10.1016/j.ijinfomgt.2008.12.006

Holmberg, K., & Thelwall, M. (2009). Local Government Web Sites in Finland: A Geographic and Webometric Analysis. *Scientometrics, 79*(1), 157–169. doi:10.1007/s11192-009-0410-6

Hsiu-Fen, L. (2010). An application of fuzzy AHP for evaluating course website quality. *Computers & Education, 54*(4), 877–888. doi:10.1016/j.compedu.2009.09.017

Huang, J. (2008).Combining entropy weight and TOPSIS method for information system selection. *IEEE International Conference on Cybernetics and Intelligent Systems (CIS 2008)*, 1281-1284. doi:10.1109/ICCIS.2008.4670971

Ivory, M. Y., & Chevalier, A. (2002). *A study of automated web site evaluation tools*. University of Washington, Department of Computer Science.

Kanellopoulos, D. & Kotsiantis, S. (2012). Evaluating and recommending Greek newspapers' websites using clustering. *Program: Electronic Library and Information Systems, 46*(1), 71-91.

Lee, S., & Leckenby, J. D. (1998). An investigation of website ranking methods, *Proceedings of American Academy of Advertising*. Retrieved from http://www.ciadvertising.org/studies/reports/measurement/3ASuckkee.html

Leonidio, U. C., Montezano, R. M. S., & Carvalho, F. A. (2011). Evaluation of perceived quality of the website of an online bookstore: An empirical application of the Barnes and Vidgen Model. *Journal of Information Systems and Technology Management, 8*(1), 109–130. doi:10.4301/S1807-17752011000100006

Li, P., & Yamada, S. (2009). Automated Web Site Evaluation – An Approach Based on Ranking SVM, *IEEE/WIC/ACM International Joint Conferences on Web Intelligence and Intelligent Agent Technologies, 3*, 34-37.

Lo, B. W., & Sedhain, R. Sh. (2006). How reliable are website rankings? Implications for e-business advertising and internet search. *Issues in Information Systems, 7*(2), 233–238.

Prom, C. (2007). *Understanding On-line Archival Use through Web Analytics*. ICA-SUV Seminar, Dundee, Scotland. Retrieved July 12, 2014, from http://www.library.uiuc.edu/archives/workpap/PromSUV2007.pdf

Richards, K. A., & Jones, E. (2008). Customer relationship management: Finding value drivers. *Industrial Marketing Management, 37*(2), 120–130. doi:10.1016/j.indmarman.2006.08.005

Scowen, G. (2007). *Increased Website Popularity through Compliance with Usability Guidelines*. (Doctoral Dissertation). University of Otago, New Zealand.

Serhat, A., & Cengiz, K. (2012). Evaluation of e-commerce website quality using fuzzy multi-criteria decision making approach. *IAENG International Journal of Computer Science, 39*(1), 69–70.

Silva, R. D., & Batista, L. (2007). Boosting government reputation through CRM. *International Journal of Public Sector Management, 20*(7), 588–607. doi:10.1108/09513550710823506

Thelwall, M., & Zuccala, A. (2008). A University-Centered European Union Link Analysis. *Scientometrics, 75*(3), 407–420. doi:10.1007/s11192-007-1831-8

Ueltschi, D. (2006). *Shannon entropy*. Retrieved July 12, 2014, from http://www.ueltschi.org/teaching/chapShannon.pdf

Wang, H. B., Ting, H. F., Chen, J. T., & Wang, D. S. (2011). Optimizing Multiple Quality Characteristics by TAGUCHI Method and TOPSIS Algorithm. *The International Journal of Organizational Innovation., 4*(2), 49–63.

Woolrych, A., Hornbæk, K., Frøkjær, E., & Cockton, G. (2011). Ingredients and Meals rather than Recipes: A Proposal for Research that does not treat Usability Evaluation Methods as Indivisible Wholes. *International Journal of Human-Computer Interaction, 27*(10), 940–970. doi:10.1080/10447318.2011.555314

Younghwa, L., & Kenneth, A. K. (2006). Investigating the effect of website quality on e-business success: An analytic hierarchy process (AHP) approach. *Decision Support Systems, 42*(3), 1383–1401. doi:10.1016/j.dss.2005.11.005

Zahran, D. I., Al-Nuaim, H. A., Rutter, M. J., & Benyon, D. (2014). A Comparative Approach to Web Evaluation and Website Evaluation Methods. *International Journal of Public Information Systems*, *10*(1), 21–39.

Zhang, H., Gu, C. L., Gu, L., & Zhang, Y. (2011). The evaluation of tourism destination competitiveness by TOPSIS & information entropy--A case in the Yangtze River Delta of China. *Tourism Management*, *32*(2), 443–451. doi:10.1016/j.tourman.2010.02.007

KEY TERMS AND DEFINITIONS

Automatic Evaluation: Is an autonomous process to assessment.

Customer Relationship Management: Is an approach to management which is focused on growing the relationship with customers enabled by Information Technology.

Information Entropy: Is a method to weight criteria without human interference, According to the amount of criterion scattering, the weight of all indices is calculated by information entropy weight.

TOPSIS: Is a multiple criteria method for identifying solutions from a set of alternatives based on simultaneous minimization of the distance from an ideal point and maximizing the distance from an exact point.

ENDNOTES

1 News websites in English translation.

2 News websites in English translation.

Chapter 11
Social Media, Customer Relationship Management, and Consumers' Organic Food Purchase Behavior

Evelyn Chronis
The University of Sydney, Australia

Qiang Lu
The University of Sydney, Australia

Rohan Miller
The University of Sydney, Australia

ABSTRACT

Extant research has been focusing on the effectiveness of social media in driving consumer engagement and interaction. However, little research has examined how social media influences firms' Customer Relationship Management. This chapter fills this gap by proposing a conceptual framework to capture the impact of social media on traditional Customer Relationship Management in the context of consumers' organic food purchasing. Specifically, this study investigates how social media influences the purchase behavior of loyalty program members and non-loyalty program members. This study also examines the effectiveness of different types of social media content on consumer purchase behavior of organic food.

INTRODUCTION

The adoption of social media into the business landscape in the past decade has transformed the nature of business communication, customer interaction and engagement. Many businesses are realizing the value of social media, but very few know how to truly harness its power. The implementation of social media strategies are becoming increasingly adopted in business boardrooms as academics debate over the

DOI: 10.4018/978-1-4666-8586-4.ch011

definition of this 'social' phenomenon joining business practices and processes. The concept of 'Social CRM' (Customer Relationship Management) has thus been introduced in the academic literature, aiming to encapsulate the essence and characteristics of social media's unique capabilities.

Social CRM is a logical extension to traditional CRM processes and approaches, drawing on a social media implementation to increase customer engagement, build customer relationships and ultimately, drive sales. Its true value lies in its facilitation of two-way flows of communication between businesses and consumers, thereby extending upon traditional CRM tools. As Social CRM becomes increasingly adopted by businesses using social media as a platform for building and enhancing consumer engagement and communication, it is becoming of increasing importance to understand its impact on firm performance and profitability.

This chapter aims to examine the impact of a Social CRM system on organic food expenditure to determine the effectiveness of Social CRM tools in driving sales. Existing research currently highlights the effectiveness of social media in driving consumer engagement and interaction (Miller & Tucker, 2013). However, research surrounding social media's influence on the purchase behavior of loyalty program and non-loyalty program members is in its infancy. As Social CRM extends upon CRM processes, it is necessary to understand its impact on loyalty program and non-loyalty program members. Furthermore, little is also known about the effectiveness of different types of social media content on sales. The research questions guiding the inquiry into this under-studied but highly relevant research area are: What is the impact of social media on the purchase expenditures of loyalty program members compared with non-loyalty program members? What different types of social media content are effective in driving organic food consumption?

The chapter is structured as follows. First, an overview of the changing nature of food consumption and increased consumer demand for organic food is provided, followed by the introduction, definition and explanation of the concept of Social CRM. Secondly, the organic food literature is discussed to give a prelude of the socio-demographic profile of the organic food consumer, and the motivations and barriers to organic food purchase, in order to set the scene for the research propositions. Third, the propositions of the research are discussed. Finally, the chapter concludes with the major contributions of the study, followed by a discussion of future research directions.

WHY THE ORGANIC FOOD INDUSTRY?

First, a note on the growing organic food or 'healthy eating trend.' Since the 1960s, food consumption has transformed alongside the breakdown of mass-consumerism in its replacement by a multi-dimensional, dynamic society (Beharrell & Crockett, 1992). Within this transformed society, individuals are constantly searching for ways to express their personal and collective identities, values and beliefs. One way in which individuals are achieving this new found self-expression is through their healthy food choices. Food consumption has essentially become an 'expression of personal identity and group affiliation within an increasingly fragmented social structure' (Beharrell & Crockett, 1992: 5).

Alongside the desire for individual and collective self-expression, external societal trends relating to the food related obesity epidemic have called upon increased inquiries into the area of healthy food choice. Obesity has overtaken smoking as the primary cause of preventable disease and illness in Australia and is now arguably, one of the most pressing issues ever facing humanity (Hoad, Somerford, & Katzenellenbogen, 2010). Fortunately, in light of the raised concerns over the obesity epidemic, many consumers are now acknowledging the connection between their diet and health, and are acting upon that knowledge through the consumption of organic food to bridge this connection (French & Hale, 2010; Langley, 2013). 'New age values' concerning individual health, diet, nature and the environment (Beharrell & Crockett, 1992) are propelling the increased demand for organic food products. This increasing consumer demand for organic food has resulted in the organic farming industry placing as one of the top three industries expected to 'fly' in 2014 (IBISWorld, 2014).

LITERATURE REVIEW

Social Media

Social media are internet-based applications that build on the technological foundations of Web 2.0 (e.g. internet forums, email, blogs, social networking sites and online communities) that have revolutionised how consumers and firms interact (Leiner, et al., 2000). As Web 2.0 has evolved to include the development of social media, businesses are using social media as a platform to disseminate information to consumers about brands, products and services. They have done so in a way that enables increased collaboration and engagement with consumers, without regard of geographical barriers. This increase in consumer collaboration and engagement with brands has dramatically changed the nature of 21st century relationship marketing (Leung, 2013). Furthermore, the nature of contemporary marketing has also fundamentally changed as a result of consumers' assuming greater control over their consumption decisions by using social media to seek information about brands, products and services (Greenberg, 2007).

At the individual level, social media has created an 'environment of unprecedented hyper-connectivity' between users (Leung, 2013). Many businesses are thus quickly learning the value of the hyper-connectivity facilitated through social media platforms and are implementing processes to monitor, respond, amplify and influence consumer behavior through these platforms (Divol, Edelman, & Sarrazin, 2012). For example, many businesses are using social media to build brand communities to monitor, respond, amplify and influence consumer behaviour, and also to disseminate information to increase consumer engagement, and ultimately, generate sales.

In today's cluttered marketing environment, many marketers believe that online brand communities are cost effective and powerful marketing tools that foster stronger consumer relationships with the brand (Algesheimer, Dholakia, & Herrmann, 2005). Online brand communities are a form of social media widely used by businesses. They are 'specialised, non-geographically bound communities based on a structured set of social relationships among admirers of a brand' (Muniz & O'Guinn, 2001). Businesses have created their own online brand communities to communicate with consumers in an inexpensive and timely fashion (Patino, Pitta, & Quinones, 2012) at each and every stage of the consumer journey (Divol, et al., 2012). Brand communities thus have the potential to positively influence elements of the customer centric model by strengthening brand loyalty, trust and engagement with brands (Laroche, Habibi, & Richard, 2013).

The creation of online brand communities has led to the rise of community-led marketing initiatives within the digital marketing strategies of businesses. This has created important implications in the area of relationship marketing as these community-driven marketing initiatives seek to enhance consumer/brand relationships, essentially transforming traditional CRM processes. Traditional CRM tools sought to manage customer relationships in a manner that aimed to extract the greatest revenue per customer throughout the customer's lifetime with the firm (Winer, 2001). This type of consumer/firm relationship management was largely dominated and dictated by the firm. However, the adoption of social media platforms, such as brand communities, has changed the nature of consumer/firm relationships. Consumers are now able to respond to firms and create their own conversations. This reciprocated engagement with the firm has therefore created consumer/firm interactions that are driven by two-way streams of dialogue and engagement. The concept of these redefined consumer/firm relationships has been introduced into the marketing literature as Social Customer Relationship Management (SCRM). SCRM draws on social media tools to engage in a strategy of consumer interaction to manage the consumer/brand relationship.

Consumers are using social media to voice their opinions, share their thoughts and experiences, seek advice and information and interact with others about brands (Smithee, 2011). Facebook is becoming an increasingly popular social media platform used by consumers to seek information about a brand or consumption activity, while feeling part of a community of like-minded consumers (Patino, et al., 2012). Social media sites, such as Facebook, are becoming increasingly popular information sources for consumers because the information disseminated via these platforms is perceived to be more trustworthy and credible. This can be explained by the less pervasive nature of social media channels in comparison to traditional marketing communications and tools (Schivinski & Dabrowski, 2013). Social media platforms facilitate dialogue with consumers as they are able to respond to brand-promoted material and participate in dialogue with the brand and other participants (Patino, et al., 2012). Social media has therefore enabled consumers to become 'expressers, informers, engagers, networkers and socialisers,' with brands and other consumers (Vinerean, Cetina, Dumitrescu, & Tichindelean, 2013).

It is the 'social' element inherent in social media platforms that extends upon traditional media, allowing consumers to seek advice and information from trusted social influences, such as friends, family or other like-minded individuals (Wilcox & Stephen, Forthcoming). As a result, the brand is no longer the only disseminator of information to consumers, rather consumers now also play a role in the creation of information on these platforms (Iyengar, Han, & Gupta, Working Paper).

The use of social media by consumers seeking information about brands raises important implications for marketers seeking to use social media to promote their brands, products and services. As social media is perceived as a trustworthy source of brand information, this insinuates that businesses can use social media as an effective marketing and communications tool. This thesis will investigate the use of social media as a platform of information dissemination by a company, and how this information impacts on consumer purchase behaviour. We will analyse a Facebook brand page that is used by the company to disseminate information about its products (organic food), and how this information impacts on the purchase expenditures of its consumers.

Customer Relationship Management (CRM)

A considerable body of academic and trade literature addresses the concept of Customer Relationship Management (CRM) approaches as a traditional marketing tool. Both academics and practitioners have explored the value and impact of building, maintaining and fostering relationships to enhance firm performance (Reinartz, 2004). The justification for CRM processes in traditional retail channels was that businesses should develop strong relationships with customers as increases in retention rates and customer longevity leads to increased firm profitability (Reichheld & Sasser, 1990).

CRM processes have also been linked to increased profitability through their capacity to enhance customer satisfaction levels and furthermore brand loyalty, which in turn results in an increase of the average revenue per customer (Dowling, 2002; Anderson, Fornell, & Lehmann, 1994;). CRM processes can also facilitate a customer-centric approach that helps businesses manage the consumer and brand relationships in order to extract the greatest value from consumers throughout the consumers' lifetime (Baird & Parasnis, 2011). However, since 2004, social tools and online processes have transformed CRM approaches. The result? Social joining the CRM- Social CRM.

What Is Social CRM?

The concept of social media, such as Facebook, joining traditional Customer Relationship Management tools and processes has been recently introduced into the academic literature as 'Social CRM' (SCRM). As the communicative empowerment of consumers is enhanced through social media, SCRM has been explained as a logical extension to traditional CRM processes, rather than a replacement (Baird & Parasnis, 2011). An extension insofar as it adds to the features, functions and characteristics of CRM tools (Greenberg, 2009).

SCRM has been defined as:

"A philosophy and a business strategy, supported by a technology platform, business rules, workflow, processes and social characteristics, designed to engage the customer in a collaborative conversation in order to provide mutually beneficial value in a trusted and transparent business environment. It's the company's response to the customer's ownership of the conversation.' (Greenberg, 2009)

The real value of SCRM therefore lies in its facilitation of two-way flows of communication between the firm and consumer, which was previously unattainable through traditional CRM tools. Through SCRM, consumers are able to engage in reciprocated conversations with the brand and other consumers and stakeholders. This has essentially changed the role of brands from 'directors' of one way streams of communications to consumers, to 'facilitators' of two way flows of dialogue between brand and consumer (Baird & Parasnis, 2011). Facebook, in particular, has received the 'lion's share of attention' in the social media space (Weinberg & Pehlivan, 2011).

As the very nature of social media enables consumers to engage and communicate with the brand on their *own* accord, in their *own* time and at their *own* control, the ownership of conversation has essentially shifted to the consumer (Greenberg, 2009). As a result, consumers are beginning to trust social media platforms as credible sources of knowledge and information acquisition as these platforms facilitate communication with like-minded consumers. Consumers are no longer the 'target' of business communications, rather facilitators of communication with other consumers and business stakeholders. This transformation has seen the demand for businesses to acknowledge this increased interaction with consumers, and accommodate it accordingly, without jeopardizing traditional business operations (Greenberg, 2009). The true value of SCRM lies in its capacity to therefore facilitate co-creation between business and consumer to arrive at a outcomes that are beneficial for both parties (Greenberg, 2009).

Social media platforms, such as Facebook brand pages, have broadened the nature of acquiring knowledge and disseminating information in real time for consumers (Seraj, 2012; Weinberg & Pehlivan, 2011). As individuals engage with brand pages online they are transforming the traditional communication mechanisms once typical of business processes (Jayanti & Singh, 2010). As individuals congregate on social media for the purpose of acquiring and disseminating information, they are simultaneously turning away from traditional advertising channels in favour of their increased control over their media consumption (Mangold & Faulds, 2009). Consequently, social media has become a popular advertising tool for businesses seeking to reap the benefits of increased consumer trust and attention (Xiang & Gretzel, 2010).

However, a question mark still remains in the boardroom surrounding social media's legitimacy in the marketing mix due to the ambiguity surrounding its economical impact on firm performance. Social media remains an 'enigma wrapped in a riddle for many executives' (Divol, et al., 2012). Many companies have adopted the social media to facilitate communications with their consumers, however the justification to devote resources to social media strategies remains a challenge for most marketing executives. The financial impact of social media as an element of the marketing mix is complex due to the qualitative, and thus nebulous, nature surrounding its financial metrics.

However, given the implementation of social media in business marketing strategies, and its popularity as a preferred, pervasive advertising medium by consumers, a stream of research has emerged investigating the return on investment of social media (Hoffman & Fodor, 2010; Kumar et al., 2013;). In particular, studies have since emerged pertaining to examine the relationship between online content and firm performance, namely as a function of sales (Goh, Heng, & Lin, 2013; Gopinath, Thomas, & Krishnamurthi, 2014). Gopinath, Thomas, and Krishnamurthi (2014) examined the impact of user-generated content (UGC) on sales by separating the volume of UGC from its valence, which has three dimensions- attribute, emotion and recommendation oriented messages. The study found that only the valence of recommendation has a direct impact on sales, indicating that UGC can be a very valuable asset to firms engaging with social media (Gopinath, et al., 2014). The study also found that the 'volume' of UGC does not have a significant impact on sales, indicating 'quality' is better than 'quantity' in terms of online WOM. Goh, Heng, and Lin (2013) found similar results in their evidence of social media contents affecting consumer purchase behavior through embedded information and persuasion. Further research has explored this positive effect as being facilitated by high quality, informative and trustworthy context providing social, intellectual and cultural value to consumers via social media platforms (Seraj, 2012; Smith, Fischer, & Yongjian, 2012).

Organic Food

What is Organic Food?

Organic food refers to 'natural,' 'wholesome' and 'healthy' food (Beharrell & Crockett, 1992) produced through renewable sources, the best environmental practices, the application of high animal welfare standards, and without the use of synthetic fertilisers and pesticides (Magistris & Gracia, 2008). The contemporary 'organic food consumer' has emerged as a result of lifestyle changes reflective of wider environmental and societal shifts towards a healthy lifestyle approach (Beharrell & Crockett, 1992). Transformed healthy eating habits since the 1960s, reflective of positive health and environmental friendliness, have influenced the trend towards organic foods as a means of individual self-representation (Davies et al., 1995). The stream of research surrounding organic food constructs a socio-demographic profile of the organic food consumer and addresses the motivations and barriers toward organic food consumption.

A Socio-Demographic Profile of the Organic Food Consumer

The increased consumption of organically produced food, coupled with the rise of environmental concerns, lead to the proliferation of research aiming to better understand the typical profile of organic food consumers and their socio-demographic characteristics (Davies, Titterington, & Cochrane, 1995; Fotopoulos & Krystallis, 2002b). Research suggests that females hold more positive beliefs toward organic food consumption (Lea & Worsley, 2005) and are the primary purchasers of organic food within the household (Fotopoulos & Krystallis, 2002b; Byrne et al., 1992). Demographic reviews of organic food consumption have further found that age (Reicks, Splett, & Fishman, 1997), disposable income and the presence of children in the household all significantly influence organic food consumption (Davies, Titterington, & Cochrane, 1995).

However, other studies identify no relationship between organic food purchase and income (Goldman & Clancy, 1991). Adopting a different approach of profiling the organic food consumer based on their levels of knowledge and awareness of organic food, Fotopoulos and Krystallis (2002) identified three types of organic food buyers: the Unaware, the Aware non-buyers and the Buyers. Ultimately, a single profile of the organic food consumer has not been achieved, which reflects the complex motivational drives behind organic food consumption.

Motivations towards Organic Food Consumption

Alongside the literature profiling the organic food consumer, there is extant research exploring the motivations underlying organic food consumption. There is generally a greater consensus surrounding the motives driving consumer purchase in comparison to attempts to profile the organic food consumer. It is generally accepted that the main drivers behind organic food consumption are health related, environmentally determined and ethically driven factors (Aertsens, Mondelaers, Verbeke, Buysse, & Huylenbroeck, 2011; Chinnici, D'Amico, & Pecorino, 2002; Davies, Titterington, & Cochrane, 1995).

Health

A considerable body of evidence argues that health related factors are the most important drivers for organic food purchases (Magistris & Gracia, 2008; Padel & Foster, 2005; Zanoli & Naspetti, 2002). Individuals' are motivated by their self-interests and the self-benefits of organic food; that is, organic food is considered as a 'way of life' representing values of wholesomeness and self-transcendence (Schifferstein & Ophuis, 1998; Lea & Worsley, 2005). The product characteristics identified with health motivation are 'better quality' and 'better taste' (Aertsens et al., 2011; Lea & Worsley, 2005), free of synthetic pesticide residues (Aertsens et al., 2011) and higher in vitamin and mineral content compared to conventionally produced food (Lea & Worsley, 2005). These strongly contribute to constructing the health motivations behind organic food consumption.

Environment

Concern over the environment has been found to be a further significant influence on organic food consumption (Schifferstein & Ophuis, 1998). It has been argued that that a concern for the environment can play a more important role in determining individual organic food consumption rather than health related motivations (Durham, 2007). Concern for the welfare of the environment has had a positive impact on organic food consumption as the process of organic farming is seen as an environmentally sustainable practice (Beharrell & Crockett, 1992). The environmental factors driving organic food consumption are motivated by the support of using renewable inputs through correct agricultural management techniques that in turn, optimize the background health of crops and maintain soil structure and fertility (Beharrell & Crockett, 1992).

Ethics

Food safety and concern for animal welfare are also considered major motivating factors towards organic food consumption (Harper & Makatouni, 2002). Ethical motivations concerning the welfare of animals have been commonly found amongst purchasers of organic food (Harper & Makatouni, 2002). The ethical dimension concerning the welfare of animals in organic food production serves to contribute to the perception of organic food being 'healthier' than conventional food, and also allows consumers to express their ethical concerns as extensions of their self-image (Harper & Makatouni, 2002)

Barriers Inhibiting Organic Food Consumption

Price

Organic food maintains a price premium compared to its conventional food counterpart, which inadvertently creates a price versus value trade-off in consumers' decision-making process to purchase organic food (Padel & Foster, 2005). This price versus value decision inhibits the consumption of organic food (Padel & Foster, 2005; Byrne et al., 1992; Roddy, Cowan, & Hutchinson, 1994; Fotopoulos & Krystallis, 2002a). However, it is also speculated that consumers may use price to inform their opinions about the taste and quality of organic food.

Availability

There can be a perception that locating specialty organic food outlets can be difficult; this lack of availability and inconvenience in turn, inhibits organic food purchases (Zanoli & Naspetti, 2002; Fotopoulos & Krystallis, 2002a). There is however, an increasing number of organic food outlets entering the market, and other food stores are also diversifying into organic foods, thereby making organic food more available for consumers.

Knowledge

Consumers' limited or lack of sufficient knowledge on the benefits of organic food consumption has been explored as another major barrier to organic food consumption (Demeritt, 2002). This lack of knowledge negatively influences organic food consumption as consumers are uninformed of the benefits of organic food, and consequently, cannot justify its price premium, leading to organic product avoidance (Padel & Foster, 2005). It is claimed that increasing consumers' organic food knowledge can in fact, positively influence organic food consumption (Magistris & Gracia, 2008; Aertsens et al., 2011) by transforming the 'unwilling consumer to a motivated organic supporter' (Fotopoulos & Krystallis, 2002a).

CONCEPTUAL FRAMEWORK

The extant research suggests consumers' lack of knowledge about organic food is a critical barrier to organic food consumption. Research suggests an increase in organic food knowledge positively influences ones likelihood to purchase and frequent use of organic food (Magistris & Gracia, 2008; Aertsens et al., 2011). As the nature of acquiring knowledge has evolved alongside the implementation of social media technologies, individuals are now engaging online to engage in knowledge transfer and information regarding products and services (Jayanti & Singh, 2010). Studies have found that social media platforms deliver value to consumers through providing intellectual value (goal driven and quality content), social value (an interactive environment for building relationships) and cultural value (a self-governed community culture that maintains trust and respect towards the community and among members) (Seraj, 2012).

The creation of intellectual value is characteristics of SCRM tools. SCRM has the capacity to facilitate the flow of information towards consumers and thereby increase consumers' knowledge on certain products or brands (Seraj, 2012; Jayanti & Singh, 2010). It therefore follows, those individuals who have 'liked' a company's Facebook page are receiving content that is rich in intellectual, social and cultural value, that can in turn, influence purchasing behavior. These individuals are also gaining knowledge about the company and its products. Facebook brand pages have been particularly praised for their ability to generate worth of mouth 'buzz' about a brand (Goh, et al., 2013), while also generating knowledge for consumers through their capability of sharing information through posts and other content, which in turn, have been proven to drive sales (Kozinets, 2002). The positive link between engagement in online brand communities and firm sales, profitability and performance has been studied and proven in the literature (Goh, et al., 2013; Gopinath, et al., 2014; Hoffman & Fodor, 2010; Kumar, Bhaskaran, Mirchandani, & Shah, 2013).

Findings from previous studies indicate that the decision making process of purchasing organic food involves various motivational factors, making it a complex psychological consumption process. Adding to this complexity is the additional array of perceived barriers to purchase, including a lack of knowledge about organic food and its benefits. Studies suggest that knowledge about organic food is an inhibitor to purchase, but when increased, pleased a pivotal role in the forming of positive attitudes towards organic food. This positive attitude formation in turn positively influences ones likelihood to purchase organic food (Magistris & Gracia, 2008).

It is therefore proposed that as social media is a trusted platform for knowledge acquisition for its consumers, it can serve to mitigate the negative effect of the 'knowledge' barrier to organic food consumption and thereby positively influence organic food sales (see Figure 1). As it has been supported that informative and high quality social media content (Seraj, 2012) can drive sales and firm profitability (Goh, Heng, & Lin, 2013; Kumar, et al., 2013; Gopinath, Thomas, & Krishnamurthi, 2014), we propose:

Proposition 1: Social media content will have a positive impact on organic food consumption

Studies in CRM literature show how CRM processes successfully yield greater average returns per consumer and thus, firm profitability (Dowling, 2002; Reinartz, 2004). In particular, streams of CRM literature have explored this link analyzing the positive impact of loyalty reward programs on increasing customer lifetime duration and share of wallet (Meyer-Waarden, 2007), repeat purchases (Taylor & Neslin, 2005) and customer retention and value (Bolton, Kannan, & Bramlett, 2000). This research supports the view a 'loyal' customer belonging the loyalty rewards program is more profitable.

Figure 1. Conceptual Framework

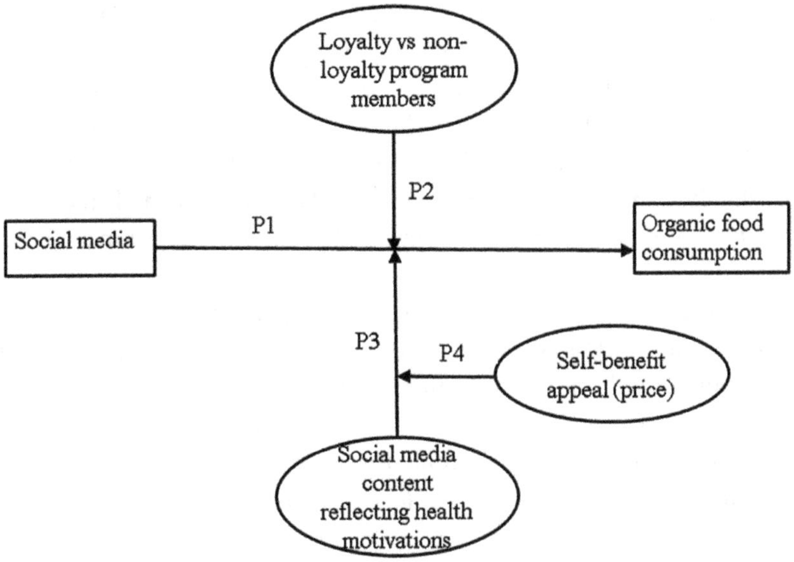

However, little is known about the effectiveness of SCRM processes in influencing loyalty program (LP) members' purchase behavior. It is accepted that LP members have existing loyalty to the company through the traditional CRM program, which begs the question- what value could SCRM processes additionally provide? SCRM processes could in fact, behave as a saturation point for these LP members, whereby additional advertising attempts via these SCRM processes will be of little to no effect on LP members. We argue, that customers who have initiated the process of joining the loyalty program recognize the benefits of organic food consumption and are frequent consumers of it. It therefore follows, that these consumers have a sufficient level of knowledge prompting them to consume organic food. We further argue that the LP members are therefore 'de-sensitised' to additional online promotion material through SCRM processes.

We further argue, that SCRM processes will therefore have a greater effect for non-members of the company's loyalty reward program. These customers are not yet fully integrated in the company's traditional CRM program and are therefore not as frequent in purchasing organic food, and perhaps, not as knowledgeable. They have however, self-selected their inclusion on the company's Facebook page, and thus have an interest in organic food.

As we have discussed the informative value of social media, these non-LP members will benefit significantly from the information and knowledge sharing nature of the organic foods' Facebook page. By keeping members of the company's Facebook community up to date with information regarding organic food, consumers will increase their knowledge and consumption of organic food. We therefore draw on organic food theory to claims an increase in consumers' knowledge about organic food will result in an increase in organic food consumption by non-LP members who are not as knowledgeable as LP members:

Proposition 2: Social media content will have a greater positive impact on organic food consumption for non-loyalty program members

Studies of social media suggest that different types of social media content have different impact on consumer engagement and sales (Goh, Heng, & Lin, 2013; Gopinath, Thomas, & Krishnamurthi, 2014). Minton et al. (2012) explored the different reasons in social media motives for sustainability in a cross-cultural study. Their findings cautioned advertisers from using generic sustainable advertising messages over social media. Instead, advertisers should target distinct sets of motives for sustainability that are industry and country specific. In individualist societies, they found responsibility and involvement motives consistently lead to organic food purchases. That is, individuals liked to feel 'responsible' for engaging in healthy eating behaviours and 'involved' with other consumers and companies in the process of doing so.

Drawing from the organic food literature, the two primary drivers of organic food consumption are health and environmental motivations. Combining this literature with the findings of Minton et al. (2012), 'health' motives are more closely in line with motives linked to a sense of responsibility and level of involvement, in comparison to environment motives, that are less individualist and more collective in nature. We therefore purport that social media content that reflect the health motivations towards organic food consumption will lead to a positive increase in organic food consumption:

Proposition 3: Social media content reflecting 'health motivations' will lead to a positive increase in organic food consumption

Health motivations refer to the individual's self-benefits of consuming organic food, which are mainly concerned with the increasing of one's personal health via the consumption of organic food (Magistris & Gracia, 2008). Health motivations are therefore reflective of 'self-benefit' appeals that promote the individual benefits of consuming organic food (White & Simpson, 2013). Should the self-benefits of organic consumption be strengthened in the social media content through an external self-benefit motivation, it therefore follows that influence of social media content on organic food consumption will be strengthened.

Social media content combining the health benefit factor of organic food consumption and a self-benefit factor external to organic food consumption, will lead to a greater significant impact on organic food consumption. Literature suggests normative appeals that activate the individual self are more responsive to self-benefit appeals (for example, cost savings) in influencing sustainable behaviours (White & Simpson, 2013). Linking to this theory, one of the most widely documented barriers to organic food consumption is the price premium of organic food products. Price acts as a barrier to organic food purchase to consumers who cannot justify the price premiums of organic food (Padel & Foster, 2005). However, it is also purported that by increasing ones knowledge about the health benefits of organic food consumption has twofold value; it creates positive attitudes regarding organic food which increases ones likelihood to purchase organic food, and, it serves to decrease the perceived barrier of price to purchase organic (Magistris & Gracia, 2008).

Ultimately, as social media platforms can act as trusted sources of knowledge acquisition for consumers as aforementioned, combining the self-benefit appeal of 'price' with the health benefits of organic food will increase ones knowledge about organic food and thus, increase organic food expenditure. The literature suggests that if the price barrier to organic food consumption be resolved in the consumers' decision-making process by promoting the health benefits of organic food consumption, the barriers effect will be mitigated. Therefore, we propose that if the price of an organic food product is included in the social media message in combination with the health benefits of the consumption of that product, there will be an increase in consumption of that product:

Proposition 4: Social media content that combines both the health benefits and price appeal of organic food will increase organic food consumption of that product

CONCLUSION AND FUTURE RESEARCH DIRECTIONS

By drawing on consumer motivations towards organic food consumption, and incorporating this theory to link a company's social media content and its effect on sales, our research is of significant contribution to the organic food literature. From a theoretical perspective, our study contributes significantly to the existing knowledge of CRM and emerging SCRM literature. It contributes to legitimizing the use of SCRM processes as new advertising tools in the marketing mix.

From a practical perspective, our research is of significant in identifying the ways in which marketers can communicate with consumers to increase healthy eating behaviors in response to the prevalent obesity epidemic. As society employs processes towards a holistic approach to health, whereby individuals are increasingly motivated to sculpt their lives through healthy eating, identifying how organic food consumption can be increased by the use of social media will have implications for organic food retailers, general food retailers at large, and policy makers who are seeking ways to reduce the effects of obesity related health issues.

While there is a considerable amount of research that addresses the impact of CRM customers on sales, there is a gap in addressing the impact of social media (SCRM) customers and CRM customers on sales. Little is also known about social media's influence on customers of a firm, and even less is understood about the effect social media has on sales. Currently, most social media tracking is done independently to sales, especially in a food retail environment, focusing on metrics such as consumer engagement and interaction. Linking social media to customer identities through a CRM program of an organic food company provides an opportunity to better understand the role of social media and CRM, relative to sales.

No study, to the best of our knowledge, has explored the link of SCRM and CRM, relative to sales, and furthermore, has not explored the impact of social media in the context of organic food. Organic food consumers represent a niche group of food consumers that have in recent years, formed a unique community to express their self-identity and values towards organic food consumption. Social media has provided a platform in which these consumers are able to promote their healthy way of living by connecting with businesses and other like-minded individuals online. We explore this niche by analyzing if these consumers are influenced by different types of social media posts that reflect typical motivations of organic food consumption, and whether this content has an effect on sales. This is just the first step to research this important area. More research is necessary to provide a full understanding of the issues in this important area.

REFERENCES

Aertsens, J., Mondelaers, K., Verbeke, W., Buysse, J., & Huylenbroeck, G. V. (2011). The influence of subjective and objective knowledge on attitude, motivations and consumption of organic food. *British Food Journal, 113*(11), 1353–1378. doi:10.1108/00070701111179988

Algesheimer, R., Dholakia, U. M., & Herrmann, A. (2005). The social influence of brand community: Evidence from European car clubs. *Journal of Marketing, 69*(3), 19–34. doi:10.1509/jmkg.69.3.19.66363

Anderson, E. W., Fornell, C., & Lehmann, D. R. (1994). Customer satisfaction, market share, and profitability: Findings from Sweden. *Journal of Marketing, 58*(3), 53–66. doi:10.2307/1252310

Baird, C. H., & Parasnis, G. (2011). From social media to social customer relationship management. *Strategy and Leadership, 39*(5), 30–37. doi:10.1108/10878571111161507

Beharrell, B., & Crockett, A. (1992). New Age Food! New Age Consumers! *British Food Journal, 94*(2), 5–13. doi:10.1108/00070709210018979

Bolton, R. N., Kannan, P. K., & Bramlett, M. D. (2000). Implications of Loyalty Program Membership and Service Experiences for Customer Retention and Value. *Journal of the Academy of Marketing Science, 28*(1), 95–108. doi:10.1177/0092070300281009

Byrne, P. J., Toensmeyer, U. C., German, C. L., & Muller, H. R. (1992). Evaluation of consumer attitudes towards organic produce in Delaware and the Delmarva region. *Journal of Food Distribution Research, 23*(1), 29–44.

Chinnici, G., D'Amico, M., & Pecorino, B. (2002). A multivariate statistical analysis on the consumers of organic products. *British Food Journal, 104*(3/4/5), 187-199. doi: 10.1108/00070700210425651

Davies, A., Titterington, A. J., & Cochrane, C. (1995). Who Buys Organic Food? A Profile of the Purchasers of Organic Food in Northern Ireland. *British Food Journal, 97*(10), 17–23. doi:10.1108/00070709510104303

Demeritt, L. (2002). *All things organic 2002: A look at the organic consumer*. Bellevue, WA: The Hartman Group.

Divol, R., Edelman, D., & Sarrazin, H. (2012). (*Producer*). Demystifying Social Media.

Dowling, G. (2002). Customer Relationship Management: In B2C Markets, Often Less is More. *California Management Review, 44*(3), 87–104. doi:10.2307/41166134

Durham, C. A. (2007). The impact of environmental and health motivations on the organic share of produce purchases. *Agricultural and Resource Economics Review, 36*(2), 304.

Fotopoulos, C., & Krystallis, A. (2002a). Organic product avoidance: Reasons for rejection and potential buyers' identification in a countrywide survey. *British Food Journal, 104*(3/4/5), 233-260. doi: 10.1108/00070700210425697

Fotopoulos, C., & Krystallis, A. (2002b). Purchasing motives and profile of the Greek organic consumer: A countrywide survey. *British Food Journal, 104*(9), 730–765. doi:10.1108/00070700210443110

French, S., & Hale, T. (2010). Are Healthy Thinkers Also Healthy Shoppers? Retrieved 22/5/14, from The Nielsen Company http://www.nielsenmediamonitor.com/content/corporate/us/en/newswire/2010/are-healthy-thinkers-also-healthy-shoppers.html

Goh, K.-Y., Heng, C.-S., & Lin, Z. (2013). Social Media Brand Community and Consumer Behavior: Quantifying the Relative Impact of User- and Marketer-Generated Content. *Information Systems Research, 24*(1), 88–107. doi:10.1287/isre.1120.0469

Goldman, B. J., & Clancy, K. L. (1991). A survey of organic produce purchases and related attitudes of food cooperative shoppers. *American Journal of Alternative Agriculture, 6*(2), 89–96. doi:10.1017/S0889189300003933

Gopinath, S., Thomas, J. S., & Krishnamurthi, L. (2014). Investigating the Relationship Between the Content of Online Word of Mouth, Advertising, and Brand Performance. *Marketing Science, 33*(2), 241–258. doi:10.1287/mksc.2013.0820

Greenberg, P. (2007). Welcome to the era of the social consumer (pp. 138-140): CRMProject.

Harper, G. C., & Makatouni, A. (2002). Consumer perception of organic food production and farm animal welfare. *British Food Journal, 104*(3/4/5), 287-299. doi: 10.1108/00070700210425723

Hoad, V., Somerford, P., & Katzenellenbogen, J. (2010). High body mass index overtakes tobacco as the leading independent risk factor contibuting to disease burden in Western Australia. *Australian and New Zealand Journal of Public Health, 34*(2), 214–215. doi:10.1111/j.1753-6405.2010.00509.x PMID:23331368

Hoffman, D. L., & Fodor, M. (2010). Can You Measure the ROI of Your Social Media Marketing? *Sloan Management Review, 52*(1), 40–50.

IBISWorld. (2014). IBISWorld reveals the industries set to fly and fall in 2014 (M. Centre, Trans.). In IBISWorld (Ed.), (pp. 1-5): IBISWorld.

Iyengar, R., Han, S., & Gupta, S. (2009). Do Friends Influence Purchases in a Social Network? Working paper

Jayanti, R. K., & Singh, J. (2010). Pragmatic learning theory: An inquiry-action framework for distributed consumer learning in online communities. *The Journal of Consumer Research, 36*(6), 1058–1081. doi:10.1086/648689

Kozinets, R. V. (2002). The field behind the screen: Using netnography for marketing research in online communities. *JMR, Journal of Marketing Research, 39*(1), 61–72. doi:10.1509/jmkr.39.1.61.18935

Kumar, V., Bhaskaran, V., Mirchandani, R., & Shah, M. (2013). Practice Prize Winner–Creating a Measurable Social Media Marketing Strategy: Increasing the Value and ROI of Intangibles and Tangibles for Hokey Pokey. *Marketing Science, 32*(2), 194–212. doi:10.1287/mksc.1120.0768

Langley, S. (2013). Australian consumers will pay more for 'eco-friendly' vegetables, study. Retrieved 29/5/2014, from Australian Food News http://ausfoodnews.com.au/2013/12/04/australian-consumers-will-pay-more-for-%E2%80%98eco-friendly%E2%80%99-vegetables-study.html

Laroche, M., Habibi, M. R., & Richard, M.-O. (2013). To be or not to be in social media: How brand loyalty is affected by social media? *International Journal of Information Management*, *33*(1), 76–82. doi:10.1016/j.ijinfomgt.2012.07.003

Lea, E., & Worsley, T. (2005). Australians' organic food beliefs, demographics and values. *British Food Journal*, *107*(11), 855–869. doi:10.1108/00070700510629797

Leiner, B. M., Cerf, V. G., Clark, D. D., Kahn, R. E., Kleinrock, L., Daniel, C. L.,.... (2000). A brief history of the internet. 2000. *Web Page. URL: http://info. isoc/org/internet-history/brief. html, 18.*

Leung, L. (2013). Generational differences in content generation in social media: The roles of the gratifications sought of narcissism. *Computers in Human Behavior*, *29*(3), 997–1006. doi:10.1016/j.chb.2012.12.028

Magistris, T., & Gracia, A. (2008). The decision to buy organic food products in Southern Italy. *British Food Journal*, *110*(9), 929–947. doi:10.1108/00070700810900620

Mangold, W. G., & Faulds, D. J. (2009). Social media: The new hybrid element of the promotion mix. *Business Horizons*, *52*(4), 357–365. doi:10.1016/j.bushor.2009.03.002

Meyer-Waarden, L. (2007). The effects of loyalty programs on customer lifetime duration and share of wallet. *Journal of Retailing*, *83*(2), 223–236. doi:10.1016/j.jretai.2007.01.002

Miller, A. R., & Tucker, C. (2013). Active Social Media Management: The Case of Health Care. *Information Systems Research*, *24*(1), 52–70. doi:10.1287/isre.1120.0466

Muniz, A. M. Jr, & O'Guinn, T. C. (2001). Brand Community. *The Journal of Consumer Research*, *27*(4), 412–432. doi:10.1086/319618

Padel, S., & Foster, C. (2005). Exploring the gap between attitudes and behaviour: Understanding why consumers buy or do not buy organic food. *British Food Journal*, *107*(8), 606–625. doi:10.1108/00070700510611002

Patino, A., Pitta, D. A., & Quinones, R. (2012). Social media's emerging importance in market research. *Journal of Consumer Marketing*, *29*(3), 233–237. doi:10.1108/07363761211221800

Reichheld, F. P., & Sasser, W. E. (1990). *Zero Defeciions*. Quoliiy Comes To Services.

Reicks, M., Splett, P., & Fishman, A. (1997). *Shelf Labelling of Organic Foods: Effects on Customer Perceptions and Sales*. The Retail Food Industry Center.

Reinartz, W., Krafft, M., & Hoyer, W. D. (2004). The Customer Relationship Management Process: Its Measurement and Impact on Performance. *JMR, Journal of Marketing Research*, *41*(3), 293–305. doi:10.1509/jmkr.41.3.293.35991

Roddy, G., Cowan, C., & Hutchinson, G. (1994). Organic food–a description of the Irish market. *British Food Journal*, *96*(4), 3–10. doi:10.1108/00070709410060998

Schifferstein, H. N. J., & Ophuis, P. A. M. O. (1998). Health-Related Determinants of Organic Food Consumption in the Netherlands. *Food Quality and Preference*, *9*(3), 119–133. doi:10.1016/S0950-3293(97)00044-X

Schivinski, B., & Dabrowski, D. (2013). The impact of brand communication on brand equity dimensions and brand purchase intention throuhg Facebook. *GUT FME Working Paper Series A, 4*(4), 1 - 20.

Seraj, M. (2012). We Create, We Connect, We Respect, Therefore We Are: Intellectual, Social, and Cultural Value in Online Communities. *Journal of Interactive Marketing*, *26*(4), 209–222. doi:10.1016/j.intmar.2012.03.002

Smith, A. N., Fischer, E., & Yongjian, C. (2012). How Does Brand-related User-generated Content Differ across YouTube, Facebook, and Twitter? *Journal of Interactive Marketing*, *26*(2), 102–113. doi:10.1016/j.intmar.2012.01.002

Smithee, B. (2011). How social media is expanding the defitions of MR, and as leaders why it is largely your responsibility. *Alert, 51*(3).

Taylor, G. A., & Neslin, S. A. (2005). The current and future sales impact of a retail frequency reward program. *Journal of Retailing*, *81*(4), 293–305. doi:10.1016/j.jretai.2004.11.004

Vinerean, S., Cetina, I., Dumitrescu, L., & Tichindelean, M. (2013). The Effects of Social Media Marketing on Online Consumer Behavior. *International Journal of Business and Management*, *8*(14). doi:10.5539/ijbm.v8n14p66

Weinberg, B. D., & Pehlivan, E. (2011). Social spending: Managing the social media mix. *Business Horizons*, *54*(3), 275–282. doi:10.1016/j.bushor.2011.01.008

White, K., & Simpson, B. (2013). When Do (and Don't) Normative Appeals Influence Sustainable Consumer Behaviors? *Journal of Marketing*, *77*(2), 78–95. doi:10.1509/jm.11.0278

Wilcox, K., & Stephen, A. T. (Forthcoming). Are Close Friends the Enemy? Online Social Networks, Self-Esteem and Self-Control. *The Journal of Consumer Research.*

Winer, R. S. (2001). A Framework for Customer Relationship Management. *California Management Review*, *43*(4), 89–105. doi:10.2307/41166102

Xiang, Z., & Gretzel, U. (2010). Role of social media in online travel information search. *Tourism Management*, *31*(2), 179–188. doi:10.1016/j.tourman.2009.02.016

Zanoli, R., & Naspetti, S. (2002). Consumer motivations in the purchase of organic food: A means-end approach. *British Food Journal*, *104*(8), 643–653. doi:10.1108/00070700210425930

ADDITIONAL READING

Cicia, G., Del Giudice, T., & Scarpa, R. (2002). Consumers' perception of quality in organic food: a random utility model under preference heterogeneity and choice correlation from rank-orderings. *British Food Journal, 104*(3/4/5), 200-213.

Claussen, J., Kretschmer, T., & Mayrhofer, P. (2013). The Effects of Rewarding User Engagement: The Case of Facebook Apps. *Information Systems Research*, *24*(1), 186–200. doi:10.1287/isre.1120.0467

Fisher, T. (2009). ROI in social media: A look at the arguments. *Journal of Database Marketing &#38. Customer Strategy Management, 16*(3), 189–195. doi:10.1057/dbm.2009.16

Hughner, R. S., McDonagh, P., Prothero, A., Shultz, C. J., & Stanton, J. (2007). Who are organic food consumers? A compilation and review of why people purchase organic food. *Journal of Consumer Behaviour, 6*(2-3), 94–110. doi:10.1002/cb.210

Loureiro, M. L., McCluskey, J. J., & Mittelhammer, R. C. (2001). Assessing Consumer Preferences for Organic, Eco-labeled, and Regular Apples. *Journal of Agricultural Resource Economics, 26*(2), 404–416.

Luo, X., Zhang, J., & Duan, W. (2013). Social Media and Firm Equity Value. *Information Systems Research, 24*(1), 146–163. doi:10.1287/isre.1120.0462

Magnusson, M. K., Arvola, A., Hursti, U.-K. K., Åberg, L., & Sjödén, P.-O. (2003). Choice of organic foods is related to perceived consequences for human health and to environmentally friendly behaviour. *Appetite, 40*(2), 109–117. doi:10.1016/S0195-6663(03)00002-3 PMID:12781160

Makatouni, A. (2002). What motivates consumers to buy organic food in the UK?: Results from a qualitative study. *British Food Journal, 104*(3/4/5), 345-352.

Patino, A., Pitta, D. A., & Quinones, R. (2012). Social media's emerging importance in market research. *Journal of Consumer Marketing, 29*(3), 233–237. doi:10.1108/07363761211221800

Rindfleisch, A., & Heide, J. B. (1997). Transaction cost analysis: Past, present, and future applications. *Journal of Marketing, 61*(4), 30. doi:10.2307/1252085

Rishika, R., Kumar, A., Janakiraman, R., & Bezawada, R. (2013). The Effect of Customers' Social Media Participation on Customer Visit Frequency and Profitability: An Empirical Investigation. *Information Systems Research, 24*(1), 108–127. doi:10.1287/isre.1120.0460

Rust, R. T., & Zahorik, A. J. (1993). Customer satisfaction, customer retention, and market share. *Journal of Retailing, 69*(2), 193–215. doi:10.1016/0022-4359(93)90003-2

Stephen, A. T., & Galak, J. (2012). The Effects of Traditional and Social Earned Media on Sales: A Study of a Microlending Marketplace. *JMR, Journal of Marketing Research, 49*(5), 624–639. doi:10.1509/jmr.09.0401

Torjusen, H., Lieblein, G., Wandel, M., & Francis, C. A. (2001). Food System Orientation and Quality Perception among Consumers and Producers of Organic Food in Hedmark County, Norway. *Food Quality and Preference, 12*(3), 207–216. doi:10.1016/S0950-3293(00)00047-1

KEY TERMS AND DEFINITIONS

Customer Loyalty: Tendency of a customer to purchase a product or service over a period of time. It is usually caused by positive previous experience.

Customer Relationship Management: A system that companies use to manage and evaluate interactions with their customers. An effective relationship management can deepen companies' relationships with their customers and build up customer loyalty.

Facebook Brand Page: A profile on Facebook which is different an actual User profile. It can used to generate worth of mouth 'buzz' about a brand and knowledge for consumers through its capability of sharing information through posts and other content.

Facebook: An online social networking website founded by Mark Zurckerberg on February 4, 2004. IT had an initial public offering in May 2012 with initial market value of $104 billion.

Loyalty Program: A reward program provided by companies to reward their loyal customers who frequently purchase from them. It also allows companies to collect detailed customer data.

Organic Food: Natural, wholesome and healthy food. It is produced through renewable sources, the best environmental practices, the application of high animal welfare standards, and without the use of synthetic fertilisers and pesticides.

Social Customer Relationship Management: A logical extension to traditional CRM processes, rather than a replacement. The real value of SCRM therefore lies in its facilitation of two-way flows of communication between the firm and consumer.

Chapter 12
The Effects of Social Media-Based Brand Communities on Brand Loyalty and Brand Equity:
Case Study - Cinere Company

Amir Khanlari
University of Tehran, Iran

Faezeh Rezaei
University of Tehran, Iran

Seyed Abolghasem Mira
University of Tehran, Iran

ABSTRACT

Nowadays, the concept of brand community is tied with media. So, the new concept of social media based brand community without constraint of geography is built. In this chapter, we investigate the effects of social media based brand community on elements of the customer centric model, brand loyalty and brand equity through its antecedents (i.e., brand loyalty, brand trust, perceived quality, brand awareness/association). An online survey with 170 users of brand community of Cinere company on facebook was conducted and path analysis technique was applied for data analysis. The results show that brand community of Cinere on social media has positive effects on all elements of the customer centric model. customer/ other customer and customer/ brand relationships have positive effects on brand loyalty with mediating role of brand trust; and loyalty, perceived quality,brand awareness/association have positive effects on brand equity. Interestingly, brand trust contributes only indirectly to brand equity. Finally, implications for practice and future research opportunities are discussed.

DOI: 10.4018/978-1-4666-8586-4.ch012

INTRODUCTION

The concept of social media in today's bussiness program is on top of all the world.Decisin makers and marketers of organizations are in an effort to identity ways and means by which companies can use social media to their best advantage.

On the other hand, the growing number of social media users is not limited to teenagers, members of Generation X, that are now 35-44 years old, increasinglypopulate the ranks of joiners, spectators, and critics(Kaplan& Haenlein,2010).It is therefore reasonable to say that SocialMedia represents a revolutionary new trend thatshould be of interest to companies operating inonline space or any space, for that matter)Kaplan& Haenlein,2010).

Due to the advantages of social media in connecting businesses to end-consumers directly, in a timely manner and at a low cost (Kaplan & Haenlein, 2010), in bringing together different like-minded people (Hagel & Armstrong, 1997; Wellman & Gulia, 1999), and in influencing customer perceptions and behavior (Williams & Cothrell, 2000), it has became the center of attention in different industries(Laroche, Habibi, Richard,& Sankaranarayanan, 2012). The highlevel of efficiency of social media compared to other traditional communication channels prompted industry leaders to state that companies must participate in Facebook, Twitter, MySpace, and others, in order to succeed in online environments(Ka- plan & Haenlein, 2010). Thus, more industries try to benefit from social media(Laroche et al., 2012). As brands are increasingly embedded in social networking sites (e.g. Facebook and Twitter) and other variant forms of social media (e.g. YouTube), the competition between brands has become a battlefield where companies co-own their brands, co-direct their brands' competitive strategies, and co-define symbolic meanings of their brands with their consumers (Heil, Lehmann, & Stremersch, 2010; Tynan,McKechnie,& Chhuon,2010).

One of the ways to participate in social media for organizations in recent years is establish of brand community. Brands such as Jeep with famous offline brand communities (Schau, Muñiz, & Arnould, 2009) try to connect with their customers and enhance their brand communities on such social networking sites as MySpace and Facebook. (as cited in Laroche et al., 2012). Perhaps the most important advantage for companies in supporting brand communities is increasing brand loyalty, which is called the "Holy Grail" for businesses (McAlexander, Schouten, & Koening,2002, p. 38) that building and maintaining it are one of the central themes of research for marketers for a very long time(i.e,Oliver& Rust, 1997; Chaudhuri & Halbrook, 2001; Bennett & Rundle-Thiele, 2002) and brand equity which is an important source of competitive advantage for the firm(Satanasavapak, 2010).Presence of company in brand communities affect these two items and their antecedents by various methods that we consider one of these ways in our research.

On the other hand, people have their own incentives to join social media and follow brands on it.They fulfill their need for belongingnessand their need for cognition with those who have shared norms, values and interests (Gangadharbhatla, 2008; Tardini &Cantoni, 2005). The Uses and Gratifications Theory confirms these incentives and argues that "audiences use media to meet their needs and fulfill their personal gratification" (Lee, 2009, p. 16). According to Sicilia and Palazon (as cited in Lee, 2009,p.17), "the gratification of individual needs in a virtual community depends on the perceived value of being a member". Virtual communities offer functional, social, and entertainment values. The functional values allude to an individual's need to give and seek information and advice. Social values cover friendship and social enhancement. Finally, entertainment values are fun and relaxation from an individual's interaction with others (Elizabeth &Bushelow, 2012).In the literature, Feeling of being socially connected is stated as acentral element in one's psychological sense of community (Sarason,1974). Although it is asserted that these feelings of belongingness would be weaker due to the absence of physical co-presence and lack of proximity in such environments (Constant, Sproull, &Kiesler, 1996; Granovetter, 1973), it has been shown that weak ties are capable of bridging people (Wellman, 1997) and encouraging member's engagement in communities to reach deep and intimate levels (Tardini & Cantoni, 2005).

Despite the importance of branding and the high adoption rate of social media(e.g.,Hsu &Tsou,2011), especially the new phenomenon of social media based brand community(Laroche et al., 2012) very few specific, empirical studies have dealt with these issues.So providing information in this field is necessary for both researchers and marketers.

In taking the perspective of brand community building (McAlexander et al., 2002; Muniz & O'Guinn, 2001),by combining models offered by Laroche, Habibi,and Richard (2013) and Loureiro(2013),our goal is to show how brand communities based on social media influence elements of the customer centric model (i.e., relationships between focal customer and brand, product, company, and other customers) and brand loyalty. And, how brand trust can contribute to brand equity and how brand awareness/association, perceived quality and brand loyalty are related to each other and contribute to brand equity. Brand community of Cinere cosmetic company on facebook is selected as a pilot to test the model. The first reason for this matter is the high level of the use of cosmetic products in Iran, such that Iranians annually spend a lot of money for purchasing different types of beauty products. So the brand community related to cosmetic market has more advocates rather than others.The second is Cinere company started its serious activity on brand community on facebook in 2012. One of the goals of this company from launching this community is to develop the company's relationships with its customers and to enhance brand loyalty and brand equity.So after a few years this company want to study the brand community effects on its brand loyalty and brand equity.

Cinereis a famouse company in cosmetic industry in Iran.It founded in 1997, AEPC Laboratories (Amalgamated Euro Products Corporation) has been producing high quality and natural-based cosmetic products to satisfy customer's needs for hair & skin care. At AEPC Laboratories (Cinere) they are devoted to developing and manufacturing a complete range of personal care and beauty care products that are truly natural in origin.

THEORETICAL BACKGROUND

Social Media

The definitions of social media are very diverse. According to Kaplan and Haenlein (2010),there is confusion among academic researchers and managers in terms of what should be included in the definition of social media. Most of these definitions are based on the elements of "sharing" and "interaction". Some definitions hilight production and the published content by users. In other definitions were implied instances of social media and identified the type of media including web sites based on user participation and user generated content,such as Linkdin, Facebook, Bookmarking and other sites focusing on user interaction (Searchenginewatch & Creativemediafarm, 2010).Safko and Brake(2009, p.6)define social media as "activities, practices, and behaviors among communities of people who gather online to share information, knowledge, and opinions using conversational media".Rheingold (1993) postulates social media to be the "social aggregations that emerge from the Net when enough people carry on those public discussions long enough, with sufficient human feelings, to form webs of personal relationships in Cyberspace." (as cited in Laroche et al., 2012).Kaplan and Haenlein(2010) defined social media by using two words of Web2.0 and the User generated content.They statedthat social media is "a group of internetbased applications that is built on the ideological and technologicalfoundations of Web 2.0, and it allows the creation and exchangeof user-generated content".

Web 2.0 is a term that was first used in 2004 to describe a new way in which software developers and end users started to utilize the World Wide Web; that is, as a platform whereby content and applications are no longer created and published by individuals(Web 1.0), but instead are continuously modified by all users in a participatory and collaborative fashion. Web 2.0 describes the evolution from the Web1.0 technologies(Laroche et al.,2012).User Generated Content (UGC) can be seen as the sum of all ways in which people make use of Social Media. The term, which achieved broad popularity in 2005, is usually applied to describe the various forms of media content that are publicly available and created by end-users(Kaplan &Haenlein,2010). With the proliferation of UGC embedded in multifarious social media contexts, consumers increasingly have access to opinions from other consumers outside their immediate social circle (Dhar & Chang, 2009).

The unique aspects of social media and its increasing popularity have revolutionized marketing practices such as advertising and promotion (Hanna, Rohm, & Crittenden, 2011). Social media has also influenced consumer behavior such as awareness, information gathering, opinions, attitudes, purchase behavior, evaluation of the product (Mangold & Faulds, 2009), brand loyalty(Laroche et al., 2013),brand equity(Loureiro, 2013; Satanasavapak, 2010) and patterns of Internet usage (Ross et al., 2009). These differences and importance are in a way that researchers are urged to treat social media as a distinct research area (Hu & Kettinger, 2008).

There are many different platforms for social media such as social networking, text messaging, photo sharing, wikis, weblogs, and discussion forums (Harris, 2009).But one of the most widely used variety of social media is the social net- working site.Social networks are social structures made by individuals or organizations with one or more users and are connected to each other. Kerpen (2011) describes social networking sites as a cocktail party where anyone can listen to what others are talking about, and can join the conversation if they wish. But what makes social networking more effective than one's average cocktail party is that instead of joining just one conversation, one has the ability to have conversations with thousands or millions of people at once.Facebook is one of the key social networks which by itself has more than 800 milion active users(Laroche et al., 2013),and483 million user logins each day(Elizabeth &Bushelow, 2012). In the recent years, it has had an important role in buisiness, culture and research (Boyd, 2007).

Facebook fan pages allow brands to create an online community of brand users on the social networking site. These public profiles, which operate in a similar manner to individual user profiles, allow a brand to share information and post updates, photos, and more (Elizabeth &Bushelow, 2012).

Brand Community

In recent years, we have seen the importance ofbranding as a strategy for business growth and development. Much has been written and researched on the concept of branding and its practical application for business success. Brands that are particularly successful seem to enjoy a strong, loyal base of customers that interact with one another and the company. These active groups have become known as brand communities(Komaromi, 2003). Brand communities are one of many options through which individuals can gather in groups to build and foster social relationships and thus to maximize their social capital.But in order to effectively understand the concept of brand community it is necessary to track its evolution along the past century and its rapid adoption during the last decade. From the philosophical interpretation of community in terms of social criticism (Muniz & O'Guinn, 2001), communalities and human collectives seem to explain social and even commercial phenomena in the field of consumer awareness and consumption behaviour. Therefore, it is not really surprising to find different, and sometimes aggressively confronted, positions towards brand community (Muñoz, 2013).To explore the mentioned evolution, table 1 summarizes keyconcepts about brand commu- nitiesextracted from top ranked articles and authors regarding marketing and social science literature(Muñoz,2013).

The concept of consumption community, first proposed by historian Daniel Boorstin.Boorstin observes that in the emerging consumer culturethat followed the industrial revolution, the sense of community in the United States shifted away from the tight interpersonal bonds of geographically bounded collectives and into the direction of common but tenuous bonds of brand use and affiliation:

The modern American, then, was tied, if only by the thinnest of threads and by the most volatile, switchable loyalties, to thousands of other Americans in nearly everythinghe ate or drank or drove or read or used. Oldfashioned political and religious communities now became only two among many new, once unimagined fellowships.Americans wereincreasingly held to others not by a few iron bonds, but by countless gossamer webs knitting together the trivia of their lives (Boorstin 1974, p. 148).

After Boorstin, Schouten and McAlexander (1995) studied subcultures of consumption and never mention the term brand community, their studies represent a paradigmatic shift within marketing research. Their findings from studying Harley Davidson motorcycle owners and their consumer behaviour had great influence in several marketing fields such as consumer behaviour, relationship marketing and brand management. Schouten and McAlexander (1995) discovered that certain Harley Davidson consumers had

Table 1. Historic Evolution of "Brand Community" in Marketing Literature. source: Muñoz, 2013

Year	Author	Concept of Brand Community
1974 - Book	Daniel Boorstin	The book describes consumption communities as a kind of "invisible new communities [...] created and preserved by how and what men consumed" (Boorstin, 1974)
1995 - Journal of Consumer Research	John W. Schouten and James H. McAlexander	The article introduced the concept of subculture of consumption to better explain the way consumers organize their lives and identities.subculture of consumption is thus an antecedent of brand community (Schouten& McAlexander,1995)
2001 – Journal of Consumer Research	Albert M. Muniz. and Thomas C. O'Guinn	"Specialized, non-geographically bound community, based on a structured set of social relationships among admirers of a brand" (Muniz & O'Guinn, 2001)
2002 – Journal of Marketing	James H. McAlexander, John W. Schouten, and Harold F. Koenig	"A brand community, from a customer experiential perspective [...] is a fabric of relationships in which the customer is situated" (McAlexander, et al., 2002)
2009 – Journal of Marketing	Hope Jensen Schau, Albert M. Muñiz Jr., & Eric J. Arnould	Brand Communities are environments where value creation is encouraged through social bonds (Schau, et al., 2009).

developed a complex subculture around the brand with established "social authorities" in a structured hierarchy.Theyfurther suggest that it is possible for a marketer who understands the structure and ethos of a subculture to establish long-lasting relationships with its members(Schouten & McAlexander, 1995; as cited in Andersson & Bertilsson, 2011). Both constructs are thus antecedents of Brand Communities within consumer behaviour literature and show the early interest of marketing, and social sciences in general, to explain the social consumption behaviour in terms of describing patterns(Muñoz,2013).

In deed this subculture, that only is antecedents of the brand community, has certain similarities with bran communities (e.g., shared ethos, acculturation patterns, status hierarchies), but important differences as well(Muniz & O'Guinn, 2001). It is not quite representative of the brand communities that describe later. For one, the Harley Davidson consum- ption subculture is characterized as having "outsider status"(Schouten & McAlexander,1995, p. 58), a significant degree of marginality, and an outlaw culture(Muniz & O'Guinn, 2001).

Afterwards, Muniz and O'Guinn (2001) officially introduce the paradigmatic shift and the construct of brand community (BC) as it is known nowadays. In their exploratory and empiric study, the authors describe the mixture of non-geographic bonds and interactions around any ascribed brand, usually those that joy of strong brand image (as cited in Muñoz, 2013, p.6).Subsequent studies leaded to add new and more transcendent arguments around social interactions within BC. In fact, McAlexander et al. (2002) proclaimed the leading role of consumer relations to effectively create value in consu- mption environments (McAlexander et al., 2002). The preponderant role of relationships among consumers and other physical, commercial and/or human entities became the centre of BC model(Muñoz, 2013) and the encouraging base for current studies.

In fact,in recent years, the concept of brand community is tied with media. Brands transcend geography because media transcend geography (Muniz & O'Guinn,2001), and technology made the constraint of geography almost irrelevant(Laroche et al.,2012). The role of social media therefore holds the key for brands to get existing and potential customers together in order to create an environment which nourishes the bond between customer and brand and to find new ways to foster this relationship, all without the constraint of geography(Kang, K.C. Lee, S.Lee, & Choi, 2007). Additionally, brand communities allow the consumer to have a greater voice and provide its members with social benefits(Elizabeth &Bushelow, 2012).

Social Media Based Brand Community

Nowadays more than ever, consumers participate in brand communities. The increasing use of the social media has influenced consumers in taking action online and following their favourite brand on the social media by, for instance, joining brand communities in social media.

Regarding the motivations for joining social media and brand communities for both people and brand managers, the concepts of social media and brand communities have become closer to each other (Laroche et al., 2013).

The intersection of brand communities and social media leads to a concept that is called social media based brand community(Laroche et al., 2013,p.77) which is a subset of the broader concept of "virtual communities" or online brand communities; but the main differentiator is their platforms. The core platform of social media is Web 2.0 plus User Generated Content (Laroche et al., 2012). Originally brand communities were established on the Web 1.0 platform, on the companies' portals or initiated by customers (Jang, 2008). However, with the popularity of social media websites, several companies are using social networking sites to support the creation of brand communities (Kaplan & Haenlein, 2010; Muniz & O' Guinn, 2001)

Unlike many traditional media where individuals consume content passively, community members in these settings create content through active participation. Such consumer-generated content shapes online brand communities' unique characteristics and influences the creation of a capital of knowledge or opinions(Annie Jin,2012).Researches demons- trate that consumers prefer recommendations from other consumers over professional reviews by critics, especially for hedonic goods (Dellarocas, Zhang, & Awad, 2007; Smith,Menon, & Sivakumar, 2005).

On the other hand, For the brand, a community allows it to share information about the brand, its history, and its culture of the brand (Muniz & O'Guinn, 2001). Further, a brand can become an informational resource for the members of the community and provide customer service. Creating a strong brand community is a key step in developing a strong relationship marketing strategy(Elizabeth &Bushelow, 2012).

Development of the Model and the Hypotheses

As mentioned earlier, the purpose of this study is to fill in the gaps of discussion in the ways in which social media based brand communities impact brand equity and it's antecedents.so we discussed these hypotheses.

Customer Centric Model of Brand Community and Social Media

Muniz & O'Guinn (2001) introduced two models of brand communities: the brand dyad relationship model (see figure 1), and the brand triad relationship model (see figure 2).

In first model Brand communities are one instrument that helps in strengthening consumer–brand relationships (e.g., Muniz & O'Guinn, 2001).second model emphasizes the importance of consumer interaction in brand communities. It suggests that consumers take an active role in creating brands through the social interaction between community members, the community, the brand, and the individual consumers (Dubois, Théophile, Westerhausen,& Uwe, 2011). In deed, a brand is viewed as a social object, which is developed and constructed by consumer feedback and consumer insight, giving the consumer an active role in the brand's development. Consumers become active loyalists who are committed to that brand(Elizabeth &Bushelow, 2012,p.6). Heding, Knudtzen and Bjerre (2009) even mention that a brand community needs interaction between at least two consumers in order to exist. In other words, brand communities have a purpose of unifying people who might share nothing in common but this brand.

It has to be noted that the sole investigation of the relationship between the customer and the brand in examining brand communities misses additional connections between the customer and other important entities.

Figure 1. The brand dyad relationship model,(Muniz&O'guinn,2001)

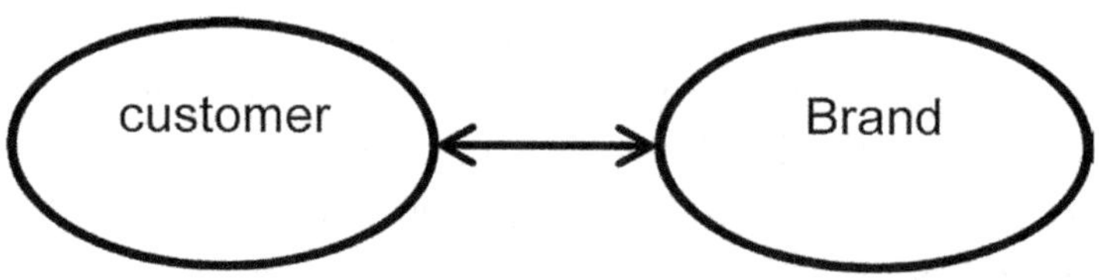

Figure 2. The brand triad relationship model, (Muniz&O'guinn,2001)

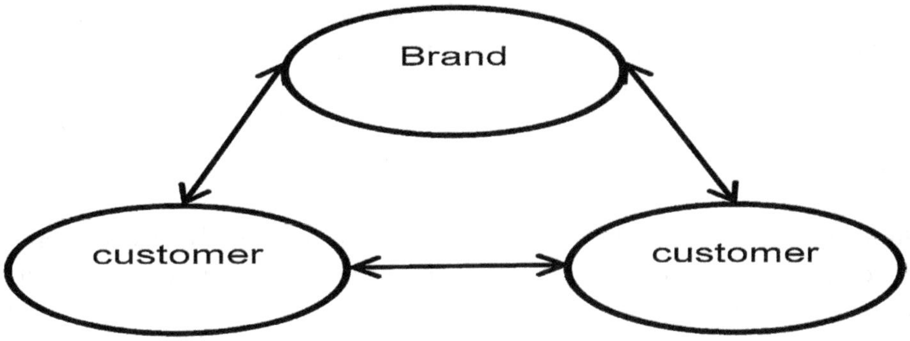

McAlexander et al. (2002) developed another model entitled the customer centric model||. In this model the customer is at the centre of the brand community in which the brand community intensity is made up of four relations between the customer and the following: other customers, the brand, the product and the company (see figure 3).

According to these researchers, brand communities nowadays have a focal consumer, instead of a focal brand. This focal consumer has relations with the brand, other consumers, the product, and the marketers.Therefore, the consumer is the centre of brand community instead of the brand itself. This caused a shift of perspective, from the brand-centric perspective as proposed by Muniz and O'Guinn (2001), to aconsumer-centric perspective as proposed by McAlexander et al.(2002), leading to a broader view of brand communities.

They believed When a member logs on a social media platform and explores the brand page, comments, shares a photo or experience, interacts with marketers, asks questions about the brand or the product or answers comments, that member is participating in the community activities and the invisible community becomes visible(Laroche et al., 2013).

Figure 3. The customer-centric model(McAlexander et al., 2002, p.39).

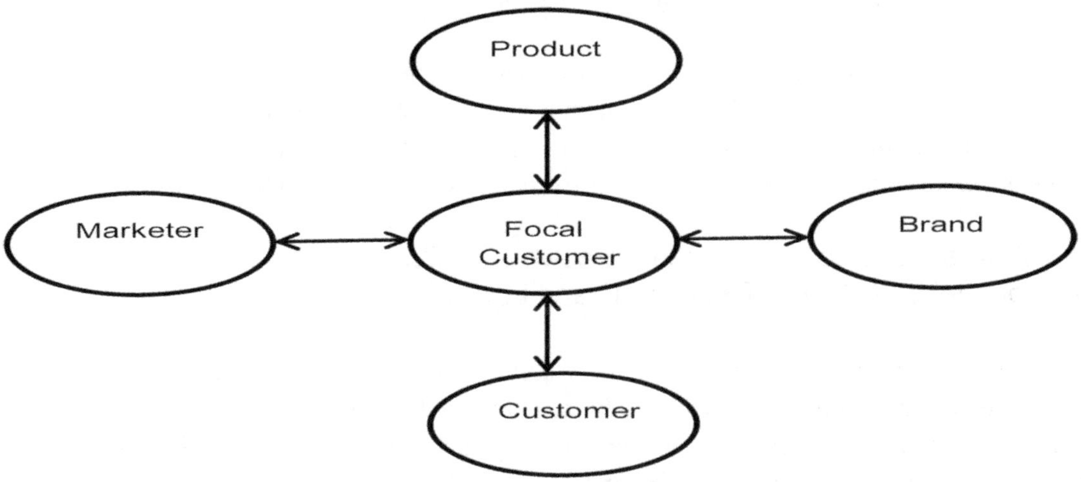

Thus, to the degree in which they support information sharing and welfare of the members, and strengthen bonds among them, brand communities based on social media – like offline brand communities– cement entities of the customer centric model of brand community, i.e., relationships between customers and brand, product, company and other customers(Laroche et al., 2013).

Now we want to test this fact in the brand community of Cinere company on facebook and see if it is true here too. So:

H_1. Social media based brand communities have positive effects on the: (a) customer/product relationship; (b) customer/brand relationship; (c) customer/company relationship; and (d) customer/ other customers relationships.

Effects of Customer Centric Model of Brand Community on Brand Trust

Trust has been studied primarily in the context of relationship marketing (Doney & Cannon,1997; Morgan & Hunt, 1997). Morgan and Hunt (1997) conceptualize trust "as existing when one part has confidence in an exchange partner's reliability and integrity". According to Blau (1964), trust is a key element in the emergence and maintenance of social exchange relationships.Brand trust is "the willingness of the average consumer to rely on the ability of the brand to perform its stated function" (Chaudhuri & Holbrook 2001, p82).

Kania (2001) and Shankar, Smith, Rangaswany (2003) propose that experience with the web; which provides online brand communities; affords consumers with enjoyable and meaningful experience with the brand which leads to brand trust. Based on these literatures and supported by involvement-commitment theory (Beatty, Homer, & Kahle, 1988; Crosby & Taylor 1983), it is proposed that participation in virtual brand community will affect customer trust in the brand and the community.

Many researchers have argued that trust is a crucial enabling factor in relations where there is uncertainty, information asymmetry,and fear of opportunism (Gefen, Karahanna,& Straub 2003; McKnight & Chervany,2002; Pavlou, Liang, & Xue, 2007), as is the case in online context. On the other hand, repeated interaction and long term relationships which are introduced as keys to building trust (Holmes, 1991; Wang & Emurian, 2005) facilitatebecause of the placeless and comprehensive nature of social media based brand communities.So we hypothesize that:

H_{2a}. The customer/product relationship has a direct positive effect on brand trust.
H_{2b}. The customer/brand relationship has a direct positive effect on brand trust.
H_{2c}. The customer/company relationship has a direct positive effect on brand trust.
H_{2d}.Customer/other customers relationships have direct positive effects on brand trust.

Brand Awareness/Association and Perceived Quality as Mediators between Brand Trust and Brand Loyalty

Formally, brand awareness refers to the customers' ability to recall and recognize the brand. Brand awareness is more than just customers knowing the brand name and having previously seen the brand, perhaps even many times. Brand awareness also involves linking the brand-the brand name,logo, symbol, and so forth-to certain associations in memory(Hoeffler& keller,2002).Brand awareness can be characterised according to depth and breadth. The depth of brand awareness concerns the likelihood that the brand can be recognised or recalled and the breadth of brand awareness relates to the variety of purchase and consumption situations in which the brand comes to mind (Keller 1993, 3; Keller 1998, 120–123).Higher depth of brand awareness leads to increased sales if consumers are more likely to think of the brand when the need arises (e.g., Coke when thirsty). Higher breadth of brand awareness leads to increased sales if consumers are more likely to think of the brand across a variety of settings when it could be employed or consumed (e.g., Coke in the morning). Two important measures of brand awareness are recognition and recall. Brand recognition is the ability of the consumer to confirm prior exposure to the brand, and brandrecall is the unaided retrieval of the brand from memory(Keller 1993, 3; Keller 1998, 120–123).

"Brand associations" describes the feelings, beliefsand knowledge that online brand community members associate to the brand. It is anything which is deep-seated in the members' minds about the brand, such as symbols, images, celebrities, etc. (Aaker 1996a; Aaker1996b)

Empirical evidence show that brand awareness and brand association can be combined into a particular dimension named brand awareness/association (Yoo, Donthu, & Lee, 2000).They are related to the strength of the brand node or trace in memory, as reflected by consumers' ability to identify the brand under different conditions(Keller,1993 Rossiter, & Percy, 1987). This awareness/association represents the favorable, strong, and unique associations in consumer "memory"(Loureiro, 2013).They play an important role in consumers' evaluations (Osselaer,2001), such as quality evaluation(Loureiro,2013).

Perceived quality is one of the main dimensions of brand equity. It is the core construct to measure brand equity (Aaker, 1996a). Perceived quality is believed to be a type of association warranting elevation to the status of a separate dimension of a brand's equity (Pappu & Quester, 2006). It is not the actual quality of the product.However, it is the consumer's subjective evaluation of the product(Zeithaml,1998). Aaker(1996a) believed that trust is the faith put into a brand with regard to its quality, consistency, etc. So, higher brand trust leads to enhance perceived quality.An other hand, The effect of high quality on brand loyalty is well known and is widely accepted as the basis of consumer satisfaction (Oliver,1981; Bitner,1990; Fornel,1992; Zeithaml, Berry, & Parasuraman,1996; Cronin, Brady,& Hult, 2000; Al-Hawari,2005;Loureiro & González, 2008; Loureiroet al., 2010)

Chaudhuri(1997) has proposed that brand loyalty is the preference of a customer for a single brand, or preference to buy a particular brand name in a product class regularly (Loureiro, 2013). Consumers' brand loyalty is strategically importantfor companies to obtain a sustainable competitive advantage, as it gives companies have some protectionfrom competition and increases their control inplanning their marketing programmes(Gounaris& Stathakopolous, 2004). The focus of marketers on building long term loyalty has led to the increasing importance of brand communities in the creation of brand equity(Dubois etal.,2011). Several empirical studies already confirmed that members of brand communities have a higher brand loyalty than non-members (Algesheimer, Herrmann, & Dimpfel, 2006). Wilimzig (2011) suggested that association with a brand community implies some sort of brand loyalty, regardless of community participation and feelings of association(as cited in Elizabeth&Bushelow, 2012,p.7). Consumers turn to online brand communities as a trustworthy and reliable source for brand related information (Punjumiemi, 2009). These online brand communities are convenient, easily accessible, and enable consumers with similar brand preferences to interact with one another. Lee (2009) concluded that loyalty to a brand community predicts brand loyalty. Therefore, participation in a brand community has a positive effect on loyalty to a brand(Elizabeth&Bushelow, 2012). It is noteworthy to mention that brand loyalty is both one of the dimensions of brand equity and is affected by brand equity (Aaker, 1991). Therefore, the other components of brand equity have an influence on brand loyalty(Aaker, 1991). A lot of researches support the positive effect of trust on loyalty in online or offline contexts (Chaudhuri & Holbrook, 2001; Chiu, Huang, & Yen, 2010; Harris & Goode, 2004; Kim, Chung, & Lee, 2011; Zhou,Jin,Vogel,Fang, &hen,2011).Accordingly, the following hy- potheses are proposed:

H_3**:** Brand trust has a positive effect on brand loyalty.
H_4**:** Brand trust has a positive effect on perceived quality.
H_5: Brand trust has a positive effect on brand awareness/association.
H_6: Brand awareness/association has a positive effect on perceived quality.
H_7: Perceived quality has a positive effect on brand loyalty.

Brand Equity and Its Antecedents

The concept of brand equity emerged in the early 1990s. It was not defined precisely, but in practical terms it meant that brands are financial assets and should be recognised as such by top management and the financial markets.An attempt to define the relationship between customers and brands produced the term "brand equity" in the marketing literature.

The concept of brand equity has been a field of interest to both firms and researchers for several years. To understand better how to build brand equity, several models and viewpoints of brand building have been put forth. One of the most widely accepted is the Farquhar's approach (1989),which defines brand equity as added value for the company, for the delivery, or for the consumer. Later, Aaker (1991),defined brand equity as a "set of brand assets and liabilities linked to a brand, its name and symbol, that add to or subtract from the value provided by a product or service to a firm and/or to that firm's customers".He classified brand equity into four most important dimensions namely brand awareness,brand associations, perceived quality and brand loyalty. For Kapferer (1998), brand equity is a reflection of the consumer and a mental image of proposed values (brand identity).Although the idea that brand equity adds value to the product or service is apparent in all definitions, two different research approaches can be perceived: a business (or financial) perspective and a customer perspective(Pappu, Ravi, Quester,2005). Keller (1998, 2001) defines customer-based brand equity as the differential effect that brand knowledge has on customer response to marketing activity. The basic premise of his model is that the power of a brand lies in what customers have learned, felt, seen, heard, and so forth about the brand as a result of their experiences over time. According to Myers (2003), the consumer perspective can also be divided in two ways: one based on consumer perceptions and the other based on his/her attitudes and behaviour(as cited in Loureiro& Miranda,2011).

In general, there are direct and indirect measures of brand equity. As for the direct approach, an attempt is made to assess the value added by the brand to the product (Farquhar,1989; Keller,2003). This approach is closely linked to the accepted definition of brand equity. The indirect approach focuses on identifying potential sources of brand equity(David,1991; Keller, 1993). However, Keller (1993) argues that the direct and indirect approaches are complementary and should be used together.Park and Shrinivasan (1994) integrated both Aaker's and Keller'sconcepts of brand equity and developed survey -based method for measuring and understanding brand equity. Krishnan (1996) extended Keller's framework using a memory-based view of brand equity to identify various associations underlying consumer-based brand equity.Yoo and Donthu (2001) developed a multidimensional consumer-based brand equity scale.

They also suggested that a potential causal order may exist among the dimensions of brand equity. Thus, the hierarchy of the effects model suggests that brand awareness and associations precede perceived quality and that perceived quality precedes brand loyalty (as cited in Loureiro,&Miranda,2011,p.477).

Researchers suggests that brand equity should be an important research domain in marketing because it is considered the combination of important consumer behavior variables.It cannot be either built or damaged in the short term. It is created in the long run through carefully designed marketing investments. Thus, brand equity is durable and sustainable. A product with strong brand equity is a valuable asset not only for the firm but also to customers(Thanh,2012). So we can conclude that one of the ways to develop and improve the brand equity, is establishing brand communities.

On the other hand, Muniz and O'Ginn(2001) noted that brand communities directly affect all four of these components of brand equity.Therefore, the strong brand community relationship would lead to greater brand awareness,brand associa- tions, perceived quality and brand loyalty(satanasavapak,2010).

As was stated brand awareness is an important component of brand equity(Aaker,1991; Keller,1993). If consumers are not aware of the brand's presence in the market, the brand will not have any meaning to the consumers (Satanasavapak, 2010). Brand awareness and associations are both positively related to brand equity. If the consumers recognize, quickly recall, and are aware of the brand, this can be a sign of quality and commitment. Thus, a buyer aware of a brand with favorable associations in her/his mind and able to recognize quality is more willing to consider this brand at the time of purchase, which leads to a favorable behavior towards the brand (Loureiro& Miranda, 2011).Another critical component of brand equity is brand loyalty(Aaker,1991; Keller,1993). High perceived quality would drive a consumer to choose the brand rather than other competing brands(Loureiro,& Miranda, 2011). Therefore, brand loyalty will increase.On the other hand, brand loyalty is considered to be the strongest path leading to brand equity (Atilgan,Aksoy, & Akinci, 2005). Brand loyalty has a positive and direct role in affecting brand equity (Atilgan et al., 2005). Nowadays, products and services sold are not only about the physicality of the products or the quality of the services but also about beliefs in the brand associated with the products or services. It indicates the critical role of the brand. As a result, brand loyalty is a concept that firms emphasize, since it may create or sustain a customers' patronage over the long-term thereby increasing brand equity(Thanh,2012).Wood (2000) states that the componenet of brand loyalty is one of the most important ones of brand equity which explains that the brand value for a company is determined by "the degree of brand loyalty, as this implies a guarantee of future cash flows"|| (p.663). Hence, this study offers the following hypotheses:

H_8: Perceived quality has a positive effect on brand equity.
H_9: Brand loyalty has a positive effect on brand equity.
H_{10}: Brand awareness/association has a positive effect on brand equity.
H_{11}: Brand trust has a positive effect on brand equity

Method and Findings

Subjects and Procedure

The research setting in this study are brand communities on social media,thus the target population is all active members of the Cinere brand community on facebook. We used the screening condition that respondents had to be an active member.

After developing the questionnaire from literature, a pilot test was conducted with ten brand community members, and four experts who had studied on social media.This test helped to purify the scale items of the questionnaire and find out if the items were well understood. Therefore, we assessed the content-related validity of the operational measures and ensure that customers understood the study's instructions and questions.

In order to collect data, company of Cinere emailed a message explaining the need to understand the user's opinion in using brand community. This invitation was also linked to a website where users could fill out an online questionnaire. We asked them answer questions as honestly as possible.

In this online survey, more than 260 invitation were sent, with incomplete responses and missing values deleted,resulting in a sample size of 170 users(39% male).Table 2 shows Survey customer profile.

With this procedure, which is consistent with previous studies in online contexts (Loureiro, 2013). the age range of participants varied between 18 and 55.

Measures

All constructs were measured with multiple item-scales and were adopted from the related literature and modified to suit the study. They was measured by a five-point Likert scale ranging from "strongly disagree" (1) to "strongly agree" (5).

- *Brand community*: Items we used for measuring the brand community developed by Srinivasan, Anderson, and Srinivasan,Anderson, and Ponnavolu (2002) and modified by Laroche et al.(2013). This scale consists of 3items. The Cronbach's alpha is 0.83.
- *Customer's relationship*: Items we used for measuring the customer's relationship with product, brand, company and other customers originally developed by McAlexander et al.(2002) and used by Laroche et al.(2013).This scale consist of 13 items with cronbach's alphas of 0.890, 0.907, 0.813, 0.861.
- *Brand trust:* Items we used for measuring the brand trust developed by Chaudhuri and Halbrook(2001).we used three out of the four items. The Cronbach's alpha is 0.830.
- *Brand loyalty*: Items we used for measuring the brand loyalty were from Delgado-Ballester, Manuera-Aleman, Yague-Guillen (2003) and Laroche et al.(2013). This scale consist of 3 items with cronbach's alpha of 0.822.
- *Perceived quality*: Items we used for measuring the perceived quality were from Satanasavapak (2010). We used 6 items.The cronbach's alpha is 0.831.

Table 2. Survey customer profile

Gender	Age	Education
Male: 39%	18-25: 35.9%	Less than 11 years: 9.4%
Female: 61%	26-32: 44.7%	Undergraduate: 18.2%
	33-55: 19.4%	Bachelor: 50.6%
		Master or PhD Degree: 21.8%

- *Brand awareness/association*: Items we used for measuring the brand awareness/association were from Yoo et al.(2000) and Yoo, Donthu(2009). This scale consist of 6 items with cronbach's alpha of0.921.
- *Brand equity*: Items we used for measuring the brand equity were from Yoo et al. (2000). This scale consist of 3 items with cronbach's alpha of0.852.

Before testing hypotheses that showed in figure 4, we first conducted the evaluation of undimensionality of the scales and then exploratory factor analysis(EFA) and convergent & discriminant validity for cheking construct validity and reliability analysis to calculate Cronbach's alpha for the scale items to ensure internal consistency (Cronbach, 1970; Laroche et al., 2013).

Undimensionality

The evaluation of unidimensionality of the proposed scales was assessed by performing exploratory factor analysis (EFA). Factors were extracted based on eigenvalues greater than 1. In addition they were required to have a significant factor loading greater than 0.4 and a high total variance explained component(Laroche et al.,2012).Based on the results only one factor was extracted for brand community, customer's relationships, brand trust, brand loyalty, brand awareness/association, perceived quality, brand equity constructs.

For determining the correlations between the variables we calculated bartlett's sphericity test and for adequacy of sampling we calculated KMO test.High value of KMO(0.828) and an small value of the significance level of Bartlet's test indicate that a factor analysis is useful with our data.Table 3 shows results.

In the EFA, we found that the items (BAW_1) and (Q_2) did not have high enough loadings on their respective factors.hence they were eliminated from further analysis.

Figure 4. Model of the effects of brand community

Note: C/P= customer/ product relationship, C/B= customer/ brand relationship, C/C= customer/company relationship, C/O= customer/ other customer relationship, BT= brand trust, PO= perceived quality, BAW/ASS= brand awareness/ association, BL= brand loyalty, BE= brand equity

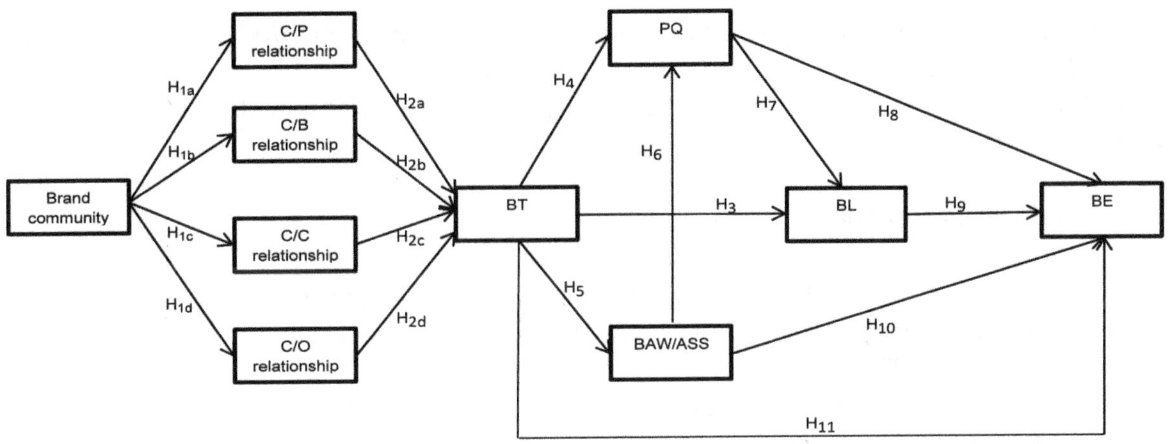

Table 3. KMO and Bartlett's test

Kaiser-Meyer-Olkin measure of sampling adequacy		0.828
Bartlett's Test of Sphericity	Approx. Chi-Square	8525.22
	Df.	496
	Sig.	.000

CFA Results

Next we conducted confirmatory factor analysis(CFA). We found that the loading of 2 items (Q5 with loading 0.09, and Q6 with loading 0.23) are less than 0.4. So, we dropped them out. The 10 scales together explain almost 79.85% of the total variance. Table 4 shows factor loadings for each item and Cronbach's alpha for each construct.

Discriminant Validity

Discriminant (also referred to as divergent) validity is evidence that a measure is not unduly related to other similar, yet distinct, constructs (Messick, 1989).

to assess discriminant validity we follow the rule that the square root of AVE should be greater than the correlation between the construct and other constructs in the model(Fornell & Larker, 1981). Table 5 shows results.

Convergent Validity

To establish convergent validity, you need to show that measures that should be related are in reality related. Referring to the CFA model and Table 4, since all the factor loadings are above 0.5, convergent validity is supported (Steenkamp & Geyskens, 2006; Laroche et al.,2012)

Reliability

Then we calculated Cronbach's alphas for each construct with a minimum of 0.70(Cronbach,1970; Nunnally, 1978). All constructs are above 0.70 and showed in Table 4.

Following these steps we test the hypotheses using path analysis and warppls 3.0 software in the next part.

Path Analysis Technique

Path analysis is an extension of multiple regression.It goes beyond regression in that it allows for the analysis of more complicated models(Streiner, 2005).The path analysis can bee seen as a special case of SEM (Maruyama, 1998).

Path coefficients were calculated by path analysis and warppls 3.0 software.

The structural results are presented in Figure 5. Thirteen path coefficients(β) are found to be significant at the $p<0.01$ level, and four are not significant.

Table 4. Shows factor loading for each construct and Cronbach's alpha for each construct

Construct	Item	Factor Loading	Cronbach's Alpha
Brand community	Ob_4: The members of this community benefit from the community	0.66	0.830
	Ob_5: The members share a common bond with other members of the community	0.76	
	Ob_6: The members are strongly affiliated with other members	0.90	
Consumer/product relationship	P_1: I love the product of the brand	0.74	0.890
	P_2: I am proud of the product	0.74	
	P_3:The product is one of my priced possessions	0.80	
	P_4:The product is fun to use	0.78	
Consumer/brand relationship	B_1: I value the heritage of the brand	0.8	0.907
	B_2: If I were to replace the product, I would replace it with another product of the same brand	0.86	
	B_3:My brand is of the highest quality	0.72	
Consumer/company relationship	Com_1: The COMPANY understands my needs	0.80	0.813
	Com_2: The COMPANY cares about my opinions	0.87	
Consumer/other customer relationship	Oo_1: I have met wonderful people because of the community	0.88	0.861
	Oo_2: I have a feeling of kinship with the other owners	0.96	
	Oo_3: I have an interest in the community because of the other owners of the brands	0.92	
Brand trust	Bt_1: My brand gives me everything that I expect out of the product	0.66	0.830
	Bt_2: I rely on my brand	0.76	
	Bt_3: My brand never disappoints me	0.90	
Brand loyalty	L_1: I consider myself to be loyal to the brand	0.93	0.822
	L_2: If the brand is not available at the store, I would buy the same brand from some othe store	0.91	
	L_3: I am willing to pay more for my brand.	0.91	
Perceived quality	Q_1: this brand is of high quality	0.82	0.830
	Q_3: the likelihood that this product would be functional is very high.	0.94	
	Q_4: the likelihood that this product is reliable is very high.	0.76	
Brand awareness/ associations	Baw_2: I can recognize this brand among other competing brands.	0.77	0.921
	Baw_3: I am aware of this brand.	0.66	
	Ass_1: Some characteristics of this brand come to my mind quickly.	0.80	
	Ass_2: I can quickly recall the symbol or logo of this brand	0.87	
	Ass_3: I have difficulty in imagine this brand in my mind	0.84	
Brand equity	Be_1: Even if another brand has same features as this brand, I would prefer to buy this brand.	0.81	0.852
	Be_2: If there is another brand as good as this brand,I prefer to buy this brand.	0.87	
	Be_3: If another brand is not different from this brand in any way,it seems smarter to purchase this brand	0.89	

Table 5. Correlation Matrix

	BC	CP	CB	CC	CO	BT	BAW	PQ	BL	BE
BC	**0.865**									
CP	0.257*	**0.870**								
CB	0.316*	0.511*	**0.919**							
CC	0.283*	0.524*	0.402*	**0.918**						
CO	0.302*	0.237**	0.087	0.211**	**0.885**					
BT	0.285*	0.257*	0.316*	0.283*	0.308*	**0.865**				
BAW	0.276*	0.305*	0.287*	0.321*	0.104	0.276*	**0.875**			
PQ	0.383*	0.440*	0.422*	0.362*	0.388*	0.383*	0.208**	**0.865**		
BL	0.373*	0.208**	0.180	0.233**	0.354*	0.373*	0.026	0.340*	**0.900**	
BE	0.295*	0.268*	0.282*	0.255*	0.103	0.295*	0.374*	0.352*	0.351*	**0.880**

Note: Square roots of average variances extracted (AVE's) shown on diagonal ;* Correlation is significant at p< 0.01,* * Correlation is significant at p<0.05;BC= brand community, CP=customer/ product relationship, CB= customer/ brand relationship, CC= customer/ product relationship, CO= customer/ other customer relationship, BT= brand trust, BAW= brand awareness/association, PQ= perceived quality, BL= brand loyalty, BE= brand equity.

Figure 5. Structural results.

Note: B is path coefficient; dashed arrows represent nonsignificant paths. BC= brand community, C/P= customer/ product relationship, C/B= customer/brand relationship, C/C= customer/company relationship, C/O= customer/other customer relationship, BT= brand trust, PO= perceived quality, BAW/ASS= brand awareness/ association, BL= brand loyalty, BE= brand equity

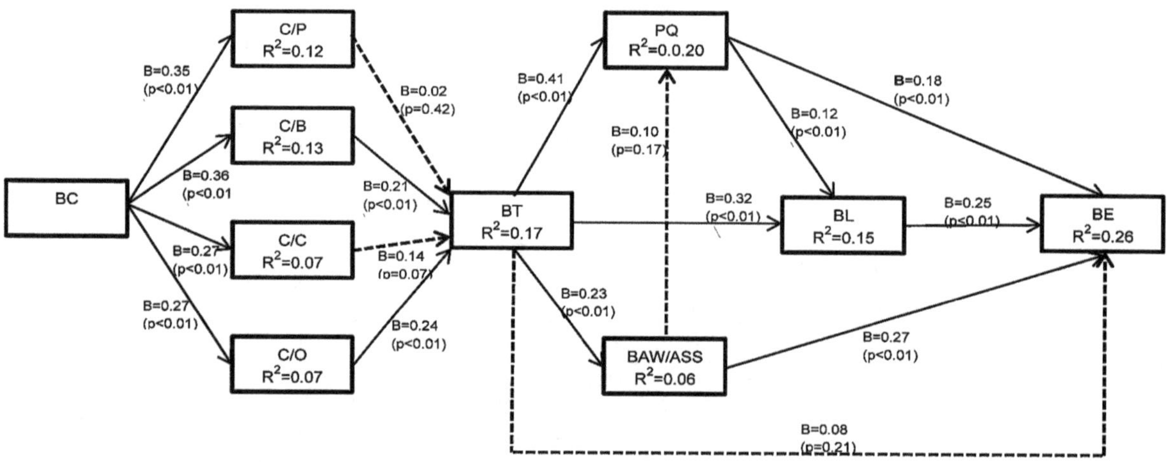

We found strong support for the effects of social media based brand community on customer-centric relationships, i.e., customer relationships with the product, the brand, the company and other customers. The path coefficients are respectively: 0.35, 0.36, 0.27, 0.27.All of these relationships are significant at p<0.01, providing support for H_{1a}, H_{1b}, H_{1c} and H_{1d}.

Only two relationships from customer centric model have significant and positive, effects on brand trust; the customer/ brand relationship (β=0.21, p<0.01) and the customer/ other customer relationship (β=0.24, p<0.01). Then only hypothe- ses H_{2b} and H_{2d} are confirmed.

The effects of brand trust on brand loyalty(H_3), perceived quality(H_4), brand awareness/association(H_5) are positive and significant. The path coefficients are respectively: β=0.32, 0.41, 0.23 and p<0.01.

The effect of perceived quality on brand loyalty is positive and significant(β=0.12), so H_7 is supported.

The effects of perceived quality, brand loyalty and brand awareness/ association on brand equity(H_8, H_9, H_{10}) are positive and significant.These hypotheses are confirmed with respectivly path coefficients:0.18, 0.25, 0.28 and p<0.01. The results show that brand awareness/association is the most important predictor of brand equity.Brand trust do not have significantly contribute to brand equity,so H_{11} is not supported.

Model Fit

The model was evaluated by path analysis technique using warppls 3.0software. Three model fit indicates are provided: average correlations path(APC), adjusted ratio significantion (ARS), average variance inflation factors (AVIF)(kock,2011).For the APC and ARS, P values are also provided.These P values are calculated through a complex process that involves resampling estimation coupled with Bonferroni-like corrections (kock,2011).This is necessary since both fit indices are calculated as average of other parame.The P values for the APC and ARS should be lower than 0.05 and the AVIF should be lower than 5(at the 0.05 level of significant).

According to the calculated numbers in table 6, the model is in an appropriate fit condition, therefore it can be used to confirm or reject the hypotheses.

CONCLUSION AND IMPLICATIONS

This research aimed to study the effects of brand communities on brand loyalty, with mediating roll of brand trust, and brand equity with antecedents of perceived quality, brand trust, brand loyalty and brand awareness/ association. In fact, we combined the models that had been proposed by Laroche et al. (2013) and Loureiro (2013) and tested it based on the brand community of Cinere cosmetic company on facebook. These results implied that the brand community of Cinere on facebook can improve customer relationship with the brand, company, product and other customers, which corroborates the findings provided by Laroche et al.(2013).Given that the motivation of people to participate in brand community is different, so all bonds are not equally strong for every community member. Therefore the relationships are of different values. Relationships with the product and the brand obtain the highest respondent scores. Despite the notion that a community is a set of social relationships, the brand community we investigate emphasize truly brand-related aspects, not more socially oriented concepts like the company or other consumers. From the author's opinion one of the reasons for this issue could be that members think the company does not pay attention to their opinions. Of course, all comments cannot be run, maybe it's better the company persuades the members that their opinions are analyzed. But in general we can conclude that brand community and social environments construct and strengthen each other.

Table 6. Model fit indices and P values

Acceptable Values	Outcome Valuees
Good if p< 0.05	APC=0.235, P<0.001
Good if p< 0.05	ARS=0.143, P<0.001
Good if AVIF < 5	AVIF=1.140

On the other hand, about half of the respondents have not met wonderful people because of the community, and don't have a feeling of kinship with the other owners. However a reason for this happening could be that the brand community is a new phenomenon and are not well stablished in Iran. Organizing group competitions, earning points for the association of Friends and sharing videos can enhance member's relationships.

Also, the research showed that the customer/brand and especially customer/other customers relationships could improve the brand trust. So the Cinere company should improve the social bonds between people and facilitate sharing the emotions and informations (Laroche et al., 2013). It means that marketers don't only engage members with brand but they should try engage them together. Given that more than ¾ of the respondents are young, probably by providing the necessary activities for enhancing ties they would support it. Even the company can use member's opinions in this field. This will also strengthen the relationships of customers with the company.

As mentioned in the literature, tendency for social interaction and answering the social feelings are one of the reasons for an individuals to take part in the community's activities. So the company should fulfill these needs. It should support them when sharing the information and respect the people's ideas and, if possible, use them.

On the other hand, increase in trust, directly improves brand loyalty, perceived quality and brand awareness/ association and indirectly improves brand equity. Brand trust is a control mechanism for facilitating the relationships with damage and uncertainty(Laroche et al., 2013).Specially in cosmetic products, that related with the important issue of beauty, custom- ers pay much more attention to the brands they know they can trust. Therefore, trust should play a big role in the strategy any cosmetic brand develop to keep and attract more customers. Because about ¾ of the respondents completely agree with this statement that they rely on their brand, we can conclude that the company has been successful in it.

Our finding is somehow consistent with other studies that found participation in virtual communities positively influences brand loyalty (Laroche et al., 2013; Brogi et al., 2013; Benson & Hedrén, 2013 ; Laroche et al., 2012 ; Kardaras, Karakostas, & Papathanassiou, 2003).

More than half of the respondents agree with these sentences "if the brand is not available at the store, I would buy the same brand from some other store", and "I am willing to pay more for my brand". This give us some indications of the positive affect online brand community could have on behavioral loyalty. To increase the brand loyalty, Cinere should also make its customers members of loyalty program and give them a feeling of true ownership in Cinere products, by making them proud to own Cinere products.

On the other hand, brand loyalty, perceived quality and brand awareness/associations confirmed as the antecedent factors in the brand equity. In fact, Consumers who are attached with the brand community would perceive that the product has more quality (perceived quality), they will have more loyalty to the brand(brand loyalty), they also learn more about the brand and its products from other members(brand awareness /associations). So, building and managing social media based brand communities would become the new challenge for marketing communication managers. But the relationship between trust and brand equity was not confirmed. However, Miller(2007) claim that internal brand-generated factors (e.g., its website) as well as external third-party factors (e.g., alliance with a well-known brand) "exert a positive influence on brand trust and consequently on its equity and consumers' willingness to behave in a favorable manner".

We also confirmed the effect of brand community on improving brand equity. This is because the community can act as a powerful tool which is effective on the customer's behavior and perception. Brand awareness/ association is known as the most important element in creating the brand equity, and it shows that the Cinere company should improve this factor through advertisement. Often direct control on these variables is not possible for a company, so perception in the casual relationship between these variables and other variables could be helpful for the company. Supporting the increase in the community's relationships can be an opportunity to enhance awareness, knowing the brand and remembering it. It can also increase the brand equity for the company. Our finding is somehow consistent with other studies that found participation in virtual communities has positive influence on brand equity (Brogi et al., 2013; Satanasavapak, 2010).

Finally, By focusing on social media, Cinere company would increase its young customer base since they are the prime users of social media networks specially in Iranian brand community Because older people in general are not as acquainted with the Internet as younger individuals and therefore prefer offline, personal communication as compared to online communication.

Limitations and Future Research

Further directions for future studies may involve an exploratory study in other commercial online contexts. Other types of variables such as culture and features of community could be examined in this concept.

The small sample size of the study might affect the results. Future research is needed to validate and generalize the findings with a larger sample size.

This study only used questionnaires to collect the data, but future researches can use interviews to achieve more accurate results.

Consider the factor of risk and the effective ways to manage the condition in the community dealing with unhappy customers. Because they can easily affect the reputationand brand equity of the company.

Conclusion

This research demonstrated the effect of brand communities established on the platform of social media on the relationships of customer centric model.This reinforced relationships leaded to brand loyalty (with mediating role of brand trust) and brand equity (with mediating roles of brand loyalty, perceived quality, brand awareness/associations).

These results show that the social media based brand communities can be effective on the customer's perception and behavior.On the other hand, With more than two thirds of the internet population connected through Social Networking sites like Facebook, Twitter and MySpace, the potential offered by this medium is tremendous.

Somarketers and researchers should pay special attention to this phenomenon and examine well established notions and theories in the brand communities based on context of social media.

REFERENCES

Aaker, D. A. (1991). *Managing brand equity: Capitalizing on the value of a brand name*. New York, NY: The Free Press.

Aaker, D. A. (1996a). *Building strong brands*. New York, NY: The Free Press.

Aaker, D. A. (1996b). Measuring Brand Equity Across Products and Markets. *Journal of California Management Review*, *38*(3), 102–120. doi:10.2307/41165845

Algesheimer, R., Dholakia, U., & Herrmann, A. (2006). The social influence of brand community: Evidencefrom European car clubs. *Journal of Marketing*, *69*(3), 19–34. doi:10.1509/jmkg.69.3.19.66363

Atilgan, E., Aksoy, S., & Akinci, S. (2005). Determinants of the brand equity. A verification approach in thebeverage industry in Turkey. *Marketing Intelligence & Planning*, *23*(3), 237–248. doi:10.1108/02634500510597283

Beatty, S. E., & Kahle, L. R. (1988). Alternative hierarchies of the attitude-behavior relationship: The impact of brand commitment and habit. *Journal of the Academy of Marketing Science*, *16*(2), 1–10. doi:10.1007/BF02723310

Bennett, R., & Rundle-Thiele, S. (2002). A comparison of attitudinal loyalty measurement approaches. *Journal of Brand Management*, *9*(3), 193–209. doi:10.1057/palgrave.bm.2540069

Bitner, M. J. (1990). Evaluating service encounters: The effects of physical surroundings and employee responses. *Journal of Marketing*, *54*(4), 69–82. doi:10.2307/1251871

Blau, P. M. (1964). *Exchange and Power in Social Life*. New York, NY: John Wiley.

Boonghee, Y., & Donthu, N. (2001). Developing and validating a multidimensioanl consumer-based brand equityscale. *Journal of Business Research*, *52*(1), 1–14. doi:10.1016/S0148-2963(99)00098-3

Boorstin, D. J. (1974). *The Americans: The Democratic Experience*. New York, NY: Vintage.

Boyd, D. M., & Ellison, N. B. (2007). Social Networks Sites: Definition, History, and Scholarship. *Journal of Computer-Mediated Communication", 13(1)*, 210-230. Retrieved fromhttp://jcmc.indiana.edu/vol13/issue1/boyd.ellison.html

Brogi, S., Calabrese, A., Campisi, D., Capace, G., Costa, R., & Pillo, F. D. (2013). The effects of online brand communit- ieson brand equity in the luxury fashion industry. *International Journal of Engineering Business Management*, *5*(32), 1–9. doi:10.5772/56854

Chang, H. H., & Liu, Y. M. (2009). The impact of brand equity on brand preference and purchase intentions in the service industries. *Service Industries Journal*, *29*(12), 1687–1706. doi:10.1080/02642060902793557

Chaudhuri,A.(1997). Consumption emotion and perceived risk: A macro analytic approach. *Journal of Business Research, 39*(2), 81-92. Retrieved from.10.1016/S0148-2963(96)00144-0

Chaudhuri, A., & Holbrook, M. B. (2001). The chain of effects from brand trust and brand affect to brand performance: The role of brand loyalty. *Journal of Marketing*, *65*(2), 81–93. doi:10.1509/jmkg.65.2.81.18255

Chiu, C. M., Huang, H. Y., & Yen, C. H. (2010). Antecedents of online trust in onlineauctions. *Electronic Commerce Research and Applications*, *9*(2), 148–159. doi:10.1016/j.elerap.2009.04.003

Constant, D., Sproull, L., & Kiesler, S. (1996). The kindness of strangers: The usefulness of electronic weak ties for technical advice. *JournalOrganization Science*, *7*(2), 119–135. doi:10.1287/orsc.7.2.119

Cornin,J.J., Brady, M.K.,&Hult, G.T.(2000). Assessing the effects of quality, value, and customer satisfaction on consumer behavioural intentions in service environments. *Journal of Retailing, 76(2)*, 193-218. Retrieved from.10.1016/S0022-4359(00)00028-2

Cronbach, L. J. (1970). *Essentials of psychological testing*. New York, NY: Harper and Row.

Cronin, J. J. Jr, Brady, M. K., & Hult, G. T. M. (2000). Assessing the effects of quality, value, and customer satisfaction on consumer behavioral intentions in service environments. *Journal of Retailing*, *76*(2), 193–218. doi:10.1016/S0022-4359(00)00028-2

Crosby, L. A., & Taylor, J. R. (1983). Psychological Commitment and Its Effects on Post-Decision Evaluation and Preference Stability Among Voters. *The Journal of Consumer Research*, *9*(4), 413–431. doi:10.1086/208935

David, A. (1991). *Managing Brand Equity: Capitalizing on the Value of a Brand Name*. New York, NY: The Free Press.

Delgado-Ballester, E., Manuera-Aleman, J. L., & Yague-Guillen, M. J. (2003). Development and validation of a brand trust scale. *International Journal of Market Research*, *45*(1), 35–54.

Dellarocas, C., Zhang, X. M., & Awad, N. F. (2007). Exploring the value of online product reviews in forecasting sales: The case of motion pictures. *Journal of Interactive Marketing*, *21*(4), 23–45. doi:10.1002/dir.20087

Dhar, V., & Chang, E. A. (2009). Does chatter matter? The impact of user-generated content on music sales. *Journal of Interactive Marketing, 23(4,)*, 300–307.

Doney, P. M., & Cannon, J. P. (1997). An Examination of the Nature of Trust in Buyer-Seller Relationships. *Journal of Marketing*, *61*(2), 35–51. doi:10.2307/1251829

Dubois, T., & Westerhausen, U. (2011). *Brand loyalty creation within online brand communities*(Master dissertation). Retrieved from http://studenttheses.cbs.dk/handle/10417/3012

Elizabeth, E., & Bushelow, E. E. (2012). Facebook Pages and Benefits to Brands. *The Elon Journal of Undergraduate Research in Communications*, *3*(2), 5–20.

Farquhar, P. H. (1989). Managing Brand Equity. *JMR, Journal of Marketing Research*, *1*, 24–33.

Fornell, C., & Larcker, D. F. (1981). Evaluating structural equation models with unobservable variables and measurement error. *JMR, Journal of Marketing Research*, *18*(1), 39–50. doi:10.2307/3151312

Gangadharbhatla, H. (2008). Facebook me: Collective self esteem, need to belong and Internet self efficacy as predictors of the I-generations attitudes toward social networking sites. *Journal of Interactive Advertising*, *8*(2), 5–15. doi:10.1080/15252019.2008.10722138

Gefen, D., Karahanna, E., & Straub, D. W. (2003). Trust and TAM in online shopping: An integrated model. *Journal of MIS Quarterly*, *27*(1), 51–90.

Gounaris, S., & Stathakopoulos, V. (2004). Antecedents and consequences of brand loyalty: An empirical study. *Journal of Brand Management*, *11*(4), 283–306. doi:10.1057/palgrave.bm.2540174

Granovetter, M. (1973). The strength of weak ties. *American Journal of Sociology*, *78*(6), 1360–1380. doi:10.1086/225469

Hagel, J., & Armstrong, A. G. (1997). *Net gain: Expanding markets through virtual communities*. Boston, MA: Harvard Business School Press.

Hanna, R., Rohm, A., & Crittenden, V. L. (2011). We're all connected: The power of social media ecosystem. *Business Horizons*, *54*(3), 265–273. doi:10.1016/j.bushor.2011.01.007

Harris, L. C., & Goode, M. M. H. (2004). The four levels of loyalty and the pivotal roleof trust: A study ofonline service dynamics. *Journal of Retailing*, *80*(2), 139–158. doi:10.1016/j.jretai.2004.04.002

Harris, R. (2009). *Social media ecosystem mapped as a wiring diagram*. Retrieved from: http://www.twitterthoughts.com/social-media-newsanalyses/ 2009/9/3/social-media-ecosystem-mapped-as-a-wiringdiagram.html?printerFriendly=true

Heding, T., Knudtzen, C. F., & Bjerre, M. (2009). *Brand management research, theory and practice*. London, UK: Routledge. doi:10.4324/9780203996171

Heil, O., Lehmann, D., & Stremersch, S. (2010). Marketing competition in the 21st century. *International Journal of Research in Marketing*, *27*(2), 161–163. doi:10.1016/j.ijresmar.2010.03.003

Holmes, J. G. (1991). In W. H. Jones & D. Perlman (Eds.), *Trust and the appraisal process in close relationships* (Vol. 2, pp. 57–104). Advances in personal relationships London, UK: Jessica Kingsley.

Hoon, K. K., Kang, S. K., Dong, Y. K., Jong, H. K., & Kang, S. H. (2008). Brand Equity in Hospital Marketing. *Journal of Business Research*, *61*(1), 75–82. doi:10.1016/j.jbusres.2006.05.010

Hsu, H. Y., & Tsou, H. T. (2011). Understanding customer experiences in online blog environments. *International Journal of Information Management*, *31*(6), 510–523. doi:10.1016/j.ijinfomgt.2011.05.003

Hu, T., & Kettinger, W. J. (2008). Why people continue to use social networking services: Developing a comprehensive model. *In Proceedings, 29th international conference on information systems*. Paris, France.

Jacobson, R., & Aaker, D. A. (1985). Is Market Share All That It's Cracked Up To Be? *Journal of Marketing*, *49*(4), 11–22. doi:10.2307/1251428

Jang, H., Olfman, L., Ko, I., Koh, J., & Kim, K. (2008). The influence of online brand community characteristics on community commitment and brand loyalty. *International Journal of Electronic Commerce*, *12*(3), 57–80. doi:10.2753/JEC1086-4415120304

Jin, S. A. (2012). The potential of social media for luxury brand management. *Marketing Intelligence & Planning*, *30*(7), 687–699. doi:10.1108/02634501211273805

Kang, I., Lee, K. C., Lee, S., & Choi, J. (2007). Investigation of online community voluntary behaviour using cognitive map. *Journal of Computers in Human Behavior*, *23*(1), 111–126. doi:10.1016/j.chb.2004.03.039

Kania, D. (2001). Branding.com: Online branding for marketing success. Chicago, IL: NTC Business Books (in conjunction with the American Marketing Association)

Kapferer, J. N. (1998). *Strategic Brand Management: Creating and Sustaining Brand Equity Long Term*. London, UK: Kogan Page.

Kaplan, A. M., & Haenlein, M. (2010). Users of the world, unite! The challenges and opportunities of social media. *Journal of Business Horizons*, *53*(1), 59–68. doi:10.1016/j.bushor.2009.09.003

Keller,K.(1993).Conceptualizing, measuring, and managing customer-based brand equity. *Journal of Marketing, 57*(1), 1-22.Retrieved from.10.2307/1252054

Keller, K. A. (2003). Brand Synthesis: The Multidimensionality of Brand Knowledge. *The Journal of Consumer Research*, *29*(4), 595–600. doi:10.1086/346254

Kerpen, D. (2011). *Likeable social media*. New York, NY: McGraw-Hill.

Kim, M., Chung, N., & Lee, C. (2011). The effect of perceived trust on electroniccommerce: Shopping online for tourism products and services in South Korea. *Journal of Tourism Management*, *32*(2), 256–265. doi:10.1016/j.tourman.2010.01.011

Kock, N. (2011). Using WarpPLS in eCollaboration Studies: Mediating effects, control and secondorder variables and algorithmchoices. *International Journal of e-Collaboration*, *7*(3), 1–13. doi:10.4018/jec.2011070101

Komaromi, K. (2003). *Building Brand Communities*. Online at: http://cdgroup.blogs.com/design_channel/brand_communities.pdf

Krishnan, H. S. (1996). Characteristics of memory associations: A consumer-based brand equity perspective. *International Journal of Research in Marketing*, *13*(4), 389–405. doi:10.1016/S0167-8116(96)00021-3

Laroche, M., Habibi, M. R., & Richard, M. O. (2013). To be or not to be in social media: How brand loyalty is affected by social media. *International Journal of Information Management*, *33*(1), 76–82. doi:10.1016/j.ijinfomgt.2012.07.003

Laroche, M., Habibi, M. R., Richard, M. O., & Sankaranarayanan, R. (2012). The effects of social media based brand communities on brand community markers, value creation practices, brand trust and brand loyalty. *Journal of Computers in Human Behavior Journal*, *28*(5), 1755–1767. doi:10.1016/j.chb.2012.04.016

Lee, J. (2009). *Effects of online brand community on brand loyalty: A uses and gratifications perspective*. Retrieved from Google Scholar.

Loureiro, J., Trávníček, P., Rauchová, J., Urfus, T., Vít, P., Štech, M., & Suda, J. et al. (2010). The use of flow cytometry in the biosystematics, ecology and population biology of homoploid plants. *Preslia*, *82*, 3–21. doi:10.1093/ aobpla/pls037

Loureiro, S. M. C. (2013). The effect of perceived benefits, trust,quality,brand awareness/association and brand loyalty on internet banking brand equity. *International Journal of Electronic Commerce Studies*, *4*(2), 139–158. doi:10.7903/ijecs.1000

Loureiro, S.M.C., & González, F. J.M. (2008). The importance of quality, satisfaction, trust and image in relation to rural tourism loyalty. *Journal of Travel and Tourism Marketing, 25*(2), 117-136. Retrieved from:.10.1080/10548400802402321

Loureiro, S. M. C., & Miranda, F. J. (2011). Brand equity and brand loyalty in the internet banking context:FIMIX-PLS market segmentation. *Journal of Service Science and Management, 4*(4), 476–485http://www.SciRP.org/journal/jssm. doi:10.4236/jssm.2011.44054

Mangold, W. G., & Faulds, D. J. (2009). Social media: The new hybrid element of the promotion mix. *Journal of Business Horizons, 52*(4), 357–365. doi:10.1016/j.bushor.2009.03.002

Maruyama, G. M. (1998). *Basics of structural equation modeling*. London, UK: Sage Publications. doi:10.4135/9781483345109

McAlexander, J. H., Schouten, W. J., & Koening, F. H. (2002). Building brand community. *Journal of Marketing, 66*(1), 38–54. doi:10.1509/jmkg.66.1.38.18451

McKnight, D. H., & Chervany, N. L. (2002). What trust means in ecommerce customer relationships: An interdisciplinary conceptual typology. *International Journal of Electronic Commerce, 6*(2), 33–57.

Messick, S. (1989). Meaning and values in test validation: The science and ethics of assessment. *The Journal of Educational Research, 18*(2), 5–11.

Monecke, A., & Leisch, F. (2012). semPLS: Structural equation modeling using partial least squares. *Journal of Statistical Software, 48*(3), 1–32. PMID:23504300

Morgan, R. M., & Hunt, S. D. (1997). The Commitment-Trust Theory of Relationship Marketing. *Journal of Marketing, 58*(3), 20–38. doi:10.2307/1252308

Muniz, M. A. Jr, & O'Guinn, C. T. (2001). Brand community. *The Journal of Consumer Research, 27*(4), 412–432. doi:10.1086/319618

Muñoz, J. A. V. (2013). *Social media lovers in Colombia: The Role of Online Brand Communities in Developing Brand Love.* (Master dissertation). University of Glasgow. Retrieved from http://www.banrepcultural.org/sites/default/files/colf_velezmunoz_jorgeandres_tesis.pdf

Myers, C. A. (2003). Managing Brand Equity: A Look at the Impact of Attributes. *Journal of Product and Brand Management, 12*(1), 39–51. doi:10.1108/10610420310463126

Nunnally, J. C. (1978). *Psychometric testing*. New York, NY: McGraw Hill.

Oliver, R., & Rust, R. (1997). Customer Delight: Foundations, Findings, andManagerial Insight. *Journal of Retailing, 73*(3), 311–337. doi:10.1016/S0022-4359(97)90021-X

Oliver, R. L. (1981). Measurement and Evaluation of Satisfaction Processes in Retail Settings. *Journal of Retailing, 57*(3), 25–48.

Pappu, R., & Quester, P. (2008). Does brand equity vary between department tores and clothing stores? Results of an empirical investigation. *Journal of Product and Brand Management, 17*(7), 425–435. doi:10.1108/10610420810916335

Pappu, R., Quester, P. G., & Cooksey, R. W. (2005). Consumer-Based Brand Equity: Improving the Measurement-Empirical Evidence. *Journal of Product and Brand Management, 14*(3), 143–154. doi:10.1108/10610420510601012

Park, C., & Srinivasan, V. (1994). A survey-based method for measuring and understanding brand equity and its extendibility. *JMR, Journal of Marketing Research, 31*(2), 271–288. doi:10.2307/3152199

Pavlou, P. A., Liang, H., & Xue, Y. (2007). Understanding and mitigating uncertainty in online exchange relationships: A principal-agent perspective. *Journal of Management Information System Quarterly, 31*(1), 105–136.

Punjumiemi, J. (2009). The revolution of brand marketing: The era of virtual consumer communities. In M. Koskela, & M. Vinnari (Eds.). In *Proceeding of the Future of the Consumer Society Conference*.

Rheingold, H. (1993). *The virtual community. Homesteading on the electronic frontier*. Reading, MA: Addison- Wesley.

Ross, C. F., Reed, D. A., Washington, R. L., Eckhardt, A., Anapol, F., & Shahnoor, N. (2009). Scaling of chew cycle duration inprimates. *American Journal of Physical Anthropology, 138*(1), 30–44. doi:10.1002/ajpa.20895 PMID:18661474

Rossiter, J. R., & Percy, L. (1987). *Advertising and promotion management*. New York, NY: McGraw-Hill Boo Company.

Safko, L., & Brake, D. K. (2009). *The Social Media Bible*. John Wiley & Sons, Inc.

Sarason, S. B. (1974). *The psychological sense of community: Prospects for the community psychology*. San Francisco, CA: Jossey-Bass.

Satanasavapak, P. (2010). The Effects of Virtual Communities on Brand Equity. *Journal of Management, 8*(1), 1–19.

Schau, H. J., Muñiz, A. M. J. Jr, & Arnould, E. J. (2009). How Brand Community Practices Create Value. *Journal of Marketing, 73*(5), 30–51. doi:10.1509/jmkg.73.5.30

Schouten, J. W., & McAlexander, J. H. (1995). Subcultures of Consumption: An Ethnography of the New Bikers. *The Journal of Consumer Research, 22*(1), 43–61. doi:10.1086/209434

Shankar, V., Smith, A. K., & Rangaswany, A. (2003). Customer satisfaction and loyalty in online and offline environments. *International Journal of Research in Marketing, 20*(2), 153–175. doi:10.1016/S0167-8116(03)00016-8

Smith, D., Menon, S., & Sivakumar, K. (2005). Online peer and editorial recommendations, trust, and choice in virtual markets. *Journal of Interactive Marketing, 19*(3), 15–37. doi:10.1002/dir.20041

Srinivasan, S. S., Anderson, R., & Ponnavolu, K. (2002). Customer loyalty in ecommerce: An exploration of its antecedents and consequences. *Journal of Retailing, 78*(1), 41–50. doi:10.1016/S0022-4359(01)00065-3

Steenkamp, J. B. E. M., & Geyskens, I. (2006). How country characteristics affect the perceived value of a website. *Journal of Marketing, 70*(3), 136–150. doi:10.1509/jmkg.70.3.136

Streiner D.L. (2005). With apologies to Albert: everything is not relative. *Evidence Based Mental Health, 8*(4), 91-93.

Tardini, S., & Cantoni, L. A. (2005). *A semiotic approach to online communities: Belonging, Interest and identity in websites' and video games' communities*. In P. Isaias, P. Kommers, & M. McPherson (Eds.). In *Proceedings, IADIS international conference e-Society*, Qawra, Malta: IADIS Press.

Thanh, N. N. D. (2012). *Relationships between brand awareness, perceived quality, trust, value, loyalty, and brand equity: A case study of Vinamilkbrand in Ho Chi Minh, Vietnam*. Available from: http://www.graduate.au.edu/gsbejournal/Journals/Dec2012/Thanh.pdf

Tynan, C., McKechnie, S., & Chhuon, C. (2010). Co-creating value for luxury brands. *Journal of Business Research, 63*(11), 1156–1163. doi:10.1016/j.jbusres.2009.10.012

Wang, Y. D., & Emurian, H. H. (2005). An overview of online trust: Concepts, elements, and implications. *Journal ofComputersin. Human Behavior, 21*(1), 105–125. doi:10.1016/j.chb.2003.11.008

Wellman, B. (1997). An electronic group is virtually a social network. In S. Kiesler (Ed.), *Culture of the Internet*. Mahwah, NJ: Lawrence Erlbaum Associates.

Wellman, B., & Gulia, M. (1999). Net-surfers don't ride alone: Virtual communities as communities. In B. Wellman (Ed.), *Networks in the global village*. Boulder, CO: Westview Press.

Wilimzig, B. J. (2011). *Online communities: Influence on members brand loyalty and purchase intent*. Retrieved from Google Scholar.

Williams, L., & Cothrell, J. (2000). Four smart ways to run online communities. *Journal of Sloan Management Review, 41*(4), 81–91.

Yoo, B., & Donthu, N. (2001). Developing and validating a multidimensioanl consumer-based brand equity scale. *Journal of Business Research, 52*(1), 1–14. doi:10.1016/S0148-2963(99)00098-3

Yoo, B., Donthu, N., & Lee, S. (2000). An examination of selected marketing mixelements and brand equity. *Journal of the Academy of Marketing Science, 28*(2), 195–211. doi:10.1177/0092070300282002

Yoon, S. J. (2002). The antecedents and consequences of trust in online purchase decisions. *Journal of Interactive Marketing, 16*(2), 47–63. doi:10.1002/dir.10008

Zeithaml, V. A. (1998). Consumer perceptions of price, quality, and value: A means-end model and synthesis of evidence. *Journal of Marketing, 52*(3), 2–22. doi:10.2307/1251446

Zeithaml, V. A., Berry, L. L., & Parasuraman, A. (1996). The behavioral consequences of service quality. *Journal of Marketing, 60*(2), 31–46. doi:10.2307/1251929

Zhou, Z., Jin, X. L., Vogel, D. R., Fang, Y., & Chen, X. (2011). Individual motivationsand demographic differences in social virtual world uses: An exploratory investigationin Second Life. *International Journal of Information Management, 31*(3), 261–271. doi:10.1016/j.ijinfomgt.2010.07.007

KEY TERMS AND DEFINITIONS

Brand Awareness/Association: Brand awareness is the ability of buyer for recall and recognize the brand and brand association is everything in customer's mind which is associated with a brand or brand benefits.

Brand Community: It is a group of fans and admirers of a brand who gather online and interact with company and other customer.

Brand Equity: Assets of a brand, like it's name and symbol, that can increase or decrease the worth of companies product or service.

Brand Loyalty: It is a preference of a special brand by customer.

Brand Trust: A brand ability in order to fulfill the promises that have been given make brand trust in a mind of customer.

Customer-Centric Model: A model of brand community in which customer is at the center and brand, company, Other customer and product are another factors which are connected to focal customer.

Perceived Quality: It is the customer's perception of the quality of product or service. It is just a judgment and different from actual or objective quality.

Social Media: Social media are computer mediated tools that were born in the Virtual world with important role of sharing and connecting people to each other.

Chapter 13
Using Social Media to Influence CRM and Loyalty: Case Study of Restaurant Industry

Rozita Shahbaz Keshvari
Islamic Azad University, Iran

ABSTRACT

This chapter explores the influence of social media in Customer Relationship Management that leads to Customer loyalty. The social media in restaurant is recognized as an essential component of the customer satisfaction and therefore it is a cornerstone of the success of CRM and customer loyalty through social media nowadays. The purpose of this chapter is to investigate how Restaurant industry can harness the power of social media by utilizing CRM that leads to Customer loyalty. The problem is approached applying both the restaurants perspective and the customer perspective. The recent explosion in social media usage, combined with the transformation of the consumer into a "consume' activist", has permanently changed the relationship between a restaurant and its customers. There were two interviews conducted for 384 restaurants collected and analyzed for the research. The results proved that Social media can be an excellent channel for building long-lasting customer relationships in restaurants.

1. INTRODUCTION

Many years ago, most businesses were local brick-and-mortars that relied on door-to-door marketing to engage the public. As technology developed rapidly, motion pictures, radio and television opened up new avenues for business marketing, eventually expanding to include direct mail, telemarketing, print advertising, trade shows and e-mail blasts. While these practices have proven successful over the years, many of today's consumers now view them as intrusive, and have consequently become quite savvy at ignoring traditional marketing attempts. Nowadays, communication has taken on new era and adapted to new mediums evolved to reflect the society in which they were developed.

DOI: 10.4018/978-1-4666-8586-4.ch013

1.1. Area of Interest

The customer experience in restaurants is paramount. It impacts retention rates, referrals, our brand, and ultimately our success or failure. Negative experiences are inevitable. It's how the restaurants handle recovery that makes all the difference. This determines if their customers will give them a second chance or embark on a negative word of mouth campaign that could reach thousands. Understanding and addressing the factors that negatively impact restaurant customer's experiences is both critical and challenging. Menuitems and promotions change regularly. Staff schedules rotate. Employees come and go. Their customers' traffic is high-volume sometimes, variable at others. And in addition to keeping tabs on day-to-day operations, franchisees must stay on top of corporate issues and cost concerns. So when it comes to effectively attracting, retaining and handling customers in restaurants to manage their needs, feedback and experiences, the need for an especially powerful and flexible solution (Utilizing social media as a powerful CRM tool) will become clear.

The social media in restaurant is recognized as an essential component of the customer satisfaction and therefore it is a cornerstone of the success of CRM and customer loyalty through social media in nowadays which is no denying the influence of social media on the way that we as human beings communicate on a daily basis. The motivation for writing this paper on the topic of social media is to gain better understanding of the phenomenon that is influencing CRM and customer loyalty, as it is needy today. Enterprises in different filed of business such as financial, banking, services, production and so on should utilize the Social Media management to provide a number of singular challenges to the restaurant owner, not the least of which is trying to stay on top of multiple platforms as they shift and dip in a seemingly constant game of musical chairs. Pinterest is on top, no Instagram, Foursquare is trending on Twitter, now it's not, wait it's changed again – and now hashtags on Facebook.

The restaurants as service industry should try to marshal their marketing resources in an effective, and fiscally practical, manner can appear nearly impossible. The authors try to find a few quick ways in which they can improve their efforts at little or no cost in restaurant industry. The other reason that motivate the author to choose this subject for this research is the restaurant field of business which is B2C (Business to Customer) & B2B (Business to Business) marketing. Further, research conducted by Dataforeningen (2010) show that businesses operating on the B2C market are experiencing an explosion in managing customer relationships on social media platforms, and on Facebook in particular (Dataforeningen, 2010). As there is limited or no academic research in the area of social media in CRM in this context, the researcher wish to address the gap by contributing to the social media research by applying marketing theory, limited to theories of customer relationship management and customer loyalty, to the concepts of social media in Iranian Restaurant industry. Moreover, the researcher attempt to show that Social media is changing customer loyalty programs also by identifying problems through monitoring what people are saying about their brands.

1.2 Key Terms and Definitions

1.2.1 Social Media

Social media tools are computer and web-based tools and softwares that people use them to share, exchange and create information and files, photos and videos in visual networks. People use computer, laptop, tablet and mobile for creating or sharing a subject, idea or picture, and sometimes other people, see that and comment their opinion or viewpoint about it. Social media is an inexpensive tool for communicate with people and promotion. You can use this tool for broadcasting news in a very short time to a large number of audiences.

Social media is defined as a new marketing channel for customer care and customer retention due to its remarkable popularity among a vast majority of both customers and enterprise. Enterprises are using social media platforms such as Facebook, Twitter and blogs as important solution to address and try to resolve any customer complaint or concerns posted on these social media sites in a timely manner to retain and improve their brand value. Customer Relationship Management performed on social media is called Social CRM (S. Mohan, E. Choi & D. Min, 2008). Social media are social software platforms that allow for two-way communication between one or many individuals, for the purpose of sharing, collaborating and interacting (Lein & Ugstad, 2011)

1.2.2 CRM

CRM or Customer Relationship Management is a field of management that uses strategies, methods and softwares to keep, manage and process customer data and records to improving and growing the quality of relation between the organization and their customers in order to keeping present customers and increasing customer loyalty. It works with recognizing the customer needs, and making products and services matching their needs, and also providing good customer services.

For any business, managing the relationship with customers is of paramount importance. According to a 2002 Goldman Sachs study, CRM is considered the second most important initiative after security for businesses (Marouan El Bernoussi, 2012). Indeed, customers are the core of businesses and the success of a company relies on customers' satisfaction degree and on its ability to manage its relationship with them. Therefore, the most important objective for any enterprise is to make their customers satisfied because the durability of their business depends on them. Customer relationship management is the use of technology in attracting, retaining and enhancing customer relationships (Berry 2002)

1.2.3 Customer

A customer of your organization is a person or organization that expect to be interested in, wants or benefits the products or services prepared by your organization. As this definition suggests, a customer is not necessarily someone who is currently purchasing from the marketer. Every person who enters the business is a potential customer. Even though they may not purchase something today, they may purchase something tomorrow.

1.2.4 Customer loyalty

Customer loyalty can be said to have occurred if people choose to use a particular shop or buy one particular product, rather than use other shops or buy products made by other companies.Customer loyalty is the key objective of customer relationship management and describes the loyalty which is established between a customer and companies, persons, products or brands. The individual market segments should be targeted in terms of developing customer loyalty.

Customer loyalty is an important metric of your business' success. It gives enterprises insight into issues ranging from whether they are serving the right customers, to the quality of their products/services, to the level of their customer service. Loyal customers also have the potential to dramatically increase the enterprises profits over time. But loyal customers don't just happen; they're cultivated as part of a conscious process that's built into the business' DNA. So, Customer loyalty is the continued and regular patronage of a business in the face of alternative economic activities and competitive attempts to disrupt the relationship (Toporek, 2014).

1.2.5 Marketing

Discovering and identifying customers' needs and make product and services according to covering their needs at the right time, right price and right place.

1.2.6 Customer service

Customer service is the act of taking care of the customer's needs by providing and delivering professional, helpful, high quality service and assistance before, during, and after the customer's requirements are met. Customer service is meeting the needs and desires of any customer.

1.2.7 Purchasing

The activity of achieving products or services from an external provider/supplier.

1.2.8 Industry

The manufacturing or technically productive enterprises in a particular field, country, region, or economy viewed collectively, or one of these individually. A single industry is often named after its principal product. Every business that can be isolated from others, is an industry.

1.3 RESEARCH OBJECTIVES

In this paper, the researcher will try to explain and critically analyze how restaurants and customers perceive their mutual virtual relationship on social media. And also in a general meaning, how social media are integrated into CRM and Customer loyalty business strategies. On the other hand, this study will help to identify factors contributing to the success or failure of utilizing social media in restaurant positioning efforts and determine the influential elements of this phenomenon on CRM and loyalty of the customers. Those factors can be used by restaurants to reposition the marketing strategy of restaurant to improve or change the restaurant revenue in the respective target market. The specific objectives of the study are:

1) To derive the dimensions of the social media in restaurant and the dimensions of CRM and Customer Loyalty towards it;
2) To examine how the Social media in restaurant affects customers' decision to return to the restaurant in the future;

3) To examine how customer satisfaction affects customers' loyalty in restaurant by enhancing social media tools;
4) To provide recommendations to the restaurant managers for increasing loyal customers through modern marketing tools especially social media.

1.4 RESEARCH HYPOTHESES

The study includes 3 hypotheses as following:

H1: By improving technology aligned with new and various social media tools, the level of CRM acceptance in customers in restaurants increase and leads to loyalty.
H2: The ability to understand customers' needs, desires, and orders and comment messages has a direct relationship with the trustworthy customer service channels.
H3: Having control on receiving needs, desires, and orders and comment of the customers through different social media communication channels in restaurant affect the acceptance of the consumers' attitude about social media as CRM tool for creating customer loyalty.

2. LITERATURE REVIEW

In this section, the author presents background information on the topic. As, the author explained before, the restaurant industry has an important role as a job creator in the Iranian economy in addition to its social impact on communities nationwide, and there are no scientific researches which concentrated on Social Media, CRM and Customer loyalty together in restaurant industry, the author focuses this industry to provide an implication of the Social Media that are of greatest importance to improve the restaurant relationship with customers through customer services and attraction of more loyal customers. On the other hand, for the restaurant business to meet the needs and desires of the targeting customers, the business must investigate the needs and desires of the customers. The information of this paper is vital not only for sustaining successful restaurant business, but also for understanding and improving CRM and Customer loyalty by using Social media.

Pontus Boström studied about CRM through Social Media and its effect on Brand Loyalty. He discussed about this fact that media is simply a communications channel. In the old days, business relationships were built one-to-one through personal communications, but 'Mad Men' took over these channels in the 50′s and used mass media to shout messages at customers to get their attention and encourage them to buy. Mass marketing has become less effective as the volume of messaging has mushroomed and overwhelmed the customer. Social Media is an evolution of the Media channel. The purpose of his research was to gain a deeper understanding of the different dimensions of attitudinal loyalty. As well to understand how mobile providers could take advantage of social media in their CRM work. A case study was chosen with four students in each focus group. One focus group had an international perspective with exchange students and the second group was made up of Swedish students. An interview was held with Telenor to receive information on how companies use social media as a customer relationship management tool. Four concepts were investigated to answer the research questions. The empirical data provides evidence that social media have an effect on attitudinal loyalty and therefore needs careful consideration from companies. Most companies are using social media to some degree and if utilized correctly it can provide a competitive advantage. In this study, he has developed a deeper understanding for the area of social media (SCRM) and the three dimensions of attitudinal loyalty (trust, commitment and recommendation). This research improved that attitudinal loyalty can be affected by SCRM to some extent. The empirical data suggest that trust and recommendation is affected by social CRM. Trust is the antecedent that social CRM have the greatest effect on. If social media is done poorly it can result in decreasing levels of trust, for example low and slow response rates. On the other side a good and efficient managed social media site where customers receive fast responses can result in a higher level of trust. This could also result in a willingness to recommend subscriptions to others. A satisfactory customer support can lead to a better overall impression of the service which has a tendency to result in customer recommendations. (Boström & Svensson, 2013)

In other study, the researchers attempted to understand the guest's needs and desires are invaluable when determining methods for improving the restaurant image. A lack of understanding of customer preference leads to problems in both product and service design (Schall, 2003). Research showed that the most successful restaurants are the ones which are fully aware of customer preferences and develop their services in line with targeted market needs. The researchers suggested restaurant operators should understand the impact of both the customers' level of satisfaction and the restaurant image on the customers' loyalty. The operators should also investigate the driving force for each component of the customer loyalty. Customers may vary in the way they become loyal to a restaurant; for some customers restaurant image may be important, whereas for others quality of service and food are more important. The results of this study regarding the customer's satisfaction level and the image attributes could help the operators of the fine dining restaurant operators to develop customers' loyalty (Victorino et al, 2005). The restaurant must focus on delivering food quality and services and a high level of dining satisfaction that will lead to increased customer return and greater market share. (Zeithaml & Bitner, 1996)

In 2012, Eric Lévy-Bencheton worked on Social CRM towards enhanced Customer Relationship Management. He mentioned the customer experience was often made public: "consum'activists" no longer hesitates to use social media to voice their views. Their views have a major impact on the purchasing decisions of others within their social circle and companies are unable to control them. This loss of management and control means that companies must change in order to stay in touch with their customers. The main idea of his research was to survive the rapid upheavals created by social media and to capitalize on these opportunities, how companies must ask themselves serious questions and update their technology accordingly to ensure they are ready for this new revolution - Social CRM. The study demonstrated that management emerged from three main perspectives: service marketing, industrial marketing, and general management. In perspective of service marketing, the way to retain customers is to improve customer service quality and satisfaction. The need for Marketing, Sales and Customer Service jobs will certainly be questioned, and these will perhaps become the first positions to come under scrutiny. But more generally, it is the entire management structure of the company that must be reconsidered. Companies must take the evolving and technological landscape of CRM into account and adopt a coherent, alert and engaging social media strategy (Lévy-Bencheton, 2012).

Furthermore, Magnini and Honeycutt studied that customer emotions play an important role in driving customer satisfaction and loyalty; they discussed the importance of face recognition and name recall to customers and its effect on customer loyalty (Magnini & Honeycutt, 2005). In 1987, Gummesson proved that in case of service providers the quality of relationships between customers and front line employees, which provides both a professional and social dimension, can strongly contribute to customers' loyalty (Gummesson, 1987). Signicant amount of work has been done on using social media data for getting insights about customers and their views about an enterprise. Monitoring and predicting user behavior and events over social media data has been explored in detail in.There has also been some recent work on analyzing social media content on brand pages for monetization purposes. Work like focuses on the former CRM process of using social data to identify potential leads for enterprises. The surge of social data has recently prompted researchers to envision conceptual models for social CRM systems that incorporate Web 2.0 technologies and user driven collaborative paradigms. Using social media data for business intelligence etc. are also relevant in this context.

In 2011 Hurtola and Jenny researched about the importance of social media in building customer loyalty. They mentioned that social media marketing was a new form of marketing that was currently generating a lot of interest. They believed the introduction of the internet and social media had changed marketing, bringing both possibilities and challenges. The ever-evolving field of social media had also challenged the use of traditional marketing models and theories. The client of their research was company which was activated as a multinational clothing company. The purpose of this article was to investigate the possibilities that social media had to offer for Company X. The company was connected to social media in many ways, and the purpose of this study was to explore the differences between the people connected to Company X via social media and those who were not connected. The aim of the questionnaire in this research was to gather information about the characteristics of the Finnish social media users who were interested in the company and to establish what their consumption patterns were in comparison with the ones who were not connected to the company via social media. They reached to this conclusion that internet questionnaire form was a successful way to gather information about social media users. The questionnaire form was accessible for a month and links were posted to several social media sites and the questionnaire form was available both in English and Finnish. As the aim was to collect data from Finnish social media users, this proved to be a wise decision; only five of the replies were in English. Respondents were also able to attend a drawing of lots for a gift certificate to Company X"s stores if they wished and this might have helped in gaining results (Hurtola & Jenny, 2011).

Marouan El Bernoussi studied the value of social media in CRM. Through this study, the researcher wanted to deeply study CRM and the value of linking social media to it. Specifically, the researcher wanted to determine if there is a potential gap between customers' and companies' perception of social CRM. He reviewed many books and manuscripts as literature review about information systems, CRM, social media and marketing, the researcher gained considerable knowledge to tackle this topic. The researcher used quantitative and qualitative approach to conduct research. Finally, he reached to these findings: Social media add value to CRM and improve companies' businesses. Social CRM will not replace the classical model of CRM. Most importantly, there is a perception gap between customers' and companies' perception of social CRM. Outcomes and implications for practice resulting from this dissertation were that businesses wanting to adopt social CRM strategies must develop a real social CRM strategy and not contenting themselves of having a presence on social media (Marouan El Bernoussi, 2012).

As mentioned before, there is on direct research that covers these research areas in restaurant industry except the ones that explained above, in following this study identifies what other researchers evolved recently (last three years ago) and compares them with each other to find the knowledge gap, and defines the perceptual model of this study. So, the researcher summarized some of the key and relevant literature in Table 1.

Table 1. Summarized of the key and relevant literature (Source: compiled by the author, 2014)

Row	Author	Area of the research	Results & Findings of the research	Year
1	Eric Lévy-Bencheton,	To study how companies survive the rapid upheavals created by social media and to capitalize on these opportunities, companies must ask themselves serious questions and update their technology accordingly to ensure they are ready for this new revolution - Social CRM.	- Companies owe CRM to themselves to be reactive by fitting into this new social ecosystem, even if this means losing control in terms of their relationships with customers and prospects. - They found four steps in the field of Social CRM: 5) E-reputation 6) Strategy & organization 7) Coaching 8) Transformation & Technology	2011
2	Shamaila Marita Lein & Mette Ugstad	To conduct an analysis of how Norwegian management consultancy firms may apply social media in customer relationship management strategies. The problem is approached applying both the company perspective and the customer perspective. For the purpose of exploring the research topic, interviews are conducted with seven Norwegian management consultancy firms.	- The application of social media in CRM can be said to be in a planning-and wait- and- see phase. - Potential for social media was identified across the CRM process - Customers seem to not be ready for application of social media in CRM today, but show positive attitudes to such application in the future. - Facebook and LinkedIn were found to be most popular social media platforms.	2011
3	Marouan El Bernoussi	To study CRM and the value of linking social media to it besides determining if there is a potential gap between customers' and companies' perception of social CRM.	- Social media add value to CRM and improve companies' businesses - Social CRM will not replace the classical model of CRM. - There is a perception gap between customers' and companies' perception of social CRM.	2012
4	Pontus Boström & Oskar Svensson	To gain a deeper understanding of the different dimensions of attitudinal loyalty. As well to understand how mobile providers could take advantage of social media in their CRM work. A case study was chosen with four students in each focus group. One focus group had an international perspective with exchange students and the second group was made up of Swedish students.	- Attitudinal loyalty can be affected by SCRM. - Trust is the antecedent that social CRM have the greatest effect on. - A satisfactory customer support can lead to a better overall impression of the service. - Social media can have positive and negative effects for the company. - The use of social media as a CRM tool can affect trust in a positive manner if used in an efficient way. - To be able to provide efficient assistance and keep up with the digital development a company needs to invest heavily on resources in their social media department.	2013
5	Raymond Menne & Desislava Halova	To investigate how companies can harness the power of social media by utilizing Social CRM. We investigated how integrating social media channels into existing Client Relationship Management platforms can influence customer service and customer loyalty.	- Integrating social media in to CRM does influence customer service and customer loyalty. - The main effects are increased opportunity to collect instant feedbacks from customers and insights into their preferences to improve the service offered even further. - Customers tend to prefer to engage and communicate more with the company when they are entertained by the content or by the way the company approaches them – in a fun, witty and friendly way	2013

3. METHODOLOGY

The author purpose is to study that social media as new communication channel with existing customer in CRM systems influence the customer satisfaction and customer loyalty. To fulfill this aim, the author chooses a research design that considers the relation between Social Media, CRM, and Customer Loyalty. As the researcher wants to test theoretical models by using them in real world situations, uses a case study which is an in depth study of a particular situation rather than a sweeping statistical survey. It is a method used to narrow down a very broad field of research into one easily researchable topic. Furthermore, the author use a mix of data collection methods (both quantitative and qualitative) in order to provide a more full perspective on how restaurants is incorporating social media into their customer relationship to achieve better satisfaction and ultimately loyalty.

The target population, (N), in this research was all the restaurants in capital of Iran (include Traditional restaurants and fast foods) operating in Tehran. The main reasons that author choose restaurants of Tehran referred to its role in PETS of the country. “PETS” is the abbreviation word defined by author; it is made of four key dimensions as foundation and developing elements of each country (P: Policy- E: Economy- T: Technology- S: Social) that each of its blames and blooms affect the other sub-dimension in country. It means, all of the new policy, economy, technology and social structure and planning was implemented initially in Tehran (due to this fact that the place, people, procedure and other needy factors of the mentioned items are exited and considered in Tehran), so we can see all of its effects and results soon in Tehran. The other reason for choosing Tehran as target population is mass of people who are living in there, “The more population is increased, the more development is created especially in social consequence.” According to statistics of 118Food website as valid source in restaurant industry, there are 2230 restaurants in Tehran. In Table 2, you can see the map of Tehran and its twenty two regions includes each regions restaurant umbers.

Table 2. Number of restaurants in Tehran regions (Source: http://www.118food.com, 2014)

Region	Number of Restaurants
1	405
2	341
3	406
4	133
5	82
6	323
7	104
8	54
9	12
10	35
11	66
12	23
13	56
14	25
15	13
16	11
17	5
18	12
19	37
20	20
21	7
22	6

The paper focus on the customer's viewpoint and how they perceive the restaurant customer relationship management, their work with social media and in turn the effect on attitudinal loyalty. For determining sample size, the author uses Cochran formula as follows:

$$n = \frac{Nz^2pq}{Nd^2 + z^2pq}$$

$$\mathrm{Z} = 1.96 \qquad \mathrm{p} = \mathrm{q} = 0.5 \qquad \mathrm{d} = 0.05$$

Regarding to the above formula, the sample size of this research is 328 restaurants in all twenty two regions of Tehran. As you see in Table 1, the numbers of restaurants are not equal in regions, so the researcher chooses randomly just one sample in each region and gather two customers opinion. This research has consisted of primary and secondary data that was collected from a number of sources. In primary research section, the author collected data from interviews, surveys and for secondary research part, most of our data was collected on the basis of literature source in the form of books, textbooks, articles, newspaper articles, internet research of news and articles published online and so on. For validity of this research, first of the author asked the viewpoint of restaurant industry plus social communication and made the questionnaire. After that, the researcher chose ten top restaurants and separated them to gain their standpoint. The data was directly exported from customers' viewpoint to SPSS. There are five clusters in the area of this study includes: social media, customer service, customer trust, customer satisfaction and customer loyalty. To test the reliability of this research, the author use Cronbach's alpha. The alpha is 0.9 that is more than 0.7 (a level considered acceptable in most science research) so, this research and constructs are reliable as shown in Table 3.

4. FINDINGS

4.1. Data Analysis for Descriptive

This section includes the data analysis and the results. The distributed questionnaires were 656 including traditional restaurant and fast foods. Table 4 provides a summary of the demographic rate. The descriptive statistics were used to identify the nature of all respondents such as demographics profiles.

Over 45% of the respondents were females. As you see in table 5, the major age group pf the respondents was between 25 to 34 years old (41.4%). There were an almost close proportion of the age groups of 18-24 years old (40.6%). The rest of the respondents were more than 35 years old and they included small portion in this research.

Table 3. Reliability Statistics

Cronbach's Alpha	N of Items
.900	27

Table 4. Result of first demographic question" What is your gender?"

		Frequency	Percent	Valid Percent	Cumulative Percent
Valid	**Female**	345	45.8	52.6	52.6
	Male	311	41.3	47.4	100.0
	Total	656	87.1	100.0	
Missing	**System**	97	12.9		
Total		753	100.0		

Table 5. Result of second demographic question "What is your age?"

		Frequency	Percent	Valid Percent	Cumulative Percent
Valid	**18-24**	306	40.6	46.6	46.6
	25-34	312	41.4	47.6	94.2
	35-44	20	2.7	3.0	97.3
	45-54	10	1.3	1.5	98.8
	More than 55	8	1.1	1.2	100.0
	Total	656	87.1	100.0	
Missing	**System**	97	12.9		
	Total	753	100.0		

Figure 1. Chart of response gender

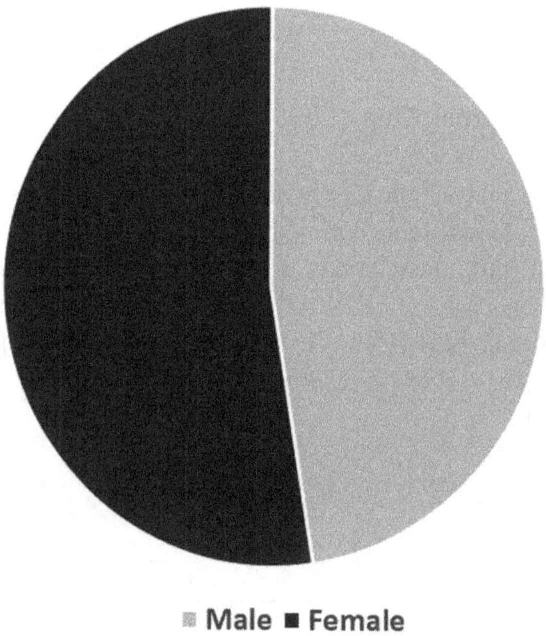

Figure 2. Chart of response age

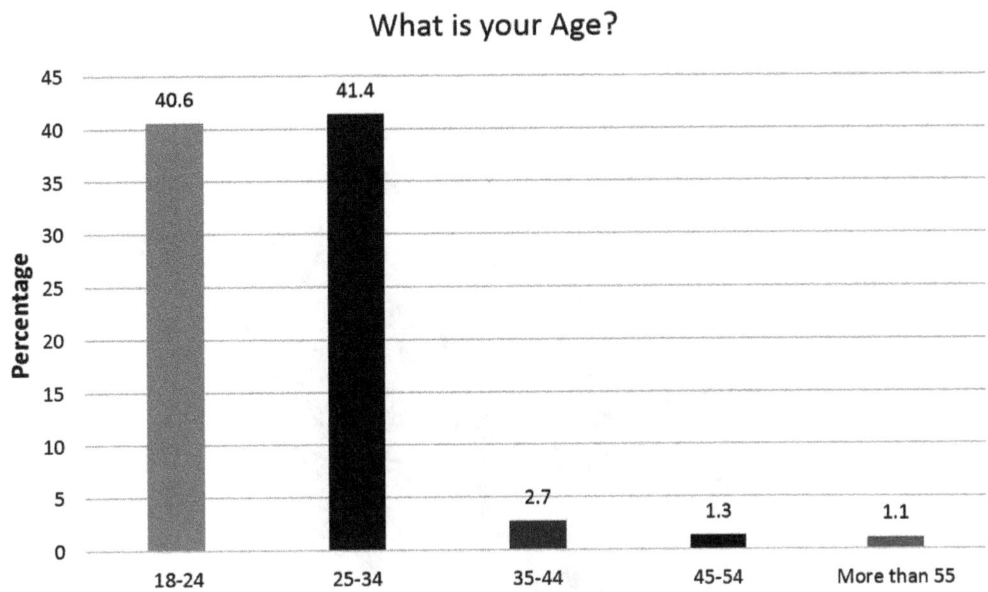

Besides the two mentioned demographic questions, the author considered two main questions in the questionnaire to analyze the customers' standpoint about their preference device for social media interaction and also asked them which of social media is included their communications channel in the restaurant? The findings (Table 6) shows the majority of the respondents were used smartphone as their preference device in social media communication (29.9%). About 20% preferred to use laptop as social media for their interactions with restaurants.

Moreover, the results (Table 7) presents that about 33% of the restaurant customers used Facebook in their communication channel with their restaurants. About 30% of them used Twitter to communicate with the restaurants. Linkedin gained the third level in communication channel in restaurants (about 13%).

Before determining the dimensions of mentioned constructs, the researcher tested the customer service channels which are the most trustworthy and the most efficient ones in social communication in restaurants. The findings represent that the trustworthy customer service channel in restaurants are

Table 6. Result of third demographic question" preference device for social media interaction"

		Frequency	Percent	Valid Percent	Cumulative Percent
Valid	**Desktop**	102	13.5	15.5	15.5
	Laptop	156	20.7	23.8	39.3
	Smartphone	225	29.9	34.3	73.6
	Tablet	173	23.0	26.4	100.0
	Total	656	87.1	100.0	
Missing	**System**	97	12.9		
	Total	753	100.0		

Figure 3. Preference device for social media interaction chart

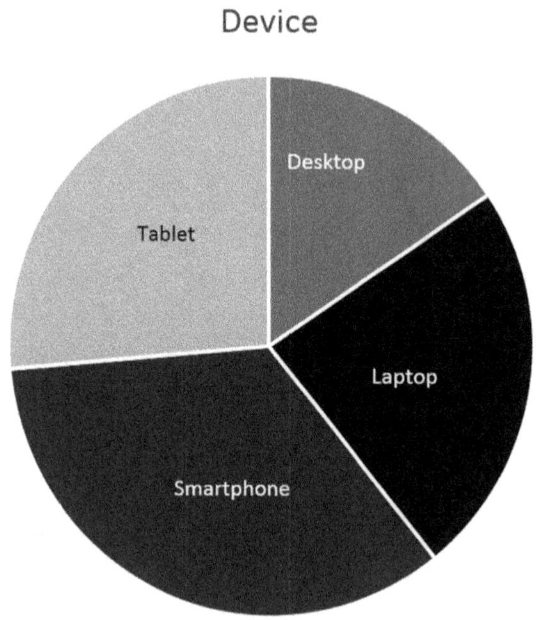

Table 7. Result of fourth demographic question "social media communication channel in restaurant"

		Frequency	Percent	Valid Percent	Cumulative Percent
Valid	**Facebook**	248	32.9	37.8	37.8
	Twitter	222	29.5	33.8	71.6
	Linkdin	96	12.7	14.6	86.3
	YouTube	68	9.0	10.4	96.6
	Google+	10	1.3	1.5	98.2
	Xing	8	1.1	1.2	99.4
	None of them	4	0.5	0.6	100.0
	Total	656	87.1	100.0	
Missing	**System**	97	12.9		
	Total	753	100.0		

telephone with 46.7%, next is email with 36.9% and the last one is social media with 3.5%. When asked the customer who of these customer services are more efficient in restaurants, 57% answered telephone is the most efficient ones, then email and finally social media (table 8) & (table 9).

In last part of analyzing, the author used the Friedman test to analyze which indexes have the most impact on each of the mentioned constructs (Table 10).

According to Table 10, each factor that have lower mean rank in comparison the others in the contacts have more value and importance in customers viewpoint. Therefore, in construct of social media:

Figure 4. Social media communication channel in restaurant chart

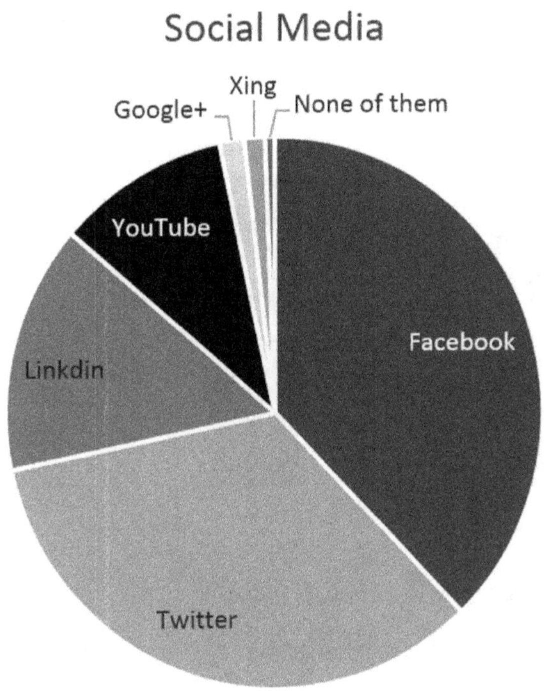

Table 8. The trustworthy customer service channels

		Frequency	Percent	Valid Percent	Cumulative Percent
Valid	***Telephone***	352	46.7	53.7	53.7
	Email	278	36.9	42.4	96.0
	Social Media	26	3.5	4.0	100.0
	Total	656	87.1	100.0	
Missing	***System***	97	12.9		
	Total	753	100.0		

Table 9. The efficient customer service channels

		Frequency	Percent	Valid Percent	Cumulative Percent
Valid	***Telephone***	433	57.5	66.0	66.0
	Email	205	27.2	31.3	97.3
	Social Media	18	2.4	2.7	100.0
	Total	656	87.1	100.0	
Missing	***System***	97	12.9		
	Total	753	100.0		

Figure 5. The trustworthy customer service channels chart

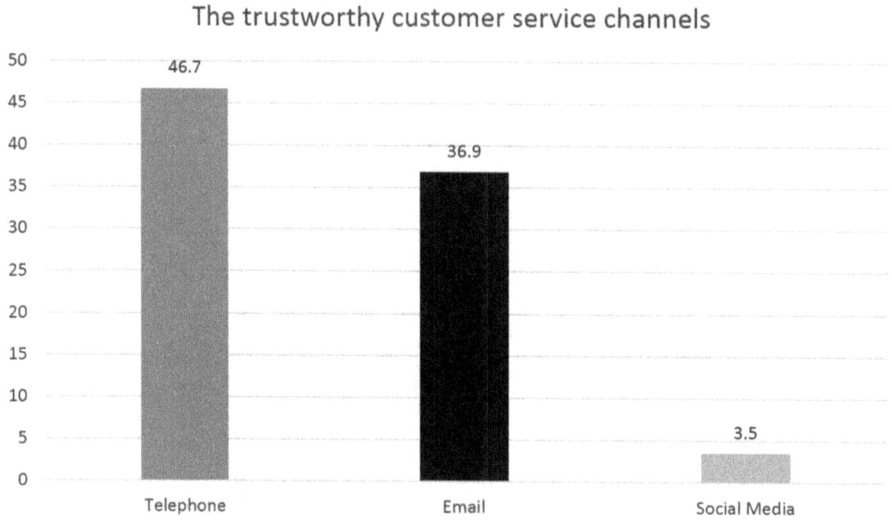

Figure 6. The efficient customer service channels chart

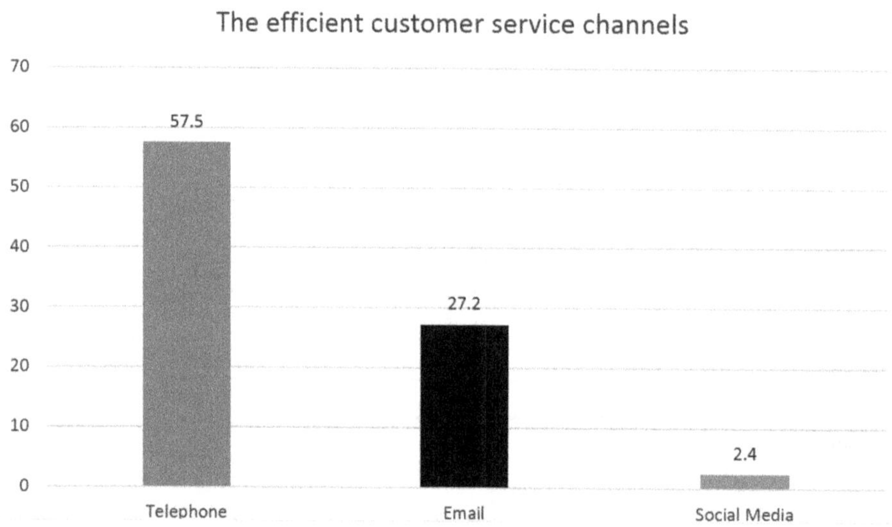

efficiency of customer service channels, simplicity and several of communication channels are the most important indexes in this group. In construct of customer service, first of all familiarity with foods, restaurants, brands and secondly customer positive image of restaurant are important. For customer trust that is influential construct is social media, there are two main factors, one is restaurant data privacy and the other is receiving the needy attention to customers issue. About customer satisfaction, presenting satisfied community in restaurants is very important for the customer. In the last construct (customer loyalty), quality of services, trust and successful CRM are the three important factors that affect directly the loyalty of the customers in restaurants.

Table 10. The most significant factors in social media construct

Mean Rank	Asymp. Sig.	Factors	Constructs
3.28	.000	Rate of interaction	*Social Media*
3.14	.000	Various of communication channel	
3.85	.000	Trustworthy of customer service channels	
3.04	.000	Efficiency of customer service channels	
3.13	.000	Simplicity	
3.42	.000	Fast response time	
4.01	.000	Fun	
3.38	.000	Friendlier communication	
4.19	.000	Transparency	
3.28	.002	Positive image of restaurant	*Customer Service*
3.65	.000	Handling the customers question/concerns quickly	
3.71	.000	Handled the customers question/concerns by network(internet)	
3.22	.001	Familiarity with foods, restaurants, brands	
3.48	.000	Access news about everything	
3.98	.001	Sharing opinion about the foods and restaurant industry	
3.78	.000	Helping to solve customers' issue	*Customer Trust*
4.16	.000	Promise to solve the issues	
3.53	.000	Receive the needy attention to customers issue	
3.39	.000	Data privacy	
3.23	.000	Providing the needy services	*Customer Satisfaction*
3.19	.000	Solving my problems/issues/questions/concerns	
2.87	.000	Satisfied community	
2.29	.000	Quality of services	*Customer Loyalty*
3.47	.000	Meet new people	
3.03	.000	Service satisfaction	
2.38	.000	Trust	
2.88	.000	Successful CRM	

4.2. Data Analysis for Research Hypotheses

The correlational research is a descriptive research method (non-trial) that examines the relationship among the variables, based on the target of the study. Correlation studies can be classified into three categories based on the target:

- Two-variable Correlation
- Regression analysis
- Covariance analysis or correlation matrix

Once the data have been collected in ordinal rankings or been inverted into ranks, Spearman's rank correlation (rs) can be used, which is a nonparametric method. One of the advantages of Spitaman's correlation coefficient over Pierrson correlation coefficient is that if one or more than one of the data is very large, compare to other numbers, since it is only the rank of them that is considered, they do not affect other data. As in the first part of the research, the model of research and hypotheses were discussed, in this section, we attempt to see whether or not the proposed factors of using social media in conceptual model of the research, have any impact on CRM and customer loyalty in restaurants?

Hypothesis 1 - By improving technology aligned with new and various social media tools, the level of CRM acceptance in customers in restaurants increase and leads to loyalty.

H_0: There is no correlation between two variables of social media tools and acceptance of CRM in customers in restaurants and loyalty.
H_1: There is between two variables of social media tools and acceptance of CRM in customers in restaurants and loyalty.

The above mentioned hypothesis test (shown in Table 11) indicates that in %95 level of certainty, since the significance value is less than level of error, therefore Hypothesis H_0 is not valid and H_1 is valid. Therefore, with the error probability %5 in the main population the sample group can also be validated and in other words, there is no enough evidence to discredit the theory of the researcher on the mentioned hypothesis, and it must be mentioned that there is a significant relationship of (%67) between Social media tools and acceptance of CRM in customers in restaurants and loyalty. By improving technology aligned with new and various social media tools such as: desktop, laptop, smartphone and tablet, the level of CRM acceptance in customers in restaurants increase and leads to loyalty. In other words, improving technology aligned with new and various social media tools have direct relation with their level of customer CRM acceptance and loyalty in restaurants. According to this percentage (67%), the majority of customers prefer to use their own smartphone to order, talk about their needs and desires. Customers want to see the new technology they use integrated into their dining experience, a new study from techonomic on consumer-facing technology shows, especially if it will speed up the process of getting their meal or paying their bill. **(Acceptance of the hypothesis H_1)**

Hypothesis 2 - The ability to understand customers' needs, desires, and orders and comment messages has a direct relationship with the trustworthy customer service channels.

Table 11. Table of the results from Hypothesis test 1

Significant Relation	α (Level of Error)	Number of Significance (sig)	Spearman Correlation Coefficient	Name of the Variables
There is a significant relationship	.05	.001	.67	**Social media tools and acceptance of CRM in customers in restaurants and loyalty**

H_0- There is no correlation between two variables of understanding customers' needs, desires, and orders and comment messages and trustworthy customer service channels

H_1- There is a correlation between two variables of understanding customers' needs, desires, and orders and comment messages and trustworthy customer service channels.

The results of testing the hypothesis 2 (shown in table 12) indicates that in %95 level of certainty, since the significance value is less than level of error, therefore Hypothesis H_0 is not valid and H_1 is valid. Therefore, with the error probability %5 in the main population the sample group can also be validated and in other words, there is no enough evidence to discredit the theory of the researcher on the mentioned hypothesis, and it must be mentioned that there is a positive significant relationship of (%53) between the ability to understand customers' needs, desires, and orders and comment messages and trustworthy customer service channels. Restaurants can understand customers' needs, desires, and orders and comment messages through trustworthy customer service channels such as telephone, email, and social media. The findings demonstrate customers trust to telephone more than other service channels not only for explaining their needs and desires, but also their orders in the restaurants. It proves that nowadays, customers seek to warm voice instead of electronic customers' service tools. On the other hand, we can conclude our restaurants in Iran should focus more on improving social media culture to increase loyalty. Restaurants offering Voice of the Customer (VoC) by expert accountable staff to reply the customers are well aware of this, as they see thousands of customer comments every day, each containing this recurring thread of common-sense logic for ensuring customer satisfaction: "Be patient and friendly. Treat customers politely and respectfully. Keep products and services in stock and up to date." **(Acceptance of the hypothesis H_2)**

Hypothesis 3 - Having control on receiving needs, desires, and orders and comment of the customers through different social media communication channels in restaurant affect the acceptance of the consumers' attitude about social media as CRM tool for creating customer loyalty.

H_0- There is no correlation between two variables of having control on receiving needs, desires, and orders and comment of the customers and the acceptance of the consumers' attitude about social media as CRM tool for creating customer loyalty.

H_1- There is a correlation between two variables of having control on receiving needs, desires, and orders and comment of the customers and the acceptance of the consumers' attitude about social media as CRM tool for creating customer loyalty.

Table 12. Table of the results of Testing Hypothesis 2

Significant relation	α (level of error)	Number of significance (sig)	Spearman Correlation Coefficient	Name of the Variables
There is a significant relationship	.05	.000	.53	**The ability to understand customers' needs, desires, and orders and comment messages and trustworthy customer service channels**

The results of testing the hypothesis 3 (shown in table 13) indicates that in %95 level of certainty, since the significance value is less than level of error, therefore Hypothesis H0 is not valid and H1 is valid. Therefore, with the error probability %5 in the main population the sample group can also be validated and in other words, there is no enough evidence to discredit the theory of the researcher on the mentioned hypothesis, and it must be mentioned that there is a positive significant relationship of (%71) between Having control on receiving needs, desires, and orders and comment of the customers and the acceptance of the consumers' attitude about social media as CRM tool for creating customer loyalty. The customers believe that the social media communication channels in restaurant such as Facebook, Twitter, LinkedIn, YouTube, Google+, Xing, then can control their needs and desires easier and faster. Using these social media communication channels as customer relationship management solution, the restaurant owner affairs representative can view a customer's complete interaction history, issues, addresses, loyalty information, and more - whether the interaction was initiated via phone, email or Web form. They can quickly identify guests, address concerns, resolve issues, and offer solutions that help to turn a negative experience into a positive one. **(Acceptance of the hypothesis H_3**)

5. CONCLUSION

Social Media is the name for the collection of tools (Facebook, LinkedIn, Twitter and many others) that any business uses to be Social via the Web. These tools are sweeping their world and are being adopted at an astonishing rate by individuals and businesses. Yet, many people still have misunderstandings about what these tools are and how they can or should be used. A common assumption is that "Facebook is for people looking to hook-up with their high school sweetheart, LinkedIn is for people looking for a job, and Twitter is for propeller heads". Do not make this mistake! All of these Social Media tools (and many that you have never heard of) are powerful tools that your competitors are using as part of their strategy to steal YOUR customers today. Businesses are using Social Media tools to re-establish and practice the old art of one-to-one communications on a global scale.

Restaurant CRM and Loyalty are two of the most important competitive survival tools for popular restaurants because loyal customers provide repeat business, higher market shares, referrals, and competitive advantages. Thereupon, it is strategically important to understand customers' standpoint and requests to attract, maintain, and satisfy those customers in order to maintain this continuous source of

Table 13. Table of the results of Testing Hypothesis 3

Significant relation	α (level of error)	Number of significance (sig)	Spearman Correlation Coefficient	Name of the Variables
There is a significant relationship	.05	.000	.71	**Having control on receiving needs, desires, and orders and comment of the customers and the acceptance of the consumers' attitude about social media as CRM tool for creating customer loyalty**

income. In this study, the researcher find out the restaurant managers should understand the impact of both the customers' level of satisfaction, customer trust, social media, and customer service on customers' loyalty. The managers should also pay attention to the driving force for each component of the customer loyalty. Customers may vary in the way they become loyal to a restaurant; for some customers restaurant image may be important, whereas for others quality of service and food are more important. The results of the present study regarding the customer's satisfaction level and customer trust, social media, and customer service could help the managers of the restaurant operators to develop customers' loyalty. The use of social media as a CRM tool can affect trust in a positive approach if used in an efficient way. While the majority of customer comments may be variations on the same theme, customers want to be heard individually and addressed personally. Restaurants who feel accountable to the people they serve will see that feedback can do more than inform and instruct. It creates a connection that drives better business practices, higher customer satisfaction and retention, and increased sales.

On the other hand, this study represents that most of Tehran restaurants customers are young with medium age of 26 years. It is good opportunity for the restaurants that utilize this group's new idea of communication to improve their services. Recommend to the restaurants to pay attention of this result that young people in Tehran have identified social media as a key element of communicating the message of the importance of safe food, new food, and various services.

Moreover, the findings indicate that new smartphone are customers' preference as social media to communicate with their favorite restaurant. Nowadays, in Tehran the number of smartphones is increasing and it will continue to increase. Everything people did online with their PCs they are doing on their smartphones. They are listening to music, reading ads, writing reviews, playing games, and looking up information. The only thing is now they are mobile. The mobile and social media revolution is well on its way. So, recommend the restaurants to update/create their profiles on google places, Facebook and other social media, optimize their website for mobile phones and tablets, and use mobile sites to educate their customers and create entertainment calendars and assign coupons.

According to findings, the author found though in Tehran the growth of using social media is increasing days in and days out, the customers trust neither are nor growth simultaneously. Most of the people preferred to use telephone to order their food to the restaurants. The main reason of this result referred to this fact that customers need warm or hot voice when calling the restaurants. They think this device is easy and efficient device to order and get services. They satiate to hear recorded voice on phone or an electronic email and response. Therefore, this study recommends the restaurants manger to consider telephone, email as CRM (Customer Relation Management) or E-CRM (Electronic Customer Relation Management) in today communication as new generation of social media communication channel.

The results proved that Social media can be an excellent channel for building long-lasting customer relationships in restaurants. Prompt and effective responses to requests for product information, praise or feedback about service, or complaints can result in improved customer support, quicker order fulfillment and faster lead qualification. Therefore, when using social media as a business tool it's important to take strategic steps to ensure restaurants can take full advantage of the opportunity. Here are some recommendations that can help you as restaurants' owner leverage the power of social media to build customer strong relationships. So far, restaurants have been slow to take to technology, there are some few recommendations and recent innovations aligned with the subject of this article that can break new ground in restaurant industry in Iran:

Select Your Social Channels Carefully in Restaurants

In addition to the old guard of Facebook, Twitter and LinkedIn, platforms such as Tumblr, Instagram and Pinterest are the new channels of digital influence, being used for everything from real-time engagement to customer service. Also don't forget that Google+ has excellent reach to the more technical audience and is also coming on strong with all the resources of Google at its disposal. This study suggests you to use Facebook initially. This may be the biggest technology leap coming in the next year, as nearly 90 percent of restaurant owners say they plan to have a Facebook presence by next year. This is a fairly low-cost add-on to make, and it has the potential to grow sales, which always gets a restaurateur's attention. Then Twitter and thirdly LinkedIn are the two most popular tools in restaurant of Iran. So, you can categorize your customers need for improving long-term relationship and offer the best choice to them and let them to choose the most prominent ones aligned with their needs, that make them happy and satisfy and trust to you easier.

Use Social Media Management Toolkits

Use tools that let restaurants quickly identify issues related to your restaurants from the massive pool of updates including blog comments, podcasts, pictures and videos. Take note of more advanced features available from toolkits including image recognition to identify photographs and videos that are relevant to your restaurants services and foods offering. As the results showed, the best social media tool that you can consider in your restaurants toolkits is supplying some application in your customers' smartphone. Digital menu boards besides smartphones are another opportunity for restaurants. Watch for fast-food restaurants to change menus more often, because digital menu boards make it so much easier than manually changing prices and items. Digital signage also allows quick-serve restaurants to provide entertainment and interactivity while you wait in.

Have an Integration Strategy

To provide value to enterprise users (e.g. sales, marketing, customer support), relevant social media content should be integrated with your CRM and other core IT systems, such as ERP, finance and logistics, creating a centralized enterprise portal. A systems integration platform with interfaces to social media and popular IT systems can provide the needed connectivity. As social media networks go in and out of favor, loosely coupled integration provided by an integration platform means that restaurants can easily add, remove or change social media channels as warranted. As you know, customers nowadays are already using social media to lodge complaints, give compliments and ask questions. It's imperative for businesses to meet their customers where they are and address any customer service or support issues as quickly as possible. A comprehensive system integration strategy and platform can help support the process and accelerate companies' ability to enjoy the benefits of social CRM.

Automate Processes Wherever Possible

Information from social media should be as actionable, such as automatically triggering alerts in cases of negative comments so they can be handled as quickly as possible. Although the processes should be automated, the interactions themselves should be personalized. Canned responses are obvious to customers and have a negative impact on the restaurants' image. Consumers want to see the new technology they use integrated into their dining experience.

Investigate Big Data Analysis and Manipulation

With so much data now at hand, there is great potential to better understand and manage customer relationships. This can include using image recognition to identify elements in posts and correlate it with other elements, but it's also key to being able to actively manage relationships with many customers and potential customers on a personal level in restaurants.

Mobile Ordering

This is one area where fast-food chains are in the forefront. Restaurants can use iPad order kiosks. Why wait in line if restaurants can file the customer's order at a kiosk immediately, and then sit down and relax? Expect more of this, since it could help prevent walk-aways and result in more orders. It's been noted that customers using a mobile ordering app tend to place larger orders than by phoning it in. Maybe it's because they have a visual guide that shows them just how delicious your fare is…kind of like having a great in-house menu and team that present an enticing vision to your in-house customers. Restaurants can't do that over the phone, and a phone book add is extremely limited at best in the amount of information they can present–but they can custom tailor your message perfectly with a restaurant ordering app. Show your customers how great your food is, give them an easy to use ordering interface, and watch your average order size grow. It really makes sense! On the other hand, when you have a mobile ordering for your restaurant, your competitors don't. It's that simple as well in the eyes of your customers. When they want to place a quick carry out or delivery order via the convenience of their mobile device, and they know that your business caters to their mobile savviness, you become the go to restaurant while your competition is left in the dark. Restaurant apps are catching on quickly in the industry, but you can still be first and lock in your position today.

Games While-U-Wait

Restaurants can project gesture-enabled games onto restaurant floors for kids to play while they wait for Happy Meals. That'll keep kids busy and we all know happy kids mean happy parents who come back to your restaurant.

Online Coupons

Restaurants should use digital coupons, and diners gobble them up. Offering online coupons for foods and restaurant's services can have numerous benefits. Restaurant can sell foods quickly, sell more foods on top of the discounted ones, and increase traffic on restaurant website. In addition, by providing internet coupons, restaurant can enhance their restaurants' brand and promote customer loyalty. Online coupons minimize advertising costs while maximizing your marketing flexibility. While a coupon business opportunity primarily advertises the restaurant, they are discounting, it can also advertise your restaurant.

Their restaurant's name, address, and other pertinent information should be featured prominently on the coupon. Doing so will have prospects perceive their restaurant as one that offers deals, leading them to visit your website for other discounts.

This study offers strategic guidelines to restaurant management. The CRM perceptions and level of satisfaction are some of the factors that helps guide the positioning and repositioning strategies of the restaurant in the local market place. The relationships among customers' satisfaction, trust, services perceptions, and restaurant loyalty determined the magnitude of their relative importance to a specific market by linking customer behavior to the restaurant loyalty. The restaurants operators should make their customers aware of their offerings. Social media should be carefully developed based on the results of ongoing research. If the target market indicates that a major personality trait is up to date, the manager should develop social media, which feature a modernized layout of furnishings, colors, and logos in various devices and channels. New customers will try the restaurant based on an initial notion of perceived quality and if they are satisfied that will enhance their further intention to revisit the restaurant. Furthermore, Managers should put more efforts to facilitate the restaurant implementation planning to respond to the changing market and customer demands. Such a system requires a mix of strategic management, marketing, motivation, innovation, training, and financial techniques in social media that will be a good subject for future research.

REFERENCES

Berry, L. L. (2002). Relationship Marketing of Services- Perspectives from 1983 & 2000. *Journal of Relationship Marketing*, *1*(1), 59–77. doi:10.1300/J366v01n01_05

Boström & Svensson. (2013). *CRM through Social Media and its effect on Brand Loyalty*. Luleå University of Technology.

Dataforeningen. (2010). *Mellomrapport; Norske virksomheters bruk avsosiale medier*. Retrieved Jun 14, 2011, from: http://www.kommunikasjon.no/Foreningen/Nyheter/_attachment/7822?=true&_ts=127f21c4f8b

El Bernoussi, M. (2012). *The value of social media in CRM: from CRM 1.0 to CRM 2.0*. Dublin Business School.

Eric Levy-Bencheton. (2012). *Practice Sales & Marketing / Customer Relationship Management*. Atos Consulting, White paper translated from the French "Social CRM: vers la Relation Client augmentée.

Gummesson, E. (1987). *Quality: The Ericsson Approach*. Stockholm: Ericsson.

Hurtola & Jenny. (2011). *The importance of social media in building customer loyalty for Company X*. Laurea University of Applied Sciences.

Magnini, V., & Honeycutt, E. (2005). Face Recognition and Name Recall, Training Implications for the Hospitality Industry. *The Cornell Hotel and Restaurant Administration Quarterly*, *46*(1), 69–78. doi:10.1177/0010880404270881

Mohan, S., Choi, E., & Min, D. (2008). Conceptual modeling of enterprise application system using social networking & web 2.0 social CRM system. In *Proceedings of the International Conference on Convergence & Hybrid Information Technology, ICHIT '08*. IEEE Computer Society. doi:10.1109/ICHIT.2008.263

Rataree, G. (2003). *Measurement of Customer Satisfaction level of Hotel Food and Beverage Service at the Westin Hotel*. (Unpublished Thesis). Oklahoma State University.

Schall, M. (2003). Best practices in the assessment of hotel-guest attitudes. *The Cornell Hotel and Restaurant Administration Quarterly*, *44*(2), 51–65. doi:10.1016/S0010-8804(03)90018-8

Shamaila Marita Lein & Mette Ugstad. (2011). *Social Media in Customer Relationship Management - An analysis of Norwegian management consulting firms*. (Master thesis). Copenhagen Business School.

Soriano, D. (2002). Customers' expectations factors in restaurants: *The situation in Spain. International Journal of Quality & Reliability Management*, *19*(8/9), 1055–1067. doi:10.1108/02656710210438122

Toporek, A. (n.d.). *What is Customer Loyalty*. Retrieved 2014, from: http://customersthatstick.com

Victorino, L., Verma, R., Plaschka, G., & Dev, C. (2005). Service innovation and customer choices in the hospitality industry. *Journal of Managing Service Quality*, *15*(6), 555–576. doi:10.1108/09604520510634023

Wu, B., Ye, Q., Yang, S., & Wang, B. (2009). A new telecom CRM framework from social network perspective. In *Proceedings of the 1st ACM international workshop on Complex networks meet information and knowledge management*. ACM.

Zeithmal, V., & Bitner, M. (1996). *Service Marketing*. New York: McGraw-Hill.

Chapter 14
Electronic Word of Mouth Marketing:
Relationship between Brand Loyalty and Electronic Word of Mouth in Social Marketing Networks

Sahra Zamanian
University of Tehran, Iran

Amir Khanlari
University of Tehran, Iran

ABSTRACT

Social networks as new form of popular and widely used communities (especially among Iranians) are considered as places to talk about brands and sharing comments, experiences, interests and help users to play more prominent role in their own and others informed choices. Purpose of this chapter is to find a logical relationship between brand loyalty on one hand, and participating in eWOM and individuals' identification through specific brands (Adidas in present chapter) on the other. Research results show a significant and positive correlation between brand loyalty, participating in eWOM and brand identification among consumers. Model presented in this chapter explains the same process. Regarding objective methodology and data collection method, this is an applied descriptive and surveying study. We used Regression approach and SPSS software to test hypotheses.

INTRODUCTION

According to the study results in the field of marketing and advertising, the traditional word of mouth marketing (WoM) is a powerful factor in shaping the consumers' attitudes and behaviors and has a much stronger effect than media advertising on consumer acceptance of the goods. In the past, the WoM was happening within a very limited and usually friendly environment in a face to face situation, including an informational source and a receiver or audience. In fact, the WoM faced with two major limitations:

DOI: 10.4018/978-1-4666-8586-4.ch014

1.Location 2.Time. However, the emergence and development of Internet as a virtual space has provided a new context for trading and business activities, both for consumers and manufacturers. Virtual community participation and User Generated Content (UGC) are the prevailing social activities in virtual spaces. Along with such trends, word-of mouth (WOM) transactions have also increased dramatically. Moore (2003) investigated the branding influence based on the word-of-mouth marketing environment. In the case of Microsoft, the number of Microsoft's Hotmail users increases rapidly by utilizing the contacts of each user. Although Microsoft spent only a small budget on marketing, its membership grew by 12 million in 18 months. Leskovec et al. (2006) proposed a model to investigate user behaviors in a large community and identified the growth and effectiveness of the social network. Richardson and Domingos (2002) utilized a probabilistic model to analyze the probability of a customer's purchasing that is strongly dependent on whether his/her friends also have purchased the same product. However, they did not focus on identifying the influencers in a customer social network to induce the potential customers with business opportunities. Several works on word-of-mouth marketing are based on social networks. Li et al. (2010) argued However, most of them focus on the observation of business situations or on the calculation of social network spreading, It is hard to acquire a practical model that can be easily and effectively applied to business strategy development.

In presence of social networks brand owners can access the largest number of their customers (actual and potential) and users are able to more actively contribute in this area and express their opinions, experiences and interests by participating in eWoM. In other words, they would be able to play a more prominent role in their own and others conscious selection. As one commentator writes: Instead of endangering millions of dollars for extensive marketing, the companies can strive as active companies on the Internet to draw the attention of millions of viewers and audiences with minimum costs through developing Web-based strategies such as making blogs and eWoM (Cheung & Thadani 2012).

On the other hand, generalization of social networks such as Meet Up, Facebook, My space and Twitter in recent years and their impact on WoM has led to the increasing importance of this issue and provided an appropriate ground to investigate this topic in different parts of the world and among different cultures.

LITERATURE REVIEW

Rise of social networking and globalization of economic activities, lead us to design new models of eWoM. Several studies have been conducted in the field of electronic word of mouth and loyalty but so far there has not been a coherent research on the impact of e-loyalty on eWoM through social networks. Research in this area can be totally divided into three main categories:

1. Researches on eWoM, role of social networks and its influential factors.
2. Researches on e-loyalty, role of social networks and its influential factors
3. Interaction between loyalty and word of mouth.

Research on Electronic Word of Mouth, Role of Social Networks, and Its Influential Factors

Social networks as new forms of popular and widely used communities, (especially among Iranians) are considered as a place to exchange personal ideas, interests and preferences with friends also brand owners can access to the largest number of their customers (potential or actual) and users are appear more actively in this area, it means that through participating in eWoM they will talk about their experiences and interests and share comments. Finally they play more prominent role in their own and others informed choices. The popularity of social networking sites including Facebook, MySpace, MeetUp, LinkedIn, and Twitter has grown exponentially in recent years and they are changing attitudes about virtual space. Then how word-of-mouth (WOM) effects on business environment need to be considered. As is well known, traditional WOM is a powerful force in shaping consumer attitudes and behaviors and can actually have greater influence on product adoption than any form of mass media advertising. However, due to the internet, the communication environment in which WOM disseminates has been unalterably changed. WOM no longer takes place in the exclusive context of face-to-face settings, involving one source and one recipient. Rather, it now increasingly occurs in the more transparent public domain of online social networks. Recognizing this trend, marketers have begun leveraging social networking sites (e.g. MySpace, Facebook, LinkedIn, and Twitter) in order to generate awareness, interest, and ultimately product purchase. Their strategy typically involves creating product-related pages, and then attempting to drive potential customers to those pages through advertising and WOM (Cheung & Thadani 2012).

As Keith et al. (2012) have described the mechanism of action, an online social networking site typically involves a collection of users profiles where registered. Members can place information that they want to share with others. Users are generally involved in creating new content (e.g. adding photos; writing messages) and consuming content that others create. On most social networking sites, users can add other users to their network of contacts. Typically one user initiates the invitation, and the other accepts or rejects it. When accepted, the two profiles become linked. The resulting network corresponds to what we refer to as a "Friend-Network". By default, the communication linkages that are established on most social networking sites (e.g. Facebook, LinkedIn) are bi-directional in nature. On others (e.g. Twitter), uni-directional linkages are established such that a user might receive information from some Friend Network members (i.e. "follow" those members), convey information to others, and interact bilaterally with yet a third Friend Network group. What distinguishes online social networking sites (e.g., MySpace, Facebook, Twitter, LinkedIn, YouTube) from other, more generic web-based communities (e.g. Yelp, Hotmail, users providing product ratings onAmazon.com) is that WOM communication typically takes place between individuals who have some form of pre-existing personal relationship with one another, because both are members of the same Friend Network. Even if that relationship is not "close", it is possible for each individual to check the background of the other by examining his or her personal profile page. In other types of online communities, this background check is not possible. In addition, online social networking sites are distinguished by the fact that they typically publish lists of those members who have elected to join the aforementioned Product-Network sub-groups. Thus, interest in (or liking of) a product becomes public knowledge. For example, depending on privacy settings, a list of those individuals who follow a particular Facebook product page (e.g. the restaurant, La Maison) is available to all site members, and the act of joining that Product Network is publicized through the individual member's "News-Feed". Conversely, in a more generic online network such as Yelp, while members may be able to see that John Doe has given La Maison a five-star rating, that information is not automatically forwarded to a sub-group of friends. Further, everyone who rates La Maison does not automatically become a member of a separate Product (La Maison) Network.

Online reviews are closely associated with word-of-mouth marketing in a Web environment. People tend to read the product reviews written by other experienced users before making a purchase decision.

In other words, these reviews are equipped with some kind of influencing power over the readers. A prior study on Amazon.com reviews suggested that reviewers may engage in experience sharing of questionable practices and promote specific agendas to build their expert identities. Examining the effect of online book reviews on the relative sales at Amazon.com and Barnesandnoble.com.

Chevalier and Mayzlin (2003) found that an improvement in reviews leads to an increase in sales. Reinstein and Snyder (2005) suggested that online movies reviews from professional critics have positive effect on increasing the customer demand. In addition, Basuroy et al. (2003) also pointed out that movie reviews have a significant impact on the performance of companies. Opinion mining can be applied to measure the influencing level of a review or comment. Zhan et al. (2007) emphasized the important role of writing and referring to product reviews on the Internet. Dobele et al. (2007) identified the key points about the success or failure of message passing in word-of-mouth marketing. By collecting and categorizing many cases about message - passing behaviors for several different products, they showed that "emotion" has more impact than "the expectation of the recipient" in the successful message passing. In general, people tend to be influ- enced by subjective expressions involving strong words and objective reaction statements are generally not considered important because they lack "emotions" to affect the purchasing decisions of others.

Industry research reports have shown that when making purchase decisions, Internet users trust online reviews posted by unknown consumers more than they trust traditional media (Cheung and Thadani, 2010). In addition, user-generated content in the form of online customer reviews was found to significantly influence consumer purchasing decisions. 91% of respondents mentioned that they consult online reviews, blogs, and other user-generated content before purchasing a new product/service, 46% of which are then influenced in the way they to purchase. It had been predicted that over 50% of total retail sales will be affected by web (e.g., online reviews) by 2014. (Channel Advisor 2010).

Thoma et al. `s (2001) Experimental results suggested that causal attributions mediate the negative WOMC1 and brand evaluation relation, receivers' attributions depend on the manner in which the negative WOMC is conveyed, and brand name affects attributions. Results also suggest that when receivers at-tribute the negativity of the WOMC message to the brand, brand evaluations decrease; however, if receivers attribute the negativity to the communicator, brand evaluations increase. Herr, et al.`s(1991) Past research in the area of consumer behavior has shown that consumers paymore attention to negative information than positive information. They also tend to weigh negative information more than positive information during evaluation and decision making. Park and Lee (2009) showed that negative eWOM has a stronger influence on eWOM effect than positive eWOM.

Cheung and Thadani conducted a general review about eWOM and focused on classifing models in this area. A total of 47 eWOM communication articles published between 2000 and 2010 were identified. Research on the impact of eWOM communication can be classified into market-level analysis and individual-level analysis. In this review, 47% (22 out of 47 articles) of the articles adopted the market-level approach, while 53% (25 out of 47 articles) focused on the individual-level analysis. As a number of researchers have already conducted a review on prior studies of market-level eWOM communication (Park & Lee, 2009; Davis & Khazanchi, 2008; Hu, Liu & Zhang, 2008).

Brown et al.(2007) To gain new insights in this important area, use a social network perspective to examine, in an online context, three key influences on the evaluation of marketing information that may explain how WOM influences consumers' decision making and attitude formation: tie strength, homophily, and source credibility. Second, the results of the field research provide strong evidence that individuals relate to Web sites as if they are primary actors in the social network and that online communities can, therefore, act as a social proxy for individual identification. they extended previous models of online social interaction and showed how online WOM has its own unique benefits and drawbacks. Shu and Haddad (2011) believe SNS[2] can facilitate WOM marketing. The effect of SNS on WOM marketing can be divided into two generic categories: (a) impact and broadcast. Impact can come from three sources: senders' attributes, receivers' attributes, and the relationship between senders and receivers. they assume that if SNS can improve these dimensions, they can improve WOM marketing: Senders' credibility, Senders' credibility, Receivers' expertise, The strength of the social network between the receiver and the sender, Similarity between senders and receivers, (b) Broadcast effect is determined by the usage and quality of the SNS platform where WOM is conducted: Perceived usefulness, Perceived ease of use, Information understandability, Information reliability, Information usefulness, System access, System usability and System navigation. But the results of their study were beyond expectation. Based on the popularity of SNS and their theoretical foundations, many would expect that SNS performance should be better but their results show the opposite. Although this study did not show SNS as preferred WOM sites, participants indicated that they would use SNS in the future. Historic data have proven users' interest in Facebook.

Research on E-Loyalty, Role of Social Networks, and Its Influential Factors

Deng et al (2010) in their research about mobile industry in an empirical study examine the determinants of customer satisfaction and loyalty of mobile instant messages. Their findings confirm that trust, perceived service quality, perceived customer value, including functional value and emotional value, contribute to generating customer satisfaction with MIM3. The results also show that trust, customer satisfaction and switching cost directly enhance customer loyalty. Additionally, this study finds that age, gender, and usage time have moderating effects. In Flavian et al. `s (2006) empirical analysis study, named "The role played by perceived usability, satisfaction and consumer trust on website loyalty", results confirmed that trust of user increases when the user perceived that system was usable and there was a consequent increase in the degree of website loyalty. In the same way, greater usability was found to have a positive influence on user satisfaction, and this also generated greater website loyalty. Finally, they found that user trust was partially dependent on the degree of consumer website satisfaction. Growing number of academic studies about online customer loyalty shows diversity, if not divergence, exists regarding the measurement and conceptualization of online loyalty. By multiplying the theoretical foundations for the study of online loyalty, researchers have identified different determinants of online loyalty and different impacts on business relationships. Toufaily et al.'s research (2012) provide an integrative model for these antecedents and consequences. This framework provides us with a cohesive view of online customer loyalty and identify potential unexplored research opportunities in this area. The model includes the determinants and the consequences observed in the empirical studies of the literature: customer characteristics, product/service attributes, company /retailer characteristics, environmental characteristics, website characteristics and consequences. In this study characteristics of customer are satisfaction, trust and motives are. Harris and Goode (2004) through both synthesizing and building on existing research into loyalty, trust, satisfaction, value, and service quality proposed a framework and tested that positions trust as a pivotal driver of loyalty. This framework presents loyalty as a consequence of direct and indirect relationships with trust, perceived value, satisfaction, and service quality. Tested model confirmed direct relationship between trust and loyalty and positive indirect relationship between satisfaction and loyalty. Harris and Goode (2004) through both synthesizing and building on existing research into loyalty, trust, satisfaction, value, and service quality proposed a framework and tested that positions trust as a pivotal driver of loyalty. This framework presents loyalty as a consequence of direct and indirect relationships with trust, perceived value, satisfaction, and service quality. Tested model confirmed direct relationship between trust and loyalty and positive indirect relationship between satisfaction and loyalty. Lin and Wang (2006) found that customer loyalty affects by perceived value, trust, habit, and customer satisfaction, with customer satisfaction playing a crucial intervening role in the relationship of perceived value and trust to loyalty. As Ùahina et al. (2012) argued brand experience has positive effects on brand satisfaction, trust and loyalty, Brand experience creates and develops trust-based relationship platform between brand and customer, brand satisfaction has a significantly positive influence on brand loyalty and brand trust has a significant effect on brand loyalty. Laroche et al. (2012) looked at the fast growing phenomenon of brand communities established on social media. They proposed a model of the effects of brand community on shared community markers, value creation practices and the way they convert to brand loyalty through brand trust by Using SEM. they found that brand communities established on social media enhance feelings of community among members and contribute to creating value for both members and the company. Furthermore, the model shows how brand loyalty is increased in brand communities. The whole model shows that value creation practices enhance loyalty through brand trust as a mediator. Contrary to their expectations, only two of the four value creation practices (brand use and impressions management) contribute to brand trust. There is one possible explanation for this finding. As Schau et al. (2009, p. 37) argue, "Practices operate like apprenticeship,'' which means that "their effects evolve over time as consumer engagement deepens and practices are integrated.'' Thus, it is possible that the effects of practices in social media based brand communities may not have evolved enough to significantly affect brand loyalty.

Interaction between Loyalty and Word of Mouth

Due to the influence of the Internet on economic activity traditional areas of study, such as satisfaction and loyalty, have received a new impulse as a consequence of the incorporation of businesses in the virtual medium. Similarly, other concepts, such as trust or usability, are acquiring a particular relevance due to the especially important part they play in the provision of services through the Internet. Despite the importance of these concepts there have been few studies that have analysed the relationship between them. (Flavian etal. 2006). Taylor and Hunter (2006) Establish Linear relationship between satisfaction, loyalty and (eWOM). Gruen et al. (2006) explore the impact of eWOM on customer economic value perceptions and loyalty intentions. They examine economic value as it accrues to the brand owner (as opposed to the firm that hosts the (eWOM) venue, and loyalty as measured by repurchase intentions and recommendations. Recognizing that marketers seek to directly influence the value of the firm's offering received by the customer as well as the customer's ongoing loyalty. They found that C2C4 know-how exchange had a direct relationship with loyalty intentions. According to previous researches, davvis et al. (1992) believe that external and internal motivations have significant effect on (eWOM) participation. but internal motivation effecta are more than external (Deci & Ryan,1985). (eWOM) participation behavior enhaces social identity among customers also when customers identify theselves by continuing to participate in (eWOM) then e-loyalty emerges. (Yoo, Sanders & Moon, 2013).

RESEARCH MODEL AND HYPOTHESES

Based on the research background, the initial designed model included the expertise factor among the users; but in the stage of data collection and after calculating the Cronbach's alpha of questions related to measure of expertise, we decided to omit the expertise structure from the model. Also, with an additional review of the research literature hypothesis # 4, which was so far questioned, was confirmed and added to the model. Considering the set of these points, the initial model was revised and following the confirmed modifications, Figure 1 was evaluated and analyzed as the final model (A more complete description regarding the model modification will be provided in the following). The definition of the sum of the structures used in the model was derived from the research background as follows.

Satisfaction

The concept of satisfaction has been widely analyzed in marketing literature However, satisfaction is a complex concept with a wide variance of definitions in previous literature. Traditionally, satisfaction can be divided into two distinct perspectives. On the one hand, the first perspective considers satisfaction as an affective predisposition sustained by economic conditions. On the other hand, the second perspective, known as non-economic satisfaction, considers the concept using more psychological factors, such as a partner fulfilling promises or the ease of relationships with the aforementioned partner. In order to propose a definitional framework of consumer satisfaction, Giese and Cote (2000) identified three general components in the concept of satisfaction: a response (emotional or cognitive); in a particular focus (a product, a consumption experience, a relationship, etc.); and at a particular time (before or after the election and consumption of a product, based on accumulated experience, etc.). Therefore, from a relational perspective (like the one used in this work), we may define satisfaction as an affective condition that results from a global evaluation of all the aspects that make up the relationship. (Casaló, 2010) According to Ùahina et al. (2012) Satisfaction is defined "as an affective response to purchase situation. Satisfaction is a positive affective reaction to an outcome of a prior experience. The satisfaction derived and

Figure 1. Research model

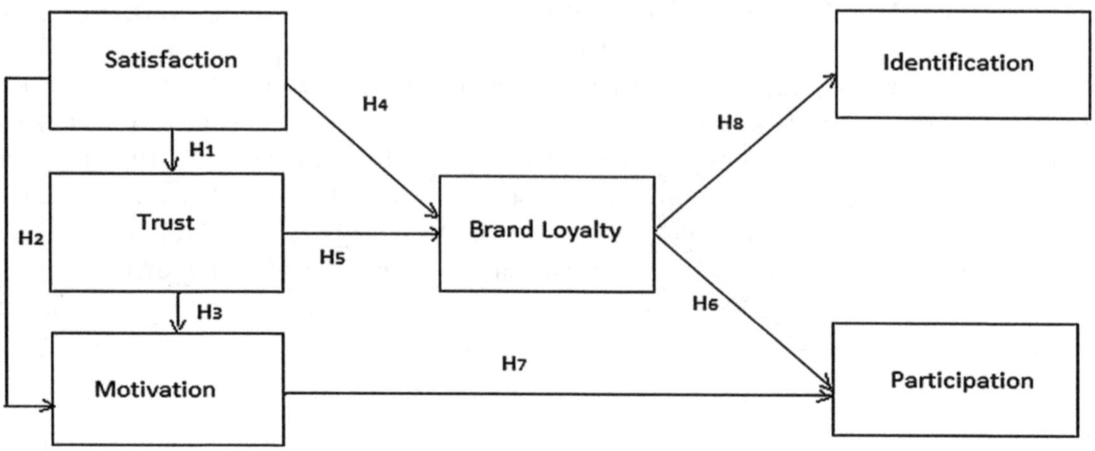

attitude formed as part of a prior experience, then impacts on subsequent purchases, completing cyclical pattern. Satisfaction has been found to lead to the long-term combination of relationships. Satisfaction is necessary but not sufficient component of loyalty. Satisfaction is an antecedent of brand loyalty, with increases in satisfaction leading to increases in brand loyalty. Customer satisfaction have been defined as overall satisfaction with customer expectations and consumption experiences. Also, overall satisfaction has been suggested to be a function of disconfirmation, which is a utility of both expectations and performance" (p.1290). The definition of customer satisfaction has been derived from customers' overall evaluation of the store experience in the retail context, and the performance of an offering to date in the service context. In the e-commerce context, satisfaction is defined as the contentment of the consumer with deference to his/her previous purchase experiences with an e-commerce firm (Chen 2012).

Trust

Trust is proposed as another important antecedent of loyalty. Trust concepts has been studied in a number of disciplines, and various definitions have been proposed. Trust is consistently related to the vulnerability of the trustor, because without vulnerability of the trustor upon the trustee, trust becomes irrelevant. In business studies, trust has been found to be important for building and maintaining long-term relationships. A commonly used definition of trust is that of Moorman et al (1992), who define it as the willingness to rely on an exchange partner in whom one has confidence. This definition is in accordance with early research, which associated trust with a "confidence in the other's intentions and motives", a definition that still holds (Brockand & Barclay, 1997).

Trust is a relationship of reliance and is also a willingness to rely on an exchange partner in whom one has confidence. It is an expectancy that the behaviors of people (or objects of trust evaluation) will follow a predetermined manner and this manner is the behaviors of others they trust. Trust can be used to indicate the strength level of relationships among people without performing a detailed investigation of intention. Munns (1995) stated that trust is a relation personal to an individual, and arises from the experiences and influences on that individual. Trust has been described as "central to all transactions" between individual or organizational actors in economics. It strengthens the motivations of people to do transactions and the benefits of each transacting target can be evaluated accordingly. Morgan and Hunt (1994) theorized, modeled, and tested the success of relationship marketing and found that commitment and trust are key factors. Brockand and Barclay (1997) studied relationships between buyers and sellers and showed that trust is based on character, motives, intentions, and role com- petence and judgment. Dunn (1988) indicated that trust is helpful for decision support in a scenario where there is uncertainty about the actions that will be undertaken by others. In other words, a trust mechanism is an important and effective component of our purchase decision, although we are not familiar with the product. The product reviews written by a trustable reviewer normally have higher impacts. On the other hand, the product reviews of an influencer should be trusted by more people. Due to these features, the trust score is a clear and appropriate pointer to potential nodes. In this research, we use a trust indicator to measure the effectiveness of our influencer identifying framework in the current study.

Trust can be defined as a consumer's confident beliefs that he or she can rely on the seller to deliver promised services, whereas a relational value can be defined as consumer's perceptions of the benefits enjoyed versus the cost incurred in the maintenance of an ongoing exchange relationship. The trust in the purchased brand may be viewed as leverage of its credibility, which in return may reinforce the consumers' repeat buying behavior (Ùahina et al. 2012)

Trust has been defined as "...the expectations held by the consumer that the service provider is dependable and can be relied on to deliver on its promises" Trust plays an important role in customer behaviour. Past studies have shown that there is a greater willingness to buy from an online retailer if trust is present Trust is also a fundamental factor influencing online purchase intentions (Schlosser et al., 2006) and web-based auction participation. Higher levels of trust result in higher loyalty to an e-service provider. As Laroche (2012) sayed Brand trust is "the willingness of the average consumer to rely on the ability of the brand to perform its stated function''. This notion is more prominent in situations of uncertainty, information asymmetry and fear of opportunism; thus, the role of trust is to decrease uncertainty and information asymmetry and make customers feel comfortable with their brand. Rate of expertise

Regarding source expertise, one of the ways people respond to a product referral is based on how the WOM information is evaluated by the message recipient relative to satisfying his or her own needs. If the recipient believes that adoption of the product or service may yield positive benefits or utilitarian, message acceptance (i.e. persuasion) WOM in on-line social networksis more likely to occur. This process is more formally known as informational influence.

Rate of Expertise

The expertise (or credibility) of the message source can determine whether a positive belief regarding utilitarian value is fostered. Individuals who are seen as being particularly knowledgeable regarding a product/service are perceived as more credible than those possessing a lesser amount of expertise. Due to their knowledge, credible sources should be better able than non-credible sources to ascertain whether a product can deliver positive benefits to the message recipient. Therefore, product-endorsement messages delivered from credible sources are more likely to be internalized. In both traditional as well as e-WOM, if the communication recipient internalizes (i.e. accepts) the message, it is expected that there will be greater product predilection, and therefore movement through the HOEs[5]. We expect the effects to be no different in regard to online social networks. Total articles discuss about marketing and advertising expertise in virtual space have 2 distinct dimensions: 1. User Knowledge on a particular brand; and 2. User Knowledge in virtual spaces and social networks. According to Brown et al. (2007) "Source expertise refers to the perceived competence of the source providing the information. It is the perceived professionalism by the receivers" (p.6). Studies have discovered that higher WOM impact comes with higher professionalism (Shu and Haddad, 2011).

In this paper, the definition of expertise rate includes the perception of readers and the comments related to a particular brand regarding the credibility of the source message to assess the quality of brands. The measures relating to this structure were extracted from articles on literature; however, after the completion of a number (50) of the questionnaires, the Cronbach's alpha value for this structure did not meet the acceptable level (0.7). According to the outputs in SPSS software and closeness of these questions to other structures, two and one questions were transferred to the structures of trust and incentive to participate in WoM, and subsequently, the expertise factor was excluded from the model.

Brand Loyalty

The concept of loyalty has been widely analyzed in the literature, especially from a marketing perspective. Loyalty implies that the consumer gives preference to a particular brand or company, although satisfactory alternatives may exist. Loyalty is defined as repeated purchase behavior exhibited over a sustained period and driven by a favorable attitude toward the subject, Although many definitions on the concept exist, it is the work of Oliver (1999) the one that provides a better explanation of loyalty "a deeply held commitment to re-buy or re patronize a preferred product or service consistently in the future, despite situational influences and marketing efforts having the potential to cause switching behavior" loyalty has 2 aspects including attitudinal and behavioral aspects (Casaló, 2010; Chang & Chen, 2008). In Wang et al. (2011) definition good customer loyalty via good and stable customer relationships can directly increase company profits. In the context of electronic/mobile commerce, customer loyalty is usually conceptualized as conative (behavioral intention) loyalty.[44] For example Srinivasan et al. (2002) and Lin and Wang (2006) defined customer loyalty as a customer's favorable attitude toward the electronic/mobile vendor that results in repeat buying behavior. Thus, customer loyalty in this study also refers to conative loyalty, which is defined as the behavioral intention to repurchase from a specific e-tailer. It must be noted that the loyalty concept considered in this paper was the traditional form of loyalty not its electronic and online form.

Electronic Word of Mouth Marketing (EWOM)

According to Gregurec et al(2012) "One interesting statement says that word-of-mouth (WOM) has been recognized as –one of the most influential resources of information transmission since the beginning of human societyWord-of-mouth relates on interpersonal communications among consumers concerning their personal experiences and evaluations of a company or its product" (p.2). It is defined as –a consumer-dominant channel of marketing communication where the sender is independent of the market. It is therefore perceived to be more reliable, credible, and trustworthy. Another definition says that WOM marketing is an action for informally sharing experiences and spreading information among consumers whenever they are satisfied or dissatisfied with specific products. Positive WOM gives brands a powerful an influential way to engage their target audience. But it is believed that the negative WOM has a stronger influence on customers' product/service/brand evaluations than positive one. e-WOM is defined as "any positive or negative statement made by potential, actual, or former customers about a product or company, which is made available to a multitude of people and institutions via the Internet" e-WOM is known to have a strong impact on purchase decisions and is a key factor in the Internet shopping market. Internet makes it easier for consumers to spread their words, and facilitates access to such opinions. Online popularity is of great importance, as it may reflect the potential demand for a product in the future and it is assumed to be even more effective than traditional, face-to-face WOM due to its greater accessibility, high reach, significantly lower costs and fast delivery (Cheung & Thadani, 2010). The power of interpersonal influence through word-of-mouth communication has been well recognized in the consumer literature. Prior studies have found that consumers perceive WOM as more trustworthy and persuasive than traditional media, such as print ads, personal selling and radio and TV advertising. The influence on purchase decision through WOM communication was further extended with the advent of the Internet, which extended eWOM communication to various additional virtual settings. On the internet, consumers can post their opinions, comments and reviews of products on weblogs (e.g.

xanga.com), discussion forums (e.g. zapak.com), review websites (e.g. Epinions.com), e-bulletin board systems, newsgroups and social networking sites (e.g. facebook.com) (Cheung & Thadani, 2010). In virtual environments, the consumers form their social networks with people who have never seen them before and exchange and share their opinions about their products and services with others. This process happens entirely in virtual communities wherein people have already relationships with each other or in discussion forums that their members have not known each other before and only refer there due to their common interests. Ewom Word-of-mouth marketing, also called viral marketing, is a new marketing method that uses electronic communications (e.g. e mail) to trigger brand messages throughout a widespread network of buyers. Dobele et al. (2005) studied several real marketing cases and analyzed why firms need word-of-mouth marketing, how to apply technology to it, and how to use it successfully.

According to Tong and Xuecheng (2010) "the eWOM has the following characteristics: (1) High efficiency and low cost (2) High reliability (3) Anonymity (4) High degree of interaction. EWOM completely overcomes the limitation of geographic space. Consumers are able to share their knowledge, experience and opinion all over the world. Besides, the search engine has revolutionized the efficiency of retrieving information and the many-to-many communication model facilitates the knowledge reservoirs in the online communication forum. More importantly, firms can spread the eWOM at virtually no cost. Similar with the traditional WOM, eWOM recommendations, as a consumer to-consumer communication form, is more influential than marketer-generated information. As far as its anonymity is concerned, the online communication can be carried out regardless of gender, age, nationalities and social status of each other. Indeed, in the online context, "no one knows you are a dog". The strong interaction is another feature of the eWOM, which is becoming more and more important due to the emergence of the web 2.0. In the web 2.0 environment, any one is both an information receiver and provider. Based on the analysis above, the nature of eWOM can be concluded. EWOM is the information about a product, service or company shared by online consumers, of which the process is efficient, low cost, reliable, anonymous and with high degree of interaction (p.249-250).

Motivation for Participation

However, the new advances are strongly based on the creation and management of networks. Although we cannot ignore the automation process associated with the development of Web, the potential of new technologies cannot be conceived without the participation of people who live, interact, learn and create via the web. Participation is essential, as it increases the involvement of customers and other stakeholders with organizations, thereby improving their reputation and marketing and also enhancing very diverse innovations that allow the creation of new business models and the upgrading of those established in the different organizations. (Fernando et al. 2012)

The main motivation for using social networks is a consequence of social influence and desire for belonging to a particular community. Yoo et al(2013) literature review showed that Motivation has been studied in a wide range of research studies and is considered an important theoretical variable. Woolfolk defines motive as a psychological state that induces, directs and maintains human behavior. (Woolfolk, 1995)

Deci and Ryan (1985) identified four types of motivation, namely, intrinsic regulation, identified regulation, introjected regulation and external regulation to account for the different reasons why individuals engage in service activities, generating their subsequent loyalty. First, intrinsic regulation refers to the customers' engagement in a service for their own feelings of pleasure and interest that derive directly from participation in the service. Identified regulation is defined as a relatively autonomous regulatory style characterized by the acceptance of a regulation as being one's own. In identifying a service as instrumentally important to a personal goal, a customer may likely participate in the service. Introjected regulation refers to a form of extrinsic motivation that is characterized by the individual internalizing external regulations. An example of introjected regulation is customers who use a service, not because they want to, but because they feel that they should (self-guilt or lack of confidence). Finally, external regulation is regarded as actions controlled by contingencies external to the individuals, such as rewards, threat of punishment and so on (Chieh et al., 2009).

Deci separates motive into intrinsic and extrinsic motives. On the one hand, intrinsic motives trigger behavior by reason of interest, enjoyment and satisfaction caused by the behavior itself. On the other hand, hand, extrinsic motives are followed by reason of compensation obtained by result of external activity. These intrinsic and extrinsic motives simultaneously influence the intention of the individual (Deci & Ryan, 1985).

Identification through Brand

The phenomenon of identification is often studied in organization research. Organization identification means that employees perceive a sense-of-connectedness to an organization and identify themselves in terms of it (Mael & Ashforth. 1992).

High suitability between person and organization reduces separation intention and increases the intention to recommend the organization. These results imply a relationship between e-WOM and identification. Bhattacharya and Sen examined the idea that a customer who has a deep involvement in a company or product becomes a supporter of that product or company (Bhattacharya & Sen, 2003).

As a result, based on social identity theory and organization identification theory, a customer identifies him/herself with a company or product in order to meet his/her self-definition, which is based on needs. Underwood et al. (2001) proposed a mechanism of combined emotions between brand and customer, which he called social identity. Social identity theory is based on the self-concept, which refers to the awareness of and feelings for individuals and consists of personal identity and social identity (Sanders & Moon, 2013). What is intended in the article includes the immaterial internal motivations.

In this paper, the identification through brand is the willingness of users to be recognized and introducing themselves and their community (virtual social networks) to others through a particular brand.

Research Hypotheses

H1: There is a direct and positive correlation between customers' satisfaction and their trust in the brand.
H2: There is a direct and positive correlation between customers' satisfaction and their motivation to participate in Electronic Word of Mouth Marketing in social networks.
H3: There is a direct and positive correlation between customers' trust and their motivation to participate in Electronic Word of Mouth Marketing in social networks.
H4: There is a direct and positive correlation between customers' satisfaction and their brand loyalty.
H5: There is a direct and positive correlation between customers' trust and their brand loyalty.
H6: There is a direct and positive correlation between customers' loyalty and their participation rate in Electronic Word of Mouth Marketing in social networks.
H7: There is a direct and positive correlation between customers' motivation and their participation in Electronic Word of Mouth Marketing in social networks.

H8: There is a direct and positive correlation between customers' brand loyalty and their willingness to be recognized through the brand in social networks.

You can see the research model in Figure 1.

RESEARCH METHODOLOGY

Regarding objective, methodology and nature, and data collection method, this was an applied, descriptive and surveying study, respectively. Due to the fact that among all active social networks around the world, Facebook is the most popular one among Iranian users, it considered as the research environment. To choose a particular brand, the world's most popular brands on social networks were initially specified through the "www.fanpagelist.com" website; then, by reviewing pages of various brands on Facebook, Adidas brand's web page was selected as the studied brand due to high number of Iranian fans and visitors. Thus, the study population included all fans of Adidas brand in Facebook social network. The number of samples, according to Morgan Law, included. Users of Adidas page with Iranian management, which were selected using simple random sampling method. The questionnaire was sent to personal page of more than 1,000 of fans of the brand, and a total of 109 responses were received. Definition and designing of the study structures were carried out with considering the research background (which was mentioned in the research literature). Also, to design the questionnaire and selecting the measures, some questions related to the same studies were used, and all the structures were examined and measured based on a 5-point Likert scale (1= strongly disagree, 5 = strongly agree) (It should be noted that the questionnaire validity was verified by experts in this area).

DATA COLLECTION

Data set for this study was collected through distributing electronic questionnaires[6] among the supporters and fans of Adidas brand page selected randomly. By providing some explanations about the purpose of the study and its applications at the beginning of the questionnaire, it was attempted to help the respondents so that they can complete the information related to demographic variables and answer the main questions with full consciousness and being ensured regarding the security and confidentiality of their information.

Examining the Questionnaire Reliability (Cronbach's Alpha)

To examine the questionnaire reliability, first, the Cronbach's alpha values of questions related to each of the structures were evaluated. However, the preliminary results showed that the Cronbach's alpha value of questions related to the expertise structure is low (0.59). In subsequent reviews and due to the similarity of this structure questions with questions of trust and motivation structures, it was decided to remove the expertise structure from the initial model. After applying the changes, the results in Table 1 were obtained.

Demographic Indices of Users

The first step to study and identify the social networks and their impact on marketing and advertising activities is to get familiar with demographic profile of the users. According to the study results, from 109 respondents, the results shown in Table 2 were obtained.

HYPOTHESES TESTING (REGRESSION ANALYSIS)

Due to the correlation nature of the relationships as well as the number of samples, five distinct regression analyses in SPSS were used to test the research hypotheses. Also according to the number of responses, the adjusted R2 outputs were evaluated for analysis of results. In hypothesis 1 (H1), the dependent and independent variables were trust in brand and customer satisfaction, respectively. After testing the hypothesis, a direct, positive and strong correlating between satisfaction and trust was found and confirmed. In hypotheses 2 and 3 (H2 and H3), the dependent and independent variables were respectively as motivation to engage in participate in WoM, and customer's satisfaction and trust that according to the results, the impact of both factors on motivation was confirmed. In hypotheses 4 and 5 (H4 and H5), the dependent variable was loyalty, while satisfaction and trust were independent variables. The results analysis confirmed the existence of a direct, strong and positive linear relationship between satisfaction and trust (as independent variables) and brand loyalty (as dependent variable); thus, H4 and H5 were also confirmed. In hypotheses 6 and 7 (H6 and H7), examining the relationship between loyalty, motivation and WoM in social networks, the WoM was the dependent variable, while motivation and WoM were independent variables that the presence of direct and positive linear relationship between two loyalty and motivation factors (as independent variables) and WoM (as dependent variable) was proved. The

Table 1. Cronbach's alpha coefficients of the research variables

Variables	Satisfaction of the Brand	Trusting the Brand	Motivation to Participate	Brand Loyalty	Participation in WoM	Consumer-Brand Identification
Cronbach's alpha coefficient	.9	.85	.77	.89	.88	.9

Table 2. Demographic characteristics of the target population

Gender		Marital Status		Education Level		Presence on Facebook		Age	
Male	61.5%	Single	91.7%	Below diploma	16.5%	Daily	73.4%	Less than 15 years	0%
Female	38.5%	Married	8.3%	Diploma & Associate's	32.1%	Weekly	%13.8	15-25	13.8%
				B.A	24.8%	Monthly	2.8%	26-35	
				M.A& Higher	26.6%	Rarely	10.1%	36-45	2.8%
								Over 45	0%

hypothesis 8 in which the dependent and independent variables were identity and loyalty, respectively, was also confirmed according to the SPSS results. Table 3 shows the results of SPSS analysis.

DISCUSSION, CONCLUSION, AND RESEARCH RECOMMENDATIONS

The present study objective was to investigate the impact of social networks on marketing processes with a focus on two main factors of brand loyalty and eWoM. Based on the research literature and background, we were looking to design a new model to explain the impact nature of customers' satisfaction and trust on brand loyalty, and also the effects of loyalty, motivation and expertise on WoM and consumer-identification through brand. Therefore, the SPSS software was used for data analysis. The analyses outputs from the beginning of the data collection process showed that the structure of expertise in this model has not the required reliability. Thus, it was omitted from the model, and a new relationship (the existence of which was confirmed during the data collection process) was added to the model. The results suggested that, although despite a linear relationship between satisfaction and trust has been questioned in previous research, but the findings of this study verified the hypothesis accuracy (Hypothesis 1). The analyses also suggested that although satisfaction and trust influence the customers' motivation to participate in WoM, but, the presence of a strong correlation and regression with a high correlation coefficient cannot be considered for them (Hypotheses 2 and 3).

In addition, a strong linear relationship between trust and satisfaction with customers' loyalty to the brand was approved in this study like previous studies (Hypothesis 4 and 5). In this model, two new relationships were also defined that either have been previously neglected or raised in some other form. The first relationship was the impact of advertising on brand loyalty on WoM (unlike previous models) (Hypothesis 6). The calculations results confirmed that brand loyalty and also the costumers' motivation have a significant positive effect on their WoM in social networks (Hypotheses 6 and 7). The second hypothesis claiming the direct and positive correlation between brand loyalty and willingness to identification through the brand (Hypothesis 8) was also fully verified. However, with detailed review of models, previous results and the current results, a remarkable and strongly recommended point for

Table 3. Multiple regression analysis and testing hypotheses

Hypothesis	Standard Coefficients		Non-Standard Coefficients	t	Sig	Result	R^2
	Beta	Std. Error	B				
H_1	.790	.040	.534	13.318	.000	Verified	.62
H_2	.286	.108	.235	2.183	.031	Verified	.3
H_3	.305	.160	.371	2.322	.022		
H_4	.632	.094	.637	6.760	.000	Verified	.645
H_5	.209	.139	.313	2.241	.027		
H_6	.630	.074	.623	8.374	.000	Verified	.545
H_7	.188	.091	.229	2.503	.014		
H_8	.767	.070	.865	12.365	.000	Verified	.584

future researchers is as follows: It would be perhaps better to establish a two-way relationship between brand loyalty and WoM; since, summarizing the results of this study and similar studies, such as Aceh Yu, Sanders and Moon (2013) studies, leads us to believe that these two factors are mutually influence each other. This means although the brand loyalty does not necessarily lead to participation in WoM, or one cannot say that the costumers participating in WoM would certainly be loyal to the brand, however, the characteristics of social networks nature and the ease in connecting with others in such environments makes it possible to use each of these factors as a predictor of future behavior of the customers. It also appears that the consumer-brand identification is also one of the factors affecting participation in eWoM, and adding this relation to the model will lead to its further enrichment. According to the results of our study and similar studies in this regard, it is quite evident that brands owners need to attend in social networks (especially Facebook) with purpose and planning. They should also identify their costumers and establish regular and constructive communication with them, those who are active in social networks. Use of Internet and social networks as a promotional tool seems to be effective to increase the sales rate of products with the lowest costs and improved quality and efficiency of the products.

As expected, Facebook members' willingness to participate in Internet research was low due to reasons such as information safety and fear of working with illegal organizations as well as and main functioning of this social network, i.e. entertaining and time-consuming feature of answering to the questions. This limitation along with the defined specific statistical population (Adidas brand fans on Facebook) increased the difficulty of collecting responses.

REFERENCES

Basuroy, S., Chatterjee, S., & Ravid, S. A. (2003). How critical are critical reviews? The box office effects of film critics, star-power, and budgets. *Journal of Marketing*, *67*(4), 103–117. doi:10.1509/jmkg.67.4.103.18692

Bhattacharya, C. B., & Sen, S. (2003). Consumer company identification: A framework for understanding consumers' relationships with companies. *Journal of Marketing*, *67*(2), 76–88. doi:10.1509/jmkg.67.2.76.18609

Brockand, S. J., & Barclay, D. W. (1997). The effects of organizational differences and trust on the effectiveness of selling partner relationships. *Journal of Marketing*, *61*(1), 3–21. doi:10.2307/1252186

Brown, J., Broderick, A. J., & Lee, N. (2007). Word of mouth communication within online communities: Conceptualizing the on line social networks. *Journal of Interactive Marketing*, *21*(3), 2–20. doi:10.1002/dir.20082

Casaló, L. V., Flavián, C., & Guinalíu, M. (2010). Relationship quality, community promotion and brand loyalty in virtual communities: Evidence from free software communities. *International Journal of Information Management*, *30*(4), 357–367. doi:10.1016/j.ijinfomgt.2010.01.004

Channel Advisor 2010 Consumer Shopping Habits Survey. Retrieved from http:// go.channeladvisor.com/rs/channeladvisor/ images/us-wp-consumer-survey-2010.pdf

Chen, S. C. (2012). The customer satisfaction–loyalty relation in an interactive e-service setting: The mediators. *Journal ofRetailing and Consumer Services*, *19*(2), 202–210. doi:10.1016/j.jretconser.2012.01.001

Cheung, C. M. K., & Thadani, D. R. (2010). The impact of electronic word-of-mouth communication: A literature analysis and integrative model. *Decision Support Systems*, *54*(1), 461–470. doi:10.1016/j.dss.2012.06.008

Chevalier, J. A., & Mayzlin, D. (2003). *The effect of word of mouth on sales: Online book reviews*. Available at Accessed on April 14, 2009, Retrived from: http://www.nber.org/papers/w10148

Coulter, K. S., & Roggeveen, A. L. (2012). Like it or not: Consumer responses to word-of-mouth communication in on-line social networks. *Management Research Review*, *35*(9), 878–899. doi:10.1108/01409171211256587

Davis, D., & Khazanchi, D. (2008). An empirical study of online word of mouth as a predictor for multi-product category e-commerce sales. *Journal of Electronic Markets*, *18*(2), 130–141. doi:10.1080/10196780802044776

Deci, E. L., & Ryan, R. M. (1985) *Intrinsic motivation and self-determination in human behavior*. New York: Plenum Press. Retrieved from: http://www.amazon.com/Intrinsic-Motivation-Self-Determination-Perspectives-Psychology/dp/0306420228

Deng, Z., Lu, Y., Wei, K. K., & Zhang, J. (2010). Understanding customer satisfaction and loyalty: An empirical study of mobile instant messages in China. *International Journal of Information Management*, *30*(4), 289–300. doi:10.1016/j.ijinfomgt.2009.10.001

Dobele, A., Lindgreen, A., Beverland, M., Vanhamme, J., & Wijk, R. V. (2007). Why pass on viral messages? Because they connect emotionally. *Business Horizons*, *50*(4), 291–304. doi:10.1016/j.bushor.2007.01.004

Flavian, C., Guinali, M., & Gurrea, R. (2006). The role played by perceived usability, satisfaction and consumer trust on website loyalty. *Journal of Information & Management*, *43*, 1–14. Retrieved from http://www.pageaccess.com/whitepapers/500ForresterUSInteractiveMktgForecast_2009_2014.pdf

Gambetta, D. (1988). *Trust: Making and Breaking Cooperative Relations*. Oxford, UK: Blackwell.

Garrigos-Simon, F. G., Alcamí, R. L., & Ribera, T. B. (2012). Social networks and Web 3.0: Their impact on the management and marketing of organizations. *Management Decision*, *50*(10), 1880–1890. doi:10.1108/00251741211279657

Gregurec, I., Tomas, B., & Coric, A. (2011). Word of Mouth Marketing within Social Networking Sites. *Proceedings of the 22nd Central European Conference on Information and Intelligent Systems Varazdin*, 227-233.

Gruen, T. W., Osmonbekov, T., & Czaplewsk, A. J. (2006). eWOM: The impact of customer-to-customer online know-how exchange on customer value and loyalty. *Journal of Business Research*, *59*(4), 449–456. doi:10.1016/j.jbusres.2005.10.004

Harris, L. C., & Goode, M. M. H. (2004). The four levels of loyalty and the pivotal role of trust: A study of online service dynamics. *Journal of Retailing*, *80*(2), 139–158. doi:10.1016/j.jretai.2004.04.002

Hennig, T., Walsh, T., & Walsh, G. (2003). Electronic Word of Mouth: Motives for and Consequences of Reading Customer Articulations on the Internet. *International Journal of Electronic Commerce*, *8*(2), 51–74.

Herr, P. M., Kardes, F. R., & Kim, J. (1991). The effects of word-of-mouth and product-attribute information on persuasion: An accessibility-diagnosticity perspective. *The Journal of Consumer Research*, *17*(4), 454–462. doi:10.1086/208570

Hu, N., Liu, L., & Zhang, J. (2008). Do online reviews affect product sales? The role of reviewer characteristics and temporal effects. *Journal of Information Technology and Management*, *9*, 201-214.

Laroche, M., Habibi, M. R., Richard, M. O., & Sankaranarayanan, R. (2012). The effects of social media based brand communities on brand community markers, value creation practices, brand trust and brand loyalty. *Computers in Human Behavior*, *28*, 1755–1767.

Leskovec, J., Adami, L. A., & Huberman, B. A. (2006). *The dynamics of viral marketing*. ACM Conference on Electronic Commerce, Ann Arbor, MI.

Li, Y. M., Lin, C. H., & Lai, C. Y. (2010). Identifying influential reviewers for word-of-mouth marketing. *Electronic Commerce Research and Applications*, *9*(4), 294–304. doi:10.1016/j.elerap.2010.02.004

Lin, C.-P., Tsai, Y. H., & Chiu, C.-K. (2009). Modeling Customer Loyalty from an Integrative Perspective of Self-Determination Theory and Expectation-Confirmation Theory. *Journal of Business and Psychology*, *24*(3), 315–326. doi:10.1007/s10869-009-9110-8

Lin, H. H., & Wang, Y. S. (2006). An examination of the determinants of customer loyalty in mobile commerce contexts. *Information & Management*, *43*(3), 271–282. doi:10.1016/j.im.2005.08.001

Mael, F. A., & Ashforth, B. E. (1992). Alumni and their alma mater: A partial test of the reformulated model of organizational identification. *Journal of Organizational Behavior*, *13*(2), 103–123. doi:10.1002/job.4030130202

Matthew, K. O., Lee, M. K. O., & Wang, C. (1995). Article. *Journal of Communications of The ACM-CACM*, *41*(3), 63–70.

Moore, R. E. (2003). From genericide to viral marketing: On "brand. *Journal of Language & Communication*, *23*(3–4), 331–357. doi:10.1016/S0271-5309(03)00017-X

Moorman, C., Zaltman, G., & Deshpandé, R. (1992). Relationships between providers and users of market research: The dynamics of trust within and between organizations. *JMR, Journal of Marketing Research*, *29*(3), 314–329. doi:10.2307/3172742

Muir, B. M., & Moray, N. (1996). Trust in automation. Part II. Experimental studies of trust and human intervention in a process control simulation. *Ergonomics*, *39*(3), 429–460. doi:10.1080/00140139608964474 PMID:8849495

Munns, A. K. (1995). influence of trust on the successful completion of a project. *International Journal of Project Management*, *13*(1), 19–24. doi:10.1016/0263-7863(95)95699-E

Park, C., & Lee, T. (2009). Information direction, website reputation and eWOM effect: A moderating role of product. *Journal of Business Research, 62*(1), 565–571. doi:10.1016/j.jbusres.2007.11.017

Reinstein, D. A., & Snyder, C. M. (2005). The influence of expert reviews on consumer demand for experience goods: A case study of movie critics. *The Journal of Industrial Economics, 53*(1), 27–51. doi:10.1111/j.0022-1821.2005.00244.x

Ribbink, D., Riel, A. C. R., Liljander, V., & Streukens, S. (2004). Comfort your online customer: Quality, trust and loyalty on the internet. *Managing Service Quality: An International Journal, 14*(6), 446–456. doi:10.1108/09604520410569784

Richardson, M., & Domingos, P. (2002). *Mining knowledge-sharing sites for viral marketing*. In *ACM SIGKDD International Conference on Knowledge Discovery and Data Mining*, Edmonton, Alberta, Canada.

Shapiro, C., & Varian, H. R. (1999). *Information rules: A strategic guide to the network economy*. Boston: Harvard Business School Press.

Shu, W., & Haddad, K. (2011). Word of mouth marketing on social network websites. *Journal of Service Science, 2* (2), 1-10.

Smith, R. E., & Vogt, C. (1995). The effects of integrating advertising and negative word-of-mouth communications on message processing and response. *Journal of Consumer Psychology, 4*(2), 133–151. doi:10.1207/s15327663jcp0402_03

Srinivasan, S. S., Anderson, R., & Ponnavolu, K. (2002). Customer loyalty in e-commerce: An exploration of its antecedents and consequences. *Journal of Retailing, 78*(1), 41–50. doi:10.1016/S0022-4359(01)00065-3

Sunderwood, R., Bond, E., & Baer, R. (2001). Service brands via social identity: Lessons from the sports marketplace. *Journal of Marketing Theory and Practice, 9*(1), 1-13.

Taylor, S. A., & Hunter, G. L. (2006). The impact of loyalty with e-CRM soft wares and e-services. *International Journal of Service Industry Management, 13*(5), 452–474. doi:10.1108/09564230210447931

Thoma, L. R., De Carlo, E., & Ramaswami, S. N. (2001). Consumers' Responses to Negative Word-of-Mouth Communication: An Attribution Theory Perspective. *Journal of Consumer Psychology, 11*(1), 57–73. doi:10.1207/S15327663JCP1101_5

Tong, W., & Xuecheng, Y. (2010). *Electronic Word of Mouth in Online Social Network. Second International Conference on Communication Systems, Networks and Applications.*

Toufaily, E., Ricard, L., & Perrien, J. (2012). Customer loyalty to a commercial website: Descriptive meta-analysis of the empirical literature and proposal of an integrative model. *Journal of Business Research, 66*(9), 1436–1447. doi:10.1016/j.jbusres.2012.05.011

Trusov, M., Bodapati, A., & Bucklin, R. (2010). Determining influential users in internet social networks. *JMR, Journal of Marketing Research, 47*(4), 643–658. doi:10.1509/jmkr.47.4.643

Trusov, M., Bucklin, R. E., & Pauwels, K. (2009). Effects of word-of-mouth versus traditional marketing: findings from an internet social networking site. *Journal of Marketing*, *73*(5), 90–103. doi:10.1509/jmkg.73.5.90

Ùahina, A., Zehir, C., & Kitapçı, H. (2012). The Effects of Brand Experiences, Trust and Satisfaction on Building Brand Loyalty; An Empirical Research On Global Brands. *Procedia: Social and Behavioral Sciences*, *24*, 1288–1301.

Wang, Y. S., Wub, S. C., Lin, H. H., & Wang, Y. Y. (2011). The relationship of service failure severity, service recovery justice and perceived switching costs with customer loyalty in the context of e-tailing. *International Journal of Information Management*, *31*(4), 350–359. doi:10.1016/j.ijinfomgt.2010.09.001

Woolfolk, A. (1995). *Educational psychology* (6th ed.). Boston, MA: Allyn & Bacon.

Yoo, C. W., Sanders, G. L., & Moon, J. (2013). Exploring the effect of e-WOM participation on e-Loyalty in e-commerce. *Journal of Decision Support Systems*, *55*(3), 669–678. doi:10.1016/j.dss.2013.02.001

Zhan, J., Loh, H. T., & Liu, Y. (2007). Gather customer concerns from online product reviews – a text summarization approach. *Journal of Expert Systems with Applications*, *36*(2), 2107–2115. doi:10.1016/j.eswa.2007.12.039

Zhu, F., & Zhang, X. (2010). Impact of online consumer reviews on sales: The moderating role of product and consumer characteristics. *Journal of Marketing*, *74*(2), 133–148. doi:10.1509/jmkg.74.2.133

KEY TERMS AND DEFINITIONS

E-WOM: Any positive or negative statement made by potential, actual, or former customers about a product or company, which is made available to a multitude of people and institutions via the Internet.

Expertise: Perceived competence of the source providing the information.

Identification: The willingness of users to be recognized and introducing themselves and their community (virtual social networks) to others through a particular brand.

Loyalty: A deeply held commitment to re-buy or re patronize a preferred product or service consistently in the future, despite situational influences and marketing efforts having the potential to cause switching behavior.

Motivation: A psychological state that induces, directs and maintains human behavior.

Satisfaction: A positive affective reaction to an outcome of a prior experience.

Trust: A willingness to rely on an exchange partner in whom one has confidence.

ENDNOTES

1 Word of mouth communication

2 Social network sites

3 mobile instant messages

4 Customer to customer

5 hierarchy of effects

6 An example of a research questionnaire after approval by experts in the scope of marketing and information technology was prepared as online (google doc) and sent to the users' personal page.

APPENDIX

Age: Less than 15 15 - 25 26 - 35 36 - 45 Over 46
Gender: Male Female
Marital Status: Single Married
Education level: Below diploma Diploma&Associate'sDegre B.A M.A & Higher
How much is your presence on social networking sites?
Daily Weekly Monthly Rarely
Answer to the following questions with:
Totally disagree Disagree No comment; Agree Totally agree

Questions

1. I am usually satisfied with Adidas products.
2. All my experiences with Adidas are satisfactory.
3. My decision to purchase from Adidas is wisely.
4. I think I am doing the right thing by purchasing from Adidas.
5. Comparing to my expectations, Adidas always produce what I want.
6. Based on my experience, I know that Adidas is quite truthful.
7. In my experience, I know that Adidas supports its customers.
8. Based on my experience, I know that Adidas is not opportunistic.
9. I think Adidas has enough experience in its working field.
10. Adidas is professional in its business.
11. Adidas is looking to fulfill its obligations.
12. What Adidas says about itself is true.
13. I think some of Adidas claims about its products are exaggerated.
14. I would like to help others in social networks using my positive shopping experiences.
15. I and my other friends in social networks try to buy from the same brands.
16. I feel good when I talk with people about my success purchase in social networks.
17. Talking with others about brands in social networks is interesting
18. People who share their opinions about brands on social networks have adequate knowledge in evaluating the quality of the brands
19. The members of social networks are quite familiar with
20. All existing brands in the case of a particular commodity
21. The members of social networks are interested to learn about brands
22. When I am asked to comment at social networks, I will recommend a particular brand to them
23. I usually post positive points about Adidas on social networks
24. I encourage my family and friends on social networks to the use Adidas products
25. I rarely miss an opportunity to give advice to others to by Adidas products
26. I prefer Adidas products to its other competitors
27. I will continue to choose Adidas
28. I love using Adidas products
29. I rarely change my favorite brand

Compilation of References

Aaker, D. A. (1991). *Managing brand equity: Capitalizing on the value of a brand name*. New York, NY: The Free Press.

Aaker, D. A. (1996a). *Building strong brands*. New York, NY: The Free Press.

Aaker, D. A. (1996b). Measuring Brand Equity Across Products and Markets. *Journal of California Management Review*, *38*(3), 102–120. doi:10.2307/41165845

Ab Hamid, N. R., & Kassim, N. (2004). Internet technology as a tool in customer relationship management. *Journal of American Academy of Business*, *4*(1/2), 103–108.

Abedin, B. (2011). Web 2.0 and Online Learning and Teaching: A Preliminary Benchmarking Study, *Asian. Social Science*, *7*(11), 5–12.

Abedin, B., & Jafarzadeh, H. (2013). Attracting and retaining customers on Facebook business pages: A Content Analysis of an Online Discussion Forum. *International Journal of Technology Marketing*, *8*(3), 304–315. doi:10.1504/IJTMKT.2013.055340

Abor, J., & Quartey, P. (2010). Issues in SME development in Ghana and South Africa. *International Research Journal of Finance and Economics*, *39*, 218–228.

Accenture. (2011). *Maximizing Customer Retention: A Strategic Approach to Effective Churn Management* [PDF document]. Retrieved from http://www.accenture.com/SiteCollectionDocuments/PDF/Accenture-Maximizing-Customer-Retention.pdf

Adebanjo, D. (2003). Classifying and selecting e-CRM applications: An analysis-based proposal. *Management Decision*, *41*(6), 570–577. doi:10.1108/00251740310491517

Aertsens, J., Mondelaers, K., Verbeke, W., Buysse, J., & Huylenbroeck, G. V. (2011). The influence of subjective and objective knowledge on attitude, motivations and consumption of organic food. *British Food Journal*, *113*(11), 1353–1378. doi:10.1108/00070701111179988

Aggarwal, C., & Zhai, C. (2012). Mining text data. *Mining Text Data*, *4*(2(63)), 889–903. doi:10.1007/978-1-4614-3223-4

Agyapong, D. (2010). Micro, Small and Medium Enterprises' activities, income level and poverty reduction in Ghana – A synthesis of related literature. *International Journal of Business and Management*, *5*(12), 196–205. doi:10.5539/ijbm.v5n12p196

Aharony, N. (2009). Web 2.0 use by librarians. *Library & Information Science Research*, *31*(1), 29–37. doi:10.1016/j.lisr.2008.06.004

Ahearne, M., Jelinek, R., & Rapp, A. (2005). Moving Beyond the Direct Effect of SFA Adoption on Salesperson Performance: Training and Support as Key Moderating Factors. *Journal of Marketing Development and Competitiveness*, *8*(1), 2014.

Ahuja, V., & Medury, Y. (2010, March23). Corporate blogs as e-CRM tools-building customer engagement through content Management. *Journal of Databases Marketing & Customer Strategy Management*, *17*(2), 91–105. doi:10.1057/dbm.2010.8

AIMIA & SENSIS. (2012). *What Australian people and businesses are doing with social media*. Retrieved from https://www.sensis.com.au/about/our-reports/yellow-social-media-report-2014

Akyene, T. (2012). Cell Phone Evaluation Base on Entropy and TOPSIS. *Interdisciplinary Journal of Research in Business*, *1*(12), 9–15.

Akyıldız, M., & Argan, M. (2011). Using online social networking: Students' purposes of Facebook usage at the university of Turkey. *Journal of Technology Research*, *3*, 95–104. Retrieved from http://www.aabri.com/manuscripts/111085.pdf

Alexa, E. L., Alexa, M., & Stoica, C. M. (2012). The use of online marketing and social media in higher education institutions in Romania. *Journal of Marketing Research & Case Studies*, 1-9. Retrieved 13 August, 2014, from http://www.ibimapublishing.com/journals/JMRCS/2012/721221/721221.pdf

Algesheimer, R., Dholakia, U. M., & Herrmann, A. (2005). The social influence of brand community: Evidence from European car clubs. *Journal of Marketing*, *69*(3), 19–34. doi:10.1509/jmkg.69.3.19.66363

Alrubaiee, L., & Al-Nazer, N. (2010). Investigate the impact of relationship marketing orientation on customer loyalty: The customer's perspective. *International Journal of Marketing Studies*, *2*(1), 155–174. doi:10.5539/ijms.v2n1p155

Anderson, E. W., Fornell, C., & Lehmann, D. R. (1994). Customer satisfaction, market share, and profitability: Findings from Sweden. *Journal of Marketing*, *58*(3), 53–66. doi:10.2307/1252310

Andzulis, J., Panagopoulos, N. G., & Rapp, A. (2012). A review of social media and implications for the sales process. *Journal of Personal Selling & Sales Management*, *32*(3), 305–316. doi:10.2753/PSS0885-3134320302

Ariely, D. (2008). *Predictably Irrational: The Hidden Forces That Shape Our Decisions*. New York, NY: Harper Collins.

Aryeetey, E. (2001). Priority Research Issues Relating to Regulation and Competition in Ghana. Centre on Regulation and Competition Working Paper Series. *Management Decision*, *41*(6), 570–577.

Ashenden, P. (October 31, 2014). Social customer service: the benefits and challenges. [Web log comment]. Retrieved from https://eptica.wordpress.com/2014/10/31/meeting-rising-customer-expectations-on-social-media/

Asnafi, A. R., & Osareh, F. (2007). A study of collaboration among Iranian News Agencies websites using Webometrics methods. *Collnet Journal of Scientometrics and Information Management*, *1*(1), 23–26. doi:10.1080/09720502.2007.10700950

Atilgan, E., Aksoy, S., & Akinci, S. (2005). Determinants of the brand equity. A verification approach in thebeverage industry in Turkey. *Marketing Intelligence & Planning*, *23*(3), 237–248. doi:10.1108/02634500510597283

Avram, G. (2006). At the crossroads of knowledge management and social software. *Electronic Journal of Knowledge Management*, *4*(1), 1–10.

Awad, E. M., & Ghaziri, H. M. (2004). *Knowledge Management*. Upper Saddle River, NJ: Pearson/Prentice-Hall.

Baird, C. H., & Parasnis, G. (2011). *From social media to Social CRM: What customers want The first in a two-part series* [PDF document]. Retrieved from http://public.dhe.ibm.com/common/ssi/ecm/en/gbe03391usen/GBE03391USEN.PDF

Baird, C. H., & Parasnis, G. (2011). From social media to social relationship management. *Strategy and Leadership*, *39*(5), 30–37. doi:10.1108/10878571111161507

Baloglu, A., & Aktas, M. S. (2010). BlogMiner: Web blog mining application for classification of movie reviews. In *5th International Conference on Internet and Web Applications and Services*, ICIW 2010 (pp. 77–84). doi:10.1109/ICIW.2010.19

Bang, J. (2005). *Understanding customer relationship management from managers' and customers' perspective: Exploring the implications of CRM fit, market orientation, and market knowledge competence.* (Ph.D. dissertation). University of Rhode Island, Kingston, RI. Retrieved May 06, 2012, from ABI/INFORM Global.

Basuroy, S., Chatterjee, S., & Ravid, S. A. (2003). How critical are critical reviews? The box office effects of film critics, star-power, and budgets. *Journal of Marketing*, *67*(4), 103–117. doi:10.1509/jmkg.67.4.103.18692

Bauer, Ch., & Scharl, A. (2000). Quantitive evaluation of Web site content and structure. *Internet Research*, *10*(1), 31–44. doi:10.1108/10662240010312138

Beatty, S. E., & Kahle, L. R. (1988). Alternative hierarchies of the attitude-behavior relationship: The impact of brand commitment and habit. *Journal of the Academy of Marketing Science*, *16*(2), 1–10. doi:10.1007/BF02723310

Beharrell, B., & Crockett, A. (1992). New Age Food! New Age Consumers! *British Food Journal*, *94*(2), 5–13. doi:10.1108/00070709210018979

Behzadian, M., Khanmohammadi, O. S., Yazdani, M., & Ignatius, J. (2012). A state-of the-art survey of TOPSIS applications. *Expert Systems with Applications*, *39*(17), 13051–13069. doi:10.1016/j.eswa.2012.05.056

Bélanger, C. H., Bali, S., & Longden, B. (2014). How Canadian universities use social media to brand themselves. *Tertiary Education and Management*, *20*(1), 14–29. doi:10.1080/13583883.2013.852237

Bennett, R., & Rundle-Thiele, S. (2002). A comparison of attitudinal loyalty measurement approaches. *Journal of Brand Management*, *9*(3), 193–209. doi:10.1057/palgrave.bm.2540069

Bennett, S., Bishop, A., Dalgarno, B., Waycott, J., & Kennedy, G. (2012). Implementing Web 2.0 technologies in higher education: A collective case study. *Computers & Education*, *59*(2), 524–534. doi:10.1016/j.compedu.2011.12.022

Benzing, C., & Chu, H. M. (2009). A comparison of the motivations of small business owners in Africa. *Journal of Small Business and Enterprise Development*, *16*(1), 60–77. doi:10.1108/14626000910932881

Beqiri, G. (2014). The impact of social media on higher education in Kosovo: The student's perspective. *Academic Journal of Interdisciplinary Studies*, *3*(2), 155–163.

Berger, J., Sorensen, A. T., & Rasmussen, S. J. (2010). Positive Effects of Negative Publicity: When Negative Reviews Increase Sales. *Marketing Science*, *29*(5), 815–827. doi:10.1287/mksc.1090.0557

Berry, L. L. (2002). Relationship Marketing of Services-Perspectives from 1983 & 2000. *Journal of Relationship Marketing*, *1*(1), 59–77. doi:10.1300/J366v01n01_05

Berthon, P., Page, M., & Pitt, L. (1996). Analysing and reducing customer defections. *Long Range Planning*, *29*(6), 821–834. doi:10.1016/S0024-6301(97)82819-1

Bharadwaj, S. G., Varadarajan, P. R., & Fahy, J. (1993). Sustainable Competitive Advantage in Service Industries: A Conceptual Model and Research Propositions. *Journal of Marketing*, *57*(Oct), 83–99. doi:10.2307/1252221

Bhattacharya, C. B., & Sen, S. (2003). Consumer company identification: A framework for understanding consumers' relationships with companies. *Journal of Marketing*, *67*(2), 76–88. doi:10.1509/jmkg.67.2.76.18609

Bitner, M. J. (1990). Evaluating service encounters: The effects of physical surroundings and employee responses. *Journal of Marketing*, *54*(4), 69–82. doi:10.2307/1251871

Björneborn, L. (2004). *Small-World Link Structures across an Academic Web Space: A Library and Information Science Approach*. Royal School of Library and Information Science, Denmark. Retrieved from http://vip.db.dk/lb/phd/phd-thesis.pdf

Blackshaw, P., & Nazzaro, M. (2004). *Consumer-Generated Media (CGM) 101: Word-of-mouth in the age of the Web fortified consumer* [PDF document]. Retrieved from http://www.brandchannel.com/images/papers/222_cgm.pdf

Blau, P. M. (1964). *Exchange and Power in Social Life*. New York, NY: John Wiley.

Blery, E. K., & Michalakopoulos, M. G. (2006). An e-CRM application in the telecommunications sector: A case study from Greece. *EUROMED Journal of Business*, *1*(2), 5–14. doi:10.1108/14502190610750135

Blohm, I., & Leimeister, J. M. (2013). Gamification - Design of IT-Based Enhancing Services for Motivational Support and Behavioral Change. *Business & Information Systems Engineering*, *5*(4), 275–278. doi:10.1007/s12599-013-0273-5

Bloom, J. Z. (2005). Market segmentation. A neural network application. *Annals of Tourism Research*, *32*(1), 93–111. doi:10.1016/j.annals.2004.05.001

Bolton, R. N., Kannan, P. K., & Bramlett, M. D. (2000). Implications of Loyalty Program Membership and Service Experiences for Customer Retention and Value. *Journal of the Academy of Marketing Science*, *28*(1), 95–108. doi:10.1177/0092070300281009

Boonghee, Y., & Donthu, N. (2001). Developing and validating a multidimensioanl consumer-based brand equityscale. *Journal of Business Research, 52*(1), 1–14. doi:10.1016/S0148-2963(99)00098-3

Boorstin, D. J. (1974). *The Americans: The Democratic Experience*. New York, NY: Vintage.

Bosch, T. E. (2009). Using online social networking for teaching and learning: Facebook use at the University of Cape Town. *Comnunicatio, 35*(2), 185–200. doi:10.1080/02500160903250648

Boselli, R., Cesarini, M., & Mezzanzanica, M. (2008). Customer knowledge and service development, the web 2.0 role in co-production. *Proceedings of World Academy of Science,Engineering, and Technology, 30*(1), 1–20.

Boston Consulting Group. (2011). *The power of social business: Lessons from Grameen experiences*. retrieved July 16 2014 from https://www.bcgperspectives.com/content/articles/corporate_social_responsibility_poverty_hunger_power_social_business

Boström & Svensson. (2013). *CRM through Social Media and its effect on Brand Loyalty*. Luleå University of Technology.

Botzenhardt, A., Witt, A., & Maedche, A. (2011). A Text Mining Application for Exploring the Voice of the Customer. In *Proceedings of the Seventeenth Americas Conference on Information Systems* (pp. 1–11). Retrieved from http://aisel.aisnet.org/amcis2011_submissions/274

Boyd, D. M., & Ellison, N. B. (2007). Social Networks Sites: Definition, History, and Scholarship. *Journal of Computer-Mediated Communication", 13(1)*, 210-230. Retrieved fromhttp://jcmc.indiana.edu/vol13/issue1/boyd.ellison.html

Boyd, D. M., & Ellison, N. B. (2011). Social Network Sites: Definition, History, and Scholarship. *IEEE Engineering Management Review, 38*(3), 16–31. doi:10.1109/EMR.2010.5559139

Bradshaw, D., & Brash, C. (2001). Managing customer relationships in the e-business world: How to personalize computer relationships for increased profitability. *International Journal of Retail & Distribution Management, 29*(12), 520–530. doi:10.1108/09590550110696969

Brady, K. P., Holcomb, L. B., & Smith, B. V. (2010). The use of alternative social networking sites in higher educational settings: A case study of the e-learning benefits of ning in education. *Journal of Interactive Online Learning, 9*(2), 151–170.

Brady, M. K., & Cronin, J. (2001). Customer Orientation: Effects on Customer Service Perceptions and Outcome Behaviors. *Journal of Service Research, 3*(3), 241–251. doi:10.1177/109467050133005

Brajnik, G. (2004). Using automatic tools in accessibility and usability assurance. In *User-Centered Interaction Paradigms for Universal Access in the Information Society (pp. 219-234)*. New York, NY: Springer. doi:10.1007/978-3-540-30111-0_18

Brockand, S. J., & Barclay, D. W. (1997). The effects of organizational differences and trust on the effectiveness of selling partner relationships. *Journal of Marketing, 61*(1), 3–21. doi:10.2307/1252186

Brodie, R. J., Hollebeek, L. D., Juric, B., & Ilic, A. (2011). Customer engagement: Conceptual domain, fundamental propositions, and implications for research. *Journal of Service Research, 14*(3), 252–271. doi:10.1177/1094670511411703

Brogi, S., Calabrese, A., Campisi, D., Capace, G., Costa, R., & Pillo, F. D. (2013). The effects of online brand communit- ieson brand equity in the luxury fashion industry. *International Journal of Engineering Business Management, 5*(32), 1–9. doi:10.5772/56854

Brown, J., Broderick, A. J., & Lee, N. (2007). Word of mouth communication within online communities: Conceptualizing the on line social networks. *Journal of Interactive Marketing, 21*(3), 2–20. doi:10.1002/dir.20082

Brown, S. A., & Coopers, P. W. (2000). *Customer relationship management: A strategic imperative in the world of e-business*. New York, NY: John Wiley & Sons, Inc.

Brugmann, J., & Prahalad, C. (2007). *Concreting business's new social compact*. Boston: Harvard Business-Review.

Bunchball, I. (2010). *Gamification 101: An Introduction to the Use of Game Dynamics to Influence Behavior*. White paper.

Burke, B. (2014). *Gamify: How gamification motivates people to do extraordinary things*. Bibliomotion, Inc.

Buttle, F. (2004). *Customer relationship management: Concepts and tools. Butterworth-Heinemann*. Amsterdam: Elsevier.

Byrne, P. J., Toensmeyer, U. C., German, C. L., & Muller, H. R. (1992). Evaluation of consumer attitudes towards organic produce in Delaware and the Delmarva region. *Journal of Food Distribution Research*, *23*(1), 29–44.

Canvas Business Model. (n.d.). Retrieved September 15 2014 from http://businessmodelgeneration.com/canvas/bmc

Cappex.com. (2010). *Establishing a benchmark for social media use in college admissions*. 2010 Social Media and College Admissions Study, Retrieved 01 July, 2014, from http://www.cappex.com/media/EstablishingABenchmarkForSocialMediaUse.pdf

Carson, D., & Gilmore, A. (2000). SME Marketing Management Competencies. *International Business Review*, *9*(3), 363–382. doi:10.1016/S0969-5931(00)00006-8

Casaló, L. V., Flavián, C., & Guinalíu, M. (2010). Relationship quality, community promotion and brand loyalty in virtual communities: Evidence from free software communities. *International Journal of Information Management*, *30*(4), 357–367. doi:10.1016/j.ijinfomgt.2010.01.004

Caudill, M. (1987). Neural Networks Premier Part I. *AI Expert*, *2*(12), 46–52.

Chai, K., Potdar, V., & Chang, E. (2006). A survey of revenue models for current generation social software's systems. Lecture Notes in Computer Science, 4704, 724-38.

Chai-Lee, G. (2013). *The use of social media in education: A perspective*. Paper presented at 2nd International Higher Education Teaching and Learning Conference. Retrieved 23 June, 2014, from http://www.curtin.edu.my/tl2013/PDF/The%20Use%20of%20Social%20Media%20in%20Education_%20A%20Perspective.pdf

Chang, A., Hsieh, S. H., & Lin, F. (2013). Personality Traits That Lead Members of Online Brand Communities to Participate in Information Sending and Receiving. *International Journal of Electronic Commerce*, *17*(3), 37–62. doi:10.2753/JEC1086-4415170302

Chang, A., Hsieh, S. H., & Tseng, T. H. (2013). Online brand community response to negative brand events: The role of group eWOM. *Internet Research*, *23*(4), 486–506. doi:10.1108/IntR-06-2012-0107

Chang, C. W., Lin, C. T., & Wang, L. Q. (2009). Mining the text information to optimizing the customer relationship management. *Expert Systems with Applications*, *36*(2 PART 1), 1433–1443. doi:10.1016/j.eswa.2007.11.027

Changchien, S. W., & Lu, T. C. (2001). Mining association rules procedure to support on-line recommendation by customers and products fragmentation. *Expert Systems with Applications*, *20*(4), 325–335. doi:10.1016/S0957-4174(01)00017-3

Chang, H. H., & Liu, Y. M. (2009). The impact of brand equity on brand preference and purchase intentions in the service industries. *Service Industries Journal*, *29*(12), 1687–1706. doi:10.1080/02642060902793557

Channel Advisor 2010 Consumer Shopping Habits Survey. Retrieved from http:// go.channeladvisor.com/rs/channeladvisor/ images/us-wp-consumer-survey-2010.pdf

Chaston, I., & Mangles, T. (2003). Relationship marketing in online business-to-business markets: A pilot investigation of small UK manufacturing firms. *European Journal of Marketing*, *37*(5/6), 753–773. doi:10.1108/03090560310465134

Chaudhuri, A. (1997). Consumption emotion and perceived risk: A macro analytic approach. *Journal of Business Research, 39*(2), 81-92. Retrieved from.10.1016/S0148-2963(96)00144-0

Chaudhuri, A., & Holbrook, M. B. (2001). The chain of effects from brand trust and brand affect to brand performance: The role of brand loyalty. *Journal of Marketing*, *65*(2), 81–93. doi:10.1509/jmkg.65.2.81.18255

Chen, C. H., Khoo, L. P., & Yan, W. (2002). A strategy for acquiring customer requirement patterns using laddering technique and ART2 neural network. *Advanced Engineering Informatics*, *16*(3), 229–240. doi:10.1016/S1474-0346(03)00003-X

Chen, M. C., Chiu, A. L., & Chang, H. H. (2005). Mining changes in customer behavior in retail marketing. *Expert Systems with Applications*, *28*(4), 773–781. doi:10.1016/j.eswa.2004.12.033

Chen, S. C. (2012). The customer satisfaction–loyalty relation in an interactive e-service setting: The mediators. *Journal of Retailing and Consumer Services, 19*(2), 202–210. doi:10.1016/j.jretconser.2012.01.001

Cheung, C. M. K., & Thadani, D. R. (2010). The impact of electronic word-of-mouth communication: A literature analysis and integrative model. *Decision Support Systems, 54*(1), 461–470. doi:10.1016/j.dss.2012.06.008

Chevalier, J. A., & Mayzlin, D. (2003). *The effect of word of mouth on sales: Online book reviews.* Available at Accessed on April 14, 2009, Retrived from: http://www.nber.org/papers/w10148

Chinnici, G., D'Amico, M., & Pecorino, B. (2002). A multivariate statistical analysis on the consumers of organic products. *British Food Journal, 104*(3/4/5), 187-199. doi: 10.1108/00070700210425651

Chin, W. W. (1998). *The Partial Least Squares Approach for Structural Equation Modeling in Modern Methods for Business Research.* Mahwah, NJ: Lawrence Erlbaum Associates.

Chiu, C. M., Huang, H. Y., & Yen, C. H. (2010). Antecedents of online trust in onlineauctions. *Electronic Commerce Research and Applications, 9*(2), 148–159. doi:10.1016/j.elerap.2009.04.003

Chiware, E. R. T., & Dick, A. L. (2008). The use of ICTs in Namibia's SME sector to access business information services. *The Electronic Library, 26*(2), 145–157. doi:10.1108/02640470810864055

Cho, J., & Adams, R. (2005). Page Quality: In Search of an Unbiased Web Ranking. In *Proceedings of the 2005 ACM SIGMOD conference* (pp.551-562), Baltimore, MD: ACM.

Chorney, A. I. (2012). *Taking The Game Out Of Gamification.* Dalhousie Journal of Interdisciplinary Management.

Christodoulides, G., De Chernatony, L., Furrer, O., Shiu, E., & Abimbola, T. (2006). Conceptualising and Measuring the Equity of Online Brands. *Journal of Marketing Management, 22*(7-8), 799–825. doi:10.1362/026725706778612149

Chung, C., & Austria, K. "Social media gratification and attitude toward social media marketing messages: A study of the effect of social media marketing messages on online shopping value," *Proceedings of the Northeast Business&Economics Association*, p581, 2010.

Chu, S. C., & Kim, Y. (2011). Determinants of consumer engagement in electronic word of mouth (eWOM) in social networking sites. *International Journal of Advertising, 30*(1), 47–75. doi:10.2501/IJA-30-1-047-075

CNN Money. (2006). *Circuit city enters second life.* Retrieved from http://money.cnn.com/2006/12/15/news/companies/bestbuy sl/index.htm

Cole, Z. (2011, December 7). Social Business: Using Marketing Mix Modeling to Maximize ROI.*Socialbusinessnews.com.* Retrieved from http://www.socialbusinessnews.com/marketing-mix-model/

Colet, E. (2000). Clustering and Classification: Data Mining Approaches. *Tabor Communications.* Retrieved from http://www.tgc.com/dsstar/00/0704/101861.html

Constant, D., Sproull, L., & Kiesler, S. (1996). The kindness of strangers: The usefulness of electronic weak ties for technical advice. *JournalOrganization Science, 7*(2), 119–135. doi:10.1287/orsc.7.2.119

Constantinides, E., & Fountain, S. J. (2008). Web 2.0: Conceptual foundations and marketing issues, *Journal of Direct. Data and Digital Marketing Practice, 9*(3), 231–244. doi:10.1057/palgrave.dddmp.4350098

Constantinides, E., & Stagno, M. C. Z. (2011). Potential of the social media as instruments of higher education marketing: A segmentation study. *Journal of Marketing for Higher Education, 21*(1), 7–24. doi:10.1080/08841241.2011.573593

Cook, P., & Nixson, F. (2000). *Finance and small and medium-sized enterprise development.* Institute for Development Policy and Management, University of Manchester.

Cornin,J.J., Brady, M.K.,&Hult, G.T.(2000). Assessing the effects of quality, value, and customer satisfaction on consumer behavioural intentions in service environments. *Journal of Retailing, 76(2)*, 193-218. Retrieved from.10.1016/S0022-4359(00)00028-2

Costa, P. T. Jr, & McCrae, R. R. (1995). Domains and facets: Hierarchical personality assessment using the revised NEO personality inventory. *Journal of Personality Assessment*, *64*(1), 21–50. doi:10.1207/s15327752jpa6401_2 PMID:16367732

Coulter, K. S., & Roggeveen, A. L. (2012). Like it or not: Consumer responses to word-of-mouth communication in on-line social networks. *Management Research Review*, *35*(9), 878–899. doi:10.1108/01409171211256587

Coviello, N. E., Brodie, R. J., & Munro, H. J. (2000). An investigation of marketing practice by firm size. *Journal of Business Venturing*, *15*(5-6), 523–545. doi:10.1016/S0883-9026(98)00035-4

Cronbach, L. J. (1970). *Essentials of psychological testing*. New York, NY: Harper and Row.

Crosby, L. A., & Taylor, J. R. (1983). Psychological Commitment and Its Effects on Post-Decision Evaluation and Preference Stability Among Voters. *The Journal of Consumer Research*, *9*(4), 413–431. doi:10.1086/208935

Culnan, M. J., Mchugh, P. J., & Zubillaga, J. I. (2010). How Large U.S. Companies Can Use Twitter and Other Social Media to Gain Business Value. *MIS Quarterly Executive*, *9*(4), 243–260.

Cunningham, M. J. (2002). *Customer relationship management: Marketing 04.04(Express Exec.)*. Oxford, United Kingdom: Capstone.

Currie, J. P. (2010). Web 2.0 for reference services staff training and communication. *RSR. Reference Services Review*, *38*(1), 152–157. doi:10.1108/00907321011020789

Dangayach, G. S., & Deshmukh, S. G. (2005). Advanced manufacturing technology implementation: Evidence from Indian small and medium enterprises (SMEs). *Journal of Manufacturing Technology Management*, *16*(5), 483–496. doi:10.1108/17410380510600473

Daniel, T. A., & McInerney, M. L. (2005). E-commerce and the 'reluctant' small business owner: How technology is changing the business model for small and medium-sized enterprises (SMEs). *The International Journal of Applied Management and Technology*, *3*, 183–206.

Das, D. (2012). PREMASA Model: An Integrated Approach To Customer Relationship Management. *IEM International Journal of Management & Technology*, *2*(1), 111–118.

Dataforeningen. (2010). *Mellomrapport; Norske virksomheters bruk avsosiale medier*. Retrieved Jun 14, 2011, from: http://www.kommunikasjon.no/Foreningen/Nyheter/_attachment/7822?=true&_ts=127f21c4f8b

Datamonitor. (n.d.). Old Spice Case Study: Using Social Media to Revitalise a Brand. Available at: http://www.datamonitor.com/store/Product/old_spice_case_study_using_social_media_to_revitalise_a_brand?productid=CM00056-004

Daugherty, T., Eastin, M. S., & Bright, L. (2008). Exploring Consumer Motivations for Creating User-Generated Content. *Journal of Interactive Advertising*, *8*(2), 16–25. doi:10.1080/15252019.2008.10722139

Davenport, T. H. (2006). Competing on analytics. *Harvard Business Review*, *84*(1), 98–107, 134. http://doi.org/Article PMID:16447373

Davenport, T. H., Harris, J. G., & Kohli, A. K. (2001). How do they know their customers so well? *MIT Sloan Management Review*, *42*(2), 63–73.

David, A. (1991). *Managing Brand Equity: Capitalizing on the Value of a Brand Name*. New York, NY: The Free Press.

Davidson, R. (2011). Web 2.0 as a marketing tool for conference centres. *International Journal of Event and Festival Management*, *2*(2), 117–138. doi:10.1108/17582951111136559

Davies, A., Titterington, A. J., & Cochrane, C. (1995). Who Buys Organic Food? A Profile of the Purchasers of Organic Food in Northern Ireland. *British Food Journal*, *97*(10), 17–23. doi:10.1108/00070709510104303

Davis, D., & Khazanchi, D. (2008). An empirical study of online word of mouth as a predictor for multi-product category e-commerce sales. *Journal of Electronic Markets*, *18*(2), 130–141. doi:10.1080/10196780802044776

Day, G. (2000). Managing market relationships. *Journal of the Academy of Marketing Science*, *28*(1), 24–30. doi:10.1177/0092070300281003

Day, S. G., & Hubbard, J. K. (2003). Customer relationships go digital. *Business Strategy Review*, *14*(1), 17–26. doi:10.1111/1467-8616.00240

DeAndrea, D. C., Ellison, N. B., LaRose, R., Steinfield, C., & Fiore, A. (2012). Serious social media: On the use of social media for improving students' adjustment to college. *The Internet and Higher Education*, *15*(1), 15–23. doi:10.1016/j.iheduc.2011.05.009

Dearstyne, B. (2007). Blogs, mashups & wikis: Oh, my! *Information Management Journal*, *41*(4), 25–31.

Deci, E. L., & Ryan, R. M. (1985) *Intrinsic motivation and self-determination in human behavior*. New York: Plenum Press. Retrieved from: http://www.amazon.com/Intrinsic-Motivation-Self-Determination-Perspectives-Psychology/dp/0306420228

Delgado-Ballester, E., Manuera-Aleman, J. L., & Yague-Guillen, M. J. (2003). Development and validation of a brand trust scale. *International Journal of Market Research*, *45*(1), 35–54.

Dellarocas, C., Zhang, X. M., & Awad, N. F. (2007). Exploring the value of online product reviews in forecasting sales: The case of motion pictures. *Journal of Interactive Marketing*, *21*(4), 23–45. doi:10.1002/dir.20087

Demeritt, L. (2002). *All things organic 2002: A look at the organic consumer*. Bellevue, WA: The Hartman Group.

Deng, Z., Lu, Y., Wei, K. K., & Zhang, J. (2010). Understanding customer satisfaction and loyalty: An empirical study of mobile instant messages in China. *International Journal of Information Management*, *30*(4), 289–300. doi:10.1016/j.ijinfomgt.2009.10.001

Deshpande, R., Farley, J. U., & Webster, F. E. (1993). Corporate Culture, Customer Orientation, and Innovativeness in Japanese Firms: A Quadrad Analysis. *Journal of Marketing*, *57*(1), 23–37. doi:10.2307/1252055

Desouza, K. C., & Awazu, Y. (2005). Maintaining knowledge management systems: A strategic imperative. *Journal of the American Society for Information Science and Technology*, *56*(7), 765–768. doi:10.1002/asi.20149

Deterding, S., Sicart, M., Nacke, L., O'Hara, K., & Dixon, D. (2011, May). Gamification. using game-design elements in non-gaming contexts. In CHI'11 Extended Abstracts on Human Factors in Computing Systems. Vancouver, BC, Canada.

Deterding, S. (2014). Eudaimonic Design, or: Six Invitations to Rethink Gamification. In M. Fuchs, S. Fizek, P. Ruffino, & N. Schrape (Eds.), *Rethinking Gamification*. Meson press.

Deterding, S., Dixon, D., Khaled, R., & Nacke, L. (2011). From game design elements to gamefulness: defining gamification. In *Proceedings of the 15th International Academic MindTrek Conference: Envisioning Future Media Environments*. Tampere, Finland. doi:10.1145/2181037.2181040

Dhar, V., & Chang, E. A. (2009). Does chatter matter? The impact of user-generated content on music sales. *Journal of Interactive Marketing, 23(4,),* 300–307.

Diamantopoulos, A., & Siguaw, J. A. (2006). Formative versus Reflective Indicators in Organizational Measure Development: A Comparison and Empirical Illustration. *British Journal of Management*, *17*(4), 263–282. doi:10.1111/j.1467-8551.2006.00500.x

Diamantopoulos, A., & Winklhofer, H. M. (2001). Index Construction with Formative Indicators: An Alternative to Scale Development. *JMR, Journal of Marketing Research*, *38*(2), 269–277. doi:10.1509/jmkr.38.2.269.18845

Divol, R., Edelman, D., & Sarrazin, H. (2012). (*Producer*). Demystifying Social Media.

Dobele, A., Lindgreen, A., Beverland, M., Vanhamme, J., & Wijk, R. V. (2007). Why pass on viral messages? Because they connect emotionally. *Business Horizons*, *50*(4), 291–304. doi:10.1016/j.bushor.2007.01.004

Dobney.com. (2008). *What is customer knowledge*. Retrieved from www.dobney.com/Knowledge/ck_definition.htm

Doherty, R. (2000). Click stream reporting & analysis for Website optimization [PDF document]. Retrieved from http://www.sascommunity.org/seugi/SEUGI2000/doherty_clickstream.pdf

Dominic, P., Jati, H., Sellappan, P., & Nee, G. K. (2011). A comparison of Asian e-government websites quality: Using a non-parametric test. *International Journal of Business Information Systems*, *7*(2), 220–246. doi:10.1504/IJBIS.2011.038513

Doney, P. M., & Cannon, J. P. (1997). An Examination of the Nature of Trust in Buyer-Seller Relationships. *Journal of Marketing*, *61*(2), 35–51. doi:10.2307/1251829

Doole, I., Grimes, T., & Demack, S. (2006). An exploration of the management practices and processes most closely associated with high levels of export capability in SMEs. *Marketing Intelligence & Planning*, *24*(6), 632–647. doi:10.1108/02634500610701690

Dorsey, P. (2012, April 13). *Social Media Is Not Social CRM, but It Can Be With These Five Steps*. Retrieved from http://www.marketingprofs.com/articles/2012/7627/social-media-is-not-social-crm-but-it-can-be-with-these-five-steps#ixzz3Pl049bv9

Dowling, G. (2002). Customer Relationship Management: In B2C Markets, Often Less is More. *California Management Review*, *44*(3), 87–104. doi:10.2307/41166134

Dubois, T., & Westerhausen, U. (2011). *Brand loyalty creation within online brand communities*(Master dissertation). Retrieved from http://studenttheses.cbs.dk/handle/10417/3012

Duffy, P., & Bruns, A. (2006). *The use of blogs, wikis and RSS in Education: A conversation of possibilities*. Paper presented at the Online Learning and Teaching Conference, Brisbane, Queensland, Australia.

Durham, C. A. (2007). The impact of environmental and health motivations on the organic share of produce purchases. *Agricultural and Resource Economics Review*, *36*(2), 304.

Educational Research Network for West and Central Africa. (2008). Graduate unemployment in Ghana: possible case of poor response of university programmes to the demands of the job market. Project report. Ghana.

Eijkman, H. (2008). Web 2.0 as a non-foundational network-centric space. *Campus-Wide Information Systems*, *25*(2), 95–104.

El Bernoussi, M. (2012). *The value of social media in CRM: from CRM 1.0 to CRM 2.0*. Dublin Business School.

Elaian, K. (1996). Employment implications of small scale industries in developing countries: Evidence from Jordan. *Science. Technology and Development*, *14*(1), 80–101.

Elizabeth, E., & Bushelow, E. E. (2012). Facebook Pages and Benefits to Brands. *The Elon Journal of Undergraduate Research in Communications*, *3*(2), 5–20.

Emarketer (2013, June 18). *Social Networking Reaches Nearly One in Four Around the World*. Retrieved from http://www.emarketer.com/Article/Social-Networking-Reaches-Nearly-One-Four-Around-World/1009976#sthash.gcLXWxbW.dpuf

Erfani, S. S., Abedin, B., & Daneshgar, F. (2013), Investigating the impact of Facebook use on cancer survivors' psychological well-being.*Proceedings of the Nineteenth Americas Conference on Information Systems*, Chicago, Illinois, August 15-17, 1-7.

Eric Levy-Bencheton. (2012). *Practice Sales & Marketing / Customer Relationship Management*. Atos Consulting, White paper translated from the French "Social CRM: vers la Relation Client augmentée.

Ernst & Young. (2012). *Driving a competitive advantage with advanced analytics* [PDF document]. Retrieved from http://www.ey.com/Publication/vwLUAssets/CAI_advanced__analytics_final/$FILE/CAI_advanced%20_analytics_final.pdf

European Commission. (2011). *Social business initiative creating a favourable climate for social enterprises, key stakeholders in the social economy and innovation. section(2011) 1278 final*. Retrieved September 8 2014 from http://ec.europa.eu/internal_market/social_business/docs/COM2011_682_en.pdf

European Union. (2012). *Financing social impact-Funding social innovation in Europe –Mapping the way forward*. Author.

Facebook (2015). *Statistics*. Retrieved on March 31, 2015 from http://newsroom.fb.com/company-info/

Fang, W. (2007). Using Google Analytics for Improving Library Website Content and Design: A Case Study. *Library Philosophy and Practice*, *9*(2), 1–17.

Fan, W., Wallace, L., Rich, S., & Zhang, Z. (2006). Tapping the power of text mining. *Communications of the ACM*, *49*(9), 76–82. doi:10.1145/1151030.1151032

Farooqi, R., & Dhusia, D. K. (2011). A comparative study of CRM and e-CRM technologies. *Indian Journal of Computer Science and Engineering, 2*(4), 624–627.

Farquhar, P. H. (1989). Managing Brand Equity. *JMR, Journal of Marketing Research, 1*, 24–33.

Feinberg, R. A., & Kadam, R. (2002). E-CRM web service attributes as determinants of customer satisfaction with retail websites. *International Journal of Service Industry Management, 13*(5), 432–451. doi:10.1108/09564230210447922

Feinberg, R. A., Kadam, R., Hokama, L., & Kim, I. (2002). The state of electronic customer relationship management in retailing. *International Journal of Retail & Distribution Management, 30*(10), 470–481. doi:10.1108/09590550210445344

Feng, T., & Tian, J. (2005). Customer knowledge management and condition analysis of successful CKM implementation. In *Proceedings of the fourth international Conference on machine learning and cybernetics*, Guanghou.

Fischer, E., & Reuber, R. (2000). *Industrial clusters and SME promotion in developing countries. (3)*. Commonwealth Secretariat. doi:10.14217/9781848597266-en

Flavian, C., Guinali, M., & Gurrea, R. (2006). The role played by perceived usability, satisfaction and consumer trust on website loyalty. *Journal of Information & Management, 43*, 1–14. Retrieved from http://www.pageaccess.com/whitepapers/500ForresterUSInteractiveMktgForecast_2009_2014 .pdf

Fornell, C., & Larcker, D. (1981). Evaluating Structural Equation Models with Unobservable Variables and Measurement Error. *JMR, Journal of Marketing Research, 18*(1), 39–50. doi:10.2307/3151312

Fotopoulos, C., & Krystallis, A. (2002a). Organic product avoidance: Reasons for rejection and potential buyers' identification in a countrywide survey. *British Food Journal, 104*(3/4/5), 233-260. doi: 10.1108/00070700210425697

Fotopoulos, C., & Krystallis, A. (2002b). Purchasing motives and profile of the Greek organic consumer: A countrywide survey. *British Food Journal, 104*(9), 730–765. doi:10.1108/00070700210443110

Foux, G. (2006, May 8). *Consumer-generated media: Get your customers involved*. Retrieved from http://www.highbeam.com/doc/1G1-145500854.html

Freire, F. C., Rogel, D. R., & Rodríguez, C. (2014). Presence and impact of Andean universities in online social networks. *Revista Latina de Comunicación Social, 69*, 571–592.

Frempong, G. K., & Essegbey, G. O. (2006). Ghana Case Study. InC. Stork and S. Esselaar (Eds.). Towards an African e-Index: SME e-Access and Usage in 14 African Countries. Witwatersrand, South Africa: Link Centre.

Frempong, G. (2007). Trends in ICT usage by small and medium scale enterprises in Ghana. *ATDF Journal, 4*(1), 3–10.

French, S., & Hale, T. (2010). Are Healthy Thinkers Also Healthy Shoppers? Retrieved 22/5/14, from The Nielsen Company http://www.nielsenmediamonitor.com/content/corporate/us/en/newswire/2010/are-healthy-thinkers-also-healthy-shoppers.html

Friedrichsen, M. (2013). Social Media in Companies. Integrated Approach for a Social Media Strategy. In M. Friedrichsen & W. Muhl-Benninghaus (Eds.), *Handbook of Social Media Management Media Business and Innovation* (pp. 25–47). doi:10.1007/978-3-642-28897-5_3

Füller, J., Matzler, K., & Hoppe, M. (2008). Brand Community Members as a Source of Innovation. *Journal of Product Innovation Management, 25*(6), 608–619. doi:10.1111/j.1540-5885.2008.00325.x

Fuloria, S. (2011). *Building Sustainable Competitive Advantage with Advanced Analytics* [PDF docment]. Retrieved from http://www.cognizant.com/InsightsWhitepapers/Building-Sustainable-Competitive-Advantage-with-Advanced-Analytics.pdf

Gambetta, D. (1988). *Trust: Making and Breaking Cooperative Relations*. Oxford, UK: Blackwell.

Gamon, M., Aue, A., Corston-Oliver, S., & Ringger, E. (2005). Lecture Notes in Computer Science: Vol. 3646. *Pulse: Mining customer opinions from free text* (pp. 121–132). Springer; doi:10.1007/11552253_12

Gangadharbhatla, H. (2008). Facebook me: Collective self esteem, need to belong and Internet self efficacy as predictors of the I-generations attitudes toward social networking sites. *Journal of Interactive Advertising*, *8*(2), 5–15. doi:10.1080/15252019.2008.10722138

Gao, Q., Dai, Y., Fan, Z., & Kang, R. (2010). Understanding factors affecting perceived sociability of social software. *Computers in Human Behavior*, *26*(6), 1846–1861. doi:10.1016/j.chb.2010.07.022

García-Murillo, M., & Annabi, H. (2002). Customer knowledge management. *The Journal of the Operational Research Society*, *53*(8), 875–884. doi:10.1057/palgrave.jors.2601365

Garnefeld, I., Iseke, A., & Krebs, A. (2012). Explicit Incentives in Online Communities: Boon or Bane? *International Journal of Electronic Commerce*, *17*(1), 11–38. doi:10.2753/JEC1086-4415170101

Garrigos-Simon, F. G., Alcamí, R. L., & Ribera, T. B. (2012). Social networks and Web 3.0: Their impact on the management and marketing of organizations. *Management Decision*, *50*(10), 1880–1890. doi:10.1108/00251741211279657

Gebert, H., Geib, M., Kolbe, L., & Brenner, W. (2003). Knowledge-enabled customer relationship management: Integrating customer relationship management and knowledge concepts. *Journal of Knowledge Management*, *7*(5), 107–123. doi:10.1108/13673270310505421

Gefen, D., Karahanna, E., & Straub, D. W. (2003). Trust and TAM in online shopping: An integrated model. *Journal of MIS Quarterly, 27*(1), 51–90.

Gefen, D., & Straub, D. W. (2005). A Practical Guide to Factorial Validity Using PLS-Graph: Tutorial and Annotated Example. *Communications of the AIS*, *16*(5), 91–109.

Gibbert, M., Leibold, M., & Probst, G. (2002). Five styles of customer knowledge management and how smart companies use them to create value. *European Management Journal*, *20*(5), 459–469. doi:10.1016/S0263-2373(02)00101-9

Gikas, J., & Grant, M. M. (2013). Mobile computing devices in higher education: Student perspectives on learning with cellphones, smartphones & social media. *The Internet and Higher Education*, *19*, 18–26. doi:10.1016/j.iheduc.2013.06.002

Gillen, J., Durkin, M., & McGowan, P. (2000). *Exploring the role of branding in the developmentof trust online.* Paper presented at the Irish Academy of Management Conference, Dublin.

Gillham, B. (2000). *Case study research methods*. London: Continuum.

Global Digital Statistics. (2014). *We are social's snapshot of key digital indicators*. Retrieved 29 November, 2014, from http://etonpreneurs.com/uploads/Global%20Social,%20Digital%20&%20Mobile%20Statistics,%20Jan%202014.pdf

Goh, K.-Y., Heng, C.-S., & Lin, Z. (2013). Social Media Brand Community and Consumer Behavior: Quantifying the Relative Impact of User- and Marketer-Generated Content. *Information Systems Research*, *24*(1), 88–107. doi:10.1287/isre.1120.0469

Goldberg, L. R. (1992). The development of markers for the Big-Five factor structure. *Psychological Assessment*, *4*(1), 26–42. doi:10.1037/1040-3590.4.1.26

Goldman, B. J., & Clancy, K. L. (1991). A survey of organic produce purchases and related attitudes of food cooperative shoppers. *American Journal of Alternative Agriculture*, *6*(2), 89–96. doi:10.1017/S0889189300003933

Gopinath, S., Thomas, J. S., & Krishnamurthi, L. (2014). Investigating the Relationship Between the Content of Online Word of Mouth, Advertising, and Brand Performance. *Marketing Science*, *33*(2), 241–258. doi:10.1287/mksc.2013.0820

Gordon-Murnane, L. (2006). Social bookmarking, folksonomies and web 2.0 tools. *Searcher*, *14*(6), 26–58.

Gounaris, S., & Stathakopoulos, V. (2004). Antecedents and consequences of brand loyalty: An empirical study. *Journal of Brand Management*, *11*(4), 283–306. doi:10.1057/palgrave.bm.2540174

Grabner-Kräuter, S. (2010). Toward a better understanding of trust in web 2.0 social networks. *AMA Winter Educators' Conference*, p313-321,

Grabner-Kräuter, S. (2009). Web 2.0 Social Networks: The Role of Trust. *Journal of Business Ethics*, *90*(4), 505–522. doi:10.1007/s10551-010-0603-1

Granovetter, M. (1973). The strength of weak ties. *American Journal of Sociology*, *78*(6), 1360–1380. doi:10.1086/225469

Gray, K., Thompson, C., Clerehan, R., Sheard, J., & Hamilton, M. (2008). Web 2.0 authorship: Issues of referencing and citation for academic integrity. *The Internet and Higher Education*, *11*(1), 112–118. doi:10.1016/j.iheduc.2008.03.001

Greenberg, P. (2007). Welcome to the era of the social consumer (pp. 138-140): CRMProject.

Greenberg, P. (2010). The impact of CRM 2.0 on insight. *Journal of Business and Industrial Marketing*, *25*(6), 410–419. doi:10.1108/08858621011066008

Greenfield, D. (2007). Social bookmarking apps provide a new knowledge management platform, eWeek.com, August 12.

Greenwood, G. (2012). Examining the presence of social media on university web sites. *Journal of College Admission*, *216*, 24–28.

Gregurec, I., Tomas, B., & Coric, A. (2011). Word of Mouth Marketing within Social Networking Sites.*Proceedings of the 22nd Central European Conference on Information and Intelligent Systems Varazdin*, 227-233.

Groh, F. (2012). Gamification: State of the Art Definition and Utilization. In N. Asaj, B. Konings, M. Poguntke, F. Schaub, B. Wiedersheim, & M. Weber (Eds.), *Research Trends in Media Informatics*. Institute of Media Informatics Ulm University.

Grönroos, C. (1994). From marketing mix to relationship marketing: Towards a paradigm shift in marketing. *Management Decision*, *32*(2), 4–20. doi:10.1108/00251749410054774

Grosseck, G. (2009). To use or not to use web 2.0 in higher education? *Procedia: Social and Behavioral Sciences*, *1*(1), 478–482. doi:10.1016/j.sbspro.2009.01.087

Gruber, H., & Pantelis, K. (2013). Competition enhancing regulation and diffusion of innovation: The case of broadband networks. *Journal of Regulatory Economics*, *43*(2), 168–195. doi:10.1007/s11149-012-9205-4

Gruen, T. W., Osmonbekov, T., & Czaplewsk, A. J. (2006). eWOM: The impact of customer-to-customer online know-how exchange on customer value and loyalty. *Journal of Business Research*, *59*(4), 449–456. doi:10.1016/j.jbusres.2005.10.004

Gulati, G. J., & Williams, C. B. (2011). Diffusion of innovations and online campaigns: Social media adoption in the 2010 U.S. congressional elections. Proceedings of*6th General Conference of the European Consortium for Political Research*, Reykjavik, Iceland. doi:10.2139/ssrn.1925585

Gulati, G. J., & Williams, C. B. (2013). Social Media and Campaign 2012: Developments and Trends for Facebook Adoption. *Social Science Computer Review*, *31*(5), 577–588. doi:10.1177/0894439313489258

Gummesson, E. (1987). *Quality: The Ericsson Approach*. Stockholm: Ericsson.

Gummesson, E., Lehtinen, U., & Grönroos, C. (1997). Comment on" Nordic perspectives on relationship marketing. *European Journal of Marketing*, *31*, 10–16.

Gupta, S., & Jain, A. (2014). *Customer Lifetime Value Analytics in Retail Banking – Staying Competitive and Profitable* [PDFdocument].Retrived from http://www.genpact.com/docs/resource-/customer-lifetime-value-analytics-in-retail-banking---staying-competitive-and-profitable

Gu, R., Oh, L. B., & Wang, K. (2011). Determinants of Loyalty for Social Networking Sites. Exploring the Grand Challenges for Next Generation E-Business. *Lecture Notes in Business Information Processing*, *52*, 206–212.

Hagel, J., & Armstrong, A. G. (1997). *Net gain: Expanding markets through virtual communities*. Boston, MA: Harvard Business School Press.

Hallowell, R. (1996). The relationships of customer satisfaction, customer loyalty, and profitability: An empirical study. *International Journal of Service Industry Management*, *7*(4), 27–42. doi:10.1108/09564239610129931

Hamari, J. (2011). Perspectives from behavioral economics to analyzing game design patterns: loss aversion in social games. In *Proceedings of the CHI 2011 Social Games Workshop*, Vancouver, BC, Canada.

Hamari, J., & Järvinen, A. (2011). *Building customer relationship through game mechanics in social games. Business, Technological and Social Dimensions of Computer Games: Multidisciplinary Developments*. Hershey, PA: IGI Global.

Hamari, J., & Lehdonvirta, V. (2010). Game design as marketing: How game mechanics create demand for virtual goods. *International Journal of Business Science & Applied Management*, *5*(1), 14–29.

Hamid, R. A., Cheng, A. Y., Akhir, R. M. (2011). Dimensions of E-CRM: an empirical study on hotels' web sites. *Journal of Southeast Asian Research. 2-15.*

Hamid, S., Chang, S., & Kurnia, S. (2009). Identifying the use of online social networking in higher education. In *Proceedings ASCILITE*. Auckland: ASCILITE. Poster presentation (pp. 419-422). Retrieved 19 January, 2015, from http://www.ascilite.org.au/conferences/auckland09/procs/hamid-poster.pdf

Hamid, N. R. A. (2008). Consumers' behaviour towards internet technology and internet marketing tools. *International Journal of Communication*, *2*(3), 195–204.

Hamill, J., & Gregory, K. (1997). Internet marketing in the internationalisation of UK SMEs. *Journal of Marketing Management*, *13*(1-3), 9–28. doi:10.1080/0267257X.1997.9964456

Han, J. K., Kim, N., & Srivastava, R. K. (1998). Market Orientation and Organizational Performance: Is Innovation a Missing Link? *Journal of Marketing*, *62*(4), 30–45. doi:10.2307/1252285

Han, J., & Kamber, M. (2006). *Data Mining: Concepts and Techniques*. Waltham, MA: Morgan Kaufmann.

Hanna, R., Rohm, A., & Crittenden, V. L. (2011). We're all connected: The power of social media ecosystem. *Business Horizons*, *54*(3), 265–273. doi:10.1016/j.bushor.2011.01.007

Hanson, C., West, J., Neiger, B., Thackeray, R., Barnes, M., & McIntyre, E. (2011). Use and acceptance of social media among health educators. *American Journal of Health Education*, *42*(4), 197–204. doi:10.1080/19325037.2011.10599188

Hansotia, B. (2002). Gearing up for CRM: Antecedents to Successful Implementation. *Journal of Database Marketing*, *10*(2), 121–132. doi:10.1057/palgrave.jdm.3240103

Harinarayana, N. S., & Raju, N. V. (2010). Web 2.0 features in university library web sites. *The Electronic Library*, *28*(1), 69–88. doi:10.1108/02640471011023388

Harper, G. C., & Makatouni, A. (2002). Consumer perception of organic food production and farm animal welfare. *British Food Journal, 104*(3/4/5), 287-299. doi: 10.1108/00070700210425723

Harrigan, P., Ramsey, E., & Ibbotson, P. (2008). E-CRM in SMEs: An exploratory study in Northern Ireland. *Marketing Intelligence & Planning*, *26*(4), 385–404. doi:10.1108/02634500810879296

Harrigan, P., Ramsey, E., & Ibbotson, P. (2011). Critical factorsunderpinning the e-CRM activities of SMEs. *Journal of Marketing Management*, *27*(5/6), 503–529. doi:10.1080/0267257X.2010.495284

Harris, R. (2009). *Social media ecosystem mapped as a wiring diagram*. Retrieved from: http://www.twitterthoughts.com/social-media-newsanalyses/ 2009/9/3/social-media-ecosystem-mapped-as-a-wiringdiagram.html?printerFriendly=true

Harris, L. C., & Goode, M. M. H. (2004). The four levels of loyalty and the pivotal roleof trust: A study ofonline service dynamics. *Journal of Retailing*, *80*(2), 139–158. doi:10.1016/j.jretai.2004.04.002

Harris, L., & Dennis, C. (2011). Engaging customers on Facebook: Challenges for e-retailers. *Journal of Consumer Behaviour*, *10*(6), 338–372. doi:10.1002/cb.375

Hartline, M. D. III, Maxham, J. G. III, & McKee, D. O. (2000). Corridors of Influence in the Dissemination of Customer-Oriented Strategy to Customer Contact Service Employees. *Journal of Marketing*, *64*(2), 35–50. doi:10.1509/jmkg.64.2.35.18001

Hayes, T. J., Ruschman, D., & Walker, M. M. (2009). Social networking as an admission tool: A Case study in success. *Journal of Marketing for Higher Education, 19*(2), 109–124. doi:10.1080/08841240903423042

Heding, T., Knudtzen, C. F., & Bjerre, M. (2009). *Brand management research, theory and practice*. London, UK: Routledge. doi:10.4324/9780203996171

Heil, O., Lehmann, D., & Stremersch, S. (2010). Marketing competition in the 21st century. *International Journal of Research in Marketing, 27*(2), 161–163. doi:10.1016/j.ijresmar.2010.03.003

Hennig, T., Walsh, T., & Walsh, G. (2003). Electronic Word of Mouth: Motives for and Consequences of Reading Customer Articulations on the Internet. *International Journal of Electronic Commerce, 8*(2), 51–74.

Hernandez, B., Jimenex, J., & Martin, M. J. (2009). Key website factors in e-business strategy. *International Journal of Information Management, 29*(5), 362–371. doi:10.1016/j.ijinfomgt.2008.12.006

Herr, P. M., Kardes, F. R., & Kim, J. (1991). The effects of word-of-mouth and product-attribute information on persuasion: An accessibility-diagnosticity perspective. *The Journal of Consumer Research, 17*(4), 454–462. doi:10.1086/208570

Hill, T., & Lewicki, P. (2007). *Statistics: Methods and Applications*. Tulsa, OK: StatSoft.

Hoad, V., Somerford, P., & Katzenellenbogen, J. (2010). High body mass index overtakes tobacco as the leading independent risk factor contibuting to disease burden in Western Australia. *Australian and New Zealand Journal of Public Health, 34*(2), 214–215. doi:10.1111/j.1753-6405.2010.00509.x PMID:23331368

Hoffman, D. L., & Fodor, M. (2010). Can You Measure the ROI of Your Social Media Marketing? *Sloan Management Review, 52*(1), 40–50.

Holmberg, K., & Thelwall, M. (2009). Local Government Web Sites in Finland: A Geographic and Webometric Analysis. *Scientometrics, 79*(1), 157–169. doi:10.1007/s11192-009-0410-6

Holmes, J. G. (1991). In W. H. Jones & D. Perlman (Eds.), *Trust and the appraisal process in close relationships* (Vol. 2, pp. 57–104). Advances in personal relationshipsLondon, UK: Jessica Kingsley.

Holotescu, C., & Grosseck, G. (2012). An empirical analysis of the educational effects of social media in universities and colleges. In *Proceedings of the 8th International Scientific Conference eLearning and Software for Education (eLSE)*, Bucharest: Editura Universitara. Retrieved 20 January, 2014, from http://www.ceeol.com/aspx/getdocument.aspx?logid=5&id=1b3dcdac-c6c7-4ea5-b1aa-de9f0fd45a23

Hoon, K. K., Kang, S. K., Dong, Y. K., Jong, H. K., & Kang, S. H. (2008). Brand Equity in Hospital Marketing. *Journal of Business Research, 61*(1), 75–82. doi:10.1016/j.jbusres.2006.05.010

Hosny, M. I., & Fatima, S. (2012). Facebok in education: Students, teachers, and library perspectives. *Journal of Computing, 4*(6), 78–86.

Hossain, M. D. M., & Aydin, H. (2011). A Web 2.0-based collaborative model for multicultural education. *Multicultural Education & Technology Journal, 5*(2), 116–128. doi:10.1108/17504971111142655

Hrastinski, S., & Dennen, V. (2012). Social media in higher education: Introduction to the special issue. *The Internet and Higher Education, 15*(1), 1–2. doi:10.1016/j.iheduc.2011.11.004

Hsiu-Fen, L. (2010). An application of fuzzy AHP for evaluating course website quality. *Computers & Education, 54*(4), 877–888. doi:10.1016/j.compedu.2009.09.017

Hsu, H. Y., & Tsou, H. T. (2011). Understanding customer experiences in online blog environments. *International Journal of Information Management, 31*(6), 510–523. doi:10.1016/j.ijinfomgt.2011.05.003

Hu, M., & Liu, B. (2004). Mining and summarizing customer reviews. In *Proceedings of the 2004 ACM SIGKDD international conference on Knowledge discovery and data mining KDD 04* (Vol. 04, p. 168). http://doi.org/doi:10.1145/1014052.1014073

Hu, N., Liu, L., & Zhang, J. (2008). Do online reviews affect product sales? The role of reviewer characteristics and temporal effects. *Journal of Information Technology and Management*, *9*, 201-214.

Huang, J. (2008).Combining entropy weight and TOPSIS method for information system selection.*IEEE International Conference on Cybernetics and Intelligent Systems (CIS 2008)*, 1281-1284. doi:10.1109/ICCIS.2008.4670971

Hui, S., & Jha, G. (2000). Data mining for customer service support. *Information & Management*, *38*(1), 1–13. doi:10.1016/S0378-7206(00)00051-3

Hunicke, R., LeBlanc, M., & Zubek, R. (2004, July). MDA: A formal approach to game design and game research. In *Proceedings of the AAAI Workshop on Challenges in Game*.

Hunter, G. K., & Perreault, W. D. Jr. (2007). Making Sales Technology Effective. *Journal of Marketing*, *71*(1), 16–34. doi:10.1509/jmkg.71.1.16

Hunter, G., & Perreault, J. W. D. Jr. (2006). Sales Technology Orientation, Information Effectiveness, and Sales Performance. *Journal of Personal Selling & Sales Management*, *26*(2), 95–113. doi:10.2753/PSS0885-3134260201

Huotari, K., & Hamari, J. (2011). Gamification" from the perspective of service marketing. *CHI 2011 Workshop Gamification*.

Hurtola & Jenny. (2011). *The importance of social media in building customer loyalty for Company X*. Laurea University of Applied Sciences.

Hu, T., & Kettinger, W. J. (2008). Why people continue to use social networking services: Developing a comprehensive model.*InProceedings, 29th international conference on information systems*.Paris, France.

IBISWorld. (2014). IBISWorld reveals the industries set to fly and fall in 2014 (M. Centre, Trans.). In IBISWorld (Ed.), (pp. 1-5): IBISWorld.

IBM. (2013). *The Case for Business Analytics for Midsize Firms* [PDF document]. Retrieved from http://www-03.ibm.com/innovation/us/engines/assets/ibm-business-analytics-case-study-1-22-13.pdf

Inmon, W. H. (2005). *Building The Data Warehouse*. Indianapolis: Wiley.

Internet World Stats. *Internet Stats and Facebook Usage in Europe*. Retrieved 29 November, 2014, from http://www.internetworldstats.com/stats4.htm

Ivory, M. Y., & Chevalier, A. (2002). *A study of automated web site evaluation tools*. University of Washington, Department of Computer Science.

Iyengar, R., Han, S., & Gupta, S. (2009). Do Friends Influence Purchases in a Social Network? Working paper

Jacobson, R., & Aaker, D. A. (1985). Is Market Share All That It's Cracked Up To Be? *Journal of Marketing*, *49*(4), 11–22. doi:10.2307/1251428

Jain, A. K., Murty, M. N., & Flynn, P. J. (1999). Data clustering: A review. *ACM Computing Surveys*, *31*(3), 264–323. doi:10.1145/331499.331504

Jang, H., Olfman, L., Ko, I., Koh, J., & Kim, K. (2008). The Influence of On-Line Brand Community Characteristics on Community Commitment and Brand Loyalty. *International Journal of Electronic Commerce*, *12*(3), 57–80. doi:10.2753/JEC1086-4415120304

Järvinen, A. S. (2009). *Games without frontiers: methods for game studies and design*. VDM Verlag Dr. Müller.

Jaworski, B. J., & Kohli, A. K. (1993). Market Orientation: Antecedents and Consequences. *Journal of Marketing*, *57*(July), 53–70. doi:10.2307/1251854

Jaworski, B., Kohli, A. K., & Sahay, A. (2000). Market-driven versus driving markets. *Academy of Marketing Science Journal*, *28*(1), 45–55. doi:10.1177/0092070300281005

Jayanti, R. K., & Singh, J. (2010). Pragmatic learning theory: An inquiry-action framework for distributed consumer learning in online communities. *The Journal of Consumer Research*, *36*(6), 1058–1081. doi:10.1086/648689

Jelinek, R., Ahearne, M., Mathieu, J., & Schillewaert, N. (2006). A Longitudinal Examination of Individual, Organizational and Contextual Factors on Sales Technology and Adoption and Job Performance. *Journal of Marketing Theory and Practice*, *14*(Winter), 7–23. doi:10.2753/MTP1069-6679140101

Jin, S. A. (2012). The potential of social media for luxury brand management. *Marketing Intelligence & Planning*, *30*(7), 687–699. doi:10.1108/02634501211273805

Johnston, R. (2008). Knowledge management in the Web 2.0 age, Associations Now, January, from: www.asaecenter.org/PublicationsResources/ANowDetail. Cfm? ItemNumber1/430024.

Johnston, M. W., & Marshall, G. W. (2006). *Churchill/Ford/Walker's Sales Force Management*. Boston: McGraw-Hill/Irwin.

Joint, N. (2009). ANTAEUS the Web 2.0 challenge to libraries. *Library Review*, *58*(3), 167–175. doi:10.1108/00242530910942027

Jones, B. (2010). Entrepreneurial marketing and the Web 2.0 interface. *Journal of Research in Marketing and Entrepreneurship*, *12*(2), 143–152. doi:10.1108/14715201011090602

Jordan, J., Lowe, J., & Taylor, P. (1998). Strategy and financial policy in U.K. small firms. *Journal of Business Finance & Accounting*, *25*(1/2), 1–27. doi:10.1111/1468-5957.00176

Jöreskog, K. G., & Wold, H. (1982). The ML and PLS Techniques for Modeling with Latent Variables: Historical and Comparative Aspects. In H. Wold & K. Jöreskog (Eds.), *Systems Under Indirect Observation: Causality, Structure, Prediction* (Vol. I). Amsterdam: North-Holland.

Jun, M. & Cai, S. (2010). Examining the Relationships between Internal Service Quality and its Dimensions, and Internal Customer Satisfaction. *Journal of Marketing Development and Competitiveness*, *8*(1), 95.

Kalman, D. M. (n.d.). Brand Communities, Marketing, and Media. Available at: http://www.terrella.com/bcmarketingwp2.pdf

Kane, G. C., Alavi, M., Labianca, G., & Borgatti, S. P. (2014). What's different about social media networks? A framework and research agenda. *MIS Querterly*, *38*(1), 274–304.

Kanellopoulos, D. & Kotsiantis, S. (2012). Evaluating and recommending Greek newspapers' websites using clustering. *Program: Electronic Library and Information Systems, 46*(1), 71-91.

Kang, I., Lee, K. C., Lee, S., & Choi, J. (2007). Investigation of online community voluntary behaviour using cognitive map. *Journal of Computers in Human Behavior*, *23*(1), 111–126. doi:10.1016/j.chb.2004.03.039

Kania, D. (2001). Branding.com: Online branding for marketing success. Chicago, IL: NTC Business Books (in conjunction with the American Marketing Association)

Kapferer, J. N. (1998). *Strategic Brand Management: Creating and Sustaining Brand Equity Long Term*. London, UK: Kogan Page.

Kaplan, A. M., & Haenlein, M. (2010). Users of the world, unite! The challenges and opportunities of Social Media. *Business Horizons*, *53*(1), 59–68. doi:10.1016/j.bushor.2009.09.003

Kapoor, P. S., Jayasimha, K. R., & Sadh, A. (2013). Brand-related, Consumer to Consumer, Communication via Social Media. *IIM Kozhikode Society & Management Review*, *2*(1), 43–59. doi:10.1177/2277975213496514

Kappen, D. L., & Nacke, L. E. (2013, October). The kaleidoscope of effective gamification: Deconstructing gamification in business applications. In *Proceedings of the First International Conference on Gameful Design, Research, and Applications*. ACM Press. doi:10.1145/2583008.2583029

Karjaluoto, H., & Leinonen, H. (2009). Advertisers' perceptions of search engine marketing. *International Journal of Internet Marketing and Advertising*, *5*(1), 95–112. doi:10.1504/IJIMA.2009.021952

Kasavana, M. L., Nusair, K. H., & Teodosic, K. (2010). Online social networking: Redefining the human web. *Journal of Hospitality and Tourism Technology*, *1*(1), 68–82. doi:10.1108/17579881011023025

Kayanula, D., & Quartey, P. (2000). The Policy Environment for Promoting Small and Medium-Sized Enterprises in Ghana and Malawi. Finance and Development Research Programme. Working Paper Series, Paper No 15. IDPM, University of Manchester.

Kaye, B. K. (2007). Web Site Story: An Exploratory Study of Blog Use Motivations. In *Blogging, citizenship, and the future of media* (pp. 127–148). New York: Rutledge.

Keller, K. (1993). Conceptualizing, measuring, and managing customer-based brand equity. *Journal of Marketing, 57*(1), 1-22.Retrieved from.10.2307/1252054

Keller, K. A. (2003). Brand Synthesis: The Multidimensionality of Brand Knowledge. *The Journal of Consumer Research, 29*(4), 595–600. doi:10.1086/346254

Kelley, L. L., Gilbert, D., & Mannicom, R. (2003). How e-CRM can enhance customer Loyalty. *Marketing Intelligence & Planning, 21*(4), 239–248. doi:10.1108/02634500310480121

Kelly, B. (2008). Library 2.0 and information literacy: the tools. In P. Godwin & J. Parker (Eds.), *Literacy Meets Library 2.0*. London: Facet Publishing.

Kennedy, G., Dalgarno, B., Gray, K., Judd, T., Waycott, J., Bennett, S., . . . Churchward, A. (2007). The net generation are not big users of Web 2.0 technologies: Preliminary findings. In *Proceedings ASCILITE*. Singapore: ASCILITE. Retrieved 23 June, 2014, from http://www.ascilite.org.au/conferences/singapore07/procs/kennedy.pdf

Kent, M. L., & Taylor, M. (1998). Building dialogic relationships through theWorldWideWeb. *Public Relations Review, 24*(3), 321–334. doi:10.1016/S0363-8111(99)80143-X

Kerpen, D. (2011). *Likeable social media*. New York, NY: McGraw-Hill.

Khong, K. W., Onyemeh, N. C., & Chong, A. Y. (2013). BSEM estimation of network effect and customer orientation empowerment on trust in social media and network environment. *Expert Systems with Applications, 40*(12), 4858–4870. doi:10.1016/j.eswa.2013.02.020

Kiehne, T. P. (2004). Social networking systems: history, critique, and knowledge management potentials, unpublished manuscript, University of Texas, Austin, TX, from: www. ischool.utexas.edu/, i385q/archive/kiehne_t/kiehne (2004)-sns.pdf

Kietzmann, J. H., Hermkens, K., Mccarthy, I. P., & Silvestre, B. S. (2011). Social media? Get serious! Understanding the functional building blocks of social media. *Business Horizons, 54*(3), 241–251. doi:10.1016/j.bushor.2011.01.005

Kımıloğlu, H., & Zaralı, H.HandeKimilogˇlu. (2009). What signifies success in e-CRM? *Marketing Intelligence & Planning, 27*(2), 246–267. doi:10.1108/02634500910945011

Kim, M., Chung, N., & Lee, C. (2011). The effect of perceived trust on electroniccommerce: Shopping online for tourism products and services in South Korea. *Journal of Tourism Management, 32*(2), 256–265. doi:10.1016/j.tourman.2010.01.011

Kim, S. H., Yang, K. H., & Kim, J. K. (2009). Finding critical success factors for virtual community marketing. *Service Business, 3*(2), 149–171. doi:10.1007/s11628-008-0059-x

Kim, Y., Street, W. N., Russell, G. J., & Menczer, F. (2005). Customer Targeting: A Neural Network Approach Guided by Genetic Algorithms. *Management Science, 51*(2), 264–276. doi:10.1287/mnsc.1040.0296

Kocak, A., & Abimbola, T. (2009). The effects of entrepreneurial marketing on born global performance. *International Marketing Review, 26*(4/5), 439–452. doi:10.1108/02651330910971977

Kock, N. (2011). Using WarpPLS in eCollaboration Studies: Mediating effects, control and secondorder variables and algorithmchoices. *International Journal of e-Collaboration, 7*(3), 1–13. doi:10.4018/jec.2011070101

Koh, J., & Kim, Y. G. (2004). Knowledge sharing in virtual communities: An e-business perspective. *Expert Systems with Applications, 26*(2), 155–166. doi:10.1016/S0957-4174(03)00116-7

Kohlbacher, F. (2006). The use of qualitative content analysis in case study research. *Forum Qualitative Sozialforschung/Forum: Qualitative. Social Research, 7*(1), 21. http://nbn-resolving.de/urn:nbn:de:0114-fqs0601211

Kohli, R., & Grover, V. (2008). Business Value of IT: An Essay on Expanding Research Directions to Keep up with the Times. *Journal of the Association for Information Systems, 9*(1), 23–39.

Kolbe, L. M., & Geib, M. (2005). Customer knowledge management. *In Proceedings of the 38th Hawaii international conference on system sciences* (HICSS).

Komaromi, K. (2003). *Building Brand Communities*. Online at: http://cdgroup.blogs.com/design_channel/brand_communities.pdf

Korn Ferry Survey. (2014, August 12). *Korn Ferry Survey: CMOs' Top Priority Remains How to Best Engage with Customers*. Reterived from http://www.kornferry.com/press/15191/

Kotorov, R. (2002). Ubiquitous organization: Organizational design for e-CRM. *Business Process Management Journal*, *8*(3), 218–232. doi:10.1108/14637150210428934

Kozinets, R. V. (2002). The field behind the screen: Using netnography for marketing research in online communities. *JMR, Journal of Marketing Research*, *39*(1), 61–72. doi:10.1509/jmkr.39.1.61.18935

KPMG. (2014). Transforming for growth: *Consumer business in the digital age* [PDF document]. Retrived from http://www.kpmg.com/Global/en/IssuesAndInsights/ArticlesPublications/global-consumer-executive-top-of-mind-survey-2014/Documents/top-of-mind-survey-2014-v2.pdf

Krafft, M. (1999). An Empirical Investigation of the Antecedents of Sales Force Control Systems. *Journal of Marketing*, *63*(July), 120–134. doi:10.2307/1251779

Krishnan, H. S. (1996). Characteristics of memory associations: A consumer-based brand equity perspective. *International Journal of Research in Marketing*, *13*(4), 389–405. doi:10.1016/S0167-8116(96)00021-3

Kukulska-Hulme, A. (2012). How should the higher education workforce adapt to advancements in technology for teaching and learning? *The Internet and Higher Education*, *15*(4), 247–254. doi:10.1016/j.iheduc.2011.12.002

Kumar, V., Bhaskaran, V., Mirchandani, R., & Shah, M. (2013). Practice Prize Winner—Creating a Measurable Social Media Marketing Strategy: Increasing the Value and ROI of Intangibles and Tangibles for Hokey Pokey. *Marketing Science*, *32*(2), 194–212. doi:10.1287/mksc.1120.0768

Kwon, O., & Wen, Y. (2010). An empirical study of the factors affecting social network service use. *Computers in Human Behavior*, *26*(2), 254–263. doi:10.1016/j.chb.2009.04.011

Lai-Chong Law, E., & Nguyen-Ngoc, A. V. (2010). Analysis of cross-cultural online collaborative learning with social software. *Interactive Technology and Smart Education*, *7*(4), 247–263. doi:10.1108/17415651011096058

Lai, L. S. L., & Turban, E. (2008). Groups formation and operations in the Web 2.0 environment and social networks. *Group Decision and Negotiation*, *17*(5), 387–402. doi:10.1007/s10726-008-9113-2

Lampe, C., Wash, W., Velasquez, A., & Ozkaya, E. (2010). Motivations to Participate in Online Communities. *Proceedings of the SIGCHI Conference on Human Factors in Computing Systems*, p1927-1936.

Langley, S. (2013). Australian consumers will pay more for 'eco-friendly' vegetables, study. Retrieved 29/5/2014, from Australian Food News http://ausfoodnews.com.au/2013/12/04/australian-consumers-will-pay-more-for-%E2%80%98eco-friendly%E2%80%99-vegetables-study.html

Larasati, A., DeYong, C., & Slevitch, L. (2012). The Application of Neural Network and Logistics Regression Models on Predicting Customer Satisfaction in a Student-Operated Restaurant. *Procedia: Social and Behavioral Sciences*, *65*, 94–99. doi:10.1016/j.sbspro.2012.11.097

Laroche, M., Habibi, M. R., Richard, M. O., & Sankaranarayanan, R. (2012). The effects of social media based brand communities on brand community markers, value creation practices, brand trust and brand loyalty. *Computers in Human Behavior*, *28*, 1755–1767.

Laroche, M., Habibi, M. R., & Richard, M. O. (2013). To be or not to be in social media: How brand loyalty is affected by social media? *International Journal of Information Management*, *33*(1), 76–82. doi:10.1016/j.ijinfomgt.2012.07.003

Laroche, M., Habibi, M. R., Richard, M., & Sankaranarayanan, R. (2012). The effects of social media based brand communities on brand community markers, value creation practices, brand trust and brand loyalty. *Computers in Human Behavior*, *28*(5), 1755–1767. doi:10.1016/j.chb.2012.04.016

Laudon, K., & Loudon, J. (2012). *Management information systems: Managing the digital firm* (12th ed.). Prentice Hall.

Laughton, P. (2011). The use of wikis as alternatives to learning content management systems. *The Electronic Library*, *29*(2), 225–235. doi:10.1108/02640471111125186

Lawson-Body, A., & O'Keefe, T. (2006). Interorganisational relationships in the context of SMEs B2B E-commerce. *Journal of Electronic Commerce in Organizations*, *4*(4), 1–28. doi:10.4018/jeco.2006100101

Lea, E., & Worsley, T. (2005). Australians' organic food beliefs, demographics and values. *British Food Journal*, *107*(11), 855–869. doi:10.1108/00070700510629797

Lee, S., & Leckenby, J. D. (1998). An investigation of website ranking methods, *Proceedings of American Academy of Advertising*. Retrieved from http://www.ciadvertising.org/studies/reports/measurement/3ASuckkee.html

Lee, J. (2009). *Effects of online brand community on brand loyalty: A uses and gratifications perspective*. Retrieved from Google Scholar.

Lee, M. K. O., Cheung, C. M. K., Lim, K. H., & Sia, C. L. (2006). Understanding customer knowledge sharing in web – based discussion boards, an exploratory study. *Internet Research*, *16*(3), 289–303. doi:10.1108/10662240610673709

Lehmkuhl, T., & Jung, R., (2013). Towards Social CRM– Scoping the Concept and Guiding Research. *proceedings of BLED 2013*, 190-205.

Leiner, B. M., Cerf, V. G., Clark, D. D., Kahn, R. E., Kleinrock, L., Daniel, C. L., ... (2000). A brief history of the internet. 2000. *Web Page. URL: http://info. isoc/ org/internet-history/brief. html, 18.*

Lempert, P. (2006). Caught in the Web. *Progressive Grocer*, *85*(12), 15–28.

Leonidio, U. C., Montezano, R. M. S., & Carvalho, F. A. (2011). Evaluation of perceived quality of the website of an online bookstore: An empirical application of the Barnes and Vidgen Model. *Journal of Information Systems and Technology Management*, *8*(1), 109–130. doi:10.4301/S1807-17752011000100006

Leskovec, J., Adami, L. A., & Huberman, B. A. (2006). *The dynamics of viral marketing*. ACM Conference on Electronic Commerce, Ann Arbor, MI.

Leung, L. (2013). Generational differences in content generation in social media: The roles of the gratifications sought of narcissism. *Computers in Human Behavior*, *29*(3), 997–1006. doi:10.1016/j.chb.2012.12.028

Levy, M. (2009). Web 2.0 implications on knowledge management. *Journal of Knowledge Management*, *13*(1), 120–134. doi:10.1108/13673270910931215

Li, P., & Yamada, S. (2009). Automated Web Site Evaluation – An Approach Based on Ranking SVM, *IEEE/WIC/ ACM International Joint Conferences on Web Intelligence and Intelligent Agent Technologies, 3*, 34-37.

Liang, B., Commins, M., & Duffy, N. (2010). Using social media to engage youth: Education, social justice, & humanitarianism. *Prevention Researcher*, *17*(5), 13–16.

Liburd, J. J. (2012). Tourism research2.0. *Annals of Tourism Research*, *39*(2), 883–907. doi:10.1016/j.annals.2011.10.006

Li, C., & Bernoff, J. (2008). *Groundswell: Winning in a world transformed by social technologies*. Boston: Harvard Business Press.

Li, D., Chau, P. Y. K., & Lai, F. (2010). Market Orientation, Ownership Type, and E-Business Assimilation. *Evidence from Chinese Firms Decision Sciences*, *41*(1), 115–145. doi:10.1111/j.1540-5915.2009.00261.x

Lin, C.-P., Tsai, Y. H., & Chiu, C.-K. (2009). Modeling Customer Loyalty from an Integrative Perspective of Self-Determination Theory and Expectation-Confirmation Theory. *Journal of Business and Psychology*, *24*(3), 315–326. doi:10.1007/s10869-009-9110-8

Lindberg, J. O., & Olofsson, A. D. (Eds.). (2010). *Online Learning Communities and Teacher Professional Development: Methods for Improved Education Delivery*. Hershey, PA: IGI Global. doi:10.4018/978-1-60566-780-5

Lin, H. H., & Wang, Y. S. (2006). An examination of the determinants of customer loyalty in mobile commerce contexts. *Information & Management*, *43*(3), 271–282. doi:10.1016/j.im.2005.08.001

Liou, J. J. H., & Tzeng, G. H. (2010). A Dominance-based Rough Set Approach to customer behavior in the airline market. *Information Sciences*, *180*(11), 2230–2238. doi:10.1016/j.ins.2010.01.025

Li, Y. M., Lin, C. H., & Lai, C. Y. (2010). Identifying influential reviewers for word-of-mouth marketing. *Electronic Commerce Research and Applications*, *9*(4), 294–304. doi:10.1016/j.elerap.2010.02.004

Lo, B. W., & Sedhain, R. Sh. (2006). How reliable are website rankings? Implications for e-business advertising and internet search. *Issues in Information Systems*, *7*(2), 233–238.

Loureiro, S.M.C., & González, F. J.M. (2008). The importance of quality, satisfaction, trust and image in relation to rural tourism loyalty. *Journal of Travel and Tourism Marketing, 25*(2), 117-136. Retrieved from:.10.1080/10548400802402321

Loureiro, J., Trávníček, P., Rauchová, J., Urfus, T., Vít, P., Štech, M., & Suda, J. et al. (2010). The use of flow cytometry in the biosystematics, ecology and population biology of homoploid plants. *Preslia*, *82*, 3–21. doi:10.1093/ aobpla/pls037

Loureiro, S. M. C. (2013). The effect of perceived benefits, trust,quality,brand awareness/association and brand loyalty on internet banking brand equity. *International Journal of Electronic Commerce Studies*, *4*(2), 139–158. doi:10.7903/ijecs.1000

Loureiro, S. M. C., & Miranda, F. J. (2011). Brand equity and brand loyalty in the internet banking context:FIMIX-PLS market segmentation. *Journal of Service Science and Management*, *4*(4), 476–485http://www.SciRP.org/journal/jssm. doi:10.4236/jssm.2011.44054

Lu, J. (2002). *Predicting Customer Churn in the Telecommunications Industry—An Application of Survival Analysis Modeling Using SAS* [PDF document]. Retrieved from http://www2.sas.com/proceedings/sugi27/p114-27.pdf

Lubbe, J., Roets, L., van Tonder, S., & Wilkinson, A. (2013). Social media: A method to recruit students into undergraduate nursing programmes. *Gender & Behaviour*, *11*(2), 5402–5411.

Luck, D., & Lancanster, G. (2003). E-CRM: Customer relationship management in the hotel industry. *Managerial Auditing Journal*, *18*(3), 213–231. doi:10.1108/02686900310469961

Lu, H., & Hsiao, K. L. (2009). Gender differences in reasons for frequent blog posting. *Online Information Review*, *33*(1), 135–156. doi:10.1108/14684520910944436

Luo, K., Hsu, M., & Liu, S. (2008). The Moderating Role of Institutional Networking in the Customer Orientation-Trust/Commitment Performance Causal Chain in China. *Journal of the Academy of Marketing Science*, *36*(2), 202–216. doi:10.1007/s11747-007-0047-z

Mabroukeh, N. R., & Ezeife, C. I. (2010). A taxonomy of sequential pattern mining algorithms. *ACM Computing Surveys*, *43*(1), 1–41. doi:10.1145/1824795.1824798

Mael, F. A., & Ashforth, B. E. (1992). Alumni and their alma mater: A partial test of the reformulated model of organizational identification. *Journal of Organizational Behavior*, *13*(2), 103–123. doi:10.1002/job.4030130202

Magistris, T., & Gracia, A. (2008). The decision to buy organic food products in Southern Italy. *British Food Journal*, *110*(9), 929–947. doi:10.1108/00070700810900620

Magnini, V., & Honeycutt, E. (2005). Face Recognition and Name Recall, Training Implications for the Hospitality Industry. *The Cornell Hotel and Restaurant Administration Quarterly*, *46*(1), 69–78. doi:10.1177/0010880404270881

Magro, M., Sharp, J. H., Ryan, K., & Ryan, S. D. (2013). Investigating ways to use Facebook at the university level: A Delphi study. *Issues in Informing Science and Information Technology*, *10*, 295–311.

Mahlouji, H., & Anaraki, N. (2009). Corporate social responsibility towards social responsible innovation: A dynamic capability approach. *International Review of Business Research Papers*, *5*(6), 185–194.

Mair J, Schoen. O. (2005). *Social entrepreneurial business models: an exploratory study*. Workingpaper. IESE Business School Madrid 610.

Malthouse, E. C., Haenlein, M., Skiera, B., Wege, E., & Zhang, M. (2013). Managing customer relationships in the social media era: Introducing the social CRM house. *Journal of Interactive Marketing*, *27*(4), 270–280. doi:10.1016/j.intmar.2013.09.008

Maness, J. M. (2006). Library 2.0 theory: Web 2.0 and its implications for libraries. *Webology*, *3*(2), 1–6.

Mangold, W. G., & Faulds, D. J. (2009). Social media: The new hybrid element of the promotion mix. *Business Horizons*, *52*(4), 357–365. doi:10.1016/j.bushor.2009.03.002

Mankelow, G., & Merrilees, B. (2001). Towards a model of entrepreneurial marketing for rural women: A case study approach. *Journal of Developmental Entrepreneurship*, *6*(3), 221–235.

Marshall, G. W., Moncrief, W. C., Rudd, J. M., & Lee, N. (2012). Revolution in Sales: The Impact of Social Media and Related Technology on the Selling Environment. *Journal of Personal Selling & Sales Management*, *32*(3), 349–363. doi:10.2753/PSS0885-3134320305

Maruyama, G. M. (1998). *Basics of structural equation modeling*. London, UK: Sage Publications. doi:10.4135/9781483345109

Maswera, T., Dawson, R., & Edwards, J. (2006). Assessing the levels of knowledge transfer within e-commerce websites of tourist organizations in Africa. *Electronic Journal of Knowledge Management*, *4*(1), 59–66.

Mathieson, K., Peacock, E., & Chin, W. W. (2001). Extending the Technology Acceptance Model: The Influence of Perceived User Resources. *The Data Base for Advances in Information Systems*, *32*(3), 86. doi:10.1145/506724.506730

Matthew, K. O., Lee, M. K. O., & Wang, C. (1995). Article. *Journal of Communications of The ACM-CACM*, *41*(3), 63–70.

Matthews, S., & Healy, M. (2008). From garage to global: The Internet and international market growth – An SME perspective. *International Journal of Internet Marketing andAdvertising*, *4*(2/3), 179–196. doi:10.1504/IJIMA.2008.017021

Matzler, K., Bidmon, S., & Grabner-Kraüter, S. (2006). Individual determinants of brand affect: The role of the personality traits of extraversion and openness to experience. *Journal of Product and Brand Management*, *15*(7), 427–434. doi:10.1108/10610420610712801

Matzler, K., Pichler, E., Füller, J., & Mooradian, T. A. (2011). Personality, person–brand fit, and brand community: An investigation of individuals, brands, and brand communities. *Journal of marketing management*, *27*(9/10), 874-890.

Mayfield, T. (2011). A commander's strategy for social media. *Joint Force Quarterly*, *60*(1), 79–83.

McAlexander, J. H., Schouten, W. J., & Koening, F. H. (2002). Building brand community. *Journal of Marketing*, *66*(1), 38–54. doi:10.1509/jmkg.66.1.38.18451

McCarthy, R. V., & McCarthy, M. M. (2014). Student perception of social media as a course tool.[ISEDJ]. *Information Systems Education Journal*, *12*(2), 38–46.

McCole, P., & Ramsey, E. (2005). E-business in professional SMEs: The case of New Zealand. *Journal of Small Business and Enterprise Development*, *12*(4), 528–544. doi:10.1108/14626000510628207

McCrae, R. R., & John, O. P. (1992). An introduction to the five-factor model and its applications. *Journal of Personality*, *60*(2), 175–215. doi:10.1111/j.1467-6494.1992.tb00970.x PMID:1635039

McGee, P., & Diaz, V. (2007). Wikis and Podcasts and Blogs! Oh, my! What is a faculty member supposed to do? *EDUCAUSE Review*, *42*(5), 28–41.

McGonigal, J. (2011). We Don't Need No Stinkin' Badges: How To Reinvent Reality Without Gamification. GDC Vault. Retrievedfrom http://www.gdcvault.com/play/1014576/We-Don-t-Need-No

McGowan, P., & Durkin, M. G. (2002). Toward an understanding of internet adoption at the marketing/entrepreneurship interface. *Journal of Marketing Management*, *18*(3/4), 361–377. doi:10.1362/0267257022872451

McGowan, P., Durkin, M. G., Allen, L., Dougan, C., & Nixon, S. (2001). Developingcompetencies in the entrepreneurial small firm for use of the internet in the management of customer relationships. *Journal of European Industrial Training*, *25*(2/4), 126–136. doi:10.1108/EUM0000000005443

McKnight, D. H., & Chervany, N. L. (2002). What trust means in ecommerce customer relationships: An interdisciplinary conceptual typology. *International Journal of Electronic Commerce*, *6*(2), 33–57.

Mead, D. C., & Liedholm, C. (1998). The dynamics of micro and small enterprises in Medium-Sized Enterprises in Developing Countries. *World Development*, *26*(1), 61–74. doi:10.1016/S0305-750X(97)10010-9

Megha Y. Patil, (2014), Social Media and Customer Relationship Management. *Journal of Business and Management*, (IOSR-JBM) PP 27-32

Mensah, S. (2004). A review of SME financing schemes in Ghana. UNIDO Regional Workshop of Financing SMEs, 15-16 March, Accra, Ghana.

Messick, S. (1989). Meaning and values in test validation: The science and ethics of assessment. *The Journal of Educational Research, 18*(2), 5–11.

Meyer-Waarden, L. (2007). The effects of loyalty programs on customer lifetime duration and share of wallet. *Journal of Retailing, 83*(2), 223–236. doi:10.1016/j.jretai.2007.01.002

Michaelas, N., Chittenden, F., & Poutziouris, P. (1999). Financial policy and capital structurechoice in U.K. SMEs: Empirical evidence from company panel data. *Small Business Economics, 12*(2), 113–130. doi:10.1023/A:1008010724051

Michelini, L., & Fiorentino, D. (2012). New business models for creating shared value. *Social Responsibility Journal, 8*.

Miller, A. R., & Tucker, C. (2013). Active Social Media Management: The Case of Health Care. *Information Systems Research, 24*(1), 52–70. doi:10.1287/isre.1120.0466

Minocha, S. (2009). Role of social software tools in education: a literature review. *Education + Training, 51* (5/6), 353-369.

Mohan, S., Choi, E., & Min, D. (2008). Conceptual modeling of enterprise application system using social networking & web 2.0 social CRM system. In *Proceedings of the International Conference on Convergence & Hybrid Information Technology, ICHIT '08*. IEEE Computer Society. doi:10.1109/ICHIT.2008.263

Monecke, A., & Leisch, F. (2012). semPLS: Structural equation modeling using partial least squares. *Journal of Statistical Software, 48*(3), 1–32. PMID:23504300

Moore, R. E. (2003). From genericide to viral marketing: On "brand. *Journal of Language & Communication, 23*(3–4), 331–357. doi:10.1016/S0271-5309(03)00017-X

Moorman, C., Zaltman, G., & Deshpandé, R. (1992). Relationships between providers and users of market research: The dynamics of trust within and between organizations. *JMR, Journal of Marketing Research, 29*(3), 314–329. doi:10.2307/3172742

Morgan, J. (2010, November 3). *What Is Social CRM?* Retrieved from http://www.socialmediaexaminer.com/what-is-social-crm/

Morgan, R. M., & Hunt, S. D. (1997). The Commitment-Trust Theory of Relationship Marketing. *Journal of Marketing, 58*(3), 20–38. doi:10.2307/1252308

Mostafa, M. M. (2013). More than words: Social networks' text mining for consumer brand sentiments. *Expert Systems with Applications, 40*(10), 4241–4251. doi:10.1016/j.eswa.2013.01.019

Mowen, J. C. (2000). *The 3m model of motivation and personality: theory and empirical applications to consumer behavior*. Kluwer Academic Publishers. doi:10.1007/978-1-4757-6708-7

Mowen, J. C., Park, S., & Zablah, A. (2007). Toward a theory of motivation and personality with application to word-of-mouth communications. *Journal of Business Research, 60*(6), 590–596. doi:10.1016/j.jbusres.2006.06.007

Muhammad, Y. (2008). *A world without poverty: social business and the future of capitalism*. Public Affairs.

Muhammad, Y., Moingeon, B., & Lehmann-Ortega, L. (2010). Building Social Business Models: Lessons from the Grameen Experience. *Long Range Planning, 43*, 308-325.

Muir, B. M., & Moray, N. (1996). Trust in automation. Part II. Experimental studies of trust and human intervention in a process control simulation. *Ergonomics, 39*(3), 429–460. doi:10.1080/00140139608964474 PMID:8849495

Muniz, A. M. Jr, & O'Guinn, T. C. (2001). Brand Community. *The Journal of Consumer Research, 27*(4), 412–432. doi:10.1086/319618

Munns, A. K. (1995). influence of trust on the successful completion of a project. *International Journal of Project Management, 13*(1), 19–24. doi:10.1016/0263-7863(95)95699-E

Muñoz, J. A. V. (2013). *Social media lovers in Colombia: The Role of Online Brand Communities in Developing Brand Love.* (Master dissertation). University of Glasgow. Retrieved from http://www.banrepcultural.org/sites/default/files/colf_velezmunoz_jorgeandres_tesis.pdf

Muntinga, D. G., Moorman, M., & Smit, E. G. (2011). Introducing COBRAs Exploring motivations for brand-related Social media use. *International Journal of Advertising*, *30*(1), 13–46. doi:10.2501/IJA-30-1-013-046

Myers, C. A. (2003). Managing Brand Equity: A Look at the Impact of Attributes. *Journal of Product and Brand Management*, *12*(1), 39–51. doi:10.1108/10610420310463126

Naqvi, S. J., & Ajiz, M. A. (2006). Attitudes toward WebCT and learning: An Omani perspective. *Issues in Informing Science and Information Technology*, *3*, 435–444.

Narver, J. C., & Slater, S. F. (1990). The Effect of Market Orientation on Business Profitability. *Journal of Marketing*, *54*(4), 20–35. doi:10.2307/1251757

Negi, R., & Ketema, E. (2010). Relationship marketing and customer loyalty: The Ethiopian mobile communications perspective. *International Journal of Mobile Marketing.*, *5*(1), 113.

Neill, W. (2013). *Gamifying Marketing: Fusing games with consumer transactions to sustain engagement and accurate choices*. Sydney: University of New South Wales.

Neuhauser, C. (2005). A five-step maturity model for on-line course design. In *Proceedings of 19th Annual Conference on Distance Teaching and Learning*. Retrieved 19 January, 2015, from http://www.uwex.edu/disted/conference/Resource_library/proceedings/03_80.pdf

Nevgi, A., Virtanen, P., & Niemi, H. (2006). Supporting students to develop collaborative learning skills in technology-based environments. *British Journal of Educational Technology*, *37*(3), 937–947. doi:10.1111/j.1467-8535.2006.00671.x

Ngai, E. W. T., Xiu, L., & Chau, D. C. K. (2009). Application of data mining techniques in customer relationship management: A literature review and classification. *Expert Systems with Applications*, *36*(2), 2592–2602. doi:10.1016/j.eswa.2008.02.021

Nguyen, B., & Mutum, D. S. (2012). A review of customer relationship management: Successes, advances, pitfalls and futures. *Business Process Management Journal*, *18*(3), 400–419. doi:10.1108/14637151211232614

Niazi, M., Wilson, D., & Zowghi, D. (2006). Critical Success Factors for Software Process Improvement Implementation: An Empirical Study. *Software Process Improvement and Practice*, *11*(2), 193–211. doi:10.1002/spip.261

Nielsen (n.d.). Facebook Users Average 7 hrs a Month in January as Digital Universe Expands. Available at: http://www.nielsen.com/us/en/insights/news/2010/facebook-users-average-7-hrs-a-month-in-january-as-digital-universe-expands.html

Nielsen (n.d.). How Social Media Impacts Brand Marketing. Available at: http://www.nielsen.com/us/en/insights/news/2011/how-social-media-impacts-brand-marketing.html

Nobel, S. (2010, August 12). *It's Time To Bury The Marketing Funnel. Forrester Research*. Retrieved from http://www.forbes.com/2010/12/08/customer-life-cycle-leadership-cmo-network-funnel.html

Noble, C. H., Noble, S. M., & Adjei, M. T. (2012). Let them talk! Managing primary and extended online brand communities for success. *Business Horizons*, *55*(5), 475–483. doi:10.1016/j.bushor.2012.05.001

Ntsika.(1999). State of Small Business in South Africa. *SARB Quarterly Bulletins; and StatsSA Releases*, South Africa.

Nunnally, J. C. (1978). *Psychometric testing*. New York, NY: McGraw Hill.

Nunnally, J. C., & Bernstein, I. H. (1994). *Psychometric Theory*. New York: McGraw-Hill.

Nyangau, J. Z., & Bado, N. (2012). Social media and marketing of higher education: A review of the literature. *Journal of the Research Center for Educational Technology*, *8*(1), 38–51.

O'Cass, A., & Weerawardena, J. (2009). Examining the role of international entrepreneurship,innovation and international market performance in SME internationalisation. *European Journal of Marketing*, *43*(11/12), 1325–1348. doi:10.1108/03090560910989911

O'Dwyer, M., Gilmore, A., & Carson, D. (2009). Innovative marketing in SMEs. *European Journal of Marketing*, *43*(1/2), 46–61. doi:10.1108/03090560910923238

O'Reilly, T. (2005). What is Web 2.0: design patterns and business models for the next generation of software, *O'Reilly Media Inc.*, 30 September, from: www.oreillynet. com/pub/a/oreilly/tim/news/2005/09/30/what-is-web-20.htm

O'Reilly, T. (2009). The war for the web. IT conversations, from: www.itc. conversationsnetwork.org/shows/detail4317.html#

O'Toole, T. (2003). E-relationships-emergence and the small firm. *Marketing Intelligence & Planning*, *12*(2), 115–122. doi:10.1108/02634500310465434

Oberer, B., & Erkollar, A. (2012). Social media integration in higher education. cross-course google plus integration sown in the example of a master's degree course in management. *Procedia: Social and Behavioral Sciences*, *47*, 1888–1893. doi:10.1016/j.sbspro.2012.06.918

Oliver, R. L. (1981). Measurement and Evaluation of Satisfaction Processes in Retail Settings. *Journal of Retailing*, *57*(3), 25–48.

Oliver, R. L., & Anderson, E. (1994). An Empirical Test of the Consequences of Behavior- and Outcome-Based Sales Control Systems. *Journal ofMarketing*, *58*(October), 53–67. doi:10.2307/1251916

Oliver, R., & Rust, R. (1997). Customer Delight: Foundations, Findings, andManagerial Insight. *Journal of Retailing*, *73*(3), 311–337. doi:10.1016/S0022-4359(97)90021-X

Organization for Economic Co-Operation. and. development (OECD). (2010). *SMEs, Entrepreneurship and Innovation*. Retrieved September 1 2014 from "http://www.oecd.org/document/16/0,3746,en_2649_33956792_44938128_1_1_1_1,00.html

Osei, B., Baah-Nuakoh, A., Tutu, K. A., & Sowa, N. K. (1993). Impact of structural adjustment on small-scale enterprises in Ghana. In A. H. J. Helmsing & T. H. Kolstee (Eds.), *Structural Adjustment, Financial Policy and Assistance Programmes in Africa*. London: IT Publications. doi:10.3362/9781780445908.004

Özgüven, N., & Mucan, B. (2013). The relationship between personality traits and social media use. *Social Behavior and Personality*, *41*(3), 517–528. doi:10.2224/sbp.2013.41.3.517

Padel, S., & Foster, C. (2005). Exploring the gap between attitudes and behaviour: Understanding why consumers buy or do not buy organic food. *British Food Journal*, *107*(8), 606–625. doi:10.1108/00070700510611002

Pallis, G., Zeinalpour-Yazti, D., & Dikaiakos, M. D. (2011). Online social networks: Status and trends. *Studies in Computational Intelligence*, *331*, 213–234.

Palmer, A., & Huo, Q. A. (2013). Study of trust over time within a social network mediated environment. *Journal of Marketing Management*, *29*(15-16), 1816–1833. doi:10.1080/0267257X.2013.803143

Palvia, S. C. J., & Pancaro, R. (2010). Promises and perils of internet based networking. *Journal of Global Information Technology Management*, *13*(3), 1–10. doi:10.1080/1097198X.2010.10856517

Panagopoulos, N. (2010). *Sales Technology: Making the Most of Your Investment*. New York: Business Expert. doi:10.4128/9781606491171

Pang, B., & Lee, L. (2008). Opinion Mining and Sentiment Analysis. *Foundations and Trends® in Information Retrieval*, 2(1–2), 1–135.

Pappu, R., & Quester, P. (2008). Does brand equity vary between department tores and clothing stores? Results of an empirical investigation. *Journal of Product and Brand Management*, *17*(7), 425–435. doi:10.1108/10610420810916335

Pappu, R., Quester, P. G., & Cooksey, R. W. (2005). Consumer-Based Brand Equity: Improving the Measurement-Empirical Evidence. *Journal of Product and Brand Management*, *14*(3), 143–154. doi:10.1108/10610420510601012

Paquette, S. (2006). Customer Knowledge Management, from http://www.fis.utoronto.ca/phd/paquette/Documents/Paquette%20%20Customer%20Knowledge%20Management.pdf

Park, C., & Lee, T. (2009). Information direction, website reputation and eWOM effect: A moderating role of product. *Journal of Business Research*, *62*(1), 565–571. doi:10.1016/j.jbusres.2007.11.017

Park, C., & Srinivasan, V. (1994). A survey-based method for measuring and understanding brand equity and its extendibility. *JMR, Journal of Marketing Research*, *31*(2), 271–288. doi:10.2307/3152199

Park, N., Kee, K. F., & Valenzuela, S. (2009). Being Immersed in Social Networking Environment: Facebook Groups, Uses and Gratifications, and Social Outcomes. *Cyberpsychology & Behavior*, *12*(6), 729–733. doi:10.1089/cpb.2009.0003 PMID:19619037

Patino, A., Pitta, D. A., & Quinones, R. (2012). Social media's emerging importance in market research. *Journal of Consumer Marketing*, *29*(3), 233–237. doi:10.1108/07363761211221800

Patton, M. Q. (1999). Enhancing the Quality and Credibility of Qualitative Research. *Health Services Research*, *34*(5), 1189–1208. PMID:10591279

Paul, R., & Chung, L. H. (2010). Brave new cyberworld: The employer's legal guide to the interactive internet. *The Computer and Internet Lawyer*, *27*(3), 1–20.

Pavlou, P. A., Liang, H., & Xue, Y. (2007). Understanding and mitigating uncertainty in online exchange relationships: A principal-agent perspective. *Journal of Management Information System Quarterly*, *31*(1), 105–136.

Payne, A., & Frow, P. (2005). A Strategic Framework for Customer. *Journal of Marketing*, *69*(4), 167–176. doi:10.1509/jmkg.2005.69.4.167

Peppard, J. (2000). Customer relationship management (CRM) in financial services. *European Management Journal*, *18*(3), 312–327. doi:10.1016/S0263-2373(00)00013-X

Peruta, A., Ryan, W., & Engelsman, R. (2013). Social media branding strategies for higher education: Comparing Facebook pages and Web sites, *The International Journal of Technology. Knowledge in Society*, *9*, 11–23.

Pew Research Internet Project. (n.d.). *Social networking fact sheet*. Retrieved 13 August, 2014, from http://www.pewinternet.org/fact-sheets/social-networking-fact-sheet/

PGreenblog. (2009, July 06). *Time to Put a Stake in the Ground on Social CRM*. Retrieved from http://the56group.typepad.com/pgreenblog/2009/07/time-to-put-a-stake-in-the-ground-on-social-crm.html

Phan, M., Thomas, R., & Heine, K. (2011). Social Media and Luxury Brand Management: The Case of Burberry. *Journal of Global Fashion Marketing*, *2*(4), 213–222. doi:10.1080/20932685.2011.10593099

Phyu, T. N. (2009). Survey of Classification Techniques in Data Mining. In International MUlticonference of Engineers and Computer Scientists (Vol. I, pp. 18–20).

Piercy, N. F., Cravens, D. W., & Morgan, N. A. (1997). Sources of Effectiveness in the Business-To-Business Sales Organization. *Journal of Marketing Practice: Applied Marketing Science*, *3*(1), 43–69. doi:10.1108/EUM0000000004320

Plakoyiannaki, E., & Saren, M. (2006). Time and the Customer Relationship Management Process: Conceptual and Methodological Insights. *Journal of Business and Industrial Marketing*, *21*(4), 218–230. doi:10.1108/08858620610672588

Porter, M. E., & Kramer, M. R. (2011). Creating shared value. *Harvard Business Review*, *89*(1), 62–77.

Prasad, P. (2011). Generating Customer Profiles for Retail Stores Using Clustering Techniques. *International Journal on Computer Science and Engineering*, *3*(6), 2506–2510.

Prom, C. (2007). *Understanding On-line Archival Use through Web Analytics*. ICA-SUV Seminar, Dundee, Scotland. Retrieved July 12, 2014, from http://www.library.uiuc.edu/archives/workpap/PromSUV2007.pdf

Punjumiemi, J. (2009). The revolution of brand marketing: The era of virtual consumer communities. In M. Koskela, & M. Vinnari (Eds.). In *Proceeding of the Future of the Consumer Society Conference*.

Qi, X., & Davison, B. D. (2009). Web page classification: Features and algorithms. *ACM Computing Surveys*, *41*(2), 1–31. doi:10.1145/1459352.1459357

Radcliff, D. (2007). Are you watching? *SC Magazine*, *11*, 40–43.

Ragins, J. E., & Greco, J. A. (2003). Customer relationship management and e-business: More than a software solution. *Review of Business*, *24*(1), 25–30.

Ram, Anbu K, & Sanjay. (2011). Responding to user's expectation in the library: innovative Web 2.0 applications at JUIT Library. *Electronic Library and Information Systems, 45* (4), 452-469.

Ram, S Paul Anbu K, J. & Kataria, S. (2011). Responding to user's expectation in the library: innovative Web 2.0 applications at JUIT Library, *Program: electronic library and information systems,* 45(4), 452-469.

Ramsey, E., Ibbotson, P., Bell, J., & Gray, B. (2004). A projectives perspective of international 'e' services. *Qualitative Market Research: An International Journal.*, *7*(1), 34–47. doi:10.1108/13522750410512868

Rapp, A., Agnihotri, R., & Forbes, L. P. (2008). The Sales Force Technology Performance Chain: The Role of Adaptive Selling and Effort. *Journal of Personal Selling & Sales Management*, *28*(4), 335–350. doi:10.2753/PSS0885-3134280401

Rashtchy, F., Kessler, A. M., Bieber, P. J., Shindler, N. H., & Tzeng, J. C. (2007). The user revolution: The new advertising ecosystem and the rise of the Internet as a mass medium [PDF document]. Minneapolis, MN: Piper Jaffray Investment Research; Retrieved from http://people.ischool.berkeley.edu/~hal/Courses/StratTech09/Lectures/Google/Articles/summary-user-revolution.pdf

Rasiah, R. (2014). Transformative higher education teaching and learning: Using social media in a team-based learning environment. *Procedia: Social and Behavioral Sciences*, *123*, 369–379. doi:10.1016/j.sbspro.2014.01.1435

Rataree, G. (2003). *Measurement of Customer Satisfaction level of Hotel Food and Beverage Service at the Westin Hotel*. (Unpublished Thesis). Oklahoma State University.

Reichheld, F. F., & Sasser, J. W. E. (1990). Zero defections: Quality comes to services. *Harvard Business Review*, *68*(5), 105–111. PMID:10107082

Reichheld, F. F., & Schefter, P. (2000). E-loyalty: Your secret weapon on the web. *Harvard Business Review*, *68*(5), 105–113. PMID:10107082

Reicks, M., Splett, P., & Fishman, A. (1997). *Shelf Labelling of Organic Foods: Effects on Customer Perceptions and Sales*. The Retail Food Industry Center.

Reinartz, W., Krafft, M., & Hoyer, W. (2004). The customer relationship management process: Its measurement and impact on performance. *JMR, Journal of Marketing Research*, *41*(3), 293–305. doi:10.1509/jmkr.41.3.293.35991

Reinstein, D. A., & Snyder, C. M. (2005). The influence of expert reviews on consumer demand for experience goods: A case study of movie critics. *The Journal of Industrial Economics*, *53*(1), 27–51. doi:10.1111/j.0022-1821.2005.00244.x

Reiss, S. (2004). Multifaceted nature of intrinsic motivation: The theory of 16 basic desires. *Review of General Psychology*, *8*(3), 179–193. doi:10.1037/1089-2680.8.3.179

Reuben, R. (2008). *The use of social media in higher education for marketing and communications: A guide for professionals in higher education*. Retrieved 23 June, 2014, from http://doteduguru.com/wp-content/uploads/2008/08/social-media-in-higher-education.pdf

Rheingold, H. (1993). *The virtual community. Homesteading on the electronic frontier*. Reading, MA: Addison- Wesley.

Ribbink, D., Riel, A. C. R., Liljander, V., & Streukens, S. (2004). Comfort your online customer: Quality, trust and loyalty on the internet. *Managing Service Quality: An International Journal*, *14*(6), 446–456. doi:10.1108/09604520410569784

Ribie`re, V. Haddad, M. & Vande Wiele, PH. (2010). The impact of national culture traits on the usage of web 2.0 technologies, *the journal of information and knowledge management systems* 40 (3/4), 334-361.

Richards, K. A., & Jones, E. (2008). Customer relationship management: Finding value drivers. *Industrial Marketing Management*, *37*(2), 120–130. doi:10.1016/j.indmarman.2006.08.005

Richardson, M., & Domingos, P. (2002). *Mining knowledge-sharing sites for viral marketing*. In *ACM SIGKDD International Conference on Knowledge Discovery and Data Mining*, Edmonton, Alberta, Canada.

Richardson, W. (2006). *Blogs, Wikis, Podcasts, and other Powerful Web Tools for Classrooms*. Thousand Oaks, CA: Corwin Press.

Rich, M. K. (2000). The direction of marketing relationships. *Journal of Business and Industrial Marketing*, *15*(2/3), 170–191. doi:10.1108/08858620010316877

Rigby, D. K., & Ledingham, D. (2004). CRM done right. *Harvard Business Review*, *82*(11), 118–129. PMID:15559450

Ringle, C. M., Wende, S., & Will, A. (2005). Smart PLS 2.0 (beta). Hamburg, Germany, Retrieved from http://www.smartpls.de

Riquelme, H. (2002). Commercial internet adoption in China: Comparing the experience of small,medium and large business internet research. *Electronic Networking Applications and Policy*, *12*(3), 276–286. doi:10.1108/10662240210430946

Rishika, R., Ashish, K., Ramkumar, J., & Ram, B. (2013). The Effect of Customers' Social Media Participation on Visit Frequency and Profitability: An Empirical Investigation. *Information Systems Research*, *24*(1), 108–127. doi:10.1287/isre.1120.0460

Ritchie, B., & Brindley, C. (2005). ICT adoption by SMEs: Implications for relationship and management. *New Technology, Work and Employment*, *20*(3), 205–217. doi:10.1111/j.1468-005X.2005.00154.x

Roddy, G., Cowan, C., & Hutchinson, G. (1994). Organic food–a description of the Irish market. *British Food Journal*, *96*(4), 3–10. doi:10.1108/00070709410060998

Rodriguez, J. E. (2011). Social media use in higher education: Key areas to consider for educators. *MERLOT Journal of Online Learning and Teaching*, *7*(4), 539–550.

Rodriguez, M., & Honeycutt, E. (2011). CRM's Impact on B2B Sales Professionals' Collaboration and Sales Performance. *Journal of Business-To-Business Marketing*, *18*(4), 335–356. doi:10.1080/1051712X.2011.574252

Rodriguez, M., Peterson, R. M., & Krishnan, V. (2012). Social Media's Influence on Business-to-Business Sales Performance. *Journal of Personal Selling & Sales Management*, *32*(3), 365–378. doi:10.2753/PSS0885-3134320306

Rohra, G., & Sharma, M. (2012). *Social CRM - Possibilities and Challenges* [PDF document]. Retrieved from http://www.tcs.com/SiteCollectionDocuments/White%20 Papers/ConnectedMarketing_Whitepaper_Social_ CRM%E2%80%93Possibilities_Challenges_0912-1.pdf

Rollins, M., & Halinen, A. (2005). Customer knowledge management competence: towards theoretical framework, *Proceedings of the 38th Hawaii International Conference on System Sciences*, Big Island, HI. doi:10.1109/HICSS.2005.180

Romano, C. (1989). Research strategies for small business: A case study. *International Small Business*, *7*(4), 5–43.

Romano, N. C., & Fjermestad, J. (2002). Electronic customer relationship management: An assessment of research. *International Journal of Electronic Commerce*, *6*(2), 61–113.

Ross, C. F., Reed, D. A., Washington, R. L., Eckhardt, A., Anapol, F., & Shahnoor, N. (2009). Scaling of chew cycle duration inprimates. *American Journal of Physical Anthropology*, *138*(1), 30–44. doi:10.1002/ajpa.20895 PMID:18661474

Ross, D. (2005). E-CRM from a supply chain management perspective. *Information Systems Management*, *22*(1), 37–44. doi:10.1201/1078/44912.22.1.20051201/85737.5

Ross, D. S. (2014). Junior college students' expectations on choosing institutions for higher education and institutions marketing strategies for admissions. *Abhinav National Monthly Refereed Journal of Research in Commerce & Management*, *3*(5), 23–27.

Rossiter, J. R., & Percy, L. (1987). *Advertising and promotion management*. New York, NY: McGraw-Hill Boo Company.

Rowley, J. (2002). Eight enhancing questions for customer knowledge management in e-business. *Journal of Knowledge Management*, *6*(5), 500–511. doi:10.1108/13673270210450441

Rowley, J. (2002). Reflections on customer knowledge management in e-business, *Qualitative Market Research. International Journal (Toronto, Ont.)*, *5*(4), 80–268.

Roy & Stavropoulos. (2007). *Customer Knowledge Management (CKM) in the e-Business Environment.* (Master`s thesis). Lulea University of Technology.

Royo-Vela, M., & Casamassima, P. (2011). The influence of belonging to virtual brand communities on consumers' affective commitment, satisfaction and word-of-mouth advertising: The ZARA case. *Online Information Review*, *35*(4), 517–542. doi:10.1108/14684521111161918

Rudman, R. J. (2010). Incremental risks in Web 2.0 applications. *The Electronic Library*, *28*(2), 210–230. doi:10.1108/02640471011033585

Ruekert, R. W. (1992). Developing a Market Orientation: An Organizational Strategy Perspective. *International Journal of Research in Marketing*, *9*(3), 225–245. doi:10.1016/0167-8116(92)90019-H

Safko, L., & Brake, D. K. (2009). *The Social Media Bible*. John Wiley & Sons, Inc.

Saini, A., Grewal, R., & Johnson, J. L. (2010). Putting market-facing technology to work: Organisational drivers of CRM performance. *Marketing Letters*, *21*(4), 365–383. doi:10.1007/s11002-009-9096-z

Salomann, H., Dous, M., Kolbe, L., & Brenner, W. (2005). Rejuvenating customer management: How to make knowledge for, from and about customers work. *European Management Journal*, *23*(4), 392–403. doi:10.1016/j.emj.2005.06.009

Samu, S., Krishnan Lyndem, P., & Litz, R. A. (2012). Impact of brand-building activities and retailer-based brand equity on retailer brand communities. *European Journal of Marketing*, *46*(11/12), 1581–1601. doi:10.1108/03090561211259998

Sánchez, D., Vila, M. A., Cerda, L., & Serrano, J. M. (2009). Association rules applied to credit card fraud detection. *Expert Systems with Applications*, *36*(2 PART 2), 3630–3640. doi:10.1016/j.eswa.2008.02.001

Sarason, S. B. (1974). *The psychological sense of community: Prospects for the community psychology*. San Francisco, CA: Jossey-Bass.

SAS. (2014). *Data Visualization: Making Big Data Approachable and Valuable* [PDF document]. Retrieved from http://www.sas.com/content/dam/SAS/en_us/doc/whitepaper2/sas-data-visualization-marketpulse-106176.pdf

Satanasavapak, P. (2010). The Effects of Virtual Communities on Brand Equity. *Journal of Management*, *8*(1), 1–19.

Saxe, R., & Weitz, B. (1982). The SOCO scale: A measure of the customer orientation of salespeople. *JMR, Journal of Marketing Research*, *19*(August), 343–351. doi:10.2307/3151568

Schall, M. (2003). Best practices in the assessment of hotel-guest attitudes. *The Cornell Hotel and Restaurant Administration Quarterly*, *44*(2), 51–65. doi:10.1016/S0010-8804(03)90018-8

Schau, H. J., Muñiz, A. M. J. Jr, & Arnould, E. J. (2009). How Brand Community Practices Create Value. *Journal of Marketing*, *73*(5), 30–51. doi:10.1509/jmkg.73.5.30

Schellong, A. R. M. (2008). Government 2.0 an exploratory study of social networking services in Japanese local government. *Transforming Government: People. Process and Policy*, *2*(4), 225–242.

Scherbaum, C. A., Cohen-Charash, Y., & Kern, M. J. (2006). Measuring General Self-Efficacy a Comparison of Three Measures using Item Response Theory. *Educational and Psychological Measurement*, *66*(6), 1047–1063. doi:10.1177/0013164406288171

Schiff, J. L. (2012). *CIO Magazine, 8 CRM Trends You Need to Watch*. Retrieved January 28, 2013, from: http://www.cio.com/article/print/699311

Schifferstein, H. N. J., & Ophuis, P. A. M. O. (1998). Health-Related Determinants of Organic Food Consumption in the Netherlands. *Food Quality and Preference*, *9*(3), 119–133. doi:10.1016/S0950-3293(97)00044-X

Schivinski, B., & Dabrowski, D. (2013). The impact of brand communication on brand equity dimensions and brand purchase intention throuhg Facebook. *GUT FME Working Paper Series A*, *4*(4), 1 - 20.

Schmitz, H. (1995). Collective efficiency: Growth path for small-scale industry. *The Journal of Development Studies*, *34*(4), 529–566. doi:10.1080/00220389508422377

Schneider, P. P., & Vogt, C. A. (2012). Applying the 3M Model of Personality and Motivation to Adventure Travelers. *Journal of Travel Research*, *51*(6), 704–716. doi:10.1177/0047287512451134

Schouten, J. W., & McAlexander, J. H. (1995). Subcultures of Consumption: An Ethnography of the New Bikers. *The Journal of Consumer Research*, *22*(1), 43–61. doi:10.1086/209434

Schroeder, A., Minocha, S., & Schneider, C. (2010). The strengths, weaknesses, opportunities and threats of using social software in higher and further education teaching and learning. *Journal of Computer Assisted Learning*, *26*(3), 159–174. doi:10.1111/j.1365-2729.2010.00347.x

Schulz, F. (August 19, 2014). *Path analysis with SAS Visual Analytics* [Web log comment]. Retrieved from http://blogs.sas.com/content/sascom/2014/08/19/path-analysis-with-sas-visual-analytics/

Schwarzer, R., & Jerusalem, M. (2004). General self-efficacy scale. In S. Salek (Ed.), Compendium of Quality of Life Instruments. Cardiff: Centre for Socioeconomic Research, Cardiff University, (Vol.6, Section 2A:1). Haslemere: Euromed Communications (CD-ROM publication).

Schwarzer, R., & Jerusalem, M. (1995). Generalized self-efficacy scale. In J. Weinman, S. Wright, & M. Johnston (Eds.), *Measures in Health Psychology: A User's Portfolio. Causal and Control Beliefs* (pp. 35–37). Windsor: NFER-NELSON.

Scowen, G. (2007). *Increased Website Popularity through Compliance with Usability Guidelines*. (Doctoral Dissertation). University of Otago, New Zealand.

Scullin, S., Allora, J., Lloyd, G. O., & Fjermestad, J. (2002, April). Electronic customer relationship management: benefits, considerations, pitfalls and trends. In *Proceedings of the IS One World Conference, Las Vegas, Nevada*. 3-5.

Secker, J. (2008). Social software and libraries: a literature review from the LASSIE project. *Program: Electronic Library and Information Systems, 42* (3), 215-231.

Selwyn, N. (2012). *Social media in higher education*. Retrieved 11 July, 2014, from http://www.educationarena.com/pdf/sample/sample-essay-selwyn.pdf

Sen, A., & Sinha, A. P. (2011). IT alignment strategies for customer relationship management. *Decision Support Systems*, *51*(3), 609–619. doi:10.1016/j.dss.2010.12.014

Seraj, M. (2012). We Create, We Connect, We Respect, Therefore We Are: Intellectual, Social, and Cultural Value in Online Communities. *Journal of Interactive Marketing*, *26*(4), 209–222. doi:10.1016/j.intmar.2012.03.002

Serantes, L. (2009). Understanding the relationship between libraries, young adults and Web 2.0: The necessity of a critical perspective. *Library Review*, *58*(3), 51–237.

Serhat, A., & Cengiz, K. (2012). Evaluation of e-commerce website quality using fuzzy multi-criteria decision making approach. *IAENG International Journal of Computer Science*, *39*(1), 69–70.

Shamaila Marita Lein & Mette Ugstad. (2011). *Social Media in Customer Relationship Management - An analysis of Norwegian management consulting firms*. (Master thesis). Copenhagen Business School.

ShamiZanjani, M., Rouzbehani, R. & Dabbagh, H. (2008). Proposing a Conceptual Model of Customer Knowledge Management: A Study of CKM Tools in British Dotcoms. *Proceedings of World Academy of Science, Engineering, and Technology*, 28, April, Rome.

Shankar, V., Smith, A. K., & Rangaswany, A. (2003). Customer satisfaction and loyalty in online and offline environments. *International Journal of Research in Marketing*, *20*(2), 153–175. doi:10.1016/S0167-8116(03)00016-8

Shao, G. (2009). Understanding the Appeal of User-Generated Media: A Uses and Gratifications Perspective. *Internet Research*, *19*(1), 7–25. doi:10.1108/10662240910927795

Shapiro, C., & Varian, H. R. (1999). *Information rules: A strategic guide to the network economy*. Boston: Harvard Business School Press.

Sherchan, W., Nepal, S., & Paris, C. (2013). A Survey of Trust in Social Networks[CSUR]. *ACM Computing Surveys*, *45*(4), 1–33. doi:10.1145/2501654.2501661

Shieh, M. D., Yan, W., & Chen, C. H. (2008). Soliciting customer requirements for product redesign based on picture sorts and ART2 neural network. *Expert Systems with Applications*, *34*(1), 194–204. doi:10.1016/j.eswa.2006.08.036

Shu, W., & Haddad, K. (2011). Word of mouth marketing on social network websites. *Journal of Service Science, 2* (2), 1-10.

Shu, W., & Chuang, Y. H. (2011). The perceived benefits of six-degree-separation social networks. *Internet Research*, *21*(1), 26–45. doi:10.1108/10662241111104866

Silva, R. D., & Batista, L. (2007). Boosting government reputation through CRM. *International Journal of Public Sector Management*, *20*(7), 588–607. doi:10.1108/09513550710823506

Simpson, M., Padmore, J., Taylor, N., & Frecknall-Hughes, J. (2006). Marketing in small and medium-sized enterprises. *International Journal of Entrepreneurial Behaviour and Research*, *12*(6), 361–387. doi:10.1108/13552550610710153

Sims, D. (2000). A new ROI for new economy CRM and just why doesn't high-tech get it? http://www.crmguru.com

Skouloudis, M. (2003, October). E-CRM vs CRM.*Magazine Ne.O*, 32-33.

Smith, A. N., Fischer, E., & Yongjian, C. (2012). How Does Brand-related User-generated Content Differ across YouTube, Facebook, and Twitter? *Journal of Interactive Marketing*, *26*(2), 102–113. doi:10.1016/j.intmar.2012.01.002

Smith, D., Menon, S., & Sivakumar, K. (2005). Online peer and editorial recommendations, trust, and choice in virtual markets. *Journal of Interactive Marketing*, *19*(3), 15–37. doi:10.1002/dir.20041

Smithee, B. (2011). How social media is expanding the defitions of MR, and as leaders why it is largely your responsibility. *Alert, 51*(3).

Smith, R. E., & Vogt, C. (1995). The effects of integrating advertising and negative word-of-mouth communications on message processing and response. *Journal of Consumer Psychology*, *4*(2), 133–151. doi:10.1207/s15327663jcp0402_03

Social Innovation Europe. (2012). *Financing social impact.* Retrieved September 1 2014 from http://ec.europa.eu/enterprise/ newsroom/cf/itemdetail.cfm?item_id=5582&lang=en

Solis, B. (2010). *Engage! The complete guide for brands and businesses to build, cultivate and measure success in the new web.* New Jersey: John Wiley and sons Inc.

Solis, B., & Breakenridge, D. K. (2009). *Putting the Public Back in Public Relations: How Social Media Is Reinventing the Aging Business of PR.* Upper Saddle River, NJ: FT Press/Pearson Education.

Soriano, D. (2002). Customers' expectations factors in restaurants: *The situation in Spain. International Journal of Quality & Reliability Management*, *19*(8/9), 1055–1067. doi:10.1108/02656710210438122

Sridharan, S. (2012). *How analytics derives customer life cycle management* [PDF document]. Retrieved from http://contentz.mkt3838.com/lp/10371/367751/How_Analytics_Drives_Customer%20Life-cycle%20Management_Nov%202012_2.pdf

Srinivasan, S. S., Anderson, R., & Ponnavolu, K. (2002). Customer loyalty in ecommerce: An exploration of its antecedents and consequences. *Journal of Retailing*, *78*(1), 41–50. doi:10.1016/S0022-4359(01)00065-3

Stake, R. E. (2000). Case studiesCase studies. In N. K. Denzin&Y. S. Lincoln (Eds.).Handbook of qualitative research, 435-453. Thousand Oaks: Sage.

Stake, R. (1995). *The Art of Case Study Research.* Newbury Park, CA: Sage.

Stavrianou, A., Andritsos, P., & Nicoloyannis, N. (2007). Overview and semantic issues of text mining. *SIGMOD Record*, *36*(3), 23. doi:10.1145/1324185.1324190

Steel, W. F., & Webster, L. M. (1991). *Small Enterprises in Ghana: Responses to Adjustment Industry. Series Paper, No. 33.* Washington, DC: The World Bank Industry and Energy Department.

Steenkamp, J. B. E. M., & Geyskens, I. (2006). How country characteristics affect the perceived value of a website. *Journal of Marketing*, *70*(3), 136–150. doi:10.1509/jmkg.70.3.136

Steinman, C., Deshpande, R., & Farley, J. U. (2000). Beyond Market Orientation: When Customers and Suppliers Disagree. *Journal of the Academy of Marketing Science*, *28*(Winter), 109–119. doi:10.1177/0092070300281010

Stoddard, J. E., Clopton, S. W. & Avila, R. A. (2006). An Analysis of the Effects of Sales Force Automation on Salesperson Perceptions of Performance. *Journal of Selling and Major Account Management*, 38-56.

Stokes, D. (2000). Entrepreneurial marketing: A conceptualisation from qualitative research. *Qualitative Market Research: An International Journal*, *3*(1), 47–54. doi:10.1108/13522750010310497

Straub, D. W. (1989). Validating Instruments in MIS Research. MIS Quarterly. *Journal of Marketing Development and Competitiveness*, *8*(1), 2014.

Street, C. T., & Cameron, A. F. (2007). External relationships and the small business: A review ofsmall business alliance and network research. *Journal of Small Business Management*, *45*(2), 239–266.

Streiner D.L. (2005). With apologies to Albert: everything is not relative. *Evidence Based Mental Health, 8*(4), 91-93.

Strong, C. (2006). Is Managerial Behaviour a Key to Effective Customer Orientation? *Total Quality Management and Business Excellence*, *17*(1), 97–115. doi:10.1080/14783360500249687

Su, C. T., Chen, Y. H., & Sha, D. Y. (2006). Linking innovative product development with customer knowledge: A data-mining approach. *Technovation*, *26*(7), 784–795. doi:10.1016/j.technovation.2005.05.005

Sunderwood, R., Bond, E., & Baer, R. (2001). Service brands via social identity: Lessons from the sports marketplace. *Journal of Marketing Theory and Practice*, *9*(1), 1-13.

Sung, Y., Kim, Y., Kwon, O., & Moon, J. (2010). An Explorative Study of Korean Consumer Participation in Virtual Brand Communities in Social Network Sites. *Journal of Global Marketing*, *23*(5), 430–445. doi:10.1080/08911762.2010.521115

Sun, T., & Wu, G. (2012). Traits, predictors, and consequences of Facebook self- presentation. *Social Science Computer Review*, *30*(4), 419–433. doi:10.1177/0894439311425978

Swift, R. S. (2001). *Accelerating Customer Relationships: Using CRM and Relationship Technologies*. Upper Saddle River, NJ: Prentice Hall.

Sykes, A. O. (2000). An Introduction to Regression Analysis. In E. Posner (Ed.), *Chicago Lectures in Law and Economics*. Chicago, IL: Foundation Press.

Symon, G. E., & Cassell, C. E. (1998). *Qualitative methods and analysis in organizational research: A practical guide*. London: Sage Publications Ltd.

Tagliavini, M., Ravarini, A., & Antonelli, A. (2001). An evaluation model for electronic commerce activities within SMEs. *Information Technology Management*, *2*(2), 211–230. doi:10.1023/A:1011417703063

Tanner, J. E., Ahearne, M., Leigh, T. W., Mason, C. H., & Moncrief, W. C. (2005). CRM in Sales-Intensive Organizations: A Review and Future Directions. *Journal of Personal Selling & Sales Management*, *25*(2), 169–180.

Tapscott, D. (2008). Viewpoint: Ten talking points for Davos. *Business Week, 16*, 1-16.

Tardini, S., & Cantoni, L. A. (2005*).A semiotic approach to online communities: Belonging, Interest and identity in websites' and video games' communities*. In P. Isaias, P. Kommers, & M. McPherson (Eds.). In *Proceedings, IADIS international conference e-Society*, Qawra, Malta: IADIS Press.

Taylor, G. A., & Neslin, S. A. (2005). The current and future sales impact of a retail frequency reward program. *Journal of Retailing*, *81*(4), 293–305. doi:10.1016/j.jretai.2004.11.004

Taylor, M., Kent, M. L., & White, W. J. (2001). How activist organizations are using the Internet to build relationships. *Public Relations Review*, *27*(3), 263–284. doi:10.1016/S0363-8111(01)00086-8

Taylor, S. A., & Hunter, G. L. (2006). The impact of loyalty with e-CRM soft wares and e-services. *International Journal of Service Industry Management*, *13*(5), 452–474. doi:10.1108/09564230210447931

Tess, P. A. (2013). The role of social media in higher education classes (real and virtual) - A literature review. *Computers in Human Behavior*, *29*(5), A60–A68. doi:10.1016/j.chb.2012.12.032

Thanh, N. N. D. (2012). *Relationships between brand awareness, perceived quality, trust, value, loyalty, and brand equity: A case study of Vinamilkbrand in Ho Chi Minh, Vietnam*. Available from: http://www.graduate.au.edu/gsbejournal/Journals/Dec2012/Thanh.pdf

Thelwall, M., Buckley, K., Paltoglou, G., Cai, D., & Kappas, A. (2010). Sentiment Strength Detection in Short Informal Text. *Journal of the American Society for Information Science*, *61*(12), 2544–2558. doi:10.1002/asi.21416

Thelwall, M., & Zuccala, A. (2008). A University-Centered European Union Link Analysis. *Scientometrics*, *75*(3), 407–420. doi:10.1007/s11192-007-1831-8

Thoma, L. R., De Carlo, E., & Ramaswami, S. N. (2001). Consumers' Responses to Negative Word-of-Mouth Communication: An Attribution Theory Perspective. *Journal of Consumer Psychology, 11*(1), 57–73. doi:10.1207/S15327663JCP1101_5

Thompson, E., & Moscardini, N. (2002). Gartner's CRM Vision: A Roadmap for customer- centric transformation. Garthner Symposium ITXPO, San Diego, California.

Tong, W., & Xuecheng, Y. (2010). *Electronic Word of Mouth in Online Social Network.Second International Conference on Communication Systems, Networks and Applications.*

Toporek, A. (n.d.). *What is Customer Loyalty*. Retrieved 2014, from: http://customersthatstick.com

Toufaily, E., Ricard, L., & Perrien, J. (2012). Customer loyalty to a commercial website: Descriptive meta-analysis of the empirical literature and proposal of an integrative model. *Journal of Business Research, 66*(9), 1436–1447. doi:10.1016/j.jbusres.2012.05.011

Trainor, K. J., Andzulis, J., Rapp, A., & Agnihotri, R. (2014). Social media technology usage and relationship performance: A capabilities-based examination of social CRM. *Journal of Business Research, 67*(6), 1201–1208. doi:10.1016/j.jbusres.2013.05.002

Trusov, M., Bodapati, A., & Bucklin, R. (2010). Determining influential users in internet social networks. *JMR, Journal of Marketing Research, 47*(4), 643–658. doi:10.1509/jmkr.47.4.643

Trusov, M., Bucklin, R. E., & Pauwels, K. (2009). Effects of word-of-mouth versus traditional marketing: findings from an internet social networking site. *Journal of Marketing, 73*(5), 90–103. doi:10.1509/jmkg.73.5.90

Tsai, W. S., & Men, L. R. (2013). Motivations and Antecedents of Consumer Engagement with Brand Pages on Social Networking Sites. *Journal of Interactive Advertising, 13*(2), 76–87. doi:10.1080/15252019.2013.826549

Tuškej, U., Golob, U., & Podnar, K. (2013). The role of consumer–brand identification in building brand relationships. *Journal of Business Research, 66*(1), 53–59. doi:10.1016/j.jbusres.2011.07.022

Tuten, T., & Marks, M. (2012). The adoption of social media as educational technology among marketing educators. *Marketing Education Review, 22*(3), 201–214. doi:10.2753/MER1052-8008220301

Twitter (2015). Twitter usage. Retrived on March 31, 2015 from https://about.twitter.com/company

Tynan, C., McKechnie, S., & Chhuon, C. (2010). Co-creating value for luxury brands. *Journal of Business Research, 63*(11), 1156–1163. doi:10.1016/j.jbusres.2009.10.012

Ùahina, A., Zehir, C., & Kitapçı, H. (2012). The Effects of Brand Experiences, Trust and Satisfaction on Building Brand Loyalty; An Empirical Research On Global Brands. *Procedia: Social and Behavioral Sciences, 24*, 1288–1301.

Ueltschi, D. (2006). *Shannon entropy*. Retrieved July 12, 2014, from http://www.ueltschi.org/teaching/ chapShannon.pdf

United Nations Development Programmed (UND) & European Research Network (EMES). (2008). Social enterprise: a new model for poverty reduction and employment generation. Retrieved August 28, 2014, from http://europeandcis.undp.org/ourwork/poverty/show/02F5569C-F203-1EE9-BD529F7FE21C9320

Van Egeren, M., & O'Connor, S. (1998). Drivers of Market Orientation and Performance in Service Firms. *Journal of Services Marketing, 12*(1), 39–58. doi:10.1108/08876049810202357

Veletsianos, G. (2012). Higher education scholars' participation and practices on Twitter. *Journal of Computer Assisted Learning, 28*(4), 336–349. doi:10.1111/j.1365-2729.2011.00449.x

Venkatesh, V., Morris, M. G., Davis, G. B., & Davis, F. D. (2003). User Acceptance of Information Technology: Toward a Unified View. *Management Information Systems Quarterly, 27*(3), 425–478.

Verhees, F. J. H. M., & Meulenberg, M. T. G. (2004). Market Orientation, Innovativeness, Product Innovation, and Performance in Small Firms. *Journal of Small Business Management, 42*(2), 134–154. doi:10.1111/j.1540-627X.2004.00102.x

Verhoef, P. C., Venkatesan, R., McAlister, L., Malthouse, E. C., Krafft, M., & Ganesan, S. (2010). CRM in data-rich multichannel retailing environments: A review and future research directions. *Journal of Interactive Marketing*, *24*(2), 121–137. doi:10.1016/j.intmar.2010.02.009

Vicari, D., & Alfó, M. (2014). Model based clustering of customer choice data. *Computational Statistics & Data Analysis*, *71*, 3–13. doi:10.1016/j.csda.2013.09.014

Victorino, L., Verma, R., Plaschka, G., & Dev, C. (2005). Service innovation and customer choices in the hospitality industry. *Journal of Managing Service Quality*, *15*(6), 555–576. doi:10.1108/09604520510634023

Vinerean, S., Cetina, I., Dumitrescu, L., & Tichindelean, M. (2013). The Effects of Social Media Marketing on Online Consumer Behavior. *International Journal of Business and Management*, *8*(14). doi:10.5539/ijbm.v8n14p66

Virkus, S. (2008). Use of Web 2.0 technologies in LIS education: experiences at Tallinn University, Estonia. *Program: Electronic Library and Information Systems*, *42* (3), 262-274.

Vock, M., Dolen, W., & Ruyter, K. (2013). Understanding Willingness to Pay for Social Network Sites. *Journal of Service Research*, *16*(3), 311–325. doi:10.1177/1094670512472729

Volkmann, Tokarski, & Ernst. (2012). Social Entrepreneurship and social business. Springer Gabler.

Vollmer, C., & Precourt, G. (2008). *Always on: Advertising, marketing, and media in an era of consumer control*. New York: McGraw-Hill.

Von Ahn, L., & Dabbish, L. (2008). Designing games with a purpose. *Communications of the ACM*, *51*(8), 58–67. doi:10.1145/1378704.1378719

Wahlberg, O., Strandberg, C., Sundberg, H., & Sandberg, K. (2009). Trends, topics and under researched areas in CRM research- a literature review. *International Journal of Public Information Systems*, *3*, 191–208.

Walsh, M. F., & Lipinski, J. (2009). The role of the marketing function in small and medium sized enterprises. *Journal of Small Business and Enterprise Development*, *16*(4), 569–585. doi:10.1108/14626000911000929

Wang, F. H., & Shao, H. M. (2004). Effective personalized recommendation based on time-framed navigation clustering and association mining. *Expert Systems with Applications*, *27*(3), 365–377. doi:10.1016/j.eswa.2004.05.005

Wang, H. B., Ting, H. F., Chen, J. T., & Wang, D. S. (2011). Optimizing Multiple Quality Characteristics by TAGUCHI Method and TOPSIS Algorithm. *The International Journal of Organizational Innovation.*, *4*(2), 49–63.

Wang, Y. D., & Emurian, H. H. (2005). An overview of online trust: Concepts, elements, and implications. *Journal ofComputersin. Human Behavior*, *21*(1), 105–125. doi:10.1016/j.chb.2003.11.008

Wang, Y. S., Wub, S. C., Lin, H. H., & Wang, Y. Y. (2011). The relationship of service failure severity, service recovery justice and perceived switching costs with customer loyalty in the context of e-tailing. *International Journal of Information Management*, *31*(4), 350–359. doi:10.1016/j.ijinfomgt.2010.09.001

Weinberg, B. D., & Pehlivan, E. (2011). Social spending: Managing the social media mix. *Business Horizons*, *54*(3), 275–282. doi:10.1016/j.bushor.2011.01.008

Wellman, B. (1997). For A Social Network Analysis Of Computer Networks: A Sociological Perspective on Collaborative Work and Virtual Community. In *SIGCPR '96 Proceedings of the 1996 ACM SIGCPR/SIGMIS Conference on Computer Personnel Research.* ACM.

Wellman, B. (1997). An electronic group is virtually a social network. In S. Kiesler (Ed.), *Culture of the Internet*. Mahwah, NJ: Lawrence Erlbaum Associates.

Wellman, B., & Gulia, M. (1999). Net-surfers don't ride alone: Virtual communities as communities. In B. Wellman (Ed.), *Networks in the global village*. Boulder, CO: Westview Press.

Werbach, K., & Hunter, D. (2012). *For the Win: How Game Thinking Can Revolutionize Your Business*. Wharton Digital Press.

Werbach, K., & Hunter, D. (2012). *How game thinking can revolutionize your business*. Wharton Digital Press.

White, K., & Simpson, B. (2013). When Do (and Don't) Normative Appeals Influence Sustainable Consumer Behaviors? *Journal of Marketing*, *77*(2), 78–95. doi:10.1509/jm.11.0278

Wikipedia. (n.d.). Facebook. Available at: https://en.wikipedia.org/wiki/Facebook

Wikipedia. (n.d.). Interpersonal Relationship. Available at: https://en.wikipedia.org/wiki/Interpersonal_relationships

Wilcox, K., & Stephen, A. T. (Forthcoming). Are Close Friends the Enemy? Online Social Networks, Self-Esteem and Self-Control. *The Journal of Consumer Research.*

Wilde, E. (2006). *Knowledge Organization Mashups.* Retrieved from http://dret.net/netdret/publications#wil06f

Wilimzig, B. J. (2011). *Online communities: Influence on members brand loyalty and purchase intent.* Retrieved from Google Scholar.

Williams, L., & Cothrell, J. (2000). Four smart ways to run online communities. *Journal of Sloan Management Review, 41*(4), 81–91.

Wilson, C. D. (2013). Making connections: Higher education meets social media. *Change: The Magazine of Higher Learning, 45*(4), 51–57. doi:10.1080/00091383.2013.806201

Winer, R. S. (2001). A Framework for Customer Relationship Management. *California Management Review, 43*(4), 89–105. doi:10.2307/41166102

Wirtz, J., den Ambtman, A., Bloemer, J., Horváth, C., Ramaseshan, B., van de Klundert, J., & Kandampully, J. et al. (2013). Managing brands and customer engagement in online brand communities. *Journal of Service Management, 24*(3), 223–244. doi:10.1108/09564231311326978

Woisetschläger, D. M., Hartleb, V., & Blut, M. (2008). How to make brand communities work: Antecedents and consequences of consumer participation. *Journal of Relationship Marketing, 7*(3), 237–256. doi:10.1080/15332660802409605

Wong, H. Y., & Merrilees, B. (2005). A brand orientation typology for SMEs: A case research approach. *Journal of Product and Brand Management, 14*(3), 155–162. doi:10.1108/10610420510601021

Woodcock, N., Green, A., & Starkey, M. (2011). Social CRM as a business strategy. *Journal of Database Marketing & Customer Strategy Management, 18*(March), 50–64. doi:10.1057/dbm.2011.7

Woolfolk, A. (1995). *Educational psychology* (6th ed.). Boston, MA: Allyn & Bacon.

Woolrych, A., Hornbæk, K., Frøkjær, E., & Cockton, G. (2011). Ingredients and Meals rather than Recipes: A Proposal for Research that does not treat Usability Evaluation Methods as Indivisible Wholes. *International Journal of Human-Computer Interaction, 27*(10), 940–970. doi:10.1080/10447318.2011.555314

Wu, B., Ye, Q., Yang, S., & Wang, B. (2009). A new telecom CRM framework from social network perspective. In *Proceedings of the 1st ACM international workshop on Complex networks meet information and knowledge management.* ACM.

Wu, M. (2011). Gamification from a Company of Pro Gamers.Retrieved from http://community.lithium.com/t5/Science-of-Social-blog/Gamification-from-a-Company-of-Pro-Gamers/ba-p/19258

Xiang, Z., & Gretzel, U. (2010). Role of social media in online travel information search. *Tourism Management, 31*(2), 179–188. doi:10.1016/j.tourman.2009.02.016

Xintong, G., Hongzhi, W., Song, Y., & Hong, G. (2014). Brief survey of crowdsourcing for data mining. *Expert Systems with Applications, 41*(17), 7987–7994. doi:10.1016/j.eswa.2014.06.044

Yang, Y., Akers, L., Klose, T., & Barcelon Yang, C. (2008). Text mining and visualization tools - Impressions of emerging capabilities. *World Patent Information, 30*(4), 280–293. doi:10.1016/j.wpi.2008.01.007

Yarquah, J. A., & Baafi-Frimpong, S. (2011). Social cost of educated youth unemployment in Ghana and its implications for education. *Centrepoint Humanities Edition., 14*(1), 122–143.

Yilmaz, C., Alpkan, L., & Ergun, E. (2005). Cultural determinants of customer- and learning-oriented value systems and their joint effects on firm performance. *Journal of Business Research, 58*(10), 1340–1352. doi:10.1016/j.jbusres.2004.06.002

Yin, R. K. (2003). Case study research: designs and methods (3rd ed.). Thousand Oaks, CA: Sage.

Yin, R. K. (2011). *Applications of case study research.* California: Sage.

Yoo, B., Donthu, N., & Lee, S. (2000). An examination of selected marketing mixelements and brand equity. *Journal of the Academy of Marketing Science*, *28*(2), 195–211. doi:10.1177/0092070300282002

Yoo, C. W., Sanders, G. L., & Moon, J. (2013). Exploring the effect of e-WOM participation on e-Loyalty in e-commerce. *Journal of Decision Support Systems*, *55*(3), 669–678. doi:10.1016/j.dss.2013.02.001

Yoon, S. J. (2002). The antecedents and consequences of trust in online purchase decisions. *Journal of Interactive Marketing*, *16*(2), 47–63. doi:10.1002/dir.10008

Youcheng, W., & Fesenmaier, D. R. (2003). Assessing Motivation of Contribution in Online Communities: An Empirical Investigation of an Online Travel Community. *Electronic Markets*, *13*(1), 33–45. doi:10.1080/1019678032000052934

Younghwa, L., & Kenneth, A. K. (2006). Investigating the effect of website quality on e-business success: An analytic hierarchy process (AHP) approach. *Decision Support Systems*, *42*(3), 1383–1401. doi:10.1016/j.dss.2005.11.005

Zafra, I. (2013, August 22). *Traditional vs. Social CRM: What's The Difference*? Retrieved from http://www.spi-global.com/blog/think-tank/traditional-vs-social-crm-whats-the-difference/

Zaglia, M. E. (2013). Brand communities embedded in social networks. *Journal of Business Research*, *66*(2-2), 216–223. doi:10.1016/j.jbusres.2012.07.015 PMID:23564989

Zahran, D. I., Al-Nuaim, H. A., Rutter, M. J., & Benyon, D. (2014). A Comparative Approach to Web Evaluation and Website Evaluation Methods. *International Journal of Public Information Systems*, *10*(1), 21–39.

Zaidieh, A. J. Y. (2012). The use of social networking in education: Challenges and opportunities. *World of Computer Science and Information Technology Journal*, *2*(1), 18–21.

Zailskaite-Jakste, L., & Kuvykaite, R. (2012). Implementation of communication in social media by promoting studies at higher education institutions. *Inzinerine Ekonomika-Engineering Economics*, *23*(2), 174–188.

Zanoli, R., & Naspetti, S. (2002). Consumer motivations in the purchase of organic food: A means-end approach. *British Food Journal*, *104*(8), 643–653. doi:10.1108/00070700210425930

Zeithaml, V. A. (1998). Consumer perceptions of price, quality, and value: A means-end model and synthesis of evidence. *Journal of Marketing*, *52*(3), 2–22. doi:10.2307/1251446

Zeithaml, V. A., Berry, L. L., & Parasuraman, A. (1996). The behavioral consequences of service quality. *Journal of Marketing*, *60*(2), 31–46. doi:10.2307/1251929

Zeithmal, V., & Bitner, M. (1996). Service Marketing. New York: McGraw-Hill.

Zeng, F., Huang, L., & Dou, W. (2009). Social Factors in User Perceptions and Responses to Advertising in Online Social Networking Communities. *Journal of Interactive Advertising*, *10*(1), 1–13. doi:10.1080/15252019.2009.10722159

Zhang, X. Z. (2007). Building personalized recommendation system in E-Commerce using association rule-based mining and classification. In *Proceedings of the Sixth International Conference on Machine Learning and Cybernetics*, ICMLC 2007 (Vol. 7, pp. 4113–4118). doi:10.1109/ICMLC.2007.4370866

Zhang, Y., Liang, R., Li, Y., Zheng, Y., & Berry, M. (2011). Behavior-based telecommunication churn prediction with neural network approach. In *Proceedings - 2011 International Symposium on Computer Science and Society, ISCCS 2011* (pp. 307–310). doi:10.1109/ISCCS.2011.89

Zhang, H., Gu, C. L., Gu, L., & Zhang, Y. (2011). The evaluation of tourism destination competitiveness by TOPSIS & information entropy--A case in the Yangtze River Delta of China. *Tourism Management*, *32*(2), 443–451. doi:10.1016/j.tourman.2010.02.007

Zhang, Z. (2011). Customer knowledge management and the strategies of social software. *Business Process Management Journal*, *17*(1), 82–106. doi:10.1108/14637151111105599

Zhan, J., Loh, H. T., & Liu, Y. (2007). Gather customer concerns from online product reviews – a text summarization approach. *Journal of Expert Systems with Applications*, *36*(2), 2107–2115. doi:10.1016/j.eswa.2007.12.039

Zhou, Z., Jin, X. L., Vogel, D. R., Fang, Y., & Chen, X. (2011). Individual motivationsand demographic differences in social virtual world uses: An exploratory investigationin Second Life. *International Journal of Information Management*, *31*(3), 261–271. doi:10.1016/j.ijinfomgt.2010.07.007

Zhu, F., & Zhang, X. (2010). Impact of online consumer reviews on sales: The moderating role of product and consumer characteristics. *Journal of Marketing*, *74*(2), 133–148. doi:10.1509/jmkg.74.2.133

Zichermann, G., & Cunningham, C. (2011). *Gamification by design: Implementing game mechanics in web and mobile apps*. O'Reilly Media, Inc.

Zichermann, G., & Linder, J. (2010). *Game-based marketing: inspire customer loyalty through rewards, challenges, and contests*. John Wiley & Sons.

Zolfaghar, K., & Aghaie, A. (2011). Evolution of trust networks in social web applications using supervised learning. *Procedia Computer Science*, *3*, 833–839. doi:10.1016/j.procs.2010.12.137

Zontanous, G., & Anderson, A. R. (2004). Relationships, marketing and small business: An exploration oflinks in theory and practice. *Qualitative Market Research: An International Journal*, *7*(3), 228–236. doi:10.1108/13522750410540236

About the Contributors

Amir Khanlari is an Assistant Professor in MBA Department, Faculty of Management at University of Tehran, Iran. He is editor of the Quarterly Journal of Business Management. He received his PhD from University of Tehran in Marketing Management in 2011. His research interests include Customer Relationship Management (CRM), Branding, and Business Intelligence. He has published his papers in the Journal of Computers & Industrial Engineering, International Journal of Human Sciences, International Journal of Engineering, Iranian Journal of Accounting & Auditing Review, and several local and international journals. Also, He has published some book chapters in IGI Global, Inc.

* * *

Babak Abedin received his Bachelor in Industrial Engineering and Master in Information Technology Management, both in Iran. He received an international scholarship from The University of New South Wales in 2006 and completed his PhD in Information Systems in 2009. Babak joined UTS in September 2013 as a Senior Lecturer and prior to that he worked at Macquarie University as a Lecturer from 2009 to 2013 and acted as the department's postgraduate coordinator from 2011 to 2012. He has published in various refereed international journals and conferences and has taught in areas of Information Systems and Accounting & Information Systems at The University of New South Wales, The University of Sydney, Macquarie University, and University of Tehran. Prior to joining academia, he mainly worked as a business analyst and IT project manager in a number of national and international projects.

Ali Acılar is an associate professor in the Department of Management Information Systems, Bilecik Şeyh Edebali University, Bilecik, Turkey. He graduated from the Department of Business Administration at Hacettepe University, Ankara, Turkey, received his MS in Operation Research and Statistics from Rensselaer Polytechnic Institute (RPI), Troy, NY, USA and obtained his Ph.D in Business Administration from Dumlupınar University, Kütahya, Turkey in 2007. His research interest includes information technology usage in SMEs, ethical use of information technology, gender issues in computer ethics, e-commerce, e-government, and social media.

George Kofi Amoako, BSc (Hons, KNUST); MBA (Marketing, UG); PhD Candidate (LondonMet) Chartered Marketer-CIM-UK Profile George Kofi Amoako, is a senior lecturer and head of department at Marketing Department of Central Business School, Central University College in Accra Ghana, an academic and a practising Chartered Marketer (CIM_UK) with specialization in Branding, CSR and Strategic Marketing. He was educated in Kwame Nkrumah University of Science and Technology in

Kumasi Ghana and at the University of Ghana and the London School of Marketing (UK). He is currently reading his PhD at London Metropolitan University UK. He has considerable research, teaching, consulting and practise experience in the application of Marketing Theory and principles to everyday marketing challenges and management and Organisational issues. He is a Chartered Marketer with The Chartered Institute of Marketing-UK. He is a past president of the Graduate Student Association of Ghana and a member of the University Council of the University of Ghana in 2000-2001. He has consulted for Public Sector and Private organisations both in Ghana and UK. He is a founding Director of Fourth Protocol firm – which was set up in 2008. He has a strong passion for branding, service quality and CSR issues in corporate world. He is a Certified Business Specialist with the Academy of Business Strategy, London and an Executive Global Partner with the same organization. George has published extensively in internationally peer-reviewed academic journals and presented many papers at international conferences.

Molood Arman is a graduate student in the field of Information Technology Management (Advanced Information Systems), at University of Tehran, Iran. She received her Bachelor in Computer engineering, from Isfahan University of Technology, Iran. She is now an IT researcher at Iran Telecommunication Research Center (ITRC).

Rebecca Baah-Ofori holds a bachelor's degree in English from the Kwame Nkrumah University of Science and Technology (KNUST), Ghana and an MPhil degree in Communication Studies from the University of Ghana. She is currently an Assistant Lecturer at the University of Professional Studies, Accra (UPSA). Prior to joining UPSA, Rebecca worked as the Publications and Communications Officer at the Institute of Statistical, Social and Economic Research (ISSER), University of Ghana and assisted in a number of research projects for the Media Foundation for West Africa, Ghana. Her research interests are in the areas of Public Relations, Advertising, Health Communications and New Media.

Ali Balapour holds a MBA degree from Faculty of Management at University of Tehran, Iran. Balapour is Quality Assurance Manager and Database Designer at PPAK Inspection Company. Previously he worked for various goods Inspection companies like Bekhrad Inspection services. His research interests include E-commerce, Social Networks, Online Consumer Behavior, web and database design for small businesses.

Evelyn Chronis holds a Bachelor of Commerce degree with Honours in Marketing obtained at the University of Sydney. Her research investigated the impact of social media on consumer purchasing behaviour. In particular, her research explored the impact of social media as an extension to traditional Customer Relationship Management tools. She is presently tutoring courses in Marketing at the University of Sydney, such as Marketing Principles and Marketing Research.

Rimantas Gatautis is the Director of Electronic Business Research Centre, at the Kaunas University of Technology. His research currently concentrates on IST influence on enterprises transformation in the transition economies, e-business models in transition economies, socio-economic aspects of IST adaptation, IST influence on governance and democracy processes, knowledge role in value creation, knowledge driven innovations, social networks and gamification.

Ali Golrokh is a PhD candidate in business management, he holds a bachelor of Information Technology and received a master in business management. The field of multidisciplinary especially by concentrating on customer behavior and study the possibility of applying technology is his main interest. He currently works as an advisor and participate in several projects in field of business development, business process analysis and design and marketing. Besides, he cooperated as a business advisor in one of the large scale customer relationship management project in one of the most famous bank of Iran.

Hassan Hajipoor is a graduate student in the field of Computer Engineering (Software Engineering), at University of Tehran, Iran. He received his Bachelor in Computer engineering, from Zanjan University, Iran.

Prerna Lal is a Lecturer in Information Management at International Management Institute, New Delhi and a published writer in journals and publications, both Indian and international. She is an engineer with an MBA degree (IIT-Roorkee). She is a SAP-certified consultant and has ITIL® V3 Foundation-level certificate in IT Service Management. She has more than 13 years of experience in academics and research with areas of interest being Data Warehousing and Data Mining, Business Analytics, Management Information System, Software Project Management, IT Service Management, Cyber Law, and Cloud Computing.

Qiang Lu is a Senior Lecturer in Marketing at the University of Sydney, Australia. He obtained his PhD in Marketing from the University of Toronto, Canada and MA in Economics from York University, Canada. His research interests are quantitative marketing, applied econometrics, consumer choice modelling and Bayesian statistics. He is also interested in big data analytics. He has published in journals such as Marketing Science, Statistical Science, and Journal of Business Research. He was awarded the 2009 ANZMAC Emerging Researcher of the Year Award. He teaches courses in Marketing such as Marketing Principles, Marketing Research and New Product Development.

Audrone Medziausiene is research associate at Electronic Business Research Centre, at the Kaunas University of Technology. Her research currently concentrates on consumer behavior in online social network, social commerce, and value creation in online social networks.

Rohan Miller holds a PhD in Marketing and Masters Degrees in Business Administration and Accounting. He is presently a Senior Lecturer in Marketing at The University of Sydney. He previously held the position as Research Director at a strategy and research company that specialises in the finance sector, and was the Research and Planning Manager at a publicly listed international gaming and technology company where he managed product planning and the global research and business intelligence program. Dr. Miller has also held academic positions at the Universities of Wollongong and Queensland. Dr. Miller's research focuses on (1) consumption with negative effects (e.g. gambling, alcohol, food), (2) marketing communications, (3) public policy, and (4) children as consumers, and miscellaneous topics of interest (including urban animal management, wool value chains, ethics, asbestos and the environment). His research has been published in various academic journals, including the Journal of Business Research, the Journal of Marketing Communications, Marketing Theory, and Public Relations Review.

He is an ad hoc reviewer for the Journal of the Academy of Marketing Science, Journal of Advertising and several other journals. Dr. Miller has served as an expert witness in several cases, including matters related to advertising, alcohol and gambling. After beginning his career was in the alcohol and media industries, Dr. Miller has extensively consulted to a variety of clients from government, the financial sector, peak industry groups, fmcg, plus others.

Seyed Abolghasem Mira is an Assistant Professor in Business Department, Faculty of Management at University of Tehran, Iran. He received his PhD from University of Tehran in International Marketing Management. His research interests include Media and Branding. He has published his papers in the International Journal of Learning & Development, international journal of Information and Knowledge Management, International Journal of Switzerland Research Park, Europen Online Journal of Natural and Social Science, Iranian Journal of Business Management, and several local journals.

Siavash Moheb holds a MBA degree from university of Tehran, he received his bachelor in civil engineering. The fields of consumer behavior and social related issues are his main interests. He currently works as a marketing planner of a major educational institute with 100 branches in Iran. He also cooperated as marketing advisor in two soil engineering services companies.

Fatemeh Najafloo is graduated from University of Tehran, Faculty of Management in the field of Information Technology Management.

Hatef Rasouli is graduated from the University of Tehran, Faculty of Management in the field of Information Technology Management.

Faezeh Rezaei holds a master degree in Marketing from Faculty of Management at University of Tehran, Iran. She received her B.S from Iran University of Science and Technology in Electronic Engineering. Her research interests include Social Media, Brand Community, and Branding.

Rozita Shahbaz Keshvari, is studying in two field in PhD level one is DBA and another is Crisis Management in Isfahan University Shakhes Pajhooh. She graduated in MBA from Sharif University. Moreover, she is marketing and management lecturer at Islamic Azad University. She also is teaching marketing and selling, CRM, Customer orientation, advertising, time management in various companies. Besides teaching she has more than ten years work experience in marketing, HR, project management. Nowadays she has more than 15 papers in ISI and scientific journals.

Mehdi Shamizanjani is Assistant Professor of IT Management at the Faculty of Management, University of Tehran, Iran. His current research interests are in knowledge management and project management. He has a bachelor's degree in industrial management, a master's degree in information technology management, and a PhD in systems management from the University of Tehran.

Mahdi Sheykhlar is a graduate of Executive Management from Islamic Azad University, Science & Research Branch, with a bachelor degree in Industrial Engineering. He has good experience in holding training seminars, HRM strategies, marketing plan in more than 50 companies in Iran. He is now the CEO of ARTIMAN Co., a company in the advertising and marketing field.

Babak Sohrabi is a Professor in the Department of Information Technology Management, Faculty of Management at University of Tehran, Iran. He received his PhD in Management Science, from Lancaster University in England. He is the Editor-in-Chief of the Information Technology Management Journal, the head of the IT Management Department of Faculty of Management, and also head of the E-learning Center at the University of Tehran. His research interests include artificial intelligence, knowledge management, e-commerce, decision support systems and organizational impact of information technology. His research has appeared in the Journal of Interdisciplinary Mathematics, International Journal of Engineering, Journal of Operational Research Society, International Journal of Production Research, Computers & Industrial Engineering, Review of Business Information Systems, Applied Soft Computing, International Journal of Engineering, International Journal of e-Collaboration, Expert System with Applications, International Journal of Applied Industrial Engineering, International Journal of Management & Enterprise Development, Behavior and information technology, International Journal of Human Sciences, and International Journal of Knowledge Management.

Sahra Zamanian, master of media management, Faculty of Management, University of Tehran, Tehran, Iran.

Index

M

N

O

P

Q

R

S

T

V

W

www.ingramcontent.com/pod-product-compliance
Lightning Source LLC
LaVergne TN
LVHW060418300926
849162LV00006B/1464